10

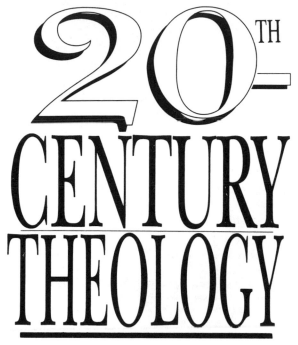

20TH CENTURY THEOLOGY

*God & the World
in a Transitional Age*

Stanley J. Grenz & Roger E. Olson

THE PATERNOSTER PRESS
Carlisle UK

InterVarsity Press
P.O. Box 1400, Downers Grove, IL 60515, USA

The Paternoster Press
P.O. Box 300, Carlisle, CA3 0QS, UK

InterVarsity Press® is the book-publishing division of InterVarsity Christian Fellowship®, a student movement active on campus at hundreds of universities, colleges and schools of nursing in the United States of America, and a member movement of the International Fellowship of Evangelical Students. For information about local and regional activities, write Public Relations Dept., InterVarsity Christian Fellowship, 6400 Schroeder Rd., P.O. Box 7895, Madison, WI 53707-7895.

All Scripture quotations, unless otherwise indicated, are from the American edition of HOLY BIBLE, NEW INTERNATIONAL VERSION®. NIV®. Copyright ©*1973, 1978, 1984 by International Bible Society. Used by permission of Zondervan Publishing House. Published in Great Britain by Hodder & Stoughton, Ltd. All rights reserved.*

USA ISBN 0-8308-1525-2 (pbk.)
UK ISBN 0-85364-590-6

Printed in the United States of America ∞

Library of Congress Cataloging-in-Publication Data

Grenz, Stanley, 1950-
    Twentieth-century theology: God and the world in a transitional
age/Stanley J. Grenz, Roger E. Olson.
        p.   cm.
    Includes bibliographical references.
    ISBN 0-8308-1761-1 (hdbk.)
    1. Theology, Doctrinal—History—20th century.   I. Olson, Roger
E.   II. Title.
BT28.G746   1992
230'.09'04—dc20   *92-8184*
                                                                      CIP

British Library Cataloguing in Publication Data

Grenz, Stanley J.
  Twentieth Century Theology: God and the
  World in a Transitional Age
  I. Title   II. Olson, Roger E.
  230

  ISBN 0-85364-529-9 (hbk)
  ISBN 0-85364-590-6 (pbk)

17	16	15	14	13	12	11	10	9	8	7	6	5	4	3	2
08	07	06	05	04	03	02	01	00	99	98	97	96	95		

To
Wolfhart Pannenberg
Scholar, Mentor, Friend

Preface

In its broad sense, theology may be defined as the intellectual reflection on the act, content and implications of Christian faith. Theology describes faith within a specific historical and cultural context, and therefore it is unashamedly a contextual discipline. Because of its contextual nature, theology poses an ongoing task. The fundamental Christian faith-commitment to Jesus as Lord and to the Triune God revealed in Christ is unchanging, of course. Yet, the world into which this confession is to be brought is in transition. Theology serves the church in each generation and in each cultural setting by assisting the people of God in reflecting on and applying the one faith of the church to the world in which contemporary disciples live and engage in ministry in Christ's name.

Consequently, theology must move among three poles—the biblical gospel, the heritage of the church and the thought forms of the contemporary world. It employs these three in seeking to articulate the unchanging confession of Jesus in a changing context and thereby to speak to the issues of succeeding generations.

Theologians in the twentieth century, like their forebears in every generation, have taken up the challenge posed by their discipline. In this volume we attempt to wade through what we perceive to be the main current of theology in this century. To this end, we survey the prominent theologians and theological movements of the recent decades. Yet these persons and movements did not arise *sui generis* nor in isolation. Therefore this volume attempts to move beyond objective survey to interpretation. Our desire is not merely to offer a synopsis of key thinkers and their thoughts, but to tell a story, the story of theology in a transitional age.

We see the twentieth century as an age of transition from so-called modern culture, inaugurated by the Enlightenment, to postmodern culture. Scholars are far from agreed on the meaning of *postmodern* as a cultural epoch, but almost no one sees the present or the future as simple extensions of those cultural forces set in motion by the Enlightenment. The twentieth century has *not* seen the full flowering and fruition of modernity but its erosion and decline. The acids of modernity have turned against modernity itself in such movements as existentialism, the new physics, feminism and deconstructionism. As none before, this century has given rise to anxiety over humanity's place in the universe, an anxiety revealed in new searches for transcendence, for a source of meaning and hope beyond the self-enclosed world described by Enlightenment science and philosophy. We see twentieth-century theology as the story of theology's struggle along with culture through this transition from modernity to postmodernity.

We believe that one significant theme that provides an interpretive tool and a means for bringing to light the unity and diversity of theology in this transitional century is the creative tension posed by the twin truths of the divine transcendence and the divine immanence. This is, of course, not the only possible interpretive key to twentieth-century theology. Nevertheless, we are convinced that the interplay of transcendence and immanence as a central theological concern has contributed greatly to determining the specific path that theology has taken over the last hundred years.

The impetus to this book lies with Dan Reid, reference book editor at InterVarsity Press, who envisioned an edited volume of essays dealing with the significant theologians of the century. His original idea quickly developed into a dual-authored interpretive treatment of the subject. Since we serve in two quite different academic contexts, we have been concerned throughout the writing of the book that it be useable in both the graduate seminary and undergraduate liberal arts contexts.

In addition to Dan Reid and the people at InterVarsity Press, our thanks go to a number of other people. Our educational institutions provided immeasurable support. Stan's work transpired during his transition from the North American Baptist Seminary in Sioux Falls, South Dakota, to Carey Theological College and Regent College in Vancouver, British Columbia. Roger's involvement was made possible in part by a six-month sabbatical granted by Bethel College, St. Paul, Minnesota. Secretarial services were provided by Joy Huisman at the North American Baptist Seminary, Elaine Dickinson and Beverley Norgren at Carey Theological College, and Janine McFarland of Bethel College. Helpful work such as checking references was provided by teaching assistants Marsha Moret Sietstra at NABS, Gerald Deguire at CTC and Tom Douglas of Bethel. And above all we each owe a debt of gratitude to our families, who patiently bore with us over the two-year gestation period of this literary "baby."

INTRODUCTION:
TRANSCENDENCE AND IMMANENCE AND MODERN THEOLOGICAL HISTORY

At its best Christian theology has always sought a balance between the twin biblical truths of the divine transcendence and the divine immanence. On the one hand, God relates to the world as the Transcendent One. That is, God is self-sufficient apart from the world. God is above the universe and comes to the world from beyond. As the Hebrew Scriptures so forcefully declare, God dwells in heaven. "God is in heaven and you are on earth," writes the Preacher (Eccles 5:2). And the seer reports seeing the Lord "seated on a throne, high and exalted" (Is 6:1).

On the other hand, God also relates to the world as the Immanent One. This means that God is present to creation. The divine one is active within the universe, involved with the processes of the world and of human history. Paul emphasized this truth in his well-known speech to the Athenians in the meeting of the Areopagus. God "is not far from each one of us," he said, " 'For in him we live and move and have our being' " (Acts 17:27-28). The related theme of God's Spirit present as the sustainer of creation is repeatedly sounded in the Old Testament, especially in the wisdom literature (such as Job 27:3; 33:4; 34:14-15; Ps 104:29-30). And Jesus himself credited the natural processes such as sunshine and rain, the feeding of the birds and the beauty of the flowers to the agency of his Father (Mt 5:45; 6:25-30; 10:29-30).

Because the Bible presents God as both beyond the world and present to the world, theologians in every era are confronted with the challenge of articulating the Christian understanding of the nature of God in a manner that balances, affirms and holds in creative tension the twin truths of the divine transcendence and the divine immanence. A balanced affirmation of both truths facilitates a proper relation between theology and reason or culture. Where such balance is lacking, serious theological problems readily emerge. Hence an overemphasis on transcendence can lead to a theology that is irrelevant to the cultural context in which it seeks to speak, whereas an overemphasis on immanence can produce a theology held captive to a specific culture.

The theology of the twentieth century, flowing as it does out of that of the nineteenth, offers an interesting case study in the attempt to balance these two aspects of the relation of God to creation. In fact, the see saw of transcendence and immanence as a significant focus provides a handle for grasping the unity and diversity of the central current of theology that flowed through the century. More specifically, the major theological proposals of this era indicate the instability introduced when transcendence and immanence are not properly balanced. As if in the ongoing course of theological history the twin truths of the divine transcendence and immanence are seeking their own proper equilibrium, twentieth-century theology illustrates how a lopsided emphasis on one or the other eventually engenders an opposing movement that in its attempt to redress the imbalance actually moves too far in the opposite direction. The attempt to reestablish an equilibrium in the face of one-sided emphases, therefore, provides a helpful vantage point from which to narrate the story of theology in that century.

Twentieth-century theology did not begin with the dawning of the new century, but rather both sometime before and sometime after the changing of the calendar from December 31, 1900, to January 1, 1901. Strictly speaking, of course, the century was inaugurated at the stroke of midnight that night. Technically, therefore, the theology of the new century began as a continuation of the basically optimistic, this-worldly mindset of the old, which emphasized the divine immanence—God at work in the world and in human affairs.

When viewed from the perspective of the flow of historical events, however, the twentieth century did not begin until the second decade of the 1900s. The unleashing of "the guns of August" in 1914 sounded not only the opening volley of World War 1 but also the death peal of the nineteenth-century world. The intellectual ethos that has characterized the 1900s was ushered in by this catastrophic event, for the First World War shattered the optimistic world view developed during the previous centuries and gave birth to the intellectual and cultural gloom prevalent during the years since 1914.

In many ways the theological agenda of our century has also been determined by the aftermath of that world-changing event. The theology of the century began with an attempt to start anew out of the ashes of the war, which devastated not only Europe but also European cultural theology. Thus it is no surprise that the theology of the new century arose first as a protest against the central themes of its nineteenth-century predecessor, including the emphasis on immanence so important for the Western mindset since the Renaissance. The theological story of the century, therefore, begins with a rebirth of the focus on transcendence, as Karl Barth and others asked again whether there was a word from the God of heaven that could be heard in the aftermath of war.

Rather than being an aberration, a minor setback in the upward march of history, as the theology of the preceding centuries would want to suggest, World War 1 was a portend of things to come. The decades since the unleashing of the war machine in central Europe have witnessed repeated and ever-worsening conflicts. The military confrontations of the century have not only taken their toll in loss of human life, but also in loss of cultural life. Despair has steadily advanced across the intellectual landscape, permeating Western culture and leaving its mark on theology as well. So significant a role has war played in the century that when taken as a whole the theology of the 1900s has been overshadowed by the question of whether we can deal with the succession of conflicts—military, political and sociological—that have buffeted our world. Such a situation eventually dashes all lingering hope, not only the hope of finding God within the world but even the hope that the voice of God might still come to us from above.

In the midst of the general cultural despair of our postmodern world, theologians in the last decades have continued to engage in their task, sometimes by recapturing the sense of immanence characteristic of the modern era, sometimes by searching for the Transcendent One. Despite their heroic efforts, by century's end theology, which began the journey of the last hundred years as "the happy science" of Karl Barth, had moved almost uncontrollably toward the unhappy cul-de-sac of deconstructionism.

Whether the events of the twentieth century will have marked the end of theology can be answered only by the twenty-first century. In any case, the lesson of the theology of the era is becoming clear. A lopsided theological edifice—one that is built on an inherently unstable foundation, whether the foundation be a one-sided emphasis on transcendence or on immanence—cannot be "fixed" simply by renovation, by adding the missing element. On the contrary, the theological construction engineer must start again from the ground up. For when the foundation is improperly laid, no cosmetic changes will lead to a durable structure.

The theology of the twentieth century began in 1914. Yet its story takes us back even farther, to the epoch that preceded it, out of which and in reaction to which the theological mind of the age emerged. As a result, the theology of this century is best understood when contrasted with the outlook of the nineteenth century, against which, chastened as it was by decades of human strife and conflict, it so vehemently reacted. Nineteenth-century theology, in turn, finds its historical context within the changes inaugurated by the great revolution in Western intellectual history, called the Enlightenment. Our story, therefore, begins with the Age of Reason.

1 THE ENLIGHTENMENT: *The Shattering of the Classical Balance*

*T*HE WAY CHRISTIANS THINK ABOUT GOD, THEMSELVES AND THEIR WORLD WAS PERMA-
nently and irretrievably altered by an era in Western intellectual history commonly
known as the Enlightenment, which marked the completion of the transition from the
ancient to the modern eras. Through its challenging of authority and its emphasis on
personal faith, the Reformation contributed to the movement out of the medieval
world. But what was merely in embryonic form in the sixteenth century took full shape
first in the Enlightenment.

No longer were thinkers willing to accept the old dogmas merely on the basis that
they belonged to the received system of church doctrine. The light of reason possessed
by each individual dethroned the ecclesiastical hierarchy as the foundation of authority. No longer would simple appeal to classical theological formulations be sufficient
to settle intellectual debates. Now thinking individuals wanted to be convinced that
what they believed was reasonable. No longer were the trendsetters of culture interested in elaborate arguments of seemingly unreasonable doctrines—such as the Trinity
and Christ's substitutionary atonement—bolstered by appeal to biblical texts and the
decisions of church councils. The intellectuals of the Enlightenment sought to stream-
line religious affirmations to those universally discernable and carrying positive moral
import. Because this era so thoroughly upset both the foundations and the orientation
of Christian theology, Christian faith since the Enlightenment has never been, and can
never be, the same. So monumental is the importance of this era that there can be
no simple going behind the Age of Reason. Christians ignore the Enlightenment only

to the peril of theology. Ignoring the great changes it inaugurated only can lead to the privatization of faith, the "ghettoizing" of Christianity and the loss of the Christian voice in modern society.

A primary change brought by the Enlightenment lies in its effect on the classic quest for a transcendent-immanent theology. This era set the stage for a far-reaching alteration of the older attempt at reaching a balance between the twin truths of the divine transcendence and the divine immanence.

The patristic era came to a climax with the grand proposal of perhaps the most influential Christian theologian of all time, Augustine, bishop of Hippo. Augustine's theology served as the standard and paradigm for all Christian theologians from his day through the Middle Ages and well into the Reformation era. Although theologians differed sharply with each other on the details, all shared a basically similar world view derived to a great degree from the heritage of Augustine.

The outlook common to these otherwise quite different eras of Western history emphasized the ordering of reality, with God at the apex, followed by the angelic hosts. Humans found their place "a little lower than the heavenly beings" (Ps 8:5), yet above the animate and inanimate things in the world.

From his lofty, transcendent position above the world, God became intimately involved in history, the theologians added. He had predestined the elect to salvation and had entered human affairs repeatedly and sporadically, but supremely in Jesus Christ. And God continued to be operative in human lives by his direction of the flow of history, but especially in the church and through the imparted grace connected with the activities of the church.

The Augustinian balance was honed and tuned in the Middle Ages, only to be reformulated in the Reformation and by the Protestant scholasticism that followed. Yet through all the tinkering this balance continued to favor God's transcendence, while seeking to avoid slighting the divine immanence. The great Gothic cathedrals that mark the high point of the Middle Ages bear silent witness to the nature of the theological synthesis, the medieval balancing act between God's loftiness and God's presence with its definite tilt toward transcendence.

The Period of the Enlightenment
In the seventeenth and eighteenth centuries, the balance developed by the theologians of the Middle Ages and honed by the Reformation was permanently and radically disrupted. A new cosmology replaced the older hierarchical ordering of reality. And with this change, the balancing of transcendence over immanence was reversed.

These two centuries form an explosive era in Western intellectual history, commonly referred to as the Enlightenment. The genesis of the Enlightenment lies in the early seventeenth century, perhaps sociopolitically in the Peace of Westphalia (1648) that ended the Thirty Years' War, and intellectually with the work of Francis Bacon (1561-1626).

Bacon stands at the beginning of the Age of Reason—marking the transition from the Renaissance to the Enlightenment—in that he was one of the first modern scientists. Even though he did not place mathematics at the center of natural knowledge as did those who came after him,[1] Bacon emphasized the method of experimentation. And he employed the fledgling scientific enterprise not only as a way of understanding the universe, but also as a means of ruling over nature. In this way he laid the foundations for modern technological society.

Historians point to the closing years of the eighteenth century as the end of the Enlightenment era. The Age of Reason had virtually run its course by the time of the publication of Immanuel Kant's *Critique of Pure Reason* (1791). This book marked both a culmination of, and an effective challenge to, many of its presuppositions. Above all, Kant weighed the primacy given to rationalism and empiricism—the elevation of the powers of human reason and the emphasis on sense experience—characteristic of the era, and the German philosopher found them wanting.

The Enlightenment Human

Despite the imprecision concerning the exact dates of its genesis and demise, historians agree that the Enlightenment carried profound and lasting importance for the development of modern Western culture. Building on the Renaissance, it signaled the victory of a fundamental change in outlook that marked a final break with the medieval mentality[2] and paved the way for the modern era.

One central, fundamental change in outlook reflected in the Enlightenment was the development of a paradoxical, even seemingly self-contradictory, understanding of the human person. This era brought an elevated status to humans and an elevated estimate of human capabilities. The Enlightenment placed humans, not God, on center stage in history. In contrast to medieval and Reformation thinking, which viewed people as important largely insofar as they fit into the story of God's activity in history, Enlightenment thinkers tended to determine the importance of God in terms of his value for the story of their own lives.[3] God, then, was shifted from his lofty position in the heavens, to which the gothic cathedrals had pointed, to the world of human affairs.

To humanity's elevated status was added an optimistic anthropology. The era attributed greater intellectual and moral abilities to humankind than traditional theology, whether Catholic or Protestant, had been willing to acknowledge. Its optimistic anthropology was evident in the Enlightenment understanding of the role of human reason in the knowing process.

Prior to this era, divine revelation was consulted as the final arbiter of truth; the task of human reason was to seek to understand the truth given through revelation. The maxim attributed to Anselm governed the quest for knowledge: "I believe in order that I may understand." In keeping with this principle, the function of human reasoning abilities was to demonstrate the rightness of revealed truths and to reconcile experience with the understanding of the cosmic drama given by the Christian faith.[4]

In the Enlightenment, however, human reason replaced externally imposed revelation as the arbiter of truth, for reason now determined what constitutes revelation. Anselm's thesis was turned on its head. The newer mindset could be characterized as declaring, "I believe what I can understand." Employing reason to systematize what was given in experience and following reason wherever it would lead rather than blindly accepting the superstitions proclaimed by external authorities became the enlightened means to obtaining knowledge.[5]

The era was similarly optimistic concerning human moral capabilities. The Enlightenment placed great emphasis on morality, not dogma. And it declared that the powers of human reason could both discover and bring about conformity to the natural moral law written within each person.

Not only did the Enlightenment elevate humankind by means of its optimistic anthropology, it also pictured the human person in a way quite different from that taught by medieval theology. In this dimension as in others, the Age of Reason built from the advancements of the Renaissance. Rather than a static being, the contemplative soul of the medieval ideal, the human creature came to be viewed as a discontented transformer of the environment. In the words of Giorgio de Santillana, the human person was "a restless wanderer engaged upon an unending adventure," for whom time was "no longer the eternal circling of the heavens, but an onrushing stream."[6]

But the elevation of humankind also extracted a heavy price. Paradoxically, when compared to traditional theology the mindset of the Enlightenment marked not only the elevation but also the deprivation of the human person. The world was no longer viewed as a cosmos in which humans enjoy a special status, as in medieval and Reformation thinking. Rather, the new science of the Enlightenment pictured the universe as a giant machine of which humans were but a small part, a minuscule cog in the giant wheel of reality. Dethroned from their lofty position at the center of creation, they likewise lost their status as a special creation of God standing above the rest of the created order.

The Foundation of the Enlightenment

The monumental shift in outlook that transpired during the Enlightenment did not occur in a vacuum. On the contrary, it came as the outgrowth of various social, political and intellectual factors that led up to this traumatic era in human history. A series of military conflicts, commonly lumped together as the Thirty Years' War, had devastated Europe in the early seventeenth century. Because of their association with rival Christian confessions, these wars led to widespread questioning of the validity of doctrinal disputes. But in addition to the religious quarrels of the century, the intellectual pathway was opened for the critical spirit of the age by two interrelated revolutions, one in philosophy and another in science.

First, the Enlightenment was the product of a philosophical revolution. Although its roots lay earlier, in the discussions of the medieval theologians, this revolution was inaugurated by the French thinker René Descartes (1596-1650), who is often dubbed the father of modern philosophy.[7] Descartes' intent was to devise a method of investigation that would lead to the discovery of those truths that were absolutely certain. Lying behind the method he proposed was the pre-eminence of mathematics that came to characterize the seventeenth century. The ascendancy of the mathematical model arose in the Renaissance out of the emphasis on the quantitative (rather than qualitative) dimensions of reality so central to the work of Kepler and Galileo.

Descartes typified the emerging Age of Reason in that he, like most of the great philosophers of the period, attempted to introduce the rigor of mathematical demonstration into all fields of knowledge.[8] His elevation of mathematical knowledge was not merely arbitrary, however. Rather, mathematics arises from the nature of reason itself, he argued, and therefore it is more certain than knowledge derived from empirical observation, which may err.

The French philosopher introduced "doubt" as the first principle of reasoning. But for him, unlike certain empiricists of the next century, the process of doubting did not lead to skepticism. On the contrary, it resulted in certainty, for as the mind doubts everything, the certainty of the existence of the doubting subject—the individual engaging in this activity—emerges. Hence the well-known adage of Cartesian philosophy: *cogito, ergo sum* ("I think; therefore, I am").

Descartes' work greatly influenced subsequent thinking.[9] From this point on, the reasoning subject and not divine revelation formed the beginning point for philosophy. The move to reason inaugurated by Descartes placed theology in a difficult predicament. Theologians sensed a need either to build on the foundation of rationalistic philosophy, thereby accepting the primacy of reason (the position of Enlightenment thinkers), or to deny that reason by itself is able to yield knowledge of eternal realities.[10] The emphasis on the voice of reason within, rather than the voice of God from above, set the stage for the orientation to immanence characteristic of modern theology since Descartes.

In addition to the revolution in philosophy, the Enlightenment was the product of a revolution in science that marked a radical departure from the world view of the Middle Ages. Central to the new thinking was a change in cosmology, prepared for by Copernicus' discovery that the earth was not the center of the universe. The shift in cosmology meant the rejection of the three-story structure of the medieval outlook, which placed heaven spatially above the earth and hell beneath it.

Perhaps even more foundational to the scientific revolution that inaugurated the Enlightenment, however, was a change in understanding of the physical world itself and the proper approach to talking about it. This change was marked by a shift from qualitative to quantitative terminology. Medieval science, following Aristotle, had focused on "natural principles," understood in terms of the "natural" tendency of every object to fulfill its own inner purpose. The Enlightenment, however, rejected the medieval discussion of "inner purpose" as metaphysical speculation.

In the Age of Reason, the earlier emphasis on final causes (the *telos,* or purpose, of objects) gave way to the mathematical, quantifying view of the scientific enterprise pioneered by Galileo (1564-1642). Precise methods of measurement and the acceptance of mathematics as the purest mode of reason formed the tools for the proper approach to the study of natural processes. Observers described phenomena in terms of laws of nature that yielded quantifiable results. Its adherence to this method meant that the Enlightenment mind treated as real only those aspects of the universe that are measurable.[11]

Enlightenment thinkers applied the new methodology pioneered by thinkers such as Descartes and Galileo to all disciplines of knowledge. Not only natural science but also politics, ethics, metaphysics and theology came under the rubric of the scientific canons. Even philosophy was affected. In fact, all fields of human endeavor became, in effect, branches of natural science.

The high-water mark of this revolution in science was reached with the work of Isaac Newton (1642-1727). The universe he described was a grand, orderly machine, whose movements could be known because they followed certain observable laws. As a result, Newton directed attention toward the explanation of the universe. He set out to show that the properties and behavior of every particle could be determined, at least in principle, by a relatively few fundamental laws. The nineteenth-century historian Alexander Pope capsulized his program and its impact in a jesting couplet:

Nature and Nature's laws lay hid in Night

God said, "Let Newton be!" and all was Light.[12]

Newton's own goal, however, was theological, not merely scientific. He believed that science enhanced human understanding of the greatness of God. The heavens declare the glory of God, he knew. His task was to discover how.

Enlightenment Principles

In essence, the revolutions in philosophy and science that spawned the Enlightenment focused on the elevation of reason over "superstition." As a result, the epoch earned the appropriate designation, the Age of Reason. While reason was surely at the center of the mindset of the age, the Enlightenment was characterized by several principles that together with "reason" formed a unified whole. Significant among these are "autonomy," "nature," "harmony" and "progress."[13]

The first principle of the Enlightenment was indeed reason. This era placed great emphasis on the human rational capability. But the Enlightenment understanding viewed reason as more than simply the human endowment itself. Reminiscent of ancient Greek and Roman Stoicism, the principle of reason meant that a fundamental order and structure lay within all reality and was evidenced in the workings of the human mind. As a result of the correspondence between the structure of reality and that of the human mind, Enlightenment thinkers concluded, the mind is able to discern and come to know the structure inherent in the external world.

The principle of reason, therefore, referred to the human capability of becoming cognizant of the foundational order of the whole universe. This objective rationality of the universe made the laws of nature intelligible and the world capable of being transformed and subdued by human activity. Likewise the consonance of the rational world and the workings of the human mind made the exercise of critical reason so important.

Closely related to the principle of reason was a second principle, "nature," the emphasis on what is grounded in or arises from "the very nature of things." The Enlightenment mind postulated that the universe was an orderly realm in which inhered the laws of nature. Nature and natural law, therefore, became the watchwords of the intellectual quest.

Enlightenment thinkers asserted that the orderliness found in "the very nature of things" was present because of the working of the grand Designer of nature. As a consequence of this belief, the enlightened mind looked to the "book of nature," which lay open for all to read, in order to find the laws of God. The universal availability of these "natural laws" transformed nature into the common court of appeal, the arbiter of all quarrels. And the goal of the human intellectual endeavor became that of bringing life into conformity with the laws of nature as discovered by reason.

"Reason" and "nature" opened the way for the third principle of the Enlightenment mindset—"autonomy." As noted earlier, in this epoch the autonomous human dethroned external authority as the arbiter of truth and action. No longer would simple appeal to the teaching office of the church, the Bible or Christian dogma be sufficient to bring about compliance in belief or conduct. The individual would now test all such external claims to authority. Immanuel Kant aptly summarized the principle of autonomy and its role in the Enlightenment:

> Enlightenment is man's release from his self-incurred tutelage. Tutelage is man's inability to make use of his understanding without direction from another. Self-incurred is this tutelage when its cause lies not in lack of reason but in lack of resolution and courage to use it without direction from another. . . . "Have courage to use your own reason"—that is the motto of enlightenment.[14]

The principle of autonomy did not give license for lawlessness, however. The Enlightenment was no antinomian era. Rather, autonomy presupposed the presence in the world of a universal natural law knowable by human reason. Rather than open the door to lawlessness, therefore, autonomy demanded that each person discover and follow the universal natural law. The way toward the discovery of the natural law lay in the use of the personal endowment of reason and conscience, rather than in mere reliance on external authorities. Thus, personal employment of reason lay at the heart of the Enlightenment emphasis on autonomy.

"Harmony," the fourth principle of the Enlightenment, built on the idea of the reasonableness and orderliness of the universe as postulated by the Age of Reason. The universe, thinkers asserted, is characterized by an overarching order, which guaranteed that despite the apparent selfish and independent activity of each person or thing in the universe the whole would turn out most adequately.

The inherent harmony of the world meant likewise that truth is a single, harmonious whole. Consequently, the Enlightenment mind elevated "proper methodology." It believed that the application of the proper method of discovery to the hitherto disjointed and seemingly contradictory disciplines of human knowledge would cleanse them of their irrational elements and bring them together into the one true philosophy.

Here again, however, the Enlightenment avoided the antinomian impulse that such an idea could generate. Harmony was not merely a characteristic of the realm of nature. It also became a type of ethical principle for the governing of human action. Humans were to act in accordance with the overarching harmony of the whole of reality.

The Enlightenment anthropology served to facilitate the desired correspondence of human life with the harmony of the cosmos. This anthropology elevated the inherent potential of the human person and set aside the Christian emphasis on depravity. If the human mind, which begins as a blank slate as John Locke had shown, could be shaped by divinely created nature, ethicists argued, then the employment of reason could indeed bring human life into harmony with the universal natural order.[15]

Finally, the Enlightenment was an era of optimistic belief in progress. Building on the work of Descartes and others, thinkers in the Age of Reason were convinced that because the universe was both orderly and knowable, the employment of a proper methodology could lead to true knowledge. So philosophers, theologians and scientists alike set forth to construct their systems, which they believed approximated truth. In fact, this era was, in the words of Isaiah Berlin, "the last period in the history of Western Europe when human omniscience was thought to be an attainable goal."[16]

But the attainment of knowledge was not merely an end in itself. According to the Enlightenment mindset, knowledge of nature's laws had practical import. Their discovery and application formed the pathway toward making humans happy, rational and free. If nature's laws could be known, the truths they teach could be implemented in personal and social life. Scientific method could change the world. Enlightenment thinkers believed that such change was just around the corner.

The optimistic belief in progress arose as well from the Enlightenment reading of history. Historians in the Age of Reason painted the Middle Ages as an era of superstition and barbarism out of which humankind was now emerging. Because of the progress they noted in their own time, Enlightenment thinkers were optimistic about the future. Despite the ebb and flow of history, they were convinced that the process was directed upward and forward. Therefore they looked to the future with hope, "as to a promised land."[17] If humans could learn to live in the light of the laws of nature, then the utopia could indeed dawn. As Isaiah Berlin rightly concluded, this age "was one of the most hopeful episodes in the life of mankind."[18]

Enlightenment Religion

The Enlightenment era challenged traditional viewpoints and reformulated thinking in every area of Western society. However, no dimension was more affected than religious belief. The Age of Reason marked the emancipation of culture from the dominance of church and Christianity.

The movement toward the autonomy of culture came as the inevitable result of the new scientific mentality of the era, which inaugurated a changed understanding of the nature of religion. Increasingly both scientists and theologians differentiated between "natural religion"—God's existence and the moral laws known to all peoples and demonstrable by reason—and "revealed religion"—doctrines as taught by the Bible and the church. As the era progressed, the latter came increasingly under attack and the former was elevated to the status of true religion. In the end, Enlightenment "natural religion" or the religion of reason replaced the focus on dogma and doctrine characteristic of the Middle Ages and the Reformation.

The intellectual path to the primacy of natural over revealed religion was paved by the British empiricist John Locke. He set forth the revolutionary thesis that Christianity, when divested of its dogmatic baggage, was the most reasonable form of religion. On the basis of Locke's views, Enlightenment thinkers constructed a theological alternative to orthodoxy—deism. The theologians of deism sought to reduce religion to its most basic elements, which they believed to be universal and therefore reasonable.[19]

Because natural religion is reasonable, the deists added, all religions, including Christianity, must conform to it.[20] Hence, the various dogmas of the church as given by revelation no longer served as the standard. Rather, all such doctrines were to be evaluated based on a comparison with the religion of reason. The result was a religion consisting of a bare minimum of dogmas to be believed:[21] the existence of God as provable by the causality of the world, the immortality of the soul and postmortem retribution for sin and blessing for virtue.[22]

Actually, the deists did not view religion primarily as a system of belief at all. More important was its ethical import. Religion's chief role, they postulated, was that of providing divine sanction for morality.[23] At the same time, the Enlightenment elevated the human capacity to attain religious truth, reducing—even eliminating—the need for revealed religion. What was truly important had been written by the Creator in the great book of nature left open for all to read.

Consequently, some Enlightenment voices were harshly critical of Christianity, claiming that it was, at least in its traditional form, a corruption of the religion of reason.[24] Enlightenment thinkers also attacked the central pillars of the Christian apologetic of the day, the appeal to fulfilled prophecy[25] and to miracles.[26] And they cast ecclesiastical authorities in the role of perpetrators of ignorance and past superstitions.

Others simply equated the two belief systems, claiming that Christianity in its purest form is but a restatement of the religion known by reason. Those who sought a continued place for Christianity carved out a niche for it by setting forth revealed religion as the necessary supplement to the religion of reason[27] or by presenting it as one historic stage in the ongoing process that would climax in the coming of the perfect, universal religion in the future.

Regardless of how Christianity was viewed, the Enlightenment elevation of the religion of reason and its emphasis on nature and nature's God constituted a victory of the new immanence—as paradoxical as this might appear—over the transcendence that epitomized the Middle Ages. The God of the deists was a far-away, radically transcendent deity. Yet the Enlightenment outlook worked to bind God closely to nature and human reason, so closely that God's transcendence came to be dissolved in the immanence of the divine within the orderly realm of creation and reason. Rather than look beyond the world to find God, the Enlightenment ultimately turned within. The shift begun in the Renaissance was now complete. And the triumph of immanence would extend into the twentieth century.

2 THE RECONSTRUCTION OF TRANSCENDENCE: *Immanence in Nineteenth-Century Theology*

A S THE EIGHTEENTH CENTURY DREW TO A CLOSE, THE ERA OF THE ENLIGHTENMENT HAD run its course, especially in England. By this time, many thinkers had abandoned the religion of reason for either skepticism[1] or religious relativism.[2] These thinkers had concluded that in the end reason is incompetent to answer the basic questions about God, morality and the meaning of life.

Although the Enlightenment had come to an end, theology would never be the same again. No subsequent theological trends could remain aloof to the developments of that epoch in the intellectual history of the West. From that point on, theologians would need to speak in terms understandable to the mindset put into place by the phenomenal changes washed up on the intellectual shores of Europe during those decades.

The closing of the Age of Reason appeared to leave religion in a predicament. It seemed that the eighteenth century had presented only two alternatives. One could opt for the traditional Christian emphasis on human sin and divine salvation, maintained by appeal to the Bible and the church. Or one was forced to follow the modern skeptical rationalism that arose as the final product of the enlightened individual mind. As McGiffert concluded in his monumental study of the pre-Kantian era, "At the close of the century the religious crisis was acute."[3]

In the nineteenth century, however, certain theologians refused to be boxed in by these options. They knew, of course, that there was no going behind the Age of Reason. Theology could never again resurrect the older belief system, because the traditional authorities of Bible and church had been dethroned forever. While agreeing that theology could not simply return to pre-Enlightenment dogmatic orthodoxy, they refused to accept post-Enlightenment skeptical rationalism as the only alternative. For this new breed of intellectuals the only way forward in the aftermath of the Enlightenment lay in incorporating its basic thrust and engaging in a search for new ways to understand the Christian faith. The theologians of the nineteenth century boldly maintained that in the face of the challenge of the Enlightenment and despite the skeptical dead end in which it had culminated, the theological enterprise could continue. Hence, they sought to move beyond the Enlightenment while incorporating the advances it had made. More specifically, they attempted to establish a new relationship between trancendence and immanence in the wake of the shattering of the medieval balance.

In the task of reconstructing theology in the post-Enlightenment world, nineteenth-century theologians had in their arsenal the weapons created by three intellectual giants. By this time the legacy of Western thought had been transferred to Germany, to which the Age of Reason had come later, but in whose theological circles it had gained a deeper rootage than in England. Consequently, all three shapers of nineteenth-century theology were German—Immanuel Kant, G. W. F. Hegel and Friedrich Schleiermacher.

These three thinkers were similar in that each sought to carve out a special domain for the religious component of life. Yet they differed sharply, for each proposed a different dimension as the essence of religion—the moral (Kant), the intellectual (Hegel), and the intuitive (Schleiermacher). The shadows of these three thinkers were cast across the intellectual landscape of the nineteenth century, competing but finally being blended together to produce what came to be known as nineteenth-century Protestant liberal theology and epitomized in a fourth German thinker, Albrecht Ritschl.

Despite the gallant efforts of its gifted thinkers, as the century moved toward its close theology discovered that it had not overcome the Enlightenment. The emphasis on the new immanence, so much a part of the human vision since the Renaissance, continued to lie at the foundation of theology's reconstructed house.

IMMANUEL KANT:
THE IMMANENCE OF GOD IN MORAL EXPERIENCE

The great thinkers of the nineteenth century attempted to move beyond the impasse that resulted from the Enlightenment by determining the special place of religion in human life. A first possible candidate was proposed by the eighteenth-century German philosopher Immanuel Kant (1724-1804). Kant proposed the practical or moral realm of life as the proper sphere of religion. By constructing theology from its proper foundation in the practical reason, he offered a new attempted balance between transcendence and immanence.

Chronologically and intellectually Kant stands closer to the Enlightenment than do

Hegel and Schleiermacher. His intellectual proximity is evidenced in his elevation of the ethical dimension of life as the central concern of religion, an understanding that lay near the heart of the ethos of the Age of Reason. Yet his method of establishing morally oriented religion differed immensely from that of the Enlightenment.

Kant's life was outwardly uneventful. He was born, studied, taught and died in the same place—the east Prussian port city of Königsberg. He served as an unsalaried lecturer at the university (1755-1770) before being elected professor of logic and metaphysics. Kant was unmarried and untraveled. His schedule was so regimented that the women of the town are said to have set their watches by his 3:30 p.m. daily walk. Not until he was fifty-seven years old did Kant produce a major work. Yet the book he did publish that year, *The Critique of Pure Reason* (1781), rocked the philosophical world and inaugurated an intellectual tidal wave, the effects of which are still being felt.

Kant's Philosophy

Immanuel Kant set into motion what he saw as a "Copernican Revolution" in philosophy. Just as the great astronomer replaced the earth with the sun as the center of the solar system, so also Kant elevated the mind to the center of human knowing (epistemology). Kant theorized that the possibility of experiencing reality was dependent on the mind.

The background to Kant's revolution lay in the grave problem of epistemology bequeathed by empiricism, the philosophical movement that came to characterize the Age of Reason in Britain. Central to empiricism's understanding of the process of knowing was what might be called "the passive mind." In his *Essay Concerning Human Understanding* John Locke, rejecting a central thesis of Cartesian philosophy, argued that the mind was a tabula rasa, an empty vessel devoid of any innate ideas. As a result, it is passive in the knowing process. It simply receives "impressions" from the external world through the senses and then formulates ideas from the impressions it has gathered.

At first glance the empiricist theory appears to be an obvious truth, a simple explanation of common, day-to-day experience. Yet the end product of this theory of knowing was the skepticism of David Hume, who showed its inadequacy as an explanation of human cognition. The empirical method, he argued, is unable to give us knowledge of certain features of reality we take for granted, most significantly, causality and substance. All we know are our perceptions, Hume declared. These perceptions include the coincidence of a sequence of events, from which we induce, but do not actually experience, a relationship of causality. Similarly, we experience a series of impressions (size, color, and so forth), but not of actual substances. Our imagination attributes these impressions to objects. According to Hume, we have no actual knowledge of substances as existing in the world. In fact, the identity of such external objects, just like causality, is not found "out there," but is merely the result of a habit of the mind.

Hume's epistemological skepticism had important consequences for religious belief, for it led to a questioning of deism, the religion built on the edifice of empiricism. He showed that the arguments for the reasonableness of natural religion are not as certain as their proponents had believed. The cosmological argument, for example, could not prove the existence of God, if causation was not an experienced phenomenon. Nor could the doctrine of the immortality of the soul survive the demise of the concept of substance. And the injustice and evil of the present undercut the case for a future realm of retributive justice on the basis of the goodness of the Creator.[4]

Kant found Hume's radical skepticism challenging. In fact, he reported that it was Hume who had awakened him from his own "dogmatic slumber." Kant's probing of the problem led him to an explanation of the limitation of the human epistemological process Hume had discovered. But unlike his British predecessor, Kant believed that this limitation did not demand a skeptical rejection of all metaphysical concepts.

In the *Critique of Pure Reason* (1781) Kant sought to set metaphysics on firm footing. To this end, he proposed a bold hypothesis: The mind is "active" in the knowing process. Knowledge of the external world, he argued, cannot be derived from sense experience alone. The senses merely furnish the raw data that the mind systematizes when actual knowing occurs. This organizing of sensations (knowledge), he added, is made possible by certain formal concepts present in the mind, which act as a type of grid or filter providing the parameters that make knowing possible.[5]

Among the various formal concepts, two are foundational: space and time. According to Kant, space and time are not properties that inhere in things. Rather, these two categories, like other formal structures, are a part of the ordering that the mind imposes on the world it encounters. Although objects may not actually exist in space and time, we simply cannot know the external world of sense experience in any other way than in terms of these two concepts, he postulated.

The hypothesis that the mind is active in the epistemological process demanded a distinction between objects present in the experience of the human knower ("phenomena") and objects lying beyond experience ("noumena"). According to Kant, a "noumenon" could be either an object as it exists apart from any relation to a knowing subject (the "thing-in-itself") or an object for which we simply lack the needed apparatus to detect. As we will see later, the category of the noumena also opened to Kant a realm beyond cause and effect in which he could ascribe freedom to the acting human moral agent.

Like Hume's, Kant's theory of knowing placed great limits on the ability of thinkers to argue from sense experience to transcendent realities, such as God, the immortal soul and human freedom. The position Kant developed in the *Critique of Pure Reason* meant that any reality that lies beyond space and time cannot be known through the scientific enterprise, because science is based on sense experience. "Pure" or speculative reason (science) can at most indicate that these metaphysical concepts are plausible, in that nothing we know in the empirical world contradicts them.

By showing the limits of empirical knowledge the *Critique of Pure Reason* placed realities that transcend space and time (such as God) beyond the realm of scientific, sense-based experience. Although at first glance this move appears to make such realities unknowable, Kant's intention was not to prove the religious skepticism of

Hume. Rather, he desired to approach metaphysical postulates from a more secure direction. He believed, as he later explained in the *Critique of Judgment,* if the reality of God were demonstrated by argument from sense-based experience, it would be difficult to view God in moral categories,[6] which was Kant's own aim. In the second edition of the *Critique of Pure Reason* he explained: "I have therefore found it necessary to deny *knowledge,* in order to make room for *faith.*"[7] For the German philosopher, "faith" belonged to another domain of human reason—reason in its "practical" aspect—which he placed in relationship to the moral dimension of human existence.

Practical Reason

By showing the fallacy of all theoretical proofs of metaphysical postulates, the first *Critique* clipped the wings of "pure" or speculative reason. But the task of establishing these postulates by some other means remained. The securing of the concepts of God, immortality and freedom came about in Kant's moral writings, especially his *Fundamental Principles of the Metaphysics of Morals* (1785), *Critique of Practical Reason* (1788) and *Metaphysic of Morals* (1797). His goal in these works was to investigate the concepts necessary to reason in its practical aspect, just as he had explored reason in its theoretical aspect in his *Critique of Pure Reason.*

At the foundation of Kant's argument is the thesis that the human person is not only a being of sense experience but also a moral being. Our relation to the world is not limited to scientific knowledge, he noted. Rather, the world is a stage on which humans act; it is a realm of moral value. Kant established the moral nature of existence by appeal to what he saw as the universal human moral experience, a sense of moral conditionedness or of "ought." Human beings are cognizant of a "pressure" placed on them to make choices that can be described only in terms of morality, he declared.

Like the theoretical, this practical or moral dimension of human existence is fundamentally rational, Kant argued. As a result, he was convinced that certain rational principles control all valid moral judgments, just as other rational principles lie at the foundation of all theoretical or sense-based knowledge. Consequently, the goal of the moral dimension of human life was to become as rational as possible. Kant spoke of this rationally moral way of living in terms of "duty."

For Kant, the way of duty culminates in the supreme principle of morality, his famous categorical imperative. Basically this principle requires that each human seek to act in accordance with whatever motivating consideration he or she as a rational being could will to be universally followed. In his words: "Act as if the maxim of thy action were to become by thy will a Universal Law of Nature."[8] As this definition indicates, the categorical imperative focuses less on specific actions and more on the motivating considerations underlying action.[9]

The Practical Postulates

The moral nature of human existence as testified to by the universal experience of moral conditionedness was foundational to Kant's reestablishment of metaphysics. On the basis of this dimension of life he argued for the certainty of the three transcendental postulates that theoretical reason could not establish. These "practical postulates" must be assumed, he argued, because they are required by the moral nature of the world.

The first two postulates, God and immortality, arose out of Kant's understanding of the *summum bonum*. The highest good for humankind, he maintained, is to live in a realm in which virtue and happiness are linked. We all know, however, that in this life virtue is not always rewarded. Therefore, Kant concluded, there must be a future life in which virtuous living is adequately rewarded, and God must exist as the one who guarantees that complete justice will indeed prevail in that realm.

Kant's argument for the postulate of freedom is especially far-reaching. Human freedom is required, he maintained, in order to account for the universal human experience of being an acting moral agent. In the phenomenal dimension humans, as physical beings, are subject to the laws of nature and therefore do not appear to be free. In the underlying noumenal realm, however, each person must be free, because moral obligation presupposes freedom. This argument served to place the human person simultaneously in two realms. Each individual must be understood both morally (as a free acting agent) and scientifically (as coming under the laws of physical causation).

Reasonable Religion

In *Religion within the Limits of Reason Alone* (1793), Kant sought to take his program one step farther, moving from morality to religion (that is, Christianity). For him this step was necessary, because religion provides the ultimate goal for morality, for it speaks of "a powerful moral Lawgiver" whose will "ought to be man's final end."[10]

This book, like Kant's work in general, marked both a continuation of and a break with the Enlightenment. He began with a discussion of "radical evil," the universal presence within us of a tendency toward evil that we cannot root out by our own powers. From the perspective of the Age of Reason, in this discussion the German philosopher had committed an unforgivable transgression.[11] He had reintroduced the specific doctrine—original sin—that had been the object of the Enlightenment's most vehement critique of Christianity.

Yet Kant had not broken completely with the Enlightenment, for he retained the basic optimism of the age. Because radical evil is found in the human person "whose actions are free," he added, "it must be possible to *overcome* it."[12]

In order to hold to both of these theses at the same time, the German philosopher differentiated between the evil principle that he saw present in our actual will and the categorical imperative that he declared coincides with our essential will. In this way Kant constructed what G. E. Michaelson, Jr., has termed "an unstable conflation of a Reformation emphasis on the fall and an Enlightenment accent of freedom."[13]

Kant's understanding of religion as essentially ethical molded his Christology. He described the goal of creation as the coming into being of a morally perfect humankind. This goal is eternally present in the divine mind as God's only-begotten Son, who is the object of our faith.[14] True to Enlightenment thinking, Kant argued that because this idea is also present in our reason, we need no "empirical example" to serve as the archetype of "the idea of a person morally well-pleasing to God." Nevertheless, in his attempt to take seriously the Christian tradition, he added that there is one historical exemplar of this ideal—Jesus—or more specifically, Jesus' disposition in the face of his suffering "for the sake of the world's highest good."[15]

The ethical essence of religion likewise shaped Kant's understanding of the importance of Christianity. In keeping with the Enlightenment, he subordinated Christianity to the universal religion of reason. For him, Christianity is but a means toward the establishment of the ethical commonwealth, a stage in the gradual coming of "pure religious faith."

The changes brought by the Enlightenment colored as well his understanding of religious authority. While acknowledging Scripture as the sole norm in the church, Kant declared that the "pure religion of reason"—which alone is authentic and universally valid—is the interpretive principle of Scripture.[16] He concluded that the moral dimension (that is, "virtue striving toward holiness") is the true meaning lying behind the biblical stories.[17] And he looked for the timeless truth of the faith lying *behind* the Christian story, namely:

> that there exists no salvation for man apart from the sincerest adoption of genuinely moral principles into his disposition; that what works against this adoption is not so much the sensuous nature, which so often receives the blame, as it is a certain self-incurred perversity . . . which the human race has brought upon itself.[18]

Finally, Kant reinterpreted the category of grace. Although he acknowledged that the biblical narrative is important, the German philosopher emphasized "that true religion is to consist not in the knowing or considering of what God does or has done for our salvation but in what we must do to become worthy of it."[19] And what we can do is simply to live morally.[20] Kant, therefore, reversed the order of grace and works central to the Reformation. "The right course is not to go from grace to virtue," he concluded, "but rather to progress from virtue to pardoning grace."[21]

Theology Grounded in Morality

The approach set forth by Kant laid an innovative foundation for theology. He did indeed infer certain central religious doctrines, specifically the reality of God and the immortality and freedom of the human person. However, in contrast to the classical theologians who argued from revelation to the attributes of God's being, Kant, not unlike Descartes, constructed his system solely on the basis of the human person as a being of reason. Thus, his method did not move from revelation to reason, but from reason to revelation. In this way Kant carried forth the Enlightenment program of delineating a purely rational faith.

Yet one important innovation separated Kant from the Age of Reason. Unlike his forebears, it was not reason in the abstract that informed his proposal. Foundational to religion is a particular dimension of human existence, the experience of moral conditionedness, he argued, which was connected to the practical aspect of reason. As a result, Kant affirmed only those metaphysical postulates that he saw as necessary to account for that dimension of human existence (such as God, immortality and freedom). By extension of this methodology, he ascribed to the divine nature only those attributes necessary for God as moral guarantor.[22] Kant, therefore, could claim no knowledge of the divine nature beyond the moral dimension. He did not ground morality in theology, as in classical Christian thinking, but theology in morality.

When viewed in the context of theological history, Kant's work marked the final demise of the deism of the Enlightenment. The Age of Reason viewed the tenets of natural religion as secure (in contrast to the shaky dogmas of revealed religion), because they were built on the appeal to the unshakable edifice of reason that employed the method of empirical investigation (what Kant termed "pure reason"). Kant, however, showed that deism's core metaphysical principles—God's existence, the soul's immortality and human freedom—could not be established by speculative reason. He thereby confirmed what the skeptics had surmised. This pathway to religion was forever blocked. The philosopher had offered a far-reaching insight into creaturely human finitude, an insight that all subsequent theology would need to take seriously.

But the dead end of Enlightenment religion did not mark the end of theology. It was possible to ground religion on some other faculty of the mind, some other dimension of the human reality. To this end Kant employed the Enlightenment emphasis on morality, but set it on firmer footing. Religion could be established, he argued, on the basis of practical reason—the ethical dimension of existence and the corresponding moral faculty of the mind. For him, the moral sphere is the proper domain of religion. There it reigns supreme, shielded from the findings of science.

Conclusion

In many respects Kant's work set the stage for subsequent discussions in both philosophy and theology. It constituted an articulate response to the Enlightenment while incorporating the major advances of that epoch. In the end, however, he was not able to overcome certain destructive tendencies of the age. He sought to establish religion as the devotion to a transcendent Lawgiver whose will ought to be the goal of humankind.

Yet the theology produced by Kant's method remained anthropocentric. And it leads inescapably to an emphasis on the divine immanence he himself so strenuously rejected. Ultimately, the "divine voice" universally heard by autonomous human reason—whether pure (the Enlightenment) or practical (Kant)—is a voice from within the self. It does not comprise a word from the transcendent "beyond." In the case of Kant's proposal, the transcendent God is easily lost in the voice of the categorical imperative found in the depths of human "practical reason."

G. W. F. HEGEL:
THE IMMANENCE OF GOD IN SPECULATIVE REASON

Immanuel Kant sought to overcome the Enlightenment and establish a new relation between transcendence and immanence by shifting the focus of religion from the domain of "pure reason" (the realm of sense-based knowledge) to that of "practical reason" (the realm of knowledge based on the experience of the human person as a morally conditioned being). A second alternative to the Enlightenment was offered by another great German philosopher, G. W. F. Hegel. Whereas Kant found the clue to the transcendent in the ethical dimension of human life, Hegel looked to the intellectual dimension for that sense of transcendence. He linked ultimate truth with the process of human history and the capability of the human mind to comprehend the meaning of that process. As humankind understands history, he boldly asserted, God comes to knowledge of himself.

Hegel's Career

The life of Georg Wilhelm Friedrich Hegel (1770-1831) spans a turbulent time in European history. This was the era of Napoleon, on the one hand, and of Romanticism, on the other. Born in Stuttgart, Hegel was raised in that part of Germany which, in the words of Carl J. Friedrich, "has been the cradle of more thinkers and poets than any other German region."[1] It is no wonder, then, that Hegel's thought blended interests in both the political and the aesthetic dimensions of human existence.

Unlike Kant who spent his entire life in the East Prussian city of his birth, Hegel's education and professional career took him to several cities of central Europe.[2] After completing his training at the University of Tübingen (where his philosophy would later have such deep impact on theological studies), he served as a tutor first at Berne, Switzerland (1791-1796) and then at Frankfurt (1796-1800). At this point in his life Hegel was concerned chiefly with his theological antecedents and the heritage of Kant.[3] A formative stage of the development of his thinking occurred during his tenure as professor at the University of Jena (1801-1806), for here he explored the full outworking of the concept of *Geist* (spirit), so central to his philosophy. At the height of his career Hegel moved to Heidelberg and then to Berlin (1818), where he labored until his death.

Hegel's Philosophy

Hegel proposed to overcome the roadblocks to the theological enterprise set up by the Enlightenment by constructing a grand joining of theology with philosophy. Therefore, in order to understand his solution to the impasse created by the eighteenth century and his importance for nineteenth-century theology, we must look to his innovative proposal for philosophy.

Hegel's philosophy marked an important break with the Age of Reason. He agreed with the Enlightenment that philosophy is related to the attainment of truth, but he redefined the focus of the philosophical enterprise. As a nonhistorically oriented epoch, the Age of Reason had reshaped philosophy into the image of natural science and thereby had hoped to find truth—and God—in the realm of nature. Nature was viewed as a static reality, a finished product. As such it was the object of human knowledge. And its delicately adjusted machinery implied the existence of a Designer.

The German philosopher agreed with the emphasis on objective, scientific knowledge championed by the empiricists of the Age of Reason. But he denied that sense experience was the only basis for knowledge or that forming ideas from sense experience was the most significant method of obtaining knowledge. Nor did he agree with his predecessors that reality is static and complete—an objective, external given that reason could grasp. Instead Hegel taught that reality is active and developing. It is an ongoing process that consists of the actual unfolding of the principle of rationality. Not only is reality logical (as the Enlightenment thinkers believed), logic is in a sense reality, he asserted, for what is rational is actual.[4]

On this basis Hegel proposed a more complex understanding of reality and human knowledge, one that focused on the structure of rational thinking. For him, the structure of thought and the structure of reality are ultimately one; both are a dynamic process.[5]

In contrast to the Enlightenment theorists, the German thinker placed philosophy above the sciences. He viewed philosophy as a means not only toward the discovery of but also toward the coming into being of ultimate truth.

In keeping with this, Hegel forged a close link between philosophy and history. In fact, as Henry D. Aiken noted, his program constituted the first "thoroughgoing attempt to view all philosophical problems and concepts, including the concept of reason itself, in essentially historical terms."[6] In seeking to answer the problem of human destiny and the meaning of existence,[7] he hoped to find God not in nature as its aloof Designer but in "the Idea," in the meaning that lies behind the process of the human story as a whole.

Three related concepts capsulize Hegel's attempt to envision reality in a new way: spirit, truth as process and the dialectic.

Spirit

The first idea central to Hegel's thought is *Geist,* which is commonly rendered in English by "spirit." Actually, no English word is an adequate equivalent for this term. It combines the concept of rationality reflected in the word *mind* with the dimension of the supermaterial bound up with *spirit.*

For Hegel, Spirit is not merely a substance (an existing thing), but an active subject, an activity, a process. Although present in humans, it is not to be equated with the human spirit, for it is the inner being of the world, the Absolute, even the sole Reality.[8] The world process, in turn, is the activity of Spirit. Through that process Spirit takes on objective form and comes to full awareness of itself. Hence, Hegel viewed all processes in nature and history as forming a unified whole and as the manifestation of a spiritual principle underlying them.

Truth as Process

The second important idea in Hegel's philosophy is his understanding of truth as process. The German philosopher did not view truth as the rational conclusions reached from the employment of the proper reasoning pattern (as was the concern of philosophy at least since Descartes). Rather, truth is the process itself. It is the whole, the ebb and flow, the twists and turns of the process of reasoning that eventually leads to resolution.

Hegel noticed likewise that the reasoning process does not view its object as external to itself, but contains that object within itself. He called this activity of reason grasping its object "conception." The ultimate conception, the gathering of all conceptions into a connected whole, Hegel termed "the Idea" or the conception of the Absolute. "Conception," therefore, involves the merging of thought and reality,[9] which is possible because reality reflects a rational structure.

Hegel linked the truth of reality with the process of history, which he viewed as Spirit coming to self-awareness. In fact, this "whole" is not merely one characteristic of reality; for Hegel it *is* reality.[10] The different epochs in human history are the stages through which Spirit passes enroute to self-discovery.[11] Hence, truth is history—viewed not as the isolated facts, but as the grand unity lying behind and revealed in the ongoing historical process. Knowledge, in turn, lies in the philosophical mastery of the patterns produced by the historical process, the grasping of the meaning of the whole.

Because of his orientation toward the ebb and flow of history, Hegel had a deep appreciation for the past. We must comprehend our heritage in order to attain true knowledge, he argued. But above all, he was interested in those dimensions that give expression to the human spirit: society, religion, ethics, art, literature and music. In the history of human culture (expressed in these activities), the human spirit encounters its own conscious life, he theorized.[12] This process, however, is no mere human activity. It is rather the activity of Spirit. Through the historical process absolute knowledge emerges. But this knowledge is Spirit knowing itself.

Dialectic

Of the various aspects of Hegel's philosophy, the most widely known is his dialectic. This dimension is related to his thesis of the dynamic nature of philosophy. In his view, philosophy is concerned with the reality that presents itself, or comes to know itself, through the ongoing process of life. Like the movement of Spirit itself, philosophy creates the various stages of its own history as it passes through them, and this activity is its truth. In each stage, the preceding stage is carried into the next as its foundation, but it is also negated. Hence, the previous stage is both preserved and suspended. Understood in this way, truth includes what it negates as it passes to the next stage of its history.

Hegel, therefore, replaced the traditional notion of static being with the dynamic concept of process. The active process of truth includes within itself becoming and passing away. And because all is in flux, the quest for truth is the study of the process in which truth emerges.

This carried an important implication for Hegel's understanding of logic. Traditional logic is based on the law of noncontradiction (A is not non-A). As such it presupposes a static outlook toward reality.

The German philosopher rejected the static outlook, turning instead to a dynamic understanding reminiscent of the ancient Greek philosopher Heraclitus. According to

Hegel, reality is in flux, and the course of development from potentiality to actuality moves through stages. As a result, thought must likewise move through a process governed by a law of dialectic. For Hegel, this dialectic is not a human construct, but is descriptive of reality as it actually is. More specifically, it is a description of the history of Spirit itself or eternal reason realizing itself in human thought. Again the close link Hegel drew between thought and reality is evident here. To know what reason must necessarily think, he asserted, is to know what must necessarily be.[13]

The Hegelian dialectic is generally described in logical terms as the triad of thesis-antithesis-synthesis. Although he might not have actually employed this schema,[14] it nevertheless provides a helpful way of understanding his proposal. First a thesis arises. This immediately generates its antithesis. The two are then merged in their synthesis. The synthesis constitutes a new thesis, and the process continues.

The contrast between thesis and antithesis that formed a part of Hegel's dialectic was not unique to him. In the *Critique of Pure Reason,* for example, Kant concluded that pure reason could lead the mind only to see the possible validity of opposing assertions concerning transcendental realities, such as God's existence, the soul's immortality and human freedom. Similarly, the Romantic thinkers spoke of a "coincidence of opposites" at work in nature and human history.

But whereas Kant concluded from this phenomenon the limits of "pure" reason, Hegel took the bold move to declare that both thesis and antithesis can be affirmed when understood in the light of a more inclusive proposition that encompasses the significance of each. This is the third aspect of the triad, the resolution of thesis and antithesis in their synthesis, in which both are canceled out, yet preserved *(aufgehoben)* in the third.

Hegel did not limit the dialectic to the movement of the human mind, however. Rather, he saw it as both a law of thought and of metaphysics. The dialectic relates to the process of reality itself, which reveals the Absolute coming to self-awareness.

The dialectic may be used to describe the triadic movement of the Absolute in several somewhat complicated ways. One focuses on the movement from indeterminate being *(Sein)* through nonbeing *(Nichts)* to becoming *(Werden)*.[15] Becoming, in turn, suspends itself in the coming to be of an actually existent something *(Dasein)*.

A related triad describes the embodiments of the conception of the Absolute.[16] The first element, the "in itself" *(an sich)*, views the conception in its bare universality. It describes the Absolute in terms of its unified essence, which forms the unity that constitutes the essence of all reality and thereby is the ground of reality. Seen in this light, it is only implicit or potential, not yet finding external expression.[17] The second aspect, "for itself" *(fuer sich)*, views the conception in its pure dispersion or differentiation. It describes the Absolute in terms of its presence in the realm of the details characteristic of the world in space and time. The resolution of these two aspects is the third element, the "in and for itself" *(das Anundfuersichsein)*, which is characterized by the conscious unity of the various differences present within the whole.

Philosophy, Theology and History

These concepts—spirit, truth as process and the dialectic—form the foundation of

Hegel's view of the relationship among philosophy, theology and history. History, he declared, reveals the gradual unfolding of the truth, for history is the field in which Spirit is active. The activities of the human spirit, especially those related to cultural and intellectual expression, are central to this work of Spirit in history. Above all, in philosophy Spirit becomes conscious of itself. Therefore in this discipline the movement of Spirit is most clearly visible.

Foundational for Hegel's appraisal of the role of religion and the significance of theology is the link he forges between God and Spirit. When viewed in religious terms, the Absolute Spirit is God, who reveals himself in the process of history.

This connection implies, of course, that philosophical understanding forms the pathway to knowledge of God. Just as in the final analysis philosophy is the history of thought, because history reveals the gradual unfolding of truth, so also in the end religion and theology are related to philosophy, for God can be conceived as existing only in the sense of his historical unfolding.

For Hegel, then, religion is ultimately thought,[18] in that it focuses on knowledge of God. Religion and philosophy seek to present the same truth, but in differing ways. Religion grasps truth in the form of images and representations, whereas philosophy apprehends the same truth in its "rational necessity." Theology is ultimately philosophical knowledge as well, for it moves beyond the images found in religion to a knowledge of their universal, philosophical significance.

Christianity

Hegel was concerned with the self-actualization of God that he found in the historical process, especially in the endeavors of the human spirit. As a result, the philosophical truth at the center of his thinking was the union of God and humanity. In theological terms, the great philosopher's entire system could be interpreted as a grand declaration of the metaphor of the Incarnation.[19]

The concern for Incarnation in turn formed the basis for Hegel's evaluation of Christianity. He claimed that as a revealed or spiritual religion, it is the synthesis of natural religion (typified in the old orient) and artistic religion (as found in ancient Greece).[20] Hegel arrived at this lofty conclusion because he saw in Christianity the religious presentation of the great philosophical truth of the Incarnation. In the rise of this historical religion with its focus on the Incarnation of Christ, humankind's hitherto implicit unity with God became explicit;[21] in this religion occurred the actual, historical coming to be of the unity of the divine and the human. As a result, Christianity marks the coming into being of the Absolute Spirit, God coming to self-consciousness through the religious activity of the human spirit.

According to Hegel, three moments of the divine reality—somewhat analogous to the divine persons bound up with the Christian concept of the Trinity—are at work in the process of the actualization of the unity of the divine and the human:[22] Essential Being, explicit Self-existence and Self-knowledge. The first moment is pure, abstract Being. The second marks the entrance of abstract Spirit into existence through the creation of the world. This "objectively existent spirit" (the world) is characterized both by being "the Son" (that which "knows itself to be essential Being") and by alienation and abandonment (evil). The third moment is the Spirit passing into self-consciousness.

This triadic process, together with the connection between God and humanity so central to Hegel's thinking (namely, in humankind God becomes conscious of himself), forms the interface between the religious story and the philosophical truth to which it points. The first moment is God in his Essential Being. In the creation of the universe, the second moment appears, as God moves outside himself, entering into relation with what is other than himself. In humanity, God returns to himself, for in the religious life in which humanity comes to know God, God knows himself.[23] This is the third moment, reconciliation within reality.

Christianity, according to Hegel, describes this process pictorially in terms of creation and redemption. He maintained that creation, as the movement into actual individual existence, necessarily includes alienation. Hence, he saw in the biblical story of the Fall an expression of the movement from innocence to self-consciousness, a movement that he deemed necessary to the establishment of humanity's independent, historical existence. Insofar as it entails estrangement, separation and alienation, Hegel agreed with traditional theology that the Fall was evil. But it was likewise positive as the necessary first step toward reconciliation (that is, the making explicit of the unity between God and humankind).

For Hegel, the significance of the Christ-event lay in the assertion that in Jesus the idea of the unity of God and humankind has been made explicit in history. In the Incarnation, the universal philosophical truth of the divine-human unity has been actualized in a particular historical individual. Because history is the actual unfolding of reality, this event has significance even for God himself. In Christ, God has actually passed from abstract idea into historical individuality, and in so doing has attained full reality. In his words, "the pure or non-actual Spirit of bare thought has become actual."[24]

According to Hegel, this truth is most clearly expressed in the crucifixion. This event speaks about God's taking on radical finitude—the highest form of which is death—and about the death of the abstract God:

> The death of the mediator is death not merely of his *natural* aspect, of his particular self-existence: what dies is not merely the outer encasement, which, being stripped of essential Being is *eo ipso* dead, but also the abstraction of the Divine Being.[25]

The death of Christ, however, is not the end. It sets the stage for the resurrection, which marks the advent of the universal or Absolute Spirit and of the kingdom of the Spirit as the goal of history and as God's full historical realization.

Philosophy and Christianity converge, therefore, in their common focus on reconciliation. The truth of both as Hegel interpreted them is, in the words of J. B. Baillie,

> that the Absolute Spirit takes upon itself and makes its own the stupendous labour of the world's history; that in so doing it infuses the component parts with spiritual significance, embodies itself in human form, and, in the process, at once eternal and in time, reconciles the world to itself and itself to the world.[26]

The Aftermath of Hegel

At the time of his death in 1831, Hegel was perhaps the most influential Christian philosopher in Germany. As the century moved on, however, many of his followers saw in his philosophy the source of a radical critique of Christianity and the seeds of the possibility of moving beyond the Christian tradition.

David Friedrich Strauss (1808-1874), for example, applied Hegelian ideas to New Testament christological studies. As a means to overcome the impasse between the supernaturalist and rationalist approaches to the understanding of Jesus' life, he developed the concept of "evangelical myth" (stories that are presented not as expressions of fact, but of theological truth). Ludwig Feuerbach (1804-1872) turned Hegel's theology upside-down, declaring God to be humankind in the condition of self-alienation. Thereby he transposed theology into anthropology, seeing talk about God as actually talk about the human state of affairs. Karl Marx (1818-1883), while agreeing with Hegel's conception of history as a self-activating totality, rejected the Hegelian spiritualism that treated empirical facts as the manifestation of a logical process.[27] In its stead, he explained human self-alienation in sociopolitical and economic terms.

Conclusion

The relationship between Christianity and philosophy that Hegel set forth provided a way out of the dilemma in which the Enlightenment had culminated, the dilemma of traditional orthodoxy versus radical skepticism. The German thinker elevated Christianity to the status of being *the* revealed religion, because it sets forth in representational form the ultimate philosophical truth concerning the unity of God and humanity.

But Hegel's reestablishment of Christianity came at great price. Christian doctrine could be shielded from the attack of Enlightenment rationalism only by moving its truth content beyond history, as it is taken up and transformed into philosophy. Although he denied that this transformation entailed a destruction of the content of religion, Hegel saw it as the only justification for the Christian religion.

As Christianity was transformed into philosophy, the transcendent God of the prophets, apostles and church fathers became the immanent *Weltgeist*, the Absolute Spirit that actualizes itself in human history. While the German philosopher saw this move as the salvation of the Christian faith, the question remains as to whether his system actually entailed Christianity's demise. Hegel offered an ingenious way of moving beyond the Enlightenment, but ultimately he could not overcome its basic theological outlook. The Hegelian system remained the "work of a radical immanentist."[28]

In a sense, this immanentism is Hegel's most important and lasting contribution to contemporary theology. Even when his speculative idealism waned or was radically reinterpreted as speculative materialism, his vision of the God-world unity remained as a powerful option for theology. Hegel asserted, "Without the world God is not God." By this he meant that God is *not* a self-sufficient being in and for himself; rather, God *needs* the world for his own self-actualization. World history is also God's history.

Hegel's view of the relationship between God and the world set the pattern for many later varieties of a theological alternative commonly called "panentheism." Subsumed under this label is any view that represents God and the world as inseparable yet distinct realities. Hence, this approach forms a middle way between traditional theism, in which God is believed to be entirely self-sufficient in relation to the world, and pantheism, which closely associates God with the world. All later expressions of pantheism follow Hegel in their own ways at this crucial point.

As the nineteenth century moved into its second half the intellectual climate of Germany witnessed a decline in the popularity of Hegelian speculative idealism and a revival of the Kantian emphasis on practical reason or moral judgments as the escape route out of human finitude. But before turning to the dominant theologian of the latter half of the century, Albrecht Ritschl, one additional piece of the nineteenth-century theological puzzle must be put into place—the thought of the greatest theological contemporary of Hegel, Friedrich Schleiermacher.

FRIEDRICH SCHLEIERMACHER:
THE IMMANENCE OF GOD IN RELIGIOUS FEELING

The theologians of the nineteenth century sought to move beyond the impasse that resulted from the Enlightenment by determining a special place of religion in human life and thereby establishing a new relation of transcendence and immanence. To this end, Kant set forth ethics or morality as the focal point of the special religious dimension. Hegel moved the focus to the intellectual or speculative realm. But more innovative than either of these proposals was the suggestion of the third great thinker of the early decades of the century, Friedrich Daniel Ernst Schleiermacher. His alternative elevated the intuitive life, a special human experience he called "feeling," to the center of religion. Hence, he looked to "feeling" for the foundation of theology.

The influence of this nineteenth-century German theologian on contemporary theology can hardly be overestimated. Although most Christians have never heard of Schleiermacher, his ideas about religion in general and Christianity in particular have trickled down to them through the theological education of their pastors, denominational leaders, favorite religious authors and college teachers. His influence is subtle but pervasive in Western Christianity. He is to Christian theology what Newton is to physics, what Freud is to psychology and what Darwin is to biology. That is to say, he may not be the absolute authority, but he was the trailblazer and trendsetter, the one thinker subsequent theologians cannot ignore.

Scholars of modern Christian thought almost universally hail Schleiermacher as the father of modern theology. He has been called a "Prince of the Church" and one of the few giants of Christian thought,[1] the most influential theologian since John Calvin[2] and the founder of modern religious and theological thought.[3] He is accorded such prominence not because he founded a particular school of theology or because all Christian theologians after him are his disciples. He did not, and they are not. Rather, Schleiermacher deserves this place of honor because he initiated a new era in theology—an era that has lasted for nearly two hundred years—the era dominated by the so-called liberal Christian theology and the various reactions to it.

Keith Clements was quite right when he said, "Over a whole range of issues Schleiermacher foreshadows approaches which we recognize as distinctively 'modern' or, as some may prefer, 'liberal.' "[4] No Christian thinker before him faced as squarely the problems posed for traditional Christianity by the scientific and philosophical revolutions of the Enlightenment. And none strove so valiantly to reconstruct Christian belief to make it compatible with the spirit of his age.

What is significant in Schleiermacher is not the particular reconstructions of Christian doctrines, but the method and approach he took in trying to disentangle Christian beliefs from conflicts with modern thought, which set the trend for theological liberals for the next two hundred years. His sympathizers as well as his opponents recognize him as the fountainhead of liberal theology because of the new *method* of achieving theological knowledge that he formulated. For this reason, our study of Schleiermacher will focus more on his theological methodology than on his specific doctrinal views, although some of the latter will be discussed to illustrate how he practiced that method.

Schleiermacher's Life and Career

It would be wrong to think of Schleiermacher as nothing more than a pioneer in theology. His contribution extends beyond the theological enterprise. During his life he was known as one of the greatest preachers in Christendom. And he was a religious and cultural leader of Germany during the first half of the nineteenth century. Schleiermacher helped found the University of Berlin and provided the authoritative German translation of Plato's works. He was noted as a patriot during Napoleon's occupation of Prussia and as a champion of political reform afterward. Consequently, his funeral in February 1834 was a public event with tens, if not hundreds, of thousands of ordinary Berliners lining the streets to watch his funeral cortege pass by.

Schleiermacher's theology is inseparable from his biography. To a very large extent his life experience gave rise to his particular reformulation of Christian thought.

Friedrich Schleiermacher was born in Breslau, Prussia (modern-day Wroclaw, Poland) on November 21, 1768. His father was a minister of the Reformed Church serving as a chaplain in the Prussian army. When young Friedrich was ten years old, the elder Schleiermacher had a deeply emotional renewal of Christian faith through the ministry of the pietist sect known as the Moravians. The Moravians (or "Herrnhuttern") were a group of deeply devout Christians from Bohemia who settled in the eastern part of Germany in the seventeenth century and were instrumental in the evangelical-pietist renewal.

The Schleiermacher family remained in the Reformed Church of Prussia, but practiced a very fervent, evangelical, religious life. At fourteen Friedrich was sent to a pietist boarding school and later to a pietist seminary to train for the ministry. Somewhere in his early education he began to develop doubts about certain of the key doctrines of orthodox Protestantism. In a letter to his father he expressed skepticism about the substitutionary doctrine of the atonement—that Christ suffered at the hands of God the just punishment for human sin. His father reacted harshly, nearly disowning his son. Although they later patched their relationship, Friedrich never fully recovered his early acceptance of the orthodox doctrines of Christianity, much to his father's dismay. However, he never lost the pietist emphasis on the "Christian affections" or devotional feelings. In a letter to his sister he affirmed much later that he was still a pietist only of a "higher order."

Schleiermacher's drift away from orthodox Protestant theology continued during his studies at the University of Halle. There he deeply imbibed the skepticism of Kant and read widely in Enlightenment philosophy in general.

In 1790 Schleiermacher was ordained to the ministry of the Reformed Church and thereafter held a series of positions in churches and noble families. His first significant position was as chaplain of the Charité Hospital in Berlin from 1796 to 1802. During these years a new movement—Romanticism—was sweeping through salon culture in Berlin, and Schleiermacher became caught up in it. Romanticism was a reaction to the cold rationalism of Enlightenment philosophy. It placed great emphasis on human feelings, imagination and intuition. Consequently, it valued poetry and music as means of self-realization and self-expression. Perhaps the movement's greatest leader during Schleiermacher's life was the great poet Johann Wolfgang von Goethe.

Schleiermacher was an attractive, bright conversationalist with a gregarious nature. He became part of a circle of friends in Berlin who were all deeply influenced by Romanticism. Although most of them were not devout Christians and even expressed reservations about religion, he formed a deep attachment to them. In fact, he wrote his first great work, *On Religion: Speeches to Its Cultured Despisers* (1799), largely because of a desire to persuade his friends that religion was not what they thought. In the book, he attempted to defend religion against the common misunderstandings that it is little more than dead orthodoxy and authoritarian moralism that stifles individual freedom and alienates people from their true humanity.

The young thinker tried to persuade religion's "cultured despisers" (the young Romanticists of Germany) that true religion is a matter of universal human "feeling" *(Gefühl)* and has little to do with dogmas. To this end the book blends together "enlightened pietism" and Romanticism to demonstrate that true religion is "an immediate relation to the living God, as distinct from submission to doctrinal or credal propositions about God."[5] Schleiermacher's *Speeches* represents one of the first truly modern studies of religion and earned its author the reputation as a youthful genius almost overnight.

In 1804 Schleiermacher was appointed professor and university preacher at Halle. During his brief tenure there he matured into a seasoned theologian, gaining great respect for his lectures, sermons and writings. When Prussia fell to Napoleon in 1806 the university closed and Schleiermacher moved back to Berlin to take up the very prestigious post of minister at the great Trinity Church. He lived out the rest of his years in Berlin helping to found the new university and becoming the dean of its theological faculty. He married the widow of a close friend in 1809, finally fulfilling his deep desire for the happiness of family life.

His life in Berlin was full of activity, including engagement in political activism that aroused the undying enmity of political conservatives. Schleiermacher preached almost every Sunday to capacity crowds at Trinity Church and confirmed hundreds of the children of Berlin's leading families, including young Otto von Bismarck, the future prime minister who united Germany into one Empire.

During his later years Schleiermacher produced a number of important works, including translations of Plato, books on ethics, philosophy and hermeneutics, and a life of Jesus. His magnum opus was a systematic theology entitled *The Christian Faith,* which first appeared in 1821-1822 and was revised in 1830. Most scholars would agree with Keith Clements that "Nothing on such a scale, and so systematic, had appeared in Protestantism since John Calvin's *Institutes of the Christian Religion* nearly three centuries earlier."[6] In this mammoth work Schleiermacher presented a system of Christian doctrine for modern times.

To traditionalists *The Christian Faith* represented a capitulation to the antisupernaturalist spirit of the Enlightenment age, a thinly disguised attempt to talk about humanity as if it were talk about God. To progressives it represented a liberation from outmoded authoritarian dogmatics and to a truly modern form of Christian faith that would not conflict with science. Its publication unleashed a hurricane of harsh criticism with charges of pantheism and the like. It also loosened a flood of revisionist theologies seeking to follow in Schleiermacher's footsteps and refashion Christianity to appeal to modern secular audiences.

Interest in *The Christian Faith* has yet to wane. New studies of it are published every year. Few if any theologians consider themselves disciples of Schleiermacher, but many recognize that nearly all theologies that deserve the label "liberal" follow the trail he blazed in this volume.

Schleiermacher died February 12, 1834, of pneumonia. His death came while he was taking communion with his family. As mentioned earlier, it evoked a great response from the people of Berlin. His funeral eulogist, H. Steffens, described the scene:

> Never has a funeral similar to this taken place. It was not something arranged but a completely unconscious, natural outpouring of mourning love, an inner boundless feeling which gripped the entire city and gathered about his grave; these were hours of inward unity such as have never been seen in a metropolis of modern times.[7]

Schleiermacher's Response to the Enlightenment

Schleiermacher's theology arose in large part as a response to the cultural and intellectual context of his time. The Enlightenment was not a comfortable era for Christianity. The spirit of the age promoted a relative indifference to religion,[8] which at times evolved into outright hostility. The French writer Voltaire, for example, attacked the church so vehemently that he was driven out of Paris and spent a time in exile. In Germany certain philosophers raised serious questions about the right of theology to occupy a place in the universities alongside the legitimate disciplines. The French Revolution led to the disestablishment of the church and the enthronement of the "Goddess of Reason" in its place.

In the intellectual sphere, the eighteenth century had elevated human reason, endowing it with almost no limits in criticizing traditional beliefs and establishing new truths in their place. As we have seen, Immanuel Kant provided the ultimate expression of reason's power by turning it on itself. According to Kant, pure reason is limited to the realm of objects of sense experience, so that what lies beyond sense experience is simply not knowable by human reason. Kant's restriction of reason to the world of sense experience presented a serious problem for any religious thought—whether traditional orthodoxy or its deistic alternative—that linked belief with reason. Schleiermacher's theology was in part an attempt to answer Kant's critique of religion while accepting the limitation he placed on reason.

During the Enlightenment, the new science of historical criticism had raised questions about the origin of the Bible and other authoritative texts of Christianity. Belief in the rule of natural law over the workings of nature discounted miracles and supernatural interventions into the course of history. And acquaintance with world religions raised questions about the uniqueness of Christianity. Is Christianity merely a historically conditioned form of religion like all other religions?

But the new situation that shaped the cultural context of Schleiermacher's theology was the Romantic movement. In part, the Romanticists were children of the Enlightenment. They shared its fear of authority and dogmatic belief systems. But they wished to recover a sense of the livingness of nature and of the power of human feeling and imagination—all of which they thought had been lost in the rationalism of their predecessors. In the Romantic emphasis on feeling Schleiermacher found his clue for reconstructing Christianity so that it would not conflict with the fundamental spirit of modern culture.

Theological Method

The English Enlightenment poet Alexander Pope succinctly expressed the spirit of modern culture: "Know then thyself, presume not God to scan, the proper study of mankind is man." But what if one could study God by studying man? What if one could truly know oneself only by knowing God and vice versa? What if it could be shown that religion in general and Christianity in particular are not inimical to humanity but essential to its true fulfillment?

Schleiermacher's ingenious and controversial project was to do just that. He sought to base theology on *human experience*—to show that religion is rooted in and even identical with an experience essential to true humanity.[9] And he attempted to reconstruct Christian doctrine so that it does not elevate God at humanity's expense, but brings the two together in an intrinsic way.

His attempt constitutes a third major endeavor to do theology in the aftermath of the Enlightenment, set alongside of Kant's attempt to base knowledge of God on practical reason and Hegel's effort to base it on a new speculative rationalism that detects the march of Absolute Spirit through history. Schleiermacher sought to provide an alternative approach through *intuition*. He looked to a fundamental, universal human feeling, the feeling of dependence on the whole of reality.

Like Kant's "turn to the subject" in philosophy, Schleiermacher's theological method might also be called a "Copernican Revolution." Just as Copernicus suggested that numerous problems in astronomy could be solved if the sun rather than the earth were to be seen as the center of the universe, Schleiermacher suggested that the impasse between rationalism and orthodoxy could be solved if human experience—specifically the feeling of absolute dependency—rather than authoritative propositions about God were to be seen as the source of theology.

Before Schleiermacher, theology was thought of in two major ways. Orthodoxy viewed the discipline as reflection on supernaturally revealed truths and thus practiced a theology "from above." Enlightenment theology (deism), viewing the enterprise as reflection on rational thoughts about God, engaged in a type of theology "from below." According to Schleiermacher (and later liberal theologians) the approach of orthodoxy led to authoritative theology, which stifled human creativity and confused the church's dogmas about God with God himself. The Enlightenment rightly rebelled against this. The deistic approach, however, led to sterile, bland natural religion that differed little from a religious philosophy. Kant had brought this to a dead end.

In the place of these two alternatives, Schleiermacher sought to reroute theology entirely by considering it as *human* reflection on human experience of God. Thus, not timeless, authoritative propositions but religious experience would become the true source of theological reflection.

The key to the success of his theological revolution lay in Schleiermacher's ability to establish religion as fundamental to human nature and not reducible to something else. In the *Speeches* he attempted to explicate the true nature of religion by mining both his own heritage in Pietism and the new cultural phenomenon of Romanticism. He tried to show that the essence of religion lies not in rational proofs of the existence of God, in supernaturally revealed dogmas or in churchly rituals and formalities, but in a "fundamental, distinct, and integrative element of human life and culture"[10]—the feeling of being utterly dependent on something infinite that manifests itself in and through finite things.

It is important to understand correctly Schleiermacher's equation of religion with "feeling." The German original, *Gefühl*, does not connote a sensation, as its English rendering would suggest, but a deep sense or awareness. "Feeling," therefore, lies on the prereflective plane of consciousness—that is, beneath and before explicit thought or sensation. Hence, the true essence of religion, Schleiermacher argued, lies in "the immediate consciousness of the universal being of all finite things in and through the infinite, of all temporal things in and through the eternal."[11] And again, "To seek and to find this infinite and eternal factor in all that lives and moves, all growth and change, in all action and passion, and to have and to know life itself only in immediate feeling—that is religion."[12]

Schleiermacher believed that such a religious feeling (which he often called "piety") is fundamental and universal in human experience. It cannot be reduced to some other aspect of human nature such as reason or conscience.[13] Although it is totally distinct from these, he argued, this religious feeling is just as essential to a full understanding of humanity. Reason and conscience give rise to science and morality; piety gives rise to religion.

Consequently, Schleiermacher was willing for religion to waive "all claims to anything belonging to the two domains of science and morality."[14] But in return he wanted religion's cultured despisers to recognize religion as *sui generis*—something human in its own right and of its own kind—and to refrain from trying to subsume it under science or ethics. Religion, he asserted, has a reality all of its own: "Piety presents itself to you as the necessary and indispensable third to science and morality, as their natural counterpart, one no less endowed with that dignity and excellence which you attribute to them."[15]

Of course, piety and religion cannot be entirely divorced from science and morality. Schleiermacher averred that all of culture rests to some extent on piety, in that culture presupposes some transcendent unity or wholeness of reality, and the inner consciousness of such unity is identical with piety.[16]

Not only did Schleiermacher wish to distinguish piety and religion from science and morality, he also wanted to distinguish them from dogmas and systems of theology. The latter are in themselves alien to true religion and are at best only human attempts to set forth piety in speech.[17] Religion can get along quite well without dogmas and concepts, he argued, but reflection on religious feeling needs and therefore creates them.[18]

After establishing the autonomy of religion and locating it in an irreducible and universal human experience, Schleiermacher turned to theology itself. In the broadest and most general sense theology is simply human reflection on religion, that is, on piety. However, he did not believe that there is any such thing as generic religion, for piety *always* expresses itself in some concrete form of religious life in and through some religious community. What Schleiermacher argued in his *Speeches* seems to be something like Aristotle's view of form and matter: piety is the essence of religion (form), but it always takes shape in some specific religious tradition (matter). In any case, he adamantly opposed the Enlightenment search for a "natural religion" divorced from any concrete religious community, theology or form of worship ("Positive Religion").[19] Therefore, reflection on religion is always reflection on some particular form of religious life.

In his great work of systematic theology, *The Christian Faith*, Schleiermacher defined theology as the attempt to set forth the Christian religious affections in speech.[20] In essence Christianity is a modification of universal human piety, the consciousness of being absolutely dependent, of being in relation to God. Schleiermacher recognized a specific form of piety that he called the Christian God-consciousness or Christian self-consciousness. This is what he meant by "Christian religious affections"—the feeling of being totally dependent upon the redemptive work of Jesus Christ for one's own relationship to God. The Christian experience of God-consciousness and self-consciousness formed and fulfilled in and through Jesus Christ is the essence of Christianity: "the distinctive essence of Christianity consists in the fact that in it all religious emotions are related to the redemption wrought by Jesus of Nazareth."[21] Rather than being the project of systematizing some supernaturally revealed set of propositions, Christian theology attempts to set forth a coherent account of the religious experience of Christians. Because that experience is fundamentally an experience of God mediated in and through Jesus Christ, all doctrines must be centered around and related to him and his redemptive work.[22]

Schleiermacher's innovation in theological method lies in his "turn to the believing subject." Not some body of divinely revealed information but the experience of believers is the subject matter and criterion for theology. For him this meant that theology must continually re-examine the doctrinal formulas of Christianity to determine their adequacy to express the Christian God-consciousness. No doctrine is sacrosanct. Everything is open to revision. Theology's critical task is to hold the church's preaching and doctrinal formulas to strict agreement with the best contemporary analysis of the Christian God-consciousness in order to determine how much of it is to be retained, how much thrown out entirely and how much revised.[23] In *The Christian Faith* Schleiermacher carried out this critical task with incisiveness and tenacity.

Schleiermacher was not content to tear down what he considered inadequate formulas of Christian belief. Besides the critical task of theology, there is also the constructive task. Consequently, he also attempted to replace inadequate formulations with what he considered better and more contemporary expressions of Christian piety.

One of his contributions to contemporary theology is his emphasis on the cultural and historical character of doctrines. Schleiermacher believed that religious experience is primary; theology in turn is secondary and must constantly be reformed in relation to the changing aspects of Christian communities. For him, "Every doctrinal form is bound to a particular time and no claim can be made for its permanent validity. It is the task of theology in every present age, by critical reflection, to express anew the implications of the living religious consciousness."[24]

Schleiermacher's theological method both incorporated the advances of the Enlightenment and sought to move beyond it. In keeping with the Age of Reason, his thinking centered around human experience, shunned authority and sought to build knowledge "from below." He followed Kant in restricting knowledge of God to what can be experienced and in eschewing speculation about "God in himself" or the ultimate nature of the universe. However, whereas the Enlightenment wished to restrict religion to the bounds of reason alone, Schleiermacher restricted it to the bounds of piety alone. His theological method appealed to the Romantic movement in its emphasis on feeling and intuitive knowledge, while avoiding Romanticism's subjectivism and irrationalism. Above all, Schleiermacher broke decisively with the Enlightenment by insisting on the uniqueness of religion as an irreducible element of human experience and on the uniqueness of Jesus Christ as the highest expression of God-consciousness.

Doctrinal Innovations
Although Schleiermacher's specific reconstructions of Christian doctrines are not as important to contemporary theology as is his method, several illustrate the effect his starting point could have on Christian beliefs. His reformulations also set the pace and

tone for many of the future developments in liberal theology.

The Bible played an important, although not central, role in Schleiermacher's theology. Christian doctrine is not to be drawn primarily or exclusively from the Bible. Rather, all doctrines, he wrote, "must be extracted from the Christian religious self-consciousness, i.e., the inward experience of Christian people."[25] The Bible is special in that it records the religious experience of the earliest Christian communities. Further, the New Testament preserves for succeeding generations the perfect God-consciousness of Jesus and its impact on the earliest Christians. The authority of Scripture, however, is not absolute. Rather, it serves as a model for all attempts by Christians to interpret the significance of Jesus Christ for specific historical circumstances.[26]

Clearly Schleiermacher did not consider the Bible supernaturally inspired or infallible. Within it he found passages and even whole books that seemed to contradict true Christian piety.[27] The entire Old Testament seemed to him to lack the normative dignity of the New.[28] Furthermore, he did not believe that the Bible could or should be considered utterly unique. Whatever the influence of the Holy Spirit was in its writing should be seen as different only in degree and not in kind from the Spirit's influence elsewhere.

For him, the Bible holds a relative authority for Christian theology insofar as and wherever it shows forth the pure model of Christ's own God-consciousness. However, it is the latter, reproduced in the self-consciousness of Christian people, and not the Bible itself, which is the ultimate criterion of truth for theology.

God

Schleiermacher's reconstruction of the doctrine of God has been one of his most controversial contributions. It was determined by the pious God-consciousness of Christian people, their feeling of absolute dependence on God. According to Schleiermacher, the attributes of God are not to be taken as actually describing God. To "describe" is to limit and divide, thereby taking away from God's infinity and implying a dependence of God upon the world. In the place of the traditional understanding, he offered what has become a classic reformulation: "All attributes which we ascribe to God are to be taken as denoting not something special in God, but only something special in the manner in which the feeling of absolute dependence is to be related to Him."[29] In other words, talk about God is always talk about human experience of God. Such statements describe not God-in-himself but a certain mode of experiencing God.

His understanding of God-talk makes it all the more clear why for Schleiermacher the test or criterion for determining the proper attributes of God is the feeling of utter dependence.[30] In drawing out the implications of that experience he concluded that God is the all-determining reality, the ultimate cause of everything—both good and evil; the one who acts but cannot be acted upon.

Schleiermacher's reformulated understanding of God presents serious problems for traditional Christian thought. For example, the German theologian was unflinching in attributing evil to God's causality. That God is the author of sin and evil is necessitated by creaturely dependence. If they could be ascribed to any other agency than God, then his omnipotence would be limited. Schleiermacher suggested that sin is ordained by God as that which makes redemption necessary.[31]

Further, Schleiermacher adamantly rejected the reality of miracles. To believe in miracles is to deny that everything that happens is ordained and caused by God. The feeling of absolute dependence requires that all of nature, in the part and in the whole, is willed, ordained and caused by God. Miracles, in the sense of special acts that abrogate the order of nature, would contradict this.[32]

Likewise, Schleiermacher denied the efficacy of intercessory prayer. To ask God to change the course of events is to imply that it is somehow independent of God *and* that God is somehow dependent on the person praying. Of course even though prayer does not change anything, *that* people pray and *that* their prayers seem to receive answers are "only part of the original divine plan, and consequently the idea that otherwise something else might have happened is wholly meaningless."[33]

It should be clear by now that Schleiermacher considered the whole notion of the supernatural to be dangerous. To him it conflicted with the proper God-consciousness of Christians. The supernatural implied that God stands over against the world, and that God and creation relate to each other through relative independence. Christian piety, in contrast, senses God as the absolute infinite power upon which everything finite is utterly dependent and which is itself absolutely nondependent.

Schleiermacher's elimination of the category of the supernatural provided a convenient solution to a pressing problem for Christianity in the age of science:

> On the whole, therefore, as regards the miraculous, the general interests of science, more particularly of natural science, and the interests of religion seem to meet at the same point, i.e., that we should abandon the idea of the absolutely supernatural because no single instance of it can be known by us, and we are nowhere required to recognize it.[34]

Thus, science and Christianity in principle cannot conflict. The former deals with proximate causes only, whereas the latter deals with the ultimate cause.

Finally, Schleiermacher found the doctrine of the Trinity problematic. He relegated it to a short conclusion at the end of *The Christian Faith*, stating coldly that it "is not an utterance concerning the religious consciousness."[35] He did not flatly deny the doctrine, but found its historical formulation so fraught with contradictions that it is virtually useless for Christian theology.

Schleiermacher's delineation of God's personhood and transcendence has formed a focal point of much controversy. Some have mistakenly charged him with pantheism, a criticism unwarranted by his exposition in *The Christian Faith*. Although it is not pantheism, there is a general consensus that his doctrine is panentheistic and thus the prototype for much later liberal Christian thought. Schleiermacher refused to separate God from the world or the world from God. God is personal, but not anthropomorphically so. That is, God is not to be thought of as a great humanlike being who rules the world from afar. But even more important, God is not to be treated as an object of any kind because to do so would be to limit and finitize God. For Schleiermacher

God is the absolute, all-determining, suprapersonal power immanent in everything but beyond all the distinctions creatureliness imposes on existence.

Christology

What of Jesus Christ? Schleiermacher rejected the traditional doctrine of the Incarnation and replaced it with a Christology based on the experience of God-consciousness. He criticized the classical doctrine of Jesus' two natures (human and divine) as illogical. Two "natures" cannot coincide in a single individual.[36] In its place Schleiermacher substituted the concept of Jesus' *Urbildlichkeit* and *Vorbildlichkeit*—his ideality and his power of reproducing it in others.[37] Jesus Christ is completely like the rest of humanity except that "from the outset he has an absolutely potent God-consciousness."[38] His God-consciousness was not a product of humanity alone; it was a product of God's activity in his life. However, it was a fully human God-consciousness. From birth on he lived in full awareness of his dependence on God. In Schleiermacher's description, "The Redeemer, then, is like all men in virtue of the identity of human nature, but distinguished from them all by the constant potency of His God-consciousness, which was a veritable existence of God in Him."[39]

According to Schleiermacher, this ideal God-consciousness that Jesus possessed is sufficient to express what the Christian calls his "divinity." It is his *Urbildlichkeit*—his being the ideal of human God-consciousness, the ultimate in perfect piety. Jesus' redemptive work lies in his communication of this God-consciousness to others. That is his *Vorbildlichkeit:* "The Redeemer assumes believers into the power of His God-consciousness, and this is his redemptive activity."[40]

Schleiermacher left no doubt about his attitude toward traditional language about Jesus as God when he endorsed what he considered to be the consistent practice of the New Testament to ascribe to him only such attributes as express exalted humanity.[41]

Evaluation

Even during his lifetime, Schleiermacher's reformulation of theology created controversy. Some of his contemporaries accused him of pantheism or even of atheism! One critic created a vicious play on his name, which in German literally means "maker of veils":

> Der nackten Wahrheit Schleier machen,
> Ist kluger Theologen Amt,
> Und Schleiermacher sind bei so bewandten Sachen
> Die meister der Dogmatik insgesamt.
>
> (To make veils for the naked truth
> is the job of clever theologians;
> all masters of dogmatics are 'Schleiermachers.')[42]

During the twentieth century controversy has focused mainly on Schleiermacher's theological method. One of his greatest detractors has been Karl Barth, who accused him of trying to speak about God by speaking about humankind in a very loud voice. In other words, Barth accused his forebear of making theology radically anthropocentric and setting the course at the end of which certain theologians of the mid-twentieth century proclaimed God to be dead.[43]

Much of Barth's criticism is well taken. Can one ever set up something purely human as the well and touchstone of truth in theology? How does one then avoid allowing anthropology to control the content of the message? How does one allow the Word of God to speak prophetically to culture? Schleiermacher began the trend within modern Christian thought toward loss of transcendence by refusing to acknowledge the possibility that God might wish to speak a word or commit an act that could not be anticipated within the horizon of human experience alone.

The weakness of Schleiermacher's theological method has serious consequences for his doctrine of God. The "feeling of utter dependence" so easily becomes a Procrustean bed onto which the Christian concept of God must be forced. Whatever will not conform must be lopped off—however crucial it is to the scriptural witness and the history of Christian thought. While the charge of pantheism is unfounded, Schleiermacher's doctrine of God suffers from an overemphasis on immanence. God's activity becomes virtually identical with nature to the extent that evil and suffering are as much God's activity as is redemption.

Furthermore it is unclear whether God has any existence above and apart from the world.[44] Schleiermacher's doctrine of God is best described as *panentheistic* in that it correlates God and the world, making them inseparable. As in all panentheistic systems, Schleiermacher's vision of the God-world relationship raises serious problems for the doctrine of grace. How can God's redemption of the world be gracious if it is not absolutely free? In tension with his emphasis on God's immanence stands Schleiermacher's emphasis on God's absoluteness, the ultimate upshot of which is the unavoidable loss of personal relationship. A true relationship with God becomes impossible because it would involve reciprocity of action and response. Schleiermacher's God, in contrast, appears strangely cold and impassive: "If, for example, to the divine nature there were to be communicated anything human in the way of capacity for suffering, in such a communication no room is left for anything divine."[45]

Perhaps this forms the Achilles' heel of Schleiermacher's doctrine of God for contemporary Christians. The horrors of the twentieth century have led to a new appreciation of the biblical language of God's identification with suffering in his own "pathos." How can Christians today have any use for a God who feels no responsive compassion and is not inwardly affected by human suffering?

Schleiermacher strove valiantly to find room within his system for the uniqueness of Jesus Christ. Ultimately he failed to do anything more than assert it. His account of Jesus' "divinity" left him on the human level, different in degree from other humans, perhaps, but not different in kind. His is the prototype of what is known today as a "functional Christology," in which Jesus' divinity is not his essential being but an activity of God in him—a way in which he functioned in relation to God and other humans. The flaw in this, of course, is that functional Christologies cannot account for Jesus' ultimacy and finality as the self-expression of God. If Jesus is ontologically (by nature) nothing more than human, why could there not come another equal to or even greater than he? It would seem that if the Christian self-consciousness is anything specific at all, it is consciousness of Jesus as Lord, something which is at best poorly expressed in a merely functional Christology.

Conclusion

Schleiermacher's greatness as a theologian is undeniable. For better or for worse, his influence has permeated contemporary theology. It is especially evident in those schools of theology labeled "liberal" that came to dominate Protestant thought toward the end of the nineteenth century. To the greatest proponent of that theology we now must turn.

ALBRECHT RITSCHL AND CLASSICAL LIBERAL THEOLOGY:
THE IMMANENCE OF GOD IN ETHICAL CULTURE

Liberal theology is notoriously difficult to define. In popular usage and in the mass media it often refers to theologies that deny traditional beliefs such as the inspiration of the Bible or the virgin birth. Its popular, generic sense is at best imprecise and relative to the theological commitments of the speaker, anyone being "liberal" if they seem to stand to his or her "left."

Historically, however, "liberalism" refers to a specific movement in Protestantism that dominated academic theology around the turn of the century. It arose first in Germany among students and followers of Schleiermacher and Hegel, and it took on its most influential form in the school of Albrecht Ritschl.

The terms "Ritschlian" and "classical Protestant liberal" are nearly synonymous. Of course, classical liberalism was also a diverse phenomenon. It is impossible to present a list of characteristics of any length that would aptly describe every liberal theologian of that era. Consequently, the best way to define classical liberal theology is to study it historically—through its major representative thinkers. Three stand out as most clearly representative of the essence of late nineteenth- and early twentieth-century liberal theology: Albrecht Ritschl, Adolf Harnack and Walter Rauschenbusch. Although not neglecting the others, our treatment will focus on Ritschl. Harnack and Rauschenbusch, for all their individual creativity, are best understood as his disciples, as two thinkers who carried his liberal agenda in new directions.

Classical Liberal Theology

Before discussing the three specific thinkers it will be helpful to give a brief description of some common features of the movement called classical liberal theology. What characteristics did these theologians share that made them a somewhat cohesive movement?

Like Schleiermacher, the liberals were committed to the task of reconstructing Christian belief in the light of modern knowledge. They believed that certain developments in culture since the Enlightenment simply could not be ignored by Christian theology, but had to be assimilated into it in a positive way. Christian theology had to adapt to the new scientific and philosophical mindset without losing itself. Liberal theology, therefore, was characterized, in the words of Claude Welch, by a "maximum acknowledgment of the claims of modern thought."[1]

A second characteristic of liberal theology was its emphasis on the freedom of the individual Christian thinker to criticize and reconstruct traditional beliefs. Negatively this entailed the rejection of the authority of tradition or church hierarchy to control theology. Not all liberal theologians were rebels or mavericks, to be sure. In fact, most of them had a profound appreciation for the communal nature of Christian truth. Nevertheless, they resolutely reserved the right to break with traditional beliefs when it seemed right and necessary.

Third, liberal theology focused on the practical or ethical dimension of Christianity. Ritschl and his followers tended to shy away from what they considered empty speculation and tried to moralize doctrine by centering all theological discourse around the concept of the kingdom of God.

Fourth, most liberal theologians sought to base theology on some foundation other than the absolute authority of the Bible. They believed that the traditional dogma of the supernatural inspiration of Scripture had been hopelessly undermined by historical-critical research. Not only church traditions but much of the Bible itself is "husk" hiding the pure "kernel" of unchanging truth lodged within it. The liberals did not dismiss the Bible as having no value, of course. Rather, they looked within it for the "gospel"—the timeless core and touchstone of truth that could not be eroded by the acids of modern scientific and philosophical knowledge. They saw the task of theology as identifying the kernel, the "essence of Christianity," and clearly separating it from the husk of cultural ideas and expressions that encased it. For many liberal theologians that husk included miracles, supernatural beings such as angels and demons, and apocalyptic events.

Finally, and perhaps unconsciously underlying the other features, liberal theology continued the drift toward divine immanence at the expense of transcendence begun by the Enlightenment and continued by the great German thinkers of the early nineteenth century. Of course, Ritschl and other liberal theologians did not self-consciously aim at a dissolution of God's transcendence in favor of his immanence—the emphasis on immanence was not Ritschl's goal as much as his legacy. But his emphasis on the kingdom of God as a historical, ethical society of love did indeed tend to elevate the *continuity* rather than the *discontinuity* between God and humankind, in keeping with the Enlightenment program. Prior to the Enlightenment, theologians emphasized the disjunction between a radically holy, transcendent God and sinful, finite humans, and they saw the Incarnation as the dramatic event whereby God bridged this gulf. Beginning in the Enlightenment and climaxing in liberalism, in contrast, theologians built from the continuity between the divine and the human as manifested, for example, in the rational, intuitive or moral capabilities. Consequently, they viewed Jesus as the exemplary human rather than as the invading Christ.

The ethos of the liberal movement has been captured by one of its leading students who says that all of its adherents "would have agreed on the necessity of giving renewed strength and currency to Protestant Christianity by adapting it to the spiritual wants of the modern man, even if much that the past had accepted without demur would have to be discarded."[2]

Albrecht Ritschl's Life and Career

The key figure in late nineteenth-century liberal theology was Albrecht Ritschl. Although he cannot be compared to Schleiermacher in terms of originality, creativity or lasting influence, he exercised such influence from about 1875 to 1925 that Ritschlianism became virtually synonymous with liberal Protestantism. Thus, whereas Schleiermacher founded an epoch in theology but not a school, Ritschl founded a school but not an epoch.

Albrecht Ritschl was born in 1822 into the family of a bishop of the Prussian Protestant church. He was musically inclined as a child and early in life showed great intellectual capability. Young Ritschl began theological studies at Bonn and continued at Tübingen and Halle, eventually returning to conclude his academic preparation at Bonn. During his university training he was influenced by Schleiermacher, Kant and the Hegelian New Testament scholar F. C. Baur.

Ritschl received his first teaching position at Bonn in 1846. In 1864 he moved to Göttingen, where he remained until his death in 1889. During his twenty-five-year tenure at Göttingen he established a reputation as Germany's leading theologian. An entire generation of Protestant pastors and teachers was deeply influenced by his lectures and writings.

Although he published many articles and books, Ritschl's most important work was a three-volume treatise entitled *The Christian Doctrine of Justification and Reconciliation*, published in stages between 1870 and 1874. Its English translator, Scottish theologian H. R. Mackintosh, said of it, "Not since Schleiermacher published his *Christliche Glaube* [The Christian Faith] in 1821 has any dogmatic treatise left its mark so deeply upon theological thought in Germany and throughout the world."[3]

Ritschl's Theological Method

Much of Ritschl's importance for modern theology, like Schleiermacher's, lies in his approach to theology rather than in his specific doctrinal proposals. In the late nineteenth century Christianity seemed constantly to be losing ground to the secular sciences. Traditional Christian theology was under siege from forces such as materialism and positivism.

Ritschl believed that the conflict between theology and science arose out of a failure to distinguish properly between "scientific" and "religious" types of knowledge. Scientific knowledge, he asserted, strives for pure theoretical objectivity, disinterested cognition of things in themselves. It attempts to grasp the inner nature of reality from a standpoint of neutrality. Religious knowledge, on the other hand, consists of value judgments about reality. It interprets reality in terms of the value things have for the knower's ultimate fulfillment. Religious knowledge has to do with the value of things for achieving the person's highest good. Another way of describing this distinction is to say that for Ritschl scientific knowledge can only be about the way things are, whereas religious knowledge is always also about the way things ought to be. Such judgments can never be disinterested or neutral. Neither should they be.[4]

According to Ritschl, conflicts between the secular academic scientific disciplines and religion arise only when people fail to observe this distinction between theoretical knowledge and religious knowledge. For him, "every cognition of a religious sort is a direct judgment of value." Consequently, we can know the nature of God and the divine in its essence only "by determining its value for our salvation."[5]

In contrast to Ritschl's viewpoint, traditional Christian theology normally incorporated some discussion of the element of metaphysics. For instance, theologians employed theoretical proofs for the existence of God to establish rational bases for Christian belief, and they generally made some attempt to describe the nature of God in himself.

Ritschl vehemently rejected any reliance of theology on metaphysics. For him such an approach was an illegitimate mingling of scientific and religious knowledge.[6] Philosophical proofs for the existence of God belong in the sphere of scientific knowledge, he argued, because they treat God as an object of theoretical interest whereas truly religious knowledge of God can never treat God as an object, merely as a part of the furniture of the world. Theology is only interested in God insofar as he affects the lives of people morally by helping them achieve their highest good.

But what is humanity's highest good? For Ritschl, Christianity is the community of people who collectively make the value judgment that humanity's highest good is found in the kingdom of God revealed in Jesus Christ. No theoretical proof of this value judgment is possible or desirable, but neither is its affirmation the product of a subjective "leap of faith." Rather, this assertion is rooted in the collective experience of Christians throughout the centuries. And its truth is supported by historical investigation into the unique calling and career of Jesus of Nazareth in whom humans find their highest ideal perfectly lived.

According to Ritschl, theology is the investigation of the collective religious and moral experience of the kingdom of God in the church. It is built on and centered around the Christian community's valuation of the kingdom of God revealed in Jesus Christ as humanity's highest good. Theology seeks to construct a system of value judgments based solely on the effects of God on Christians' lives and the worth of those effects for their highest good. To this end, it makes use of historical research into the self-consciousness of Jesus and the original effects his preaching of the kingdom of God had on the earliest Christians. Such historical research, Ritschl maintained, would preserve theology's value judgments from becoming mere flights of subjective fancy and give it its own kind of scientific character.

In short, for Ritschl theology seeks to determine the true essence of Christianity as distinct from its merely outward forms and expressions. Furthermore, it attempts to represent all doctrines in systematic relation to that essence as their controlling force.[7]

What is the source and norm of theology? According to Ritschl it is not the Bible as a whole but the "apostolic circle of ideas" as determined through sound historical critical research.[8] Ritschl was sure that such research would show the kingdom of God to be that essence of Christianity—the kernel in the husk—and the heart of the apostolic circle of ideas.

Ritschl's theological method bears a striking affinity to Kant's philosophy. The latter was mediated to Ritschl through a philosopher at Göttingen, Hermann Lotze, who tried to ameliorate Kant's skepticism while holding to his basic epistemology. Although much controversy has revolved around the question of the influence of Kant and Lotze on Ritschl, this much can be said with certainty: Ritschl followed Kant in trying to expunge metaphysics from theology and in bringing religion into the closest possible connection with ethics. He eschewed all speculation into the nature of God himself apart from his effects on humans (although here he appealed to Luther more than to Kant). Ritschl differed from Kant, however, in that he claimed that God *really is known* in his effects. And he disliked Kant's separation between the "phenomenal" and "noumenal" realms. In responding to Kant, Ritschl relied heavily on Lotze for the idea that a thing (in this case, God) is present and manifest in its effects (in this case in revelation and salvation).[9]

God and the Kingdom of God

Ritschl's doctrine of God was profoundly affected by his theological methodology. The first and most striking evidence of this is that he had very little to say about God in himself. He asserted that Christian theology is only interested in God's effects on people and in the value judgments appropriate to those effects.

Ritschl said little about the Trinity, for example, because he viewed it as a doctrine about God's inner being above and apart from God's relation to the world, and therefore it could not be articulated as a value judgment. Similarly he saw no positive role for the traditional metaphysical attributes of God, such as omnipotence, omniscience and omnipresence. While not explicitly denying them, he seemed to dismiss the attributes as lying in the realm of theoretical rather than religious knowledge. For Ritschl, the primary Christian theological affirmation is "God is love."[10] To this he added that Christian faith requires that God be personal and transcendent or "supramundane."[11]

Ritschl was much more interested in the kingdom of God than in God himself. Jesus had proclaimed the kingdom of God, which, according to Ritschl, is the unity of humanity organized according to love.[12] Christian faith grasps this kingdom revealed in Christ as humanity's highest good. Faith, therefore, knows the God proclaimed by Jesus as love. Apart from this, it has no interest in any "being of God."

For Ritschl, the kingdom of God is not only humanity's highest goal and good, it is also God's own highest goal and good.[13] Perhaps the most striking thing about Ritschl's doctrine of God lies here. For him God's own self-end, his reason for being, so to speak, is the same as ours—the kingdom of God.

In spite of his acknowledgment of God's transcendence, this identification of God's being with the progress of his kingdom in the world bends Ritschl's theology in the direction of immanence. Certainly later liberal theologians drew this conclusion, and overall the emphasis of liberalism's doctrine of God fell on the divine immanence within history rather than on his transcendence over it.

Sin and Salvation

For Ritschl the kingdom of God is also the inner meaning of the doctrines of sin and salvation. Because the kingdom of God is judged by Christian faith as the highest good, theology must understand sin as the opposite of that kingdom.[14] Sin is not primarily a willful wrong act, for this understanding trivializes the concept. Nor is sin an inherited disposition, a view that robs it of the element of responsibility. In place of the traditional doctrine of original sin Ritschl posited the existence of a "kingdom of sin," a "whole web of sinful action and reaction, which presupposes and yet again increases the selfish bias in every man."[15] Sin is primarily selfishness. Its essential character lies in its contradiction of the ideal of human unity centered around love, which is the kingdom of God. However, sin is not inherited. It is universal, but no other reason can be given for its universality than that all individuals do sin.

Throughout Ritschl's theological writings the kingdom of God appears to have two foci—a religious one and an ethical one. The religious focus is justification, the moment of salvation in which God declares the sinner forgiven. The ethical focus lies in the assertion that God calls reconciled men and women to fulfill the ideal of love toward the neighbor. For Ritschl "salvation" must include both of these foci.

In his doctrines of sin and salvation the revolutionary this-worldly aspect of Ritschl's theology is most clearly evident. He believed that salvation is not primarily a matter of achieving a state of blessedness in some afterlife—although he never denied such a state. Rather, salvation is primarily the full fruition of the kingdom of God on earth. Consequently, Christianity is not an otherworldly religion but a religion of world transformation through ethical action inspired by love.

Christology

Perhaps the most controversial aspect of Ritschl's theology is his Christology. Once again the kingdom of God is the controlling center of his doctrine, and Ritschl used it to replace those aspects of the traditional doctrine that he considered speculative and metaphysical.

Classical Christology, following the Creed of Chalcedon (A.D. 451), affirms that Jesus Christ was and is one person possessing two distinct natures—the human and the divine. His "divinity," then, consists in his divine nature. Ritschl firmly rejected this traditional formula for Jesus' divinity on the ground that it is scientific rather than religious.[16] It is not, he argued, a judgment of Jesus' value but a disinterested assertion of something Jesus is supposed to have possessed before and apart from any affect he had on people. The truly religious estimate of Jesus, he asserted, is interested in his historical conduct, religious convictions and ethical motives, and not in his supposed inborn qualities or powers, "for not in the latter but in the former does He exert an influence upon us."[17] Therefore, the affirmation of Jesus' divinity, Ritschl argued, is a value judgment Christians make based on the worth of his life in effecting their salvation. Because he came as the unique bearer of the kingdom of God he is judged to have the value of God for Christians.

Ritschl was sensitive to the charge that he reduced Jesus Christ to a "mere man." He spent many pages anticipating and defending himself against this criticism. Ritschl interpreted Jesus' divinity as the unique "vocation" given to him by God his Father to be the perfect embodiment of the kingdom of God among humans—a vocation he fulfilled to perfection. Because he took this life task as his exclusive vocation and realized it perfectly, his very person became the historical influence that makes possible the achievement of God's and humanity's highest good. Thus Christians confess Jesus to be "God," for this is a value judgment based on his life's worth for both God and humanity.[18]

Ritschl refused to discuss the origin of the uniqueness of Jesus' "Kingly Prophethood." Such inquiry, he claimed, would lead into empty metaphysical speculation and away from the sphere of value judgments. However, he could not restrain himself from discussing the concept of Christ's preexistence. Here more clearly than anywhere else he fell into inconsistency by allowing an element of metaphysics to influence his thought. Apparently he simply could not settle for the conclusion that Jesus' accomplishment was a product of his own initiative and effort. Rather, it had an eternal source in the mind and will of God:

> . . . as Founder and Lord of the Kingdom of God, Christ is as much the object of God's eternal knowledge and will as is the moral unification of mankind, which is made possible through Him, and whose prototype He is; or rather, that, not only in time but in the eternity of the Divine knowledge and will, Christ precedes His community.[19]

In other words, for Ritschl Christ "preexisted" only in the sense that he and his work are eternally known and willed by God. This affirmation of Christ's ideal preexistence seems blatantly to transgress Ritschl's own self-imposed limits on theology. It introduces an element of metaphysics or ontology that cannot be supported solely by historical research into Christ's worth for human salvation. This affirmation goes beyond the sphere of value judgments and asserts the reality of a transcendent ground and origin of Christ, a sphere Ritschl marked off as speculative in his criticism of the classical doctrine of Christ's divine nature.

Central to Ritschl's theology is Christ's accomplishment of salvation for humankind. But how does this occur? Here Ritschl introduces the concept of Jesus' "vocational obedience" to the Father: Jesus perfectly fulfilled the way of life appropriate for the kingdom of God. His sinless life and voluntary death not only revealed the kingdom of God in history but released it as a power for transforming the world.

It appears that Ritschl's main interest lay in Christ's historical life as a moral example carrying an impact on history. Although he explicitly rejected any doctrine of the atonement that would make Christ the bearer of divine punishment for the world's sins, Ritschl did not deny the special significance of Christ's death.[20] The death of Jesus was simply part of his vocation of utter loyalty to the cause of God's kingdom.

Ritschl had little to say about Jesus' resurrection or exaltation. For all practical purposes Ritschl represented Jesus' continuing influence on the world as that of a powerful moral image that continually energizes the community of the kingdom of God.[21]

Evaluation

Ritschl's reputation as a modern theologian of lasting importance passed under a cloud during the middle of the twentieth century, mainly as a result of withering criticism from neo-orthodox thinkers like Karl Barth and Emil Brunner. The fairness of that criticism is a matter of dispute today, and there was talk of a "Ritschl Renaissance" in the 1960s and 1970s.[22] Most recent critics agree that Ritschl's contributions lay in his effort to extricate Christian faith from unnecessary conflicts with post-Enlightenment science and philosophy and in his "moralizing of dogma." In an era in which Christian theology was increasingly accused of being irrelevant to ethical progress due to its concentration on another world, Ritschl brought his spiritual and intellectual powers to bear on drawing out the moralizing power of the central Christian truth of God's redemption of humanity in the kingdom of God. As a result of his influence an entire generation of Christian pastors and teachers developed the "social gospel."

Any critical evaluation of Ritschl's theology must raise the question, Is it possible to make an absolute distinction between theoretical or scientific judgments on the one hand and religious or value judgments on the other? Much of his theology is based on just such a distinction; yet critics have repeatedly pointed out that he himself failed to adhere to it consistently.

Ritschl was not alone in attempting to free Christian theology from overpowering control by philosophical systems of thought and supposedly objective natural theologies. The central problem in his theological method lies in the adamant way he tried to rule out all discussion of God in himself, as well as his own failure to avoid such talk entirely. James Richmond correctly criticized Ritschl for too severely limiting the scope of theological inquiry: "Theologians are right to fear stirring up a science-religion conflict from which religion has nothing to gain and everything to lose, but they ought to prevent this fear from producing a form of intellectual paralysis."[23]

Ritschl's limitation of theological inquiry to the realm of value judgments is problematic in several ways. For example, it cannot admit a full understanding of the divine transcendence. If theology cannot discuss the inner reality of God's being, it will naturally appear that God exists only in relation to humans. God will become dissolved in his effects, until only his effects are considered important. To a certain extent this danger appears already in what some critics have seen as Ritschl's near identification of God with the kingdom of God.[24]

In addition to the problem of transcendence, Ritschl's limitation of theology to value judgments raises serious problems for the public nature of theology. In spite of his intentions, Ritschl's theology seems open to the accusation of subjectivism. As Richmond notes, "at points Ritschl's theology does *seem* to withdraw religion into a restricted area of its own, and abandon to 'irreligious' (i.e., profane) science or philosophy the wider realm of 'human knowledge.' "[25] While there is no doubt that Ritschl would react in horror to the common habit of modern Christians to divorce "faith" from "facts," there is equally no doubt that he is partly responsible for the development of this fallacy.

Perhaps no dimension of Ritschl's thought has evoked more criticism than has his Christology. Why did he discard the ancient Christian doctrine of the divine and human natures of Jesus Christ in such an apparently cavalier manner? Part of the reason lies in what has already been seen to be an illegitimate and inconsistent rejection of ontology, his unwillingness to engage in discussion of the substance or being of things behind their appearances and effects.

Another cause is more ulterior. Richmond pinpoints the problem: "Ritschl and his nineteenth-century contemporaries did not understand Christ's deity in terms of *substance,* nor of *consubstantiality* with God, simply because such terms had become in post-Enlightenment Germany unintelligible, not to say meaningless."[26] In other words, Ritschl, like other liberal thinkers, tended to accept the consensus of modern, educated, post-Enlightenment society as a norm for theology. This led Barth and other critics of liberal theology in the twentieth century to level at Ritschl the rather harsh but somewhat deserved label of "culture Protestantism."

Not only were the reasons for Ritschl's rejection of classical Christology dubious at best, but the understanding of Jesus that he put in its place can only be considered reductionistic. In spite of all his disclaimers, he reduced Jesus to the religious and ethical ideal of humanity.[27] However strongly he asserted Jesus' special status in the divine work of salvation, Ritschl effectively closed the impassable gulf between Christ and the rest of humanity.[28] As a result, there remains no basis for belief that Jesus is God's unsurpassable self-revelation.

The only answer Ritschl had to this objection is that any equal to Christ who might appear in history would stand in dependence on him and would therefore be subordinate to him.[29] Our natural response is, of course, Why? Ritschl's account of the person of Christ, like that of most liberals, falls far short of the high incarnational Christology of the church that dates back to the New Testament itself. In no sense is his Christ "God with us." Even a sympathetic critic like James Richmond cannot help but label Ritschl's Christology "impoverishingly restrictive."[30]

Adolf Harnack

As noted earlier, Ritschl's theology gave rise to an entire school of liberal theologians whose influence permeated the major Protestant churches of Europe and America around the turn of the century. Two members of the Ritschlian school stand out because of the creative ways in which they built on his foundation: the German scholar Adolf Harnack and the American professor of German descent Walter Rauschenbusch.

Adolf Harnack was perhaps the most brilliant and popular advocate of liberal Protestant theology at the turn of the century. He was professor of church history at the

University of Berlin from 1888 until retirement in 1921. His lectures drew hundreds of students, and his scholarly writings (approximately sixteen hundred titles) brought him great acclaim from the academic world. Harnack was a close confidant of Kaiser Wilhelm of Germany, who placed him in charge of several important cultural institutions, including the Royal Library in Berlin. He was knighted by the Kaiser in 1914. Harnack, who wrote Wilhelm's speech to the German people announcing the beginning of World War 1,[31] strongly supported the Kaiser's war policies. This was one factor that turned his most notable student, the Swiss theologian Karl Barth, against him. After the war Harnack was offered the post of ambassador to the United States by the new government—an honor he respectfully declined. He died in 1930. Today a major government building in Berlin, the "Adolf von Harnack Haus," stands as a memorial to this towering figure in modern theology.

Harnack's widest influence came through the publication of a series of lectures given at the University of Berlin in 1899 and 1900, which were taken down verbatim by a student and presented to the professor. In 1901 these lectures were published in America under the title *What Is Christianity?* The volume went through numerous editions and was widely read and quoted by liberal preachers and authors for the next thirty-five years.

In these sixteen lectures Harnack attempted to identify the central kernel of authentic Christianity, which he calls the "Gospel," and to separate it from the husk of cultural forms in which it is communicated in the New Testament and historical traditions of Christendom.[32] He set forth the thesis that Jesus proclaimed a message about God the Father, not about himself: "The Gospel, as Jesus proclaimed it, has to do with the Father only and not with the Son."[33] According to Harnack, this gospel is simple and sublime, consisting of three interrelated truths: the kingdom of God and its coming, God the Father and the infinite value of the human soul, and the higher righteousness and the commandment of love.[34]

Harnack found little of the gospel in the Old Testament. Even in the New Testament it is encrusted with fantastic stories of miracles, angels, devils and apocalyptic catastrophes. Throughout its history, he argued, the church has been overlaid with husks of alien philosophical concepts such as the Greek identification of the *Logos* with Christ.[35] For Harnack, in spite of all this the gospel has survived wherever Jesus' pure and simple message of the kingdom of God has been accepted as the highest and most glorious ideal known to humanity. This ideal is "the prospect of a union among men, which is held together not by any legal ordinance, but by the rule of love, and where a man conquers his enemy by gentleness."[36]

Walter Rauschenbusch

Harnack stopped short of applying the ideal of the kingdom of God to specific political agendas; he even harshly criticized those who would use it to fuel revolutionary reform movements. Walter Rauschenbusch, in contrast, spent most of his creative energy as a theologian doing just that.

Rauschenbusch was the son of a German Lutheran minister who became a Baptist shortly after immigrating to the United States. Walter had a profound conversion experience when he was only nine years old. Having sensed God's call to be a minister, he attended Rochester Seminary in New York, where his father had become a professor in the German-speaking department.

The young pastor's first position was in Hell's Kitchen, a particularly impoverished section of New York City. There he became involved in the growing socialist movement and helped to found a religious socialist newspaper.

In 1891 Rauschenbusch spent several months studying New Testament in Germany where he came under the influence of the Ritschlian emphasis on the ethical kingdom of God as the heart and soul of the gospel. When he returned to the United States he threw himself into the budding "social gospel" movement, becoming its most theologically able exponent and leading prophet.[37] In 1897 he became professor of church history at Rochester Seminary and through his writings and lectures promoted the political and economic transformation of America until his death in 1918.

Rauschenbusch's books, which were mostly written for popular consumption, are not weighty theological tomes, but practical applications of the ethical aims and ideals of the kingdom of God to concrete social life. The most influential work and one which catapulted him into the public limelight was *Christianity and the Social Crisis,* published in 1907.

This work set forth in stark language the extreme gap between wealth and poverty in America and asserted that being a Christian in this social crisis meant working for the salvation of economic structures that perpetuate poverty. The essential Christian task, he wrote, is not so much to abolish drunkenness and adultery, but "to transform human society into the Kingdom of God by regenerating all human relations and reconciling them in accordance with the will of God."[38] He specifically singled out laissez faire capitalism as a part of the Kingdom of Evil in American life and called on American Christians to lead a new revival, in which not only individual souls but entire corporate entities and social structures would repent and be saved.

In 1912 Rauschenbusch published his second major book, *Christianizing the Social Order.* In it he offered specific suggestions for the revival he envisioned. He called for the socialization of major industries, support for labor unions and the abolition of an economy centered around greed, competition and the profit motive. All these changes he equated with the gradual Christianization of the social order—a progressive approximation of the kingdom of God in human society.

Rauschenbusch published what became the systematic theology for the social gospel movement, *A Theology for the Social Gospel,* in 1917. Here he attempted to redefine every major Christian doctrine in terms of the social and historical reality of the Kingdom of Love, which he equated with "humanity organized according to the will of God."[39] While Rauschenbusch did not explicitly deny the classical doctrines of the Christian faith, he reinterpreted them in light of the central unifying theme of the kingdom of God. For example, the main significance of Jesus lay in the new concept of God that he offered to humanity. Instead of portraying God as a monarch, Jesus "democratized the conception of God" by taking him by the hand and calling him "Father."[40]

Rauschenbusch then defined salvation as the "voluntary socializing of the soul."[41]

The American social gospel movement represented the most practical and concrete expression of classical liberal theology. Most of its underlying theological methods and themes go back to Ritschl, but it combined them with an evangelical fervor for social reform absent in European liberal theology.

Although liberalism remains a force to be reckoned with, to a great extent the First World War swept away classical liberal theology and with it the social gospel. For the next decades a new form of Protestant theology, neo-orthodoxy, would hold sway. The new movement was harshly critical of the liberal theology of thinkers like Ritschl, Harnack and Rauschenbusch. One of the exponents of the newer thinking, H. Richard Niebuhr, penned the now classic condemnation of liberalism: "A God without wrath brought men without sin into a kingdom without judgment through the ministrations of a Christ without a cross."[42]

Underlying all other dissatisfactions with liberal theology was neo-orthodoxy's fear that its emphasis on the kingdom of God within history would dissolve God into the world. Human effort would then replace divine sovereignty, and a not-so-subtle apotheosis of humanity would replace the worship of the holy God. The neo-orthodox reaction against this immanentalist impulse of the older liberalism marks the beginning of twentieth-century theology. To it we now turn our attention.

Natural theol.

3 THE REVOLT AGAINST IMMANENCE: *Transcendence in Neo-orthodoxy*

*T*HE GUNS OF AUGUST 1914 SOUNDED THE DEATH KNELL OF THE NINETEENTH-CENTURY intellectual ethos. World War 1 marked the end of the progressivism of the century of optimism and set the stage for the underlying current of pessimism characteristic of the ensuing years. In the same way, the end of the theology of optimism that pervaded the nineteenth century was signaled by the publication of a commentary on the book of Romans written by the pastor residing in an obscure, small town in Switzerland, Karl Barth.

The reaction to the prevailing liberalism that Barth set in motion itself came to dominate the theological scene well past the midpoint of the twentieth century. Although thinkers in the wake of his pioneering work would chart their own individual courses, the Swiss theologian did indeed father a new movement in theology. This new direction is generally termed "neo-orthodoxy."

The neo-orthodox movement was characterized by the attempt of theologians to rediscover the significance for the modern world of certain of the doctrines that had been central to the older Christian orthodoxy. Consequently, its proponents stood in a complex relationship to the liberalism that preceded the newer thinking. On the one hand, neo-orthodox theologians followed the older liberalism in viewing the Enlightenment as a given, and as a result with their liberal forebears they accepted biblical criticism. On the other hand, the younger thinkers rejected what they saw as the culture Christianity of liberalism, which arose out of the emphasis on natural theology. They were gravely concerned that Protestant liberalism had been so intent on making the Christian faith palatable to the modern mindset that it had lost the gospel. The Word of God—the voice of the Transcendent One—no longer thundered the good news of reconciliation to humankind lost in sin. Neo-orthodoxy sought to reassert these forgotten themes to a world that once again needed to hear God speak from beyond.

In the quest to reassert themes such as human sin, divine grace and personal decision, twentieth-century neo-orthodoxy drew inspiration from a hitherto unheeded nineteenth-century voice who had spoken out against the dominant thinking of his day. That voice was the "melancholy Dane," Søren Kierkegaard.

 Søren Kierkegaard was born in Copenhagen in 1813, the son of a wealthy Lutheran businessman, and died in 1855. His was an unhappy childhood; he suffered from a crooked back and was physically frail. Despite being educated for church ministry, completing his studies in 1840, his actual interest lay in philosophy and literature. Young Kierkegaard's unhappiness was exacerbated by his thwarted love relationship with Regina Olsen. Although the couple was engaged in 1841, Kierkegaard found it necessary to break the tie. But he spent much of the remainder of his short life pining for his lost love.

Kierkegaard was a prolific writer. His literary career came in three stages. In the first, he dealt mainly with his relationship with Regina Olsen. The second stage followed his conversion experience in 1848 and focused on the difficulty of being a Christian. A funeral oration in January 1854, in which a bishop of the Danish state church praised a departed colleague who had in fact lived a worldly life, launched the third stage in Kierkegaard's output. He waged a bitter attack on the state church, exposing the disparity between early Christianity and the contemporary Danish version.

Lying behind Kierkegaard's diatribes was his fundamental controversy with the Hegelian philosophy accepted by the intellegensia of his homeland. The Danish philosopher rejected the reigning view that reason was able to answer the basic religious questions of life. And in contrast to the collectivism that arose from the Hegelian link between human spiritual progress and the historical self-development of Absolute Spirit, Kierkegaard emphasized the individual.

In the place of the conventional wisdom of his day, Kierkegaard offered a new understanding of the nature of truth, at least as he has been interpreted in the twentieth century. Truth is not impersonal, not attained by dispassionate thinking.[1] Rather, truth is subjectivity; it arises when the personal subject wholeheartedly wills to be in the truth. Consequently, the beginning point in the quest for truth does not lie in the detached contemplation of universals; rather, truth begins with the concrete individual in the concrete situation of life.[2] Hence Kierkegaard's well-known definition of truth: "An objective uncertainty held fast in an appropriation-process of the most passionate inwardness is the truth."[3]

 In *Philosophical Fragments*, Kierkegaard outlined his famous distinction between Christianity and Socratic religion. The latter, "Religiousness A," is the religion of immanence, because it presupposes that truth is present within the individual. What

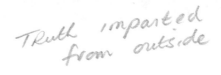
Truth imparted from outside.

is required for truth to emerge is merely that someone act as a midwife, helping the knowing subject to give it birth. But in the religion of Jesus—"Religiousness B" or the religion of otherness—the student is destitute of truth, or even worse, exists in a state of error. The individual therefore requires a teacher who brings the truth and even provides the condition necessary for its reception. Such a teacher is Savior and Redeemer, and his coming is "the fullness of time."[4]

For Kierkegaard, this teacher of course is Jesus the Christ. But the Christian confession of Jesus as the Christ involves a double paradox. It asserts that God has become human, that the Eternal has become temporal. And it declares that our eternal happiness has its foundation in a historical event, the historicity of which is only probable and not fully certain. Because it is a paradox, the truth of Christianity is grasped only by faith and not by reason. Being a Christian, therefore, involves a willingness to venture forth in faith where reason cannot take us. Its essence lies in passionate concern and holy fear and trembling, not in complacent certitude, Kierkegaard concluded.

Themes announced by the nineteenth-century Danish philosopher—the transcendence of the God who speaks the ineffable divine truth to the individual in the moment of divine encounter—became the foundation on which the theologians of neo-orthodoxy in the twentieth century built and the theses that they expanded in their theological deliberations.

KARL BARTH:
TRANSCENDENCE AS GOD'S FREEDOM

When future historians of theology look back on the twentieth century there is little doubt who they will name as its single most influential Christian thinker: Karl Barth. Widely recognized during his own lifetime as a modern church father, he is often classed together with Augustine, Aquinas, Luther, Calvin and Schleiermacher because of his massive, original contribution to theology. Virtually all twentieth-century theologians have sensed a compulsion to respond to him in some way. Decades after his death new articles and books dissecting his theology continue to appear in Europe and America. Scholarly conferences are held regularly to discuss Barth's continuing significance, and special meetings of theologians were held in 1986 to commemorate the one hundredth anniversary of his birth.

While there is no formal "school" of Barthian theology, a number of leading European and American theologians consciously identify with Barth's basic program and seek in their own ways to continue it. His stature was in no way exaggerated in the conclusion of one of his most noted students, Eberhard Jüngel, who wrote in 1982,

> Karl Barth is the most significant Protestant theologian since Schleiermacher, whom he sought to overcome and to whom he nevertheless remains indebted in many ways. Barth's personal and literary influence profoundly changed the shape of Christian theology across confessional boundaries, significantly altered the direc-

tion of the Protestant church, and also left an unmistakable imprint on the politics and cultural life of the twentieth century.[5]

Barth's Life and Career

Karl Barth was born in 1886 in Basel, Switzerland. His father was a lecturer at a college for preachers (similar to a seminary) and identified with a fairly conservative group within the Reformed Church of Switzerland. When Barth was two years old his father accepted a much more prestigious position as an assistant lecturer at the University of Bern. Barth's family life was strict but generally happy, and he later remembered respecting his father very greatly and being deeply attached to his mother.[6]

On the eve of his confirmation in 1902 Barth resolved to become a theologian, not so much with preaching and pastoral care in mind, he later wrote, as with the hope of reaching a proper understanding of the creed, to replace the rather hazy ideas of it that he had at that time.[7] He studied theology at the universities in Bern, Berlin, Tübingen and Marburg, eventually arriving at a theological position within the Ritschlian school of liberal thought. In Berlin he came under the influence of Harnack, and at Marburg he became a disciple of the great Ritschlian theologian Wilhelm Herrmann. Later, of course, he radically repudiated this theology, much to the dismay of his teachers.

Barth never completed a doctorate, although later in life he was showered with honorary degrees from many great universities. In 1908 he was ordained to the ministry of the Reformed Church and took a position as assistant pastor in Geneva. There he occasionally preached in the same great hall in which Calvin had lectured three and a half centuries earlier. Like most assistant pastors he found the work unfulfilling and moved in 1911 to a small parish in Safenwil, a village on the border between Switzerland and Germany. It was in Safenwil that theological history was made. There Barth created a revolution in theology.

Many factors led to Barth's radical break with liberal theology. Two, however, stand out as especially noteworthy. First, Barth found that liberal theology was useless in his weekly task of preaching the gospel to the people of Safenwil. As a result, he undertook a careful and painstaking study of the Scriptures and through it discovered "The Strange New World Within the Bible," to employ the title of one of his earliest articles. In the Scriptures he found not human religion, not even the highest and best thoughts of pious people, but God's Word: "It is not the right human thoughts about God which form the content of the Bible, but the right divine thoughts about men."[8] Barth found a relevant message for his parishioners in the transcendent Word in Scripture and not in the philosophical theology of the liberal school of neo-Protestantism in which he had been trained.

The second factor that turned Barth away from liberal theology was an event. In August 1914 he read a published statement by ninety-three German intellectuals supporting Kaiser Wilhelm's war policy. Among them were nearly all of his theological teachers, whom he had until then religiously honored. Their support of German imperialism led Barth to believe that something must be terribly wrong with their theology, if it could be so quickly compromised in the face of the ideology of war. Disillusioned by his teachers' conduct, Barth concluded that he could no longer "accept their ethics and dogmatics, their Biblical exegesis, their interpretation of history."[9] For him, the entire liberal theology of the nineteenth century had no future, and he turned his considerable but hitherto hidden theological talent toward its demolition.

During the war Barth began work on a commentary on Paul's epistle to the Romans. Published in 1919, it unexpectedly created a furor because of its harsh criticism of liberal Protestant theology. According to one theologian of the time, *Der Romerbrief (The Epistle to the Romans)* fell like a bombshell on the playground of the theologians. In it Barth affirmed the validity of *both* the historical-critical method of studying Scripture *and* the doctrine of verbal inspiration, and he stated that if he were forced to choose between them he would choose the latter.[10] Barth criticized liberal theology for turning the gospel into a religious message that tells humans of their own divinity instead of recognizing it as the Word of God, a message that humans are incapable of anticipating or comprehending because it comes from a God utterly distinct from them.[11] In essence Barth was calling for a revolution in theological method, a theology "from above" to replace the old, human-centered theology "from below." Throughout the commentary he emphasized the wholly otherness of God, the gospel, eternity and salvation. These great truths, he argued, cannot be built up from universal human experience or reason, but must be received in obedience from God's revelation.

Because of its emphasis on the confrontation between God and humanity, *Der Romerbrief* won for Barth's theology labels such as "dialectical theology" and "theology of crisis." "Dialectical" placed Barth in the sphere of Kierkegaard's philosophical method rather than Hegel's. For Kierkegaard, because of human sinfulness and the wholly otherness of God, God's truth and human thought can never be smoothed out into a rational synthesis. Instead, the paradoxical truths of God's self-revelation must be embraced in a leap of faith by the finite human mind. In his preface to the second edition of *Der Romerbrief* (1922) Barth admitted his indebtedness to Kierkegaard:

> ... if I have a system, it is limited to a recognition of what Kierkegaard called the "infinite qualitative distinction" between time and eternity, and to my regarding this as possessing negative as well as positive significance: "God is in heaven, and thou art on earth." The relation between such a God and such a man, and the relation between such a man and such a God, is for me the theme of the Bible and the essence of philosophy.[12]

Within a few months of its publication, *Der Romerbrief* became the focus of heated debate. Some liberal biblical scholars and theologians dismissed it as the rantings of a religious enthusiast, while others hailed it as a recovery of the true spirit of the Reformation. Some of Barth's own teachers, including Harnack and Herrmann, were puzzled by its unhistorical and uncritical approach to the Bible. In spite of the furor, however, numerous pastors, teachers and theologians found it a badly needed corrective for Christian theology moving into the twentieth century. So influential was *Der Romerbrief* that many scholars date the end of nineteenth- and beginning of twentieth-century theology with its publication in 1919.

Largely because of the success of *Der Romerbrief* Barth was offered a position as professor of Reformed theology at the University of Göttingen in Germany in 1921. Shortly after arriving he fell into serious conflict with the disciples of Ritschl, the great liberal thinker, who had taught there in the late nineteenth century and was still revered. Barth continued to write articles and books setting the Word of God over against human reason and accusing liberal neo-Protestantism of succumbing to the culture of Enlightenment rationalism. He argued that the greatest danger to the gospel was not that it be rejected, but that it be peacefully accepted and made harmless by becoming merely another possession of human reason and culture. In his eyes, for a century German liberal theology had been subverting the gospel by making it respectable. Naturally, such polemics won Barth few friends among the reigning theological elite.

In 1925 Barth was offered a professorship at the University of Münster, where he stayed only five years, moving on to the University of Bonn in 1930. During this period a decisive shift of emphasis began to appear in his writing. While not forsaking his rejection of liberal theology, he began to emphasize God's "Yes" to humanity in Jesus Christ more than the "No" that he had been pronouncing for over a decade.

Barth discarded his first attempt at a systematic theology *(Prolegomena to Christian Dogmatics,* 1928). He saw that it was too corrupted by existentialist philosophy, and he wished to produce an absolutely *theological* and therefore totally *biblical* theology free from dependence on any human system of thought. Further, he wanted to emphasize the objectivity of God's revelation more than the subjectivity of human faith.

In 1931 Barth wrote what many scholars consider his most important statement of his mature theological method: *Fides quarens intellectum* (faith seeking understanding), a study of the medieval scholastic theologian Anselm of Canterbury. Contrary to many interpretations of Anselm, Barth argued that the great churchman was not a rationalist but a devout scholar seeking to bring reason into the service of faith. Anselm's ontological argument for the existence of God was not an attempt to prove God apart from faith but an attempt to understand with the mind what is already believed by faith.

For Anselm, Barth argued, all theology is to be done in the context of prayer and obedience. This means that *Christian* theology cannot be an objective, dispassionate science, but must be the understanding of God's objective self-revelation in Jesus Christ made possible by grace and faith alone. What is required for finding theological answers is "a pure heart, eyes that have been opened, child-like obedience, a life in the Spirit, rich nourishment from Holy Scripture."[13] In other words, Barth asserted, the presupposition of correct theology is a life of faith, and its mark is unwillingness ever to set itself in explicit contradiction to the Bible, "the textual basis of the revealed object of faith."[14]

Until the writing of his treatise on Anselm, Barth's theology emphasized the *negativity* of the encounter between God and humanity. Beginning with this book his theology began to emphasize the *positive* knowledge of God in God's self-revelation in Jesus Christ. The negative element remained, in that Barth always opposed every form of natural theology—the attempt to gain knowledge of God from nature, culture and philosophy. However, his emphasis had shifted toward the possibility of true knowledge of God in Jesus Christ as grasped by faith.

Shortly after completing his book on Anselm, Barth began work on a systematic theology, the *Church Dogmatics,* which was left unfinished at thirteen volumes when he died in 1968. The most noticeable feature about it (besides its sheer size) is the lack of any traditional prolegomena or philosophical introduction. Barth consciously omitted it because he was convinced that true theology must be the explication of God's Word and nothing else. Any attempt to ground the truth of God's Word in human reasoning, however devout and sincere, inevitably leads to theology being subverted by human, historical modes of thought and thus to "anthropocentric theology," the evil against which Barth fought so hard.

The presupposition of Barth's entire effort in *Church Dogmatics* is that God establishes an analogy between himself and humanity in Jesus Christ. Barth contrasted this "analogy of faith" with the older concept of the "analogy of being." Knowledge of God is not an innate capacity within human nature or experience, but is possible only because God graciously gives it in Jesus Christ who is both God and human. One either "sees" Jesus Christ as the Way, the Truth and the Life or one does not. There is no proving this truth. In fact, every attempt to prove Christ borders on idolatry, for it calls God and his revelation before the bar of human reason.

During the early 1930s Barth became deeply involved in the anti-Nazi Confessing Church movement in Germany. In 1934 he helped write the Barmen Declaration, which stated that Jesus Christ is the only Lord for Christians and thereby leveled an implicit criticism of the German Christians' elevation of Hitler to the status of a messiah. Barth saw the German Christians' acceptance of Nazi ideology as a form of culture Christianity, the normal outcome of natural theology, and he gave great encouragement to those dissidents within the state church who opposed the Nazis. Because of his refusal to give the Hitler salute at the beginning of his lectures or to sign an oath of loyalty to Hitler, in June 1935 the German government summarily dismissed Barth from his teaching position at Bonn. He was offered the position of professor of theology at the University of Basel and returned to the city of his birth, where he lived and taught the rest of his life.

Throughout his twenty-seven years of teaching at Basel, Barth worked on his *Church Dogmatics* and numerous other books and articles, preached regularly at the city prison and attained a reputation as a Mozart scholar. Students from around the world came to hear his lectures and participate in his seminars. So many students arrived from England and America that Barth began to hold a weekly English-speaking seminar. In 1962 he retired from full-time teaching at the age of seventy-five and immediately embarked upon his first trip outside of Europe, spending seven weeks traveling around the United States lecturing, sightseeing and meeting people. *Time* magazine honored him with a cover story, and the University of Chicago bestowed an honorary doctoral degree on him.

The last few years of life were extremely difficult for Barth, as his health failed and he found himself the object of harsh criticism from both the left and the right.

He was dismayed by the rise of secular theology and the theology of the death of God, as well as by less radical movements. But he was greatly encouraged by the changes within the Roman Catholic Church during the Second Vatican Council (1962-1965), at which he was an invited observer. Karl Barth died at home in Basel sometime during the night of December 9, 1968. His death marked the passing of a theological giant.

Theological Method

As we have already seen, Barth's theological method had both a negative and a positive pole. Negatively, he eschewed any form of natural theology and never tired of analyzing and trumpeting the ways in which it subtly and inevitably leads to the cultural subversion of the gospel:

> Christian natural theology very respectfully and in all humility re-casts revelation into a new form of its own devising. But for all that its behavior is so respectful and forbearing, for all that it subordinates itself so consciously and consistently, natural theology has already conquered it at the very outset, making revelation into non-revelation. This will certainly show itself in what it does with the revelation that has been absorbed and domesticated by it.[15]

Barth attempted to demonstrate how the subversion of the gospel had taken place in classical Roman Catholic theology, classical liberal Protestant theology and even in the German Christians' openness to the ideology of Nazism. From the history of theology and his own discernment of the sovereignty of God in the gospel message Barth concluded that

> the logic of the matter demands that, even if we only lend our little finger to natural theology, there necessarily follows the denial of the revelation of God in Jesus Christ. A natural theology which does not strive to be the only master is not a natural theology. And to give it place at all is to put oneself, even if unwittingly, on the way which leads to this sole sovereignty.[16]

Barth summarized his own position by declaring, "The possibility of knowledge of God's Word lies in God's Word and nowhere else."[17] This statement expresses the positive as well as the negative side of his theological method. In spite of the unreadiness of humanity for God and the impossibility of true knowledge of God through reason, nature and culture, in his sovereign freedom and grace God has revealed himself in human history and made possible the miracle of knowledge of himself. The single event in history in which God is revealed, according to Barth, is the event of Jesus Christ. And in Christ God reveals *himself*, not merely information or a way of life. For Barth this means that "the eternal God is to be known in Jesus Christ and not elsewhere."[18]

But how can one know that this is true? Barth responded, "The proof of faith consists in the proclamation of faith. The proof of the knowledge of the Word [of God] consists in confessing it."[19] In other words, faith in Jesus Christ as the self-revealed truth of God is self-authenticating. For the Christian this is the fundamental fact on which everything else rests and which itself rests on nothing else. Faith is a gift of God.

God's Word and the Bible

For Barth the only source of Christian theology is God's Word. This Word, however, consists of three forms or modes. The primary form is Jesus Christ and the entire history of God's acts leading up to and surrounding his life, death and resurrection. This is revelation proper, the gospel itself. The second form is Scripture, the privileged witness to divine revelation. Finally, the church's proclamation of the gospel forms the third mode. The latter two forms are God's Word only in an instrumental sense, for they become God's Word when God uses them to reveal Jesus Christ.

The Bible, consequently, is not statically God's Word. God's Word always has the character of *event;* in a sense it is God himself repeating his being in action. The Bible *becomes* God's Word in an event: "The Bible is God's Word to the extent that God causes it to be His Word, to the extent that He speaks through it."[20]

Barth's view of Scripture caused much controversy and criticism. Liberals accused him of elevating the Bible to a special position that nearly equaled the traditional doctrine of verbal inspiration, thus removing it from historical critical inquiry. Conservatives, on the other hand, assailed Barth's subordination of Scripture to a nonpropositional event of revelation and his explicit denial of its inerrancy, some going so far as to label his theology a "new modernism."

Actually, both criticisms fall near the target, but miss the mark. On the one hand, Barth did deny Scripture the status given it in classical orthodoxy. He distinguished between the Bible and the Word of God, affirming that "what we have in the Bible are in any case human attempts to repeat and reproduce this Word of God in human words and thoughts and in specific human situations."[21] On the other hand, he warned sternly against the danger of concluding that Scripture's divine inspiration—its special status as privileged witness to Jesus Christ—is merely a human value judgment. Its inspiration, Barth said, is not a matter of our own estimation or mood or feeling:

> Certainly it is not our faith which makes the Bible the Word of God. But we cannot safeguard the objectivity of the truth that it is the Word of God better than by insisting that it does demand our faith, and underlie our faith, that it is the substance and life of our faith. For in so doing we maintain that it is the truth of the living God, beyond which there is none other, the power of which we are not allowed to doubt in face of the forces of human subjectivity, which we have therefore to know and recognise as such. But if this is true, then it stands that we have to understand the inspiration of the Bible as a divine decision continually made in the life of the Church and in the life of its members."[22]

That the Bible is the Word of God, then, in no way depends on the subjective experience of the individual or on scholarly conclusions based on internal and external evidence. For Barth, the Bible is the Word of God because again and again, apart from any human decision or initiative, God uses it to produce the miracle of faith in Jesus Christ. The church's proper attitude toward Scripture is one of obedience and submission because the only authority above it is Jesus Christ himself. The Bible mediates Christ's authority to the church. Furthermore, the Bible has authority over the church, because "it is a record, indeed historically it is the oldest extant record, of the origin and therefore of the basis and nature of the Church. . . . Therefore Holy Scripture has always in the Church a unique and in its way singular authority."[23]

Clearly, Barth held the Bible in high regard, placing it over every human authority while subordinating it to Jesus Christ himself. Throughout his *Church Dogmatics* he treated the Bible *as if* it were verbally inspired and doctrinally infallible. He never appealed to some other authority over against Scripture. On the contrary, he boldly asserted that under Jesus Christ and in complete agreement with him it is normative for Christian belief:

> What finally counts is whether a dogmatics is scriptural. If it is not, then it will definitely be futile, for we shall definitely have to say regarding it that in it the church is distracted, i.e., it is busy about other matters and is not doing justice to the scientific task set for it by the problematic nature of its proclamation.[24]

Christocentric and Trinitarian Theology   *God of 3 modes revealed in Jesus*

The structure of Barth's theology is thoroughly *christocentric*. The beginning, center and end of every doctrine is the event of Jesus Christ—his life, death, resurrection, exaltation and eternal union with God the Father. At every juncture of theology Barth asked, What is the proper understanding of this in the light of God's act in Jesus Christ? This christocentric structure provides the coherence and unity that makes Barth's massive theology a system.

For the Swiss theologian, Jesus Christ is the singular and unique *self-revelation of God*, the Word of God in person. From this basic affirmation of faith Barth deduced the deity of Jesus Christ: "revelation is the self-interpretation of this God. If we are dealing with His revelation, we are dealing with God Himself and not . . . with an entity distinct from Him."[25] One of Barth's basic axioms is that behind the actuality must lie the corresponding possibility.[26] Thus, if Jesus Christ is who faith says he is—the unsurpassable *self*-revelation of God—then he must be in some way identical with God himself and not merely an agent or representative of God. Behind and within the actuality of the event of revelation, then, lies its possibility—the Triune God.

Barth understood the doctrine of the Trinity as the only possible Christian answer to the question, Who is the self-revealing God? He asserted, "Thus it is God Himself, it is the same God in unimpaired unity, who according to the biblical understanding of revelation is the revealing God and the event of revelation and its effect on man."[27] In direct contradiction to Schleiermacher's approach, Barth placed the doctrine of the Trinity at the beginning of his theology. He argued,

> The doctrine of the Trinity is what basically distinguishes the Christian doctrine of God as Christian, and therefore what already distinguishes the Christian concept of revelation as Christian, in contrast to all other possible doctrines of God or concepts of revelation.[28]

According to Barth, then, God's revelation is God himself. God *is* who he reveals himself to be. Consequently, Jesus Christ, as the unique and unsurpassable self-revelation of God, is identical with God and therefore both truly human and truly divine: "Jesus Christ is not a demigod. He is not an angel. Nor is he an ideal man."[29] Rather, "the reality of Jesus Christ is that God Himself in person is actively present in the flesh. God Himself in person is the Subject of a real human being and acting."[30]

Barth made it clear that in talking about Jesus Christ he was talking about the Incarnation of the second "mode of Being" *(Seinsweise)* of God. He preferred "mode" over "person," because to modern ears the word *person* inevitably implies "personality" and God has only one personality.[31] If Jesus Christ were another personality different from the Father he could not be the Father's *self*-revelation. In Barth's estimation, Father, Son and Holy Spirit are the divine ways of being that eternally subsist within God in absolute unity. Yet their distinction forms the precondition for God's revelation in Jesus Christ and his spiritual presence within the life of the church. Thus, when Barth said that "God is Jesus Christ and Jesus Christ is God"[32] he meant this to be understood within the context of the Trinity: Jesus Christ is the second mode of being of God, the reiteration of the Father's own personality.

God as "He Who Loves in Freedom"

freedom for transcendence
love immanence

Although the doctrine of the Trinity is the center and heart of his doctrine of God, Barth devoted most of an entire volume to the attributes or perfections of God's being *(Church Dogmatics* 2/1). He defined the Being of God as "The One Who Loves in Freedom" and divided the divine perfections into two categories, the perfections of the divine loving and the perfections of the divine freedom. This rubric replaced the traditional duality of God's immanence and transcendence.

Barth claimed that God's love and freedom must be equally emphasized and balanced in order to do justice to the God of Jesus Christ. God's love is his freely chosen creation of fellowship between human beings and himself in Jesus Christ.[33] God wills to be ours and wills us to be his.[34] This is revealed above all in God's gracious identification with sinful humanity in the cross of Jesus Christ: "The Way of the Son of God into the Far Country."[35] The perfections that express this great love of God are grace and holiness, mercy and righteousness, patience and wisdom.[36]

Without in any way qualifying God's being as love, Barth proceeded to emphasize the *freedom* of this love. While God's love for the world is real and eternal, it is not necessary. God would still be love even if he did not choose to love the world.[37] Barth was clearly thinking of liberal theology, especially that influenced by Hegel, when he warned: "If we are not careful at this point we shall inevitably rob God of his deity."[38] God has perfect love and fellowship within himself—in his triune life—before and apart from his love for and fellowship with the world.[39] Only in this way can pantheism be avoided and God's love for the world be truly gracious, Barth argued. If God needed the world as the object of his love, then his would not be purely gracious love and the world would be necessary to God's being. God would then be robbed of his deity.

In contradiction to the entire drift of liberal thinking about God since Schleiermacher and Hegel, Barth affirmed God's absolute transcendence over the world, which he conceived of in terms of God's freedom: "The loftiness, the sovereign majesty, the holiness, the glory—even what is termed the transcendence of God—what is it but this self-determination, this freedom, of the divine living and loving, the divine person?"[40]

In fact, God is God only because he is absolute in relation to the world: "God confronts all that is in supreme and utter independence, i.e., He would be no less and no different even if they all did not exist or existed differently."[41] The perfections of God's freedom are unity and omnipresence, constancy and omnipotence, eternity and glory—all of which Barth creatively reinterpreted.[42]

In spite of his emphasis on God's freedom, Barth did not interpret God's love for humanity as a mere whim, as something that adds nothing to the divine life and about which God actually has little concern. Rather, God's fullness of life within himself "leans toward" unity with creaturely life.[43] Furthermore, God does not remain a prisoner of his freedom, but freely chooses to go out of himself into real fellowship with the world that reaches its deepest unity in Jesus Christ. In fact, this desire and decision for union with creatures in Jesus Christ was for Barth the ground and basis of the creation of the world itself. God created the world for no other reason than to enter into covenant fellowship with it in the Incarnation, death and resurrection of Jesus.[44]

Thus, Barth recognized no hidden God behind the God of love revealed in Jesus. Even though God could have reserved his life and love for himself alone and withheld it from the world, "He does not will to be God without us . . . and creates us rather to share with us and therefore with our being and life and act His own incomparable being and life and act."[45]

Doctrine of Election

According to Barth, the supreme event of God's entry into human history is the cross of Jesus Christ, in which the Son of God goes into the "far country" to take onto himself the divine wrath and rejection so richly deserved by sinful humanity. Thus, Jesus Christ is the one elect and reprobate (damned) man, all other humans being included in and represented by him: "The rejection which all men incurred, the wrath of God under which all men lie, the death which all men must die, God in his love for men transfers from all eternity to Him in whom He loves and elects them, and whom He elects at their head and in their place."[46]

Like his theology in general, Barth's doctrine of election is "christomonistic." Jesus Christ is for him the only object of God's election and damnation. No terrible decree of double predestination divides humankind into the saved and the damned. Rather, all are included in Jesus Christ, who is both the electing God and the elected human, and the benefits of his saving work extend to them all. Only he suffers the rejection of God, and of course he is God rejecting himself: "in the election of Jesus Christ which is the eternal will of God, God has ascribed to man . . . election, salvation and life; and to Himself He has ascribed . . . reprobation, perdition and death."[47] Thus, for Barth predestination means that from eternity God decided to acquit humanity at great cost to himself.[48]

But to whom does God's acquittal extend? Barth made absolutely clear that Jesus Christ is the only truly rejected person and that all humans are elect in him.[49] People may try to live a godless life in rejection of God, but "their desire and undertaking were nullified by God before the world began. . . . What is laid up for man is eternal life in fellowship with God."[50]

Does this amount to the doctrine of *apokatastasis* or universalism? In his written responses to this question Barth refused to give a straight answer: "I do not teach it, but I also do not not teach it"![51] Nevertheless, we can guess what the answer must be. As Catholic scholar Hans Urs von Balthasar pointed out, "it is clear from Barth's presentation of the doctrine of election that universal salvation is not only possible but inevitable. The only definitive reality is grace, and any condemnatory judgment has to be merely provisional."[52]

Evaluation

Barth's theological career began with controversy. It comes therefore as no surprise that controversy has surrounded his own theological method. Heirs of the liberal theology that he so vehemently rejected have often dismissed his approach as fideistic, as requiring modern believers to sacrifice reason and return to the tutelage of religious authority.[53] However, these critics have not been very successful in answering Barth's accusation that their approach to theology leads to the cultural subversion of Christianity.

Some conservative Protestant theologians have echoed the charge that Barth's theology is fideistic. In their estimation it jeopardizes Christian witness and evangelism by undermining any possibility of apologetics.[54] Other conservatives, however, have endorsed Barth's basic theological method as the best response to the Enlightenment's inflation of autonomous reason and its challenge to orthodox Christianity.[55]

The strength of Barth's theological method lies in its total reliance on revelation. Because of this, his theology is truly "theological," being free from dependence on philosophical systems or cultural, intellectual fads. Consequently, Barth's theology is able to take a prophetic stance toward the world, a strength clearly demonstrated in his early denunciation of Nazism as a form of idolatry arising out of natural theology. The theological nature of his approach also allows his to be a theology of proclamation, that is, a theology for preaching. Because they are built entirely on revelation, the great themes of the gospel remain free from being reduced to mere representations of philosophical truths.

Overall, then, Barth's theological method preserves theology's autonomy over against other disciplines. Theology remains the irreducible science of God's Word.

Theology's greatest strength is also the source of the greatest weakness of Barth's theological method, a weakness that arises from the extreme to which he takes theological autonomy. His refusal of every kind of rational justification of the truth of revelation leads theology beyond autonomy into isolation. If there are no intelligible bridges connecting theology with other disciplines or with common human experience, how can Christian belief appear to outsiders as anything but esoteric? It is one thing for Barth to reject liberal theology's reduction of Christian belief to what can be anticipated within the horizon of human experience; it is another thing for him to eliminate any connection between belief and experience.

Wentzel van Huyssteen summarized this problem:

Barth is justified in rejecting the reduction of the object of theology to mankind's religious consciousness. . . . But the assumed axiomatic datum of God and His revelation offers no escape . . . because the positive quality thus given to revelation can offer no alternative to subjectivism in theology. A positivistic theology of revelation that adopts a highly esoteric method makes it extremely difficult to convince others that the basic tenets of theology—God, revelation, Holy Scripture, inspiration, etc.—are not the constructs of subjective whim, whether personal or directed by an influential tradition.[56] *— Christ only —*

A second controversial point of Barth's theological method is its alleged *christomonism.* Some of Barth's critics have used this term to describe the extreme concentration on Jesus Christ present throughout his entire theology. Not only did Barth make Jesus Christ the center and heart of his theology, thereby being "christocentric," but he also restricted knowledge of and about God to what is revealed in Christ. Hans Urs von Balthasar described Barth's thought as an intellectual hourglass "where God and man meet in the center through Jesus Christ. There is no other point of encounter between the top and bottom portions of the glass."[57] The problem with such a move is that it leads to the denial of any general revelation, that form of revelation which seems to form the core of Paul's entire argument in the first chapter of Romans.

The accusation of christomonism arises as well from Barth's use of the person of Jesus Christ as the foundation and organizing principle of his entire theology. Every doctrine is turned into a form of Christology. This is clearly illustrated in Barth's doctrine of election. Jesus Christ is both the subject and object of predestination. But exactly where are God the Father and human beings in this scheme?

Perhaps *christomonism* is too strong a term to serve as a fair description of Barth's theology. Certainly he did not deny the distinction between the Son, the Father and the Holy Spirit. And he certainly did not blur the distinction between Christ and the world. Furthermore, the term is too polemical to do justice to Barth's great contribution in bringing Christ back into the center of Christian thinking, where he belongs. Nevertheless, the Swiss theologian's extreme concentration on Christology gives his theology the appearance of being one-sided and of neglecting the roles of the Father, the Spirit and human beings in salvation history.

Barth's doctrine of Scripture has been the object of considerable criticism from both liberal and conservative theologians. Liberals accuse him of ignoring the results of higher criticism and treating the Bible as if it were verbally inspired. Conservatives on the other hand accuse Barth of making too radical a distinction between "God's Word" and the Bible and denying the Bible's doctrinal infallibility.[58] Both sides tend to ignore the difference between Barth's theory of Scripture and his use of it. Liberals focus on his use of Scripture and ignore his strong statements regarding the human nature of the Bible. Conservatives focus on his theory and ignore the way in which Barth treats Scripture as if it were an absolute authority in theology.

The apparent inconsistency in Barth between theory and practice does indeed deserve criticism. Would it have been possible for Barth to spin out his magnificent modern exposition of classical Christian belief if he had held consistently to his theory of Scripture? Simply stated, his assertion of a tension between God's Word and the doctrinal propositions of the Bible hardly lends itself to such a highly systematized propositional exposition of biblical teaching.

One of Barth's greatest contributions to twentieth-century theology is his recovery of the doctrine of the Trinity from obscurity. Liberal theology from Schleiermacher onward had treated this doctrine as a relic of early Christianity's supposed "Hellenization" and had failed to see any ethical relevance in it. Under Barth's influence theology has returned to serious consideration of the doctrine of the Trinity, even if it has not reached any consensus concerning it.

Yet his handling of the doctrine of the Trinity has not met with universal agreement. Some critics have argued that Barth's treatment is implicitly modalistic; it reduces God to a single subjectivity by identifying God's one essence with his "person" and by employing the term *modes of being* for the trinitarian distinctions.[59] This criticism has a degree of validity in regard to the first volume of the *Church Dogmatics,* in which Barth derived the triunity of God from the concept of divine self-revelation and emphatically identified God's personhood with his single essence or nature.[60] Yet even there he rejected modalism by affirming "the ultimate reality of the three modes of being in the essence of God above and behind which there is nothing higher."[61] In later volumes Barth made absolutely clear his rejection of modalism and asserted the eternal and irreducible distinction between Father, Son and Holy Spirit by affirming an order of obedience within the eternal being of God (while rejecting any subordinationism).[62]

Conclusion

In terms of the flow of the theological history of the twentieth century, one of the great strengths of Barth's theology lies in its recovery of the transcendence of God. Only if God's love toward the world is radically free can it be gracious. The graciousness of God's relation with the world is at the very heart of the Christian gospel.

In his zeal to protect God's freedom and transcendence, however, Barth may have sacrificed too much on the human side of the God-world relationship. This is most clearly illustrated in his doctrine of salvation. Here God's triumphant Yes! in Jesus Christ makes null and void every human No! As G. C. Berkouwer, one of Barth's most sympathetic critics, correctly concluded, "In Barth's theology the triumph of grace makes vague the seriousness of the human decision, just as the kerugma *[sic]* is threatened with becoming a mere announcement without any vital exhortation."[63]

We may be tempted to say that whereas Schleiermacher made the mistake of trying to talk about God by talking about humankind in a very loud voice, Barth made the mistake of trying to talk about humanity by talking about God in a very loud voice. Perhaps Barth's error is the slightest, but to make neither one would be far better.

EMIL BRUNNER:
TRANSCENDENCE IN DIVINE-HUMAN ENCOUNTER

It is not unusual in any field of scholarship to find a true giant overshadowed by the colossi. Emil Brunner's stature and influence in twentieth-century theology would be indisputable were it not for Barth and Bultmann who overshadowed him. Together these three formed a triumvirate of dialectical theologians who revolutionized the discipline by reasserting the classical themes of the Protestant Reformation in the twentieth-century context. Despite their early alliance, they came to diverge quite radically from one another, especially during the years immediately after World War 2, which marked the height of their influence in the English-speaking world.

Although Barth became more famous and controversial than Brunner, the latter first exposed the new theology of God's transcendence to England and America. Brunner studied in England immediately before World War 1 and in America immediately after it. He also gave lecture series in the two countries during the 1930s, 1940s and 1950s, and some of his books were translated and widely read before those of Barth. He produced popular as well as scholarly works in theology and actively participated in interdenominational groups. All of these activities made him an early leader of the dialectical theology among English-speaking theologians.

The sheer mass and weight of Barth's theological production, however, gradually pushed Brunner's reputation into the background, much to his dismay. Nevertheless, Brunner's influence continues to be felt through the use of his *Dogmatics* (systematic theology) in British and American seminaries. Many theologians secretly prefer Brunner to Barth because of the clarity of his writing and the breadth of his vision of Christian truth.

Brunner's Life and Career

Emil Brunner was born two days before Christmas, 1889, in Zurich, Switzerland. He was raised and educated in the Reformed tradition of Zwingli and Calvin and earned a doctorate in theology from the University of Zurich in 1913. Most of his life was spent teaching theology at that same university, where Brunner held a chair from 1924 until his retirement in 1955. He taught at Princeton University in the United States for one year (1938-1939) and at the Christian University of Tokyo from 1953 to 1955. He preached frequently in the great cathedral of Zurich, where Ulrich Zwingli had thundered during the Reformation, and he welcomed international students, many from America, into his classes as well as into his home. A significant number of American evangelical theologians came to Zurich, and through them his influence on American theology continued into the 1960s and 1970s. Brunner died in his home city of Zurich in April 1966, after a long illness that had seriously affected his ability to work beyond retirement.

Brunner was a prolific author, penning numerous treatises and articles on theology, social ethics and Christian living. These include *The Mediator,* a full-length treatment of the person and work of Christ; *Man in Revolt,* a Christian anthropology; *The Divine Imperative,* a system of Christian ethics; and *Revelation and Reason,* a study of theological method. Toward the end of his career he summed up his entire life's work in a three-volume *Dogmatics.* These volumes contain his mature thought about all major Christian beliefs as well as many of the controversies of twentieth-century theology. A notable feature is his constant effort to distinguish his own theology from that of the man under whose shadow he struggled for recognition—Karl Barth.

Theological Concerns

Nearly every theologian is influenced by a concern about the wrong directions in which that person sees theology moving. Clearly Brunner's main concern was to counter the drift of nineteenth- and early twentieth-century theology into the type of immanence that, in the words of Paul Jewett, "regards man and God as metaphysically, epistemologically and ethically continuous, so that man may arrive at the true knowledge of God within the framework of his own innate possibilities."[1] Such a theology of immanence was epitomized in the various branches of Hegelian thought and was implicit in the entire theological methodology of classical Protestant liberalism at the turn of the century.

Although he is mentioned only occasionally, Schleiermacher seems to have been the object of much of Brunner's scorn as the paradigm of Christian theologians who make knowledge of God a natural capacity of humanity. Brunner's theology is a sustained attack on all attempts to grasp God with natural reason independent of revelation or to make any sort of human philosophy the necessary framework for understanding God's Word. He echoed Tertullian, Pascal and Kierkegaard in asserting, "If God is what . . . philosophical Theism says He is, then He is not the God of the Biblical revelation, the sovereign Lord and Creator, Holy and Merciful. But if He is the God of revelation, then He is not the God of philosophical Theism."[2]

In addition to his struggle against the theology of immanence Brunner faced two more opponents, "orthodoxy" and Karl Barth. As is often the case among thinkers, Brunner saw in his closest allies his greatest enemies. In many ways his theology parallels that of the Protestant orthodox theologians. He nevertheless vilified them for their virtual identification of the words of Scripture with the Word of God. As will be shown, Brunner was never more vehement or unfair than in his criticism of Protestant orthodoxy's doctrine of Scripture. He held no personal animosity toward Barth, who lived only a few miles away from him and whose theology gradually came to overshadow his own. However, Barth was never more vehement or unfair than in his attack on Brunner's doctrine of general revelation in the booklet *Nein!* (No!).[3]

After their disagreement in the mid-1930s, Brunner and Barth snubbed one another until the 1960s, when their American students arranged a reunion. Throughout his *Dogmatics* Brunner emphasized his disagreements with Barth in a somewhat exaggerated way. To the end he remained highly critical of Barth's doctrine of election, which he saw as leading inevitably to universalism and thus to the neglect of the necessity of a personal decision for or against Jesus Christ.[4]

Biblical Personalism

Brunner's theology ought not to be defined by what he opposed. To a great extent his concerns about the course theologians were tracking dominated the directions he took and the particular emphases he chose. However, his contribution to contemporary theology has its positive and original side. This contribution begins with his identification of revelation with the "I-Thou Encounter" between the individual and God.

In setting forth what he saw as the biblical definition of the truth of revelation,

Brunner borrowed heavily from two twentieth-century existentialist thinkers, Ferdinand Ebner and Martin Buber. Brunner referred to Ebner, who died in 1931, as an "eccentric genius" and acknowledged his own indebtedness to Ebner's epoch-making significance.[5] But it was the Jewish theologian and philosopher Martin Buber who most directly influenced Brunner in his "discovery" of the biblical concept of truth as divine-human encounter. Buber developed this insight most fully in his book *I and Thou*,[6] and Brunner explicated its significance for a Christian doctrine of revelation in *Truth as Encounter*.[7]

In order to grasp the nature of divine revelation, Brunner, following Buber, argued, one must first distinguish between two kinds of truth and knowledge: "it-truth" and "Thou-truth." The former is appropriate to knowledge of the world of objects, whereas the latter speaks to the world of persons. A fundamental difference exists between persons and objects; failure to recognize this difference and carry through its consequences in all areas of life lies at the foundation of the errors of philosophy.

Consequently, building on Ebner and Buber, Brunner asserted that any theology that treats knowledge of God as analogous to knowledge of objects (for example, distant planets or subatomic particles) is fundamentally wrong-headed. The very essence of Christianity lies in the eventfulness of encounter between God and humanity. Knowledge of God is personal in the sense that it transcends the plane of objects and the subject-object dualism inherent in knowledge of objects, calling instead for personal decision, response and commitment:

> Truth as encounter is not truth about something, not even truth about something mental, about ideas. Rather is it that truth which breaks in pieces the impersonal concept of truth and mind, truth that can be adequately expressed *only* in the I-Thou form. All use of impersonal terms to describe it, the divine, the transcendent, the absolute, is indeed the inadequate way invented by the thinking of the solitary self to speak of it—or, more correctly, of Him.[8]

According to Brunner, because God is personal, truth about him and knowledge of him must be the kind that is appropriate to the "Thou." Consequently, Christian truth must be truth as encounter, truth that happens in the crisis of the meeting between God and the human person in which God speaks and the person responds. Only such truth does justice to the freedom and responsibility of persons; only such truth preserves the heart of the gospel, namely, the personal relationship with God: "This truth comes to man as a personal summons; it is not a truth which is the fruit of reflection; hence it is truth which, from the very outset, makes me directly responsible."[9] Building from his concept of revelation as I-Thou encounter, Brunner's entire approach to theology has been designated "biblical personalism." He did indeed elevate this insight, and his attempt to center everything around it stands as his greatest contribution to modern theology.

Brunner believed that most of the problems of modern theology stem from the type of thinking that set the subject and object of knowledge over against each another and then subordinated one to the other. This model of knowledge was drawn from the sphere of impersonal objects. As a result the natural sciences became the standard of truth, and autonomous reason became the only appropriate method of knowing reality. But this naturally leads to a distortion of faith into some form of objective knowledge, whether knowledge of doctrines or of the timeless truths of reason. In either case, the personal character of faith and revelation is violated, he argued.

Revelation as Encounter

According to Brunner, words and propositions about God can never have the status of revelation because they inevitably objectify God and fall back within the sphere of "it-knowledge." In fact, "No speech, no word, is adequate to the mystery of God as Person,"[10] he declared. Revelation proper, then, is always an event of personal relationship-in-encounter that overcomes the subject-object division and truly communicates God to the human person: "Revelation is . . . never the mere communication of knowledge, but it is a life-giving and life-renewing communion."[11]

The type of nonpropositional revelation Brunner emphasized occurs in two events: historically in the Incarnation of God in Jesus Christ and presently in the *testimonium spiritus internum*, the inner witness of the Holy Spirit to Jesus Christ that makes the believer contemporary with Christ:[12]

> Only in this Word of the Holy Spirit does the Divine revelation in Jesus Christ become the real, actual word of God to man, in which the parabolic term of the historical revelation, *Deus dixit* [God spoke] becomes *Deus dicit* [God speaks], which is to be taken literally.[13]

The main point of Brunner's doctrine of revelation is that in it God does not communicate something about himself, but himself.[14] An obvious and often repeated criticism of this view is that one cannot receive a communication of a person without knowing something about the person. Can revelation be completely nonpropositional?[15] Brunner agreed that propositional knowledge about God naturally and necessarily arises out of the divine-human encounter that is revelation proper. However, he maintained that such propositional knowledge must be distinguished from revelation itself. He declared, "The spoken word is an indirect revelation when it bears witness to the real revelation: Jesus Christ, the personal self-manifestation of God, Emmanuel."[16] And, "the Word which has been formulated in human speech is now only revelation in an indirect sense; it is revelation as witness to Him."[17]

What Brunner was trying to avoid was the heresy of "Theologismus"—putting doctrine or theology in the place of personal faith.[18] To be sure personal faith arising out of the I-Thou encounter with God through Jesus Christ gives rise to reflection and words about God, he asserted. But these are never to be confused with revelation; otherwise belief in them will come to replace true faith. Even the apostles' witness to Jesus Christ, as indispensable as it is to faith, is not the object of faith itself. Doctrine, which is rational reflection on the apostles' witness and teaching, is even further from the heart of faith. Doctrine lies in the realm of "it-truth" and not "Thou-truth." Consequently, it cannot be the object of faith, and belief in it cannot replace true faith. Nevertheless, Brunner averred, these secondary instruments of revelation are indispensable to faith.[19]

What then is the status of the Bible? Brunner offered a twofold attitude toward Scripture. On the one hand, it is the absolutely indispensable witness to Jesus Christ. Therefore it is the source of both faith and theology. But on the other hand, Scripture is not God's verbally inspired, infallible propositional Word to humanity.

Brunner steadfastly refused to identify revelation with the words of Scripture. Scripture is a unique vehicle and instrument of revelation in that it contains the primary witness to the revelation of God in Jesus Christ.[20] But this meant to him that not everything in Scripture is of equal value or even true:

> The Scripture—first of all the testimony of the Apostles to Christ—is the "crib wherein Christ lieth" (Luther). It is a "word" inspired by the Spirit of God; yet at the same time it is a human message; its "human character" means that it is coloured by the frailty and imperfection of all that is human.[21]

The doctrine of verbal inspiration was the special focus of Brunner's attack. He railed against it for its supposed "disastrous results," including sterile intellectualism and confusion of revelation with "revealed doctrines."[22] Nevertheless, he held to a very high view of Scripture's authority as the indispensable witness to the original revelation—Jesus Christ—and the instrument of present revelation—the I-Thou encounter with God in which the believer becomes contemporaneous with Jesus. As a consequence of this function of Scripture, Brunner said, the Bible is the basis and norm of Christian doctrine: "Christian doctrine is legitimate, is truly based upon revelation, and the faith which is based upon it is the true knowledge of faith, in so far as this doctrine and this faith agree with the teaching of the Bible."[23]

After making such a positive assessment of the Bible's authority, Brunner seemed to worry that he may have come too close to the traditional orthodox doctrine of Scripture and thereby risked equating it with revelation itself. Therefore he worked his way back to Jesus Christ himself as the only real norm and authority for Christian faith, relegating both the apostolic testimony and the Bible that contains it to secondary, relative authorities open to criticism and correction:

> The word of Scripture is not the final court of appeal, since Jesus Christ Himself alone is this ultimate authority; but even while we examine the doctrine of Scripture, we remain within the Scriptures not, it is true, as an *authority*, but as the *source* of all that truth which possesses absolute authority.[24]

Brunner desired to avoid any hint of immanence in his doctrine of revelation. On the one hand, he wished to eliminate the immanence of revelation in natural human knowledge and experience, while preserving the transcendence of revelation by equating it with the unique Word of God in Christ, the apostolic witness to Christ and the present I-Thou encounter between the individual and God. This led him to a complete and unequivocal rejection of any "natural knowledge of God." On the other hand, he also wished to eliminate any immanence of revelation in human propositions—even divinely "inspired" ones. To equate revelation with human words would deny its transcendent quality over against everything finite, conditioned and temporal, as well as its personal quality over against everything in the "it-realm."

At the same time, Brunner could not bring himself to discard any objective source and norm for Christian doctrine. Rather, he located that source and norm in Scripture. Nevertheless, Brunner denied that the Bible is an ultimate norm. It is, at best, penultimate or proximate.

This raises a question hinted at earlier: How can knowledge—such as theology claims to be—have a purely nonpropositional norm? And can Scripture function as the kind of norm Brunner clearly wanted it to be (at least some of the time) without something like verbal inspiration? Paul King Jewett, who studied with Brunner in Zurich, has argued that Brunner's doctrine of revelation and Scripture is fundamentally incoherent.[25] Rather than being able to maintain the authority of Scripture apart from the doctrine of verbal inspiration, Brunner has simply swung back and forth between a form of "theopneusty" (divine inspiration) and abandonment of scriptural authority altogether.[26] Instead of transcending the orthodox-liberal antithesis regarding Scripture, Jewett said, Brunner has simply alternated between the two, "now making assertions which involve the identification of the Word of God with the words of men, now relativizing the function of Scripture as a vehicle of revelation to the point of losing its normative character altogether."[27] Jewett criticized Brunner's absolute distinction between "it-truth" and "Thou-truth" as impossible to maintain. If divine revelation is to serve as a norm for Christian doctrine, as Brunner intended, then it cannot be entirely devoid of propositional content. Otherwise there is no way from revelation to confession, from personal encounter to doctrine.

At times Brunner himself seemed to recognize this difficulty. He acknowledged the disciples' confession of Jesus as the Son of God as the testimony of the Spirit of God in human words.[28] In other words, even for Brunner, the confession "Thou art the Christ, the Son of the Living God" is the Word of God in human speech; it is divinely inspired testimony.[29] Once Brunner admitted this one instance of an identity between human speech and God's Word, the "dimensional divide" between propositional truth and divine revelation itself was broken down.[30] Brunner slipped at this point because even he recognized that without any sort of propositional element, divine revelation cannot serve as a "source and norm" of Christian doctrine. Revelation remains only a subjective experience.

In spite of his awareness of this, Brunner continued to insist on the nonpropositional nature of revelation and the nonidentity of God's Word with the human words of the Bible. Jewett, therefore, was surely right when he concluded that "Brunner halts his break with the tradition short of a complete abandonment of the authority of the Bible, only by an act of will."[31] Only by occasionally falling into sheer inconsistency with his own doctrine of revelation could he provide any sort of objective norm or criterion for doctrinal truth.

Brunner should have maintained his valuable distinction between Thou-truth and it-truth while providing greater insight into their mutual interdependence, thereby doing greater justice to his own dialectical approach to theology. Theology simply cannot be guided and controlled by a divine revelation that has no aspect of it-truth, even if that propositional element must be seen as secondary to the experience of I-Thou encounter.[32]

Controversy with Barth

As already mentioned, Brunner sought to distinguish his own contribution to theology from Barth's by emphasizing two major differences: the status of "general revelation" and the doctrine of God, especially of election and predestination.

A famous altercation between the two neo-orthodox giants took place in the mid-1930s over the issue of general revelation and natural theology. Brunner published an essay entitled "Nature and Grace" in which he argued that Barth was wrong to deny any sort of genuine revelation of God in nature, because

> the Word of God could not reach a man who had lost his consciousness of God entirely. A man without conscience cannot be struck by the call "Repent ye and believe the Gospel." What the natural man knows of God, of the law and of his own dependence upon God, may be very confused and distorted. But even so it is the necessary, indispensable point of contact for divine grace.[33]

Against Barth, Brunner presented a view of general revelation that he believed was fully consistent with the New Testament and the Protestant Reformers, especially Calvin and Luther. He eschewed any notion of a "natural knowledge of God" in the sense of proofs of the existence of God while maintaining that the image of God in humanity—the human person's capacity for receiving God's Word—remained in spite of the fall.[34] Recognition of such a bare, minimal awareness of God, he believed, is indispensable to the missions of church and theology, because it calls them to articulate the faith in a way that can be understood. While human thoughts and questions cannot determine the content of the gospel that the church proclaims, they must be taken into account in determining its manner of proclamation.[35]

Barth responded to Brunner's essay with a thunderous "Nein!": "I have to reply with a 'No!' to Brunner and the whole chorus of his friends and disciples and those who share his opinions."[36] The tone of Barth's essay was harsh, perhaps because he was at that time teaching in Germany and struggling with the Nazi temptation into which many "German Christians" were falling, as he saw it, because of their openness to natural theology. Barth accused Brunner of giving aid to that "theology of compromise" which was leading to the subversion of the German church to Nazi ideology.[37] Furthermore, he accused Brunner of implicitly denying salvation by grace through faith alone and falling back into the Catholic or (worse yet!) the neo-Protestant (liberal) theology of salvation by advocating a cooperation between grace and human effort.[38] Turning to an analogy, Barth asked,

> If a man had just been saved from drowning by a competent swimmer, would it not be very unsuitable if he proclaimed the fact that he was a man and not a lump of lead as his "capacity for being saved"? Unless he could claim to have helped the man who saved him by a few strokes or the like! Can Brunner mean that?[39]

Barth rejected Brunner's minimal "natural theology," which really amounted to nothing more than acknowledgment of a point of contact for the gospel in every person, as a definite turn away from the gospel of grace and toward compromise with the natural thinking of modern humans. The gospel, he asserted, stands in no need of any point of contact other than the one created by the Holy Spirit, which is always a miracle.[40] And the question concerning the "How?" of proclamation and of theological and ecclesiastical activity should be rejected at the outset, he added, because "only the theology and church of the antichrist can profit from it. The Evangelical Church and Evangelical theology would only sicken and die of it."[41]

Brunner was deeply and personally injured by Barth's harsh attack. Throughout his career he continually referred back to it, attempting to clarify his own position and to criticize Barth's. In 1949 he wrote in the first volume of his *Dogmatics* that

> Barth, in the defense of his main concern—with which we are in entire and un-
> hesitating agreement—in his great "Spring-cleaning" has cleared out and thrown
> away a great deal that had nothing to do with Natural Theology, but was an integral
> part of the truth of the Bible; owing to the one-sided way in which he has defended
> his cause, he has injured the legitimate claims of Biblical theology, and has thus
> created unnecessary hindrances for the promulgation of his ideas.[42]

Although the two giants of dialectical theology became reconciled shortly before their deaths, the rift they created (for which Barth must bear most of the blame) will be remembered as one of the most unfortunate and ironic conflicts in contemporary theology. One result of it was Brunner's attempt to search out and expose every actual or potential heresy he could detect in Barth's theology.

A primary object of Brunner's criticism was Barth's doctrine of election, which he considered highly speculative and saw as leading inexorably into universalism. Perhaps he was attempting to return some of Barth's venom when he wrote that his doctrine of election "is in absolute opposition, not only to the whole ecclesiastical tradition, but—and this alone is the final objection to it—to the clear teaching of the New Testament."[43]

Brunner worked out his own doctrine of divine election in conscious opposition to both Barth and the classical Calvinist doctrine of double predestination. The problem with both, he averred, is that in speculating into the eternal background of God's gracious election they move beyond anything stated or directly implied in divine reve-lation.[44] Brunner rejected any "logically satisfying theory" of election[45] in favor of what he considered a thoroughly dialectical, and therefore biblical, understanding:

> To believe in Jesus Christ and to be of the elect is one and the same thing, just as
> not to believe in Jesus Christ and not to be of the elect is the same thing. There
> is no other selection than this, there is no other number than that which is con-
> stituted by the fact of believing and not believing.[46]

Brunner's Contribution to Contemporary Theology

There is little doubt that Brunner deserves greater acclaim as a giant of twentieth-century theology than he receives.[47] Unfortunately, radical originality is often consid-ered the sine qua non of the truly great theologian. Brunner did not attempt to be either radical or original in the usual senses. Instead, he was interested in providing a contemporary restatement of classical Reformation theology that would avoid the errors of both extreme conservatism and extreme liberalism.

Conservatives have often learned from Brunner to avoid any simplistic equation of divine revelation with the words and propositions of the Bible and to embrace a more personalistic understanding of revelation. Liberals have often learned from him to avoid any simplistic equation of divine revelation with the best and highest thoughts of humans about God and to remain open to the transcendent Word of God, which in the divine-human encounter breaks through the constraints of human reason with sovereign unpredictability.

RUDOLF BULTMANN:
TRANSCENDENCE OF THE KERYGMA

Unlike the other major articulators of neo-orthodoxy, Rudolf Bultmann was not primarily a systematic theologian, but a New Testament scholar. His chief concern was to make biblical, Christian faith understandable to the modern mindset. He did so by employing an existentialist interpretation of the New Testament, which views the message of the ancient document as God's Word addressed to the individual and calling for an individual faith response. Yet he refused to acknowledge any deep chasm between exegesis and systematic theology, claiming instead that the task of both is to explicate human existence in relation to God by listening to the Word of God that addresses the individual through the New Testament.[1] Because of his contribution to this wider issue of theological method, Bultmann has been a formidable voice in the realm of systematic theology as well as of New Testament studies.

Despite certain differences between the two, Bultmann regarded himself as an ally of Karl Barth in the neo-orthodox challenge to liberalism. Nineteenth-century theology, he believed with Barth, had made the human person, rather than God, the center of theology.[2] Like Barth, he declared that we can know God only in response to God's revelation, which comes in the divine Word, the *kerygma*, addressed to the individual human. At the same time, he went beyond Barth. Bultmann interpreted the divine address solely in terms of the human situation, which he, following the existentialist philosopher Martin Heidegger, saw as characterized by anxiety and even despair.[3]

Bultmann's Career and Its Setting

Rudolf Bultmann was heir to a grand ecclesiastical tradition.[4] He was the oldest son of a Lutheran pastor in the northern German province of Oldenburg. His fraternal grandparents were missionaries to Africa, and his maternal grandfather had been a pastor in pietistic southern Germany. Bultmann was educated at the leading universities of Germany—Tübingen, Berlin, Marburg. His teaching career took him to Breslau and Giessen, before his return to his alma mater (Marburg) in 1921, where he served until his retirement (1951).

Unlike many of his colleagues, Bultmann was not forced to leave his teaching post during the Hitler regime. Perhaps this was partly because, as he suggested, he never directly or actively participated in political affairs,[5] although he did speak out against certain aspects of the Nazi program.[6]

Like Barth, Bultmann launched his scholarly career at an important juncture in modern theological history. The liberal consensus of the nineteenth century was eroding, and the theology that would come to dominate the first half of the twentieth century was just beginning to take shape. During that transitional period, several fundamental issues confronted scholars both in New Testament studies and in theology. Bultmann's importance lies in his response to these problems. Although his basic theological approach had taken form prior to his encounter with Martin Heidegger, he steadfastly looked to the insights of existentialist philosophy as providing the way forward in treating the difficult problems of the day.

Faith and the Historical Jesus

A first problem confronting New Testament scholars as the nineteenth century drew to a close was the question of the historical Jesus. The historical-critical method, which during the nineteenth century had come to dominate biblical studies in general and New Testament research in particular, stripped away the older unified picture of the life of Jesus. This research revealed the differing emphases and representations of Jesus present among the authors of the New Testament documents. As a result, scholars could no longer simply equate the history of Jesus with the portrait presented in the Gospels. This change of viewpoint raised a difficulty for theology: Which is normative, the Christ proclaimed in the New Testament texts or the real historical Jesus lying behind the texts?

Building from the legacy of Schleiermacher, liberalism had opted for the second of these alternatives, setting forth as normative for theology the Jesus of history, especially the personality of Jesus that they believed could be reconstructed on the basis of his teaching, conduct, inner development and impression on his contemporaries.[7] In keeping with this orientation, scholars launched what has come to be called "the quest of the historical Jesus," the attempt to move behind the Gospels to determine exactly what Jesus himself had said and done.

As the century ran its course, however, some scholars began to question this program. In his monumental work, *The Quest of the Historical Jesus* (1906), Albert Schweitzer concluded that the search had ended in failure. The person of Jesus that researchers had reconstructed from the texts was nothing more than a reflection of their own image. In contrast to this liberal portrait, Schweitzer claimed that the real Jesus of history was an apocalyptic preacher who proclaimed the nearness of the end of the world. As such, he was completely foreign to modern humanity and therefore could have no message for our day.

Martin Kähler moved in a direction somewhat different from Schweitzer. In *The So-called Historical Jesus and the Historic, Biblical Christ* (1896), he argued that the key to the meaning of the New Testament does not arise through the history it portrays and the historical method of study, but through the message proclaimed by the church. "This real Christ is the Christ who is preached," he asserted.[8]

Bultmann entered this foray on the side of Kähler and in a sense radicalized Kähler's position. In this context he is well known for his thoroughgoing application to the Gospels of a technique termed "form criticism." Bultmann the New Testament scholar arrived at largely negative conclusions concerning what could be known about the Jesus of history. The materials in the Gospels presented a Jesus who had already been covered over with the thought forms of the Hellenistic context in which they were written, he asserted. In fact, the New Testament is not concerned with the Jesus of history. Its focus is on the Christ of faith.

For Bultmann, however, this lack of knowledge concerning the Jesus of history was not a detriment to the Christian faith. Rather than the history of Jesus, he argued, it is the *kerygma* or message of the early church that is central to faith. This conclusion arose out of two considerations. Even the New Testament itself, as a document of the proclamation of the early church, focuses its concern on the Christ of the *kerygma*, not on the facts concerning the historical Jesus, he argued. Further, this conclusion is in keeping with the nature of faith as Bultmann, building from the categories of existentialism, understood it. Faith does not arise out of the results of historical research. The key issue in faith is not one's ability to gain knowledge about the Jesus of history, but a personal confrontation with the Christ in the present. As a result, the Jesus of history holds little relevance for faith. Faith is not knowledge of historical facts, but a personal response to the Christ confronted in the gospel message, the proclamation that God had acted in Jesus.

In this way, Bultmann claimed to be applying the Lutheran theme of justification by faith to the realm of knowledge and thought. His program, he asserted, "destroys every longing for security," whether based on good works or "objectifying knowledge." We have nothing at our own disposal on which to build faith; we are, "so to speak, in a vacuum."[9] In this situation, faith can only be the gift of God's grace that comes to us in the *kerygma*.

This does not mean that occurrences in the past are totally inconsequential for faith, however.[10] Bultmann did not maintain that Christianity could exist apart from the past event of the cross, for example.[11] What he refused to assert is that faith can be shored up by historical investigation, for no such activity can prove that God has acted in any past event. In fact, history forms a closed continuum of cause and effect. God's action in historical events, therefore, is not determined through historical research, but is open only to the eyes of faith.

In keeping with his radical skepticism concerning the possible results of historical research, Bultmann maintained that the historical Jesus himself is not to be viewed as the focus of God's revelation. At this point he remained a faithful representative of the kerygmatic understanding of revelation characteristic of neo-orthodoxy. God's revelation, he argued, lies in the present encounter of an individual with the preaching concerning Christ. What is important about the past events is only *that* in Jesus, God acted redemptively. In Bultmann's estimation, any details of God's action that research into the life of Jesus could provide are unimportant to faith. For this reason, he placed Jesus' own preaching within the context of Judaism, not early Christianity,[12] and set forth his well-known assertion, "The message of Jesus is a presupposition for the theology of the New Testament rather than a part of that theology itself."[13]

Eschatology

A second issue tackled by Bultmann was that of eschatology. The nineteenth century was an era of optimism. Although they acknowledged the presence of apocalyptic elements in the New Testament documents (such as the expectation of a catastrophic end of the world), the theologians of the liberal movement dismissed such statements as an unimportant appendage to the true message of Jesus. For the religious signif-icance of Jesus, liberal thinkers looked instead to the eternal truths he taught and to his impressive personality. And the importance of the New Testament, they claimed, is focused in the religious insights it offers.

As the century drew to a close, this aspect of the liberal program was likewise called into question. Scholars rediscovered the centrality of apocalyptic in the New Testament. Instrumental in this rediscovery were Johannes Weiss and Albert Schweitzer, who argued convincingly that apocalyptic themes were not merely peripheral to Jesus' proclamation; rather, his message was thoroughly apocalyptic or eschatological in orientation. In Schweitzer's estimation, however, this discovery served to discredit the New Testament, in that its central content, the belief in an imminent end of the world, had been proven false.

Bultmann built on the findings of Weiss and Schweitzer. He agreed that Jesus and the early Christian community anticipated the soon arrival of the kingdom of God, a hope that was not fulfilled.[14] But rather than being forced thereby to a negative con-clusion concerning the relevance of the New Testament message, he reinterpreted the eschatology of the New Testament. Bultmann moved behind the temporal sense in which that message had been given to what he perceived to be its true existential meaning. Yet his reinterpretation of the temporality of the New Testament message was not arbitrary. Rather, Bultmann claimed that both Paul and John pointed in this direction, for they themselves had spoken of the eternal life received in faith as a present, existential reality, and not a future, temporal anticipation.[15]

Mythology

Bultmann's career occurred at a time when biblical and theological scholars were wrestling with a third problem, mythology. As a result of historical-critical studies of the New Testament documents, scholars had come to see the presence of mythological influences in these writings. This was especially observable in the christological themes employed by the early church. Theorists, including Bultmann, claimed that the New Testament reflected the use of the myths of the mystery religions, especially the myth of the descent of a redeemer god, to describe the work of Jesus the Christ.

Liberal theology had responded to this discovery by advocating a cutting away of the mythology in order to view the eternal truths present among the myths. Bultmannn rejected such a move. Removing the myth, he claimed, could not be accomplished without also losing the *kerygma,* the real message of the New Testament. Liberal theology, he argued, had lost that message, for it had reduced the *kerygma* to principles of religion and ethics and thereby had transformed Christianity into a nonhistorical religion. Bultmann therefore advocated not removal but interpretation of myth, in order to see the true meaning of the documents expressed in this literary form. This is what he meant by the term *demythologizing*. He did not aspire to rid the texts of their mythical elements, but rather to understand these elements correctly, that is, in accordance with their underlying existential meaning.[16]

Such a reinterpretation was necessary, Bultmann maintained, because of the great gulf between the world view in which the ancient texts had been written and the modern mindset.[17] He defined myth as the form of thought that represents the transcendent reality in this-worldly terms. But this definition could readily lead to the conclusion that any talk about an act of God belongs to the order of myth, a viewpoint that Bultmann strongly refuted. To avoid this possibility, he offered another understanding of *myth*, using the term to refer to any expression that is de facto excluded by the orientation toward natural science characteristic of the modern mentality.[18]

According to Bultmann, demythologizing properly understands the mythological terminology. Myth is problematic not only because it makes the Christian message unacceptable to the modern mind, but because it also distorts the message itself, inhibiting genuine encounter with the *kerygma*. The program of demythologizing is justified, Bultmann argued, for it facilitates the gospel in its task of addressing humans today. Bultmann's overriding concern is that each hearer of the gospel be confronted existentially with the reality of the transcendent God. The program of demythologizing is vital because it facilitates this encounter.

But demythologizing also carries biblical precedence, Bultmann added. The development of this enterprise is noticeable already in the New Testament itself, specifically in the writings of Paul and John.[19]

Hermeneutics
The problem of mythology that Bultmann tackled was related to a corresponding theological problem, that of hermeneutics. Historical-critical study had led to an awareness of the existence of a great gulf between the intellectual world of the biblical writers and that of the modern world. Bultmann responded to this issue as well.

Liberal theology sought to bridge the gulf between the ancient texts and the modern mind by the discovery of the "timeless" truths found in the documents, the most important of which were the ethical principles taught by Jesus. Again at this point Bultmann rejected the liberal approach. He found this response naive, in that it assumed the presence within the texts of universal, eternal principles waiting to be discovered by objective hermeneutical means. Bultmann, in contrast, argued that the relationship of the reader to the text is far more complicated. The question we bring to the text, he declared, determines the answer we receive from it, and our relation to the subject-matter determines our question.[20]

Bultmann maintained that the gulf between the ancient text and the modern world could be overcome only as we employ an appropriate "pre-understanding" in our exegetical quest. For him, the question that unites the ancient text with the modern reader is that of human existence.[21] Despite their mythological cosmology—in fact, expressed through that mythical way of viewing the world—the biblical authors were raising the question of personal existence, the same question that lies at the heart of the human quest in any age. For this reason, Bultmann concluded, existentialism offers the proper pre-understanding for approaching the biblical documents, for it provides "the most adequate perspective and conceptions for understanding human existence."[22] By bringing the crucial question of human existence to the texts, we are able to hear the Word of God addressing us through the biblical *kerygma* and thereby be confronted with the Transcendent One.

God's Transcendence

A final problem for which Bultmann sought an answer lay in the doctrine of God. As we saw in the previous chapter, the theology of the nineteenth century placed great emphasis on God as immanent. In the early years of his work, Karl Barth launched a campaign against this emphasis, based on Kierkegaard's concept of the "infinite qualitative distinction" (God is qualitatively different from creation, so that philosophical reason cannot provide knowledge of God). Thereby Barth reintroduced the transcendence of God. Bultmann joined Barth in this endeavor. In fact, Bultmann sought to employ a radical and thoroughgoing application of the idea of God's transcendence to the entire spectrum of religious thought.

In one sense, however, the concept of transcendence that Bultmann offered differed from that presented in the biblical documents.[23] According to his reconstruction, the ancient peoples held to a spatially oriented, three-story universe, with God and heaven above and hell located beneath the earth. This cosmology, Bultmann argued, is simply incompatible with our modern, scientific world view. God's transcendence, therefore, can no longer be understood in spatial terms. In its stead, Bultmann offered a nonspatial understanding. But this was based on another dimension of the biblical outlook. In contrast to the Greek conception of divine transcendence as timelessness, as mind over against the material and sensual world, biblical transcendence refers to God's absolute authority, he argued.[24] As a result, Bultmann set forth an existential understanding. Transcendence means that God stands before us in the existential moment of decision, addressing us with his Word and confronting us with the challenge of responding in faith, thereby creating authentic existence.

This understanding of God, however, meant that we can never speak of God objectively, but only in terms of what he does in us.[25] God is unknown apart from the individual faith response to the divine self-disclosure in his Word. This self-disclosure is not the communication of truths about God, not a body of knowledge, but an occurrence that calls the individual to response. Thus, we cannot speak *about* God, he argued—we cannot speak in detached, impersonal, objective terms—we can only speak *of* God. All theoretical talk about God, which according to Bultmann requires a position of neutrality vis-à-vis God on the part of the speaker, is precluded. In the same way, Christ is the Word of God, not as a body of ideas, but as God's Word addressed to the individual.

Further, Bultmann posited a reciprocal relationship between statements concerning God and those concerning the human individual. In making this assertion he did not simply reduce theology to anthropology, as some of his critics have maintained,[26] but rather made the two inseparable. Theological statements are possible only when they are also anthropological statements.

Existentialism and Theology

As already indicated, Bultmann's theological approach focuses on the harnessing of existentalist philosophy in the theological task. We must now look more closely at his existentialist theological program.

Every use of a specific philosophy in service to theology raises the question concerning the choice of a philosophical foundation made by the theologian. In Bultmann's case this question arises in terms of existentialism: Why did Bultmann deem existentialist philosophy profitable for theology?

Bultmann disciple Schubert Ogden offered a rationale in keeping with the German scholar's sympathy with the goals of neo-orthodoxy. The primary motivation, he suggested, lay in Bultmann's concern to preserve the absolute transcendence of God: Existentialism "enables him to express more adequately than any other conceptuality he knows the underlying conception of God and man which he is primarily concerned to convey."[27] Others locate the source of this move in the hermeneutical problem Bultmann sought to overcome, namely, the impossibility of approaching any text without asking questions of it and bringing to bear on it certain known concepts. Bultmann simply viewed the question of human existence as the only adequate hermeneutical principle.[28]

It would seem that we ought not to reduce Bultmann's motivation to any one problem he addressed. Rather, he apparently found in existentialism a fruitful key for dealing with the entire gamut of problems to which he addressed himself: the problem of divine transcendence, the hermeneutical problem and the problems of mythology, eschatology and the historical Jesus. But the beginning point for him clearly lay in the question raised by neo-orthodoxy as a whole, namely, how God addresses humankind today. Bultmann's response employed the concept of human existence, which he found both in the New Testament itself and in existentialist philosophy. God addresses the individual from his transcendence as the Wholly Other, and the divine Word calls forth a radical, life-changing response. Therefore theology, which by definition is discourse about God, cannot but speak about human existence at the same time.

Heidegger and the New Testament

Bultmann found the categories of the existentialist philosophy of Martin Heidegger to be helpful in clarifying what he perceived to be the fundamental meaning of the biblical message. Heidegger provided him with an alternative to traditional ontologies that could offer only what he termed an "objectivized" view of humankind, that is, that view the human person in universal terms that focus on one's place in the realm of nature, rather than in terms of historicity, in terms of concepts that focus on each human as an individual who determines one's personhood through personal deci-sions.[29] Yet Bultmann did not see himself foisting Heidegger's interpretations on the New Testament.[30] Rather, he saw existentialism as a means of providing a necessary "pre-understanding" in order that the true message of the New Testament itself could be understood. Nor did he choose existentialism because it was the reigning philos-ophy of the day. Instead, he was convinced that the basic orientation found in exis-tentialism lies within the structures of faith as found in the New Testament. Thus Bultmann did not view existentialism as exerting an external influence on theology, but as reflecting the very heart of the New Testament message itself.[31] He incorporated this philosophy as a helpful tool in the theological task, because it provided both the basic manner of raising the question that the gospel message answers and the system of basic concepts in which this answer must come, namely, the realm of human ex-istence.[32]

The Categories of Existentialism
Heidegger's writings provided Bultmann several concepts, which he employed with great success in developing his theological program. A first helpful existentialist cate-gory is that of "existence" itself. For Heidegger, existence is never focused on the general or universal, but always on the individual and personal, on the person as possessing the capability of decision. He viewed human existence, therefore, not in the scientific but in the existentialist sense, as dealing with personal existence and personal choice. As a result, existence is a punctiliary event—it occurs in each moment—rather than a linear develop-ment. It is determined by the decisions an individual makes in any given moment. In keeping with this understanding, Heidegger distinguished be-tween the being of a human and the being of all objects in the world. The former he termed "existence," whereas the latter is merely "extant."[33] As an outworking of Hei-degger's influence, a dichotomy between "existence" and "world" lay at the heart of Bultmann's theology.

Bultmann also built on Heidegger's understanding of historicity. Each individual is a historical being, he declared. This means that we are to view each person in relation to history, rather than in relation to the eternal structures of nature. But beyond this, each one is historical in the sense of being one's own particular history. What is significant about each individual, Bultmann argued (following Heidegger), is the per-son's capacity for responding to the happenings that occur throughout the course of his or her life, which are actually historical encounters. These responses, and not some fixed essence, determine what the individual is.[34] One's life, therefore, is to be viewed as arising out of the future, rather than the past, and is molded by personal decisions.[35]

Authentic Existence
Related to the concepts of existence and historicity is the important dialectic between authentic and unauthentic existence. According to Heidegger, there are two modes of being. People develop an *authentic existence* whenever they accept the challenge of being thrown into the world. On the other hand, people develop an *unauthentic existence*

whenever they lose the distinction between self and the world.

Bultmann employed this schema to understand the distinction between the biblical terms *sin* (which for Bultmann is basically "unbelief") and *faith.* Unauthentic existence, he maintained, consists in the search for security and satisfaction in the "world," that is, in the realm of the tangible, in one's own achievements or in the past. This is sin— understanding oneself in terms of self and apart from God. Authentic existence, in contrast, is the refusal to base one's life on the "world," but rather on intangible realities, coupled with a renunciation of self-centered security and an openness to the future. It is living in the world, but at the same time living over against the world, seeing the world "as if not," to employ Bultmann's phrase. This is faith—personal commitment to God. And through faith a new self-understanding emerges, for faith is an act of response to God in which the individual finds his or her own being.

History

Another major existentialist concept employed by Bultmann is that of "history." Here he followed Heidegger and broke with the outlook of the nineteenth century. History is not merely the science of facts concerning the past pursued in a nonpersonal, detached manner. Rather, truly significant historical knowledge is always existential knowledge; it leads to personal encounter and comes about through engagement in history.

Foundational to his thinking concerning history is the differentiation between *Historie* and *Geschichte,* which Bultmann apparently accepted from Martin Kähler.[36] Bultmann himself employed the adjectives corresponding to these two terms to refer to two different methods of approach to history, understood as the field of human actions and the types of events that result from them.[37] Detached, neutral observation leads to factual information of the past as a chain of cause and effect *(historisch).* When the events are approached from the perspective of the question of human existence, however, they are no longer merely past occurrences but become present events *(geschichtlich)* that can disclose one's own personal existence. More important than the simple facts, therefore, is meaningful history, the events as they continue to have influence or significance. To be relevant, therefore, history must be meaningful, or interpreted, event.

Bultmann declared that such meaning cannot be found by observation from some vantage point outside of the flow of history. Rather, one can begin only with one's own personal history. As a result, one's primary concern when engaging in historical studies can only be the question of human existence. And what is of final importance is personal, individual history, that is, personal authentic existence.

Related to this outlook toward history is Bultmann's understanding of temporality, which he derived from Heidegger's threefold structure of "care." Bultmann found the common division of time into past, present and future problematic, insofar as it results in the "present" becoming a dimensionless mathematical point separating the past and the future. Heidegger's existentialist understanding of time, in contrast, focused on the present as the point of decision. Rather than merely referring to what has happened once for all, "the past" is significant because of its relationship to the realm of inauthenticity. This arises in that the past represents the lack of decision or lack of possibility. Because the past is now fixed, it no longer holds out possibility. The inauthenticity connected to one's past is to be taken into personal existence by the acceptance of its guilt.

In like manner "the future" is more than the "not yet." It is the realm of possibility that demands decision. In one's present existence the individual is confronted with the future, the realm of possibility. As a result, each person is called to live from the future. "The present," in turn, is not merely the "now"; it is the situation of responsible decision, namely, the decision to unite past and future into authentic existence.

Faith and the Gospel

At this crucial juncture Bultmann parted company with his existentialist mentor; for here he introduced the Christian *kerygma* as a necessary component. In contrast to Heidegger, who held out hope that authentic existence was within the grasp of the unaided individual, Bultmann claimed that authentic existence was solely the product of the response of faith to the grace of God offered in the Christian proclamation, which response itself was a miracle wrought by God.[38]

This, however, brings us again to Bultmann's understanding of the Christian *kerygma* and its relationship to faith. Following Paul, he maintained that the *kerygma* is the preaching of the cross and the resurrection as the salvation-event, an event that forms an inseparable unity.[39] But by this he did not mean merely the objective "facts" of what happened to Jesus of Nazareth. As we have noted, for Bultmann meaningful history cannot be equated with the uninterpreted brute facts of the past. Already early in his career he rejected all theories that seek to prove that the death and resurrection of Jesus have atoning and forgiving power.[40] What is important is the meaning of the cross and resurrection, that is, their continued significance as God's Word addressed to individuals today. As we respond to the *kerygma,* the cross and resurrection become our experience.

Understood in this manner, the cross (which Bultmann did accept as a fact of Jesus' history) is God's liberating judgment on humankind.[41] The resurrection (which Bultmann refused to speak of in terms of an event of past history)[42] refers neither to the return of a dead man to life in this world nor to the translation of Jesus to a life beyond.[43] Rather, it signifies the elevation of the Crucified One to the status of Lord. As a result, "faith in the resurrection is really the same thing as faith in the saving efficacy of the cross," Bultmann asserted.[44]

The proclamation of this Christian message gives rise to faith, Bultmann declared. By "faith" he meant the willingness to understand oneself as crucified and risen with Christ. The *kerygma,* therefore, is the place where Jesus Christ is confronted and becomes for the hearer the "eschatological event." Through the *kerygma* the Living Lord brings the end of the (old) world for the believer. As already noted, for Bultmann the confrontation is not dependent on personal knowledge of Jesus' earthly life. Thereby Christian faith is freed from dependency on the shifting sands of critical historical scholarship.

Critique

For decades Bultmann's program provided an immeasurable service to many thinking Christians by offering them a way of integrating the ancient gospel with the modern mentality. At the very heart of his outlook is a worthwhile emphasis on the necessity of the Christian message to speak to questions raised by contemporary humans, important because Christians often find themselves answering questions that people in the world are not asking. Likewise helpful is his assertion that truth is not merely objective, but that to be fully received truth must "grip the soul" of the hearer.[45] And finally, Bultmann set forth a laudable attempt to reestablish the transcendence of God, supplying a needed polemic against the overemphasis on the immanence of God found in liberalism.

Despite these and other contributions, Bultmann's program has been highly controversial.[46] Conservatives concluded that the German scholar had jettisoned biblical authority and were squeamish about his application to the Bible of the category of myth. Confessionalists averred that at many doctrinal points his interpretations are at variance with traditional understandings. Young's summarization highlights this situation:

> According to Bultmann, the history of Israel is not history of revelation for the Christian; Jesus is not the Christ event in world history but becomes such in the proclamation and hearing of the Word; the *extra nos* feature of God's act is retained only in a special sense; the resurrection of Christ is not an event in history following the crucifixion but is the dimension of meaning of the cross; and so on.[47]

Other critics focused on his understanding of myth, which subsequent scholars have deemed narrow.

Apart from the question of proper doctrinal formulations and criticisms related to various aspects of his position, a major theological problem lies at the center of Bultmann's program. This problem is evidenced in three major weaknesses. The first relates to exegesis, the second to the life of faith and the third to the nature of God.

One-sided Exegesis

First, Bultmann's application of the grid of existentialism to New Testament studies resulted in a tendency toward oversimplified exegesis leading in turn to a one-sided theology. His claim that the New Testament *kerygma* is essentially existential address, while reflecting a vital concern of the documents, is a truncation of what the documents themselves present. Many texts simply do not deal with the issue of human existence as formulated by Bultmann, but focus on other themes. As a result, theology cannot be reduced to soteriology, as his program seems to demand. Bultmann admitted as much, but then employed the existentialist orientation he found in Paul and John as a type of "canon within the canon."

The grid of human existence likewise resulted in an overly radical separation of past historical events and the contemporary experience of faith. In his attempt to free faith from dependency on the findings of historical research, Bultmann went too far. While retaining the importance of Jesus' cross for faith, he nevertheless made the content of Jesus' life irrelevant, and this because he viewed faith solely as the response to the message that God had acted in Christ. But as Moltmann correctly pointed out, this viewpoint "omits to note that concrete historicity is always disclosed, made possible and limited through history that really happened, and not vice versa."[48] Rather than produce the history of Jesus as its expression, our faith owes its existence to that history.

Privatized Faith

Second, Bultmann's theological approach, with its too narrow understanding of the gospel message, readily results in a too narrow, privatized faith. For him, faith is personal decision in the matter of authentic living, understood in a highly individualized fashion. This does encapsulize a dimension of the New Testament *kerygma* and understanding of faith. But the biblical message is more than this. It is directed beyond the private domain of individual decision to address the whole of life.

Bultmann's existentialist emphasis runs the risk of excluding the corporate and social dimensions of Christian faith.[49] He placed little emphasis on the outworking of faith in the life of the believer or on the corporate life of believers in community. Nor can we find in his program the foundation for Christian involvement in the wider society. On the contrary his existentialist orientation fosters an inwardness that readily can lead to an overlooking of the social and political implications of the gospel.

In theological terms, Bultmann's program underscored the necessity of personal justification (the decision of the individual to be transformed from inauthenticity to authenticity), but it did not lead to sanctification, to the dynamic of actual Christian living and spiritual growth as disciples of the Lord in community with one another and in the world. It is likewise not insignificant that his writings seldom speak concerning the church. From the vantage point of subsequent theological developments, we can only conclude that Bultmann's theology provides a helpful, partial soteriology, but lacks a satisfying ecclesiology.

Truncated God

Finally, under the influence of his existentialist grid Bultmann's radical application of the theme of the infinite qualitative distinction led to a truncated understanding of God. His limitation of theological discourse to the dimension of human existence served to eliminate assertions concerning both God's eternal reality and God's actions in the world.

The German scholar's intention is laudable. In the face of the immanentist theology of liberalism he rightly sought to elevate God as the Transcendent One, the Wholly Other standing over against the individual human. But Bultmann erred in maintaining that this God can be known only as he acts in me, that is, as he creates authentic existence, so that theology becomes the reflection on the experience of the encounter that leads to authentic existence. It would be mistaken to claim that Bultmann thereby reduced theology to anthropology, a charge that he himself dismissed,[50] but it does mean that no statement can be made about God that does not at the same time speak about the human person.

Bultmann's claim that we can speak about God only insofar as we are at the same time speaking about ourselves places God's eternal nature beyond the boundary of human theological assertion. Thereby God is made unknowable in the divine eternal reality. Bultmann claimed that this situation is in keeping with the purpose of faith: "Not what God is in Himself, but how he acts with men, is the mystery in which faith is interested."[51] While it points toward an important truth, this reduction of what theology can assert is simply too narrow when compared to both the New Testament and theological history. Central to the classical theological quest is the desire to make assertions about the eternal reality of the Godhead not limited by, but also lying beyond, who God is to the individual believer.

Not only are statements about the divine reality reduced in scope, but Bultmann's position works to preclude statements about God's action in the world. While classifying as mythological most statements about God's acting, Bultmann resolutely maintained that God has acted in Christ "once for all on behalf of the world."[52] And he consistently sought to show how affirmations concerning this divine action are to be understood in terms of human existence. But as John Macquarrie pointed out, not all biblical assertions concerning God's mighty acts, grace, revelation or the uniqueness of Jesus can be formulated in accordance with the existentialist hermeneutical criterion. Hence, not all statements concerning transcendence can be translated into assertions about the self, as Bultmann's program would seem to require.[53]

His strict existentialist orientation placed undue limitations on christological affirmations as well. Bultmann himself was forced to limit assertions of God's actions to the simple statement that "a particular historical event, that is, Jesus Christ, is to be understood as the eschatological 'once for all.' "[54] This statement, however, with its attendant rejection of the propriety of assertions concerning the status of the historical Jesus as the eternal *Logos*,[55] is in the final analysis simply inadequate to the manifold understanding of Jesus' significance and the significance of the action of the transcendent God in Jesus as affirmed by the New Testament and by the church.

Conclusion

Bultmann was motivated by a concern to allow the gospel to speak to the modern mind unencumbered by the myths of the ancient world. He believed that because people had cast off all mythological concepts they could no longer speak in terms of supernatural acts within the chain of cause and effect. By relegating statements of God's action in history to the realm of faith, he hoped to allow the true scandal of the gospel to encounter people today. To do so required that he follow Kant's lead and draw an impenetrable line between the realm of the autonomous natural world and the transcendent realm of faith. Subsequent advances in science and philosophy have indicated how unfortunate and unnecessary a move this was.[56] The "autonomous natural realm" as a closed chain of cause and effect has itself been exposed as a myth. And the dangers of any theology that banishes God to the realm of private belief have become increasingly apparent.

In short, Bultmann engaged in a noble attempt to reassert the transcendence of God in the face of the emphasis on immanence found in nineteenth-century liberal theology. But his radical program of demythologizing in accordance with categories of existentialism, set forth as an attempt to bring the ancient message to the modern mind, led him to a truncated description of the very transcendence he desired to maintain. Because in Bultmann's system God cannot be spoken of except in relation to the human person and God cannot act in the world except in the private realm of personal faith, the broader dimensions of God's transcendence vis-à-vis creation are eliminated from the purview of the theologian. Despite his helpful attempts to provide an existential basis to reconstruct theology in the modern world, Bultmann simply could not escape the problems set forth by the Enlightenment and left unresolved by the nineteenth-century theology to which he so vigorously responded. He was simply unable to reaffirm the transcendence of God in its full, biblical sense.

REINHOLD NIEBUHR:
TRANSCENDENCE REVEALED THROUGH MYTH

Reinhold Niebuhr never saw himself as a theologian.[1] Above all he was, in the words of his wife, a preacher and a pastor;[2] he was likewise a social ethicist, an apologist and a "circuit rider" among the nation's colleges and universities.[3] Because his education was interrupted by family needs following the death of his father and by his "boredom with epistemology,"[4] Niebuhr never gained the usual academic theological credentials. The highest degree he completed was the M.A. from Yale. Nevertheless in terms of impact, he has been hailed as the most influential American theologian of the first half of the twentieth century. His influence was felt beyond the Christian community, for his activities and writings carried impact in the entire nation. As D. R. Davies noted,

> One of his greatest achievements is that he has made theology a science of secular urgency and significance. He is one of the very few theologians to whom secular and humanist thinkers pay attention, as much as they pay to their own publicists. This is a most rare achievement, of which few theologians can boast.[5]

His shadow was especially felt in the social-political realm. Over a decade after his death, Paul Jersild concluded: "It is difficult to find a theologian in the twentieth century who has exerted more influence on a nation's political life than has Reinhold Niebuhr.[6]

One cannot say that Niebuhr was an innovative theological thinker. His mission was not that of setting forth a creative, new theology, but of applying the Christian faith as he understood it to the social dimensions of life. Yet his efforts in this area resulted in his becoming a dominant, shaping voice in the American religious community during the middle decades of the twentieth century. This influence has insured for Niebuhr a place of great importance for the theological history of the century.

Scholars have frequently categorized Niebuhr as a "neo-orthodox" theologian.[7] Yet he rejected this designation, for he equated the label with the thought of Barth, whom he repeatedly criticized.[8] Nevertheless his importance in the story of theology lies in his connection to the protest movement against liberalism which, because of the rediscovery of classical Christian doctrines it entailed, is generally termed "neo-ortho-doxy." By being the most influential American spokesman for the growing rejection—pioneered by Barth—of nineteenth-century theology, Niebuhr became a vehicle for the dissemination of certain central emphases of neo-orthodoxy into American theology.

Niebuhr's Career and Intellectual Development

Niebuhr's upbringing, like that of Walter Rauschenbusch, with whom he shared certain affinities (despite Niebuhr's explicit rejection of the social gospel movement), occurred in the context of an environment bathed in pietistic Christianity. His father was a pastor in the Evangelical Synod (now part of the United Church of Christ), the roots of which lay in the union of Lutheran and Reformed traditions in Prussia. After finishing high school in Lincoln, Illinois, Reinhold attended Elmhurst College and Eden Seminary before heading for Yale in 1913, where he completed a B.D. and then an M.A. in 1915.

Niebuhr's professional career began in Detroit. Again the similarity of his story to that of Rauschenbusch is striking. Upon graduation from Yale he became the pastor of a congregation consisting largely of assembly-line workers at the Ford Motor plant. Here he gained firsthand exposure to the plight of those who were being exploited by the industrialists of the nation, an experience that had a profound influence on both his social orientation and his theology. Just as Rauschenbusch's pastorate in New York's "Hell's Kitchen" set him on a course toward socialism, the young pastor Niebuhr became an advocate of a similar proposal for social change.

Yet at one crucial juncture Niebuhr's path departed from that of the German Baptist. Rauschenbusch's experiences led him to a swing leftward in theology—in the direction of the "social gospel," a movement that employed certain central elements of theological liberalism. In contrast, Niebuhr's metamorphosis, in a manner reminiscent of Karl Barth, eventually led to a movement to the right—to a rediscovery of orthodoxy. The social upheaval he saw during his years in the pastorate forced him, in his words, "to reconsider the liberal and highly moralistic creed which I had accepted as tantamount to the Christian faith."[9] Yet the shortcomings of liberalism extended beyond the social to the personal realm as well: "In my parish duties I found that the simple idealism into which the classical faith had evaporated was as irrelevant to the crises of personal life as it was to the complex social issues of an industrial city."[10] In short, in Detroit he came to see that the liberal theology of his seminary training was insufficient to meet the challenge of twentieth-century pastoral ministry in all its dimensions.

His activities as a Detroit pastor catapulted Niebuhr to national prominence. As a result, in 1928 he was called to teach ethics at New York's Union Theological Seminary, at that time the most prestigious Protestant seminary in America. Here he taught until his retirement in 1960. A high point in his life occurred when Niebuhr was invited to deliver the prestigious Gifford Lectures at Edinburgh in 1939. These were subsequently embodied in what has become his most widely read work, *The Nature and Destiny of Man.*

Perhaps because of the intellectual revolution he underwent in the pastorate, Niebuhr was never afraid to change and develop his thinking. Openness to and involvement in change was for Niebuhr an unquestioned, assumed dimension of life—as is evident in the popular little prayer that he composed in 1934 and would have discarded, had not a friend requested from him a copy: "God, give us grace to accept with serenity the things that cannot be changed, courage to change the things that should be changed, and wisdom to distinguish the one from the other."[11]

Niebuhr scholar Ronald H. Stone divides his life into four phases: those of liberal, socialist, pragmatist and finally pragmatic-liberal.[12] Yet these phases are woven together into a whole. In all of them Niebuhr wrestled with his liberal heritage in terms of the relation between the ideal and the real, which he found in the religion of the Bible.[13] How do the realities of life in the present, tainted as they are by evil and sin, fit together with the ideal for humanity? Niebuhr found the answer to this question, as put forth by the theological and social liberalism of his day, to be naive, ill-advised and unworkable. In its stead he sought to bring the biblical gospel to the specific historical situation in which he found himself and thereby to discover how to apply that gospel to Western civilization as a whole.[14]

Practical Christianity

Throughout his writings three interrelated themes predominate, all of which fall under Niebuhr's basic, central task. First, he was intensely interested in the practical implications of Christian faith. His fundamental goal was that of setting forth the insights of the Christian tradition within the modern situation and in living out in his own life the convictions that his faith inculcated in him. His goal was always "to establish the relevance of the Christian faith to contemporary problems."[15] As a result, he refused to limit his endeavors to abstract theological discussions, but became an activist, seeking to apply theological insights to realms as diverse as politics, international affairs, human rights and economic systems. In each, however, he consistently sought to act as a prophetic preacher, encountering contemporary social life with the critique provided by Christian faith.

In so doing, he functioned as a type of apologist, for he sought to show the significance and value of Christian faith in a society that had largely rejected the gospel, or in his words, he was interested "in the defense and justification of the Christian faith in a secular society."[16] But his apologetic employed an approach far different from the classical appeal to the intellectual reasonableness of Christianity. Niebuhr attempted to set forth the Christian faith as providing the meaning of life, but he maintained that "no ultimate sense of the meaning of life is rationally compelling."[17] In fact, the two central propositions of Christianity, that God is person and that God has taken historical action to overcome the alienation between humankind and God, "are absurd from a strictly ontological standpoint."[18] Whereas the reigning liberal theology of his day had sought to reduce the absurdity of the faith by reducing the biblical message to a set of "eternal principles" of ethics or ontology, Niebuhr advocated an apologetic that would make clear the ontologically ambiguous status of the concepts of personality and history.[19] In the midst of such ambiguities, we must leave room for the nonrational,[20] so that the message of God's relationship to creation as evidenced in the symbols of the Bible can be spoken.

Lying behind this drive was a conviction that D. R. Davies rightly described as "the principle of the relevance of an absolute, transcendent gospel to a relative situation: the applicability of Christianity to every social situation."[21] For Niebuhr, the relevance of Christianity relativized other outlooks, chief of which was the inadequate, optimistic view of the human person and human society prevalent in his day. He repeatedly assailed the two articles of the modern faith: the idea of progress and the idea of the perfectibility of humankind.[22] So poignant was his critique that one contemporary declared, "No single thinker has done more than Niebuhr to reveal the bankruptcy of secular illusions and ideals in our time."[23]

Proximate Justice

Second, present throughout his writings is a continual emphasis on "proximate justice." Niebuhr set forth a prophetic declaration concerning the reality of the human situation in the world. Regardless of our good intentions, we can hope to find in human society only a partial experience of justice, he said. Perfection is an impossible goal, "the impossible possibility" that nevertheless confronts us in the present.[24] According to Niebuhr, this situation is rooted in the unalterable reality of the human situation itself. As humans we always stand under infinite possibilities and are potentially related to the totality of existence; but we are nevertheless always creatures of finiteness.[25]

Thus, we ought not to believe naively that the solutions we propose to social ills or our fervent efforts to alter society will inaugurate the perfect human order. Our attempts to redress evils in society will breed other injustices. The best we can hope for is a more just situation today than was present yesterday. In theological terms, the kingdom of God is an unachievable goal, a standard we can never reach but that continually stands as judge over human society. It does not come within history, that is, by human action, but is God's gift from beyond.

Christian Anthropology

Third, as indicated above, Niebuhr's writings continually explore the human situation lying behind the impossibility not only of creating a fully just society but also of attaining the ideal in any form in the realm of the real. His quest to understand this impossibility led Niebuhr to classical Christian theology, specifically anthropology, the doctrine of the nature of the human person. In fact, not only did anthropology lie at the center of his magnum opus, *The Nature and Destiny of Man,* his understanding of the human predicament is a constant thread present in and tying together virtually all of his writings. The constant presence of anthropology in Niebuhr's writings led one commentator to conclude:

> Niebuhr's most significant contribution to the restatement of Christian theology in our generation is his exposition of the doctrine of man. Unlike systematicians like Aquinas or Barth who cover the whole corpus of Christian truth by the method of

a *Summa,* Niebuhr makes one doctrine, brilliantly plumbed to its depths, the basis of his whole thought.[26]

Although this comment is an overstatement,[27] it does underscore the centrality of anthropology to Niebuhr's thinking.

Niebuhr was drawn to the doctrine of humanity because he discovered a profundity in the classical Christian understanding lacking in liberalism. Actually it was, in his view, the rejection of the biblical anthropological themes by the reigning liberal tradition, which replaced them with the false doctrines of the perfectibility of humankind and the idea of progress,[28] that was responsible for the central problems of the day. In liberalism, he maintained, "the 'sin' of Christian orthodoxy was translated into the imperfections of ignorance, which an adequate pedagogy would soon overcome."[29] In contrast to what he saw as liberalism's naive optimism, emphasis on human reason and faith in education, the Bible presents a realistic picture, Niebuhr argued. As a result, his own anthropology reflected that of classical Christianity, insofar as he sought to emphasize the two-sidedness of the present human situation. He affirmed the high stature of humanity as created in the image of God as well as the biblical theme of universal human sinfulness.

The Human Contradiction

At the center of Niebuhr's anthropology is his understanding of the contradiction that characterizes the human situation. Humankind, Niebuhr argued (following the book of Genesis and the apostle Paul), entails both a potential and a problem, two realities that cannot be separated. In *The Nature and Destiny of Man* he summarized the biblical anthropology in three theses.[30] First, the human person is a created and finite existence in both body and spirit. Thus, all dualistic anthropologies—viewpoints that divided the human person into body and soul—were to be rejected. Second, humans are to be understood primarily from the standpoint of God (that is, as the image of God), rather than in terms of their rational faculties or in relation to nature. Thus, each human is a self that is able to stand outside of itself and the world and that cannot find meaning in itself or in the world. Third, humans are sinners. And because of sin, they are to be loved but never trusted.

Niebuhr, then, was not interested in the human person as such—not the ideal human or the abstract human. As a result he rejected philosophies that spoke of humankind in ontological categories. Instead, similar to other neo-orthodox theologians, he was interested in the human person as a historical being.[31] Thus his writings focused on humans in terms of their double relation to God and to each other in society.[32]

Human Sin

Of the three dimensions of the biblical anthropology Niebuhr found the concept of sin most lacking in the modern mindset. Therefore he repeatedly raised the issue of human sin. Yet this dimension of the biblical understanding of the human reality was intricately related to the other two. In contrast to dualistic anthropologies, he found sin to be rooted in the very heart of the human person, in the misuse of the capacity that constitutes human uniqueness—self-transcendence.[33] According to Niebuhr, this is the point of the biblical story of the Fall.[34] Through the misuse of our capability of self-transcendence, we refuse to acknowledge our creatureliness. Betrayed by our ability to survey the whole, we imagine ourselves to be the whole. Niebuhr, therefore, in good Reformation fashion and in contrast to what he perceived to be the tendency in liberalism, viewed sin as an act of the whole person, so that no realm of the human reality can be exonerated from complicity in our rebellion against God.[35] As a result of this thoroughgoing nature of our creaturely rebellion, the human problem is not how finite humans can know God, he argued, but how sinful people can be reconciled to God.[36]

Christian orthodoxy developed the doctrine of original sin as the explanation of the universality of this human rebellion. In his Gifford lectures Niebuhr set forth the profound truth that he found within the classical doctrine[37] (although in retirement he conceded the error of his earlier attempt to revive its vocabulary;[38] consequently he shifted his language and spoke of the human contradiction in terms of self-seeking/self-giving).[39] Sin is universal and inevitable, but not necessary, so that we are nevertheless responsible for it. The truth of original sin, therefore, is that it declares that the potential to err is rooted in each self. Niebuhr, however, rejected the traditional interpretation of original sin as an inherited taint, looking instead to Kierkegaard's concept of anxiety to explain the universal experience of the rise of sin.[40] The paradox of freedom and finitude characteristic of the human situation leads to insecurity, he declared. We are involved in the contingencies of the natural process of life (finitude). But we are able to stand outside of them and foresee their perils (freedom). By nature we are bound and limited; yet we are also free, endowed with the capability of rising above nature. The resultant sense of insecurity inimical of this situation brings anxiety. In the state of anxiety, we are tempted to turn to sinful self-assertion—to transmute our finiteness to infinity, our weakness into strength, our dependence to independence—rather than to trust in the ultimate security of God's love. Put in biblical terms, we are capable of sin or of faith.

For Niebuhr, then, sin ought to be understood in relationship to faith. Faith is the acceptance of our dependence on God, whereas sin is the denial of our creaturehood. This sin comes in two forms, two ways by which we seek to escape anxiety. The first is sensuality, the attempt to deny human freedom by retreating into the animal nature.[41] More basic and universal is the second approach, the denial of our human limitations by asserting independence. This is the sin of pride, which can take several forms:[42] the pride of power (grasping for power as an attempt to experience security), the pride of knowledge (claiming as final and absolute what is only finite knowledge) and the pride of virtue (claiming absolute status for one's own relative moral standards), leading to spiritual pride (endowing our partial standards with divine sanction).

Not only is pride present in individuals, Niebuhr added, it is even more pronounced in groups, for "the group is more arrogant, hypocritical, self-centered, and ruthless in the pursuit of its ends than the individual."[43]

Modified Neo-orthodoxy

Anthropology lay at the center of Niebuhr's interests as a theologian-ethicist-preacher. At the same time, his understanding of the human reality was embedded in a broader theological context that incorporated certain themes articulated by European neo-orthodox luminaries such as Karl Barth and Emil Brunner, while at the same time evidencing important differences from them. The central difference lay in the degree of rejection of liberalism. Concerning American neo-orthodoxy, of which Niebuhr is often cited as the most significant voice, Edward Carnell declared, "its own retreat from liberal immanence is less ambitious."[44]

Niebuhr was less severe in his rejection of liberalism than Barth and others, because he proposed a less restricted understanding of the relation of God to the world. On this central issue he agreed with the main emphases of Continental neo-orthodoxy without being as thoroughgoing in the focus on the disjunction between God and the world as were the theological giants of Europe. He saw in the Bible an emphasis on the transcendence of God, but one that is balanced with an emphasis on God's "intimate relation to the world."[45]

Therefore Niebuhr affirmed a twofold revelation from God.[46] Private (or "general") revelation is "the testimony in the consciousness of every person" that one's life touches a transcendent reality beyond the system of nature in which each person exists. This private revelation in turn gives credence to the second dimension of revelation, namely, public, historical ("special") revelation.

Thus, whereas Barth found no point of contact between God and the human person, Niebuhr found whole areas of contact.[47] While agreeing that humans are sinners, he nevertheless saw the human potential, even the potential to see oneself as a sinner.[48] While emphasizing divine transcendence, he did not remove God so far as to eliminate the possibility of knowing God. He agreed that revelation was an offense to reason, but not so as to make human recognition of truth impossible. Nor was natural theology fully erroneous so as to make eternity irrelevant to history. Rather, the wisdom of God discerned by faith is never in complete contradiction to human experience, and as a result the truth of the gospel can be confirmed by experience, even though it is not derived from experience.[49]

In short, while joining in the neo-orthodox critique of liberalism, he refused to shift to the other extreme, and this for the sake of theology: If time and eternity are totally disjunctive, then meaningful speech about God is precluded. And a crucial point of intersection Niebuhr found lay in the realm of personality. He saw this as "a serviceable analogical concept" to help us understand God's transcendence and immanence, for "person" connotes both freedom over and relation to the life process.[50]

Although Barth was the main object of his criticisms of neo-orthodoxy, Niebuhr also expressed reservations concerning the alternative to Barth presented by Rudolf Bultmann.[51] In addition to their differing orientation points for the academic discipline (Bultmann came to theology from the perspective of New Testament studies, Niebuhr approached the task from social ethics), the major point at which the two parted company lay in their understanding of myth. Bultmann sought to demythologize the

New Testament message in order to make it comprehendible to the modern non-mythological mindset. Niebuhr, in contrast, sought to show how biblical myths still speak to the modern situation with its own (and often false) myths. He criticized the German scholar for failing to make a sufficiently sharp distinction between prescientific myths (which "disregard what may have always been known or have now become known, about the ordered course of events") and permanent myths (those which "describe some meaning of reality, which is not subject to exact analysis but can nevertheless be verified in experience"). Because of this failure, Niebuhr concluded, Bultmann was negligent "to guard the truth in the *kerygma.*"[52]

Rejection of Liberalism
This broad outline of Niebuhr's thought and his complex relationship to neo-orthodoxy offers a perspective from which to look more closely at his rejection of liberalism. As a result of his experiences in the pastorate and his study of the Christian sources, Niebuhr offered a devastating critique of the reigning theological and social outlook of his day, while remaining appreciative of the liberal heritage. In fact, he even came to criticize its expression in the social gospel movement with which he retained great affinities.

Central to his critique was his sense that in its naive optimism liberalism had lost the biblical message, especially the realistic biblical understanding of human nature. At first (in the 1930s), however, Niebuhr attacked liberalism from a Marxist-socialist perspective. Although throughout his life he found Marxism helpful, Niebuhr came to see that it too was flawed, and this at similar points as was liberalism itself. It posited no transcendent God of judgment, and it set forth a romantic anthropology that failed to take seriously the Fall of humankind. On both counts he later discovered in Augustine an understanding more reflective of the actual situation, with the result that his attack on the liberal tradition came to be launched from an Augustinian perspective (in the 1940s).

Niebuhr crystallized his early dissatisfaction with liberalism in a book, *Moral Man and Immoral Society* (1932). This work was not his first literary attempt; yet it established him as a major theologian. Although he later modified certain of its points, Niebuhr never wavered from the book's central thesis: "that a sharp distinction must be drawn between the moral and social behaviour of individuals and of social groups."[53] Whereas individuals may be moral insofar as "they are able to consider interests other than their own in determining problems of conduct," human societies and social groups are more susceptible to "unrestrained egoism."[54]

Contrary to what the title of his book might suggest, Niebuhr was no naive romanticist concerning the morality of individuals. Rather, he maintained that each human is endowed not only with an unselfish but also with a selfish impulse.[55] This evil impulse finds even less restraint in social groups than in individuals. As a result, all human self-help programs, such as those proposed by Niebuhr's liberal forebears and contemporaries, are doomed to fall short of the ideal.

On the basis of his analysis, Niebuhr proposed a "double focus of the moral life," consisting of two different perspectives and two corresponding ethical ideals. For the inner life of the individual the ideal is unselfishness. But human social life requires another ideal, which can only be that of justice.[56] This theme was developed further in his subsequent work, which continued his attack on liberalism, *An Interpretation of Christian Ethics* (1934). Here Niebuhr set forth the thesis that whereas "love may be the motive of social action . . . justice must be the instrument of love in a world in which self-interest is bound to defy the canons of love on every level."[57]

Beginning in *An Interpretation of Christian Ethics* and continuing in subsequent writings, Niebuhr broadened his critique of liberalism to include insights he gained from the study of the biblical faith and Augustine, afforded him by his presence on the faculty at Union.[58] He rejected what he termed "the moralistic utopianism"[59] and sentimentality of the liberal church, finding at its root the mistaken conception that love is a simple historical possibility, rather than "an impossible possibility."[60]

Liberal moralism was sentimental for three reasons, Niebuhr maintained.[61] First, in keeping with his anthropological differences with liberalism, he saw in it a lack of awareness of the depth and power of sin. This lack of awareness fails to meet the needs both of individual spiritual pilgrims and of justice in society. Second, liberal moralism fails to delineate the religious heights disclosed in the gospel. In response to the human predicament it merely sets forth the command to love God and neighbor, without proclaiming the mercy of God revealed in Christ as the source of both forgiveness of sin and power for overcoming sin. Third, insofar as liberalism misunderstood the radical disjuncture between the ideal and the actual—the radical way that love transcends all human ideas and achievements—it lacked political and social realism.

Niebuhr's Alternative

Niebuhr not only offered a critique of liberalism, he proposed an alternative that he found more in keeping with "Christian realism." In this program he looked to the faith of the Bible, and primarily its Hebraic roots, for assistance. He maintained that Western culture was indebted to this religious tradition for its two foundational emphases, "the sense of individuality and the sense of a meaningful history."[62] In keeping with this heritage, he attempted to reestablish these emphases in the contemporary situation.

Like other neo-orthodox theologians, Niebuhr's constructive proposal drew from a dialectical understanding of the relationship between time and eternity.[63] The eternal is revealed in the temporal, but not exhausted by it. He found this thesis presented in the Bible in terms of the meaningfulness of life. History and human existence are meaningful, but their source and fulfillment lie beyond history.[64] As a result, this relationship can be expressed only in symbolic terms. Thus, the dialectical relationship between eternity and time opens the way for the use of myth.

Myth

According to Niebuhr, myth is necessary because certain aspects of reality, such as the nature of the human predicament and the transcendent source of the meaning of history, are paradoxical and therefore cannot be comprehended in terms of scientific or rational categories.[65] The meaningfulness of life requires a source beyond itself, he asserted. But because the center of reality transcends both immediate experience and the categories by which we seek to describe it, in the search for the transcendent, purely rational approaches are inadequate. The transcendent can be spoken of only by means of the use of myths, which serve as symbols of ultimate truth. Thus, Niebuhr found in the Christian symbols a way of referring to the transcendent source of meaning.

In this understanding Niebuhr set himself apart from both liberalism and traditional orthodoxy. In its love affair with the scientific method, the purely rationalistic approach to life and the contemporary mindset, liberalism had rejected the myths of the Christian faith, he argued. Equally problematic, however, is orthodoxy's "sin of profanity": "It has insisted on the literal and historic truth of its myths, forgetting that it is the function and character of religious myth to speak of the eternal in relation to time, and that it cannot therefore be a statement of temporal sequences."[66]

Rightly understood as declarations of the relationship of the eternal to the temporal, the myths of the Christian faith are significant for our age, Niebuhr asserted. One such myth is that of the Fall. As we have already seen, its importance for Niebuhr did not lie in its use as a literal description of an event that occurred at the beginning of human history. Rather, he viewed it as a profound statement concerning the universality of sin as arising out of human finitude and freedom. The Fall, then, is a powerful statement concerning the human predicament throughout history and in every situation.

The Life of Faith

For Niebuhr, however, the central Christian message moves beyond human sin to divine salvation, although his understanding of sin forms the context for his view of this dynamic. Like neo-orthodoxy in general, he rejected the rationalistic attempt to see salvation in terms of knowledge of God, choosing rather to describe it in terms of the life of faith in the midst of the contradictions of existence in the world. Thus, according to Niebuhr faith "must remain a commitment of the self rather than a conclusion of its mind."[67] Although admitting that a limited rational validation of the truth of the gospel is possible as it is correlated with truths known through science and philosophy,[68] ultimately faith cannot be validated; it can only be lived.[69]

Faith, then, entails facing realistically the insecurities of life and realizing that they can be overcome only by God. Such faith protects against pride, for God and God alone is looked to as the source of security. Faith likewise lays hold of the meaning of the whole of life and of history,[70] and thereby "touches the realm of mystery beyond rational comprehension."[71] This relationship with God, however, rests on God's forgiveness, not on our own righteousness.

The Cross

For Niebuhr, however, the focal point of the Christian faith is the cross, for Christianity proclaims a gospel for which this event is central. In keeping with his rejection of the rationalist approach to the mystery of reality, he cautioned that the meaning of the cross does not follow logically from the observable facts of history,[72] but is visible only to the eyes of faith, just as the finality of the gospel as the meaning of human history is not provable by rational analysis.[73]

The cross is important because it is revelatory; it discloses the profound truth about humankind and about God. On the one hand, it speaks about the human situation. The cross is at one and the same time the revelation of our essential nature and of our sin. At the cross we see what we are essentially, albeit not in terms of a present possession but only as what we are to be, and we learn as well the depth of our own self-contradiction.[74] As a result, this event shows the depth of the human predicament and that human perfection is simply not attainable in history.[75] The cross declares that because of the power of sin, love lives in history as suffering love. In short, the cross is a declaration of divine judgment on human sin. On the other hand, this symbol proclaims the divine love and forgiveness for sin. It is "a revelation of the love of God," yet only to those "who have first stood under its judgment."[76]

For Niebuhr, the event of the cross stands as the climax of the biblical revelation of God's sovereignty over history. It discloses the divine love, which is able to overcome the evil of the human heart and likewise takes the evil of history into and upon itself.[77] The cross, therefore, provides the clue to the meaning of history, which lies in love, for it is "the myth of the truth of the ideal of love."[78] At the same time, the truth revealed in the cross becomes the basis of a new wisdom, Niebuhr argued, through the Christian faith-affirmations that Jesus is the Son of God and the Second Adam,[79] two symbols that for him indicate that Jesus "discloses the ultimate mystery of the relation of the divine to history."[80]

In its classic form, Christian theology explicates the meaning of the cross in the doctrine of the atonement, a doctrine that is an embarrassment and a stumbling block to the modern mindset. But against those who would eliminate the atonement as an "incomprehensible remnant of superstition" or set it forth as a "completely incomprehensible article of faith,"[81] Niebuhr sought to understand the significance of the doctrine. To him, it offered the final key to the understanding of history. It declares that history is incapable of providing its own meaning and therefore points to the judgment and mercy of God for its fulfillment. God's judgment, in turn, is symbolic of the seriousness of history and the ultimate significance of good and evil. God's mercy, in contrast, speaks of the incompleteness and corruption present in all historical actions, but also of the divine love that takes evil into itself.

The Divine Transcendence

Niebuhr's understanding of the nature of meaning and its disclosure to humankind resulted in what was perhaps his deepest and most thoroughgoing critique of the contemporary mindset. In his view the modern age was guilty of substituting "the God of reason and nature for the God of revealed religion."[82] Thereby it had forgotten the finiteness and creatureliness of humankind. As a result it had lost the sense of the transcendent, that is, it could not "subject human righteousness to a transcendent righteousness, the righteousness of God."[83]

In the face of the modern denial, Niebuhr sought to reaffirm the biblical idea of divine transcendence as a basis for both the judgment and the overcoming of the human predicament. For him, this dimension is set forth in the concept of the kingdom of God that has come in Christ and is to come as the culmination of history. On the one hand, only the idea of a transcendent God and the kingdom of God standing over against history and humankind could provide the needed point of judgment to check the human tendency toward self-assertion and pride, whether in individuals or in groups.[84] The Christian proclamation of the final meaning of history as arising from the *Alpha* and the *Omega* of history stands as a check on all humanly devised provisional meanings, judgments and fulfillments of history.[85] At every moment, the kingdom of God remains an unattainable ideal.[86]

On the other hand, the concept of the transcendent establishes that the meaning of history is disclosed to the present, illuminating "the darkness of history's self-contradictions,"[87] and it offers hope for a final completion of history.

Niebuhr saw this hope expressed through the three major eschatological symbols found in the Bible, none of which were to be understood literally, but were nevertheless to be taken seriously.[88] The symbol of the return of Christ is an expression of faith in the sufficiency of God's sovereignty and in the final supremacy of love. The last judgment affirms the seriousness of the distinction between good and evil. And the resurrection implies "that eternity will fulfil and not annul" the variety found in the temporal process and that the dialectic of finiteness and freedom has no humanly devised solution.[89]

Ultimately, the disclosure of the meaning of history, while perceived by faith, likewise serves the life of faith and the Christian witness in the world. Niebuhr concluded his magnum opus, *The Nature and Destiny of Man,* on this note. To live in faith means to find "ultimate security beyond all the securities and insecurities of history,"[90] that is, in the transcendent God of history, he declared. In 1939 Niebuhr expressed optimism that this type of life of faith could dissuade others "from the idolatrous pursuit of false securities and redemption in life and history."[91]

Critique

By means of a more profound understanding of the height of divine transcendence and the depth of the human predicament, Niebuhr sought to insert a note of realism into what he sensed was a naively optimistic cultural and religious climate. This attempt has been both lauded as his greatest contribution and condemned as his greatest weakness. Without a doubt Niebuhr's concept of realism was influential in the realm of American politics, especially in shaping United States foreign policy in the years immediately following World War 2.

Concerning Niebuhr's legacy two critical comments are in order, however, both of which relate to his understanding of time and eternity and to the nature of transcendence offered by his theological orientation.

Unreal Symbols

First, like the other theologians of the neo-orthodox movement, Niebuhr was concerned with the question of how the myths and symbols of Christianity can be applicable to the modern mind. His response to this issue marked a positive step beyond Bultmann, for Niebuhr viewed such myths as revealing the transcendent meaning of history. But despite this important contribution, Niebuhr's proposal has proven itself to be less than completely satisfying. Simply stated, although providing a way of taking the symbols seriously—but not literally—he removed them from the realm of actual history.

Like Bultmann, Niebuhr argued that the clue to the meaning of history could not be found within history, but was disclosed only to the eyes of faith, to the one who could perceive beyond the process of life its transcendent meaning. But any such proposal raises certain crucial theological questions.

One such question is that of fideism.[92] Can any mythological approach to the understanding of salvation history move beyond subjectivism? For Niebuhr the events that disclose the meaning of history, insofar as they are revelatory events, are essentially suprahistorical. They disclose the meaning of history not insofar as they are literal, historical events. Rather, they become events of disclosure only to faith. But how can such events actually offer the needed clue to the meaning of history? Is it not possible that the clue they provide is, in the final analysis, placed there by the believing observer?

Another such question concerns God's working in history. How can Niebuhr's view, with its emphasis on the "beyond history," speak of God's redemptive activity within history? [93] Paul Lehmann directed this question to Niebuhr's Christology:

> Despite its insistence upon the Cross as the standpoint from which it is possible to make sense out of the manifold and complex dynamic of history, Niebuhr's Christological thinking does not sufficiently stress "the mighty acts of God" as transforming events which, having actually occurred, serve as beacon lights in a sea of historical relativity whereby the channel to the fulfilment of human destiny is charted . . . the Incarnation and the Atonement express more than faith's apprehension of this dynamic [of history]. They point to the facts that something has occurred and does occur. God has become man. Jesus Christ has been crucified. In consequence of these events, other events happen.[94]

Lehmann and others traced this problem in Niebuhr's thinking to a deeper theological difficulty, namely, to a truncated pneumatology. Niebuhr simply did not develop the relationship of the Holy Spirit to the affirmation of Christ as the Second Adam nor to his understanding of our being in Christ.[95] As a result his theology was, in the final analysis, "binitarian."[96]

Perhaps what several critics detected on the christological level was pervasive in Niebuhr's doctrine of God. By moving the revelatory events of history into the realm of myth, he appeared to have eliminated the ability of such events to disclose the reality of a transcendent God who is truly able to act in the world.

Dark Transcendence

Second, subsequent theological history has suggested that Niebuhr's choice of the cross as the central theological symbol was in need of augmentation. Because it was moved by the cross, his vision of the Christian story focused on what Paul Jersild termed "the tragic character of the struggle between divine love and human resistance."[97] It is therefore not without some credence that Niebuhr was dubbed a pessimistic theologian and that many critics claimed that his central theological motif was human sin. Although such portrayals easily become mere caricatures, they do point out an important dynamic at work in the implications of his thinking. In the final analysis, Niebuhr's proposal does lead to a certain type of pessimism.

Niebuhr's emphasis on the cross functioned as the theological foundation for his call to a long-suffering struggle in an attempt to attain what in the end cannot be attained. He saw this dynamic operative in the personal, but more importantly in the social realm. Because of the persistent presence of evil in the world, Christians can only hope for historical renewal, rather than for historical fulfillment.[98] On the basis of this perspective, Niebuhr offered a realistic, and yet largely negative, apologetic for democracy: "Man's capacity for justice makes democracy possible; but man's inclination to injustice makes democracy necessary."[99] In the end, his cross-centered theology disclosed only a dark transcendence, the reality of an *impossible* possibility standing in judgment over all human action.

Subsequent history has confirmed that while such a theology from the cross speaks an important word, it must always be coupled with a theology from the resurrection.[100] This means that the emphasis on self-criticism must be coupled with a sense of optimism and self-appreciation.[101] To our cry of repentance, which arises when we become aware of our sinfulness, must be added the word of absolution. Added to the declaration of the impossibility of the task of the kingdom of God, we need likewise to hear a message of divine promise and of divine power active in the transformation of the world. And to Niebuhr's distrust of all social groups must be added the promise of Christ's presence in the community of faith as it struggles by the power of the Holy Spirit on behalf of Christ's lordship in the world. In short, to Niebuhr's removal of eschatology to a realm beyond history must be added the hope of the fulfillment of history within history—in part in the present and in its fullness beyond the final day.

Conclusion

Reinhold Niebuhr sought to call Western society back from its flight into the immanence of God, a flight that resulted in a naive, unrealistic optimism concerning what human beings could accomplish. In its stead he sought to provide a theological understanding characterized by a balance between transcendence and immanence. This is his greatest legacy for the theological history of the twentieth century. Yet he accomplished this task at a great cost. Niebuhr's proposal worked to remove the activity of God in history—whether past or future—to a realm beyond history. Thereby he left his followers little hope of finding the transcendent God in actual events, whether in salvation history or in the consummation of history.

4 THE DEEPENING OF IMMANENCE: *Reformulations of the Liberal Tradition*

*T*HE NEO-ORTHODOX REVOLT AGAINST CLASSICAL PROTESTANT LIBERALISM DOMINATED theology from the 1920s until about 1960. Yet even before it had completely run its course certain voices had begun to articulate dissent. Some thinkers were suspicious that neo-orthodoxy had done too thorough a job in exorcising the ghost of the one-sided emphasis on immanence they had detected in liberalism. Was it possible that Barth and company had inadvertently gone too far in reaffirming the divine transcendence?

Uneasiness about the possible excesses of neo-orthodoxy produced thinkers who sought to offer alternatives to the dominant theology in the wake of the demise of the older liberalism. They could not avoid taking seriously the critique of immanental theology. But they also believed that only the reestablishment of the emphasis on immanence could provide a proper understanding of the reality of God needed to meet the ongoing challenge to Christianity posed by the modern mindset.

Thus, these thinkers sought to reformulate and deepen the immanental theology of the older liberalism. They did not advocate a simple return to the now discredited older culture Christianity, of course. Rather, they sought to employ themes borrowed from the newer philosophies, such as existentialism, or to incorporate the advances gained by recent scientific endeavors as a means of restating the Christian belief in God in a way that twentieth-century people could understand and accept.

Examples of the new liberalism abound, including John Macquarrie's existentialist theology and the empirical theology of Nelson Wieman (1884-1975). Yet paradigmatic of the whole thrust of the twentieth-century renewal of liberalism are the two varieties chosen for discussion in the following pages. Paul Tillich provides perhaps the most lucid example of a neo-liberal who chose existentialism as theology's conversation partner. And the broad movement that utilized the philosophical theme of process illustrates the attempt to correlate theology with the emphasis on change and evolution characteristic of modern science.

The theologians discussed in these pages were liberals, therefore, but not in the classical sense. They are perhaps best called "chastened liberals." The liberalism, the rebirth of which they advocated, was one that had gone through the fires of neo-orthodoxy. As a result, theirs was to be a deepened liberalism, one that was characterized by a more profound sense of the immanence of God within the processes of creaturely life.

PAUL TILLICH:
THE IMMANENCE OF THE "GOD ABOVE GOD"

More than any other twentieth-century theologian Paul Tillich deserves the title "apostle to the intellectuals."[1] In a manner reminiscent of second-century Christian apologists such as Justin Martyr he sought to communicate the essential truths of the Christian faith to the intellectuals among his contemporaries in their own thought forms. Toward the end of his life he acknowledged this overriding apologetic purpose and passion by confessing, "My whole theological work has been directed to the interpretation of religious symbols in such a way that the secular man—and we are all secular—can understand and be moved by them."[2]

Tillich's theological contribution is comparable to Barth's in terms of overall influence and impact, although it is quite opposite in terms of approach. Like Barth he produced a massive system of theology that influenced an entire generation of Christian thinkers and was granted the notice and acclaim of secular society as well. Unlike Barth, he strove for positive correlation, if not synthesis, between modern secular philosophy and Christian theology.

Although Tillich died in 1965, his legacy endures into the last decades of the century and probably will be felt well into the twenty-first. An international society of philosophers and theologians called the North American Paul Tillich Society continues scholarly discussion of his work. The centennial of his birth in 1986 saw a number of conferences devoted to his theological contribution and its enduring significance. In 1977 a published study of North American theologians identified Tillich as the single most important influence upon American systematic theology.[3]

During his own lifetime Paul Tillich was recognized by secular culture as one of the greatest minds Christian theology has ever produced. Few theologians have ever received the honor and recognition accorded Paul Tillich by politicians, governments, universities and foundations. Even the media, as was symbolized by his appearance on the cover of *Time* on March 16, 1959, recognized the significance of his achievement.

Tillich's Life and Career

Paul Tillich was born into the family of a Lutheran pastor in the German town of Starzeddel near Berlin on August 20, 1886.[4] He seems to have had a serious interest in theology and philosophy from an early age—possibly even as young as eight—and began moving toward a career in ministry at the age of eighteen. Like most university students in Germany at the time, Tillich studied at several major German universities including Halle and Berlin, coming under the influence of critical philosophy, theology and biblical studies. During his education for ministerial ordination he determined to become a professor of theology and eventually received not only ordination in the Protestant state church but also appointment as *Privatdozent* (tutor) at the University of Halle.

Tillich's studies were interrupted temporarily by World War 1, in which he served as a chaplain. He spent time in the front lines of battle and not only officiated at the funerals of many soldiers—including some of his best friends—but also helped bury them with his own hands. His encounters with mass death and destruction became a turning point in his personal life and faith. He suffered two nervous breakdowns and underwent a severe crisis of doubt that transformed his view of God.

After the war Tillich accepted a teaching position at the prestigious University of Berlin and became involved in radical socialist politics. He was instrumental in the formation of the religious socialist movement, eventually publishing a major book on the subject, *The Socialist Decision*. During the 1920s Tillich became a well-known figure in German academic circles. He left Berlin first for Marburg, then to the Dresden Institute for Technology, finally landing at the University of Frankfurt. During his tenure as professor of philosophy at Frankfurt he came into open conflict with the Nazis and was condemned as an "enemy of the state" when they came to power. His book *The Socialist Decision* was burned publicly on May 10, 1933, and in October of the same year the Gestapo began to follow him everywhere.

Had he stayed in Germany Tillich may have ended his life in a concentration camp. He was spared that fate by the invitation of Columbia University and Union Theological Seminary in New York City to move there in 1933. Tillich had a difficult time adjusting to life in the United States, and learning the English language proved especially troublesome at first. However, with the special help of friends like Reinhold Niebuhr he and his wife Hannah made the transition to American life, becoming citizens in 1940.

Tillich remained at Union Theological Seminary until his retirement in 1955. During his twenty-three years there he gained great fame for his sermons, many of which were published, and for his theological reflections on all areas of contemporary culture. In 1940 he was given an honorary doctorate by Yale University and was cited as a "philosopher among theologians and a theologian among philosophers."[5]

During World War 2 he secretly delivered radio addresses to the German people for the Voice of America and met with President Roosevelt at the White House in 1944.

In the years immediately after the war he traveled widely, giving numerous lectures to enthusiastic audiences so that, in the words of his biographers, "only a few years before his retirement from the seminary, Tillich acquired a wide and enthusiastic public which clamoured to hear him."[6] In 1951 Tillich published the first volume of his *Systematic Theology*, in which he expounded his views on theological method, reason and revelation, and God. The second volume, which dealt with the human predicament and Christ, appeared in 1957. Volume three, which did not appear until 1963, focused on the theme of life and the Spirit, as well as on history and the kingdom of God. His other publications, including *The Courage to Be* and *The Dynamics of Faith*, appealed to a more popular audience, as did his sermons and lectures.

Upon retiring from the seminary Tillich accepted the invitation of Harvard University to become "University Professor"—perhaps the most prestigious academic position in America. He was entitled to teach any course he wished and had great freedom to travel, research and write. His lectures were tremendously popular among students; hundreds filled the lecture hall an hour early to be assured of seats. A sort of personality cult formed around Tillich, with students lining the sidewalk to the building in order to see him walk past. His lectures at other universities drew hundreds and even thousands of listeners, in spite of the fact that many critics claimed that his talks were nothing more than "unintelligible nonsense."[7]

Tillich received an invitation to John F. Kennedy's inauguration in 1961 and was seated on the platform with a small group of special guests. He received twelve honorary doctorates from major American universities and two from European universities including the University of Berlin. After retirement from Harvard in 1962 he became Nuveen Professor of Theology at the University of Chicago Divinity School and served as distinguished theologian in residence. Tillich's death on October 22, 1965, was noted in the *New York Times* with a brief editorial and front-page obituary.

Certainly few theologians have ever received the public acclaim Tillich did. He was truly a "legend in his own time." However, his life as a Christian theologian was marked by great ambiguity. He was beset by doubts about his own salvation and feared death greatly.[8] He promoted socialism while enjoying the benefits of an upper-middle-class lifestyle.[9] He was renowned as a great ecumenical Christian and yet rarely attended church[10] and apparently lived a fairly promiscuous lifestyle.[11]

Such ambiguities illustrate well his descriptions of the destructive tensions that Tillich believed are inherent in finite existence. For him, doubt is a necessary element in faith, and alienation and estrangement lie at the very root of human life. The Power of Being—God—can help us gain courage to face the inevitable threat of nonbeing and to accept that we are accepted, but it cannot completely overcome these tensions and ambiguities in existence.

In order to understand these themes, which were so central to Tillich's theology, we must make clear certain elements of his basic presuppositions and theological method.

Tillich's Presuppositions

One of Tillich's basic assumptions was that theology should be apologetic. It must formulate and communicate its concepts in a way that truly speaks to the modern situation. By "situation" Tillich meant the particular questions and concerns of people in culture, "the scientific and artistic, the economic, political, and ethical forms in which they express their interpretation of existence."[12] He was harshly critical of theologies, such as fundamentalism and "kerygmatic theology" (neo-orthodoxy), which neglect the role of this situation and try, in his words, to throw the Christian message at people like a stone instead of attempting to answer the questions put to it by contemporary culture.[13] For Tillich, in contrast, theology must be "answering theology"; it must adapt the Christian message to the modern mind while maintaining its essential truth and unique character.

Apologetic theology presupposes some common ground between the Christian message and the contemporary culture in which it is being expressed. The existence of such a common ground is another basic assumption of Tillich's theology. At the very least, he believed, the questions implicit in contemporary existence can and must be answered by theology as it draws on divine revelation. If this were not possible, theology would be obsolete, because it simply cannot answer questions that are not being asked. Fortunately, Tillich believed, the fundamental questions raised by contemporary existence are indeed answered, specifically in the symbols of divine revelation.

A third basic presupposition of Tillich's theology is the crucial role played by philosophy in theology's apologetic task. In direct contrast to Barth, he believed that philosophy is indispensable to theology, because it formulates the questions that theology answers, and because it provides much, if not all, of the form that those answers must take. Consequently, Tillich held philosophy in high regard: "No theologian should be taken seriously as a theologian, even if he is a great Christian and a great scholar, if his work shows that he does not take philosophy seriously."[14] Against the fideism of thinkers such as Pascal, he remarked, "The God of Abraham, Isaac and Jacob and the God of the philosophers is the same God."[15]

Closely related to the third presupposition is a fourth. The particular kind of philosophy most useful to theology is ontology, especially existentialist ontology. In fact, Tillich defined philosophy so as to make it virtually synonymous with ontology: Philosophy is "that cognitive approach to reality in which reality as such is the object,"[16] and ontology is the "analysis of those structures of being which we encounter in every meeting with reality."[17] Tillich would not settle for any definition or use of philosophy that stops short of ontology, because it is the true center of all philosophy[18] and its questions and concerns are implicit in every other approach to philosophy.[19]

At its root, then, philosophy is ontology—the study of being. It raises ontological questions such as what it means to say that something *is,* what is ultimately real beyond all appearances, what is being itself beyond all particular things that have being and what structures are inherent in everything that has being? Hence, he declared, "Philosophy asks the question of reality as a whole; it asks the question of the structure of being. And it answers in terms of categories, structural laws, and universal concepts. It must answer in ontological terms."[20]

For Tillich, ontology's usefulness to theology lay in the questions it raises more than in the specific answers it proposes. A helpful example is his delineation of the question of "nonbeing," with which the ancient Greek philosophers wrestled and which twentieth-century existentialist philosophers have revived, although in a different way. For Tillich, this continued interest in nonbeing was not surprising, because "anxiety about non-being is present in everything finite."[21] It is natural for humans to wonder about their own status in relation to being, because in their moments of deepest thought they realize that they are finite, transitory, temporal. They might "not be" just as easily as "be." In fact, nonbeing belongs to their existence, for they are faced with the threat of nonbeing every moment.

Nonbeing raises the question of a power of being that overcomes the threat of nonbeing and upholds and sustains finite beings. Such a power cannot be finite, but must be "being itself" or the "ground of being." Without it, finite existence would sink into nonbeing or nothingness. In short, the ontological question of nonbeing and the power of being raises the question of God, Tillich believed. In fact, without the ontological question, he argued, the answer theology sets forth—"God"—cannot be understood. In his words, "Only those who have experienced the shock of transitoriness, the anxiety in which they are aware of their finitude, the threat of non-being, can understand what the notion of God means."[22]

Ontology, then, is absolutely crucial to contemporary apologetic theology. This is especially the case given the dominance of existentialist philosophy in the twentieth century. In fact, existentialist ontology, Tillich said, is the "good luck of Christian theology,"[23] because it raises questions that theology, drawing on divine revelation, is particularly suited to answering. In this way, questions and answers concerning ontology form the common ground of philosophy and theology: "The structure of being and the categories and concepts describing this structure are an implicit or explicit concern of every philosopher and of every theologian. Neither of them can avoid the ontological question."[24] Of course the approaches of philosophy and theology to the question of being differ considerably. Philosophy takes the attitude of detached objectivity while theology looks at ultimate being, the power that overcomes the threat of nonbeing, with "passion, fear, and love."[25] Nevertheless, in order to deal adequately with ontological issues and concerns, Tillich averred, one must take on both roles— that of philosopher and that of theologian. Every creative philosopher is some of the time a theologian,[26] and every theologian must also play the role of philosopher in order to analyze the existential situation of humanity and the questions implied therein. Philosophy and theology are two distinct but inseparable and interdependent "moments" or aspects of a fully orbed ontology.

A final presupposition of Tillich's theology is the special nature of human existence in ontology. This is best expressed in the assertion, made several times in *Systematic Theology,* that "man is microcosm."[27] By this Tillich meant that the powers and structures of being appear in the human in a way not true of any other creature. Human beings are open to and participate in the structures of being both below and above themselves, so that their being provides special clues to ultimate reality: "Man participates in the universe through the rational structure of mind and reality. . . . He participates in the universe because the universal structures, forms, and laws are open to him."[28] Therefore, ontological reflection must turn to humanity, not to nonhuman nature, if it is to formulate questions and answers about ultimate reality or being itself.

These presuppositions underlay and informed Tillich's entire thought. But they were also highly controversial and have been the source of much scholarly debate. Most philosophers, especially in the English-speaking world, have reacted negatively to his identification of philosophy with ontology and even more negatively to his assertion of the inseparability of philosophy and theology.[29] Many theologians, on the other hand, have criticized him for making Christian theology the prisoner of "ontological specu-lation," thus jettisoning both the autonomy of theology and biblical personalism.[30] Per-haps the most damaging criticism is that close inspection of Tillich's ontology reveals that it is eclectic. It attempts to combine totally incompatible strands of philosophy, namely, traditional ontology rooted in Plato, Augustine and the German idealist philos-ophers and modern existentialist ontologies formulated by Heidegger and Sartre.[31]

The Method of Correlation

Building on these presuppositions, Tillich proceeded to propose a method for theology that would be both faithful to the original Christian message and contemporary in expression—the method of correlation. This approach determined the entire structure and form of his systematic theology and is often considered one of his most enduring contributions to modern theology.

Tillich offered his method of correlation, which "explains the contents of the Chris-tian faith through existential questions and theological answers in mutual interdepend-ence,"[32] in conscious rejection of three inadequate alternatives. The first method, the "supernaturalistic," is followed by many Protestant theologians. For Tillich it is inade-quate because it ignores the questions and concerns (the "situation") of humans who are to receive the message and expect the Word of God to create the possibility for understanding and accepting its truth.[33] According to Tillich, in contrast, "man cannot receive answers to questions he never has asked."[34]

No doubt Tillich was thinking of both fundamentalism and Barthian neo-orthodoxy here. Of course the conservative theologians might respond, "What if human beings, because of their fallenness, never come up with the right questions?" Tillich simply believed that the right questions *are* present in our very existence as humans.[35]

The second inadequate traditional alternative, the "naturalistic" or "humanistic" method, is the exact opposite of the first, for it attempts to derive theological answers from the natural human state. In this method, typical of much of liberal theology, "Everything was said by man, nothing to man."[36] Tillich accused the humanistic meth-od of overlooking the estrangement of human existence and the fact that revelation (which contains the answers) is something spoken *to* humans, not by them to them-selves.[37]

Finally, Tillich rejected the "dualistic" method, which tries to combine supranatural with natural. Here he was referring to traditional natural theology, such as what has been common in Catholicism since Thomas Aquinas. It posits two kinds of theological answers—those derivable from nature alone, such as the existence of God, and those which must be supranaturally revealed. The problem with this method is that it tries to derive the answer (God) from the form of the question. In its place Tillich proposed the method of correlation, which resolves natural theology into the analysis of existence and supranatural theology into the answers given to the questions implied in existence.[38]

The method of correlation, then, is a form of *fundamental theology* that substitutes for natural theology. Tillich's approach replaces the proofs of the existence of God that traditionally form a large part of natural theology with the question of God implied in human existence as analyzed by ontology.

The method of correlation revolves around questions and answers. The questions are raised by philosophy through careful examination of human existence. The theologian must function as a philosopher in this first step of theology. The second step is uniquely theological, as the theologian draws on the symbols of divine revelation to formulate answers to the questions implied in human existence that philosophy can discover but not answer. The overall task of the theologian in both steps is to bring the questions and the answers together in critical correlation.[39] The answers theology presents must be derived from revelation, but they must be expressed in a form that will speak to the existential concerns of human beings. The theologian's task is to interpret the answers of revelation so that they remain faithful to the original Christian message while becoming relevant to the questions asked by modern secular men and women.

According to Tillich "God" stands as a preliminary example of how the method of correlation works:

> God is the answer to the question implied in human finitude. However, if the notion of God appears in systematic theology in correlation with the threat of non-being which is implied in existence, God must be called the infinite power of being which resists the threat of non-being. In classical theology this is being itself.[40]

The *Systematic Theology* follows this method. In the first part Tillich analyzed the nature of human reason under the conditions of existence, discovering that it contains the question concerning something that transcends reason while fulfilling it. Thus, reason itself, as analyzed by ontology, raises the "quest for revelation." Tillich then proceeded to interpret divine revelation as that which answers the questions raised by reason. A similar pattern is followed in the other four parts of the theology. In each case the answer takes its form from the question, and its content, Tillich claimed, is derived entirely from revelation.

Tillich's method of correlation has received mixed reviews. Although some found it extremely helpful in presenting theology in a way that is both faithful and relevant, critics chided Tillich for giving philosophy too much independence from and authority over revelation. Tillich did restrict philosophy to the tasks of formulating the questions for theology and of determining the form of the answers. But does not even this nevertheless accord to secular philosophy too large a role in theological construction? In defining the method of correlation Tillich did not require philosophy to be transformed or converted before launching into its task, thereby leaving philosophy "autonomous"—to use his categories—rather than truly "theonomous" or healed.[41] How can such a discipline, disrupted by the tensions inherent in finite reason, be trusted to formulate the right questions in the right manner? Might not the substance and form of the questions serve as a confining prison or Procrustean bed onto which the answers of revelation must fit? As Christian philosopher George Thomas has asked,

> Can a philosophical reason which has not been fully "converted" by the Christian faith correctly formulate the "structure" and "categories" of Being and raise the deepest "questions" implied in existence? If not, will not the Christian "answers," whose form is determined by the nature of the "questions," be distorted or obscured?[42]

A common criticism leveled against Tillich is that his employment of the method of correlation did not match his idealistic description of it. In spite of his intention to allow the content of the theological answers to be determined entirely by divine revelation, in actual practice the content as well as the form became influenced, if not determined, by the philosophical questions. Thomas raised this with regard to Tillich's doctrine of God, in which he describes God not as *a* being or *a* person but being itself and the ground of everything personal. In keeping with his own understanding of the Christian message as declaring that God *is* himself personal, Thomas asked whether "Tillich's statement of [the Christian view] has not been weakened at points by the intrusion into his thinking of an impersonal philosophy alien to the spirit of Christianity."[43] Theologian Kenneth Hamilton concluded that the method of correlation as actually practiced by Tillich takes nothing from the Christian message and everything from the ontological system of thought from which it begins. In actual practice, he argued, Tillich did not truly "correlate" questions and answers but interpreted the language of Christian faith so as to make it conform to his preconceived ontological system.[44]

Truly the single most significant weakness in Tillich's theology is that it is a sophisticated form of the "Procrustean bed syndrome." Procrustes, the evil innkeeper of ancient Greek lore, forced his tall or short guests to fit the bed they slept in by torture or mutilation, stretching or amputating whatever portion of their anatomy did not reflect the dimensions of their host's resting place. This has often been used as a metaphor for systems of thought that predetermine truth by forcing data to fit their preconceived structures. Theologian John Jefferson Davis expressed this aspect of Tillich's method concisely:

> While the idea of a method of correlation is valuable and even necessary, as Tillich developed it modern culture rather than the Christian tradition was really the controlling factor. As a result the modern mind was addressed but not *confronted* by a biblical message demanding a truly radical conversion of the heart and mind to the Living God.[45]

The accuracy and fairness of this critique of Tillich's method, however, can be determined only on the basis of the actual outworking of his systematic theology. Because a complete exposition of it would go far beyond the scope of this discussion, only a cursory presentation of a few of its major themes, namely, his concepts of revelation, God and Christ, will be attempted.

Reason and Revelation

The first part of Tillich's systematic theology attempts to establish a correlation between reason and revelation. In this section, Tillich tried to uncover conflicts and questions inherent in reason that drive it beyond itself toward revelation. His goal was to show that "revelation is the answer to the questions implied in the existential conflicts of reason."[46] In contrast to those who see reason and revelation as opposed to one another, Tillich believed that "reason does not resist revelation. It asks for revelation, for revelation means the reintegration of reason."[47]

In order to understand Tillich's concept of reason it is necessary to grasp something of his fundamental ontology of "essence and existence." This ontological distinction underlies much or all of his theology and makes its first significant appearance in his treatment of the nature of reason. According to Tillich, reality as we know and experience it must be differentiated into two realms: essence and existence. Essence is the potential, unactualized perfection of things. It has ontological reality but not actual existence. Existence, on the other hand, is actual and "fallen" from essence. Because it is cut off from its perfection while still being dependent on it, it is not itself.

The philosophical background of Tillich's distinction between essence and existence lies in Platonic thought.[48] Plato believed in an ideal world of "forms" or perfect patterns of things and a world of individual, existing things that are imperfect copies of the forms. Tillich adapted the Platonic ontology to fit his own purposes. Nevertheless Plato's general ideas of essence and existence serve as the background to Tillich's use of these terms.

For Tillich, "existence" refers to what is both finite and fallen. It is limited as well as disrupted and distorted by the condition of being cut off from its true being. This is true of actual reason, or what he calls "the predicament of reason in existence"; it is fallen from the "essential nature of reason" and therefore suffers certain conflicts that it cannot solve itself.[49]

Essential reason, or reason itself, is transcendent. It is the "structure of the mind which enables the mind to grasp and to transform reality."[50] It also includes the mind's capacity for logical reasoning, discovering means toward ends. Ultimately essential human reason depends both on a rational structure of the universe (the "logos of being") and on the fit between it and the mind's structure. Reason itself, then, is not merely finite.[51] It is that function of both the universe and humanity which makes knowledge and discovery possible. Therefore, it transcends everything merely finite.

Actual reason, or reason in the predicament of existence, is different. Like everything that exists it is limited and estranged from its true essence, which gives rise to conflicts. This estrangement shows itself in reason's polarities that belong together, but under the conditions of existence fall into conflict and contradiction—polarities such as autonomy versus heteronomy, relativism versus absolutism and formalism versus emotionalism. Through a careful analysis of these polarities Tillich attempted to show that although reason itself cannot solve the conflicts, they nevertheless cry out for reconciliation. Tillich concluded that the conflicts produced by these polarities lead inevitably to either a desperate resignation of truth itself or the quest for revelation, "for revelation claims to give a truth which is both certain and of ultimate concern—a truth which includes and accepts the risk and uncertainty of every significant cognitive act, yet transcends it in accepting it."[52] In other words, reason needs to be "saved" or "healed." It cannot heal itself, but it does reach out beyond itself for a power that will reunite it with its essential structure and thus fulfill it.

According to Tillich, the uniting of the polarities of reason is the task of revelation. It reestablishes the essential structure of reason under the conditions of existence "fragmentarily, yet really and with power."[53] Consequently, he defines revelation formally as "the manifestation of the ground of being for human knowledge."[54] Revelation is the manifestation of the power that reunites what is tragically and destructively separated, thereby saving, healing and bringing harmony out of conflict. It is the unveiling of the mystery of being, the "self-manifestation of the depth of being and meaning."[55]

Like many twentieth-century theologians, Tillich rejected the concept of revealed words or propositions. Revelation is never the communication of information. Rather, it is event and experience that can happen through many different media, including nature, history, groups and individuals, and speech. In fact, anything can become a bearer of revelation if it becomes transparent to the ground of being.[56] Words and doctrines are not revealed, but whenever the depth of being manifests itself through language something sounds through, which is "the Word of God" or revelation. Belief in revelation as spoken or written words from God is "*the* Protestant pitfall," Tillich claimed.[57]

The Bible, then, is not the "Word of God." In fact, according to Tillich, "Probably nothing has contributed more to the misinterpretation of the biblical doctrine of the Word than the identification of the Word with the Bible."[58] The "Word" is God manifest. However, Tillich did find a role for the Bible in revelation. It "participates" in revelation as the document that records the event of final revelation in Jesus the Christ.[59]

Tillich differentiated revelation into "actual revelation" and "final revelation." The former designates all events and experiences that manifest the power of being wherever and whenever they may happen. The latter designates the ultimate, unsurpassable event of the healing power of the New Being to which all other revelatory events and experiences point.

What ultimately distinguishes Christianity from other religions is its claim "to be based on the revelation in Jesus as the Christ as the final revelation."[60] Of course it cannot prove this claim to be true. However, Tillich attempted to show that this revelatory event—the appearance in a particular person in history of the universal healing power of the New Being—is final and unsurpassable, because it heals or saves reason by overcoming its conflicts. It is the answer to the question of revelation raised by the structure of reason under the conditions of existence.[61] The existential conflicts of reason call for a power that is both universal and concrete, absolute and relative, a power that negates the finite while preserving it. Only such a reality can heal reason by reestablishing the essential harmony of its poles.

As the being who is determined in every moment by God and as the finite individual who sacrificed himself completely to the infinite while maintaining his individuality, Jesus the Christ fulfills the double test of finality of revelation.[62] By his life and death he revealed the power of self-negation, in that he presented a picture or symbol of something finite that does not claim to be final in its own right. Such a self-sacrificing finite being defeats the demonic conflicts of existential estrangement and creates true "theonomy," which cancels out autonomy and heteronomy while preserving the truth in both. This power of self-negation, or New Being, is "the Christ."

Jesus was the finite individual who Christians believe became the Christ by his self-sacrificing life and death. He did so because he refused the demonic temptation inherent in finite existence to claim finality for himself. This sacrificing of himself to the Christ made Jesus of Nazareth the medium of the final revelation.

For Tillich, this means that any Jesus-centered religion is a complete perversion of Christianity: "A Christianity which does not assert that Jesus of Nazareth is sacrificed to Jesus as the Christ is just one more religion among many others. It has no justifiable claim to finality."[63]

We will discuss Tillich's Christology more fully later. However, the decidedly Gnostic tone of this assertion cannot be passed over without comment. The Christology of the Gnostics was more often dualistic than docetic.[64] Certain Gnostic sects required members to curse Jesus in order to demonstrate their knowledge of the Christ as someone separate from him. (This is probably the background of Paul's condemnation of those who cursed Jesus [1 Cor 12:3]). To be sure, Tillich did not encourage or condone cursing Jesus. However, his radical distinction between Jesus of Nazareth and the "Christ" who is not a person but a power of New Being echoes the Gnostic view.[65]

The "God Above God"

Tillich believed that he had successfully correlated reason and revelation by showing that revelation fulfills reason without destroying it and that reason raises the question of revelation, without which it would be a meaningless answer. Throughout his discussion of reason and revelation, however, he referred to what is revealed as the power of being, the New Being, the ground of being, or God. What is revealed in final revelation, and to a lesser extent in universal revelation, is God, the religious word for the ground of being.[66] God is the power of love that heals reason by reunifying its polar elements, which in existence have fallen into conflict.

Tillich's doctrine of God has created more controversy than any other area of his theology. Much of the discussion has arisen out of his well-known assertion: "God does not exist. He is being itself beyond essence and existence. Therefore to argue that God exists is to deny him."[67] Some of the furor arose entirely from a simplistic misunderstanding of Tillich's technical use of the term *existence,* which gives rise to the impression that Tillich was an atheist. However, even some astute critics have argued that in spite of all his talk about God as being itself, Tillich *was* an atheist.[68]

It would be impossible here to give adequate consideration to all the nuances of Tillich's doctrine of God or to the various interpretations of it. However, we will attempt to show that while he may not have been an atheist, his doctrine of God places such a strain on the immanence and the transcendence of God that the follower of Tillich must choose between them. Further, opting for the nearly total immanence of Tillich's "God above God"[69] is most consistent with his overall viewpoint. Mark Kline Taylor is correct in noting that Tillich risked "tracing out God's transcendence so deep in the fabric of existence . . . that the meaning of 'transcendence' was stretched beyond recognition."[70]

If God is the answer, then, what is the question? As we have already seen, for Tillich the question must precede the answer and determine its form. Simply stated, God is the answer to the question implied in being: "What is being itself?"[71] According to Tillich, finitude is a mixture of being and of nonbeing.[72] Therefore, he engaged in a complex and subtle ontological analysis of the structure of finitude in order to show that it raises the question of a power of being or being itself that can overcome the threat of nonbeing inherent in itself. The ontological question arises in human existence because of finite beings' awareness that they are not the ground of their own being, an awareness that comes to its most intense expression in the "metaphysical shock" that occurs when a person becomes existentially threatened by nonbeing.

If God is the answer to the question implied in human finitude, Tillich argued, he cannot be a being, even the highest or most supreme being, but must be conceived as the "power of being," "power of resisting nonbeing," "infinite power of being" or ultimately "being-itself."[73] Now this power of being (that answers the question of nonbeing) by definition cannot "exist"[74] because "existence" is a mode of finite being—the condition of fallenness or estrangement. Every particular being participates in nonbeing, which is what makes it finite and in need of a power of being to uphold it in being. If God were *a* being he could not be the object of ultimate concern and the power that answers the question of finitude. Something else would then be God. This is what Tillich meant by "the God above God." The God who is being itself or the ground and power of being is superior to the supposedly finite God of traditional Christian theism who is thought of as a person and a being.

Tillich struggled to express the transcendence of being-itself, while maintaining its immanence. He asserted that being-itself is not the universal essence of everything, the underlying substance of the world, because being-itself transcends the essence/existence split to which all things in the world are subject due to their element of nonbeing. Being-itself does not participate in nonbeing and therefore infinitely transcends everything finite.[74] For Tillich this meant that because God is absolute and infinite, unconditioned and free, nothing can be said about him that is not symbolic except that he is being-itself.[76] All other assertions about or descriptions of God are purely (not merely!) symbolic.

After affirming the transcendence of God so strongly, Tillich turns to God's immanence. God and the world participate in one another. Everything finite participates in being-itself, which is the structure of being in which everything is grounded.[77] Conversely, God participates absolutely and unconditionally in everything that is, as its ground and aim.[78] God includes everything finite within himself in a dynamic, living process. In fact, it would seem that this "life" of God necessarily includes the world with all of its nonbeing.[79]

For Tillich, then, God transcends the world and the world transcends God. God is immanent in the world and the world is immanent in God.[80] Paradoxically, God may be unconditioned, but so long as there is a world he cannot be outside of it or it outside of him, otherwise he would not be truly infinite and unconditioned, but limited and conditioned by something other than himself. Therefore, the world exists "within" (nonspatially) the life of God, and God is the being (but not the substance) of the world.

It should be clear why critics have not been completely pleased with Tillich's position. Even as sympathetic an observer as Mark Kline Taylor concluded, "Tillich's understanding of transcendence was so thoroughly immanental that many remained perplexed about his meaning of God's 'otherness' or 'transcendence.' "[81] One of Tillich's most astute critics, Adrian Thatcher, went farther, arguing that he failed to explicate the transcendence and immanence of God coherently, so that he risked positing two separate ideas of God.[82]

Overall, it would seem that the "God above God" is really beneath and within everything. Of course these are metaphorical characterizations borrowed from spatial reality to describe something nonspatial. Nevertheless, however different being-itself, the power of being or the ground of being may be from particular finite things or even their totality, it cannot be transcendent in any traditional sense. This is especially true in light of Tillich's emphasis on the mutual participation between God and the world. God is the being of the world. Transcendence simply means that he is not subject to the limitations and conflicts to which finite things are subject. He includes these limitations and conflicts in himself, and this contributes to his life. Concerning this, Tillich wrote,

> In this view the world process means something to God. He is not a separated self-sufficient entity who, driven by a whim, creates what he wants and saves whom he wants. Rather, the eternal act of creation is driven by a love which finds fulfilment only through the other one who has the freedom to reject and to accept love. God, so to speak, drives toward the actualization and essentialization of everything that has being. For the eternal dimension of what happens in the universe is the Divine Life itself. It is the content of the divine blessedness.[83]

That this is a form of panentheism is beyond dispute. At the end of his system of theology, Tillich himself used the word to describe his view.[84] God and the world are not identical, but they are intimately and inextricably linked. One is reminded of Hegel's assertion, "Without the world God would not be God."[85]

Language such as this raises the problem of how a person relates to the being of the world, to the ground of being that is not *a* being, or *a* person. On the one hand, Tillich stated, "The personal encounter with God and the reunion with him are the heart of all genuine religion."[86] But on the other hand, he asserted that the protest of atheism against a heavenly, completely perfect divine person is correct. Such a being would "exist" and therefore could not be being-itself.

Still, Tillich did not want to say that God is *impersonal*. He explained that " 'Personal God' does not mean that God is *a* person. It means that God is the ground of everything personal and that he carries within himself the ontological power of personality. He is not a person, but he is not less than personal."[87] Can one "encounter" and have any real relationship with the "ground of everything personal"? Tillich was well aware of this objection and the entire line of biblical personalism that underlies it. He strove to solve this dilemma by synthesizing ontology and biblical personalism. Ultimately, however, he failed. In the end he could only express his synthesis in a paradox: "Our encounter with the God who is a person includes the encounter with the God who is the ground of everything personal and as such is not *a* person"![88] Surely this satisfies neither reason nor religious experience.

Tillich believed that the God above God who does not exist but is being itself provides the final answer to the questions implied in human existence.[89] One cannot avoid the suspicion, however, that he allowed the form of the question to determine the content of the answer. Being-itself simply cannot be the transcendent, righteous, holy and personal God of Abraham, Isaac and Jacob, the Father of Jesus Christ.

Christology

Tillich's Christology is similarly determined by the form of the question with which it is correlated. In "Existence and the Christ," the third part of his systematic theology, he presented a powerful and controversial phenomenology of human existence. At its foundation is his interpretation of the Fall of humanity, which he viewed as the universal transition from essence to existence that "is not an event in time and space but the transhistorical quality of all events in time and space."[90] The Genesis story of the sin of Adam and Eve is not to be taken literally, he argued, but as a symbolic expression of the predicament of humanity, our inevitable estrangement from essential humanity and therefore from God, the ground of being.

Although he denied that the Fall is ontologically necessary, Tillich averred that it is identical with "actualized creation."[91] In other words, the transition coincides with our exercise of free will. As soon as humans actualize their freedom, they fall from the state of dreaming innocence (a concept he borrowed from Kierkegaard), which marks their essential being in union with God, and enter into estranged existence. This gives rise to tensions, anxieties, conflicts, despair, guilt and all sorts of evils in human life.

According to Tillich, we ought not to understand the Fall as an occurrence either in the history of the race or of the individual, but as a symbol for the universal human situation.[92] At the same time, it is not a necessary structural feature of humanity. It cannot be derived from the human essence, but has the nature of an irrational leap for which humans are responsible.[93] This is, of course, Tillich's version of "original sin."

Critics have suggested that Tillich's view "ontologizes sin," or makes it necessary, because it represents it as identical with creation. This interpretation is supported by his assertion that "man is caught between the desire to actualize his freedom and the demand to preserve his dreaming innocence. In the power of his finite freedom, he decides for actualization."[94] It appears, then, that the only alternative to "falling" would be to remain unactualized—to be only potentially human—in dreaming innocence. As soon as humanity actualizes itself it falls into estranged existence. Critics rightly question whether this does not indeed make sin a necessary feature of human actuality. In any case, Tillich made it clear that the Fall, the transition from essence to existence, is the "original fact" about humankind as we know it. Ontologically the Fall into existence precedes everything that happens in time and space.[95]

Tillich believed that his analysis opened the door for a truly Christian Christology. Universally implied in human existence is the quest for a New Being that will break through estrangement and overcome anxiety and despair by reuniting us with our essence. For Tillich, then, Christ is the answer. The Christian symbol of Christ is the symbol of a New Being appearing under the conditions of existence yet conquering the gap between essence and existence.[96]

Christians believe that this New Being appeared in the life and death of Jesus of Nazareth. For Tillich, however, the name and the details of his life are relatively unimportant. He argued that if historical criticism should ever happen to come to the conclusion that the man Jesus of Nazareth never lived, faith in the presence of the New Being would not be affected. "Participation, not historical argument," he explained, "guarantees the reality of the event upon which Christianity is based. It guarantees a personal life in which the New Being has conquered the old being. But it does not guarantee his name to be Jesus of Nazareth."[97]

In what sense was Jesus special, then? Tillich flatly denied that Jesus was "God become man." The doctrine of the Incarnation must be reinterpreted to mean that Jesus Christ was "essential man appearing in a personal life under the conditions of existential estrangement."[98] He also suggested that one could indicate the divine presence in Jesus by speaking of "essential Godmanhood" appearing in him.[99] In other words, for Tillich, Jesus was not "divine" and did not have a "divine nature." Rather, he manifested in and through his humanity an entirely new order of being—essential humanity under the conditions of existence participating in but conquering estrangement. In him humanity became "essentialized" within existence, which is of course a paradox. The original unity of God and humanity was restored in Christ, although under the conditions of existence. No traces of estrangement between Jesus and God can be found in the biblical picture of Jesus as the Christ.[100] In fact, this overcoming of estrangement *is* his Christhood. In this way Tillich replaced the traditional two natures Christology with this understanding of Jesus as the New Being, and thereby substituted a dynamic relation for the older concept of a static essence.[101]

What made Jesus the Christ? Here Tillich's Gnostic tendencies resurfaced. He said that Jesus "proves and confirms his character as the Christ in the sacrifice of himself as Jesus to himself as the Christ."[102] This clearly implies a dualistic Christology that separates Jesus and Christ from one another. Tillich claimed that he was trying to develop a constructive contemporary Christology that would preserve both the "Christ-character" and "Jesus-character" of the event,[103] but he seemed to drive a wedge between them.

It should not come as any surprise that Tillich denied the bodily resurrection of Jesus. He preferred instead the "restitution theory": The effect of the New Being on the disciples led to the "restitution of Jesus to the dignity of the Christ in the minds of the disciples" after Jesus' death.[104] Similarly Tillich attempted to "de-literalize" the symbols of Jesus' preexistence as the *Logos* and his virgin birth, ascension and parousia.[105]

Again we must ask whether Tillich allowed the form of the question to determine not only the form of the theological answer but also its content. His rather dubious analysis of human existence led to the need for a concrete yet universal power of essentialization, a "New Being," in history to reunite humans with their essential being. This power must be *from* God, but cannot *be* God, because God, the ground of being, cannot appear under the conditions of existence. Yet Tillich admitted that even the appearance of the essential human being under the conditions of existence is a paradox.[106] Nevertheless, for Tillich, Jesus the Christ cannot be truly human and also God—and this because of the way he defined both and ruled out the two natures doctrine.[107] Therefore, Jesus must have been a human being who achieved a union with God that belongs essentially to every human being.

The questions this formulation raises are numerous. How can Tillich avoid falling into the ancient christological heresies such as adoptionism, docetism, Nestorianism and Monophysitism? Although these viewpoints are totally incompatible, Tillich has managed to combine them without transcending them. His view of Jesus is adoptionist: Jesus was nothing more than a man who achieved something. His view of Christ is docetic: "Christ" is not identical with the man Jesus and needed not even be Jesus at all, for the humanity and particularity of Jesus seem unnecessary to Christ. Tillich's overall picture of Jesus as the Christ appears Nestorian in that the theologian divides the two. Yet at the same time it smacks of the Monophysite heresy, for Tillich makes Christ something purely spiritual and not tied to the historical personality of the man Jesus. George Tavard was correct when he concluded,

> Paul Tillich has failed to account for the biblical picture of Jesus and for the Christological dogma as the Church has always believed it. He has paid lip-service to the dogmas. . . . But when he himself tried "to find new forms in which the Christological substance of the past can be expressed," the Christological substance vanished. The divinity of Christ has been rejected for fear of a Christological metamorphosis. And the humanity of Christ has been declared unknowable. Thus both the Christ-character and the Jesus-character of Jesus the Christ have been lost. Where the Council of Chalcedon, spearheading the Church, follows a ridge between two chasms, the Christology of Paul Tillich falls into two chasms one after the other.[108]

Critical Evaluation

The ultimate judgment on Tillich's theology is clear. In spite of the basic soundness of his theological method and his good intention to carry it out faithfully, he went too far in allowing the form of the questions to determine the content of the theological answers. The overall ontological system became a Procrustean bed that not only set the agenda for making theology contemporary but also constrained and mutilated the Christian message so that it became barely recognizable.

Most crucially, however, while attempting to solve the problem of God's transcendence and immanence, Tillich actually tore them apart. Thereby, his phrase "God above God" became a more literal description of his doctrine than he intended. But which "God" was Tillich's God? Was it the absolute God, "Being itself," untouched by existence, or was it the God intrinsically involved in the process of the world with all its conflicts and tensions? As we have already seen, the overall cast of his theology favors the latter. It leans heavily toward panentheism and thus, in the final analysis, must be judged to be a case of radical immanentism. This explains why certain proponents of "Christian atheism" in the 1960s proclaimed him as their mentor.

PROCESS THEOLOGY:
IMMANENCE WITHIN THE PROCESS

The mid-twentieth century witnessed the rise of two major alternatives to the neo-orthodox response to liberalism. The proposal of Paul Tillich did not look for God in the transcendent realm beyond, but rather in the depth of existence. He called us to become transparent to the divine ground of our being as exemplified by Jesus the Christ, who is the "New Being." In this way Tillich deepened the theme of immanence found in liberalism on the basis of the mid-twentieth-century infatuation with existentialism. Although Tillich enjoyed wide influence during his lifetime and has had a lasting impact on many of his students, his theological orientation never developed into a school of theological thought.

Paralleling Tillich's work and outlasting his proposal in terms of ongoing influence is an approach that has developed into a prominent school of thought: process theology. Although a twentieth-century phenomenon, its roots lie early in the Western intellectual tradition, in the choice, made by the ancient Greek philosophers, of Parmenides rather than Heraclitus—Being rather than Becoming—as the foundational metaphysical concept.

The champion of Being was Parmenides (c. 515-450). He viewed reality in terms of what remained the same despite the appearance of change in the realm of sense experience. He argued that Being is eternal and that change is impossible, because it entails the coming to be of something that was not.[1] Parmenides' chief rival was Heraclitus (c. 540-475), who emphasized Becoming. "You cannot step twice into the same rivers; for fresh waters are ever flowing in upon you," he declared.[2] According to Heraclitus all reality is involved in incessant change. It is always subject to new modifications,[3] with the pattern of change produced by the interaction or tension of opposites.[4] Change, therefore, was his fundamental metaphysical concept.

The predominance of Parmenides' position in Western philosophy remained largely unchallenged until the nineteenth century, when the industrial revolution and developments in science inaugurated a shift away from the mechanistic view of the world.[5] The changes in science were ignited by thinkers such as Einstein, who replaced the static concepts of Newtonian physics with a world view focusing on organic relationships. Although still indebted to the older mechanistic cosmology and the dream of the conquest of nature, Darwin aided this scientific revolution by placing the idea of dynamic change at the heart of biology.

The philosophical way for the shift in thinking was prepared beginning with Schleiermacher and Hegel. They spoke of the Absolute in terms of the Whole that contains and is contained in each part, thereby ascribing finiteness and freedom to ultimate reality. Henri Bergson (1859-1941) and William James (1842-1910) advanced the organic view of reality by introducing into philosophy and psychology the idea that relations are internal and capable of being experienced. Bergson gave a purposive and adventuring dimension to evolution, for he spoke of God as the driving force of its processes and postulated an open future in which the details are decided moment by moment.[6] James viewed consciousness as a stream whose later moments are able to grasp their predecessors.[7] These developments served to challenge Descartes' emphasis on the static ego.[8]

The changes in philosophy and science filtered into the outlook of society in general. Modern life came to be characterized by a new sense of contingency, transience and relativity.[9]

The ultimate goal of process theology is to indicate the relevance of the Christian faith, especially its conception of the relation of God to the world, in a culture imbued with the sense of Becoming.[10] To this end process theologians employ the new dynamic outlook, which declares that to be actual is to be in process and that every actual entity is an integration of opposites—inner plus outer, past plus future, self plus other.

The Basic Outlook of Process Theology
Foundational to the revelancy process thinkers envision is the reconciliation of theology and science.[11] Thus, they reject the older division of life into the religious sphere and the secular or scientific sphere. Theology must speak to all of life, process theologians maintain. This is "eschatological talk," the attempt to see the present world in the light of what it will become.

According to process theology, not only must the concept of God not contradict scientific thinking, it must move from a naturalistic starting point, which is completely open to scientific investigation. Process thinkers therefore reject what they believe to be antiquated concepts of God—the Cosmic Moralist, the Unchanging and Passionless Absolute, the Controlling Power or the Sanctioner of the Status Quo.[12] In place of these, they substitute a new (and for them relevant) understanding of God that views the deity as a participant in the temporal process.[13] To facilitate this goal, process thinkers generally set forth a new natural theology that incorporates into itself evolution as foundational to all reality and thereby attempts to bring together immanence and transcendence into a new balance.[14]

Enroute to a new balance between immanence and transcendence, process thinkers reject the older concept of static transcendence, the view of reality that postulates a higher and a lower realm. In its stead, they substitute what may be termed an evolutionary transcendence. Lying behind this concept is an understanding of growth reminiscent of Hegel, in which a prior state is not abandoned but rather fulfilled by the subsequent state. They view transcendence in temporal rather than spatial metaphors. It is the "advance into the future," especially the "ultimate future."

Although sharing certain common features, the broader stream of twentieth-century process thinking reflects two somewhat different traditions—those of Teilhard de Chardin and Alfred North Whitehead. More dominant is the latter approach, which more widely carries the specific label "process theology."

Teilhard's Career
The life of the French Roman Catholic thinker Pierre Teilhard de Chardin (1881-1955) was consumed by two burning devotions, the church and the scientific study of humanity.[15] In obedience to the first, at the age of eighteen he entered the Jesuit order. By the time he was ordained to the priesthood (1911), he had become proficient in both theology and geology, especially paleontology (the science of early forms of life as recorded in the fossil records). Subsequent studies placed him under the influence of the leading archaeologists of his day and sparked in him an interest in what would be the topic of his life's work, human evolution.

Teilhard's interest in human prehistory took him to China in 1923. On his return, he learned that because some of his beliefs were considered unorthodox by his superiors, he was forbidden to teach at the Institute Catholique in Paris. As a result he lived a type of exile in the Far East from 1926 to 1946. There he engaged in paleontology, including involvement in the discovery of prehistoric human remains (the Peking Man), and continued his literary activities, which by church order remained unpublished. Again thwarted in his attempt to assume a teaching post in France during the years 1946 to 1951, he finally moved to New York, where he remained until his death in 1955. His several manuscripts, including his magnum opus, *The Phenomenon of Man* (completed in 1938), were published posthumously.

Science and Christianity
Teilhard's thought was motivated by his conviction that science and Christianity are two phases of the same act of complete knowledge.[16] This conviction was based on the distinction he drew between the "without" and the "within" of all things. The "without" refers to the external nature of reality, the material realm explored by the scientist.[17] Equally significant, however, is the "within"—the immeasurable dimension of things, the underlying "spiritual" realm of purpose and unity—so often ignored by researchers but discussed by theologians. Teilhard dedicated himself to the task of demonstrating the convergence of these two. He saw the hope for the future of the world to lie in "the conjunction of science and religion."[18] Only in this way could the entire "phe-

nomenon of man," and thus the most scientific understanding of humankind, come into view.[19]

His research into the evolution of the world led Teilhard to conclude that this process followed what he termed the "law of complexity and consciousness."[20] Some degree of consciousness is present at every level of reality, being bound up with the "within." But evidenced as well is the tendency for the organization of matter through time to become increasingly complex, centered and conscious, a process that climaxes in the advent of humankind. He accounted for this tendency in the universe by appeal to what he termed "radial energy," the spiritual force permeating all reality and drawing it forward.[21] On this basis he postulated that the process of evolution was not driven by blind chance but by positive purpose ("orthogenesis").

Teilhard set forth a dialectical schema of cosmic history. The first stage is characterized by divergence or explosion, the production of diverse "gropings" for advancement. Next comes the stage of convergence or implosion, as things regroup around certain of these "gropings" and thereby create "thresholds." This situation leads to the stage of emergence, the breakthrough of a "new creation" surpassing the previous state.

The French thinker is perhaps best known for his application of this schema to the long process of evolution, leading to its crowning achievement, humankind. The first epoch included the various primordial geological developments that prepared the earth for the task of sustaining life.[22] Next came the advent of the cell and the resulting evolution of the various life forms and the encircling of the earth's surface (the "biosphere"). The goal of this process was the emergence of humankind.[23]

According to Teilhard, the uniqueness of humankind lies in the capacity for reflection, in the ability not only to know but "to know that one knows."[24] In humans, therefore, consciousness, which permeates all reality, becomes centered. The appearance of humankind marked what Teilhard called "noogenesis" (from the Greek word *noos*, mind), leading to the development of the "noosphere" (the encircling of the earth with the self-conscious species).

At this point, Teilhard moved from theorist to visionary, for he sought to extrapolate from the entire process of evolution a vision of the future. The French thinker believed that a high point was reached with the advent of "the modern earth," beginning at the end of the eighteenth century. Its advent, however, has thrust on us a grave responsibility. Since the discovery of evolution, the discovery that we are "nothing else than evolution become conscious of itself,"[25] he wrote, "we have become conscious of the movement which is carrying us along, and have thereby realized the formidable problems set us by this reflective exercise of the human effort."[26] Lying yet before us is the final stage of the evolutionary process, the uniting of all people together into a "mega-synthesis,"[27] which he termed the Omega point. Rather than entail the loss of personal consciousness, freedom and individuality, this situation will constitute the growth of consciousness into "hyper-reflection" or "hyper-personalisation."[28] In view of this possibility, Teilard called on humankind to forego the tendency toward isolation and move in the direction of "planetisation,"[29] that is, the bringing together of individuals in what we would refer to as "the global village."

The Omega Point and the Future

The Omega point fulfilled a crucial function in Teilhard's thinking. Although he viewed it as the last in the evolutionary series, it nevertheless stood outside that series. It offered a type of fixed, transcendent reference point, as well as being the driving force for the entire process.[30]

Yet even the Omega concept could not provide him with more than an ambiguous understanding of the final reality. In *The Phenomenon of Man* he offered two possible scenarios for the ultimate future. The first followed the utopian vision of the nineteenth century, anticipating a reduction of evil on the earth. The second was more in keeping with the apocalyptic fears of the first and the twentieth centuries. In this scenario evil will continue to grow alongside good, leading eventually to a catastrophic finale.

In Teilhard's later writings, the apocalyptic vision predominated. Perhaps as a result of his contemplation of the eventual running down of the universe predicted by the second law of thermodynamics, he replaced his earlier monism of spirit-matter with a vision of humankind breaking free from matter and rising to a new level of spirit-oriented life. In 1946 he wrote:

> Mankind, at the end of its totalization, its folding-in upon itself, may reach a critical level of maturity where, leaving Earth and stars to lapse slowly back into the dwindling mass of primordial energy, it will detach itself from this planet and join the one true, irreversible essence of things, the Omega point. . . . An escape from the planet, not in space or outwardly, but spiritually and inwardly, such as the hyper-centration of cosmic matter upon itself allows.[31]

In 1947 (and again in 1952) he suggested that this could entail a breaking through of "the material framework of Time and Space."[32]

The Significance of Christianity

Teilhard's description of cosmic evolution formed the context for his view concerning the significance of Christianity. The Christian faith stands in close relationship to the Omega point. While remaining the goal of cosmic history, the Omega is manifested to us and is active among us as the one who is responsible for the process itself.[33] According to Teilhard, the presence of Omega within the process is indicated in various dimensions of Christianity,[34] including its affirmation of a personal God and of a redeeming Incarnation. More significantly, the Omega is present in the church, which as the embodiment of Christ's work in drawing together a worldwide community of love sets forth a new state of consciousness encircling the globe. The Christian vision concludes by speaking of the end of the world and the final unity of all things in Christ, which Teilhard termed "Christogenesis." His employment of these themes indicates that the French thinker's concept of Omega developed from a purely scientific analysis of evolution and a future convergence of humankind to a specifically Christian assertion that this point of convergence is none other than the Christ of Christian faith.[35]

Whitehead's Metaphysics

Teilhard has been especially influential in Roman Catholic circles. The dominant tradition of process theology, however, finds its philosophical foundation elsewhere, primarily in the thinking of Alfred North Whitehead (1861-1947).[36] Whitehead was a mathematician in his native Britain until 1924, when he accepted a professorship of philosophy at Harvard University. At Harvard he "produced the most impressive metaphysical system of the 20th century," to cite the appraisal of William Reese.[37]

Whitehead's overarching goal was to reestablish the importance of metaphysics in the context of a scientifically oriented, antimetaphysical environment. Science is necessary, he maintained, but it must be based on a proper cosmology, for every science tacitly presupposes a metaphysic.[38] Consequently, he saw himself as engaging in what for him was the traditional task of speculative philosophy: "the endeavour to frame a coherent, logical, necessary system of general ideas in terms of which every element of our experience can be interpreted."[39]

Whitehead attempted to develop an understanding of reality that would fit the modern scientific theories that had replaced Newtonian physics. Newton presupposed that real things have a simple location in space and time independent of all other things and that the relation of a thing to others was external and accidental. The new physics replaced the idea of simple location with the concept of energy—work done—and it described reality in terms of power, so that in time all things are connected through the history of efficient causation. Whitehead sought to work out the underlying metaphysics of this newer view.[40] But he rejected the modern reduction of causality to efficient causation. He claimed that the physicists' notion of physical energy was but an abstraction of a more complex energy found in every event.[41]

Whitehead referred to his approach as a "philosophy of organism,"[42] because of its emphasis on "feeling," dynamic movement and "being present in another entity."[43] He placed himself within the philosophical tradition from Descartes to Hume,[44] which found in the human subjective experience the clue to the fundamental nature of reality.[45] Yet Whitehead moved beyond that tradition by asserting that the subjective or emotional experience ("feeling") is present not only in humans but in all reality.[46] His system can also be classified as a modified monism, for the fundamental building blocks of reality ("actual entities") are all alike. Hence, "God is an actual entity, and so is the most trivial puff of existence in far-off empty space."[47] And because the macroscopic and microscopic processes mirror each other, the nature of all reality can be depicted by any one entity.

The Building Blocks of Reality

According to Whitehead's metaphysics reality is built from four ultimate concepts—actual occasions, eternal objects, God and creativity.[48] Unlike Plato, he did not view the latter three categories as existing realities.[49] Rather, the world consists of the actual occasions[50] with the other three functioning as formal categories that give shape to the world.[51]

For Whitehead, reality is not static essence, but process. Alluding to the maxim of Heraclitus, he wrote, "The ancient doctrine that 'no one crosses the same river twice' is extended. No thinker thinks twice; and, to put the matter more generally, no subject experiences twice."[52]

The fundamental elements of this process are the "actual entities." These are not permanently enduring things, but transient "occasions of experience" or "drops of experience."[53] They are not neutral, objective, purely material substance, but are value-oriented, for each is a striving toward the realization of some value.[54] Each occasion is an activity of becoming, a bringing together into a unity of "feeling" (which Whitehead called "satisfaction") responses to the relevant past and the reachable future. Hence, each is dipolar, consisting of a "physical" pole (the past) and a "mental" pole (the achievable possibility). And each creates itself in the process of experiencing.[55]

While self-creative, each occasion is also embedded in a stream of occasions on which it is dependent.[56] Each is partially the product of past occasions of experience, for it accepts and rejects dimensions from its antecedent.[57] Whitehead used the term *prehension* to speak of the movement from past to present, that is, of the relatedness of each occasion to the antecedent universe.

An actual occasion is a fleeting reality. Once it has attained a unity of experience, it passes from the "privacy" of becoming to its "public" function as an object to be used by others in their becoming. It "perishes." Yet it is prehended by its successor and ultimately by God, obtaining thereby "objective immortality." Whitehead termed the process whereby an actual occasion becomes an object for subsequent entities *superject*. In order to emphasize this movement from subject to object he referred to the actual entity as a "subject-superject."

Prehension insures a continuation of past into present. Yet each occasion is also unique and new, for it arises from what is already given without being limited to that given. It is free to accept or reject prehensions from the past. This aspect introduces the concepts of the eternal entities and of God.

Not only does each occasion prehend antecedent occasions, it also selects and rejects eternal objects in the process of creating itself. Eternal objects are patterns and qualities—geometric relationships, colors, emotions, pleasures, pains—somewhat similar to Plato's Forms.[58] They are the "pure potentials"[59] that an actual occasion could reflect.

In the entire process of its becoming, each occasion is confronted by an "initial aim,"[60] consisting of the best possible combination for the now-forming occasion, which it is free to accept or reject. By means of this initial aim the occasion seeks to create an enjoyable experience and to be creative of the future by making a contribution to the enjoyment of others. This initial aim, according to Whitehead, is provided by God. God has another function as well. Once an occasion arises, it immediately perishes. Yet it is not lost.[61] It not only forms the predecessor for the next occasion but also adds to God's experience, where it remains imbedded forever ("objective immortality"). Hence, God is integral to the process that constitutes the world.

God as an Entity
Central to Whitehead's elaborate understanding of the deity is the presupposition that God is an entity among the other entities in the world.[62] Like all actual entities, God is dipolar, consisting of a primordial and a consequent dimension.[63] The primordial nature (the nontemporal, "mental" pole) refers to God as the principle of the process

of the world.[64] God envisages the infinite variety of eternal objects, functions as the primordial valuation of all possibilities[65] and supplies the lure to the actual entities in the process of becoming.[66] Hence, God contains the entire range of possibilities[67] and is thereby the foundation of novelty.

Yet in the primordial nature God is not complete. God's feelings "lack the fullness of actuality." As a result, another dimension of God is also necessary. As "God consequent" (the temporal, "physical" pole) God prehends the temporal world, functioning as the location of all perishing actual entities and thereby forming the world into a unity. In this way God retains the novelties achieved as the future becomes the present and vanishes into the past.[68] This activity completes God's nature in "a fullness of physical feeling."[69] Thus God becomes "the great companion—the fellow-sufferer who understands."[70]

These two dimensions of the divine reality produce an integral relation between God and the world. Both need the other, and both are bound up with the other. As Whitehead concluded, "each temporal occasion embodies God, and is embodied in God."[71]

Occasions that share a common element tying them together into a self-sustaining whole form a "society of occasions."[72] Societies come in various types, including "living societies,"[73] but the most unique is that of the human person. Each human is a society that can remember its past, anticipate its future and weave the two together. Yet a human remains a finite society, for its experience incorporates a limited past and a limited future. God, in contrast, is the unbounded society[74] who remembers all experiences and envisions all possibilities and who weaves past and future together in a never-ending process.

Behind the whole is another ultimate concept, creativity.[75] Creativity is not another existing "thing," but is rather the principle of unity behind the multiplicity of the actual entities. It is likewise the principle of novelty displayed by each of the actual entities and the source of the individuality of each as a participant in the "creative advance" characteristic of the process as a whole.[76]

The Process Theology

His metaphysic of process led Whitehead to a specific theological orientation. Three postulates provide a summary of this theology. First, God is not aloof from, nor unaffected by, the world; rather God and the world are interdependent. Whitehead's emphasis, therefore, clearly is on the divine immanence, for God is "an actual entity immanent in the actual world."[77] God is also transcendent, of course, but only insofar as the divine being is logically, not chronologically, prior to the world. Nor is God's transcendence unique. Transcendence characterizes every actual entity, for each "in virtue of its novelty, transcends its universe, God included."[78] God's transcendence refers to the divine inexhaustibility, enduring faithfulness of purpose and ability to utilize even evil for good ends.[79]

Second, God works in the world primarily through persuasion, rather than coercion. God provides the lure, of course, but each occasion has the prerogative to accept or reject it. Thus, when Whitehead offered images of God and the world, the two he chose were "tender care" and "infinite patience."[80] Process thinker Lewis Ford has drawn out the implications of this understanding: "Faith in this sense is reciprocal. Just as the world must trust God to provide the aim for its efforts, so God must trust the world for the achievement of that aim."[81]

Third, we ought not to view God in terms of omnipotence, but as the one who suffers with the world. Whitehead rejected the classical understanding of God as the divine despot, claiming that in this way, "the Church gave unto God the attributes which belonged exclusively to Caesar."[82] Nor is God omniscient in the classical sense of knowing the future. Like humans, God knows the future only as possibility, never as actuality.

John Cobb's Process Theology

Whitehead's metaphysics exercised a profound influence on theology in the twentieth century. Themes from his system are evident in the writings of many theologians. But beyond this general employment of process ideas, some thinkers have become disciples of the British philosopher, finding in the Whiteheadian model a foundation for the reformulation of Christian theology.[83] Perhaps the most prominent articulator of the school of Whiteheadian process theologians is John Cobb, Jr.

In 1990 Cobb retired after a prestigious career as Ingraham Professor of Theology at the School of Theology and Avery Professor at Claremont Graduate School, Claremont, California. The son of Methodist missionaries to the Orient and himself a member of the clergy, Cobb attended the University of Michigan and the University of Chicago. The latter has been one of the major centers for the advancement of Whiteheadian process theology.

Cobb has been a prolific writer. His works include titles dealing with pastoral theology, political theology, ecology, and the relationship between Christianity and Buddhism. But most important, he has provided a contemporary articulation of process theology, the theological orientation that lies behind his engagement with all other issues.

Foundation in Whitehead

The overriding motivation for Cobb's entire enterprise was the desire to launch a challenge to the modern mentality. His goal was nothing less than the construction of a vision of reality for the postmodern world.[84] This vision would in turn provide the intellectual underpinnings for the transforming power of the Christian faith.

For this monumental task, Cobb employed Whitehead's philosophy as the foundation on which to develop a new Christian natural theology. Although acknowledging that the theological enterprise is linked to a faith community,[85] Cobb appealed to the presence of theologizing outside that community as the rationale for the employment of "something like natural theology" in the work of the theologian.[86] He found in Whitehead's process philosophy the best possible philosophical basis for the development of a new Christian natural theology that could assist him in the theological task.[87] Cobb based this choice on what he perceived to be the intrinsic excellence of Whitehead's structure of thought and its congeniality to faith.[88]

On the foundation of Whitehead, Cobb constructed an understanding of God that he claimed to be more in keeping with biblical personalism and more compatible with contemporary science than the various conceptions found in classical Christian theology. This union of Whitehead and the Bible was facilitated by the convergence Cobb observed between the preaching of Jesus concerning the coming kingdom of God and the scientific picture of an evolving universe. Human experience includes the sense that we are being called forward, he argued, but this experience cannot be explained solely by a mechanistic model that views all events as arising from a cause found in the prior conditions. Rather, humans have a sense of being "lured" beyond what the past dictates, of being directed to something beyond.

This experience of being lured to the future, Cobb added, is not limited to humans. Rather, all nature is being called forward toward ever new possibilities. The source of this "teleological pull," he concluded, must be conceived of in terms of personality (that is, as will and love), in other words, as God. In short, both Jesus' message and the scientific cosmology point to the same conception of God, namely, God as "the One Who Calls."[89]

Cobb, therefore, employed Whitehead in his attempt to replace the classical view of God as the controlling power over the world. In its stead he introduced the idea of God as Creative-Responsive Love,[90] who relates to the world through persuasion, not coercion. According to process philosophy, the initial aim God provides can be chosen or rejected. Cobb interpreted this to imply that the outcome of the process is unknown and that God undergoes risk and adventure in the cosmic experiment, while remaining the source of unrest in the world.

Christology

The Claremont theologian utilized process philosophy to reformulate Christology as well,[91] albeit in a manner that stands in the tradition of classical *Logos* Christology. Lying behind his understanding is the "incarnational" relatedness of actual entities he found in Whitehead's cosmology. According to process thinking, present occasions incorporate into themselves both past experiences and the initial aim offered to them. In a sense, therefore, the past is incarnate in the present.[92]

The process understanding of the primordial nature of God providing the lure for each occasion formed the grist for Cobb's christological mill. The theologian linked the Christ with the divine primordial nature (the *Logos*) and thereby found the key to understanding both the universal presence of the *Logos* in creation and his special presence in believers. The Christ, Cobb argued, is the incarnation of the divine primordial nature as the initial aim in all occasions of experience. While present universally, the work of the Christ is most discernible in higher creatures, especially in humans. The Christ is present in them to the extent that they "decide for" the *Logos*, that is, insofar as they are receptive to that presence.[93]

As the Incarnation of the *Logos*, the Christ is the source of novelty in the world. Hence, Cobb preferred to speak of the Christ as "creative transformation."[94]

As a Christian, however, Cobb remained committed to speaking about the special relationship between the *Logos* and Jesus of Nazareth. Jesus is the Christ, he argued, because Jesus brought into history a distinctive structure of existence, in that the Incarnation of the Christ in him constituted his very selfhood. Jesus revealed the basic truth about reality, which, if we accept it, opens us to being creatively transformed as well.[95] In this way, Cobb offered what some have termed an "exemplification christology."[96] He places greater emphasis on Jesus' role of exemplifying what is universally divine than on the qualitative uniqueness of Jesus' work in salvation. Christians, in other words, put their faith in a Jesus who exemplifies a more universal principle, namely, that which characterizes the primordial nature of God.

Finally, Cobb drew on process thinking in order to articulate a vision for the future. Foundational to that vision is the process emphasis on the indeterminate nature of the future. Because the future is open, progress can occur, he argued. However, this same openness means that the opposite of progress remains a possibility as well; we may choose self-annihilation. There is, in short, no future kingdom of God that is destined to come as the climax of the process. Nevertheless, the kingdom remains for Cobb the ideal toward which we are to direct our hope and our actions. The radical openness of the future, consequently, demands that we act as co-creators with God for the sake of the betterment of the world.

Cobb's writings are somewhat vague concerning the content of the anticipated future. Basically he echoed Teilhard's call for new human communities characterized by mutual participation.[97]

Practical Questions

As his career unfolded, Cobb eventually became dissatisfied with grappling with issues of metaphysics and turned to problems of a more practical nature.[98] Yet even as he became engaged by these issues, he repeatedly looked to process thinking for a foundation from which to speak.

One problem he tackled was that posed by the religious pluralism characteristic of the contemporary world. Cobb advocated entering into dialog with non-Christians with the goal of mutual transformation and growth in truth.[99] Of special interest to the Claremont theologian has been the dialog with Buddhism, which is not surprising given his background on the Asian missionary field. Cobb attempted to show that a mutual transformation could arise by bringing together the Christian concept of God with the Buddhist understanding of emptiness. The emphasis on the ultimacy of this great Eastern tradition dovetailed nicely with the Whiteheadian vision of God. God is totally open to the ongoing process, even to the point of being constituted by that process.[100]

The dialog with other traditions was an important endeavor in Cobb's estimation. However, a trio of current problems took on even more pressing importance for him. The challenge posed by liberation and feminist thinkers led him to close ranks with them. Consequently, Cobb came to view, in the words of one of his books, process theology as political theology.[101]

Cobb was especially disturbed by the growing ecological crisis. In the face of this menace Whitehead's metaphysics, with its emphasis on the organic unity of all reality, offered help. The process understanding of the connectedness of all occasions through the concept of prehension provided a philosophical foundation for the emphasis on holism and the idea of the web of life set forth by proponents of the ecology movement.[102]

His concern for ecology led Cobb to turn his attention to economics as well. In *For the Common Good*[103] he and his coauthor sought to move beyond the individual-centered Enlightenment view to one that focuses on "person-in-community" and hence on relationality. Economics, therefore, must lift our eyes beyond the individual until it brings into focus a vision of "the Great Economy" that sustains the total web of life.

The Process *Telos*

Although Cobb's writings are not totally devoid of a discussion of eschatology, this doctrine did not receive the degree of attention he devoted to Christology. Thus, Cobb left to other process thinkers the challenge of providing a more complete reinterpretation of classical Christian doctrine of the last things.

In contrast to the Omega point of Teilhard's cosmology, Whiteheadians tend to anticipate no end to history, no time at which the process will come to rest.[104] Whitehead was concerned with the problem of the "perishing" of actual entities, which he resolved through the concept of "objective immortality" (the objectified entities are taken into the divine life).

What Whitehead postulated of actual entities, process theologians have extended to humans and to the cosmic struggle against evil. Because God is not omnipotent, there can be no guarantee that good will triumph. As a result, the overcoming of death and the triumph over evil cannot occur in history, but only in the divine experience "that accomplishes our redemption from evil."[105] Our task is to add to the enjoyment of God, for as we are "remembered by God," we are "taken up into God's life," which in process theology is "resurrection."[106]

General Characteristics of Process Theologies

Despite the differences among various process theologians and between Teilhardians and Whiteheadians, they all share several characteristics. All tend toward a similar order of theology. The givenness of some dimension of the world (that is, its dynamism and a metaphysical understanding of the world process), rather than revelation, functions as a type of natural theology and forms the starting point for the theological enterprise. The human person, in turn, is an illustration of, or the product of, the dynamic process at the center of all reality. The basis of the dynamism of the world is God, whose presence is in everything and in every act[107] and who is the source of the movement of all things toward convergence, whether in Omega (Teilhard) or within the divine experience (Whitehead). Process Christologies are preoccupied with Christ, not Jesus. The Incarnation of the *Logos* is important in that it results in the transformation of the world into something sacred (that is, "pleromatization").

Because the motivation lying behind the process cosmology is to give due regard to the experience of human freedom, process anthropologies reflect an optimistic outlook concerning human capabilities. The cooperation of the creature as a co-creator with God is a constant theme in the writings of process thinkers. To make room for human involvement and to insure that the future is indeed open, process theologians reconceptualize God as the divine persuader, whose power and control over the future of the universe is limited, not merely by divine choice but rather in God's very being. As a result, God is not absolutely perfect in all respects, but relatively perfect, in that God's perfection is a dynamic and continually growing one. Instead of absolute perfection, process theologians ascribe "surpassingness" to God. God is continually surpassing God's prior perfection and is always more perfect than creatures.[108]

The implications of such reformulations of Christian concepts are far-reaching. Although it would be incorrect to term process theology pantheistic (for it does not simply equate the world with God), its *panentheism* (to use the term preferred by process theologian Charles Hartshorne) moves in that direction. In process thinking the world, especially humankind, acts as a co-creator not only of itself but also of God. As a result, one cannot conceive of God apart from the world.[109] And the vision of the eschaton anticipated by process theologians tends toward a consummation beyond history, whether as the nonhistorical redemption in the experience of God (Whitehead) or as some spiritualized reality beyond the demise of the physical universe (Teilhard).

Problems with Process
Emphases such as these have led sympathizers and opponents alike to note problematic areas in process theology.[110] Some critics attack its very foundations, namely, its appeal to process philosophy, especially that of Whitehead. Contemporary postmodernists, for example, view this philosophy as but another example of the now disgraced approach of the modern era called "foundationalism," in which reason is looked to as capable of arriving at truth independently of outside assistance.[111] Similarly, contrary to its basic intent, process philosophy is deemed incompatible with modern scientific understandings (such as the theory of relativity)[112] and as actually presenting a stunted ontology when compared not only to classical supernaturalism, which it has sought to replace, but also to the complex world science is now discovering.[113]

Other critics attack the edifice by moving from the theology to its outworking. They reject process thought as offering an inadequate basis for ethics.[114] The source of its truncated ethic lies in two related themes of the process system: its overly optimistic view of humankind and its underemphasis on the reality of evil. Both Teilhard and Whitehead sought to move beyond the naive optimism of liberalism.[115] Yet the question remains as to the extent to which their proposals truly present evil in its full seriousness. For both thinkers evil is a by-product of the process, even a necessary part of the world's movement toward God,[116] rather than an alien intruder into the world, as classical theology sees it.

Process theologies have also been tested on the basis of their ability to illumine central Christian doctrines concerning God such as the doctrine of the Trinity. The dipolar conception of the deity presented by Whiteheadian thinkers like Cobb has been especially vulnerable. Process theists tend to equate God the Father with the whole of the Godhead and then look for a place for the other two Trinitarian persons.[117] Cobb, for example, identified the Son with the primordial nature and the Spirit with the consequent nature. This has led critics such as Wolfhart Pannenberg to suggest that this view is merely a form of the ancient heresy of dynamic monarchianism[118] (that Jesus is divine in that God's power rested on him).

Of the various reformulations of process theology, however, its understanding of God's relationship to the world has been most central in critical discussions. Some critics question the loss of God's unchangeableness. If God is ever-changing, they ask, how can process theologians assert that God is always loving or that God is morally different from a world characterized not only by goodness but also by evil?[119]

Other critics find that process thought links God too closely to the world.[120] Implicit in Teilhard, but more explicit in Whitehead, is an emphasis on the importance of human cooperation in the process of creation. God seeks to persuade us to make the best possible decisions enroute to the future. But in the end this means, in the words of Huston Smith, that "God is not completely in charge." Sympathetic critic Joseph Bracken noted the dire consequences of this move: "there is no way to legitimate the traditional understanding of God as Creator within the Whiteheadean scheme of things."[121]

This criticism has been echoed by others. In Jürgen Moltmann's estimation the exclusion or reduction of the doctrine of creation out of nothing, which he finds inherent in process theology,[122] leads to an unfortunate "divinization of the world."[123] Similarly, Ted Peters holds that in the process concept of creation an "immanent creativity" replaces the classical Christian transcendent understanding.[124]

While the process view fits well with the contemporary secular outlook, Smith's probing question, Why should secularity be made the final court of appeal?[125] haunts all modern theologies, including process thought. Actually, the process conception may be out of step with contemporary concerns for liberation. In the final analysis it offers less hope than the classical vision that God's program will triumph.[126]

Taken together, these criticisms point toward the central weakness of the process conception of God. In its laudable interest to set forth God's immanence in the world, process theology runs the risk of losing sight of the divine transcendence.[127] This danger is evident in several ways. First, it places God within the process as one example of the principles of its cosmology. Classical theism, in contrast, contends that God lies beyond metaphysical principles as derived from normal experience and science. Through this change, process thought gives too little place to the radical otherness of God.[128]

Second, process theology focuses on God's suffering with the world (and this in an insufficient manner)[129] and relegates the overcoming of evil solely to the divine experience. As a result, it provides an all too minute understanding of the holiness of God as the one who rejects sin and evil to the point of actively working to gain the victory over them on behalf of the world. As Ted Peters so aptly declared, "The 'God the Father Almighty' confessed by the creeds is either replaced or reinterpreted by a deity who is strong on persuasion but weak on potency."[130]

Conclusion

By salvaging the positive features of the liberal tradition of the nineteenth century—especially the affirmation that the natural processes are the location of God's redemptive work[131]—process theology attempted to reestablish the vitality of theology in the context of the twentieth-century scientifically orientated world. To this end, it utilized the dynamic nature of reality set forth by the new scientific theories of physics and biology as the central plank in a new natural theology foundation for the edifice of Christian theology. In this way it sought to provide an alternative to the radical rejection of philosophy found in the dominant strand of theological thinking in the first half of the century—neo-orthodoxy.

While continuing the liberal tradition in a new setting, process theology has been unable to avoid the major difficulty inherent in its nineteenth-century predecessor. In the end, transcendence is swallowed up by immanence, and the process God is but the mirror of the human striving for unity. Process theology, in short, has not been able to overcome the central problem of theology since the Renaissance.

5 IMMANENCE WITHIN THE SECULAR:
The Radical Movement

*T*HE DECADE OF THE 1960S WAS A PERIOD OF FERMENT AND RAPID CHANGE IN THE THEO-logical history of the century.[1] For several decades neo-orthodoxy in its various forms had determined the theological climate, giving to theology a distinctively transcendent emphasis. In the 1960s, however, the predominance of neo-orthodoxy was challenged from many quarters, as younger theologians groped for new expressions of, and new approaches to, the theological task in which the immanence of God could once again reemerge.

Neo-orthodox theologians had set out to eradicate what they saw as the naive optimism of nineteenth-century liberalism. Their "existential pessimism" included a cautionary stance toward what could be accomplished through human efforts, including technology and politics. The younger generation of theologians, however, reacted against the reigning pessimistic mood. They were less melancholy—more optimistic about the human experiment, more open to celebrating the emerging secular culture and to engaging in political action.

At the beginning of the decade, the sharp reaction to and quest for an overturning of the older approaches gave the theological discussion an appearance of anarchy, due to the presence on the theological scene of what Martin Marty and Dean Peerman poignantly referred to as "iconoclasts, exorcists, prophets, and muckrakers."[2] The anarchy and confusion became most apparent in the death-of-God phenomenon. But by mid-decade a renewed hunger for some type of order reemerged,[3] as evidenced in the quest for the role of the church in the secular city and later in the emergence of the theology of hope.

Despite the wide variety of attempts and probings to devise a truly new theology, theologians in the decade generally evidenced certain common characteristics. The most obvious similarity among them was their more "world-centered" rather than church-centered approach and concern.[4] In the 1960s, thinkers struggled with the meaning of "the secular" and its significance for theology. As a result, the doctrine of God became central to their musings, as evidenced by, but by no means limited to, the radical death-of-God movement. And they reopened the question of the meaning of the category of "religion," so emphatically answered by Karl Barth.

Contributing to the ferment of the 1960s was the retirement of the theological giants of previous decades—Barth, Niebuhr, Tillich. Their passing from the scene occurred at a time when no voices of their renown and stature emerged to replace them (although the 1960s did witness the launching of the careers of several younger theologians). This situation was partly due to World War 2, which interrupted the academic process and diverted the energies of the churches, especially in Germany but also in the Western nations.

In the ferment of the 1960s no single theological orientation surfaced. Rather, the decade saw the rise and disappearance of several theological "fads," which despite their short lifespan have exercised lasting influence, even into the present. Among the fads that most epitomize the 1960s as an iconoclastic, antitraditional, challenging and probing decade were several probings that together formed what has been termed "radical theology." The radical theologians of the decade responded to the emphasis on transcendence they inherited from their neo-orthodox teachers by launching a new quest for the immanence of God, finding the presence of the divine reality within the temporal reality of modern life.

The background to the radical theology of the 1960s actually lay in the neo-orthodoxy it sought to overcome. But more than any others, the theologians of the new immanence found their inspiration in the legacy of Dietrich Bonhoeffer, the acquaintance of Karl Barth who had served as a leader in the Confessing Church in Germany during the Third Reich and subsequently was martyred for his opposition to the Hitler regime. It is, therefore, with Bonhoeffer that the story of the immanental theology of the early 1960s must begin.

DIETRICH BONHOEFFER:
TRANSCENDENCE IN THE MIDST OF LIFE

Without a doubt the life of no theologian in the twentieth century has captured the fascination of more people than has that of the young German victim of the Nazi regime, Dietrich Bonhoeffer. And no decade of the century provided a more hospitable context for a postmortem revival of interest in the legacy of Bonhoeffer than the turbulent 1960s.

The interest in the martyr of Nazism was especially acute in the United States. In this nation "the 60s" marked the high point for the varied expressions of the exuberance of youth. This exuberance touched every dimension of society. Even politics felt the power of youth, a power that came to be symbolized by the rise of the Kennedys to national political prominence. But youthful America also witnessed the dark side of life in the 1960s. At the height of their protest against the establishment, the lives of several of its heroes were snuffed out by assassins' bullets. It is understandable, therefore, that the story of a young protester killed by the most demonic regime of recent history would find a receptive place in the hearts of young thinkers in that decade.

Bonhoeffer's Life and Martyrdom

Dietrich Bonhoeffer was born in Breslau on February 4, 1906, the son of a university professor, Karl Ludwig Bonhoeffer, who was an authority on psychiatry and neurology.[5] As was true of several other leading twentieth-century theologians, a tradition of theology was to be found in Bonhoeffer's family. His maternal great-grandfather, Karl-August van Hase, was one of the most distinguished nineteenth-century German church historians, and his grandfather, Karl-Alfred, had been a chaplain to the Emperor. His father's family, which had migrated from Holland to Würtemberg in the fifteenth century, also could boast several theologians.[6]

The Bonhoeffers moved to Berlin in 1912. At the age of twelve, Dietrich became interested in reading theology. His education included Tübingen at the age of seventeen and Berlin at eighteen (1924), where he studied under the leading liberal thinkers of the day, including Adolf von Harnack, Karl Holl and Reinhold Seeberg. His dissertation, *Sanctorum Communio: A Dogmatic Investigation of the Sociology of the Church,* received the praise of one of the rising theologians of Europe for whom Bonhoeffer had gained great admiration—Karl Barth.

Following his studies (1927), Bonhoeffer served a German-speaking congregation in Barcelona, Spain, for a short time, before returning to Berlin (1929). There at the age of twenty-four and after completing his inaugural dissertation, *Act and Being: Transcendental Philosophy and Ontology in Systematic Theology,* he became lecturer in systematic theology at the University of Berlin (1930). To prepare himself further for the work of teaching, Bonhoeffer spent a year at Union Theological Seminary in New York, where he became impressed with the concern for the poor he found among many American students, but bemoaned their lack of interest in theology.[7] On his return to Germany in 1931, he developed two relationships that subsequently became vital for his life and work, the first with Karl Barth and the second with the ecumenical movement.

Hitler's rise to power in 1932 changed the course of Bonhoeffer's life. In fact as Eberhard Bethge remarked, it was "robbed of its initiative by Nazi history."[8] This event triggered a crisis within German Lutheranism. The young theologian aligned himself with the Confessing Church, which broke ranks with the state church over the issue of Nazi ideology. Bonhoeffer's academic career was short-lived, becoming a victim of the religious and political turmoil in his homeland. In 1933, having come to believe that his career had lost its proper meaning,[9] Bonhoeffer abandoned academia, taking a leave of absence from the university and moving to London, where he served two congregations as pastor. Here he attempted to explain to British Christians and the World Alliance of Churches the nature of the struggle that was developing in the German church.

In 1935 Bonhoeffer returned to Germany to direct an illegal seminary for training ministers for the Confessing Church. This renowned school, which eventually was located in Finkenwalde, followed the innovative format of engaging in theological education within the context of a close-knit community. In addition to studying the normal academic disciplines, the participants in the school sought to learn to live the Christian life in genuine brotherhood and in total dedication to the Lord.

While at Finkenwalde, Bonhoeffer met the young woman, Maria von Wede, to whom he later became engaged. But all too soon the existence of the school became known to the Gestapo. In 1940 the secret police closed it, yet not before Bonhoeffer was able to record the principles employed in the innovative experiment in two books, *The Cost of Discipleship* (1937) and *Life Together* (1939).

As war appeared inevitable Bonhoeffer left Germany in 1939 at the urging of his American friends, to avoid the problems that his pacifism would cause him. But he soon sensed a compulsion to return to the oppressed Christians in his homeland. "I shall have no right to participate in the reconstruction of Christian life in Germany after the war," he wrote Reinhold Niebuhr, "if I do not share the trials of this time with my people."[10] Upon returning to Germany, Bonhoeffer was forbidden to speak anywhere in the Reich. He served as a courier in the German Military Intelligence Service and from this position was able to work with the resistance movement (with which he had made contact already in early 1938), even traveling to Geneva and Britain on its behalf. In 1942 he was the one appointed to communicate to the British government the terms of surrender outlined by the underground. When this offer was rejected, many in the movement came to the conclusion that there was no alternative but the assassination of the Führer. The dilemma with which he struggled at this time led Bonhoeffer to set aside his earlier pacifism and to become involved in a daring plot to murder Hitler.

On April 5, 1943, the Gestapo arrested Bonhoeffer, together with his sister Christel and her husband Hans von Dohnanyi, in his parents' house on suspicion of involvement with the underground. Although the planned attempt on Hitler's life had not yet occurred, evidence of Bonhoeffer's complicity had already been unearthed. During the next eighteen months he was incarcerated in Tegel Military Prison in Berlin, where he wrote the documents subsequently published in his famous *Letters and Papers from Prison*.

Like his theological career, Bonhoeffer's prospective marriage fell victim to the events in Germany. His engagement to Maria von Wede came just prior to his arrest. Yet his fiancée was a faithful visitor and a source of joy and encouragement to him during the dark days of imprisonment.

In September 1944, the Gestapo discovered certain documents that confirmed the involvement of Bonhoeffer and others in the assassination plot. As a result, he was transferred to the Gestapo prison on Prinz Albrecht Street for torture. Then, in early February 1945, Bonhoeffer was secretly moved to Buchenwald. On April 3, with the sound of Allied guns in the distance, he and several others were trucked to the Bavarian Forest, which hid an extermination camp in Flossenburg. For a time he was imprisoned in Schoenberg. When his name was called out for transport to Flossenburg, Bonhoeffer declared to his friend, "This is the end—for me the beginning of life." During the night of April 8-9, a court martial met and sentenced him to death. Early in the morning Dietrich Bonhoeffer was executed, just days before the Allies liberated the camp. His composure in the face of death led the camp doctor to remark, "In the almost fifty years that I worked as a doctor, I have hardly ever seen a man die so entirely submissive to the will of God."[11]

From an early age, Bonhoeffer had sensed an interest in theology. In the end, however, he discovered that he had been called to a different vocation, that of sacrificing his life for the faith. As Leibholz rightly concluded, "Bonhoeffer's life and death belong to the annals of Christian martyrdom."[12]

Christ the Center

Bonhoeffer was a theologian, but not a systematic theologian in the traditional sense. Not only his life but with it his work was interrupted and finally cut short by the tragic events in Germany in the 1930s and 1940s. As was his life, so also his writings are fragmentary. Two of his most important treatises, *Christ the Center* and *Ethics*, are reconstructions, the first from lecture notes recorded by his students and the second from incomplete manuscripts concealed from the Gestapo. As a result, as Heinrich Ott rightly concluded, "neither as a whole nor in its parts is Bonhoeffer's work something completed."[13]

Further, Bonhoeffer did not live long enough to systematize his own thinking. Rather, he continued to grow, develop and change in accordance with his experiences. The most striking example of a profound change is his setting aside his earlier pacifism in order to join in the plot to assassinate the chancellor of his country.

His student and friend, Eberhard Bethge, divided Bonhoeffer's intellectual pilgrimage into three periods: academic teaching at the University of Berlin, the church struggle and teaching in the Confessing Church, and opposing the Hitler regime.[14] In the first period, Bonhoeffer's central concern was that the church understand itself as community. His concern in the middle period was for costly discipleship. And at the end of his life, he focused on "worldly holiness."[15] Yet one theme provides a unifying thread throughout Bonhoeffer's varied theological writings. Central to the whole is Christology. As Ott concluded, "Christology was at all stages of his pilgrimage the inward law of his thinking, the definitive thought."[16] During the course of his entire life Bonhoeffer wrestled with the question, "Who is Jesus Christ?"[17]

The formulation of this central christological question is crucial for an understanding of the thinking of the German theologian. Bonhoeffer never debated the *presence* of Jesus Christ. He sensed this presence in the manifold and varied situations in which he lived.[18] But at different stages in his pilgrimage he wrestled with differing focal points of Christ's presence and reality. At the beginning of his academic career, for example, he developed the ecclesiological focus, finding the presence of Christ in the church, understood in terms of community.[19] This thesis formed the basis for Bonhoeffer's repeated emphasis on the Christian life as involvement in the messianic sufferings of Christ.[20] The theme of the presence of Christ in the church was joined at the end of his life by another, which became his legacy for subsequent theology. As his *Letters and Papers from Prison* indicates, while a captive of the Hitler regime he engaged in an intense struggle with the question of the presence of Christ in the world.[21]

Break with Liberalism

Bonhoeffer was influenced by several theologians. But he found in Karl Barth his closest kindred spirit. Kenneth Hamilton offered an apt, though perhaps overstated, indication of the depth of this theological relationship: "If there is one key that opens the door to his theology more than any other, it is the recognition that at all stages of his career he consciously formed his own concepts with Barth in mind more than any other living theologian."[22]

Like Barth, Bonhoeffer sought a decisive break with the liberalism of his theology teachers. Specifically, he rejected the concept of a "religious a priori." This idea had its basis in Schleiermacher's theology, but was mediated to Bonhoeffer by his teacher, Reinhold Seeberg. Liberalism had employed the assumption of an innate human ability to sense the infinite in order to develop a point of contact between God and humanity and thereby to establish natural theology.[23] Similar to Barth, Bonhoeffer believed that God's revelation comes only in and through Jesus Christ and that this divine self-disclosure (and thus Christology) is the heart of theology and ethics. Further, he assumed the absolute contrast between the divine self-disclosure and religion as the human attempt to reach God, so indicative of Barth's theology. In fact, this maxim forms part of the background for several of his profound but undeveloped phrases and comments, including his radical call for a "religionless Christianity."

Despite his deep appreciation for Barth, already at the beginning of his career Bonhoeffer rejected the radicality of Barth's view. To him it seemed to make the Word of God so epistemologically transcendent that it could not be found concretely in time.[24] Bonhoeffer drew a closer link than did Barth between Christ and the church, maintaining that the revelation in Christ is an ecclesiological reality. Yet his affinity to Barth is evident in his rejection of the concept of the church found in liberalism, which views it in terms of a religious community. Bonhoeffer argued that the nature of the church cannot arise from a general concept of religion, but must be determined solely from God and the divine revelation.[25] Later in life, his differences with Barth were to surface again and deepen, as Bonhoeffer came to struggle even more consciously with the "world come of age" and the presence of Christ in that world.

Struggle with Modernity

More so than Bonhoeffer's christological ecclesiology and his rejection of the liberal heritage, however, his struggle with modernity has constituted his continued legacy for theology. This struggle was present throughout his life. But it was especially evidenced in a series of letters to Eberhard Bethge written during Bonhoeffer's incarceration in the Tegel Prison. Sprinkled within his writings are several striking phrases that he did not live to systematize fully, but were rediscovered and expanded by the secular theologians of the 1960s.

One widely used phrase arises from a book written during the middle period of Bonhoeffer's life. In *The Cost of Discipleship* he vividly contrasted "cheap grace" and "costly grace." Cheap grace refers to what we might call "churchianity," the type of religion that believes that salvation comes easily, by means of the belief of doctrines. In Bonhoeffer's words, "Cheap grace is the preaching of forgiveness without requiring repentance, baptism without Church discipline, Communion without confession, absolution without contrition."[26]

Costly grace, in contrast, declares that salvation is costly. It cost God his Son. And it demands obedience, that is, a life of discipleship. Luther discovered costly grace when he returned from the cloister to the world, Bonhoeffer declared, for he learned that "the only way to follow Jesus was by living in the world."[27] This thesis, following Jesus into the world, became a central theme of Bonhoeffer's prison musings.

Throughout most of his life, but especially in prison, Bonhoeffer struggled with the idea of discipleship—not with the kind that results in detachment from the world, but, building on the theme set forth in *The Cost of Discipleship*, the discipleship that leads the Christian to follow Christ back into the world.

This radical discipleship, he believed, was demanded by the contemporary experience of a world "come of age." His musings on this situation, found in his prison letters, did not mark a decisive break from his earlier thought, but arose out of his central christological emphasis. Bonhoeffer himself indicated this continuity in a statement written on April 30, 1944. Before introducing his reflections on the contemporary situation as a time of "no religion at all," he articulated his driving concern: "The thing that keeps coming back to me is, what is Christianity, and indeed what is Christ for us to-day?"[28]

By the phrase, "the world come of age," Bonhoeffer meant that the church now finds itself in a world in which humans operate autonomously, without sensing a need to refer to either divine grace or divine truth. In the world come of age, people no longer require God as a working hypothesis, whether in science, in human affairs in general or increasingly even in religion.[29]

Actually, the older view of God was a false view, Bonhoeffer maintained. It referred to the God-of-the-Gaps, the God who was called in to be responsible for what could not be explained by some other means. God was used as a stop-gap for the incompleteness of human knowledge. This erroneous use of God was not limited to science, however, but was extended as well to the wider human problems of guilt, suffering and death. In the face of scientific advances, theology proclaimed God as the answer to life's problems.[30] As this process reached its culmination and God was pushed out of increasingly larger dimensions of life, Bonhoeffer concluded, Christian theology turned to the inner life of the individual, attempting to retain at least this realm as the domain of the God who had been driven out of the world.

Bonhoeffer's concern was for the implications of the contemporary situation—the world come of age—for the church and Christian proclamation. "What is the significance of a Church . . . in a religionless world? How do we speak of God without religion, without the temporally-influenced presuppositions of metaphysics, inwardness, and so on?" he asked.[31]

This concern was heightened by the failure of theologians to offer what he thought to be a helpful response to the adulthood of the world. In fact, in Bonhoeffer's estimation the various attempts to accommodate the Christian message to the growing maturity of the world evidenced a common difficulty. They all build from the premise that individuals can be addressed as sinners only after their "weaknesses and meannesses have been spied out."[32] Such approaches demand that the apologist be able to point out to individuals that they are riddled with problems, needs and conflicts. For Bonhoeffer, however, this strategy is self-defeating, for it entails a denial of the maturity of the world.

Bonhoeffer argued that Christianity must abandon all such approaches and adjust its witness. It can no longer attack "the adulthood of the world," for this attack is pointless, ignoble, and unchristian.[33] Rather than polemics and apologetics, Bonhoeffer called for Christians to understand the world come of age better than it understands itself, namely, on the basis of the gospel and in the light of Christ,[34] and this because the autonomous world cannot truly understand itself unless it recognizes its relation to Christian faith. "We should not speak ill of man in his worldliness," he concluded, "but confront him with God at his strongest point."[35]

Religionless Christianity

To this end, Bonhoeffer advocated a "religionless Christianity." This phrase was intended to set forth his understanding of the true Christian faith in the midst of the false religion he had already rejected earlier in his career. The concept of religion he criticized was religion as built on an apologetic that begins with the assumption that all human beings are naturally religious. Like Barth he attacked as well the kind of religion that was merely speculative metaphysics, for this was but the human search for God. He likewise dismissed the privatistic understanding of religion, which limited religion to the "spiritual" realm or was solely otherworldly in orientation. This approach made religion "magical," with God acting from the outside at the whim of humans. Finally, the kind of religion Bonhoeffer rejected was the attitude that introduces God as the completion of a person's life, added at the boundaries of human need.[36]

According to Bonhoeffer, the situation of the world come of age demands "a non-religious interpretation of biblical terminology."[37] He suggested that the erroneous theological conceptions widespread in the church ought to be replaced with an understanding that sees God as "the Beyond in the midst of our life."[38] We are to find God in what we know, he argued, not in what we do not know.[39] Further, in the contemporary world come of age we must view God as weak and powerless in the world, the one who "allows himself to be edged out of the world and on to the cross." Only in this way can God be with us and help us.[40] Thus the beginning point for a nonreligious interpretation of biblical terminology, in Bonhoeffer's understanding, lies with a rejection of human religiosity, which in distress looks to the power of God in the world. We must abandon this imagery in favor of the God of the Bible "who conquers power and space in the world by his weakness."[41]

Holy Worldliness

For Bonhoeffer this understanding of God is coupled with a radical Christian discipleship characterized by "holy worldliness." To understand the "worldliness" he advocated, we must get clear in our minds what he was rejecting. Throughout his life, the German theologian struggled with the question concerning where Christ is to be found, concluding that he is in the world, not merely in some special, religious sphere. The call for a Christian "worldliness" is the application of this christological axiom to the life of discipleship. Bonhoeffer saw the chief temptation faced by Christians as the lure to withdraw out of the world into pious enclaves, to erect private spheres of religiosity or to view religion as one activity or dimension of existence in addition to the others.

The gospel is not a call to be religious in this sense, Bonhoeffer asserted. Thus he rejected any suggestion that Christians should strive for a detached, disengaged piety that was viewed as elevating them above humankind. To be a Christian, he argued, does not entail cultivating asceticism.

Rather, to be a Christian means to participate in the life of the world, to serve God in the world, and not merely in some sterile religious sanctuary or in an isolated, sheltered Christian enclave. The church is "to stand in the center of the village," he argued, and the Christian life is to be lived in the world.[42] He found this call to be based on the nature of the Christian hope itself, which is not directed toward an escape from the present situation into a better world beyond the grave, but rather sends believers back to life on earth in a wholly new way. We must "drink the earthly cup to the lees," he declared, for only in so doing is the crucified and risen Lord with us.[43]

Participation in life on earth means, on the one hand, affirming life and the goodness given in life for us to enjoy. "I am sure we ought to love God in our *lives* and in the blessings he sends us," Bonhoeffer wrote. "If he pleases to grant us some overwhelming bliss, we ought not to try and be more religious than God himself. For then we should spoil that bliss by our presumption and arrogance."[44]

On the other hand, this participation as a Christian means sharing in the sufferings of God in the life of the world. This conception, more than the former, constituted the culmination of Bonhoeffer's thinking.[45] The Christian living in the world come of age, he argued, must accept full responsibility for the world's history.[46] Above all, sharing God's sufferings means living as a true disciple—becoming vulnerable in service to the world, following in the steps of "the man for others." For "the Church is her true self only when she exists for humanity."[47]

Hence, the Christian is to aspire to be a human being, not a "saint." In Bonhoeffer's poignant words:

> It is only by living completely in this world that one learns to believe. One must abandon every attempt to make something of oneself, whether it be a saint, a converted sinner, a churchman (the priestly type, so-called!) a righteous man or an unrighteous one, a sick man or a healthy one. This is what I mean by worldliness— taking life in one's stride. . . . It is in such a life that we throw ourselves utterly into the arms of God and participate in his sufferings in the world."[48]

Nevertheless, the radical discipleship Bonhoeffer proposed did not mean a complete overturning of classical Christian piety. Being a worldly Christian does not give license for an immoral or indulgent lifestyle. Rather, it requires stretching oneself to the limit in the attempt to participate in the suffering of God in the world. It therefore necessitates living "close to the presence of God," that is, living "in Christ," to use the Pauline phrase that Bonhoeffer found so helpful. Only in this way can the believer become strong to face the challenges of life. Bringing together ethical and strenuous living, Bonhoeffer declared, "Christ does not only make men good: he makes them strong too."[49]

The Ultimate and the Penultimate

Bonhoeffer combined these two aspects of Christian discipleship by an insightful employment of the concept of "the secret discipline" and its partner concept, the integral relationship between the "ultimate" and the "penultimate." The latter idea is more readily understood.

For Bonhoeffer there is a close connection between the eternal reality and the present world. This relationship means that the Christian must avoid the twin errors of total rejection of, or complete sanctioning of, the present world (that is, the penultimate).[50] Christians are to live as those who belong wholly to this penultimate world. In so doing, however, they must always keep in view that Christ is the Lord of the world[51] and that the activity of God is manifested in everyday life. The realm of the ultimate is what gives meaning to the penultimate. Bonhoeffer, therefore, called Christians to engage in life in the world with a vision of the ultimate reality, namely, God and God's intention to offer justification to the believer. In this way, Christian life in the world becomes "participation in the encounter of Christ with the world," and this in that "in Christ the reality of God meets the reality of the world."[52]

The Secret Discipline

Bonhoeffer's undeveloped use of the "secret discipline" is more difficult.[53] In the ancient church the secret discipline was the restraint laid on the baptized person not to reveal to outsiders certain deeper realities of the Christian faith. In the prison letters Bonhoeffer called for an application of this reserve appropriate for the contemporary situation.[54]

The foundation of the use of this concept in the prison letters is found in Bonhoeffer's early writings. In his discussion of Matthew 6 in *The Cost of Discipleship*, he suggested that there is a hiddenness in the way of discipleship in the world. Christians are to avoid both taking notice of themselves and seeking self-display in the presence of others. Instead they are to give place to God to make visible the hidden realities.[55] The secret discipline, then, refers to the life of discipleship in the world as it is sustained by the believer's connection to the Lord, as believers place their faith in God and allow God to work righteousness in them. In Finkenwalde, Bonhoeffer looked for a secret discipline in the corporate devotional life of the worshiping community, which provided the sustenance for engagement in the world.

In his later writings Bonhoeffer seemed to find that the secret discipline had implications beyond the personal and corporate life of piety. In fact, the principle articulated earlier appeared to have value for the matter of the crucial relationship between the ultimate and the penultimate. Christians live in the penultimate world and engage in service to others; but they derive the power to love others from the divine grace at work in them. They do not proclaim that they possess goodness by virtue of their adherence to certain doctrines or their practice of prescribed forms of piety. To do so would be to shift their basis of trust from God to religion. The secret discipline seeks to maintain Christians in the proper attitude in the midst of their life in service of the world.

The most far-reaching and debated application of the secret discipline, however, is its significance for church proclamation and theology in the context of the world come of age. In the contemporary situation in which talk about God has lost its meaning, Bonhoeffer concluded, traditional churchly language must remain silent, so that Christian speaking can be reborn out of praying for and working on behalf of others.[56] In this way, he proposed a reestablishment of a secret discipline that gave the Christian a proper restraint in proclaiming a traditional and unconformable theology in a world that could no longer understand the older categories. Bonhoeffer valued the traditional exposition, but sought to insure that "the *mysteries* of the Christian faith are preserved from profanation."[57]

Transcendence

Like the neo-orthodox theologians, Bonhoeffer sought to reestablish the transcendence of God in the face of the immanental theology of liberalism. Yet his understanding of transcendence was not that of the in-breaking Word, characteristic of the early Barth, nor that of the omnipotent God who comes to the world in power, set forth in traditional orthodoxy. For him, the transcendent God is "the Beyond in the midst of the world," the reality of the ultimate that gives meaning to the penultimate, the presence tapped by means of the secret discipline that gives sustenance to the believer and the church in their task of being in the world. In a book he had in mind but was unable to write, Bonhoeffer planned to set forth his understanding:

> Transcendence consists not in tasks beyond our scope and power, but in the nearest Thou to hand. God in human form, not, as in other religions, in animal form . . . nor yet in abstract form—the absolute, metaphysical, infinite, etc.—nor yet in the Greek divine-human of autonomous man, but man existing for others, and hence the Crucified.[58]

Unfortunately Bonhoeffer never lived to expand, systematize and fill out these themes. Yet his embodiment of them in his life and in his death set forth an illustration of his theological orientation that is perhaps more profound and more vivid than any subsequent treatise might have been. By sacrificing his life in the task of living the kind of radical discipleship that participates truly in the suffering of God in the world, Bonhoeffer bequeathed to others the task of constructing the systematic theological edifice for which he laid the foundation.

Several such constructive attempts came in the 1960s in the work of secular and radical theologians who gained their inspiration from the German martyr.

SECULAR THEOLOGY:
THE SUBMERGENCE OF GOD WITHIN THE MODERN WORLD

The early 1960s witnessed a renaissance of interest in the writings of the martyred German theologian, Dietrich Bonhoeffer. In that decade, his works, but especially *Letters and Papers from Prison,* came to have far-reaching impact on the Anglo-American theological world. Many thinkers were intrigued by the insightful but undeveloped ideas Bonhoeffer had penned in his musings in Tegel Prison. And the catch-phrases he had coined caught the imagination of certain post-Barthian theologians in Britain and the United States. These thinkers set themselves to the task of carrying to completion the program suggested by Bonhoeffer. The result of this renewed interest in what was perceived to have been Bonhoeffer's call to the church was a conglomeration of new and radical movements in theology that experienced a short yet lastingly important life in the radical 1960s.

In many ways this phase of twentieth-century theological history arose as both a response to and a deepening of certain themes in the theology of Karl Barth, to which each of the leading voices of the movement was indebted.[1] Barth had set the stage for the emergence of the radical theologies through the sharp distinction he had drawn between Christian faith, viewed as God's search for humankind, and religion, which he rejected as the human search for God. The theological developments of the 1960s reacted against but also continued this aspect of Barth's theology.[2]

On the one hand, the insurmountable gulf between Christian faith and human religion Barth created effectively removed God from the realm of everyday life. In so doing Barth had exalted transcendence to the loss of immanence, except for the immanence of God in the revelatory Word. This removal of God from the world was apt to trigger a renewed search for the presence of God in the world. John Macquarrie, therefore, hit on a central point in finding in the radical theologians "a rebellion against, and then an overcompensation for, the Barthian exaggeration of God's transcendence and the corresponding deprecation of man's 'natural' achievements."[3]

On the other hand, the radical theologies were built on Barth's distinction between true faith and human religion. The dichotomy he established resulted in a rejection of the division between religious and secular life. Rather than being called to perform a few religious actions, Barth declared, Christians are to serve God "in the whole range of their humanity,"[4] and thus in the world or the secular sphere.[5]

The positive influence of Barth as providing a foundation for the radical theologies was important. To his name could be added that of the German theologian, Friedrich Gogarten.[6] But more significant than Barth or any other predecessor, these theologians saw their efforts as an explicit and conscious attempt to employ the insights of Dietrich Bonhoeffer. This proved to be a difficult task, however, given the incomplete nature of Bonhoeffer's musings. Critics of the theologians of the 1960s have repeatedly chastised them for their *misuse* of the German martyr's statements. Macquarrie's evaluation is typical: "But the trouble is that Bonhoeffer's views are not treated as the tentative and obscure gropings that they were meant to be. They are invoked, together with the glamour of their author's martyrdom, for confident assertions that may have been very far from Bonhoeffer's mind."[7]

Regardless of the actual degree of their fidelity to their predecessors and despite important differences among them, the radical thinkers were united by certain common features. All of them found inspiration in Bonhoeffer's call for a "religionless" Christianity. All were decidedly christocentric, advancing the legacy of Barth and Bonhoeffer beyond what even their theological mentors envisioned. All desired to remove from Christianity the traditional emphasis on the "otherworldly." And finally they all sought to come to grips with what is absolutely basic in the language of "belief."

The Death-of-God Movement

Chronologically seen, the first significant stream of radical thought in the 1960s was what has come to be termed the death-of-God movement. This phenomenon arose in the opening years of the decade, then disappeared, only to be resurrected after it was posthumously discovered by the secular press. Despite its publicity, the death-of-God theme never gained a wide following. Rather, it remained virtually a two-man show[8] consisting of William Hamilton and Thomas J. J. Altizer. These two thinkers proposed a thoroughgoing radical accommodation to the world come of age. As their response to Bonhoeffer's call for a secular interpretation of the gospel they examined the phenomenon of the "death of God" in the modern secular world.

Perhaps no contemporary theological expression has created as much controversy as the "death of God." The popular media picked up on it and turned it into a cultural phenomenon almost overnight. *Time* magazine featured it in a cover story entitled "Is God Dead?" in October 1965. Numerous other magazines and newspapers, as well as radio and television, jumped on the bandwagon to popularize the most radical theology of "theothanatology." Conservative Christians wrote choruses with the refrain "God's not dead" and printed bumper stickers with the slogan "My God's Not Dead—Sorry About Yours!"

The catalysts of this uproar, William Hamilton and Thomas Altizer, were taken aback by it.[9] They were concerned that more often than not the popular press had distorted their message, and they sensed a compulsion to publish a number of books and articles interpreting it for educated Christian laypersons because, as Hamilton wrote, "It is important not to be satisfied with the news magazines, the weekly religious journals and *The New Yorker*."[10] However, the more they wrote and spoke on the subject, the more clear it became that the slogan "Death of God" was highly ambiguous—even to them. Was it a historical event? A linguistic event? A cultural event? Or was it an affirmation of the divinity of humankind—the deepest expression of the immanence of God? All are possible interpretations of the intent of Hamilton and Altizer.

In order to dispel any misconceptions about its radicality, Hamilton made absolutely clear in a 1966 essay that their intent was to deny belief in the traditional God of Christian theism:

> This is more than the old protest against natural theology or metaphysics; more than the usual assurance that before the holy God all our language gets broken and diffracted into paradox. It is really that we do not know, do not adore, do not possess, do not believe in God. It is not just that a capacity has dried up within us; we do not take all this as merely a statement about our frail psyches, we take it as a statement about the nature of the world and we try to convince others. God is dead. We are not talking about the absence of the experience of God, but about the experience of the absence of God.[11]

And yet, Hamilton averred, the death-of-God theology was not just "a complicated sort of atheism dressed in a new spring bonnet" but a truly *Christian* form of theology. With this Altizer chimed in by asserting that only a Christian can truly affirm that God is dead.[12] For both of them this is because Jesus Christ remains the best place to stand alongside suffering humanity *against* all dehumanizing and alienating powers, including the transcendent, sovereign God of Christian theism.

William Hamilton

William Hamilton was a professor of church history at the Baptist-related Colgate Rochester Divinity School in the early 1960s.[13] His theological education included studies under Reinhold Niebuhr and Paul Tillich at Union Theological Seminary. He received his doctorate in Scotland under the renowned theologian Donald M. Baillie. One of his first books was *The New Essence of Christianity* (1961), in which he began to introduce the concept of the death of God, building on the ideas of Nietzsche, Camus and Tillich. Essentially the book was a protest against the concept of divine providence ruling history and a call for Christians to stand in the midst of a culture without God and not to wait for some reappearance of the divine. For Hamilton, the true essence of Christianity is to live active, worldly lives without God in the place defined by Jesus— alongside the neighbor, participating in her struggles and sufferings.[14]

During the sixties Hamilton continued to speak and write on the death of God. He appeared to become even more radical and self-consciously atheistic. In 1966 he coauthored *Radical Theology and the Death of God* with Altizer, who called him "the most articulate leader of the death-of-God movement in America."[15] This volume marked the high point of the movement, after which it began to lose focus and power.

Hamilton lost his teaching position at Colgate Rochester and moved into the secular academic world, focusing especially on themes related to the demise of God in English literature. In 1974 he published a book building on this research entitled *On Taking God Out of the Dictionary*.[16] He has also published works on Herman Melville and the symbolism of God's death in *Moby Dick*.

In his books and in interviews Hamilton has suggested that he sees belief in God as dangerous. The task of the death-of-God theologians in the sixties was that of the detective—to discover and interpret the deadly body of God in modern culture. The task of the theologian today is that of the killer—to capture and abolish God. In 1989 Hamilton affirmed that "people with Gods are dangerous. And one of the things you can do to help your brothers and sisters is to take Gods away from people so their weapons won't be quite so sharp as they are with monotheism."[17] Nevertheless, Hamilton still considered himself a Christian, based on his firm commitment to Jesus Christ as the one who shows the way to be human.[18]

Thomas Altizer

In spite of his own words elevating Hamilton, Thomas Altizer is generally considered the leading exponent of the death-of-God theology or "Christian atheism" in the 1960s. During the height of the controversy he was associate professor of Bible and religion at the Methodist-related Emory University in Atlanta. Since that time he has turned to English studies and especially the school of deconstructionism.

Altizer rose to prominence with the publication in 1966 of his manifesto of the death-of-God theology entitled *The Gospel of Christian Atheism*.[19] In the same year he coauthored *Radical Theology and the Death of God* with William Hamilton. A number of books followed his involvement in the movement and paved the way for his later participation in a new form of radical theology that draws on deconstructionism.

Altizer's writing style does not lend itself to easy interpretation. Hamilton might have been praising him when he wrote that "Altizer is all *élan*, wildness, excessive generalization, brimming with colorful, flamboyant, and emotive language."[20] But that style is a major obstacle to understanding him. Another obstacle is his eclecticism. Altizer draws on a vast array of thinkers to concoct his own unique recipe of thought. Among the most prominent influences are the philosophers Hegel and Nietzsche, but he also calls on the mystical poet William Blake. These three, Altizer said, formed the primary sources for his theology. However, the indelible marks of Bonhoeffer and especially Tillich are clearly visible in his thought as well. Hamilton and Altizer dedicated their book *Radical Theology and the Death of God* to Tillich, and in his preface to *The Gospel of Christian Atheism*[21] Altizer cited him as "the modern father of radical theology."

The overall theme of Altizer's Christian atheism is the absolute immanence of God in humanity "dissolving even the memory or the shadow of transcendence."[22] The passage through this death of God into radical immanence, he argued, is the "one clear portal to the twentieth century."[23] That is why it is necessary for theology—because theology must come to terms with the modern consciousness of humanity's full liberation and responsibility as articulated by its prophets who are the modern world's secular, profane minds: Freud, Marcuse, Sartre, Blake, Hegel and Nietzsche. These are the sources of Christian theology, according to Altizer, because they reveal the histor-ical destiny of humanity in our time, "a time in which simply to share the universal condition of man is to take upon oneself a life without God."[24]

Altizer viewed the death of God as an event in history and not just a symbolic expression of modern humanity's autonomy. He labeled this event the "self-annihila-tion of God" and interpreted it as the ultimate act of kenosis or self-emptying symbol-ized in the doctrines of the Incarnation and cross. This kenotic act of divine self-annihilation took place in Jesus Christ, so that God became identical with humanity by negating his own objective existence through finite life and death:

> The God who acts in the world and history is a God who negates himself, gradually but decisively annihilating his own original Totality. God is that Totality which "falls" or "descends," thereby moving ever more fully into the opposite of its orig-inal identity. God or the Godhead becomes the God who is manifest in Christ by passing through a reversal of His original form: thus transcendence becomes im-manence just as Spirit becomes flesh.[25]

Thus, Altizer says, "the Christian proclaims the God who has totally negated or sac-rificed himself in Christ."[26]

For Altizer, this self-sacrifice of God is an act of grace for the sake of the creature. By wholly and entirely identifying with creaturely existence, God affirms its being. Maintaining his independent existence in transcendence would destroy humanity's freedom and responsibility. Altizer saw this radical immanence of God as leading to an important and necessary practical conclusion: the one who affirms the death of God can overcome all forms of "No-saying" to life and say "Yes" to this world and to life in it.[27]

Critique

Needless to say, Altizer's critics from across the theological spectrum were quick to condemn his radical vision of the absolute immanence of God in humanity. Some charged it with sheer paganism, while others shrugged it off as the ravings of a con-fused genius. Two of the most positive responses appeared in 1969 from sociologist Peter Berger and theologian Langdon Gilkey. Berger explored the "signals of tran-scendence" in ordinary human experience in *A Rumor of Angels.*[28] He suggested that modern society has the resources for a rediscovery of the supernatural.

Gilkey, a leading theologian at the University of Chicago, raised the possibility of a renewal of God-language in a secular culture in *Naming the Whirlwind.*[29] He criticized the death-of-God theologians for falling prey to a basic inconsistency. "Without God-language," he wrote, "this theology cannot consistently hold onto the category of the Lordship of Jesus." It thereby relinquishes its sole touch with the Christian tradition and its claim to be a Christian theology.[30] Furthermore Gilkey argued that Christian atheism's claim that contemporary human existence is entirely godless is "neither a true nor an illuminating picture of our secular life as it actually is."[31] To demonstrate this he explored in great depth and detail the "dimensions of ultimacy," such as freedom and hope in human experience. Both Berger and Gilkey concluded that this theology fundamentally misinterpreted human experience by ignoring its openness to a transcendent "beyond."

Devastating criticisms from theologians of both the left and right brought about the death of the death-of-God theology in the late 1960s. It was rejected as too radical in its absolute immanence and its elimination of transcendence. However, its most important legacy lies in its challenge to late-twentieth-century Christian theologians to rediscover and reconstruct the transcendence of God in a way that will speak with power to the increasingly secular modern mindset. In one way or another most of the theological movements of the latter half of the century, including "secular theology," can be interpreted as responses to this challenge.

John A. T. Robinson

Between the emergence of the death-of-God phenomenon and its resurrection in the popular media arose another expression of radical theology. More so than Hamilton and Altizer, who sought to discard all talk of God and hence to undermine the theological task as it had been traditionally conceived, other radical theologians attempted to salvage theology in the midst of secular culture. The short-lived movement they formed has come to be known as the "secular Christianity" movement. Theologians who danced to the beat of this drum celebrated the rise of the secular era and were concerned with the church's response to the modern situation. In their opinion, the church ought to be "God's avant-garde," to use Harvey Cox's designation, claiming secularity as the work of God and participating in the building of the new humanity, the new secular city of humankind.

Several theologians were at work in the early 1960s seeking to develop Bonhoeffer's call for a secular faith, a rethinking of Christianity in the midst of the world come of age. One significant early statement of the theme of Christian secularity came in 1963, in Paul van Buren's book, *The Secular Meaning of the Gospel.*[32] More important for the church as a whole and as providing the major impetus that triggered the debate over radical theology, however, was the publication that same year of the controversial book *Honest to God*, written by John A. T. Robinson,[33] at that time bishop of Woolwich in the Church of England. Although he was a trained New Testament scholar[34] and not a theologian, his book was instantly popular and enjoyed widespread influence beyond what its author had anticipated.[35]

Honest to God was motivated by Robinson's position as a bishop, as one entrusted with the task of serving as a guardian and defender of church doctrine, at a time when, in his words, "there is a growing gulf between the traditional orthodox supernaturalism in which our Faith has been framed and the categories which the 'lay' world (for want of a better term) finds meaningful today."[36] Thus, while sensing with Bonhoeffer the reality of a world come of age, he found the adulthood that the German theologian noted not merely in the world but within the believing community itself. On behalf of this constituency, Robinson set himself to the task of engaging in a radical questioning of the established religious frame of reference. His overarching goal, then, was pastoral, not explicitly theological. Reminiscent of Bonhoeffer, Robinson sought to make a contribution to the task of the church, which he saw as "to equip Christians, by the quality and power of its community life, to enter with their 'secret discipline' into all the exhilarating, and dangerous, secular strivings of our day, there to follow and to find the workings of God."[37]

In the book, Robinson brought to convergence various strands in contemporary thinking. Three were most significant: Tillich, Bonhoeffer and Bultmann.[38] Paul Tillich had articulated the problem of God in philosophical terms. Rudolf Bultmann was responsible for setting forth the problem of biblical interpretation (given the use of myths in the Bible), which he answered with his program of demythologizing. And Bonhoeffer had turned attention to the questions of God, Christ and the nature of the church. In their individual ways, each of the three called into question the traditional understanding of transcendence, which viewed God as a being, a separate entity beyond the world. Under differing terminology each rejected the older images of the faith as mythological (Bultmann), supranaturalist (Tillich) or religious (Bonhoeffer).[39] Likewise, Robinson claimed that such imagery was outmoded and a stumbling block to faith.[40]

Robinson's God

According to Robinson, God is not to be seen as "up there" or "out there," whether in spatial or in metaphysical and spiritual terms. Instead of this supernaturalism, the bishop sought to build on the work of his mentors in order to reformulate the Christian doctrine of God in a way palatable to the modern mindset. This was to be accomplished, however, not simply by substituting an immanent for a transcendent deity. Rather, Robinson hoped to "validate the idea of transcendence for modern man" by restating its reality in nonmythological terms.[41] To this end he looked to personal freedom and love as the chief categories of transcendence,[42] a thesis he developed further in subsequent writings.

In *Honest to God* Robinson argued that God is what gives meaning and direction to the world, and especially to human relationships in the world. Following Tillich, he spoke of God as "in here," in the depth of our being, and declared that statements about God are statements about the "ultimacy" of personal relationships.[43] As a result, to acknowledge the transcendence of God means to recognize the unconditional in the conditioned relationships of life and to respond to it "in unconditional personal relationship."[44]

Armed with Tillich's conception of God, Robinson pursued Bonhoeffer's christological axiom, Christ as the man for others, and his understanding of the life of the Christian as "worldly holiness." Anticipating a theme Harvey Cox would develop further, he called for a new understanding of the holy and the secular. The holy, Robinson asserted, is not to be set over against the profane, but is "the 'depth' of the common," in the same way that the "secular" is not a godless section of life but the world "cut off and alienated from its true depth."[45] Worship, in turn, is intended to make us more sensitive to the presence of Christ in the common realities of life, so that we may indeed see the Beyond in our midst.

While breaking no new ground, *Honest to God* was significant. It popularized the perspectives of the three theologians to whom Robinson appealed, especially Bonhoeffer. It likewise symbolized the right of Christian leaders and thinkers to discuss and question in a frank and open way the most central doctrines of the faith as traditionally formulated by the church.

Further Questionings

The pastoral concerns Robinson raised in *Honest to God* were developed with a view toward the church in his 1965 book, *The New Reformation?* Here the Anglican bishop explored further his proposal for a secular gospel, drawing inspiration once again from Bonhoeffer's christological and ecclesiological theses.

The beginning point for *The New Reformation?* lay in the author's perception that the question central to the first Reformation, How can I find a gracious God? has been reformulated into, How can I find a gracious neighbor?[46] In this contemporary situation, Robinson argued, the church must follow in the footsteps of its Lord who was the man for others.[47] To do so, it must be prepared to meet people where they are and to accept them as they are.[48] In this way they can make it possible for people to be met by Christ where they are in the world.[49] For this to happen, however, the church "must take shape round the needs of the world,"[50] he argued.

Again in 1967 in *But That I Can't Believe!* Robinson posed the question of belief and unbelief in the world come of age. Despite his questionings, he concluded his study of various problematic Christian doctrines on an optimistic note. A secular proclamation of the gospel is possible, he asserted, because Christians share with people around them several key concepts, focal points and experiences: integrity, justice, solidarity, responsibility, the importance of the person and an emphasis on quality of relationship.[51] With these points of contact in view, he expressed confidence that Christians can indeed "come alongside" others in the world and point them toward the Christ in the midst of life.

Transcendence within Immanence

Throughout his writings, Robinson struggled with the basic theological problem of immanence and transcendence. Despite his attempt to maintain the traditional category of transcendence, he found that the contemporary situation required that the idea of immanence take precedence in Christian discourse, which must move from immanence to transcendence.[52] Even ten years after the publication of *Honest to God*, he reiterated the same theme: "Yet, whether specific 'God'-talk is a help or a hindrance, it is 'transcendence *within* immanence' that we have somehow to articulate and express."[53] In keeping with this maxim, he described the task of theology as that of finding "a projection which enables us to represent the divine initiative as *in* the processes of nature rather than as acting on them from without, as exercised through the events of secular history rather than in some sacred super-history."[54]

Robinson's search for a viable alternative theological model was rewarded, as he became enamored with the program of Teilhard de Chardin. Robinson found an important point of convergence between the secular theology movement and Teilhard's process theology in their mutual concern that the transcendent not be abolished into pure naturalism. Both orientations claim that the apprehension of the transcendent is given "in, with, and under the immanent."[55]

The Anglican bishop found in the panentheistic personalism he saw in the French Jesuit both the solution to the theological problem of transcendence and immanence and a way of maintaining the traditional emphasis on God as person. For Robinson, the personal remained "the central interpretive category of the whole of reality," but he sensed no commitment to the particular image that represents the category of the personal as a divine being.[56] Rather than view God as a bigger Individual or as the collective Personality, Robinson opted for speaking of God in terms of the "interpersonal field" that was both in and beyond all things and persons, unifying them into a living whole. This unity, he added, has the character of personal love rather than impersonal mechanism. In the divine field, "the finite *Thous* are constituted what they are in the freedom of a wholly personalizing love." Robinson credited Teilhard as being the thinker who had taken this view "to its most daring limits."[57] Personalistic panentheism, he concluded, was essentially an incarnational theological model and therefore fundamentally appropriate for Christianity.[58]

After his tenure as bishop of Woolwich, Robinson returned to the academic setting at Cambridge University. Here he was able to complete the book on Christology he had wanted to write for several years.[59] In *The Human Face of God* he continued the immanental theme articulated ten years earlier in *Honest to God*.

For Robinson, what is important is the immanental presence of God in the world, and this concern shaped his Christology. Christ is the one in whom the transcendent, that is, "the unconditional," is visible, the one in whom the Christian sees divinity "in man," he asserted. In this way, Jesus is the "preliminary sketch," "the prototype of the new humanity."[60] In the end, it was not Jesus' divinity that captured Robinson's imagination, but his humanity, for this dimension of Jesus' reality leads to Christian living in the world. Thus, his entire study concludes with an eisegesis of Bonhoeffer: "whatever may be the ultimate truth of our belief, living has to be done in the anonymity and secularity of the penultimate, where the one who is 'God for us' *is* a 'bare man' . . . to be served and loved for his sheer humanity."[61]

Christianity and the Secular

The theological reflection that followed in the wake of *Honest to God* crystallized into what has been termed the secular Christianity movement. Theologians of the movement baptized the secular and sought to show how the church ought to become enmeshed in the building of the new humanity, the new secular city of humankind.

Foundational to the call issued by proponents of the new Christian secular theology was a specific understanding and positive appraisal of the concept of the *secular*. This term was employed to refer to a specific point of view, a mood or an outlook toward the world.[62] Harvey Cox, for example, summarized "the style of the secular city" in terms of pragmatism and profanity, that is, the secular person's orientation toward the question, Will it work? and toward a wholly terrestrial horizon and away from religious questions.[63]

Thus, the secular point of view emphasizes the temporal rather than the eternal and focuses on "this-worldly" realities rather than the "otherworldly" dimension. The secular mood finds meaning in everyday activities rather than in pious, traditional religious disciplines. It highlights secular knowledge—knowledge gained by human endeavor and useful to ordinary living—not theology and metaphysics. And the secular outlook looks to the autonomous person, not the life of faith, as the source of whatever significance the human enterprise may have.[64]

In promoting the secular mood, the secular Christianity movement adamantly held to a distinction between *secularity* and *secularism.* The former term refers to the outlook characterized by the attitudes of modern science and this-worldly concerns. The secular theologians hailed secularization as basically a liberating development. It delivered society and culture, in the words of Harvey Cox, "from tutelage to religious control and closed metaphysical world-views."[65] *Secularism,* in contrast, is the attitude that asserts that only through science is any trustworthy knowledge attainable and only the tangible and human affairs of the world are important. This attitude is dangerous, because it too readily becomes a new closed world view that can even function like a religion.[66]

The secular theologians fought against the secularist attitude, claiming it to be an idolatrous deprecation of the true secularity promoted by the God of the Bible. In the words of William O. Fennell,

> Secularism results from the inevitable tendency on the part of fallen man to make some aspect of his creaturely existence in the world an absolute which serves him in the place of God. Or man himself assumes the status of the absolute and becomes the object of a devotion, hope and service "religious" in quality and extent.[67]

While opposing secularism, these theologians claimed that the secular outlook is legitimate and has its foundations in the Bible.

As a result of their distinction between *secular* and *secularism,* the proponents of the new theology attempted to bring God back into the world, because this is where God is to be found, while avoiding the false ideas of the age. Reminiscent of a theme articulated by Bonhoeffer, Fennell described "the theology of true secularity" as calling humans "from an idolatrous secularism to a believing secularity."[68] To this end the secular theologians called for an erasing of the traditional line between church and world, on the basis of the reconciling work of Christ. Again Fennell drank deeply from the well of Bonhoeffer and spoke for the entire movement:

> But since Jesus Christ is the one in whom *the world* is reconciled to God, the community seeks no separate existence for itself as a religious community in radical separation from the world. Rather, like its Lord, and in him, it exists for the sake of the world. It seeks in speech and action and attitude to interpret to the world the foundation in God of its true rather than false worldliness.[69]

Harvey Cox

Although several theologians jumped on the bandwagon of this theological "fad," it was epitomized and popularized by a young Baptist professor, Harvey Cox, in what became the most influential articulation of the secular theology movement, his widely read book *The Secular City* (1965). Trained at Yale and Harvard, Cox taught at Andover Newton Seminary before joining the faculty of Harvard Divinity School in 1965. During the 1960s his secular theology found practical application through his activism both in inner-city ministry and in the civil rights movement.

The foundational thesis of *The Secular City* is that the process of secularization, rather than being destructive of Christian spirituality, actually is in profound agreement with the Christian faith. This agreement arises out of the fact that secularization is simply "the legitimate consequence of the impact of biblical faith on history."[70] In fact, secularity is dedicated to what is truly authentic and basic to the gospel, namely, liberty and responsibility. The call of the gospel to conversion, therefore, is an admonition to the acceptance of "adult responsibility."[71] In keeping with this evaluation, Cox, in words reminiscent of Bonhoeffer, challenged Christians to find God in contemporary movements of secularization:

> Rather than fighting and opposing secularization, we would do better to discern in it the action of the same One who called an earlier people out of endless toil, in a land where the taskmasters were cruel, and into a land flowing with milk and honey.[72]

Cox's main concern was to draw out the implications of his thesis concerning secularization for the church. He asserted that the proper basis for a doctrine of the church (ecclesiology) lies in a theology of social change, even revolution,[73] symbolized by the image of the "secular city." Because of its juxtapositioning of two significant terms, *secular* and *city*, for Cox this symbol represents the positive goals of the gospel call: "The idea of the secular city exemplifies maturation and responsibility. Secularization denotes the removal of juvenile dependence from every level of a society; urbanization designates the fashioning of new patterns of human reciprocity."[74] As a result he found in the image of the secular city as the "commonwealth of maturity and interdependence" an apt symbol for the biblical idea of the kingdom of God.[75]

Out of the image of the secular city Cox delineated a new understanding of the traditional threefold mission of the church.[76] Its *kerygmatic* function consists of "broadcasting the seizure of power." The church announces the coming of a new era, the era of freedom from every restraining force and personal and social responsibility. Its *diakonic* function is "healing the urban fractures," as the church engages in reconciling the profound ills of urbanized existence and struggles, together with people of no faith, for the wholeness and health of the city. Finally, the *koinonic* function of the church is that of "making visible the city of man." This task refers to the church's responsibility to demonstrate visibly what it proclaims (the kerygma) and to what it points (diakonia). According to Cox, however, such demonstrations pointing to the kingdom of God are not the sole prerogative of the church. Rather, "wherever cogent and tangible demonstrations of the reality of the City of Man appear today, these are signs of the Kingdom."[77]

Finally, drawing from Bonhoeffer[78] and Gollwitzer and not unlike the death-of-God theologians, Cox turned to the thorny issue of speaking about God in the secular context.[79] His solution is based on the thesis that in secular society politics, understood in the Aristotelean sense of the science of the *polis*, functions in the way that metaphysics once did, namely, as the source of unity and meaning for human life and thought. As a result Cox called for a theology that oriented itself toward this new language. Following Paul Lehmann, he declared, "What God is doing in the world is politics, which means making and keeping life human." Consequently, "Theology today must be that reflection-in-action by which the church finds out what this politician-God is up to and moves in to work along with him."[80]

For Cox, this meant a revised understanding of transcendence. God comes to us today, he asserted, in the events of everyday life and of social change. In these events God is both the foundation of freedom and the basis of the experience that not everything is pliable and capable of being "transmuted into extensions of ourselves."[81] God lies behind the stubbornness of the realities that confront us.[82] But above all God comes as our work partner, who wants us to be interested in others, not in God. This idea led Cox to offer the climactic suggestion of the book, namely, that we might need to lay aside the word *God* in favor of another designation of the reality that confronts us in the secular city, a new name of God's own choosing that would emerge in God's own timing.

The Demise of Secular Christianity

Like *Honest to God, The Secular City* proved to be an immensely popular book. Its attractiveness arose out of its ability to pull together two competing dimensions of the needs felt by the younger church members in the turbulent 1960s. The work reflects the revolutionary spirit of the decade while providing a means to remain responsible and active Christians.[83] Yet the ability of the radical theology as a whole to provide a satisfying alternative was short-lived.

Already by mid-decade theologians had become disenchanted with the "pop theology." David L. Edwards, editor of the collection of responses to Robinson, *Honest to God Debate,* called for someone to write a book with the title *Beyond the Secular.*[84]

Criticism came from beyond the theological community as well. In the eyes of its opponents, the radical theology had not performed the apologetic purpose its designers had envisioned. Secularist thinkers were not impressed with the newer attempts toward accommodation with the mindset of the age, some even expressing preference for the older theism or neo-orthodoxy.[85]

Even the more conservative approach of Cox did not escape the chastisement of its audience. Critics sensed a gnawing suspicion that he as well had moved too far toward accommodation with the contemporary mindset and had failed to retain the chastened insights gained by the previous generation of theologians. Despite the intentions of the secular theologians to take Barth seriously,[86] readers such as Charles C. West feared that Cox's book would be misinterpreted as "a return to the robust liberalism of the days before Reinhold Niebuhr" and therefore would "undergird the good conscience and thereby the insensitivity and pride, of technicians, managers, statesmen and revolutionaries."[87] West faulted the book for neglecting the gulf between "the highest achievements of human goodness and the minimum necessary to bring health and peace to the world."[88]

In the older theologies, the chastened realism that critics feared had been over-shadowed by Cox's optimistic emphasis on human maturity and responsibility were given expression by the crucifixion of Christ. This theme was sorely lacking in *The Secular City*.[89] Cox, however, was not oblivious to the importance of the symbol for Christian living in the world. In a book based on lectures he delivered to a youth conference in 1963, Cox called on Christians by virtue of their baptismal experience "to see the world as the place in which the crucifixion of Jesus goes on . . . day after day . . . and to participate in this continuing crucifixion."[90]

His sympathizers also were unsure of Cox's solution to the problem of Christianity in a secular age. Daniel Callahan, for example, indicated that *The Secular City* had been guilty of overkill in its attempt to rid theology of metaphysics. Against Cox he raised a crucial question: "Can secular man, after all, afford to ignore metaphysics? Can he really get away with a purely pragmatic solution to his socio-historical problems?" Callahan's answer was a resounding No: "Man is not just a political and historical creature; he does not live by social reconstruction alone."[91] The loss of the ontological had left readers with the impression that Cox had so enveloped God in the world that the radical theologian had lost the distinction between the human and the divine.[92]

Cox's Subsequent Odyssey

While never fully forsaking it for some new and foreign territory, even Cox himself did not simply settle down in the secular city for any great length of time, but rather set out on a theological odyssey that would have him repeatedly catch the cresting wave of new experiments in theology. From the festivity of the late 1960s,[93] through a phase akin to narrative theology,[94] back to the activism of liberation theology[95] and eventually into the dialog with other religious traditions[96]—his successive books indicate anew that Harvey Cox has been a theologian in search of a theology.

In his response in *The Secular City Debate* Cox began his reevaluation of the work. Under the force of his critics he admitted a continuing need for myth and metaphysics in the secular city, although he strongly maintained that these elements could never again exercise the absolute claims of the past.[97] Four years later, Cox attempted to provide a balance for what he had come to see as the one-sided activism of the earlier work.[98] Radical theology, he declared in *The Feast of Fools*, had elevated present experience to divine status.[99] To counter this mistake, he called for a "theology of Juxtaposition" that would begin with radical theology's focus on the present crisis of faith, but unite it with the emphasis on the past found in traditional theology and the orientation toward the future of the then-rising star of the theology of hope.[100]

The vantage point of a ten-year interval allowed Cox to gain a perspective on the writing of *The Secular City*. He acknowledged that it was composed during a reactionary phase of his life, when he was living in the "heady ecstasy of escape" from the small town in which he had been raised.[101] As the twenty-five-year anniversary of its publication arrived, Cox found that *The Secular City* had not only been a harbinger of things to come, perhaps even of postmodernism, but also implicitly reaffirmed the traditional Christian concept of providence. The seasoned theological maverick could conclude, "To live well instead of badly we need discontinuous experiences, somehow it all eventually makes sense. But *we* don't need to know the *how*. There is someone else, even in the secular city, who sees to that."[102]

Already in the mid-1960s Cox glanced about for a viable direction in which to move. As a possible solution to the problem of God he immediately lighted upon the new ontology that was just beginning to appear on the horizon of Continental theology. The waves that were to lap on the shores of American theology from Germany in the second half of the 1960s were created by the shift toward the future that was to follow the rise in popularity of Teilhard de Chardin and the introduction into theology of the philosophy of Ernst Bloch. Cox was one of the early visionaries to see the rolling tide.[103]

Conclusion

The question that the radical theology set out to answer was, in the words of Harvey Cox, "How . . . do we maintain an affirmation of transcendence in a culture whose mood is radical and relentlessly immanentist?"[104] Despite their graplings with this problem, theologians in the early 1960s were unable to provide a lasting solution to it. Those critics who accused Cox and others of thoroughgoing immanentalism[105] may have overstated the case. Nevertheless in reacting to the radical transcendence of neo-orthodoxy, they did indeed dissolve the transcendence of God too completely into the world. In this way immanence once again overshadowed transcendence.

In spite of its devastating shortcomings, the radical theology of the first half of the decade opened the door to a creative renewal of transcendence that avoided the spatial dualism the radical theologians found so abhorrent. It is to Harvey Cox's credit that he was able to herald the dawning of the next theological movement, the theology of hope, and its orientation to the future as a way out of the impasse of secularism and the death-of-God theology.

6 THE TRANSCENDENCE OF THE FUTURE:
The Theology of Hope

[handwritten: Look out for POLITICAL Theology]

T HE DECADE OF THE 1960S WAS AN ERA OF CONFUSION IN WHICH MANY PEOPLE WERE searching for new answers. In Europe and America the decade witnessed unprecedented demonstrations against war and for new forms of social life emphasizing individual freedom, social responsibility and world peace. At the same time theology was falling into turmoil as its great giants retired and died, and their successors talked about the demise of God and the world setting the agenda for the church. No previous decade had witnessed such rapid secularization combined with new, intense hopes for humanity. No previous decade had witnessed such rapid decline into despair for traditional theology.

"Protest atheism," with its arguments against belief based on the overwhelming evidence of gratuitous evils on a massive scale, gained great strength during the sixties. Atheists pointed to the Holocaust and Hiroshima to disprove the existence of the God of Christian theism. They also argued that the God of traditional Christianity excluded human freedom and the sense of responsibility for *this* world. They based hope for the future on purely secular and humanistic principles.

Theologians of accommodation responded by embracing the atheistic agenda, often reducing traditional Christian beliefs to symbols of human aspirations. Their "God" either dwindled away into near-complete immanence, as in process theology, or disappeared altogether, as in "Christian atheism." Theologians of reaction responded to the growing forces of secularization and atheism by retreating into fortresses of anti-intellectual emotion, mysticism or confessionalism that satisfied itself with condemning the "spirit of the age." Their God floated away from human problems into irrelevance, making appearances only in supernatural events of the distant past or the near future—as in dispensationalism—or in ecstatic events of the present—as in the charismatic movement.

Neither accommodation nor reaction, however, proved satisfactory as a theological answer to the revolutionary hopes and despairs of the times. In the middle of the confusion a book appeared from a virtually unknown young German theologian, which seemed to many to provide the needed new approach for theology in the latter half of the century. The book was *Theology of Hope*[1] written by a thirty-nine-year-old professor of systematic theology at Tübingen, West Germany—Jürgen Moltmann. In this work Moltmann called for a shift to eschatology, to the traditional doctrine of last things but reinterpreted and understood afresh, as the foundation for the theological task.

Moltmann's efforts were paralleled or augmented by several other theologians. The most significant of these thinkers were Moltmann's colleague Wolfhart Pannenberg, the German Roman Catholic scholar Johannes Metz, and in America Carl Braaten, all of whom were initially—whether correctly or incorrectly—associated with a new theological movement generally called the "theology of hope."

According to Braaten, the theologians of hope were interested in responding to the third of three questions posed by Immanuel Kant in his *Critique of Pure Reason:* What can I know? What ought I to do? And, What may I hope? Braaten reported that modern philosophy had occupied itself primarily with the first of these questions and to a much lesser extent with the second. Now the time had come, however, to devote theological attention to the third, and thereby to set forth a point of contact with the secular human.[2]

In part the theology of hope was the outworking of several developments in twentieth-century thought. One important precursor was a rediscovery that had been surfacing in New Testament studies since the turn of the century. Scholars had come to realize that eschatology had been a central feature of Jesus' proclamation and of the New Testament as a whole. Yet these discussions had not yet moved from exegesis to application.

Consequently, the theologians of hope sought to move beyond the question, What did Jesus and the early church hope? to discover in what way past eschatologies can be addressed to humankind today. Hence, Kant's question, What may I hope? and the more foundational query, What does it mean to hope? were among the issues they sought to address. In this way, the theology of hope looked for a point of contact in contemporary culture for the eschatology of hope that characterized the early church.[3]

The theological rediscovery of eschatology indicative of the theology of hope came likewise as an attempt to provide an alternative to the influence in Christian thought of the Greek concepts of circular time and salvation as escape from time. The younger thinkers found remnants of this outlook in the theology of Karl Barth. But even more important, they sought to supply an alternative to the concept of existential time that had been set forth by Rudolf Bultmann. The theologians of hope desired to take seriously the biblical emphasis on the linearity of time, in contrast to what they saw among their Barthian and Bultmannian colleagues.

The other important development that opened the way for the theology of hope was the modern problem of the existence of God. In the 1960s many theologians were agreed that modern atheism had correctly put its finger on certain insurmountable difficulties arising out of the traditional concept of God as a being who exists outside of and throughout time. Such a God left no room for human freedom and provided no solution to the pressing problem of evil.[4] The theologians of hope were not content to opt in the direction of immanental theology rampant during the turbulent decade of the 1960s. They followed neither the radical theologians, who spoke of the death of God or who subsumed God within the secular realm, nor the process theologians who relegated God to the task of moving with humankind through the ebb and flow of the ongoing movement of time.

Instead, these thinkers sought to reestablish the transcendence of God, albeit not by employing the spatial categories of the past that pictured God as the one who dwells in the heavens above the earth. In their quest to understand afresh the divine transcendence, the theologians of hope set forth a bold thesis: Rather than spatiality, temporality may serve as the beginning point for the quest for God as the Transcendent One. As a result, they spoke of God as the "power of the future," the "coming God" who casts his shadow over history from his abode in the "absolute future" of his yet-to-appear sovereign reign.

JÜRGEN MOLTMANN:
THE TRANSCENDENCE AND IMMANENCE OF THE FUTURE

Although Moltmann was not the only prophet of the new, eschatologically oriented approach to theology, through translations of his many books and numerous articles he quickly became its best-known expositor in the English-speaking world. He also made frequent trips to Great Britain and America, serving as visiting professor at Duke and Emory universities and delivering the prestigious Gifford Lectures in Scotland in 1984-1985.

Throughout all of Moltmann's voluminous writings one theme stands out as central: hope for the future based on the cross and resurrection of Jesus Christ. The hope that he writes and speaks about is a realistic hope grounded in history and experience. It answers the deepest aspirations of secular as well as religious people. For this reason, his theology struck a chord with audiences in the turmoil and confusion of the 1960s. And it has continued to draw interest, as Moltmann has unfolded his theology through a series of books that reconstruct the central Christian doctrines in the light of God's promises for the future.

Moltmann's Life and Career

Jürgen Moltmann was born in Hamburg, Germany, in 1926.[5] He was raised in a liberal Protestant home where he received more knowledge of Lessing, Goethe and Nietzsche than of the Bible. Like nearly all young German men, he fought in World War 2. He was captured by the British in Belgium in 1945 and held as a prisoner of war until 1948. Like Tillich, war brought about a crisis of faith in Moltmann's life. The result was different from Tillich's, however:

> In the camps in Belgium and Scotland I experienced both the collapse of those things that had been certainties for me and a new hope to live by, provided by the Christian faith. I probably owe to this hope, not only my mental and moral but physical survival as well, for it was what saved me from despairing and giving up. I came back a Christian, with a new "personal goal" of studying theology, so that I might understand the power of hope to which I owed my life.[6]

At Göttingen, Moltmann studied theology under teachers strongly influenced by Barth. Initially he became an ardent fan and disciple of the great master of dialectical theology. In fact, one of his earliest publications was a scholarly study of the beginnings of dialectical theology.[7] Although the influence of Barth remained in the fundamental tenor of Moltmann's theology, he later became highly critical of the great Swiss theologian's neglect of the historical nature of reality and the eschatological nature of theology.[8]

Moltmann received his doctoral degree in theology in 1952 and served as pastor of a small Reformed church until 1957, when he became a teacher of theology at an academy *(kirkliche Hochschule)* operated by the Confessing Church at Wuppertal. There he came into contact with Wolfhart Pannenberg, who became the other leading spokesman for eschatological theology in the 1960s. Who exercised the greater influence on whom remains a matter of no little disagreement between the two theologians and their students. After a brief stint at the University of Bonn, Moltmann was offered the prestigious position of professor of systematic theology at the University of Tübingen and except for visiting professorships in the United States has remained there since.

Since the publication of *Theology of Hope* in 1965 Moltmann has continued his exploration of the Christian faith with eschatology as his central theme. His major works include *The Crucified God* (1973), *The Church in the Power of the Spirit* (1975), *The Trinity and the Kingdom* (1980), *God in Creation* (1985), which is based on his Gifford Lectures, and *The Way of Jesus Christ: Christology in Messianic Perspective* (1990).

In addition to writing, lecturing and teaching, Moltmann has been involved in ecumenical dialogs with Catholics, Orthodox Christians and Jews. He also participated in the Christian-Marxist dialogs of the late 1960s and has probably done more than any other Western theologian to build bridges between Christians and revisionist Marxists. His critical engagement with liberation theologians of all kinds has made him a major influence in revolutionary and political theologies of the latter half of the century around the world.

According to Moltmann, the real heart of Christianity, and therefore the true cen-

History is Real
Suffering is Real } *God gives meaning to history*
Highlights Reality

terpiece of theology, is hope for the coming of God's "Kingdom of Glory," the divinely promised fulfillment of God's glory in the full freedom and community of humans as well as the liberation of creation itself from bondage to decay. Every part of his theology is permeated by this central motif. He maintains that eschatology has too often served as a useless appendage to theology, and even where it has been emphasized it has not been allowed full play. Instead of the traditional approach, he wishes to let the eschatological Kingdom of Glory in which God will be "all in all" determine the correct formulation of every Christian doctrine: "From first to last, and not merely in the epilogue, Christianity is eschatology, is hope, forward looking and forward moving, and therefore also revolutionizing and transforming the present."[9] He asserts that this reorientation toward the future is not only biblically sound but also points the way to solutions to the problems and impasses of contemporary theology.[10]

Eschatological Ontology and Theology

One of Moltmann's primary concerns in theology is to employ eschatological or "messianic" theology to overcome the conflict between God's immanence and transcendence through a creative reconstruction of the doctrine of God. He believes the concept of God as the "power of the future" will also help overcome the modern conflict between classical theism and atheism. Moltmann is also concerned to overcome the destructive separation between theological theory and Christian practice by providing a "critical theory of God" that will have direct social application.

In his eschatological reorientation of theology Moltmann draws on several sources. While he is by no means a fundamentalist and is highly critical of "literalistic biblicism," his theology is biblically grounded. Through their studies of the centrality of the categories of history and apocalyptic for Hebrew and early Christian thought, Old and New Testament scholars such as Gerhard von Rad and Ernst Käsemann influenced the German theologian. His theological influences include Barth and a lesser-known thinker, Hans Joachim Iwand, who emphasized the eschatological and social dimensions of God's reconciling act in Christ's cross and resurrection.[11]

Besides these Christian sources, Moltmann draws heavily from his critical interaction with a revisionist Marxist philosopher at Tübingen, Ernst Bloch. Bloch produced a massive utopian philosophy based on a blending of Christian eschatology and Marxist scientific social analysis, entitled *Das Prinzip Hoffnung* ("The Principle Hope"). For Bloch, hope for a perfect "homeland" where the individual overcomes all alienation and is at one with oneself is a fundamental human instinct and one that drives history through revolutionary change toward utopia. The philosopher developed an ontology of "not-yet-being" in which the as-yet-unrealized utopia exerts power over the present and past, giving rise to human "transcending without transcendence."[12] *EXPECTATI*

Jewish hope for homeland

Moltmann borrows much from Bloch's ontology of the future, but adds a powerful critique of "transcending without transcendence." He sees Bloch's belief that humanity can face the future in hope and transcend its circumstances toward utopia without God to be an illusion:

> A historical future without heaven cannot be a forecourt of hope and the motivation

Handwritten top margin: Hope in Escaton

for any historical movement. A "transcending without transcendence" such as Bloch proposed turns infinity into indefinite endlessness and makes the striving for fulfillment merely an "on and on."[13]

We can interpret much of Moltmann's thought as an attempt to provide an answer to Bloch without negating his valuable contribution to Christian theology. On the one hand, he finds in Bloch's "atheism of hope" a challenge to Christian theology to make eschatology the medium of its thought.[14] On the other hand, he warns that Christian hope, while utilizing insights from Bloch, must resist the religious reductions inherent in the atheism of hope.[15] Bloch appreciated Christianity's apocalyptic vision of a future kingdom of God while harshly criticizing its dependence on "heavenly transcendence" as unrealistic and abstract. Throughout his writings Moltmann attempts to show that Christian hope is anything but unrealistic and abstract and that in fact hope without God is groundless and shallow. As Marcel Neusch reports, against Bloch

> Moltmann maintains that Christian hope is in fact not an abstract utopia but a passion for the future that has become "really possible" thanks to the resurrection of Christ. By entering into history the resurrection of Christ introduces a *novum* which gives substance to hope and opens up to it a definitive horizon (an *ultimum*) that does not signal the end of history but is rather a real possibility for human life and for history itself.[16]

Moltmann is not an accommodationist theologian. He does not allow a secular philosophy such as Bloch's atheism of hope to predetermine or control his reconstructions of doctrines. Yet together Barth and Bloch form the "odd couple" of Moltmann's theological background. Barth's dialectical theology provides the theological raw material, whereas Bloch provides the stimulation and the philosophical conceptuality for Moltmann's new interpretation of Christianity's hope.[17]

Handwritten margin note: Use phil. only

Although Moltmann has written on virtually every conceivable subject within the scope of theology, his greatest contributions lie in the doctrine of God. Before discussing this crucial area of his thought, however, it is necessary to examine briefly his ideas of theological method and of divine revelation.

Revelation as Promise

By his own confession Moltmann intends his theology to be "biblically founded, eschatologically oriented, and politically responsible."[18] However, his methodology is somewhat more complex. In fact, there is reason to doubt whether he has a coherent theological method in any traditional sense. This lack of systematic approach arises partly from his lack of interest in correct doctrine. "I am not so concerned," he writes, "with correct but more with concrete doctrine; and thus not concerned with pure theory but with practical theory."[19] He sees the task of theology not so much as to provide an interpretation of the world as to transform it in the light of hope for its ultimate transformation by God.[20]

Another reason for Moltmann's lack of systematic methodology lies in his belief in the provisionality of human knowledge in light of the incompleteness of reality short of its eschatological fulfillment. Only when the Kingdom of Glory promised by God

Handwritten bottom margin: Theol of hope - not political Theol world transformed by view of future

arrives will we "know as we are known" and "see as we are seen." Until then all thought about God must be full of tension.[21] Contradiction lies at the heart of reality as history because the future, if it really is future and not just more of the same, contradicts the present and the past.

If anything is axiomatic for Moltmann it is that the future is new, and not merely an extension of the past. This "eschatological ontology" runs as a common thread throughout his entire corpus, tying it all together. For him, reality is not a predetermined or self-contained system of cause and effect, but is historical in nature, and "hope has a chance of a meaningful existence only when reality itself is in a state of historic flux and when historic reality has room for open possibilities ahead."[22] This means that the future is not completely inherent in the present.[23] Rather, the future (and for the Christian, the God of the future) is the ground and origin of reality's new possibilities, working them into the present and in this way having mastery over it.[24]

In his ontology, then, the future is not determined by the present but itself determines the present. The future is "ontologically prior" to the present and the past. It is not *becoming* from the present, but *coming* to it, drawing it forward into totally new forms of reality. This means that theological categories and concepts must be open-ended, always ready to be superseded and revised in the light of the future as it occurs.

Because he holds to such an eschatological epistemology it is no wonder that Moltmann does not elevate rigid consistency and systematic coherence as theological virtues. Dialectical thinking about the future's contradictions of the present cannot help but give rise to paradoxes, and it often ends in doxology rather than logical conclusions. For Moltmann, then, "theological concepts become not judgments which nail reality down to what it is, but anticipations which show reality its prospects and its future possibilities."[25]

Moltmann is not an irrationalist who rejects any sort of methodology, however. He does not merely throw out ideas with no ground or interconnection. Although he does not specifically mention Tillich's method of correlation, his theology seems to aim at the same sort of answering function. But its concepts are not derived from nature, human existence or anything of the world as it already is. On the contrary, Moltmann explicitly rejects "natural theology" (in which he includes "anthropological theology"), because it presupposes that God is already manifest in the existence or order of the world *as it is.* For Moltmann, the present world is clearly "out of order," so to speak; only in the future Kingdom of Glory will God be manifest, because he will then be "all in all."[26] Yet even though God's being cannot be proved by reason or evidence, anticipatory knowledge of God from "traces of God" in nature is possible for those who know God.[27]

Moltmann's rejection of natural theology as any sort of preamble to Christian theology is almost as complete as Barth's. However, unlike Barth, he holds out real hope for theology's ability to speak relevantly to secular people by drawing on revelation's answers to meet their needs and questions. Moltmann describes theology's task in a way similar to Tillich: "If it is correct to say that the Bible is essentially a witness to the promissory history of God, then the role of Christian theology is to bring these remembrances of the future to bear on the hopes and anxieties of the present."[28] The basis for a true natural theology, then, lies not in "proofs" of God from the world as it is, but in the sighs and groans of creation for redemption. Ultimately, only Christian hope, based on God's revealed promises for the future, can make happiness in the present possible, because "hope makes us ready to bear the 'cross of the present.' It can hold to what is dead, and hope for the unexpected."[29]

Concern for meeting the questions of the present with answers drawn from God's revelation of the future, therefore, lies at the center of Moltmann's theological method. But what is "revelation?" Once again, Moltmann provides no simple, once-for-all definition, for his thinking develops over time. However, the single most important category for understanding revelation is "promise." Through a meticulous examination of Scripture he discovered that both Israel and the early church regarded the primary form of God's presence and appearance among them as promise for the future.[30]

The religion of promise, however, is to be distinguished radically from "epiphany religions" that interpret God's presence and appearance as unveilings of what exists eternally in some heavenly realm. Such an interpretation of revelation, Moltmann claims, serves to provide comfort in the midst of troubling change by annihilating history and to provide sanction to the political and cultural status quo by linking it with the eternal.[31] For him the epitome of epiphany religion is Greek philosophical theology with its obsession with timelessness (Parmenides) and with an eternal realm of forms of reality (Plato). But this theology is not merely a relic of the dead past, for Moltmann traces its effects in philosophy and religion throughout two millennia of thought up to and including Karl Barth's concept of revelation.[32]

In contrast to revelation as epiphany, Moltmann argues that Israel experienced God's word and presence as a history of promise and faithfulness to his promises. This experience of revelation fundamentally altered conceptions of history and the status quo: "Under the guiding star of promise this reality is not experienced as a divinely stabilized cosmos, but as history in terms of moving on, leaving things behind and striking out towards new horizons as yet unseen."[33] Rather than the religious sanctioning of the present, the experience of revelation led the ancient people of God to "a break-away from the present towards the future."[34] Thus revelation-as-promise gave rise to Israel's unique concept of history as linear and initiated its prophetic tendencies, which constantly called for greater righteousness in the light of God's faithfulness and future kingdom.

Moltmann finds the same idea of revelation at work in the New Testament church. It experienced Christ as an event of promise and proclaimed his death and resurrection as promises of God's future kingdom.[35] It also experienced the Holy Spirit as the "earnest" of the promised future of Christ. In the resurrection of the crucified Christ and in the sending of the Spirit God promised his own righteousness in history, life overcoming death in the general resurrection of the dead and a kingdom of God in a new totality of being.[36] Based on these promises the early church lived in hope with a view toward the future and toward mission, experiencing the faithfulness of God while remaining restless for the coming of God's kingdom of righteousness.

Revelation-as-promise does not impart facts, but kindles faith and hope. Nevertheless, Moltmann averred, there is a kind of knowledge engendered by promise, the knowledge of things hoped for, a prospective, anticipatory, provisional and fragmentary knowledge that always remains open and strains beyond itself.[37] In Moltmann's view this knowledge is not the same as futurology, which seeks to predict the future based on present trends and tendencies. Instead, it is knowledge of the future based on the promise of God in Christ. More specifically, "it knows the future in striving to bring out the tendencies and latencies of the Christ event of the crucifixion and resurrection, and in seeking to estimate the possibilities opened up by this event."[38]

For Moltmann, the Bible is not itself revelation and is not verbally inspired, but it is a witness to the promissory history of God.[39] In a way reminiscent of Barth and Brunner, he described the Scriptures as human responses to the promises of God, while at the same time being God's testimony to himself. The Bible contains the narratives of God's promises and human responses to the promises, but its primary value lies in pointing beyond itself to the coming kingdom of God: "In these accounts of the past we encounter the promissory history of the future of God. We find the future in the past, see the future revealed and anticipated in the past, and find ourselves taken up into this history of liberation."[40] Thus, the authority of the Scriptures is instrumental: God uses the Bible and the Spirit to bring about his kingdom and is glorified in them. Like everything else, however, the Scriptures themselves are not already perfect, but "will be fulfilled in perfection in the kingdom of the coming glory."[41]

Moltmann's driving desire to provide an alternative to "transcendence theology" and "immanence theology" is evident already in his doctrine of revelation. Instead of conceiving of revelation as a supernatural incursion into history from beyond or as a natural capacity of humans in history, he described it as the promise of totally new and unexpected events in the future that can be anticipated in the present. The futurity of the events signals the transcendence of revelation, which contradicts the present and opens it to a new totality of being not already inherent in it.[42] Revelation is not the unveiling of already existing truth, but the "apocalypse of the promised future of the truth."[43] Even their historical fulfillments do not exhaust God's promises: "In every fulfillment the promise, and what is still contained in it, does not yet become wholly congruent with reality and thus there always remains an overspill."[44]

Revelation, therefore, is transcendent in the way that the future is transcendent. But it is also immanent in the way that the future is imminent to the present. The future Kingdom of Glory does not yet exist, but it is not absent from the present either. It is "present" in its effect:

> As compared with what can now be experienced, it brings something new. Yet it is not for that reason totally separate from the reality which we can now experience and have now to live in, but, as the future that is really outstanding, it works upon the present by awaking hopes and establishing resistance.[45]

The Futurity of God

Moltmann's new approach to transcendence and immanence based on futurity is

perspective

crucial to his doctrine of God. The German theologian drew the closest possible link between God's own being and the future Kingdom of Glory in which God will be fully present and manifest in the world. Consequently, "God is not 'beyond us' or 'in us,' but ahead of us in the horizons of the future opened to us in his promises," so that "the 'future' must be considered as mode of God's being."[46] Moltmann is fully convinced that if God already fully existed, whether "above us" or "in us," reality could not be truly historical. History would fall back into meaninglessness or annihilation, as in the epiphany religions. Furthermore, the evil and inhumanity of history would by necessity be a reflection on God, insofar as either God can but does not want to overcome it, or he cannot and therefore is not really God.

Absolutely crucial for Moltmann is the reality of history as what is to be contradicted. *Real* Because of the evil and suffering in it, he argued, "God is not the ground of this world and not the ground of existence, but the God of the coming kingdom which transforms this world and our existence radically."[47]

God's transcendence, then, does not lie in his being the Creator and Sustainer of a world that already exists. Transcendence is God's being the power that transforms the present world from the perspective of its future by negating what is negative in it and by drawing it into the Kingdom of Glory. Similarly, God's immanence is his imminent futurity impinging on every moment, contradicting its contradictions of the glory of the kingdom.

Moltmann did not conceive of this dualistically, however. For him, the future does actually penetrate into the present and past, releasing events that work to propel it forward into its future. These proleptic or anticipatory events are works of God in which he himself is truly present in suffering and power, and hence he is immanent in the world. The greatest among these occurrences are the events of Jesus Christ, especially his crucifixion and resurrection, and the sending of the Holy Spirit.

Consequently, Moltmann conceives of God's presence in the world trinitarianly. If God's transcendence lies in his *coming* ("Adventus") out of the future to the world, contradicting its negativities, his immanence lies in his *becoming* together with the world in the trinitarian history of the kingdom within the world. His vision of God's transcendence and immanence as the presence of the future constitutes Moltmann's doctrine of God as "eschatological, trinitarian panentheism." As will be seen, he regards the immanence of God as a real history of the triune God within world history. At the same time he sees this history not as development or evolution but as prolepsis and anticipation.

The Trinitarian History of God

Christocentric view

Moltmann explored the connection between the doctrine of the Trinity and eschatology in two major books, *The Crucified God* and *The Trinity and the Kingdom*. For him the key to understanding God's identity as historical—and thus immanent—is the doctrine of the Trinity as understood from the event of the cross of Jesus Christ. Through a penetrating analysis of the cross, Moltmann concluded that this event not *back* only has an effect on humanity in the dynamic of reconciliation, but also on God. The *as well*

Right time - Stressi future -
projection of God

cross is the occasion in which God constitutes himself as Trinity within history: "What happened on the cross was an event between God and God. It was a deep division in God himself, in so far as God abandoned God and contradicted himself, and at the same time a unity in God, in so far as God was at one with God and corresponded to himself."[48]

Consequently, for Moltmann, the "Trinity" is simply a shorter version of the passion narrative of Christ. The basis and ground of the Trinity is the separation-in-unity God experienced within himself in this event, and the cross cannot be understood apart from the Trinity.

From his interpretation of the cross Moltmann drew several radical conclusions. Because it is linked intrinsically to the event of the cross, the Trinity is historical; it is constituted in and through suffering and conflict, and it takes different forms throughout the history of God's kingdom on the way to the future. Moltmann radically rejected the idea of an immutable, impassable God removed from the sufferings and conflicts of history. What happens in history happens "in God," because the cross opens God to the world:

> If one conceives of the Trinity as an event of love in the suffering and the death of Jesus—and that is something which faith must do—then the Trinity is no self-contained group in heaven, but an eschatological process open for men on earth, which stems from the cross of Christ.[49]

Moltmann's account of the "historical being of God" in *The Crucified God* began a project of reinterpreting the nature of God, which differs radically from both traditional Christian theism and process theology while preserving elements of both. Although the project remained incomplete in that book, he took it up again in two later books. Moltmann's reinterpretation broke boldly from classical theism by asserting on the basis of God's suffering the death of the Son in the event of the cross the real historicity of God. Consequently, the cross is not extrinsic to God's own being, as if God would be exactly who and what he is without it; rather it constitutes God's being as Trinity through the dialectic of the separation and unity between Father and Son. In Moltmann's words, "This means that God's being is historical and that he exists in history. The 'story of God' then is the story of the history of man."[50]

At the same time, Moltmann's program differed from process theology. The German theologian rejected any idea of development in God, and he asserted that the historicity of God is an act of God's free and gracious choice. God's experiences of conflict, pain and suffering in history are not due to some inherent interdependence between God and the world. Consequently, Moltmann's passionate, trinitarian God is not Whitehead's fellow sufferer who understands, but is the Father of Jesus Christ who "has decided from eternity for seeking love, and in his decision to go outside of himself lies the conditions for the possibility of this experience."[51]

Furthermore, Moltmann's God not only understands, as in process thinking; he also helps. His trinitarian suffering in the cross releases into the world the Spirit of the unity of Father and Son that works toward its transformation. But above all, unlike process theology, Moltmann kept in view at all times the transcendent future of God's Kingdom of Glory, which is the final consummation of history—God's and the world's. Against process theology he asserted, "If there is no new creation of all things, there is nothing that can withstand the Nothingness that annihilates the world."[52]

A major key to understanding Moltmann's doctrine of God in its distinction from classical theism and process theology is his idea of God's self-limitation. Without question Moltmann posited a reciprocal relationship between God and the world. In his immanence God is in some way dependent on the world, although the world's dependence on God remains greater. God's life history is the triune history of Father, Son and Spirit in the progress of the kingdom through world history. Events such as the cross, resurrection and sending of the Spirit actually constitute God's being who he is.

But why? For Moltmann this is so because of God's overflowing love expressing itself in compassionate involvement with the world. Is such involvement with the world necessary for God? Moltmann suggested that in God "necessity" and "freedom" are transcended by love. Consequently, God does not feel any compulsion; yet

> the self-communication of his goodness in love to his creation is not a matter of his free will. It is the self-evident operation of his eternal nature. The essential activity of God *is* the eternal resolve of his will, and the eternal resolve of his will *is* his essential activity.[53]

While God is not compelled to relate to the world in the way that he does, his relationship is the natural outworking of his love, which is his nature. Moltmann concluded quite paradoxically, "This does not mean that he cannot but love the world eternally; nor that he could either love it, or not."[54]

God's loving and gracious choice to allow his own life to be constituted by the history of the world entails self-limitation. Moltmann explained, "In order to create a world 'outside' himself, the infinite God must have made room beforehand for a finitude in himself."[55] Similarly, in order to redeem the godforsaken world God enters the godless space created by his self-limitation and suffers it, thus bringing it within his divine life in order to conquer it. This, then, is the point of the trinitarian history of the cross in which God constitutes himself through suffering and death: "By entering into the Godforsakenness of sin and death (which is Nothingness), God overcomes it and makes it part of his eternal life: 'If I make my bed in hell, thou art there.' "[56] So God's self-limitation preserves both his transcendence and his immanence. Because he is limited, he is vulnerable and historical and includes the pain and suffering of the world while conquering it. Nevertheless because this limitation is self-chosen and not imposed by his nature (apart from his will) nor by anything outside himself, he remains transcendent. God's self-limitation is not a matter of metaphysical necessity or fate.

According to Moltmann, then, God's relationship to the world cannot be expressed either in the terms of classical theism, which pictures God as immune to and invulnerable to the imperfections of the world, or in the categories of process panentheism, which pictures him as a pathetic, finite being trapped in endless codependence with the world.

Moltmann labeled his own view "trinitarian panentheism" and claimed that it preserves and deepens the truths in both views while avoiding their weaknesses.[57] Whether that is indeed the case is debatable. The entire structure of his concept of God depends on the coherence of its foundation, which lies in the idea that God's love unites freedom and necessity while transcending them. Moltmann argued that God did not have to create and enter into the world and history, but at the same time he asserted that there could be no "otherwise." Although the German theologian found such talk merely an example of theology's "creative antitheses," to some of his readers it appears nothing less than a sheer contradiction.

Trinitarian Panentheism

Given Moltmann's adamant insistence that Jesus' cross and resurrection as well as the sending of the Spirit to the church constitute the trinitarian life of God,[58] his "trinitarian history of the cross" naturally raises a crucial question: Would God be trinitarian apart from the events of world history?

In *The Crucified God* Moltmann seemed to deny any eternal triune life of God already constituted apart from the event of the cross: "Anyone who really talks of the Trinity talks of the cross of Jesus and does not speculate in heavenly riddles."[59] This appears to be a thorough rejection of the traditional doctrine of the immanent or ontological Trinity, which views God as existing in triune heavenly perfection from all eternity. To support his own position Moltmann quoted Catholic theologian Karl Rahner: "The economic Trinity *is* the immanent Trinity, and the immanent Trinity *is* the economic Trinity."[60] The reader is thereby left to conclude that Moltmann does not believe that God would be trinitarian without his historical interaction with the world, even though this would move his doctrine of God even farther away from classical Christian theism toward a pantheistic dissolution of God in history.

Moltmann developed his trinitarian panentheism farther and attempted to redress the pantheistic implications of *The Crucified God* in *The Trinity and the Kingdom*.[61] Here he set forth a social doctrine of the Trinity, in order to overcome the "disintegration of the doctrine of the Trinity in abstract monotheism"[62] and to link God intimately with the world and its history while preserving and deepening the divine transcendence. In this work Moltmann criticized all interpretations of trinitarian doctrine that reduce the three persons to modes of a single subjectivity, because this inevitably sets God over against the world and implies a hierarchical, monarchical relation between them. Against all reductions of "Christian monotheism," Moltmann affirmed the distinct subjectivities of Father, Son and Holy Spirit:

> The history in which Jesus is manifested as "the Son" is not consummated and fulfilled by a single subject. The history of Christ is already related in trinitarian terms in the New Testament itself. So we start from the following presupposition. *The New Testament talks about God by proclaiming in narrative the relationships of the Father, the Son and the Spirit, which are relationships of fellowship and are open to the world.*[63]

Moltmann described these relationships through an analysis of the various stages of the histories of the Son and the Spirit as their work toward the glorification of the Father in the kingdom of God. He moved beyond his earlier focus on the cross as the

All have works to do.

central event constituting God as Trinity to discuss various events, including the resurrection and sending of the Spirit, in which the kingdom of God develops by being handed over from one divine subject to another and thereby changing its pattern. As a result, the Father is not the only subject of trinitarian activity toward the kingdom. In his work the Father is dependent on the sending, surrender and glorification of the Son and the Spirit. The intertrinitarian being of God consists of these changing, historical patterns of relationships, with the common thread being the kingdom of God as the goal of the entire divine activity.

Again in this discussion Moltmann seems to import history into the being of God. God develops through the activities of the three distinct persons toward the kingdom. Even God's perfect unity is eschatological and therefore historical. In history there is no single pattern of divine interdependence, but a variety of ways in which the persons contribute to the kingdom in relation to each other. Their unity is one of *goal,* not *origin,* formed by the process of "perichoresis" (interpenetration) in which "the trinitarian persons form their unity by themselves in the circulation of the divine life."[64]

This raises to an intense pitch the question of whether God would be trinitarian, and therefore God, without the world. In *The Trinity and the Kingdom,* Moltmann valiantly attempted to answer this question with a more carefully nuanced interpretation of the immanent Trinity and the economic Trinity. Although continuing in his rejection of any concept of an immanent Trinity in eternity untouched by the events of salvation history, the German theologian was now willing to admit some validity to the concept of an inner life of the Trinity distinct from the constitution of the Trinity in history.[65] He reaffirmed Rahner's thesis of the identity of the immanent Trinity and the economic Trinity; yet he interpreted the connection not as absolute identity without distinction but as reciprocity and interdependence. In other words, while there may be an intratrinitarian life that is not *wholly* constituted within history, it is stamped by the cross and the other events of salvation history.[66] The cross of the Son and the joy of love in glorification through the Spirit put their impress on the inner life of the triune God from eternity to eternity.[67]

Moltmann asserted that the immanent Trinity—which is eschatological—exerts the primary influence in this reciprocal relationship between the immanent Trinity and the economic Trinity.[68] How that primary determination is felt or known he left unexplained. He simply asserted it, perhaps to divert further criticism that his doctrine of the trinitarian history of God dissolves the Trinity into world history. Ultimately for Moltmann the immanent Trinity is completed and perfected only when the history of salvation is completed and perfected. In his words, "When everything is 'in God' and 'God is all in all,' then the economic Trinity is raised into and transcended in the immanent Trinity."[69]

It seems that Moltmann could and should have brought his eschatological ontology into play more effectively in explaining from the eschatological perspective the significance of the immanent Trinity for the economic Trinity and salvation history. In the end he seemed only to pay lip service to it. This, however, raises serious questions about his commitment to the transcendence of God.

Extreme Immanence (handwritten)

The Shift to Immanence

Whereas he began his doctrine of God in *Theology of Hope* with a strong emphasis on transcendence—to the point of implying the supernaturalness of the future—throughout his books Moltmann moved steadily toward an overemphasis on God's immanence within history. In *God in Creation,* for example, he underscored the "perichoretic relationship" between God and the world—a relationship of fellowship, mutual need and mutual interpenetration,[70] and he strongly suggested a model of the world as God's body.[71]

How can we explain this gradual shift from the transcendence of the God who has futurity as mode of being to panentheistic immanence of God in the world and the world in God? A possible answer lies in Moltmann's growing political denigration of power and hierarchy and his emphasis on community, fellowship, equality and interdependence. Somewhere during his theological sojourn he became convinced that hierarchy and power are intrinsically evil and set about to erase all vestiges of lordship from his doctrine of God. Even the future Kingdom of Glory, which always played a constitutive role in his theology, was reconceived as a fellowship of liberated nature, humans and God existing in harmony on an equal footing, instead of the monarchy of the glorious Lord of creation over all.

(handwritten in left margin: John fellowship IN)

Toward the end of *God in Creation* Moltmann discussed the kingdom of God as the "Sabbath" in which God rests from his creative works and enjoys their fruits:

> On the sabbath the resting God begins to "experience" the beings he has created. The God who rests in the face of his creation does not dominate the world on this day; he "feels" the world; he allows himself to be affected, to be touched by each of his creatures. He adopts the community of creation as his own milieu.[72]

Reigning, lordship, judgment and praise of God are all muted if not absent from Moltmann's later works. God's goal for persons is not that they be his servants or children, the German theologian came to see, but his friends, and "in friendship the distance enjoined by sovereignty ceases to exist."[73]

(handwritten in left margin: No! just perspective)

We must conclude that Moltmann's social and political antipathy to hierarchy distorted his otherwise creative and insightful approach to theology. It led him to overemphasize the immanence of God to the detriment of God's transcendence, and it resulted in his outright denial of monotheism and possible fall into the heresy of tritheism.

In *The Trinity and the Kingdom,* for example, Moltmann provided a criticism of "political and clerical monotheism," which made clear that he considered the traditional doctrine of the Trinity a justification for political and ecclesiastical forms of totalitarianism: "The notion of a divine monarchy in heaven and on earth, for its part, generally provides the justification for earthly domination—religious, moral, patriarchal or political domination—and makes it a hierarchy, a 'holy rule.' "[74] *(handwritten: Fem The)*

Moltmann intended his own emphasis on the distinct personhood of the three subjects of the trinitarian history of God to function as a social and political statement. He elevated his doctrine of the Trinity to the status of being a "critical principle" for theology in its messianic mission of transforming the world. Because societies reflect

Christian Koinonia - fellowship (handwritten at bottom)

their gods in the way they organize themselves, he explained, it is important for Christian cultures to rediscover the biblical concept of God's triunity as community and fellowship among three equal persons, not a monarchy of one person over the others and the world.

But does Moltmann's social doctrine of the Trinity actually rest on biblical and theological grounds, or is it merely a product of social and political considerations? If the latter, it opens itself to the criticism that it is merely an example of creating God in the image of a theologian's ideal of an egalitarian society. Thereby it reinforces Feuerbach's thesis that the concept of God is nothing more than the projection into the heavens of the idealized human essence. *— Assuming truth*

Moltmann's doctrine of God begs the question as to whether it is so one-sided in its rejection of monarchy that it falls into the opposite error of tritheism. If his view does indeed harbor a latent tritheistic tendency, then it must be judged as unbalanced and perhaps even heretical.

Critical Evaluation

No final evaluation of Moltmann's theological contribution can or should be made, given his tendency to shift his thinking. Nevertheless, a few preliminary judgments are in order, however tentative they may be.

Moltmann's theology introduced several powerful new images and concepts into late-twentieth-century Christianity. No other theologian has done as much to explore the implications of eschatology and of the cross of Christ for the being of God. Taking his cue from Bonhoeffer's statement that "only the suffering God can help," Moltmann opened up a veritable new chapter in theology, in which the suffering of God is almost a new orthodoxy that few have seriously questioned.

Furthermore, Moltmann has done more than anyone since Karl Barth to revitalize the doctrine of the Trinity in contemporary theology. Especially in his earlier works he helped give birth to the entire eschatological orientation in theology that provided creative new ways of conceiving God's transcendence and immanence.

At the same time, Moltmann's theology is riddled with tensions. The eschatological ontology on which it is based has yet to receive full explanation. For example, left unexplained is how the future, which is still open, can impinge on and influence the present. Is God, who is present and active in history, future to himself? And how real are the agonies, sufferings and victories of the present, if the future Kingdom of Glory is assured by God? Does that assured future reality not imply something like an "epiphany," which Moltmann so vehemently rejects?

But most significantly, in spite of his intention of providing a new approach to the traditional problem of the transcendence and immanence of God, Moltmann ultimately abandons them to a tension. He speaks of the God of the eschatological future, the "power of the future," the God with futurity as a mode of being who *comes* out of the future to contradict and transform the world. But he also talks about the suffering, struggling God of history whose unity as Father, Son and Spirit is still future to himself. How exactly these pictures of God cohere Moltmann leaves unexplained.

1. John.

In the end, Moltmann's theology falls prey to the perennial temptation of contemporary theology to emphasize God's immanence to the detriment of his transcendence. By linking God's intertrinitarian being so closely with historical events, the German theologian calls into question the deity of God. As one of Moltmann's sympathetic interpreters admits concerning this theology, "World history is taken up into the inner-divine history in such a way that the deity of God is made ontologically dependent upon world history and God only truly comes to himself through the completion of world history."[74]

WOLFHART PANNENBERG: TRANSCENDENCE IN REASON AND HOPE

A German thinker who with Moltmann was hailed in the 1960s as a proponent of the emerging theology of hope is the Munich systematic theologian Wolfhart Pannenberg. Pannenberg has never been keen on accepting for himself that label. His aversion is correct, in that his program moves beyond the original intent of the theology of hope. Nevertheless, the inclusion of Pannenberg within this historical movement, while not exhausting his contribution, remains appropriate. His rise to theological prominence occurred in the context of the advent of the theology of hope. And he shares the central orientation of the movement, namely, the emphasis on the future or the eschaton as the point of transcendence.

Pannenberg's Early Theological Development
Wolfhart Pannenberg was born in 1928 in a part of northeast Germany that now belongs to Poland. The basic outlook that drives his theological program came to be shaped quite early in life. A crucial factor in this molding process was the path he followed in coming to faith, for this was at the same time the path that led to his choice of theology as his life's pursuit. A series of experiences was crucial in launching him in this direction.[1]

The first experiences occurred when he was about sixteen years old. While browsing through the public library, Pannenberg happened on a book by the atheist philosopher Friedrich Nietzsche. Thinking it was a work on music, Pannenberg's "first love" at that time, he read it. Nietzsche's writings convinced young Pannenberg that the influence of Christianity was responsible for the disastrous shape of the world. Yet they also sparked his interest in issues of philosophy.

At about the same time, what Pannenberg has termed "the single most important experience"[2] of his life occurred. While walking home through the woods during sundown one winter afternoon, he was attracted to a light in the distance. When he approached the spot, he found himself flooded—even elevated—by a sea of light. The theologian now sees in this experience Jesus Christ making claim to his life, even though he was not yet a Christian. Over the ensuing years this experience has become the basis for Pannenberg's keen sense of calling.

Pessimistic of World (handwritten annotation)

His first positive experience with Christianity itself came in his final school years through his *Gymnasium* (high school) literature teacher, who had been a lay member of the Confessing Church during the Third Reich. Pannenberg saw in this teacher a contradiction to his earlier view that Christianity was responsible for the distortions of human life. Because he was wrestling with the question of the deeper meaning of reality, he decided to look more closely at the Christian faith, and this by studying theology and philosophy. From his inquiry he concluded that Christianity is the best philosophy, a conclusion that launched Pannenberg's life both as a Christian and as a theologian.

Soon after his experience of light, the Pannenberg family left their home in the wake of the Soviet offensive. Two years later he began studies at the university in Berlin. His initial fascination with Marxism gave way to opposition to it, as he subjected the system to intellectual scrutiny. His firsthand exposure to the evils of two human social orders—Nazi Germany and Stalinist Eastern Europe—forms a part of the background to Pannenberg's conclusion that no human political system can ever fully mirror the perfect human social structure that one day will come as a divine gift in the kingdom of God.[3]

Theo of (handwritten annotation)

While in Berlin Pannenberg became impressed with the work of Karl Barth. He saw *Hope* (handwritten annotation) in Barth's early writings an attempt to establish the sovereignty of God and to claim all reality for the God of the Bible. But study in Basel with Barth himself beginning in 1950 resulted in Pannenberg becoming uneasy, not with this goal but with what he perceived to be a dualism in his teacher's thought between natural knowledge and the divine revelation in Christ. Out of this reaction to Barth grew another important aspect of Pannenberg's theological program,[4] the attempt to show that God's revelatory work does not come as a stark contradiction to the world, but is the completion of creation. Pannenberg seeks to draw out the religious implications found in all secular experience,[5] claiming a continuity between redemption and creation, a continuity he came to find in the historical process.

In 1951 Pannenberg moved to Heidelberg, where he studied under such scholars as Peter Brunner, Edmund Schlink, Hans von Campenhausen and Gerhard von Rad.[6] During the years as a student in this great German university, his thinking concerning the nature of revelation took shape, in part through ongoing discussions with a group of students from various disciplines, which came to be known as the Pannenberg circle. The conclusions of the group were subsequently published as *Revelation As History.*[7]

In 1955 Pannenberg completed his academic training. After teaching at the Lutheran church seminary in Wuppertal (1958-1961) and the University of Mainz (1961-1968), he moved to the University of Munich in 1968, the site of the bulk of his academic career.

The Intent of Pannenberg's Theology

Pannenberg is a theologian of both the church[8] and the public sphere. His program is directed toward the unity of the church and the place of the one church in a secularized world. As a result, he has been an untiring supporter of ecumenism. But his understanding of the goals of the ecumenical movement have made him no friend of the political orientation that characterized the World Council of Churches for many years.[9] Such activities take away from what he sees as the central task of ecumenical endeavors, the establishment of eucharistic fellowship among the churches, leading to Christian unity. Unity, he believes, is the only way by which the church's voice can speak with credibility in the contemporary secular society.[10]

His concern, however, does not end with church unity but moves beyond to include the future of humanity. Pannenberg sees the function of the church in the world to be a witness to the temporality of all human institutions prior to the coming of the kingdom of God. As it gives expression to fellowship among humans and between them and God, especially in the Eucharist, the church becomes the sign of God's eschatological kingdom,[11] which is the hope of the world. Theology is in part a servant to this task.

Loss of † voice in Society.

Theology and Truth

Despite this broad intention lying behind Pannenberg's work, its central importance lies in his understanding of the nature of theology itself and of the truth to which theology is related. Simply stated, he is attempting to change the course of contemporary theology, to combat what he perceives to be a widespread privatization of religious belief in general and of theology in particular.

We must put this quest in the context of Pannenberg's assessment of the trajectory of modern theology. In 1975 he indicated his perception of the failure of theology in an autobiographical remark given to a group of students in Denver: "Perhaps if you have heard anything about my work, you have learned that I am accused of being a rationalist by some people. Others call me a fundamentalist. . . . But . . . there is one thing I am certainly not; I am certainly not a pietist."[12]

Underlying this remark is Pannenberg's conviction that in seeking to deal with the Enlightenment, the intellectual revolution that drastically altered the understanding of the basis of the Christian faith, the theology of the last two centuries has to its detriment turned to a pietistic emphasis on a decision of faith.[13] Prior to the Enlightenment the salvation-historical events, which were seen as providing the foundation for faith, were accepted on the basis of what was claimed to be the authoritative witness of God, mediated either by the teaching office of the church (the Roman Catholic view) or by the Bible as the product of the divine inspiration of the prophets and apostles (the Reformation position). In keeping with this the Reformers posited a connection between three aspects of faith—*notitia* (knowledge), *assensus* (assent) and *fiducia* (trust).

In the Enlightenment, however, the understanding of an authoritative testimony to historical knowledge, taught by Augustine and Luther, was replaced by science and a newer historical methodology that sought to reconstruct past events by employing scientific and critical tools. As a result, the historicity of events became uncertain, and the historical basis for faith was called into question. Thus, in the post-Enlightenment world, humanity lives without revelation, understood in the sense of a word from beyond history by means of which reality can be viewed through the eyes of God.

To avoid making faith uncertain and dependent on historical research, post-Enlightenment theology moved the foundation for faith away from historical events to the experience of conversion, which is seen as providing its own certainty. In other words, a shift has been made from the older view, which began with a rational appeal to historical fact, to the modern approach, which moves from the subjective experience of the believer.

This modern position has given birth to two distinct yet equally erroneous alternatives. Some theologians dismiss the historical content of the Christian tradition as irrelevant. This is the position of the radical pietists, in whose ranks Pannenberg includes Rudolf Bultmann. Others follow the path of what he terms "conservative pietism," in which the plausibility of the historical aspects of the faith is grounded in the experience of faith. Thus, for example, personal conversion is made the basis for the certainty of the events of Jesus' history, such as his miracles and the resurrection.

At the heart of Pannenberg's alternative to this development is Luther's thesis that by nature faith cannot be derived from itself, but only beyond itself in Christ.[14] From this Pannenberg concludes that faith is dependent on a historical basis. Specifically, the historical revelation of God must form the foundation for the act of trust, if faith is to be trust in God and not in itself. He admits that the revelation that grounds faith remains contestable in this world. But he nevertheless adamantly declares that only the field of argument, and not a nonrational decision of faith, can meet the philosophical and historical challenge to the Christian claim to knowledge of God.

According to Pannenberg, then, theology is necessary because actual truth must underlay faith, if faith is to be valid.[15] His theology, in turn, is an attempt to place Christian faith on firm intellectual footing once again, and thereby to provide an alternative to the subjectivist approach of much modern theology.

In one sense Pannenberg's understanding of theology follows the classical model. As in the older view, he sees theology as a public discipline related to the quest for universal truth. For him the truth question is to be answered in the process of theological reflection and reconstruction. He criticizes any attempt to divide truth into autonomous spheres or to shield the truth content of the Christian tradition from rational inquiry. Theological affirmations must be subjected to the rigor of critical inquiry concerning the historical reality on which they are based. Theology, in other words, must be evaluated on the basis of critical canons, just as the other sciences, for it also deals with truth. And the truth of the Christian faith must be measured according to the coherence criterion,[16] that is, insofar as it fits together with—even illumines—all human knowledge.[17]

At one crucial point, however, Pannenberg's understanding of theology moves beyond the classical tradition. He declares that truth is not found in the unchanging essences lying behind the flow of time, but is essentially historical and ultimately eschatological.[18] Until the eschaton, truth will by its own nature always remain partial and truth claims debatable. Therefore, theology, like all human knowledge, is provisional. It simply cannot pack into formulas the truth of God. The future alone is the focal point of ultimate truth. As a result, one must treat all dogmatic statements as hypotheses to be tested by means of their coherence with other knowledge. This, he claims, is in accordance with the Scriptures, which declare that only at the end of history is the deity of God unquestionably open to all.[19]

Reason and Hope

Pannenberg's understanding of the nature of the theological task gives rise to a theology oriented toward two intertwined focal points—reason and hope.[20] The significance of the term *reason* is obvious from what has already been noted—theology is a rational undertaking. The term *hope* capsulizes the thoroughgoing eschatological orientation of his program. Since his entire systematic theology focuses on the eschaton we may characterize it as a theology of hope. Foundational to the whole of Pannenberg's theology is the concept of the kingdom of God understood as the glory of the Trinity demonstrated in God's rulership over creation.

Pannenberg does not follow nineteenth-century theology in understanding the kingdom in terms of an ethical community. Rather, his view accords with the exegetical discoveries of the twentieth century, which find the source of this term in the apocalyptic movement and the teaching of Jesus.[21] The biblical message of the kingdom is thoroughly eschatological in orientation, for it proclaims the final lordship of God over creation, which has already broken into history in the appearance of Jesus. Enroute to the eschaton, the Christian community lives in hopeful expectation of the final consummation of the lordship of God over the entire world. Only then will the glory and reality of the triune God be fully demonstrated.

The theme of hope, however, leads back again to the rational dimension of Pannenberg's theological enterprise, with which it is intertwined. As a public discipline, theology's purpose is that of giving a "rational account of the truth of faith."[22] This orientation to "rational accounting" is foundational to the mandate of the church itself, as he understands it. As a people of hope whose eyes are directed to the eschatological consummation in the kingdom of God, the Christian community dares not retreat into a privatized ghetto of individual or familial piety. Rather, it is called to remain in the world, where the struggle for truth occurs, and there to engage in the theological task. Because the theological task is linked with the quest for ultimate truth—the truth of God—theology is a public and rational endeavor.

Systematic Theology and the Doctrine of God

Following the classical tradition, Pannenberg asserts that the whole of systematic theology is essentially the doctrine of God. In fact, God is the all-inclusive object of theology.[23] Even though Christian dogmatics moves beyond the doctrine of God to include anthropology, ecclesiology and so forth, these belong to that one overarching topic.

The starting point from which we can talk about God is the commonly held "semantic minimum" concerning "God," which views God in terms of power. God is "the power on which all finite reality depends"[24] or "the power that determines everything." From this basic premise, however, Pannenberg draws a far-reaching assertion: The deity of God is connected to the demonstration of God's lordship over creation.[25]

This thesis implies that the idea of God, if it corresponds to an actual reality, must be able to illumine not only human existence but also our experience of the world as a whole. In his words, "It must be made plausible that all finite reality depends on him, not only human beings and the course of their history, but also the world of nature." This can be done, Pannenberg adds, only by presenting "a coherent model of the world as God's creation."[26] This is why he believes that the overarching task of systematic theology is to show the illuminating power of the Christian conception of God.

In addition, however, the thesis that God's deity is connected to his lordship over creation means that only the final salvation of God's creatures can ultimately demonstrate the assertion of God's existence. This realization, of course, serves to shift the emphasis of theology to history and eschatology. "It is only in the event of final salvation," Pannenberg argues, "that the reality of God will be definitively established." Consequently, the entire process of history climaxing in the consummation constitutes "a self-demonstration of God's existence."[27] Systematic theology is an explication of this self-demonstration.

The Starting Point for Theology

In keeping with his thesis of the current debatable nature of the assertion of God's existence,[28] Pannenberg argues that theology cannot merely launch into the doctrine of God, but must win its starting point. To accomplish this, he builds on an anthropological observation that in turn provides a link between philosophical and revealed theology, namely, that humans are in a certain sense naturally religious.[29] By this he means that the structure of the individual human person and of corporate human life is pervaded by a religious component. In theological terms, the destiny of humanity is existence in the image of God, a destiny visible in human "openness to the world."[30] This understanding of humanity's basic religious nature builds from the early Schleiermacher and a reinterpretation of Descartes' concept of the infinite. Its background, however, lies earlier, in the medieval discussions of what is first, albeit dimly, known to the human mind. Pannenberg finds this question illumined by means of two contemporary concepts. The first is "exocentricism," the thesis that each human must ground personal identity outside oneself, Although this concept has been disseminated by twentieth-century philosophical anthropology, Pannenberg finds its foundation in Luther's understanding of faith. The other concept is Erik Erikson's well-known idea of "basic trust."

Religious awareness, Pannenberg explains, arises out of the rudimentary consciousness of the difference between "I" and "world" found already in the act of trust, which is then augmented by one's presence in the family. As a person experiences finitude and temporality in everyday life, an intuition of the infinite develops. To this, however, Pannenberg adds an innovative thesis. The intuition of the infinite does not itself comprise explicit knowledge of God. Rather, such knowledge is mediated by religious traditions. This subsequent knowledge allows the individual to reflect on the earlier immediate experiences and to conclude that therein lay an "unthematicized knowledge" of God. In other words, that this basic intuition of the infinite relates to the theme of God is a conclusion drawn only by reflection on the process of religious history.

In this way Pannenberg connects this basic religious phenomenon to the experience of God found in the religions, which come to an awareness of the activity and essence of God through the works of creation. This connection, in turn, opens the way for him to view the rivalry of the religions as the location of the revelation of truth.[31]

With Barth, Pannenberg asserts that revelation occurs only as God gives himself to be known. But he argues that the focal point of this revelation is the historical process. For Pannenberg this history is the history of religions. On the world historical stage conflicting truth claims, which are at their core religious and are ultimately attempts to express the unity of the world, are struggling for supremacy. The religious orientation that best illumines the experience of all reality will in the end prevail and thereby demonstrate its truth value.

In this context, Pannenberg finds significance in the religious history of Israel. In Israel came the breakthrough to monotheism, which allowed for an understanding of the world as a unity, and the breakthrough to the future orientation of God's activity in history. These discoveries formed the context for the message of Jesus, which Pannenberg declares to be the focus of the revelation of the nature of the eternal God. Jesus is the prolepsis—the historical preview—of God's self-disclosure, which ultimately lies at the end of history. For this reason, Pannenberg develops out of the life of Jesus the Christian doctrine of God.[32]

The Christian Conception of God: The Triune One

At the heart of Pannenberg's theology is the doctrine of God. And at the heart of the Christian conception of God, he argues, is the doctrine of the Trinity.[33] It comes as no surprise, therefore, that God as the Triune One forms the center of Pannenberg's systematic theology.

In contrast to theological practice since the Middle Ages, Pannenberg's systematic theology moves from the concept of revelation immediately to an explication of the doctrine of the Trinity and only then to the delineation of God's unity and attributes.[34] The traditional attempt to derive the plurality of the trinitarian persons from a concept of God as one being, he asserts, can only lead to problems, because in such approaches God remains a single subject, rather than the three persons.

In moving away from the older methodology, Pannenberg's doctrine of God offers an intriguing proposal for the contemporary question of the link between the immanent Trinity (God's eternal essence) and the economic Trinity (God as active in salvation history).[35] The link he forges arises from the foundational thesis that all systematic theology is but the explication of what is implicit in God's own self-disclosure. Consequently, he seeks to ground the doctrine of the Trinity on revelation, that is, on the economy of salvation—on the way that the Father, Son and Spirit appear in the event of revelation—as is presented in the life and message of Jesus. Only then does he move to the discussion of the unity of God found in the divine attributes. In this way Pannenberg grounds the doctrine of God in the divine economy, and as a result the understanding of the immanent Trinity flows from the economic Trinity.

Crucial to Pannenberg's development of this doctrine is his concept of self-differentiation.[36] The essence of person, he argues, is to give oneself to the counterpart; hence, the concept of person includes the idea of dependency. All three Trinitarian persons are mutually dependent on the others, he asserts.

In this way Pannenberg offers an alternative to the subordination of the Son and the Spirit to the Father that he finds so detrimental to traditional theology. He brings this mutual dependency into the process of salvation history and emphasizes the eschatological completion of the divine program in the world as the focal point for the revelation of the unity of the divine being. The unthematicized infinite comes to be named by the purposeful activity of the three trinitarian persons in the world.

Transcendence and Immanence

Whereas in the earlier stages of his career Pannenberg was noted for his attention to Christology, when he set himself to the task of delineating his full systematic theology the importance of pneumatology or the doctrine of the Spirit became increasingly evident. In fact, central to Pannenberg's entire dogmatics is his attempt to develop a new pneumatology. The tendency in theology is to reduce the role of the Spirit to that of offering an explanation in situations in which all rational suggestions fail; he intends to replace this with a much broader and more biblical doctrine of the Spirit. But in so doing, he develops as well the key to and understanding of the divine transcendence and immanence.

Crucial to his pneumatology is Pannenberg's understanding of spirit as "field," a conception related to but not to be equated with the field theory introduced in nineteenth-century science.[37] Actually, the roots of the idea lie much earlier—in the ancient Stoic philosophers who developed a doctrine of a physical *pneuma* (spirit). However, the theologians of the patristic era rejected this idea in favor of the conception of God as spiritual mind.

This new pneumatology of field is central to Pannenberg's doctrine of God.[38] In agreement with the atheistic criticism of Feuerbach and others, he rejects as a mere projection the classical understanding of God as reason and will (that is, mind). The divine essence, Pannenberg maintains, may be better described in terms of the "incomprehensible field"—that is, dynamic spirit—which likewise comes forth as the third person of the Trinity, the Holy Spirit.

In addition to field/spirit as characterizing the divine life, Pannenberg sets forth a profound assertion of the Spirit's all-pervasive, creative presence in creation and in human life, climaxing in the new life of the believer and the church.[39] In this way the same concept that describes the divine essence functions as the principle of the relation of God to creation and as the principle of the participation of creation in the divine life.

Crucial here is the connection Pannenberg draws between the Christian assertion of the Spirit as the source of life in creation and the biological discovery that "life is essentially ecstatic."[40] Each organism lives in an environment that nurtures it. And each organism is oriented by its own drives beyond its immediate environment toward its future and the future of its species. This is the sense in which creatures participate in God through the Spirit, Pannenberg asserts. Hence, we can understand the Spirit as the environmental network or "field" in which and from which creatures live.

The Spirit is also the "force" that lifts creatures above their environment and orients them toward the future. This work of the Spirit ultimately leads to the self-transcendence that characterizes the human person and forms the basis for the special life beyond the self in Christ, found in the believing community of the church.

The concept of field also forms the foundation for Pannenberg's anthropology. The human person, he argues, is not to be seen in terms of an "I" that preexists experience of the world.[41] Rather, he has a more complicated understanding of the formation of personal identity. Important for identity development is the immediate perception of the totality of a person's existence,[42] which Pannenberg terms "feeling,"[43] or the "field" in which a person lives.

Because this totality of existence is an eschatological concept related to the meaning of reality that only arises when the flow of life is completed, Pannenberg views the biblical concept of the image of God as eschatological as well; it is realized at the end of human history, not at the beginning. He likewise defines sin in terms of the idea of the building of personal identity. Sin is "self-love," the "I" as it fixates on its own finiteness, rather than finding its identity from fellowship with God, that is, via existence *extra se* in Christ.[44]   *outwardly focussed,*

Lying behind this understanding of God and the world is a specific theological interpretation of space and time that parallels the concept of the religious nature of humankind outlined earlier.[45] Pannenberg argues that it is impossible to imagine the parts of space and time without presupposing both space and time as undivided wholes that form the background or context for these parts. This intuition of infinite space points to the immensity and omnipresence of God, whereas the intuition of time as a whole points to God's eternity.[46]

God, then, is the "field" in which creation and history exist. In Pannenberg's words, "the presence of God's Spirit in his creation can be described as a field of creative presence, a comprehensive field of force that releases event after event into finite existence."[47]

As the comprehensive field, God is both immanent in the world and also transcendent over it. His immanence is obvious. All creation and all events live from their environment, which is the divine field, the source of life. And the immanent Spirit is what animates creatures in raising them beyond themselves to participate in some measure in the divine life. Yet in the process of life God is not only immanent; he also remains always transcendent. God is more than the chain of the finite parts of time and space. And the divine life is more than the sum of the lives of finite creatures.

Above all, however, transcendence arises from the future orientation inherent in the relation between God and the world. As Spirit, God functions as the whole that provides meaning to the finite events of history. This meaning is profoundly future, for only at the end of history do we find the meaning of history and the connection of each event with that meaning. The end, then, transcends each moment, as that glorious reality toward which all history is moving. In this way time and eternity are interrelated, for, Pannenberg writes, "it is through the future that eternity enters into time."[48]

Jesus and the Son

The doctrine of the Trinity lies at the heart of Pannenberg's systematic theology. It remains, however, to round out the picture by indicating the main themes of Pannenberg's doctrine of Christ. For in Jesus, eternity—the future—has entered profoundly into time.

Issues of Christology have always been of central concern to Pannenberg. In fact, the first of his works translated into English was the monograph *Jesus—God and Man*.[49] This book contains his controversial delineation of the centrality of the resurrection for Jesus' history and his important emphasis on the historicity of this event. Here Pannenberg argues that the resurrection of Jesus is God's confirmation of the appearance and mission of Jesus, for through this event Jesus experienced in the midst of history that eschatological transformation to which humanity is destined.

As a monograph, the earlier work presupposed the reality of God and unfolded solely in terms of a Christology "from below." However, Pannenberg admits that such an approach is incomplete when Christology is pursued within the context of systematic theology. Such a discussion must occur in the context of a specifically Christian anthropology, undertaken with an awareness of the doctrine of God.

To accomplish this in his systematic treatment, Pannenberg reintroduces the classical theological concept of *Logos* understood as the principle of the unity of the world. But to this traditional idea he adds an interesting twist. The *Logos* represents the order of the world as history. Consequently, Jesus is the *Logos,* not as some cosmic abstract principle, but in his human life as Israel's Messiah and as the one who brings to light the proper relationship of the creature to the Creator.

Foundational to Pannenberg's proposal is the assertion that we do not view the connection between Jesus and God directly in terms of the unity of the preexistent *Logos* with humanity, but rather indirectly, via Jesus' relationship to the Father as unfolded in Jesus' own history.[50] As the one who was obedient to the Father to the point of death, Jesus is the eternal Son, the *Logos,* for the attitude that humbly differentiates oneself from God and places oneself in the service of God is the way to participation in life.

As the one who was obedient to his divinely given mission to the point of death, Jesus is God's reconciliation. He acted as our substitute in that he shared our situation (death) and thereby altered it. Pannenberg calls this view "inclusive substitution." Through faith we can participate in the new life brought by Christ. In our voluntary subordination to God we enjoy communion with God and will participate in God's eternal life beyond our own finitude and death.[51]

Pannenberg and His Critics

The program that Wolfhart Pannenberg undertook is perhaps the most ambitious attempt since Barth to set forth a complete systematic-theological delineation of Christian doctrine. Not only does he systematize the teaching of the church, he seeks to outline an approach for Christian engagement with the philosophical underpinnings of contemporary society's movement away from its religious roots. In this bold undertaking Pannenberg has refused to be dissuaded by the many voices today who reject the mere idea of attempting a truly systematic theology in the contemporary context and by those who have sought to shift the focus of the theological task in other, less ambitious directions.

As a result Pannenberg's work has been rigorously criticized and at times dismissed *in toto* as no longer relevant. However, when viewed from the prospective of theological history as a whole, he emerges as a modern heir to the classical understanding of theology viewed in terms of the reasonable demonstration of the Christian truth claim and the Christian conception of God. Whatever problems are present in his proposal, Pannenberg ought not to be faulted for attempting to "do" theology. Rather, critical discussion with his proposal must focus on questions concerning the correctness and adequacy of his theological method.

Revelation and the Bible

Pannenberg offers an important contemporary restatement of the traditional attempt to ground theology on revelation. Although not minimizing other focal points of revelation, classical Protestant theology emphasizes the Bible as the deposit of divine revelation. Pannenberg diverges from this traditional approach.[52] He does not adhere to the older Protestant doctrine of verbal inspiration,[53] but bases his understanding of the nature of Scripture in the relation of the history of religions to revelation. For him the history of religions is the location of a dispute among rival religious truth claims. In this history the religion of Israel leading to the advent of Christianity is crucial because of the insights developed through this process. The Bible is the sourcebook for this tradition, and thereby it retains a central importance for theology, even in the post-Enlightenment situation.

Pannenberg's criticism of the older Protestant doctrine of inspiration must be taken seriously. In the contemporary world simple appeal to the Bible as an unquestioned authority is no longer possible. Pannenberg rightly points out that in the present context the doctrine of Scripture can no longer simply be set forth at the beginning of theological reflection. Therefore, his suggestion that the authority of the Bible is to be the goal rather than the presupposition of theology stands as a valid challenge to the classical Protestant approach.

Nevertheless, agreement with his perception of the contemporary loss of biblical authority does not require agreement with his appraisal that modern textual criticism destroys the doctrine of inspiration. Nor for that reason can we simply set aside Scripture, as even Pannenberg implicitly acknowledges. Pannenberg's doctrine of reconciliation contains a promising basis for a renewed doctrine of Scripture in the thesis that the apostolic proclamation became the vehicle for the ongoing speaking of the risen Lord. Unfortunately the German theologian has not made the step from this idea to a full-orbed doctrine of Scripture.

Revelation and the Spirit

Pannenberg's emphasis on the historical nature of revelation leads to the related question as to how the observer comes to see this revelation, that is, to the question of the role of the Spirit in illuminating history. He sees himself as attempting to develop an understanding of the unity of revelation in the face of the bifurcation of the concept. For this reason, Pannenberg tolerates no suggestion that some additional inspired word or some supernatural working of the Spirit must be added to events; meaning arises out of the events themselves.[54]

Although he does not mean to suggest that the Spirit has no role in the process of faith, at times Pannenberg appears to minimize the role of the Holy Spirit in the epistemological process of grasping the revelation of God in history. The question therefore remains. How is it that some respond positively to the hearing of the report, whereas others reject the message?

Whatever that answer may be, Pannenberg refuses to ground the solution to the problem of faith and unbelief in the mystery of the action of the Spirit, an approach often found in traditional theology. Why a person comes to faith or remains in unbelief resides in the mystery of human personhood, which he sees as a gift of God.

In his systematic theology Pannenberg comes to a more profound understanding of this dynamic than is found in his earlier works. Here he acknowledges the brokenness of the knowledge of revelation in the era before the consummation, with the result that the apostolic proclamation is of utmost significance for the understanding of revelation in history. This marks a helpful development in his thought. While he continues to maintain that no inspired word must be added to events, the acknowledgment of the brokenness of knowledge opens the way for an affirmation of the mysterious aspect in the epistemological process in this era of the contestability of truth claims.

Reason and Piety

The orientation to the future characteristic of Pannenberg's thought and its attendant revision in ontology could appear to call into question certain aspects of traditional Christian piety. His theology seems to lay no foundation for the traditional emphasis on God's presence as an existing being in the here and now and for talk of current events as in some sense divinely preordained before the world was created.

More problematic than the lack of these themes in his theology, however, is Pannenberg's apparent thoroughgoing rationalism and hard-nosed rejection of any attempt to base theological conclusions on a faith-decision that has not been through the fire of rational reflection and challenged by alternative viewpoints. Before drawing any conclusions concerning this dimension of his theology, however, we must place his perceived bent toward rationalism in the context of Pannenberg's understanding of himself as a theologian called to serve the church in the setting of the public marketplace of ideas.

Pannenberg's intent is to articulate a solid intellectual foundation for Christian faith in an age in which any religious commitment is often prematurely rejected as unreasonable or even irrational. In response to what he sees as a wrong turn made by theology at the post-Enlightenment fork in the road, Pannenberg is seeking to return to a balanced understanding of the role of reason in establishing faith. He readily admits that in the present truth claims can be only provisional; consequently, the quest for truth must orient itself to the eschaton, when truth in its fullness will emerge. Although prior to the eschaton only a provisional, controversial answer can be made to the question of life's meaning, people of faith can obtain a greater degree of certainty than is often admitted. They have good reasons to affirm their faith, which need not be based on an irrational decision.

Although he admits that humans do not live only on the basis of reason and cautions against thinking that through rational arguments people will be brought to faith, Pannenberg points out that if the reasonableness of Christianity is not indicated, the step to faith is made difficult. In the midst of irrational barriers, he sets himself to the task of changing the climate that presupposes that Christianity fails the test of reason.

At the same time, Pannenberg is also convinced that in the public testing of ideas, a rational delineation of the Christian faith, more so than personal piety, is the chief weapon of the church. Despite the fundamental correctness of his intent, he has overstated the case. As important as the rational discussion may be, the piety of conscious Christians also provides an important apologetic for the truth of the faith.

In spite of this cautionary word, we must admit that Pannenberg's emphasis on the illuminating power of the idea of God for our experience of the world as a whole challenges those who would reduce the faith to the private world of personal piety. The German theologian invites us to see that Christian theology ought to have an impact on all dimensions of life and the entire range of disciplines connected with the pursuit of faith.

Eschatological Ontology

Central to Pannenberg's theological vision is his eschatological ontology and the corollary understanding of God as Spirit. The German theologian identifies God, the all-determining reality, with the divine field that works upon the world from the future. Like Moltmann, he has attempted to reconceive transcendence and immanence in temporal rather than spatial terms. God's transcendence is his futurity and wholeness, and in this ontology, the future has power over every present, not only defining it but also determining it in its depth. These ideas, however, have raised a storm of criticism.

One area of criticism concerns the ethical vision that Pannenberg's eschatological ontology undergirds. In contrast to Moltmann, who stood at the headwaters of the political theology movement, the Munich thinker has been an unrelenting opponent of left-wing political theologies, especially of liberation theology. Critics, however, wonder why he cannot recognize the natural affinity between his theology and those who call for political revolution in the name of justice.[55]

Another area of criticism focuses on the issue of reverse causality. Pannenberg has been repeatedly criticized because his eschatological ontology appears to be deterministic.[56] Although the German theologian has sought to respond to the charge of determinism, it and other questions simply have not gone away: Can the future, which is in some sense truly open, have an effect on the present? Is retroactive causality conceivable? Does the temporal category of futurity actually solve the problems of divine transcendence that plagued the traditional spatial imagery?

Pannenberg's ontology also raises the question of God's personhood. Does the imagery of God as the divine field working upon the world from the future allow us to conceive of God as truly personal? Does the language of "field," coupled with Pannenberg's aversion to traditional notions of God as mind and will, imply an impersonal or suprapersonal God, a God who is the whole that is greater than the sum of the world's parts but not a gracious, completely free and self-sufficient divine person?

Critics who raise questions such as these await the full development of Pannenberg's theology for clearer answers. No doubt in the future he will address these concerns. In the meantime, however, many readers continue to have reservations about Pannenberg's commitment to God's personhood and freedom over the world, as well as about the cogency of his highly creative ontology of the future.

Conclusion

Despite the reservations stated here, Pannenberg must be lauded as providing an alternative both to the dominant existentialist bent characteristic of German theology throughout much of the twentieth century with its emphasis on an existentialist transcendence and to the resurgence of immanental theology found in much of American theological thinking. He offers a quite different proposal, focusing attention again on the classical quest for ultimate truth in the midst of the contemporary, post-Enlightenment situation.

Following the theology of hope, Pannenberg reintroduces the concept of the divine transcendence—and this in the mode of the future as standing over against the present. Yet he tempers the radical transcendence delineated in Moltmann's early writings and the radical immanence that developed in Moltmann's later writings. For Pannenberg, God's transcendence does not so much contradict the present as bring it to completion, and God's immanence through the divine Spirit does not so much imprison him as give opportunity for his love freely to increase the bountiful unity of creation. More so than Moltmann, Pannenberg has been able to link salvation with creation, thereby developing a creative understanding of the relation of the world to its transcendent/immanent Source.

7 THE RENEWAL OF IMMANENCE IN THE EXPERIENCE OF OPPRESSION: *Liberation Theologies*

*T*HE 1960S WERE A TURBULENT AND RADICAL ERA. MANY NEW THEOLOGIES WERE BORN, vied for attention and died out. But none achieved dominance, even though several have enjoyed lasting significance. As the decade began drawing to a close, its radical tendencies were channeled in a direction quite different from what had predominated since the advent of the death-of-God movement, that radical fad with which the preceding ten years had begun.

The newer radicals had grown tired of the attempts of the 1960s to deal with the intellectual challenge of atheism. Instead they were concerned about the challenge posed by the various examples of social and economic oppression experienced by peoples in the present. In fact, many of these voices were highly critical of all previously articulated modern theology, claiming that theologians had contented themselves with focusing only on the first phase of the Enlightenment critique of Christianity, the intellectual challenge of atheism. The time had come, they asserted, to move on to the second phase of the Enlightenment, the challenge to the socioeconomic status quo posed by thinkers like Karl Marx.

The post-1960s radicals issued a far-reaching call to the theological discipline. Theology had long enough afforded itself the luxury of withdrawing into its "ivory tower" to debate the intellectual arguments for the existence of God in the face of the atheist critique, they claimed. The time had come for theology to join forces with the oppressed and down-trodden in society and engage in a struggle with them and on their behalf. Only in this way could theologians discover the reality of God.

The varied attempts to respond to contemporary experiences of oppression—which for the new radicals formed a deeper critique of the Christian faith than did intellectual atheism—all appealed to the theme of liberation. If God is real, then this God must be involved in the struggles of the present to bring about liberation from oppression. And if Christianity is true, then its message must be one of liberation. Because of this common theme of liberation from oppression, the various strands of the new radicalism are generally united under what has come to be known by the broader category of "liberation theology."

Several strands of liberation theology found their beginning point in the critique of the intellectualism characteristic of both traditional and modern North Atlantic theology. Of these, three stand out as typical and as most significant for the story of twentieth-century theology: Black theology, Latin American liberation theology and feminist theology.

In a sense all three attempted to offer an antidote to what the new radicals perceived to be a shift toward a one-sided emphasis on divine transcendence in much contemporary theology, including the thought of persons such as Moltmann and Pannenberg. Rather than waiting to find the Transcendent One—the "power of the future"—in the final consummation of history, they looked for the Immanent One—the "power of liberation"—in the present circumstances of life. In seeking this counterbalance, however, they moved the pendulum too far in the opposite direction of the divine immanence, thereby failing to create the biblical balance between God as transcendent and as immanent.

BLACK LIBERATION THEOLOGY:
IMMANENCE IN THE BLACK EXPERIENCE

Persons of African descent living in the United States enjoy a rich religious heritage. Their experience, born as it was out of the era of slavery and the social and economic oppression that followed, gave rise to a unique religious tradition that included expression through the medium of "Negro spirituals."[1] The traditional Black religious outlook included several abiding themes: the equality of all persons (or the impartiality of God),[2] the justice of and therefore the ultimate triumph of the cause of the Black community and the present experience of frustration.[3]

The civil rights movement of the 1960s sparked a revival of interest in and gave an intensification of meaning to the religious themes that had characterized the history of Blacks in America.[4] This movement instilled a new self-consciousness among them, which in turn called for the development of a view of the gospel specifically for their situation, one that was in harmony with the new consciousness of Black identity. The response of Black theologians to this need came in the form of "Black theology."

Although it participated in the ethos of the era, the Black theology voiced in the 1960s and 1970s differed from the various radical theologies that mushroomed and died away in this turbulent time. Like they, Black theology was in part born out of a renaissance of interest in Dietrich Bonhoeffer.[5] But unlike the radical theology of the academic theologians that looked to Bonhoeffer for its inspiration, Black theology was not concerned with the intellectual problems of secularized culture; its concern lay instead with the realities of the experience of Blacks in America. As a result, Black theologians did not debate the question as to how the idea of God could be made palatable to the modern mindset, for this was not an issue among their people. They sought rather to harness the biblical imagery for the goal of the advancement of the Black community.

While differing with other radical movements, on another level Black theology shared one point of similarity with them. It too struggled with the central problem confronting all theologians in the 1960s, how the idea of God could remain a valid and powerful symbol in the contemporary world. Whereas the radical theologians debated the intellectual relevance of God, Black thinkers struggled with the relevance of the Christian conception of God for a people who were oppressed, often by persons who claimed to be Christian. For this reason, Black theology is generally classified among the theologies of liberation.

Black Theology and Liberation Theologians
In 1969 a group of Black church leaders set out a concise description of the new theology. Their description indicates the orientation to contextualization characteristic of all liberation theologies:

> Black Theology is a theology of black liberation. It seeks to plumb the black condition in the light of God's revelation in Jesus Christ, so that the black community can see that the gospel is commensurate with the achievement of black humanity. Black Theology is a theology of "blackness." It is the affirmation of black humanity that emancipates black people from white racism, thus providing authentic freedom for both white and black people. It affirms the humanity of white people in that it says No to the encroachment of white oppression.[6]

As this description indicates, the classification of Black theology as a type of liberation theology is appropriate. Like all such theologies, it focuses on activity, not on contemplation. It desires to change the world, not merely to reflect on the nature of reality. Hence, Black theology employed at least implicitly the methodology explicitly developed by other liberation theologies, namely, the view of theology as primarily the critical reflection on "praxis," as reflection on action in the struggle for liberation.

Black thinkers in the United States carried out their initial work in isolation from and without awareness of similar currents in the Third World.[7] As a result, one major theological difference—that of background and sources—set Black theology at its inception apart from the theological currents that arose among oppressed peoples elsewhere. Many of the Latin Americans were Roman Catholic thinkers trained in Europe. Their teachers included some of the leading European exponents of the rising theology of hope and the political theology movement. As a result, at its inception Latin American liberation theology was a Roman Catholic phenomenon and constituted in part a response to European thinking.

Black theology, in contrast, has been a North American, Protestant phenomenon. Its leaders were trained in North American Protestant seminaries. Their writings reflected their engagement with the liberalism or neo-orthodoxy of their teachers. It is not surprising, therefore, that Black theologians have never seen their task as including the construction of a response to the theology of hope to the extent characteristic of Latin American liberation theologians.[8] Black thinkers have written with an awareness of newer German theological currents (especially of Moltmann and Metz). But Black thinkers found them less helpful in developing a language for Black theology than they originally expected, in part because of what James Cone termed the European "tendency toward theological abstractions."[9]

Rise and Development

Black theology arose out of a specific historical context—the 1960s—and therefore must be understood within that context. The decade of the 1960s was marked by several far-reaching events for Black people in the United States. It witnessed the activities of Martin Luther King, Jr., who more than any other leader came to personify the civil rights movement. He remained the undisputed spokesman for the Black religious community in its social aspirations until his untimely assassination in 1968. The air was filled with more radical voices as well, including that of Malcolm X, whose autobiography enunciated the call for Black power.

By mid-decade, the rising Black consciousness had begun to produce broadsides, consensus statements and even book-length treatments concerning the Black religious experience. On the basis of this literary output, Wilmore and Cone suggest that Black theology developed in three stages.[10] The first developmental stage (1966-1970) signaled the end of the subordination of the Black churches to White Protestantism. During these years, Black theology emerged out of the civil rights and Black Power movements, as Black clergy debated issues such as integration, love and the use of violence with their White colleagues.[11] This period, therefore, was characterized by a distrust between White and Black religious leaders.

In the second stage, the focus shifted away from the Black church and toward academic institutions, as professional theologians entered the foray.[12] Black thinkers set themselves to the task of defining Black theology and engaged in a lively debate with White academicians concerning the validity and goals of Black theology. The crucial points at issue among Black proponents at this stage included the relationship between liberation and reconciliation and the question of theodicy and suffering.[13]

Several factors gave impetus for the transition to the third stage, which began around 1977.[14] A resurgence of conservatism was sweeping the nation. Some Black theologians were coming to perceive that their internal debates were academically sterile. And Black thinkers were beginning to encounter other liberation movements.

At issue in this period has been the relationship of the Black American experience to that of other oppressed groups and the economic and political implications of liberation. This stage has also been marked by a decisive return to an emphasis on the importance of the Black church and on cooperation among Black denominations.[15] In keeping with this new mood, Black theologians have once again focused on the task of serving the church through the training of future leaders, seminars for church people and writings for the church audience.[16]

An Early Voice

One important early treatise that paved the way for the rise of Black theology was the study by Joseph R. Washington, Jr., *Black Religion: The Negro and Christianity in the United States* (1964). Washington offered an unflattering sketch of the history and current situation of Black religion in America. Rejecting the thesis of earlier studies that viewed Black religion as one aspect of the broader category of North American Protestantism, Washington asserted that it was actually a distinctive phenomenon in North American religious life.[17] But he viewed that distinction negatively. Washington claimed that the socioeconomic disinheritance of Blacks took a tragic toll even in the religious dimension of their lives, for Black religious communities had been turned into "a status symbol of racial-class identity."[18]

Washington advocated a radical move on the part of the Black church in the face of its theological poverty and because it had outlived its usefulness as a community center, a usefulness based on the older segregation model.[19] As a step toward "assimilation beyond integration," the "pattern of authentic acceptance"[20] that formed the only hope for the future, he challenged Black congregations to "go out of business" and Black Christians to enter the White congregations *en masse*.[21] Only by voluntarily giving up their segregated worship life and demanding assimilation in the Christian community, Washington argued, could the material gains Blacks were attaining "be matched by spiritual growth."[22]

Growing Militancy

The optimism toward the possibility of assimilation proclaimed by Washington was soon dispelled. As the decade wore on, the Black quest for integration gave way to Black militarism and a growing attack on the White churches and their leaders.[23] The new militarism affected the thinking of Black pastors and church executives. Pastors, who preached in the ghettos each Sunday, sought to understand the relevance of the gospel for Black liberation and thereby hammered out the first tenets of the new theology.[24]

One of the first theological statements of the new Black militancy was a book of sermons published in 1968 by Albert B. Cleage, Jr., pastor of the Shrine of the Black Madonna, a United Church of Christ congregation in Detroit. Cleage spoke as a Black man to Black people. He claimed that only a "resurrection of a Black Church with its own Black Messiah" could serve as the unifying center for Black people. He called on all Blacks to shake off their slave identification with the White oppressor and to sacrifice for the sake of the Black Nation, even if this meant leaving prestigious jobs in White-owned businesses.[25] To facilitate this call, Cleage applied biblical election imagery to the Black community. The Bible, he claimed, had been written by Black

Jews[26] but had been corrupted by Paul in his attempt to make the original message concerning a Black Messiah palatable to the heathen Europeans.[27] Cleage's goal was to move his congregation to take responsibility to change the world, rather than to choose the easier course of simply waiting "for the Son of man to come back in clouds of glory."[28] In Gayraud Wilmore's evaluation,

> Cleage may have gone too far, but no one made a greater contribution to the decolonization of the minds of Black Christians, and no institution has sought more seriously to demonstrate the implications of Black Theology for local congregations than his Shrine of the Black Madonna.[29]

Cleage's efforts were followed in 1969 by a phenomenal occurrence. Together with several colleagues, he had been instrumental in founding the Interreligious Foundation for Community Organization. In April of that year Detroit played host to an IFCO-sponsored conference on Black economic development. The attendees at this meeting formulated a document, the Black Manifesto, in which they demanded from White churches, synagogues and "all other racist institutions" reparations for the past mistreatment of the Black people. The minimum amount to be paid was five hundred million dollars, or "15 dollars per nigger."[30]

The statement itself would have created only a small stir had it not been for a most dramatic move on the part of one of its major architects, James Forman. On Sunday, May 4, 1969, the Black leader walked down the aisle of Riverside Church in New York City and hurled a series of demands at its minister and people. One month later, Wilmore offered this assessment:

> That dramatic confrontation with one of the historic symbols of White middle class Protestantism has precipitated perhaps the most serious crisis in the American religious establishment since the bitter polemics and antagonisms which divided it prior to the Civil War.[31]

The attack had been directed against mainstream Protestantism not only because of its traditional role as the custodian of public righteousness but also because of the perception among Black leaders that through its involvement in the civil rights movement the White religious establishment had stimulated a climate of unrealistic expectations on the part of the Black community.[32]

Despite professed sympathy for the economic plight of Blacks, the mainline churches did not respond in a tangible way to the manifesto. (An appeal to the World Council of Churches, however, was instrumental in the establishment of its controversial Program to Combat Racism.)[33] The attack on the White churches characteristic of the first stage of the development of Black theology continued into the 1970s, but its effectiveness clearly waned.[34]

As Black thinkers sought to provide a theology for the new Black self-consciousness, division within their ranks began to emerge.[35] At issue was the question of the purpose of Black theology. Was its goal the liberation of Blacks from White oppression or the reconciliation among the communities—between oppressed and oppressor? The discussion was not limited to thinkers of any single orientation, but included representatives of the entire theological spectrum, including Black evangelicals.[36]

The issue of theological purpose was related to a second purpose, that of the content of Black theology: Is it concerned solely about the specific Black experience in America or is its topic the universal history shared by all humans? This latter issue intensified during the second half of the decade of the 1970s. Black theologians sought to place themselves within the context of other liberation movements and to find lines of correspondence with liberation theologies articulated in other contexts, such as in Africa, Latin America and the struggles of feminists and Native Americans.[37]

James Cone

In the ferment of the 1960s and 1970s many voices began to speak to the issues surrounding the experiences of Black people in the United States. But perhaps the most widely-known and representative Black theologian is James H. Cone, Charles H. Briggs Professor of Systematic Theology at Union Theological Seminary, New York. Cone was able to emerge as an important voice for the new Black theology in part because he shared the plight of oppressed Blacks through his upbringing in the South. This qualified him to understand their feelings and to speak on their behalf. At the same time, his voice was significant because he had obtained the academic credentials necessary to gain a hearing in the largely White-dominated theological circles.[38]

Black Power and Black Theology

Cone's sketch of the systematic theology that could serve the needs of the emerging Black consciousness appeared in 1970 with the publication of *A Black Theology of Liberation*. However, the way was paved for it by his *Black Theology and Black Power*, published a year earlier. The author's goal in his earlier book was to bring together the aspirations of the Black Power movement with what he saw as the central message of Christianity—liberation—thereby setting forth in a preliminary way the agenda for Black theology.

Cone's polemic was directed primarily against the White church, of course. But at the same time, his insistence on the applicability of the Christian faith in the cause of liberation set him at odds with the more radical advocates of Black power who completely rejected Christianity as a religion solely of the White oppressor. In contrast to both groups, Cone claimed that Black power is not the antithesis of Christianity, but rather is "Christ's central message to twentieth-century America."[39]

In seeking to bring the two together, Cone defined both Black power and Black theology. His description of the former as the "complete emancipation of black people from white oppression by whatever means black people deem necessary"[40] left the door open for the use of violence in the task of Black liberation.[41] But the goal he charted for the movement was clearly not lawlessness. Cone also described Black power as "an *attitude,* an inward affirmation of the essential worth of blackness."[42] And he declared that the freedom for which Blacks were struggling "is not doing what I will but becoming what I should."[43]

With this goal in view, Cone set forth an understanding of Black theology. It is the analyzing of the Black condition in the light of God's revelation in Jesus, in order to create a sense of Black dignity and to provide in Black people the "soul" necessary to destroy White racism.[44]

Black theology, then, was clearly ethnocentric, that is, a theology for Blacks alone. As a result, Cone elevated the Black experience of oppression to the status of ultimate authority. Hence, he could forthrightly state, "Black Theology is not prepared to accept any doctrine . . . which contradicts the black demand for freedom now."[45] This meant that for Cone the fundamental form of sin is racism. Yet he did not mean racism in general, for Cone himself was avowedly racist in a certain sense, but specifically *White* racism with its oppressive tendencies. Further, Cone affirmed with Cleage that Christ is Black, and therefore the church must become Black with him.[46]

Despite the radical positions of the book, as he drew *Black Theology and Black Power* to a close, Cone backed away from a purely ethnocentric understanding of the gospel. He concluded that being Black was ultimately not a matter of skin color, but of the heart, soul and mind. Blackness entailed finding one's identity with oppressed Blacks, rather than with White oppressors.[47]

A Black Liberation Theology

A Black Theology of Liberation has been Cone's most influential and widely read treatise. This work deepened the meshing of Black aspirations toward liberation and the Christian faith begun in *Black Theology and Black Power*. The author's task was to set forth the liberating activity of God as the central motif for a presentation of theology. Theology is not simply the rational study of the being of God, Cone asserted, but the study of God's liberating activity in the world, so that the oppressed will "risk all for earthly freedom, a freedom made possible in the resurrection of Christ."[48]

To carry out the theological task, Cone explored how the key doctrines of classical Christianity appear under the rubric of Black theology. To provide the proper foundation for this description, however, Cone felt constrained to delve into the prior question of theological norm. In a lengthy discussion of this issue, he moved from Barth's thesis of the event character of revelation, but turned that thesis on its head. Cone asserted that "revelation is a black event, i.e., what black people are doing about their liberation."[49] From this understanding, he concluded that revelation was more than merely divine self-disclosure, being instead God's self-disclosure to humankind in a situation of liberation.[50] As a result, Cone, in a way somewhat reminiscent of Paul Tillich, set forth two focal points as the norm for Black theology. The task of theology, he declared, is to keep in constant tension the biblical and the modern communities of faith, in order thereby to speak meaningfully in the contemporary situation.[51]

Armed with this norm, Cone turned his attention to the central doctrines of the Christian faith. The book follows a basically Barthian structuring that begins with divine revelation and proceeds to explicate an understanding of God, humanity and Christ, before concluding with the church and eschatology.[52] Cone elevated as the core tenet of Black theology the biblical God who is related to the Black struggle for liberation.[53] This means that God is Black: God has joined in the oppressed condition and is known wherever people experience humiliation and suffering. The essence of the nature of God, therefore, is found in the concept of liberation.[54]

Cone's doctrine of God flowed into his anthropology. Just as he did not speak of a disengaged, universal God, so also he refused to view humanity in abstraction from the concrete experience of oppression and liberation. In keeping with his view of God as the one who engages in liberation, Cone rejected the classical and neo-orthodox understandings of the image of God (the image as rationality or as the divine-human encounter). Instead he declared that the divine image consists of humans involved in the liberation struggle against the structures of oppression.[55] And because God is Black, to be free as a human means likewise to be Black, to identify with the oppressed and to participate in human liberation.[56]

In outlining his Christology, Cone drew heavily on the New Testament documents, which he saw as presenting Jesus "as the Oppressed One whose earthly existence was bound up with the oppressed of the land."[57] On this basis Cone argued that Jesus is the Black Messiah and the revelation of God. For Cone, the concept of the Black Messiah expresses the concrete presence of Christ in the contemporary situation and the idea that the Black revolution is "God's kingdom becoming a reality in America."[58] Thus, he viewed salvation and the role of the church primarily in terms of liberation from injustice in this world, rather than merely in relationship to the hope of a better life in the next.

Revisions

Beginning with the publication of his two early works, Cone has provided leadership to the Black theological movement. His efforts since the explosive years of the late 1960s have been directed toward the correction of his earlier proposals, toward engagement in dialog with other liberation movements—Latin American, African, Asian and feminist—and toward chronicling the development of Black theology.

In the 1970s and 1980s Cone sought to revise his program in view of what he acknowledged as the most telling deficiency of his first two books. Critics claimed that his version of Black theology was defined by White concepts (specifically those of Barth), so that he had not actually utilized Black history and culture as the primary source in defining Black theology.[59] While admitting the validity of the criticism, Cone has continued to affirm the importance for the Black experience of certain Barthian emphases—the centrality of Christ in the gospel message, the primacy of the Bible as the source for knowlege of Jesus and God and the preaching of the Word of God[60]— as well as the neo-orthodox emphasis on truth as not being equated with words or propositions, but as encounter (albeit for Cone in social rather than individual existence).[61] Nor has Cone strayed from his understanding of the nature of Christian theology as "language about the *liberating* character of God's presence in Jesus Christ as he calls his people into being for freedom in the world."[62]

What has changed since 1970 is that Cone has sought to deepen his understanding of the Black experience as a foundational source, together with Scripture,[63] for the task of the Black theologian. Lying behind his fuller employment of the Black experience is Cone's acknowledgment (arising out of his acceptance of the thrust of the point made by his critics) that social matrix determines the form and content of one's theological vision.[64]

This deepened understanding and his interest in other liberation theologies have resulted in Cone's theology becoming increasingly directed toward the sociopolitical dimension of the gospel.[65] In fact, he faulted the earlier Black theology for failing to employ the tools of the social sciences in order to articulate a social and economic analysis of the deeply rooted sources of White racism. Since those early attempts, however, Cone and others have rejected their former appeal to "the morality of the oppressor" and their naive belief in the goodness of humankind, seeking to replace these ideas with a due recognition of the Christian doctrine of sin.[66]

Immanence and Transcendence

During the 1960s and 1970s Black theologians struggled with the question of the presence of God in an oppressive situation. As a result, Black theology came to be characterized by an emphasis on the immanence of God. James Cone described this traditional theological concept as meaning that "God always encounters us in a situation of historical liberation."[67]

At the same time, Black thinkers, not unlike the radical theologians before them, did not want simply to eliminate the concept of the divine transcendence. But they did find it necessary to reinterpret it. Cone, for example—like John A. T. Robinson before him—argued against any kind of spatial understanding of the term. Instead the Black thinker chose to link transcendence with the idea of a higher purpose. "Transcendence" refers to the purpose of humankind in the struggle for liberation "as defined by the infinite."[68] But apparently his Christian rootage would not allow him to settle for such a human-oriented definition. So Cone added a divine reference. Transcendence likewise means that the reality of the God who is involved in the struggle for liberation is not limited to any one particular human liberating experience.

Critique

Black theology played an important role in the development of a new self-consciousness and sense of identity for the Black church in the 1960s and 1970s. It formed a conscious attempt to relate the Christian gospel to the situation of the Black community in America. Despite these and other contributions, it was not without problems, however.

First, Black theology was problematic because it was ethnocentric. Prior to the 1960s theologians, regardless of their theological orientation, perceived their efforts and their discipline in terms of the engagement in the quest for truth on behalf of all humankind. Black theologians, in contrast, openly asserted that their task was properly limited to their own ethnic community. It was a theology by Blacks and for Blacks.

Second, Black theology elevated experience to the status of norm for theology. In this way, it merely reflected the methodology characteristic of the earlier liberalism, of course. But Black theology took this approach one step farther. Its norm was not universal human experience, but the specific experience of the Black community described in terms of oppression. As a result, Black theology became a massive reinterpretation program. The traditional Christian narrative of salvation and the theological categories traditionally used in its articulation (God, sin, salvation, and so forth) were cast in political-economic-social and specifically ethnic (that is, Black) terms, in contrast to the spiritual-cosmic and universally human die that beautified classical theology.

But the major flaw in Black theology, like that of other theologies born in the 1960s, was its failure to balance immanence and transcendence. Simply put, Black thinkers elevated the concept of the divine immanence to the overshadowing of the divine transcendence, resulting in a lopsided theology. The problem was not that Black theology had no concept of transcendence. Cone and others used the term. But they offered a substandard reinterpretation of it. Transcendence meant that God was not limited to a particular experience of liberation.

As theological trends since the heyday of Black theology—such as narrative theology and the new mysticism—with their quest for the transcendent have confirmed, a truncated understanding of transcendence, which arises whenever transcendence is overshadowed by immanence, is finally unsatisfying. Because of their inherent instability due to the loss of transcendence, theologies of liberation eventually give way to theologies of spirituality.

LATIN AMERICAN LIBERATION THEOLOGY: *IMMANENCE IN LIBERATION*

In 1968 the bishops of the Roman Catholic church in Latin America, gathering in the city of Medellín, Columbia, initiated a theological revolution. This was the second meeting of CELAM, the Latin American Episcopal Conference, often referred to as CELAM II or simply Medellín. The bishops shocked the world by condemning the church's traditional alliance with the ruling powers of Latin America and by describing the situation in that part of the world as "institutionalized violence" against the people.

CELAM II is often considered the true beginning of "liberation theology." According to one North American theologian of liberation, it "initiated a revolution in Latin American church life that will finally mean a revolution in Latin American history."[1] Then in 1971 a volume appeared that was destined to become the textbook of the new movement: *A Theology of Liberation,* written by a Peruvian priest and theology professor named Gustavo Gutiérrez.

The CELAM conference and the publication of Gutiérrez's theology unleashed a flood of reflection and criticism that dominated theological circles throughout the decade of the 1970s. Were Catholic bishops and theologians advocating violent revolution in Latin America? Was Jesus a revolutionary like Che Guevara or Camillo Torres?

In 1979 the bishops met again to discuss the social and economic situation in Latin America and to reconsider the theology of liberation spawned by CELAM II. The leaders of the church intended CELAM III, often referred to as "Puebla" after the Mexican city where the bishops met, to provide a balance to the radical positions taken earlier. However, their intentions were not realized. By giving theological endorsement to the idea of God's "preferential option for the poor," and by criticizing the military dictatorships of Latin America while praising the "base communities" of Christians that had sprung up during the previous decade, the conference only served to lend even further impetus to the fledgling movement of liberation theology.[2]

What Is Liberation Theology?

Fundamentally liberation theology is a theological movement arising out of Latin America and other third world countries that takes as its point of reference the experience of the poor and their struggle for liberation. However, not every theology that expresses concern for the poor or that proposes a program for helping them qualifies for this label. Rather, liberation theology is a radical new approach for the theological task that begins with the poor, especially the poor classes of the third world, and recognizes God's presence in their struggle to throw off oppression. In the words of its greatest exponent, "The theology of liberation is rooted in a revolutionary militancy."[3] One Latin American evangelical offered a fuller definition:

> Liberation theology is an allegedly biblical and profoundly christological quest for genuine Christian orthopraxy. Such orthopraxy results from the juxtaposition of a critical reflection on the church's pastoral activity and its historical interpretation in the light of divine revelation.

The roots of liberation theology lie in both the far and the recent past. Many of its advocates refer back to Bartolomé de Las Casas, a sixteenth-century Spanish priest in South America who defended the Native Americans against the Conquistadors who often considered them nonhuman. Las Casas argued to the emperor of Spain that the native inhabitants of South America were humans, created in God's image, and therefore deserving of respect and justice. He linked salvation inextricably with social justice and pointed out that the Spaniards were placing their own salvation in jeopardy by treating the Indians so cruelly and unjustly.[4]

The more recent roots of liberation theology lie in secular and religious events and movements of the mid-twentieth century. During the 1960s a development closely linked with Moltmann's theology of hope emerged in Europe, known as "political theology." Its leading exponent was Johannes Metz, a colleague of Moltmann's at Tübingen, who laid some of the groundwork for liberation theology's distinctive method with his writings on the role of political "praxis" (committed involvement) as the starting point of theological reflection.[5]

Important as well was the Second Vatican Council, which met in Rome from 1962 to 1965. The council revolutionized many aspects of the Roman Catholic church and, in the opinion of many scholars, opened the doors to radical social and political involvement by Catholic laity and clergy.

A third taproot of liberation theology lay in the concrete situation of Latin America. In the late 1950s and early 1960s there arose an increasing disenchantment with the concept of economic development as an adequate means for eliminating poverty in the region. Paulo Freire, a Catholic educator in northeastern Brazil, argued that the poor themselves must take the first steps in dealing with their plight. He engaged in a program he termed *concientization* or "making aware." Because poverty is caused by a few privileged persons defending their status, Freire declared, the poor must liberate themselves from their "dominated-conditioned mentality" and free the rich from their "dominating-conditioned" mindset.

During the 1960s and 1970s several particularly harsh regimes came to power that suppressed the efforts of people such as Freire and crushed moderate as well as left-wing movements for social justice. Thousands of political activists disappeared, were tortured or killed. The gap between the rich and the poor, already wide, rapidly became a gaping chasm. This situation, which the bishops at Puebla labeled "institutionalized violence," gave rise to a "second violence"—revolutionary movements to overthrow the oppressive regimes. Much of liberation theology is reflection on this "revolutionary situation" and what roles Christians should play in it.

Without question liberation theology has been the most influential form of theology in Latin America in the late twentieth century. It has also been the most controversial. Much of the controversy arose from its involvement in the violent overthrow of the Somoza regime in Nicaragua and the role it played in the Sandinista regime, which ruled during the decade of 1979-1989. Several liberationist priests, including Miguel D'Escoto and Ernesto Cardenal, served as officials in the semi-Marxist Sandinista government, in spite of Pope John Paul II's orders against such activity.

In September 1984 the Vatican released a document critical of liberation theology. The piece, entitled "Instruction on Certain Aspects of the 'Theology of Liberation,' " was written and signed by Joseph Cardinal Ratzinger, the conservative head of the Sacred Congregation for the Doctrine of the Faith, Rome's office for identifying and correcting heresy within the church. Ratzinger warned Catholic Christians against the alleged defects inherent in liberation theology, especially its supposedly uncritical acceptance of concepts borrowed from Marxist thought.[6]

The next year Cardinal Ratzinger and the Sacred Congregation "silenced" a leading Brazilian liberation theologian, Leonardo Boff, for one year. The order meant that Boff, one of liberation theology's most articulate spokesmen, could not lecture in public or publish anything during that time. About the same time the Vatican investigated another leading liberation theologian, Gustavo Gutiérrez of Peru. However, the investigation led to no condemnation or silencing. On the contrary, the Vatican's position on liberation theology appeared to have softened somewhat since the first instruction in 1984. This was evident in a second Ratzinger instruction, dated April 1986, the "Instruction on Christian Freedom and Liberation." Although it also criticized some aspects of liberation theology, the overall tone and thrust of the instruction gave more comfort than concern to Latin American liberation theologians.[7]

Despite such moves toward accommodation, the struggle over liberation theology continues. It seems that every year dozens of new books and articles pour forth analyzing the movement, either praising it or criticizing and condemning it.

Liberation Theologians

Like most contemporary theological movements, liberation theology is diverse. Its voices are many, and they reflect the different countries and religious backgrounds of its proponents. However, there is an observable unity of spirit and a surprising lack of internal criticism within the movement. A consciousness of unified purpose overrides differences of detail. Most of its leading spokesmen (as yet there are no leading women in the movement in Latin America) are Catholic. They include Gustavo Gutiérrez of Peru, Leonardo Boff and Hugo Assmann of Brazil, José Miranda of Mexico, Juan Luis Segundo of Uruguay and Spanish-born Jon Sobrino of El Salvador. Because Latin America is predominantly Catholic, it is not surprising that there are few Protestant liberation theologians. The most notable one is Methodist José Míguez Bonino of Argentina.

Latin American liberation theology has spawned a number of North American defenders and expositors. Although it would not quite be fair to label him a "liberation theologian," Robert McAfee Brown, Professor Emeritus of Theology at the Pacific School of Religion, is certainly its most articulate, if somewhat uncritical, North American observer and interpreter.[8]

Although the movement has many dimensions, our discussion will focus almost exclusively on the consensus themes of Latin American liberation theology as illustrated through the writings of two of the spokesmen mentioned above, the Roman Catholic theologian Gustavo Gutiérrez and his Protestant counterpart José Míguez Bonino.

Because of his early lectures and the important book from which the movement derives its name, Gustavo Gutiérrez is often considered (against his will) the "father of liberation theology." He was born in Lima in 1928 of a relatively poor family. In 1959 he received his Ph.D. in theology from the University of Lyon in France and was ordained to the priesthood.

Gutiérrez's early career was spent ministering to a poor parish in Lima and teaching theology and social sciences at the Catholic University there. During the 1960s he served as chaplain to the National Union of Catholic Students of Peru, and through this work he came into contact with revolutionaries such as Che Guevara and Camilo Torres. Torres had been a Catholic University chaplain himself, until he renounced his priesthood and joined a guerilla group in Bolivia where he was killed fighting with government forces.

Many of the most influential books and articles of the theology of liberation came from Gutiérrez's pen, including *The Theology of Liberation*[9] and *The Power of the Poor in History*. He has taught and lectured at universities and seminaries around the world and is a frequent keynote speaker at conferences of liberation and third world theologians. A man of modesty despite his world renown, Gutiérrez lives in a small apartment above the cramped headquarters of his Bartolomé de Las Casas Center, a liberation theology think-tank in Rimac, a Lima *barrio* or slum.

José Míguez Bonino was born in Santa Fe, Argentina, in 1924. His parents were Methodists. Although he was raised in a middle-class family, he had many contacts with the poor people of Argentina and gradually gained a social concern that led him to identify with socialism. He pursued theological studies at a Protestant seminary in Argentina and received his licentiate in 1948. Later he studied at Emory University in Atlanta, Georgia, and Union Theological Seminary in New York City, receiving his Ph.D. in 1960.

Míguez Bonino's ecumenical commitment resulted in his serving as a special Methodist observer at the Second Vatican Council in Rome and as president of the World Council of Churches. His academic career has included being professor of theology at two Protestant institutions in Argentina as well as visiting professor at theological institutions in England, Costa Rica, France and the United States.

Míguez Bonino has been a major defender of the Christian use of Marxist social analysis. In his book *Christians and Marxists: The Mutual Challenge to Revolution*[10] he explained how it is possible for a Christian to be a Marxist and for a Marxist to be a Christian. His most influential book, however, is *Doing Theology in a Revolutionary Situation*.[11] In it he set forth the basis for a theology of liberation, calling the church to overcome its attitude of privatization or identification with the status quo and to become involved in revolutionary struggle on behalf of the poor. Míguez Bonino developed the theoretical and ethical basis for such involvement in *Toward a Christian Political Ethic*.[12]

Even though Gutiérrez is Catholic and Míguez Bonino is Methodist, their agreement on the basics of theology, ethics and Christian mission is substantial. We will attempt to describe in a sympathetic yet critical way this consensus of liberation theology and illustrate it with references to these two thinkers' works.

Contextual Theology
A theme implicit in all liberation theology is that theology must be contextual. This is, however, more a presupposition than an explicitly stated thesis. It means that theology must be intrinsically linked with a specific social and cultural situation. In fact, building on the "sociology of knowledge," liberation theologians would argue that all theologies always are linked with and shaped by a specific social and cultural milieu. In the words of Dermot A. Lane, "Knowledge is not neutral or value-free. Instead all knowledge tends to embody the social circumstances and conditions of its time."[13] In other words, knowledge always tends to reflect the vested interests of the knower. Vested interests vary considerably from one society and culture to another; consequently, knowledge will reflect this variance.

Such a theory of knowledge can and sometimes does lead to relativism—the idea that knowledge is so conditioned by social, political and economic realities that it is impossible to rise above them. Liberation theologians do not embrace this kind of deterministic and reductionist view, however. While accepting the basic insights of the sociology of knowledge, they embrace another, often closely related view associated with twentieth-century Marxist thought: In order to rise above the self-enclosed "knowledge" of class and race interest, people can and must exercise "critical consciousness" or "dialectical thinking." This means that each person must gain awareness of one's own vested interests and subject them to scrutiny and criticism. By becoming suspicious and critical (dialectical) in relation to the dominant thought-forms of one's own culture, a person's knowledge can rise above this social-environmental conditioning.[14]

If knowledge arises from the conditioning process of the social environment, then of course all knowledge is necessarily contextual. Both the "knowledge" conditioned by the dominant class, which is really "ideology," and the critical knowledge that arises among those who stand over against that class are bound up with the unique situation in which each of these different "knowers" lives and thinks.

Liberation theologians assert that this is as true for theology as for any other discipline. Consequently, in their eyes, the theologies of Europe and North America are simply unsuitable for the social situation of Latin America. In the words of Gutiérrez:

> Here faith is lived by the poor of this world. Here the theological reflection seeking self-expression has no intention of being a palliative for these sufferings and refuses integration into the dominant theology. Here theology is ever more conscious of what separates it from the dominant theologies, conservative or progressive.[15]

So, theology is always contextual, never universal. What is developed in one place, whether Rome or Tübingen or New York, cannot be imposed on every other place. Such theology "from above" is anathema to the liberation theologians. They seek a truly indigenous Latin American theology that arises out of an involvement in its unique sociopolitical realities.

According to Gutiérrez, a major difference between European and North American theologies on the one hand, and Latin American theology on the other, arises from their different "interlocutors." The North Atlantic theologies, whether liberal or conservative, have been shaped by the questions of modern Western nonbelievers. The main question they ask focuses on how to speak of God in a secular world. The task of Latin American theology, in contrast, is not conditioned by the nonbeliever's questions, but by the question of the "nonperson": "the human being who is not considered human by the present social order—the exploited classes, marginalized ethnic groups, and despised cultures."[16] "Our question," Gutiérrez explained, "is how to tell the nonperson, the nonhuman, that God is love, and that this love makes us all brothers and sisters."[17]

Míguez Bonino was similarly adamant in his assertions of the contextuality of theology. In fact, *Doing Theology in a Revolutionary Situation* is a defense of the right of Latin American liberation theologians to adopt and adapt Marxism for *their* theology in *their* context. Against all criticisms that bind them to the authority of European or North American theologies, he boldly asserted concerning liberation thinkers: "they will refuse to be subject to the academic theology of the West as a sort of *norma normans* to which all theology is accountable. And they will reject a theological debate which proceeds as if abstracted from the total situation in which reflection takes place."[18]

Of course the thesis of the contextuality of theology forms a major point of conflict between the Latin American theologians and their counterparts in Rome. Because the unity of the church and its theology is a pillar of Roman Catholic teaching, church leaders cannot help but worry that this basic presupposition of liberation theology may lead to schism. Similarly, European and North American Protestant theologians who have wanted to enter into critical dialog with this new form of theology have often felt rebuffed, because they are considered outsiders, if not oppressors.

Despite such concerns, virtually no one today questions the presupposition of the contextuality of all theological discourse. Consequently, the assertion of liberationists that the Latin American context is unique and that it will inevitably color the theology that arises within it stands unchallenged.

Latin American Poverty

The second major theme of liberation theology is the specific nature of the Latin American context. If theology is intrinsically linked to its social, political and economic context, with what context does Latin American theology have to deal? Liberation theologians agree that the single most significant feature of Latin American society is poverty. This poverty is not the same as poverty in Europe or North America because it is endemic, pervasive and imposed. The poverty that crushes the humanity of the majority of people in Latin America is no accident, according to liberation theologians; it is the result of sinful structures of society that work to maintain the extreme wealth and power of the few at the expense of the very humanity of the majority.

Statistics cannot give a human face to this poverty, but they can help we who are outside the situation understand something of the radical nature of the solutions proposed by militants. According to Robert McAfee Brown, over half of the children born in Peru die before reaching age five.[19] In Brazil the top 2 per cent of the landowners control 60 per cent of the arable land, whereas 70 per cent of the rural householders are landless. Similar statistics hold true in other Latin American countries. In Peru workers who used to support six persons must provide for eight with less than half the income they had formerly. In El Salvador a family of six needs $333 per year to survive, but over half the population earns less than that.

Throughout Latin America poverty has reached catastrophic levels. The toll on the young is most appalling. Many of the larger cities teem with unwanted, abandoned children who beg and often are abused. One priest turned liberation theologian said that he is in constant daily contact with persons "who simply live by competing with the swine and the vultures for what they can find in the garbage dumps."[20] As the poor of Latin America grow poorer, the rich prosper more than ever. Many who protest this situation are mysteriously killed or simply disappear. A classic example is Archbishop Oscar Romero of El Salvador, who was assassinated by a death squad while saying mass a day after he publicly called for young Salvadoran soldiers to refuse orders to shoot their fellow countrymen.[21]

And yet the majority of people in Latin America, both rich and poor, both powerful and powerless, are confessing Christians. The Catholic church is the officially established church in most countries, and even where it is not established it is tremendously powerful. Gutiérrez is harshly critical of the church's traditional use of its influence, which, he charged, "has contributed, and continues to contribute to supporting the established order."[22] One of the most incisive and controversial theses of liberation theologians is that contrary to its claims the church is not "neutral" in terms of sociopolitical involvement, but actually has always taken the side of the oppressors; only now is it beginning to switch sides. In their opinion, of course, the church has a long way to go.

The analysis of the causes of Latin American poverty given by liberation theologians is simple, yet hotly debated. First, they assert that Latin America suffers from an *external* situation of economic dependence imposed by European and North American countries and multinational corporations and an *internal* situation of institutionalized violence against the poor perpetuated by ruling oligarchies and military regimes. Foreign dominance and internal oppression work hand-in-hand. When Latin America gained its political independence from Spain and Portugal in the early nineteenth century, it did not gain economic independence. Its economies have always remained under the control of foreign nations and companies, giving rise to neocolonialism. Of course Europe and North America have pretended to help Latin American countries through various "development" projects, but liberation theologians claim that development has always come with strings attached and has served only to deepen the situation of domination and dependence.

Míguez Bonino minced no words in his assessment: "Latin American underdevelopment is the dark side of Northern development; Northern development is built on third-world underdevelopment. The basic categories for understanding our history are not development and underdevelopment but domination and dependence."[23] Gutiérrez concurred, concluding that "there can be authentic development for Latin America only if there is liberation from the domination exercised by the great capitalist countries, and especially by the most powerful, the United States of America."[24]

The external situation of dominance and dependence, which in the eyes of liberation theologians amounts to pillage and plunder of Latin America's resources, is exacerbated by an internal situation that Medellín labeled "institutionalized violence." Latin American countries are ruled by small groups of powerful people, who are usually related to each other, known as "oligarchies," or by military regimes that cooperate with multinational corporations in return for Northern support. These regimes rule with an iron fist. Under the pretence of "national security" they ignore human rights, civil liberties and basic human dignity.

In El Salvador alone, over seventy thousand people have allegedly died or disappeared at the hands of the government or the death squads that serve it. Even where the statistics are not so egregious, institutionalized violence is said to exist in the very living conditions imposed on the majority by the ruling minority. Gutiérrez summarizes the conditions in which he labors:

> What we are faced with is a situation that takes no account of the dignity of human beings, or their most elemental needs, that does not provide for their biological survival, or their basic right to be free and autonomous. Poverty, injustice, alienation, and the exploitation of human beings by other human beings combine to form a situation that the Medellín conference did not hesitate to condemn as "institutionalized violence."[25]

According to both Gutiérrez and Míguez Bonino the Latin American situation of structural poverty and institutionalized violence is the product of international capitalism. Consequently, it can be changed only through a radical break with the status quo.[26] Such a break, they add, is already in the works. Latin America is experiencing revolutionary ferment, so that, in the words of Gutiérrez, "A broad and deep aspiration for liberation inflames the history of humankind in our day, liberation from all that limits or keeps human beings from self-fulfilment, liberation from all impediments to the exercise of freedom."[27] The question, therefore, is not whether the church should "get involved in politics" or "take sides." The question, according to the theologians of liberation, is whose side will it take in the present revolutionary situation.

God's Preferential Option for the Poor

The third central theme of liberation theology is that all theology and mission arises out of the preferential option for the poor. In the present revolutionary situation characterized by class struggle and conflict, the church must cast its lot with the oppressed, because in history God himself is on the side of the poor. Gutiérrez explained: "the poor deserve preference not because they are morally or religiously better than others, but because God is God, in whose eyes 'the last are first.' This statement clashes with our narrow understanding of justice; this very preference reminds us, therefore, that God's ways are not ours."[28] Míguez Bonino was no less clear: "Poverty . . . is a scandalous fact which must be eliminated. God himself is engaged in the struggle against it; he is clearly and unequivocally on the side of the poor."[29]

But what does it mean to assert that God is on the side of the poor? Is God prejudiced, a respecter of persons? A broad and careful reading of liberation theology's treatment of this theme makes clear that the "preferential option for the poor" does *not* mean that poor persons automatically stand in right relationship with God and will go to heaven simply because of their disadvantaged economic situation. Actually, most liberation theologians do not think in terms of who will be saved eternally and who will not, for there is a strong universalist tendency among them. Preference for the poor means that even though God loves all people, he identifies with the poor, reveals himself to the poor and sides with the poor in a special way. Above all, it means that in the class struggle God sides with the poor against every oppressor who would exploit or dehumanize them.

The liberation theologians' claim that the church must also side with the poor has received substantial support from the leadership of the Catholic church, including Pope John Paul II. But the concrete outworking of this preferential option is a matter of great controversy. Does it entail armed revolution? Or is it something more nebulous, identifying with the poor intellectually or seeking to live in "solidarity" with their plight?

Liberation theologians may disagree at times on these matters, but they agree that siding with the poor is not an option for the Christian or the church. According to Robert McAfee Brown, it means commitment to the poor in the attempt to build a more just society: "To the degree that the cries of the poor are heard, and are given priority over the complaints of the rich, there can be movement toward a more just society."[30]

Such involvement, whatever form it takes—such "liberating praxis"—is for liberation theologians the starting point for all genuine theology.

Theology as Critical Reflection on Praxis

The fourth theme of liberation theology is methodological: Theology is "a critical reflection on Christian praxis in light of the word of God."[31] Gutiérrez coined this definition of theology, which has caught on among other liberation theologians. It expresses the belief that theoretical reflection should be the "second act" following theology's "first act," which is "praxis."

For Gutiérrez, theology begins with and arises out of commitment to the liberation of the poor. That active commitment is "praxis." Theological reflection, in turn, is the bringing of the Word of God to bear on such Christian involvement for the poor, in order to purify and support it. Consequently, theological reflection is never detached, merely theoretical or objective. In many ways this understanding forms an exact reversal of classical theological method, which has often placed ethics or mission second to reflection. Gutiérrez and others, therefore, are staging a Copernican revolution in theological method involving an "epistemological break" with tradition. Míguez Bonino expressed it this way:

> Theology, as here conceived, is not an effort to give a correct understanding of God's attributes or actions but an effort to articulate the action of faith, the shape of praxis conceived and realized in obedience. As philosophy in Marx's famous *dictum*, theology has to stop explaining the world and to start transforming it. *Orthopraxis*, rather than orthodoxy, becomes the criterion for theology.[32]

Liberation theologians give various reasons in support of their shift in theological method.

One reason is philosophical, relating to the sociology of knowledge referred to earlier. Knowledge, so it is claimed, is never a detached, objective grasp of truth in itself. All human knowledge arises out of some specific encounter with social reality. Consequently, in order to find "truth" we do not attempt to escape the conflicts and commitments of social reality, but we purpose to stand within them and reflect scientifically and critically on them.[33] We do not find truth by thinking instead of acting, but by thinking or reflecting on acting. In all forms of knowledge, therefore, acting (praxis) is the first act, and reflection is the second.

The second reason for this new approach to theological method is religious. Liberation theologians believe that knowledge of God comes in and through obedient commitment to God's own project for the poor: "To know God is to work for justice. There is no other path to reach God."[34] Liberating praxis, therefore, provides privileged cognitive access to God and hence must precede reflection. This does not mean that theology can do without reflection, however. Reflection, according to Gutiérrez, brings the Word of God to bear on praxis in order to orient or guide it.[35] But it never stands back objectively to criticize it, for that would be to fall back into sterile and arid intellectualism.

What role do divine revelation and the Bible play in liberation theology? For liberation theology, revelation is clearly more than the Bible. It encompasses rather the entire historical project of God's liberating activity.

Liberation theology links God closely with history, avoiding any speculation about God in himself. According to Gutiérrez, God's liberation of his people from bondage and oppression in the Old Testament forms the "theophany of God." God appears and actually enters into history in the great events such as the exodus. In the New Testament a new dimension of God's relationship with history appears: "In Jesus Christ God not only reveals himself in history, he becomes history."[36] Of course Gutiérrez did not mean that God and history merge into one. He was speaking here of the Incarnation as the ultimate point of revelation.

Although liberation theologians have not worked out any detailed, systematic doctrine of Scripture, it is clear that the Bible functions as the primary and normative record of the revelatory liberating experiences of God's people. However, we cannot restrict revelation to the distant past. God's historical activity on behalf of the poor is continuing. This also constitutes revelation in and through the praxis of the church. That is not to say that God is revealing any "new things" today that supercede or contradict what God revealed in the past. Gutiérrez sought to avoid such a conclusion as well as any other misinterpretation of the primacy of praxis:

> The ultimate norms of judgment come from the revealed truths that we accept by faith and not from praxis itself. But the "deposit of faith" is not a set of indifferent, catalogued truths; on the contrary, it lives in the church, where it rouses Christians to commitments in accordance with God's will and also provides criteria for judging them in the light of God's word.[37]

So, according to liberation theology, theology is bipolar. It involves two distinct but interdependent poles, between which it constantly moves: praxis and theory. But the primacy belongs to praxis.

Theology and Marxism

Fifth, liberation theology sets forth Marxism as an aid to Christian praxis. More controversy has surrounded this theme than any other dimension of liberation theology. Indeed, nearly all liberation theologians use Marxist social analysis to understand the particular situation of poverty in Latin America, as well as to provide solutions to that problem. The nearly unanimous opinion among them is that capitalism is inherently evil, and that socialism, though far from the kingdom of God, is the ideal form of economics. According to Gutiérrez, tearing down the present system and building a new socialist society is the best way to fulfill Jesus' command to offer a cup of cold water in his name, because

> to offer food or drink in our day is a political action; it means the transformation of a society structured to benefit a few who appropriate to themselves the value of the work of others. This transformation ought to be directed toward a radical change in the foundation of society, that is, the private ownership of the means of production.[38]

Gutiérrez's statement embodies two key characteristics of liberation theology's use of

Marx: as a "tool of social analysis" and as a program for changing society. Both Gutiérrez and Míguez Bonino agree that because labor is part of essential human identity, forcing people to sell the fruits of their labor for less than full value, as in capitalism, leads to alienation and exploitation. The person who owns the means of production, such as a mine or a factory, exploits the workers by taking away the "surplus value" of their labor. This exploitation alienates the workers from the their labor, and hence from themselves. Exploitation and alienation eventually ignite a struggle between the classes, climaxing in revolution, especially in situations of extreme poverty such as Latin America.

Liberation theologians claim that Marx's analysis illumines the causes of the injustice and extreme poverty of Latin America. And they are convinced that their use of his ideas in theology is no different than the use of pagan philosophers like Plato by the church fathers or Thomas Aquinas's use of Aristotle. Of course they also assert that Christian use of Marx's philosophy must be critical and transformative. Míguez Bonino, who is perhaps the most articulate defender of a critical Christian use of Marx, offered this explanation:

> Features like class-struggle, the dictatorship of the proletariat or the role of the Communist Party are in part a piece of analytic theory which, with all due correction and revision, have to play a part in a Christian's articulation of his love-seeking-for-justice. But they are also ideological slogans which bear the mark of a conception of man and history which the Christian cannot fully accept. The Christian alliance with Marxist socialism is therefore always an uneasy alliance, in which the fundamental divergence about the source and power of solidary love results in constant questioning in the realm of practice. But it is important now to emphasize that the source of this criticism is not a rejection of Marxism as social theory but a radical questioning of the philosophical foundation of its ethos—the rejection of the Triune God of Love.[39]

Salvation as Integral Liberation

A sixth common theme of liberation theology is salvation as "integral liberation." Gutiérrez, who considered salvation to be the central theme of Christianity, offered his version of liberation theology as a reconstruction of the doctrine of salvation.[40] In the past, he argued, the church wrongly concentrated on salvation as "quantitative"—as "guaranteeing heaven" for the greatest number. Today, especially in Latin America, salvation must be reinterpreted in qualitative terms—as commitment to social transformation, for this is "the only way to have a true encounter with God."[41] For Gutiérrez and other liberation theologians, there can be no purely spiritual, otherworldly encounter with God. God is either encountered in and through "conversion to the neighbour" or not at all.[42]

Although Gutiérrez virtually equates salvation with liberation, he emphasizes that the liberation that truly saves the individual and society is "integral"; it involves all dimensions of human existence. He is clearly not interested in questions about the minimum requirement for entrance into heaven. We could search the literature of liberation theology in vain looking for discussion of such purely individualistic, spiritual salvation.

Salvation is the activity of God and humans working together within history to bring about the full humanization of all relationships. The concern of liberation theologians is that we become "sisters and brothers,"[43] that is, that we abolish unjust social systems that oppress, exploit and alienate people.

Christian Mission as Liberating Praxis

Finally, liberation theology sets forth Christian mission as liberating praxis. The mission of the church in Latin America is to transform society toward the kingdom of God, they argue. Solidarity with the poor in their struggle, teaching them to understand the true causes of their poverty ("conscientization") and supporting and encouraging popular efforts to throw off oppression are all means of salvation. In the final analysis, of course, the kingdom of God is a gift that God alone can and will give at the end of time. Only then will total liberation take place. Within history, however, the church of Jesus Christ is charged to promote the growth of the kingdom, to bring about concrete approximations of its final perfection through building a just society. All actions that work toward this goal, Gutiérrez claimed, may carry the label "liberating": "Any effort to build a just society is liberating. And it has an indirect but effective impact on the fundamental alienation. It is a salvific work, although it is not all of salvation."[44]

A question often put to liberation theologians is whether "any effort to build a just society" might include violence. Can violent overthrow of existing orders be baptized as Christian mission? Can the work of salvation include armed conflict? This question became especially poignant during the Sandinista revolution in Nicaragua, in which liberationist priests participated. The heroic status of the guerilla priest Camilo Torres raised the issue as well.

Gutiérrez and Míguez Bonino agree that while violence is never ideal, as a last resort it may prove to be a necessary means of bringing about justice—even for Christians. The main difference between them lies in their attitude toward it. Míguez Bonino clearly considers violence at best a necessary evil. Nonviolent resistance to institutionalized violence is always preferable to armed revolt.[45] While Gutiérrez himself does not prefer revolution, he refuses to criticize those who, like Che Guevara and Camilo Torres, find it necessary to participate in armed struggle against the violence of the established order: "We cannot say that violence is all right when the oppressor uses it to maintain or preserve 'order,' but wrong when the oppressed use it to overthrow this same order."[46] Both theologians agree that the main tools of Christian mission are the nonviolent means of prophetic denunciation of oppressive structures of society and annunciation of God's will for total liberation from all that dehumanizes people—especially poverty.

Critical Evaluation

Liberation theology has generated a tremendous amount of criticism. Some of that criticism is polemical and generates more heat than light. Nevertheless, both conservative and liberal theologians have offered thoughtful, sympathetic critiques of liberation theology that have challenged the movement to explain its views more carefully and cogently.

Liberation theologians themselves have not been eager to engage in dialog with their critics; they assert that the best way to judge a theology is by its fruits, not by the strength of its intellectual arguments.[47] Their defenders sometimes impute evil motives to those who question the orthodoxy of liberation theologians. Robert McAfee Brown, for example, charged, "The church can suffer fools gladly, but it has a harder time with prophets, particularly when they threaten to interfere with profits."[48] Despite McAfee Brown's caution, the task of bringing to light some of liberation theology's weaknesses as well as its strengths remains crucial, for it prods adherents of the movement to clarify, and even perhaps purify, their positions.

Without a doubt liberation theology has brought to the Christian world's attention the plight of the suffering poor in Latin America. It has inspired hope and courage in the hearts of millions and prophetically denounced the apathy and injustices lying at the root of their plight. The movement also has brought to the church's attention the need for a new "social appropriation of the gospel" in a world of social and economic conflicts between entire nations of "haves" and "have nots."

Despite the positive role liberation theology has played in raising awareness, it has laid itself open to serious questions that cannot be dismissed merely by pointing out the good the movement has accomplished nor by impugning the motives of its critics.

Some observers have rightly questioned whether theology can be totally contextual. Would not a fully contextualized theology eliminate the basis on which to launch a worldwide condemnation of injustices such as apartheid or torture?[49] Others have questioned whether the blame for Latin American poverty can be so entirely and exclusively laid at the feet of northern governments and corporations. Is it not possible that some, if not much, of it is the result of conditions within specific countries? In any case, there seems to be more than enough blame to go around, and many experts believe some responsibility should fall on the economic policies of Latin American governments themselves.[50] Yet other critics question whether it is biblically or theologically sound to say that God "favors" the poor, solely because they are poor. Sam Portaro warned that "when we accept the idea of a divine bias, we are being unfaithful to our ministry to the whole people of God."[51]

Many critics have objected to liberation theology's use of Marxism. Marxist categories cannot serve as a tool of social analysis without being drawn into its attendant atheistic view of history and humanity, they warn. Marxism's understanding of the economic causes of human alienation, for instance, cannot be separated from Marx's view of the human person as a product of one's own self-creation through work rather than as a creature of God.[52]

The most serious objections, however, have been raised against liberation theology's method and its view of the God-human relationship. J. Andrew Kirk, a British evangelical sympathetic to liberation theology, asked quite rightly whether its method is even possible. Can theory and reflection be made secondary to praxis? Does not "right praxis" presuppose some view (theory and reflection) of what is right and what is wrong? And does not this mean for the Christian that Scripture, not praxis, must be the ultimate norm?

Kirk argued that in order to avoid a new ideologizing of the Christian message, Gutiérrez's theological method must be turned around. Some pre-understanding of right praxis versus wrong praxis will set the stage for theological reflection, he noted. And if our pre-understanding is not drawn from Scripture, it will come from some particular human ideology. Kirk concluded,

> For this reason, we insist that the task of modern theology should be a consciously critical reflection on God's Word in the light of a contemporary praxis of liberation. If this is not the order of our methodology then the phrase (in Gutiérrez' definition), "in the light of God's Word," ultimately becomes emptied of content.[53]

Kirk's point is well taken: "Right praxis ultimately depends on right theory."[54] Liberation theologians appear to acknowledge this themselves when they make judgments about the value of their praxis and that of others, commending the one while condemning the other.

Liberation theology's view of the relationship between God and humanity is highly ambiguous. Its theologians affirm the transcendence of God and never fail to pay lip service to the need for personal repentance and faith. Yet their emphasis causes concern. For Gutiérrez, God is to be encountered and known *only* within history through liberating action on behalf of the neighbor. "Since the incarnation," he wrote, "humanity, every human being, history, is the living temple of God. The 'profane' . . . no longer exists."[55] Left unclear, however, is whether for Gutiérrez the truly "sacred" any longer exists either. In spite of his denials and those of his defenders like Robert McAfee Brown, is seems that Gutiérrez's almost total neglect of the transcendent dimensions of grace, heaven and the eschatological kingdom of God, and of the personal relationship with God through the living Jesus Christ makes his a form of secular theology. Does God have any existence above and apart from human history? Does sin lie deeper than does participation in sinful structures of existence? Does salvation mean anything more than participation in a liberation movement?

Liberation theologians have yet to answer adequately these and other questions. If they wish to avoid being accused of theological reductionism, they must rise to the challenge and explain the roles played in their theology and their view of Christian life by traditional theological truths such as God's freedom and transcendence, original sin and personal conversion to Jesus Christ through repentance and faith. Until that occurs the suspicion will remain that for them "God" and "salvation" function as little more than ciphers for the power of liberation and involvement in social action on behalf of the poor.

FEMINIST THEOLOGY:
THE IMMANENCE OF GOD IN WOMEN'S EXPERIENCE

A group of Christian women gather in a suburban living room to worship, pray and share their stories of oppression at the hands of the male-dominated society and churches. They pray to God the Father and Mother Goddess and sing nonsexist hymns. Then they gather around a small table with a bell, a candle and a Bible. The worship leader reads passages from the Bible that oppress women and the group cries out in unison "Out, demons, out!" At the close of this ritual "Exorcism of Patriarchal Texts" a woman proclaims, "These texts and all oppressive texts have lost their power over our lives. We no longer need to apologize for them or try to interpret them as words of truth, but we cast out their oppressive message as expressions of evil and justifications of evil."[1] This is a Woman-Church, a local expression of a growing force within contemporary Christianity.

The Women-Church movement is only one expression of a growing alienation from traditional Christianity and its theology among feminists. In the words of one leading feminist theologian, "The more one becomes a feminist the more difficult it becomes to go to church."[2] Those who have chosen to stay within the institutional church have pressed for inclusive language in worship so that humankind is not identified as "man" and God is not always the Father but sometimes Mother as well. Church art is also affected. A sculpture of "Christa"—Christ as a woman on a cross—hangs in a cathedral in New York.

What Is Feminist Theology?

In the last third of the twentieth century theology became increasingly affected by a growing feminist consciousness. But beyond the general awareness, beginning in the late 1960s female theologians and students of theology developed a new genre of contemporary Christian thought known as feminist theology. In one sense, this theology is an outworking of and closely akin to the feminist movement that developed in the wider North American society.

The roots of late twentieth-century feminism actually lie a hundred years earlier. During the abolitionist movement that preceded the Civil War in the United States, certain activists came to realize that the emancipation of slaves and the rights of women shared the same biblical basis. This phase of the women's movement climaxed in the passage of the Nineteenth Amendment to the U.S. Constitution, which gave women the right to vote.

In the 1960s several factors contributed to a reemerging of the feminist impulse. The decade began with the appointment of the President's Commission on the Status of Women. Two years later (1963), Betty Friedan's monumental book, *The Feminist Mystique,* hit the bookstores of the nation. But as in the nineteenth century, it was perhaps the renewed awareness of Black Americans in the civil rights movement that played the leading role in rekindling a consciousness of the oppressed status of women. Several activist women responded to the situation by forming the National Organization for Women (NOW). The church was among the institutions that fell under the scrutiny of the movement, initially through impassioned works such as Mary Daly's *The Church and the Second Sex* (1968) and *Beyond God the Father* (1973).

Late twentieth-century feminist theology shares certain similarities with North American Black theology and Latin American liberation theology. Like they, it begins with a situation of oppression, thereby becoming critical reflection on praxis—the experience of oppressed persons freeing themselves from domination. It focuses on socio-political dimensions of sin and salvation, and makes use of sociological more than philosophical categories. The chief difference between feminist theology and Latin American liberation theology lies in the identification of the primary oppression. While the latter sees it in terms of enforced poverty, the former argues that the most basic oppression of all is sexism or, more specifically, patriarchy—the deeply engrained cultural domination of women by men.

Not all feminist theology is Christian. There are Jewish feminist theologians, and non-Christian feminists advocate a new form of paganism through worship of the "Mother Goddess." We will focus exclusively on Christian feminist theology, which according to Pamela Dickey Young "tries to articulate adequately the Christian witness of faith from the perspective of women as an oppressed group."[3] As we will see, significant diversity exists among Christian feminist theologians, but the bonds of sisterhood hold strong among them and lead to a unity of perspective.

Pamela Dickey Young has identified four fundamental unifying themes that define the movement: Traditional Christian theology is patriarchal (done by men and for men); traditional theology has ignored or caricatured women and women's experience; the patriarchal nature of theology has had deleterious consequences for women; and therefore women must begin to be theologians and equal shapers of the theological enterprise.[4] A fifth common theme might be added: Women's experience, as defined by feminists, must be the source and norm for any serious contemporary Christian theology. Anne E. Carr spoke for all in stating,

> While women can make no claim to a unique knowledge of God, they can trust that their experience and understanding of God provide an important and necessary corrective to an imagery and understanding derived from an over-masculinized church and culture. And in the Christian context, the experience and insights of women allow for a genuinely critical retrieval of traditional and contemporary ways of understanding God.[5]

While all feminist theologians agree on these five themes, they diverge on several significant points. There is no unanimity, for instance, on whether women should remain within the traditional Christian churches to try to reform them or leave the church and find fellowship with other women and sympathetic men in Women-Churches. They also disagree over the authority of traditional sources of Christian theology, such as the Bible and church tradition.

Many attempts have been made to categorize feminist theologians according to distinct approaches to these and other questions, but most such schemes prove useless. Feminists repeatedly shift their own positions, and the term *feminist* itself has taken on new and narrower connotations. At one time anyone who advocated absolute equality for women in the church would have been considered a Christian feminist. In this sense, one could speak of "evangelical feminism" or "biblical feminist." Toward the end of the twentieth century, however, "Christian feminist theology" came to be used almost exclusively for a movement that seeks sweeping revision in theological foundations and beliefs.

Feminist Theologians

Among the leaders of the mainstream of feminist theology are three especially influential and outspoken advocates of change: Elisabeth Schüssler Fiorenza, Rosemary Ruether and Letty Russell. Elisabeth Schüssler Fiorenza, a professor at Harvard Divinity School, previously taught at the University of Notre Dame. She is the author of several influential articles and books on feminist theology, church history and New Testament studies. Her best-known work is *In Memory of Her: A Feminist Theological Reconstruction of Christian Origins* (1984), a massive study of the "lost memory" of women in the early church.[6] Letty Russell is professor of theology at Yale Divinity School and author of several books on hermeneutics and theology, including *Human Liberation in a Feminist Perspective—A Theology* (1974)[7] and *Household of Freedom: Authority in Feminist Theology* (1987).[8] Perhaps the most influential feminist theologian is Rosemary Ruether, professor of historical theology at Garrett-Evangelical Theological Seminary, which is associated with Northwestern University in Evanston, Illinois. An articulate and persuasive speaker as well as a prolific writer, Ruether has done more to promote the cause of feminist theology and Women-Churches than any other single person. Among her books are *Sexism and God-Talk: Toward a Feminist Theology* (1983) and *Women-Church: Theology & Practice* (1986).

Feminist theology developed in three distinct steps. These remain permanent moments or aspects of its ongoing work.[9] Feminists begin with a critique of the past—a "recovery of the dangerous memory of women's oppression" by the male patriarchal church and culture. The second step or moment seeks alternative biblical and extra-biblical traditions that support, in the characterization of Ruether, "women's personhood, her equality in the image of God, her equal redeemability, her participation in prophecy, teaching, and leadership."[10] Finally, feminists set forth their own unique method of theology, which includes the revisioning of Christian categories. In the words of Pamela Dickey Young, "Every theological doctrine and concept had to be examined anew in light of the growing awareness that women had been oppressed in the church at least as systematically as in other parts of society."[11]

That this foundational step came last is no accident, for feminist theology, like Latin American liberation theology, sees theology as reflection on praxis. Theological method, then, is reflection on the process of reconstructing Christian belief and life on the basis of women's experience. Ruether outlined the task of feminist theology as clarifying the vision of the feminist community of faith and clarifying the criteria for testing what is authentic. Such reconstruction is necessary, she explained, because the primary source of the feminist faith cannot be the church, church tradition or Scripture. Rather,

> the patriarchal distortion of all tradition throws feminist theology back upon the primary intuitions of religious experience itself: namely, the belief in a divine foundation of reality which is ultimately good, which does not wish evil or create evil, but affirms and upholds our autonomous personhood as women, in whose image we are made.[12]

Critique of Christian Tradition

As feminists look back over two thousand years of Christian history and even further back into the history of the Hebrews they see something quite different from what others have seen. They see a dark history of patriarchal oppression of women. For them, the entire history of Judeo-Christian tradition is marked by the invisibility of women, the subjugation of women and their enforced domination by men. Many of them see a history of violence against women that has denied them not only equality but humanity. Old Testament passages that imply female "uncleanness" after child-birth and during menstruation, New Testament texts that deny women the right to speak in church and imply their subordination to men in the "chain of being," church fathers who called women "defective males" and blamed them for men's sins—feminists see all these moments of "sacred history" as anything but sacred.

According to Ruether, this awakened and raised consciousness of female oppression at the hands of patriarchal religion and culture comes as a severe shock that largely defines "women's experience" today. When women with a feminist consciousness look back at Christian tradition, "an entire social and symbolic universe crumbles within and outside them. They recognize in the familiar the deeply alien."[13]

Feminist theologians approach their critique of Christian tradition dialectically, that is, both negatively and positively. The negative dimension involves exposing and condemning the evils of androcentrism, patriarchy and misogyny, all of which, they conclude, are deeply imbedded in the fabric of Christianity and Western culture. The deepest and most pervasive evil of all is androcentrism, the world view "in which men possess all dignity, virtue, and power in contrast to women who are seen as inferior, defective, less than fully human, the alien or 'other' in relation to the male human norm." And its presence in the church is obvious: "Insofar as Christianity has given to the symbolism of father and son a central, determinative role in shaping its theology and practice, it is androcentric."[14] In fact, its presence permeates the whole. Ruether charged,

> Starting with the basic assumption that the male is the normative human person and, therefore, also the normative image of God, all symbols, from God-language and Christology to church and ministry, are shaped by the pervasive pattern of the male as center, the female as subordinate and auxiliary.[15]

Androcentrism manifests itself socially in patriarchy. According to feminists, patriarchy cannot be reduced merely to sex-based structures. It is not only the subordination of females to males. Rather, it includes "the whole structure of Father-ruled society: aristocracy over serfs, masters over slaves, king over subjects, racial overlords over colonized people."[16] Thus, patriarchy is found in all forms of domination-submission, all hierarchies of power and control. Insofar as the Christian tradition includes and affirms it, that tradition is corrupt and in need of prophetic denunciation and radical revision.

The practical result of androcentrism and patriarchy is a deep-rooted misogyny or hatred of women in Christian tradition. Feminist theologians believe that the sin of misogyny is manifested throughout the Bible and church history in the suppression of the roles of women among the people of God and in identifications of sin with femaleness. As Ruether pointed out, Augustine identified maleness with the image of

God, Thomas Aquinas regarded females as "misbegotten males" and the Reformers did nothing to change the status of women in the church. Even Karl Barth considered woman second to man in the covenants of nature and grace.[17] Feminists conclude that their analysis of Christian tradition illustrates its need to be purged of sexism before it can be useful.

The positive aspect of the feminist approach to the Christian tradition is the recovery of the lost memory of women. No one has done more to rediscover the roles and contributions of women in Christian tradition than Elisabeth Schüssler Fiorenza. Although her methods and conclusions might be considered speculative, the Harvard professor claims that the earliest Christian movement was thoroughly egalitarian and that the patriarchal pattern of male domination came late into the first-century church as an accommodation to Roman culture. Consequently, "the woman-identified man, Jesus, called forth a discipleship of equals that still needs to be discovered and realized by women and men today."[18] Other feminist church historians have attempted to uncover the stories of great women of faith and courage in the Christian tradition as a means of overcoming its patriarchal cast.[19]

We should not assume that the feminist critique of tradition involves only a condemnation of blatant sexism and recovery of lost stories of women. Rather, as Ruether pointed out, it aims at a total revolution against hierarchically structured culture: "Culturally, sexism defines the whole system of reality, from 'matter' to 'God.' One cannot challenge sexism without the dethronement of the cultural universe as an authentic and good model of life."[20]

Feminist Theological Method

All feminist theologians agree that women's experience, as defined by feminists, must be the center of theological reflection. They do not, however, agree entirely on what this means or on what role other sources and norms of theology play in a feminist theology. Nevertheless, Anne Carr expressed a general consensus: "The cultural situation to which Christian tradition must be correlated today is the growing and questioning experience of women in the church."[21]

Tillich's method of correlation forms the background for Carr's statement. Theology must combine the questions of contemporary culture with the answers of revelation, and the form of the answers must be determined by the cultural setting. At the very least, therefore, women's unique experience of being the "second sex," the oppressed half of humanity, must play a determinative role in theological formulation.

But what is "women's experience?" Pamela Dickey Young discovered five dimensions of women's experience wherein it differs significantly from men's: Women experience their bodies differently, in that they are more closely related to the cycles of nature; women have different socialized experiences, in that they are taught by culture to submit to men and to appeal to men sexually; women now have feminist experience in which they become conscious of their gender-oppression and of unjust structures of society that dehumanize them; women have a different historical experience in and through the recovered "lost history" of women; and women have different individual experiences that can be catalysts for change.[22] Anne Carr expressed the view of many feminist theologians when she described women's nature as different from men's in being more "transformative and person-centered."[23] Other theologians have identified the unique experience of women as relationality, nondualism, intuitiveness and communality. Despite the differing descriptions, all feminists agree that the primary experience of women, whether they are aware of it or not, is oppression at the hands of patriarchal society.

But why should either gender's experience be determinative for theology? Should not theology's norms be neutral and universal, rather than gender-specific? Rosemary Ruether vehemently rejected this suggestion with the retort that all theology that has thus far been considered standard and orthodox has been male-oriented. Men's experience has not only colored theology, it has determined the content and form:

> The use of women's experience in feminist theology, therefore, explodes as a critical force, exposing classical theology, including its codified traditions, as based on *male* experience rather than on universal human experience. Feminist theology makes the sociology of theological knowledge visible, no longer hidden behind mystifications of objectified divine and universal authority.[24]

Feminist theologians take three distinct approaches to explicating the role of women's experience in relation to classical norms of theology.[25] Elisabeth Schüssler Fiorenza rejects any aspect of classical Christianity as a norm for theology, because it is so thoroughly patriarchal and therefore inimical to women. She does not consider even Jesus himself an authoritative norm for theology, because his life was so intrinsically interwoven with the oppressive culture of which he was a part. Fiorenza advocates Women-Church as the normative community for Christian theology. Articulating a radical application of what Ruether calls the "feminist critical principle" or "the promotion of the full humanity of women,"[26] she asserted that what counts as "word of God" is what women identified with other women in community decide is liberating for women.[27] According to Fiorenza, Women-Church will decide what this means in terms of the theological validity of tradition and theology. Even Jesus' own life and teachings are not immune to such critical evaluation.

Rosemary Ruether finds the source of the feminist critical principle in the "prophetic-liberating tradition" of Scripture. In her estimation, theology makes use of numerous sources—Scripture, non-Christian pagan religions, marginal and "heretical" movements within Christianity, philosophies such as liberalism, romanticism, and Marxism, and contemporary stories of women's oppression and liberation. However, the ultimate norm for interpreting what is divine revelation lies in the prophetic-liberating tradition of which Jesus was the historical paradigm. Thus, "Feminist readings of the Bible can discern a norm within Biblical faith by which the Biblical texts themselves can be criticized. . . . On this basis many aspects of the Bible are to be frankly set aside and rejected."[28] The prophetic-liberating tradition is the vision of a completely egalitarian, nonhierarchical society unmarked by patterns of domination and submission. The employment of this norm for theology will result in an explicit critique of patriarchy, as well as the deepening and transformation of all "the liberating prophetic visions" so that they include what they did not include—women.[29]

In contrast to the other two leaders, Letty Russell looks to the future for the theological norm.[30] The future she envisions is a utopia of complete equality and freedom that she calls the "Household of Freedom," which is Russell's metaphor for what is traditionally called the eschatological kingdom of God. "If there were a household of freedom," she wrote, "those who dwelt in it could find a way to nurture life without paying the price of being locked into roles of permanent domination and subordination."[31]

Although her vision of utopia is fully consistent with women's experience, Russell actually derived it from Jesus' ministry and lifestyle. According to her reading of the Gospels, Jesus was a feminist, in the sense that he refused to exercise his authority through power-relationships that dominate or coerce people. He rejected such authority and the hierarchical structures that support it, while establishing relationships of interdependence and community among his followers. Jesus proclaimed the future kingdom of God and used parables and metaphors that portray it as egalitarian rather than patriarchal.

This future Household of Freedom, which is "creation mended," becomes for Russell the norm of all theology. Even Scripture must be judged by it. Because the language of domination and subordination that reinforces patriarchal political institutions is found in the Bible,[32] the Bible must be used against itself. That is, feminist interpreters must "appeal to God whose authority works through the power of love, against God who rules through the patriarchal power of domination."[33]

All feminist theologians agree, then, that Scripture alone—*sola scriptura*—cannot serve as the principle of authority for theology, because the Bible is thoroughly permeated by patriarchy. In addition, divine revelation is an ongoing process; we cannot restrict it to the past, even if we recognize some historical events such as Jesus Christ as paradigmatic for future revelation. One must also recognize women's (feminist) experience as divine revelation and elevate it as a primary source and norm for contemporary Christian theology, if theology is to be credible to women and liberated men. The key to feminist theological methodology, in short, is the primacy of feminist-defined women's experience in theological formulation.

Even Ruether and Russell, both of whom appeal to some aspect of Christian tradition for support, in actual practice look to the feminist critical principle as the ultimate hermeneutical norm for detecting the Word of God in the past. William Oddie was quite right in concluding, concerning this theological movement, that " 'feminist consciousness' is the channel for the primary revelation, by which all others are to be judged."[34]

Feminist Reconstruction of Christian Belief

Feminist theology reaches its climax in a thoroughgoing revision of traditional Christian doctrines and symbols. Anne Carr expressed the sentiment of all feminist theologians in declaring that "the truth of theological formulation lies in its effects,"[35] and that given the past history of the oppressive effects of Christian doctrines and symbols, they cannot be used any longer without radical negation and retranslation.

The central tenet needing transformation is the doctrine of God. Ruether believes that this primary Christian idea has been dominated by male-oriented dualism arising out of patriarchal images of society. "Dualism" divides what essentially belongs together and sets them over against each other in hierarchically arranged orders of good and evil, domination and subordination.[36] While claiming that males are not intrinsically evil in the sense of having unique, evil capacities that women do not share,[37] Ruether argued that men display a marked tendency toward psychic and sociological dualisms that women do not.[38] Insofar as theology has been dominated by male-oriented thinking, it has been characterized by a set of dualisms that have served to subjugate and dehumanize women, including nature/spirit, transcendence/immanence, soul/body, creation/redemption, male/female, good/evil.

According to Ruether this dualistic approach has led to the identification of women with the "lower nature" and of males with the "higher nature." Consequently, women are correlated with matter, body, creation, immanence, evil; maleness, in contrast, is identified with spirit, soul or reason, transcendence, redemption, good. Because dualism leads to all manner of evils against women in theology, it must be rooted out, beginning with the doctrine of God.

Ruether is not satisfied to criticize the traditional imagery of God as male. She considers it so obviously oppressive that it hardly needs discussion. Most feminist theologians would agree with her that because "God is both male and female and neither male nor female," inclusiveness can occur only as we speak of the deity by employing female as well as male metaphors.[39] But she wishes to go beyond the critique of the Father image of God and argue that any parent image of God is patriarchal, because it implies dualism and hierarchy: "Patriarchal theology uses the parent image for God to prolong spiritual infantilism as virtue and to make autonomy and assertion of free will a sin."[40]

In searching for a nondualistic reference for God, Ruether turned to Tillich's concept of God as the ground of being, which she prefers to call the "primal Matrix" or "God/ess." For her, God/ess is not a transcendent, personal being, but "the transcendent matrix of Being that underlies and supports both our own existence and our continual potential for new being."[41] God/ess is no more to be identified with spirit, transcendence or maleness than with matter, immanence, and femaleness. In fact, God/ess is no more to be identified with humankind than with nature. On the contrary, God/ess embraces all such dualities in a dynamic unity, so that there is no "great chain of being" with the divine at the top and inanimate nature at the bottom. Because of its unity with God/ess, all reality is radically equal.[42]

With its use of concepts borrowed from Tillich, Teilhard de Chardin and process theology, Ruether's vision of God clearly emphasizes the divine immanence. She has little place for images of God as powerful, sovereign or free. Despite her intentions, however, what she seems to have accomplished is not a liberation of theology from dualism but the creation of a new dualism that is the opposite of the one she finds inherent in male theology. Instead of linking the divine and the good with transcendence, spirit, freedom, power and maleness, she identifies them with immanence, matter, impersonal energy and femaleness.

At the same time, Ruether's theology also suggests monism. Her account of God/ess is only a hairsbreadth from the nature-personification Mother Goddess of the radical feminists who worship the earth and themselves. This impression is reinforced by Ruether's identification of God/ess with the liberated self of the feminist woman: "The liberating encounter with God/ess is always an encounter with our authentic selves resurrected from underneath the alienated self."[43]

In all fairness we must acknowledge that sheer monism is not Ruether's intention. She prefers to think of her theology as dialectical—affirming the dynamic unity of all reality. But of course "dialectical" thinking is notorious for falling into either monism or a subtle form of dualism. In Ruether's case it appears to fall into both at different times.

Few theologians have attempted to develop a feminist Christology. In fact, one of the biggest problems facing feminist theology is to explain how a male savior can be of benefit to women. Most Christian feminist theologians regard Jesus Christ as a paradigm of true humanity—humanity freed of the evil of patriarchal attitudes and behavior patterns. Letty Russell, for example, sees in Jesus nothing more than God's representative of true humanity, and her emphasis falls not on Jesus' uniqueness but on the ability of other humans to become representatives of true humanity like he was.[44]

Once again it is Ruether who has provided the most profound feminist reinterpretation. However, hers is hardly original, but is basically a feminist appropriation of Tillich's Christology of Jesus as the New Being. Like Tillich, Ruether rejects the classical Christology of Chalcedon that, she said, is neither a consistent evolution of Jewish messianic hope nor "a faithful rendering of the messianic announcement of Jesus of Nazareth and his views of the coming Reign of God."[45] In its stead, in a manner reminiscent of classic liberalism, she elevated her rendition of the historical Jesus. "Once the mythology about Jesus as Messiah or divine *Logos,* with its traditional masculine imagery is stripped off," she asserted, "the Jesus of the synoptic Gospels can be recognized as a figure remarkably compatible with feminism."[46]

In Ruether's account, Jesus was the liberator who denounced the power and status relationships that defined privilege and deprivation.[47] He did not proclaim himself, but pointed beyond himself to the new humanity to come, the redemptive humanity enjoying perfect community free of dualisms and hierarchies. Ruether identified the new humanity with "Christ." Thus, Jesus was the Christ only in the sense that he represented the new humanity and served as its forerunner. Consequently, "Christ, as redemptive person and Word of God, is not to be encapsulated 'once-for-all' in the historical Jesus. The Christian community continues Christ's identity."[48]

The radical nature of Ruether's theology is spelled out in a "Feminist Midrash" (interpretive story) at the beginning of *Sexism and God-Talk.* This story is a highly imaginative account of the history of salvation involving a female deity, "The Queen of Heaven," who is above Yahweh, and a figure who appeared to Mary Magdalene after

Jesus rose and disappeared—a figure "taller and more majestic [than Jesus] . . . regal and yet somehow familiar, a woman like [Mary] herself."[49] The figure tells Mary that she is now the "continuing presence of Christ" who will "continue the redemption of the world."[50] The midrash closes with what cannot be brushed off as mere "story" because it clearly intends to provide its interpretation in theological idiom: "With Jesus' death, God, the heavenly Ruler, has left the heavens and has been poured out upon the earth with his blood. A new God is being born in our hearts to teach us to level the heavens and exalt the earth and create a new world without masters and slaves, rulers and subjects."[51]

Feminist theologians offer creative reinterpretations of other central themes of Christianity such as sin, salvation, the church and eschatology. The exposition of feminist interpretations of God and Jesus Christ provided here should suffice, however, to demonstrate that this theological movement is much more than simply a development within orthodox Christianity committed to the goal of women's equality. On the contrary, in the eyes of its leading speaker, it necessarily includes radical, sweeping revisions in every area of Christian theology and life.

Critical Evaluation

It is crucial that we distinguish between the movement for women's equality within the churches and "feminist theology." The former has gained a wide recognition and has won agreement within a broad spectrum of Christian denominations and theological commitments. Insofar as it has remained rooted in the biblical, Christian tradition, the quest for equality in the church has made a genuine contribution to twentieth-century Christian thought and life. A consensus is developing among both evangelical and liberal Protestants that there is no compelling biblical reason to deny full participation of women with men in both ministry and the home.

But if the direction in which mainstream feminist theology has been drifting is the norm, the movement for women's equality can no longer be called *Christian feminism.* For the sake of preventing confusion, we may best reserve that term for the thorough theological revision centered around women's experience, as exemplified by Ruether and others.

Feminist theology has done a great service to the Christian community by pointing out the evils of androcentrism, patriarchy and misogyny. Its theologians have often helped the church to become more inclusive and therefore truer to the image of God as both male and female and to the universality of the gospel. In spite of the gains it has offered, however, feminist theology goes too far in its radical revision of the Christian symbols, and it threatens a new schism within the body of Christ by its support and encouragement of the Women-Church movement.

The heart of the difficulty lies in feminist theology's view of authority, a view that actually amounts to the rejection of any authority except that exercised by feminist consciousness. In order for any Christian theology to be truly prophetic, it must have some means of self-criticism as well as criticism of the culture around it. Feminist theology is adept at exposing the evils of the patriarchy deeply rooted in society and the church. But what norm does it recognize for criticizing its own principles and practices? This is a serious problem for any theology that raises a "critical principle" drawn from the consciousness of a particular group of people—whether philosophers or the oppressed—and uses it to determine what is and what is not normative in Scripture.

Feminist theology stands at the end of a long line of such theologies going back to Schleiermacher. But in contrast to Schleiermacher and his followers, feminists dismiss any attempt to discover a "universal human experience"—a religious a priori—that can be determinative for theology. At present, anyway, they claim that gender-specific experience is the touchstone of theological truth.

Evangelical theologian Donald Bloesch was accurate in his assessment that feminist theology is not nearly as acute in discerning its own ideological basis as in identifying and criticizing that of patriarchal thought.[52] "When a theology becomes consciously ideological, as in some forms of feminist and liberation theologies," Bloesch noted, "it is bound to lose sight of the transcendent divine criterion, the living Word of God, by which alone it can determine the validity of its social valuations."[53]

Critics of feminist theology have not been alone in recognizing this flaw in its methodology. Pamela Dickey Young, a self-identified Christian feminist, argued that in spite of its great service in recovering women's experience as a source of theology, feminism has by and large gone too far in cutting itself loose from the Christian tradition. It has allowed principles from outside that heritage to become the controlling norms for its account of what is truly "Christian." The problem with this is obvious:

> Basically the person employing the term *[Christian]* can use it however he or she wishes. This means, then, that whereas feminist theologians may claim the use of "Christian" for whatever liberates women, if there is nothing that can be derived from the tradition itself that can be used normatively to argue that this is what Christianity is all about, then others can use the tradition in less liberating ways.[54]

In other words, even though feminist theologians such as Ruether and Russell appeal to the person of Jesus as warrant for their doctrinal reformulations, they sacrifice the right to call their theologies "Christian" when they hold women's experience—as defined by feminists—as a norm that controls what in his life and teachings is normative and what is not. This is, in Bloesch's terms, sheer ideology. As Young perceptively suggested, the feminist method of determining "Christian" doctrine leads directly into relativism: "If one appeals only to a member's self-identification as a criterion for deciding what is or what is not part of a given religious tradition, one is left with a relativism that must accept all without judgment or discernment."[55] Women's experience, in short, cannot serve as the ultimate norm for something that claims to be a form of Christian theology. Without the objective norm of the transcultural Word of God, Christianity becomes whatever any individual or group says it is.

Feminist theology's doctrines of God and Christ illustrate the inherent weakness in its methodology. Their reformulation of neither doctrine holds anything substantial in common with classical Christianity. Because hierarchy is assumed to be patriarchal and patriarchy is evil, God (or God/ess) cannot be Father or even Parent. Because dualism is a male-oriented, oppressive way of regarding reality, God (God/ess) and the world cannot be absolutely different. Elizabeth Achtemeier, a noted biblical scholar and theologian, argued that this identification of God or God/ess with the world will ultimately lead feminist theology into another religion different from Christianity, if it has not in fact done so already:

> No religion in the world is so old as is this immanentist identification of God with creation. It forms the basis of every nonbiblical religion, except Islam; and if the church uses language that obscures God's holy otherness from creation, it opens the door to corruption of the biblical faith in that transcendent God who works in creation only by his Word and Spirit. Worshippers of a Mother Goddess ultimately worship the creation and themselves, rather than the Creator.[56]

Feminist theology must rediscover transcendence in both its methodology and its doctrines of God and Christ if it is to exercise a lasting, positive impact on Christian theology.

8 THE TRANSCENDENCE OF THE HUMAN SPIRIT: *The New Catholic Theology*

*T*HE PROBLEM OF TRANSCENDENCE AND IMMANENCE HAS OCCUPIED THE ATTENTION OF twentieth-century Roman Catholic theologians as much as their Protestant counterparts. They have offered some of the most intriguing and fruitful paths toward solving the dilemma. The turn of the century witnessed the rise of a new school of Catholic thought labeled "modernism." Its leading proponents practiced higher biblical criticism, questioned some of the stricter tenets of the church and called for greater adaptation of Catholic theology to modern culture. In many ways it paralleled the phenomenon of classical liberal theology in Protestantism. Just as the latter gave rise to a conservative reaction, so Catholic modernism was opposed by a movement called "integralism," which emphasized the integrity of the great tradition of the church and tended to react negatively to any accommodation with modern culture.

Several popes worked to crush modernism, and for decades it was considered virtually anathema in the church. Its leading theologians were silenced or even deposed from their teaching positions, and a mood of fear settled within the theological community. Innovation was considered dangerous at best, evil at worst.

In 1959 a new pope was elected by the cardinals of the Roman Catholic church, who took the name John XXIII. In spite of the fact that he was old and was expected to be a "caretaker" pontiff, John XXIII set about reforming the church to bring it up to date, a process called *aggiornamento*. His main achievement was to call a new council of the church, the Second Vatican Council, commonly known as "Vatican II." The council, which met at the Vatican City in Rome from 1962 to 1965, produced significant changes in the life of the church. In many people's eyes it threw open the windows of the church and let the fresh breezes of the modern world blow in. Vatican II was the beginning of a new era for Roman Catholics around the world.

Two of the leading Catholic theologians at Vatican II were Karl Rahner of Innsbruck and Hans Küng of Tübingen. The former was already an elder statesman of Catholic theology, and after the close of the council he produced a progressive, modern interpretation of the faith. The latter was a "young Turk" of Catholic theology just beginning to show his colors. In the wake of Vatican II, he styled himself as a modern Luther continuously challenging the church to continue farther and faster in the direction of change. While both could be considered progressives in contemporary Catholic theology, Rahner would certainly be the more conservative of the two.

Rahner and Küng both sought to bring heaven and earth together without losing the distinction between them. That is, the search for transcendence in immanence consumed much of their theological energies. They believed that traditional Catholic theology had been too dualistic in its approach to this problem, tending to separate the supernatural from the natural, grace from nature, transcendence from immanence. In their own ways each sought to overcome this perceived dualism and do justice to the presence of the Spirit of God in the world.

The influence of Rahner, Küng and other progressives fostered tremendous changes in European and American Catholic theology after Vatican II. However, under Pope Paul VI (1963—1978) a reaction began to set in. The conservative reaction has become more powerful and intense during the tenure of the popular Pope John Paul II, which followed John Paul I's short, thirty-three-day reign in 1978. John Paul II appointed a conservative reformer, Karl Ratzinger, as head of the powerful Sacred Congregation for the Doctrine of the Faith in Rome. Some have charged that under Ratzinger the church established a new inquisition. Others believe he has treated progressives fairly and leniently.

In the midst of all of this turmoil and confusion in the church, Rahner and Küng have stood out. They have been regarded as visionaries and trailblazers courageously pointing the direction for the future. Moderates look to Rahner. More liberal and radical progressives look to Küng.

KARL RAHNER:
THE TRANSCENDENCE OF HUMAN SUBJECTIVITY

Karl Rahner has been criticized for the high level of abstraction many find in his theological reflections. He once received an anonymous cartoon that depicted him as a "theological nuclear physicist" lecturing to a group of fascinated multipliers, one of whom takes his message in the next frame to a group of popularizers. After the lecture, one of the popularizers stands in a pulpit and expounds the message to a congregation. Jesus stands to the side listening and saying, "I don't understand." The intended point was that Rahner's theology is too difficult to explain—even to the one it is supposed to be about. Something inevitably gets lost in the translation. Rahner's response when reminded of this humorous criticism was, "That's just the way it is when you're a theology teacher."[1]

Rahner's Significance

In spite of the abstruse nature of much of his theology, Rahner has become the most influential Roman Catholic theologian of the twentieth century. According to one of his interpreters, he functions as "a kind of universal god-father to contemporary Roman Catholic theology."[2] He has been compared to Thomas Aquinas, Friedrich Schleiermacher, Karl Barth and Paul Tillich. By the time of his death in 1984 his influence had reached into nearly every Catholic seminary and university theology faculty in the world, as well as into the Vatican itself. It is impossible to understand the changes taking place in Catholic theology in the latter half of the twentieth century without paying attention to the role played in these changes by Karl Rahner.

One example of that role is found in Rahner's influence on the Second Vatican Council held in Rome from 1962 to 1965, which brought sweeping changes into the life of the church. While he was virtually unknown outside of academic theological circles before 1962, his activities on the council gained him a worldwide reputation. Although he worked mainly behind the scenes on theological committees and panels, his ideas and even certain of his unique terms worked their way into several of the sixteen declarations passed by Vatican II. Rahner came to be recognized as "the most powerful man at the Council."[3]

Rahner's theology is a form of "mediating theology." It seeks a middle ground between two extremes that have been at war with one another in the Catholic church for over one hundred years. Many people are attracted to his thought precisely because of this mediating tendency.

One extreme Rahner worked hard to avoid is integralism—the approach that seeks to preserve the integrity of the traditional theology of Roman Catholicism at all costs. While integralism provides a safe harbor for theology in the storms of modernity, Rahner found it a haven of false security and irrelevance. At the other extreme is modernism—the approach that seeks to make theology relevant to the modern mind to the point of accommodation to secular culture. Rahner strived valiantly to steer his theology between these two extremes. In an interview he expressed the essence of his own approach: "Theology must be so presented that it encourages a genuine dialogue between the best of traditional thought and exigencies of today."[4]

Rahner's Life and Career

Karl Rahner was born on March 5, 1904, in the Black Forest city of Freiburg, Germany. His family was rather large, middle class and devoutly Catholic. Like his older brother Hugo, Karl decided to become a priest and specifically a member of the Jesuit order. The order assigned him to become a professor of philosophy and sent him to several schools, eventually to the University of Freiburg where he studied under the famous existentialist philosopher Martin Heidegger. His doctoral dissertation on Thomas Aquinas' theory of human knowledge was rejected by the Catholic faculty, because they found it to be too heavily influenced by Heidegger. Eventually it was published as *Spirit in the World* (1939), his first philosophical book, and received high acclaim as a work of genius.

Rahner began his teaching career on the theological faculty of the University of Innsbruck, Austria, in 1937. Although the school was closed by the Nazis during World War 2, he eventually returned and continued lecturing there until 1964. In that year he moved to the University of Munich to succeed the famous Catholic apologist Romano Guardini in the chair of Christian Worldview. After a falling out with the other faculty members, Rahner relocated to the University of Münster to teach dogmatic theology. He retired from full-time teaching in 1971 and returned to Munich, where he remained until near his death. Rahner died in Innsbruck in 1984.

Even in retirement Rahner was extremely active. He traveled extensively both before and after his retirement, speaking, participating in interreligious, ecumenical and Marxist-Christian dialogs, and giving advice to theological councils, conferences, cardinals and popes. The size of his written legacy rivals Barth's and Tillich's. By 1984 over 3,500 books and articles had appeared in print under his name. His most important articles were collected and published in a twenty-volume set entitled *Theological Investigations,* which contains over eight thousand pages in the German edition. Fortunately, he produced a one-volume systematic theology near the end of his life, *Foundations of Christian Faith* (1978), which provides an excellent introduction to his life's work by concisely summarizing its method and major themes. When asked to formulate briefly the purpose and theme of the book, Rahner provided an exquisitely succinct summary of his entire theology:

> I really only want to tell the reader something very simple. Human persons in every age, always and everywhere, whether they realize it and reflect upon it or not, are in relationship with the unutterable mystery of human life that we call God. Looking at Jesus Christ the crucified and risen one, we can have the hope that now in our present lives, and finally after death, we will meet God as our own fulfilment.[5]

The Transcendental Method

Rahner's theology can be interpreted appropriately as a response to the secular loss of the transcendence of God, even though he completed most of his writings before the radical theologies of the 1960s. The forces of extreme immanence that led to such phenomena as "Christian atheism" and "secular theology" were recognized by Rahner long before their full manifestation in the "death of God" movement. His entire career was a struggle against the competition between transcendence and immanence, which led theologians to believe they had to choose between the majesty and sovereignty of God on the one hand and the autonomy and freedom of humans on the other. He capsulized his lifelong conviction by declaring that "The dilemma of the 'immanence' or 'transcendence' of God must be overcome without sacrificing the one or the other concern."[6]

Rahner's theological method reflects this conviction. He strives to show that ordinary, universal human experience is unintelligible without the transcendent, holy mystery called "God," and that the Holy Mystery of God must be encountered and known in and through the historical environment people experience in daily life. The key to understanding Rahner's approach to theology, therefore, is his "transcendental method." Because this method is heavily philosophical, it is best to look first at his attitude toward and use of philosophy.

Like Tillich and unlike Barth, Rahner considered philosophy an essential moment or aspect of the task of theology. The place for the involvement of philosophy in theology lay in what Rahner called "fundamental theology," which "comprises the scientific substantiation of the fact of the revelation of God in Jesus Christ."[7] In other words, fundamental theology constructs the foundations for dogmatic or systematic theology by rationally justifying belief in God's self-revelation in Jesus. It attempts to show through philosophical reflection that belief in this revelation is not arbitrary or a sheer "leap of faith" but rests on sound intellectual grounds. Ultimately, then, fundamental theology's purpose is to make Christian belief possible with intellectual honesty.[8]

Rahner employed "transcendental reflection" as a philosophical tool to show that the human being is by nature "spirit," by which he means "open to receive revelation." Humans are not only parts and products of the natural world; they are also oriented toward an infinite, mysterious horizon of being that Christians know as God. In other words, they are transcendent.[9] Rahner argued that humans transcend nature and themselves in every act of questioning and thinking. They are not closed in on themselves, but are open toward, oriented to and receptive of divine revelation. To demonstrate this philosophically was Rahner's great task, one that consumed most of his theological energy.

Rahner's tool in demonstrating this truth was transcendental reflection. Although he saw it as perfectly consistent with the philosophical theology of the great medieval Catholic thinker Thomas Aquinas, he borrowed this tool primarily from modern philosophers such as Kant, Maréchal and Heidegger. Transcendental reflection seeks to discover the necessary conditions for facts. It asks, given the undeniable reality of a particular thing, What must be real in the mind or the universe for it to exist? What are its necessary a priori conditions?

A crude illustration of this mode of reflection, drawn from the physical sciences, may help in understanding its much more subtle and abstract use in philosophy. Long before astronomers actually saw the planet Neptune, they deduced its existence in the solar system from observing certain irregularities in the movements of Uranus that could be explained only by the existence of another planet. Through a kind of transcendental thought process, they actually knew about Neptune, before seeing it through a telescope in 1846.[10] The point of transcendental reflection in philosophy is similar: to discover the preconditions for human knowledge and experience, or, in Rahner's words, to ask "What is the *a priori* transcendental condition for the possibility of [human] subjectivity?"[11]

According to Rahner, an objective investigation of ordinary, universal human experience, focusing on what he called "transcendental experiences," shows that humans are naturally oriented toward the holy mystery that Christians call God. That is to say, God is not alien to human nature, but an intrinsic part of it as the necessary condition for human subjectivity. In *Hearers of the Word* Rahner focused on the phenomenon of human cognition—the experience of knowing a thing as a thing—in order to establish metaphysically that some relationship to the infinite necessarily precedes any knowledge of a finite thing as its precondition. Forming any intellectual judgments about things—drawing conclusions about them—necessarily involves setting things apart from oneself and yet seeing them in relation to oneself. It also involves separating them from yet in relation to the whole of reality. To know a thing, which is different from simply seeing or feeling it, is to transcend both oneself and the thing in an act of abstraction.[12]

Abstraction, then, is the uniquely human intellectual act of forming concepts about things. It is not merely sensing them or remembering them (which animals are capable of doing) but also recognizing them as particular cases of classes of things. One sees a number of beings and interprets them as "humans" or questions their "humanity." For Rahner, that phenomenon is a mysterious human capacity that signals something transcendent—a relationship to Being itself, to the whole of reality. The necessary background for such an act is the whole of reality. But the "whole of reality" is not a thing. It cannot be comprehended, but exists only as an infinite horizon toward which humans move in their subjectivity.

What Rahner was attempting to establish in *Hearers of the Word* was a unique and mysterious capacity of humans. He spoke of it as

a *capacity* of dynamic self-movement of the spirit, given *a priori* with human nature, directed towards all possible objects. It is a movement in which the particular object is, as it were, grasped as an individual factor of this movement towards a goal, and so consciously grasped in a pre-view of this absolute breadth of the knowable.[13]

Because the "absolute of the knowable" cannot be known by ordinary human cognition except as a mysterious absolute horizon, it must reveal itself. Otherwise it remains a sheer mystery, and the meaning of particular things remains ultimately unintelligible.

At this point Rahner introduced God into his fundamental theology. Metaphysical-transcendental reflection on human subjectivity was not meant to be any sort of proof of the existence of God. It was designed, however, to be a proof of a human capacity for divine revelation. Without the self-revelation of the infinite horizon of knowing and being toward which the human person is inwardly oriented, all things would be ultimately meaningless. Rahner considered his phenomenology of human transcendence proof that human nature is spirit, as well as matter, and that a certain openness to God forms the inner core of that spiritual nature.[14] From this, Rahner drew the conclusion that "man is at least the one who must listen for a revelation from a free God speaking in *human words.*"[15]

Rahner called the natural transcendence of humanity its *"potentia oboedientialis"*— obediential potency—for a possible revelation.[16] He believed that a purely philosophical transcendental inquiry into the structure of human experience could show that it is naturally inclined toward receiving God's Word. The *potentia oboedientialis* means that "man is that existent thing who stands before the free God who may possibly reveal himself."[17] So strong is this potency that Rahner considered it a kind of knowledge of God imbedded within human nature itself. In every act of cognition, in every transcendental experience in which humans reach out beyond themselves and their finite world toward an infinite horizon of meaning, hope and love, they show that they always already know God implicitly.[18] However, this implicit knowledge of God is unthematic and nonreflexive; it is preconscious, latent and often dormant or even rejected. Nevertheless, it remains a knowledge of and relationship to God that is intrinsic to human nature.[19]

The purpose of Rahner's highly sophisticated philosophical anthropology was to provide rational support for Augustine's claim that humans are created restless until they find their rest in God. In more popular jargon, all humans have a "God-shaped empty place" in their beings that can be filled only by God. Rahner believed that the proof of this could be found through transcendental inquiry into the a priori conditions for human knowledge.

But what is the value of such inquiry? Why did Rahner go to such torturous lengths, such heights of subtle abstraction, to discover this implicit knowledge of God called the *potentia oboedientialis?* The answer lies in the secular impulse of the modern world and its overwhelming tendency to place God and humanity in either tension or identity. Rahner sought to show that contrary to the accusations of such modern secular philosophers as Nietzsche and Sartre, God is not a threat to human self-fulfillment. Rather, God is the necessary horizon of human subjectivity and therefore belongs essentially to human nature. And contrary to pantheists who would identify God with humanity, he attempted to show that there is a radical difference between the finite and the infinite, signaled by the ultimate mysteriousness of the absolute horizon of human subjectivity. The human person is intrinsically, inwardly related to a holy mystery in and through human subjectivity. Yet the holy mystery remains transcendent— even to the transcendence of the human subject that reaches out toward it. If that holy mystery is to be known, it must make itself known.

Transcendental Revelation

The purpose of Rahner's fundamental theology was to establish the readiness of human subjectivity for divine revelation. Humans are by nature potential hearers and obeyers of God's Word. Some critics have argued that his anthropology obviated the need for any special divine revelation, because it implied that humans already know God by nature. This would be the heresy of "ontologism," and Rahner vehemently rejected any such interpretation of his theology.

More cautious critics have argued that his transcendental anthropology predetermines what revelation can say to humans, in that God can reveal only what they are by nature capable of perceiving. George Vass, a Jesuit colleague and former student of Rahner's, warns, "The weight and emphasis he attributes to this anthropological approach could prejudice man's genuine listening to the genuine word of God that surprises him in history."[20] If Vass and other critics are correct, Rahner's theology stands squarely in the tradition of Schleiermacher and Tillich and therefore runs the risk of the same radical immanentism that plagued their theologies.

The critical issue, however, is not how much stock Rahner placed in the human capacity for revelation, but how much authority he accorded special revelation, which comes from outside of and beyond our natural human capacity. He strived mightily to avoid the immanentist implications of the liberal tradition. In *Hearers of the Word* he cautioned against that tradition: "The 'place' of a possible revelation by God may not be determined in such a way as to restrict the possibilities of such a revelation in advance."[21] And he reiterated, "He who is essentially open to being cannot by his own capacities set limits to the possible object of a revelation."[22] Fundamental theology, then, must be restricted to the status of being a preparation for the gospel and not become a predetermination of it.

But what has Rahner gained, if his fundamental theology merely establishes that humans are by nature open to God's Word? Has he avoided the danger of immanentism only to fall into the opposite extreme of making God and his revelation so transcendent that it comes to the human receptor as something completely alien and extrinsic? Contemporary theology knows this as the problem of transcendence and immanence. Traditional Catholic theology speaks of it as the problem of nature and grace: How can the human being be naturally open to God's self-communication in revelation and salvation without that in any way preconditioning or limiting the freedom of that self-communication? In other words, what good is divine self-communication if it cannot convey something unanticipated and radically new? On the other hand, what good is the openness of nature if God's self-communication can and does contradict nature? Why not then simply say with Barth that God's revelation and salvation completely create their own "point of contact?"

Rahner called the position that divine self-communication contradicts human nature "extrinsicism" and the position that it is captive to human nature "intrinsicism."[23] The former is the scourge of traditional theology, the latter of contemporary modernist and liberal theology. He sought to overcome this polarity of extremes with a mediating concept: the "supernatural existential."

Because the supernatural existential is perhaps the central concept of Rahner's entire theology we must explain it in some detail, beginning with several basic definitions. Michael J. Buckley defined *existential* as "a generic term applied to those characteristics or capacities of human existence which make it specifically human and distinguish it from other modes of existence."[24] Rahner borrowed the term from Heidegger. If something is a permanent, universal characteristic of human existence that sets it apart from other beings, then it is a human existential—whether or not it is considered necessary to human nature itself. Self-awareness and freedom are examples of such human existentials.

Supernatural does not necessarily mean "miraculous." That may be the popular connotation, but in especially Catholic theology it has a somewhat different meaning.

It designates whatever transcends nature; whatever cannot be included in the reality of the purely natural. A fundamental axiom of Catholic theology is that God's gracious self-communication to humans must be supernatural. Otherwise it is in some sense merited or compelled by nature and thus not free; if it is not free it is not a gift and therefore not truly grace. In order to preserve the unmerited and free nature of grace Catholic theology tended to emphasize its extrinsic nature.

Rahner wished to overcome that extrinsicism while doing justice to the freedom and transcendence of God in his self-communication to humanity. Consequently, he emphasized the concept of the supernatural existential. According to Rahner, not only are humans always by nature open to God *(potentia oboedientialis),* they are also always supernaturally elevated by God in that transcendental openness so that such elevation becomes an actual experience of God in every human life. God, Rahner claimed, actually communicates himself to every human person in a gracious offer of free grace, so that God's presence becomes an existential, a constitutive element, in every person's humanity.[25] Without the supernatural existential, humans would remain a question struggling for an answer, open to something beyond themselves, a holy mystery, an infinite horizon, unknown and completely transcendent. But because of the supernatural existential, humans find the terminal point of their transcendence within themselves as gracious, personal, loving presence.[26]

The universal presence of God in humans is "the light that lights everyone coming into the world," but it is not a part of their natural equipment. Although it is an "existential," it is not "natural." It is completely gracious and therefore supernatural. Rahner took great pains to make this absolutely clear, and thereby to avoid any hint of the heresy of radical immanentism. He clarified the matter in this way: "This communication is not to be understood in a pantheistic or gnostic way as a natural process of emanation from God. It is to be understood rather as the freest possible love because he could have refrained from this and been happy in himself."[27]

Although it is supernatural, the divine presence is not extrinsic. The whole point of the supernatural existential is to overcome extrinsicism and intrinsicism. It does not contradict human nature, because it comes as an elevation of transcendental openness of that nature to God.

According to Rahner, therefore, humans are not only beings open to Being and divine revelation, they are also recipients of God's gracious self-communication. "Man," he wrote, "is the event of a free, unmerited and forgiving, and absolute self-communication of God."[28] This is the first kind of divine revelation—original experience of God in and through the prevenient grace of the supernatural existential. Like the *potentia oboedientialis,* however, it is transcendental, not "categorical" (specific, concrete, historical). It does not communicate special knowledge of God, but exists within the human person as an offer of personal knowledge of and a relationship with God. By itself it remains unthematic and nonreflexive, but it does provide a "point of contact" for thematic, reflexive knowledge of God in special revelation.[29]

At this point many students of Rahner wonder what the difference is between the *potentia oboedientialis* and the supernatural existential, and they ask why both are necessary to his theological methodology and anthropology. Admittedly, Rahner is not entirely clear on this point, for he describes both in terms of the unthematic, nonreflexive knowledge of God that provides a point of contact within the human person for special revelation.

Concerning this apparent discrepancy, two statements are in order. First, for Rahner the *potentia oboedientialis* is part of the natural equipment of human beings. It is a philosophical-anthropological fact discovered through transcendental inquiry. The supernatural existential, in contrast, is not part of human nature but comes as a real self-communication of God to it. It is added, as it were, to every human person's natural humanity. Therefore, it cannot be discovered through a purely transcendental-philosophical inquiry, but neither does it in any way contradict it. According to Rahner, "it is the most self-evident thing of all, and at the same time it cannot be logically deduced from anything else."[30] Second, the *potentia oboedientialis* contains no real presence or knowledge of God. It is the human striving toward God in all things. Whatever "knowledge" it provides is only the knowledge that comes in the form of a question. The supernatural existential, on the other hand, conveys real knowledge and experience of God as an offer of redeeming grace. It is more than just a question; it conveys an offer, even though it still does not bestow the gift of redeeming grace itself. Only together, therefore, do the *potentia oboedientialis* and the supernatural existential do any good for the human person or the theologian.

This raises a serious question for Rahner's entire theological enterprise. Has he actually overcome the dangerous dualism of extrinsicism and intrinsicism? Has he indeed provided a key to solving the dilemma of transcendence and immanence? Given the subtlety and complexity of Rahner's theology, it would be difficult to give a clear and unequivocal answer. Everything depends on the viability of the concept of the supernatural existential, which in spite of its supposed "self-evident" nature seems to be a highly debatable and idiosyncratic idea. Rahner's supernatural existential cannot be established either philosophically or biblically, nor is it a traditional concept of Catholic thought. Furthermore, the supernatural existential is a highly unstable concept. If the theologian emphasizes the universal aspect denoted by the term *existential,* the concept may easily fall into intrinsicism and become little more than another religious a priori like Schleiermacher's God-consciousness. If one puts forward the supernatural aspect, the supernatural existential may easily fall into extrinsicism and become little more than another theological assertion about the transcendence of God's self-revelation.

Rahner himself used the concept in both ways. This gave rise to an odd juxtaposition of intrinsicism and extrinsicism, or immanence and transcendence, in his theology. For example, he strongly asserted that whoever freely cooperates with the gracious presence of God in the supernatural existential can and will be saved—apart from any special revelation. Such persons Rahner called "anonymous Christians."[31] Of course this raises our question, that has plagued every immanentist theology since Schleiermacher, to an intense pitch: Why do humans need any special, historical revelation?

Of course, Rahner clearly did not intend to fall prey to radical immanentism. Therefore, he also asserted that the supernatural existential is an absolutely free activity of God in human persons and that it requires categorical revelation in order to arrive at its own fulfillment.[32] To the extent that this emphasis is to be taken seriously it is clearly extrinsicist and stands in serious tension with the first emphasis. We can only conclude that Rahner's key concept—the supernatural existential—is highly ambiguous and of dubious value in solving the dilemma of transcendence and immanence in contemporary Christian theology.[33]

Categorical Revelation

Rahner distinguished between two types of revelation. The first has just been described. Our natural and supernatural orientations toward God constitute "transcendental revelation." This revelation, mediated through transcendental experiences, provides an implicit knowledge of God that always remains unthematic and nonreflexive. It communicates God, but not specific information about God that could be formulated conceptually and reflected on. Transcendental revelation reaches out toward a holy mystery that remains for it infinite, indefinable and ineffable.[34] God is present therein as question, not as answer.

Transcendental revelation forms the a priori basis for reflexive and thematic knowledge of God. This, however, can be achieved only through the second type of revelation, which Rahner called "categorical" or "real" revelation, specific revelation in history through events, words and symbols. These two aspects of revelation—transcendental and categorical—are distinct, yet interdependent. Both are necessary to revelation.[35]

Rahner defined categorical revelation as that self-revelation of God which
> is not simply given with the spiritual being of man as transcendence, but rather has the character of an event. It is dialogical, and in it God speaks to man, and makes known to him something which cannot be known always and everywhere in the world simply through the necessary relation of all reality in the world to God in man's transcendence.[36]

Categorical revelation discloses the inner reality of God that cannot be discovered through transcendental revelation alone. That inner reality includes the personal character of God and his free relationship to spiritual creatures.[37] This categorical revelation of God occurs throughout history and across cultures whenever and wherever people by God's grace actualize their natural and supernatural transcendentality and "break through," as it were, to a reflexive knowledge of God.

Every religion is an attempt at such a "break through." Consequently, Rahner believed that "in all religions there are individual moments of such a successful mediation . . . when the supernatural, transcendental relationship of man to God through God's self-communication becomes self-reflexive."[38] In such moments, people of any religion or no religion become anonymous Christians. However, because of human depravity every such event of revelation remains partial and intermixed with error.

Because universal categorical revelation remains partial and fallible, Rahner posited the existence of a second, higher type of categorical revelation, which he described as "public, official, particular and ecclesially constituted revelation."[39] By this he meant the prophetic revelation found primarily in the Old and New Testaments on which the Christian church is based. This revelation is different in degree, rather than in kind, from universal revelation: "Something comes to expression in the prophets which fundamentally is present everywhere and in everyone, including ourselves who are not called prophets."[40] Hence, the particular, historical revelation contained in the Bible is not a "bolt out of the blue," but a fulfillment and completion of the universal self-communication of God, both transcendental and categorical.[41]

Finally, Rahner arrived at the highest revelation of all, revelation in an absolute sense. Because in him we find the Incarnation of God, the unsurpassable climax of all revelation is Jesus Christ. As absolute revelation, Jesus Christ provides a touchstone for interpreting the entire universal history of revelation. But even here Rahner denies an absolute break with the rest of revelation. The Incarnation of God in Jesus Christ is simply the highest point of God's self-communication, the most intense mediated immediacy of God's presence in human history and experience. For Rahner, the entire history of the cosmos, including evolution, contains the seed of God's absolute self-communication, which comes to fruition in the Incarnation. Even the divine-human reality of Jesus Christ is not for him a "bolt out of the blue"; rather it too is the fulfillment of the self-transcendence of creation itself, the "omega point" toward which all things in creation gravitate.[42] Nevertheless, it provides a touchstone for distinguishing the particular and official revelation from the universal and incomplete revelation in history.

God as the Absolute Person

We have already shown that for Rahner God is ultimately mysterious in himself. God is "absolute mystery" to natural human transcendentality; God is "holy mystery" to supernatural transcendentality. Even with the help of the supernatural existential, humans are unable to know God as other than the mysterious, indefinable, holy terminal point of their transcendence. God is immanent within human experience as the transcendent mystery that cannot be comprehended in spite of its absolute nearness.

But what more can be said about God than this? Rahner provided little in the way of a systematic treatment of God's attributes, but lengthy, subtle and detailed discussion of God's relationship to the world is scattered throughout his writings. Here it will be possible to touch on only a few key points—God's personhood, God's relationship to the creation and God's triunity.

For Rahner, God's infinity is axiomatic. As the Infinite One, God is never an object for human scrutiny and must not be treated as one. Therefore, one cannot conceive of him as an individual.[43] However, he is not impersonal either,[44] despite all the problems of attributing personhood to him. Creaturely personhood simply cannot be derived from something impersonal. The impersonal gives rise to the impersonal; only personhood gives rise to the personal. God's personhood, however, must be both analogous to yet completely transcendent above human personhood. That is, we cannot conceive of God as a human, or even as an angelic person, however great. In the end, the statement that God is a person, though necessary, must be left open to the "ineffable darkness of the holy mystery."[45] Hence, we must confess God as "the absolute person" who stands in absolute freedom in relation to everything else, including human persons.

Rahner affirmed the Christian doctrine of *creatio ex nihilo*. But for him this does not necessarily imply any belief about a temporal beginning of the world. Rather, it describes the God/world relationship: Everything that is not God is totally dependent on God. For Rahner, the key element in this doctrine is that "God does not become dependent on the world, but remains free vis-à-vis the world and grounded in himself."[46]

Such a statement should unequivocally rule out any pantheism or panentheism from Rahner's theology. Then how could the charge of "dangerous immanentism" ever arise against it? George Vass, for one, accuses Rahner of dangerous immanentism because of "the incapacity of his philosophical theology to keep God and the world apart."[47] This appears, according to Vass, in Rahner's critique of dualism and in his affirmation of an "element of truth" in pantheism.

In large part Rahner's doctrine of God is a protest against dualism, in the same way that his doctrine of revelation is a protest against extrinsicism. The two are inextricably linked. In spite of his strong affirmation of the transcendence of God in his treatment of *creatio ex nihilo*, he cautioned that the doctrine must not be interpreted in a dualistic sense. The difference between God and the world is not the same sort of difference as exists between two categorical (finite, particular) realities. A God who existed and operated as an individual existent alongside others—even alongside the world as a whole—would be a false God. Rather, Rahner averred that "the difference between God and the world is of such a nature that God establishes and is the difference of the world from himself, and for this reason he establishes the closest possible unity precisely in the differentiation."[48]

Vass calls this a "hardly translatable statement."[49] Apparently what Rahner meant is that the source of the difference between God and the world lies in God himself, and therefore the difference is not absolute. The element of truth in pantheism, according to Rahner, is that God is the absolute reality, the original ground and the ultimate goal of everything. Nothing exists in free, autonomous independence alongside of or over against him.[50] In the light of his earlier statement about God's freedom and independence from the world, we should not read anything sinister into these warnings against dualism, by which Rahner apparently meant deism, or into this affirmation of the "element of truth" in pantheism. Clearly, for Rahner, God and the world exist in a unity-in-difference and difference-in-unity established freely by God himself in which God remains independent of creation. To this extent he kept the transcendence and immanence of God in careful balance.

Rahner wrote several treatises on the doctrine of the Trinity, including a book entitled simply *The Trinity* (1974). Perhaps his most lasting contribution to contemporary trinitarian thought, and certainly the one most relevant to the present study of transcendence and immanence, is his development of what has come to be known as "Rahner's Rule": "The 'economic' Trinity is the 'immanent' Trinity and the 'immanent' Trinity is the 'economic' Trinity."[51]

It is customary in trinitarian theology to distinguish between God's threefold activity toward what is outside himself in history—the economic Trinity—and the threefoldness of God in himself in eternity—the immanent Trinity. Rahner believed that throughout the long history of Christian reflection on the doctrine of the Trinity these two aspects of the Trinity had gradually become separated, so that theologians speculated on the intratrinitarian relations completely apart from any salvation-historical activity of the three persons.

For example, some theologians suggested that any one of the three persons of the Trinity could have become incarnate, not only the Son, and that all activities of the Trinity in the world are activities of the entire Trinity. Rahner vehemently rejected this thesis. It falsely separates God-in-himself (or "in-themselves") from history, and it seems to make the Incarnation superfluous to God's inner being, which would then remain unaffected by it. In such a case, there could be no real self-communication of God to creatures in history.[52]

Once again, Rahner was protesting against extrinsicism and false dualism—this time as they appear in the traditional tendency to divide the immanent Trinity from the economic Trinity. He argued that there is no warrant for making any statements about the intratrinitarian relations (the immanent Trinity) apart from what God actually is and does among us in history and that the economic activity of the three persons in human history for our salvation must be recognized as the real presence of the immanent Trinity.

His thesis, however, raises the question of God's immutability. If the economic Trinity *is* the immanent Trinity and vice versa, does God change in and through his relations with history? The doctrine of the immanent Trinity, whatever its defects, was meant to guard against a dissolution of God in history. Rahner's answer was typically ambiguous: "God can become something. He who is not subject to change in himself can *himself* be subject to change *in something else*."[53] The creature—especially the human creature—was created by God in such a way *(potentia oboedientialis)* that it is a proper vehicle for God's own becoming in self-expression. The creature is "the grammar of God's possible self-expression."[54] By emptying himself in assuming human nature to himself, God "becomes" without changing.

According to Rahner, this is a proper, "dialectical" interpretation of God's immutability. In his relationship with creatures God remains true to himself without being static. God himself actualizes potentialities in both creation and himself in such a way that he does not lose himself and the world does not become God. Yet both "become" something in and through their relation with the other; they enter into a real history with each other without merging.

For Rahner, therefore, the immanent Trinity and the economic Trinity are joined in history in the event of the Incarnation, which is the primary event of God's "becoming." In Jesus Christ the *Logos*, the second person of the Trinity, became a human person. This becoming could not have left the intratrinitarian being of God untouched. The Incarnation signals a true history in God. Yet even in this event God remained the same. He became in and through another to which he emptied himself and which he added to himself.

In order to explicate this idea further we will need to investigate Rahner's doctrine of the Incarnation.

The Absolute Savior

Predictably, Rahner's doctrine of the person of Jesus Christ is "transcendental Christology." It inquires about the transcendental preconditions for the appearance of such a God-man or "absolute Savior," as Christians claim Jesus of Nazareth was and is. Rahner cited as the central question, "Is something like an absolute saviour or a God-man . . . an idea which is intelligible to some extent, prescinding from the question whether and where this idea has been realized?"[55] Rahner's answer was "Yes." Through an inquiry into human transcendental experience he concluded that searching for a God-man within history is a basic human activity.[56]

Whether Jesus Christ is indeed such an absolute Savior is another question. Although transcendental Christology cannot prove Jesus' absolute saviorhood, it can provide a point of contact between anthropology and Christian faith in Jesus as the Savior of the world. Rahner found the ultimate basis for the Christian claim that Jesus is the absolute Savior in the historical combination of Jesus' self-consciousness and his resurrection. Jesus claimed to bear in himself a "new and unsurpassable closeness of God which on its part will prevail victoriously and is inseparable from him."[57] This closeness Jesus called the "coming and the arrival of God's kingdom," and he challenged people to accept or reject this God who had come close in himself. From this Rahner offered this conclusion:

> Jesus, then, is the historical presence of this final and unsurpassable word of God's self-disclosure: this is his claim and he is vindicated in this claim by the resurrection. He is of eternal validity and he is experienced in this eternal validity. In this sense in any case he is the "absolute saviour."[58]

What of the church's claim that Jesus was and is not only the absolute Savior of the world—the fulfillment of the deepest human aspirations—but also God incarnate? Rahner believed that the ontological divinity of Jesus Christ could be established from his function as absolute Savior. An absolute Savior, he argued, must be more than merely a human prophet. Only God himself in self-communicating grace can save absolutely. Any merely human mediation of a message from God would fall short of the real presence of God transforming and "divinizing" the world. Furthermore, Rahner argued, an absolute event of salvation must be an event in the very life of God himself.[59]

We can understand these assertions properly only against the background of Rahner's view of final and ultimate—"absolute"—salvation. Such salvation, which human transcendentality strives toward, involves much more than a "message" from God. It necessarily includes the real presence of God in the very depths of creaturely existence, transforming it in grace toward higher union with God. In a word, it is "divinization." Absolute salvation brings a grand result: "Now God and the grace of Christ are present as the secret essence of every reality we can choose."[60] Such a union of God and humanity, which preserves their distinction, cannot be produced by a mere prophet. If Jesus was and is the event of absolute salvation, as Rahner believed his resurrection established, then he could not have been less than God present in a man—Immanuel, "God with us."

Rahner affirmed and defended the classical christological doctrine of the "hypostatic union," which states that Jesus Christ is one person in two natures—human and divine. His defense rested on transcendental and historical grounds. If Jesus' entire consciousness was indeed permeated by radical and complete surrender to God, and if what he accomplished by his life, death and resurrection constituted the final and absolute event of salvation, then he could be no other than God incarnate.[61]

But would that not contradict his true humanity? Rahner adamantly rejected any hint of docetism—the view that Jesus' humanity was unreal or a mere "livery" of God. Jesus was as much a human as anyone else, Rahner argued, even to the extent of being fallible in his own consciousness about many things.[62] His divine consciousness was apparently transcendental and therefore unthematic and nonreflexive during his formative years. And it never overwhelmed or displaced his finite human consciousness. How can the finite creature, in this case Jesus' humanity, and the infinite being of God unite in a single entity such as the person of Jesus? That is the mystery of the hypostatic union, a mystery that has never been satisfactorily solved. Rahner believed he had an insight that would open up the mystery. The clue lay in his concept of humanity as the "cipher of God."

Humanity as the "Cipher of God"

According to Rahner's anthropology, humans are not merely creaturely, immanent, closed in upon themselves and nature. Rather, as we have seen, we are transcendent while remaining finite. That human nature is transcendentally open to God is a fundamental philosophical fact. Theologically, in view of the Incarnation, one must say that our human God-openness is intended by God as the potential for divine self-expression. In other words, the human person is the creature that is incomplete without Incarnation. God is the mystery of humanity, and humanity is the cipher of God. Humanity is the question; God is the answer. Just as the question participates in the answer and the answer participates in the question while transcending it, so God and humanity belong essentially together. God has decided it will be so.[63]

"When God wants to be what is not God, man comes to be."[64] This is one of the most telling statements in Rahner's entire theology. It indicates that for him, the purpose for the creation of humanity, if not the cosmos as a whole, is the Incarnation. Humankind is created so as to be the "cipher of God," the symbol and vehicle of God's self-expressive presence. Consequently the Incarnation does not contradict true humanity, but brings it to its greatest possible fulfillment. According to Rahner, the assumption that in order to be a true human person Jesus had to have some independent, autonomous existence over against God is fundamentally mistaken, because "closeness and distance, or being at God's disposal and being autonomous, do not vary for creatures in inverse, but rather in direct proportion."[65] Therefore, Jesus Christ could be the most radically human, autonomous and free precisely because his humanity was made closest to God by its assumption into eternal union with the *Logos* in the Incarnation.

For Rahner, then, the Incarnation was the ultimate accomplishment and fulfillment of both God and humanity. In it God's desire to express himself outwardly through what is not God came to fulfillment. At the same time, the Incarnation comprises fulfillment of the human search for an absolute Savior and human radical openness toward God.

All things, therefore, in heaven and on earth were fulfilled in Jesus Christ.

Critical Evaluation

Our discussion has already raised several critical questions about Rahner's theology. Despite our concerns about his views on certain topics, there can be no doubt that Rahner will continue to have a profound and lasting effect on contemporary, especially Catholic, theology. He provided a mediating approach that bridged the gap between two extremes that threatened and still threaten the unity of the church. He interacted positively and powerfully with modern thought, while remaining doggedly faithful to the rich heritage of Catholic theology. He refused to be intimidated by the modern prejudice against abstract philosophical and theological speculation and, for many people, recovered a sense of the beauty and grandeur of the mind's ability to grasp something of the mystery of God. Rahner may have provided the greatest impulse and path for faithful renewal of Catholic theology since Thomas Aquinas in the thirteenth century.

But what of his approach to transcendence and immanence? Was he able successfully to untie the Gordian knot that has so baffled contemporary theology? Unfortunately, like Alexander the Great in the Greek myth, Rahner did not untie the knot; he cut it. The concepts he employed for the purpose of providing a renewed understanding of immanence and transcendence ultimately fail, and this because of their ambiguity. They are, as George Vass said, "eel-like"; one just cannot pin them down.[66]

Yet Rahner did affirm the transcendence and immanence of God equally, often in very creative and innovative ways that provide new avenues of thought.

The ambiguous nature of Rahner's concepts of the supernatural existential and the unity-in-difference of God and creation has already been noted. Left to be explored is his concept of the Incarnation, which contains the clearest expression of his vision of the God/world relationship. In Jesus Christ, God's transcendence and immanence meet and become one. Or, it might be better to say, this event reveals the essential unity of the divine transcendence and immanence.

Speaking analogously, of course, Rahner taught that God wanted from all eternity to express himself outwardly in what is not God. The Catholic theologian did not speculate on why that is so, however, leaving its explanation in the mystery of God's love. Because immanence in the other is a basic desire and impulse in God himself, he created something inwardly oriented to God's own presence and brought it to consciousness—a consciousness entirely dependent on his own secret and mysterious presence (potentia oboedientialis). Then he graced the creature with his own self-communication in its innermost being (supernatural existential) without fully uniting with it. God's creation remained yet incomplete, striving and yearning for more. Finally, God chose one particular historical instance of that creation and stepped into it by an act of self-emptying identification, expressing himself through it to all others. By their intrinsic connection with it they too began to be divinized—to receive the presence of God.

In this way, the immanence of God that had been in the creature all along received the transcendence. The telos (ultimate goal and purpose) of the transcendence was achieved by the immanence, and the telos of the immanence was achieved in the transcendence. In the interconnection of Jesus Christ both God and humanity "happened" together, while remaining distinct.

Rahner's account forms a beautiful story. Whether it solves the dilemma of transcendence and immanence, however, is another story. In this vision, as in so many similar visions that are based on metaphysical speculation, the specter of a panentheistic interdependence of God and creation lurks in the background. Rahner did assert that God could remain God without the world and his involvement in it. Yet his overall theory of humanity as the "cipher of God" implies that God needs the world and especially humanity as the mode of his self-expression. It implies as well that the creation is not truly good until the Incarnation unites it with God.

The specter that haunts Rahner's theology begins to look more and more like the ghost of Hegel, whose panentheistic philosophy of the "true infinite" that includes the finite in itself blurred the distinction between God and humanity. The house of contemporary theology has been haunted by Hegel's ghost ever since the great German philosopher lectured at Berlin, and Rahner's theology has not been completely exorcised of it.

HANS KÜNG:
STRIKING THE BALANCE BETWEEN IMMANENCE AND TRANSCENDENCE

On December 18, 1979, Professor Hans Küng was on a skiing vacation in the Austrian Alps when the message arrived: The Vatican had declared him not a Catholic theologian. This was the culmination of a decade-long struggle between the world-famous Tübingen theologian and Rome's Sacred Congregation for the Doctrine of the Faith. Rarely does such a theological controversy make headlines around the world, but in this case the secular media had made Küng out as a modern-day Martin Luther challenging the monolithic giant of the Catholic establishment.

Küng rushed back to Tübingen to save his teaching position and contact his publishers to be sure that his current book would not be held up by the news. He need not have worried. The news only enhanced his prestige and position both at Tübingen and around the world. His books' sales increased dramatically, and he received calls to speak to audiences everywhere. Overnight Küng became a martyr and the leading spokesman for reform in the Roman Catholic church.

Küng's Life and Career

Hans Küng was born on March 19, 1928, in the small town of Sursee in the Catholic part of Switzerland. His father owned a shoe store and a small inn. Together with his younger brother and five younger sisters, Küng grew up in a secure, stable and devout environment, with most of the privileges of any middle-class Swiss family. At the age of twenty he went to Rome to begin his studies toward the priesthood, a vocation he had settled on rather quietly during his last years in *Gymnasium* (high school). In Rome he received a traditional theological education at the prestigious Gregorian University.

At first Küng strongly supported the traditional authoritarian approach to church life, theology and society taken by Pope Pius XII, who was determined to stamp out any revival of modernism or liberalism within the Catholic church. In 1950, while Küng was studying in Rome, the pope issued an encyclical entitled *Humani generis* that condemned certain supposedly humanistic trends in theology. The papal act inaugurated a wave of suppression of new ideas within Catholic theology, which lasted until Vatican II in the early 1960s. Several leading French Catholic theologians, including Teilhard de Chardin and Henri de Lubac, were silenced or deposed from their teaching positions, a movement of "worker priests" was suppressed and the Dominican Order was purged of free thinkers and alleged mavericks.

Throughout the 1950s, Küng became more and more uncomfortable with the heavy-handed approach to well-intentioned adaptations of Catholic thought and life to modern society. At first, he kept his concerns to himself and broadened his own horizons with rigorous intellectual engagement with such non-Catholic thinkers as the atheist existentialist Jean Paul Sartre and the Protestant Karl Barth. He later confessed that both served as liberators of his own philosophical and theological thought.

Küng was ordained a priest and celebrated his first mass in St. Peter's Cathedral in Rome in October 1954. Shortly afterward he moved to Paris to work on a doctorate in theology. There he came under the influence of several leading Catholic moderate theologians, including the patristics scholar Yves Congar and Hans Urs von Balthasar, a fellow Swiss, who further encouraged Küng in his studies of Karl Barth. His tenure in Paris set him on the basic course that he would follow as a Catholic theologian, a course marked by ecumenical openness, progressive, critical orthodoxy and positive dialog with secular science, philosophy and world religions.

Küng's first book was a revision of his doctoral dissertation on Karl Barth's doctrine of justification. *Justification: The Doctrine of Karl Barth and a Catholic Reflection* was published with a brief "letter to the author" by Barth himself in 1957. It created a small stir because of its main thesis, Küng's claim that "on the whole there is fundamental agreement between the theology of Barth and that of the Catholic Church."[1] Although

Barth did not necessarily agree with this thesis, he embraced its author as a younger colleague and friend and invited him to hold dialog in his seminars at Basel. The Catholic hierarchy was less enthusiastic in its response. Only later did Küng discover that the Sacred Congregation for the Doctrine of the Faith, the office in Rome that investigates heresies in the church, opened a file on him shortly after publication of this book.

In 1960, on the eve of the Second Vatican Council, Küng was invited to take a chair in fundamental theology at the University of Tübingen—a most unusual invitation for a thirty-two-year-old scholar. He has remained a professor there in spite of controversy and conflict with both the Vatican and the German bishops of the Catholic church and routinely draws huge crowds of students to his lectures. In the early 1960s he gained a reputation as a progressive reformer through his lectures, articles and books, and he played a significant advisory role at Vatican II. Even before the council opened, just as he was arriving at his new post in Tübingen, Küng was already explaining what this council should accomplish. In his second book, *The Council, Reform and Reunion* (1960), the young reformer articulated high hopes for the conclave and called for it to move the splintered Christian churches toward visible unity. Much of his later career as a theologian can be interpreted in the light of his disappointment over the outcome of the council.

During the 1960s Küng was primarily concerned with challenging and reinterpreting Catholic teachings about the nature of the church. In *Structures of the Church* (1962), *The Church* (1967) and *Infallible?* (1970) he presented devastating biblical, historical and theological criticisms of the hierarchical authority operative in the Roman Catholic church, its resistance to change, and especially the dogma of the infallibility of the pope.

The reformer called, for instance, for the recognition that only God is infallible and that the church may be "indefectible" in its overall vision of truth but never free from any taint of error, even when its human head speaks *ex cathedra*. In place of infallibility, Küng substituted the thesis that the church is kept in truth by God "in spite of all erring and misunderstanding."[2] His reasons for rejecting the traditional dogma of infallibility were twofold. The first was ecclesiological. Küng considered the infallibility doctrine rationally indefensible; it is impossible to reconcile absolute infallibility with the actual mistakes and contradictions of Catholic history. The second reason was theological. According to Küng's biographer Robert Nowell, "There is [in Küng] a Barthian insistence on the absolute primacy and otherness of God."[3]

Besides calling for a radical revision of the dogma of infallibility, Küng also criticized the church's position on numerous practical matters of church order and ethics, such as birth control and priestly celibacy.

Küng's writings on the church gained him the undying enmity of powerful leaders in Rome and caused even some of his friends to defect from the ranks of his supporters. His early mentor Hans Urs von Balthasar sharply criticized his former student's more radical views, and Karl Rahner called him a "liberal Protestant"—a charge Küng would find especially hard to disprove.

The Vatican launched a serious investigation of his writings and called him to Rome for interrogation about his theological views. Rather than submit meekly, Küng resisted, because he considered the action of the hierarchy unjust, lacking in the kind of due process provisions necessary to any fair legal procedure. The investigation dragged out for a decade and intensified with every book Küng wrote.

During the 1970s Küng's main interest lay in the area of apologetics. While the Vatican and the bishops of the German Catholic church were investigating him for heresy regarding teachings about the church, he was busy publishing books in which he sought to establish positive dialog with secular audiences. "Apologetics" and "dialog" are not often equated. In Küng's mind, however, true Christian apologetics must take seriously the secularism, and even the atheism, of modern Western culture and attempt to communicate Christian belief in a way that will speak to people of that mindset. His approach to apologetics is similar to Tillich's "method of correlation."

In 1970, just before *Infallible?* appeared, Küng published a massive study of Hegel's Christology, entitled *The Incarnation of God,* on which he had been working for years. It drew little attention outside of scholarly circles. The average reader was no doubt daunted by its nearly six hundred pages of fine print! Even scholars found it difficult to read because of the technical detail with which the author analyzed and interpreted Hegel's thinking. Küng, however, considers it his finest and most fundamental theological contribution.[4]

Küng published his most popular book, *On Being a Christian,* in 1974. It is a massive exposition of basic Christian belief and ethics written for educated lay audiences. The seven hundred pages did not prevent it from becoming a bestseller in German bookstores. Although less enthusiastic than in Germany, its reception in England and America was nevertheless wider than that enjoyed by most theological books. In *On Being a Christian* Küng articulated a progressive account of Christian doctrine based on a thoroughly modern, scientific world view. His discussion of the person of Jesus Christ became a focus of major criticism by conservative Catholics and led the German bishops to side with the Vatican against him. One especially harsh critic charged that he represented Jesus as a maverick reformer courageously standing up against the religious establishment of his time and thus as "the man who would be Küng!"

In 1978 Küng published what many critics consider his magnum opus: *Does God Exist? An Answer for Today.* At a length of over eight hundred pages in English translation, it constitutes a comprehensive theological analysis of and response to modern atheism.

The controversy between Küng and the Vatican culminated in 1979 with the withdrawal of his *missio canonica,* his privilege to instruct Catholic ministerial students in the faith. He was declared *not* a Catholic theologian, much to the dismay of his family, students and friends around the world. Over a thousand students demonstrated in the public square in Tübingen. Newspapers and scholarly societies around the world published editorials and declarations condemning the Vatican's act as a "new inquisition."

Küng's reputation and career were greatly enhanced by the event. His book sales skyrocketed, and invitations to speak and teach poured in from around the world. The

University of Tübingen set up a special institute for Küng to head and kept him as a professor, in spite of the fact that Catholic students could no longer take his courses for credit toward their ministerial licenses. Küng himself, now freed from any restraint, embarked on a crusade against what he considered the backwardness of the Vatican. When asked in 1989 what he thought of the popular Pope John Paul II, he replied, "We'll just have to wait for him to die" and expressed hope that the next pope would carry out the reforms begun by Vatican II.[5] In 1990 he published an especially biting critique of Rome, "Longing for John XXIV: In Memory of Pope John XXIII."[6]

During the 1980s and into the 1990s, Küng turned his interest primarily to theological method and interreligious dialog. He spearheaded a landmark conference of theologians on "paradigm change" in theology at Tübingen in 1983, and in 1987 he published a major work on the subject, entitled in English *Theology for the Third Millennium: An Ecumenical View*. He also held many conferences and engaged in dialogs with representatives of major world religions, coauthoring with them several books, including *Christianity and the World Religions* (1985).

Because his theology is so closely tied up with his adult biography, it is essential to deal with Küng's life and career in some detail. In terms of exposure in the secular media, he has been without question the most visible theologian of the twentieth century. That exposure, together with his treatment by the Vatican, cannot help but have exercised great impact on his theology.

Küng's "Critical Rationality"

Is Küng a liberal Protestant in Roman Catholic disguise? There is no question that he— like Erasmus during the Reformation—wishes to remain within the Roman Catholic church and change it from within. His theological method, however, is much more akin to that of contemporary Protestant theology than to classical Catholic thought. Küng stands in the tradition of Schleiermacher and Tillich while also drawing heavily on Barth. In fact, one might correctly say that his entire project is an attempt to mediate between the Catholic and the Protestant streams of contemporary theology.

To analyze Küng's theological method we must look first at his basic epistemological starting point, which he calls "critical rationality," then inspect his view of the rationality of belief in God, before moving to his proposal for a new postmodern paradigm. Finally, we will consider his view of theology's sources and norms.

In *Does God Exist?* Küng defended the rational credentials of basic Christian theism against the onslaughts of such modern atheists as Feuerbach, Marx, Nietzsche and Freud. Through careful analysis of the grounds of their objections to belief in God, he discovered that, although atheism cannot be conclusively refuted, neither can it be conclusively substantiated. His assessment of Nietzsche is typical: "If we look dispassionately behind the mask of the prophet, visionary, emotional thinker, preacher, his atheism also was *not really justified, but assumed as a datum*."[7] Laboriously, Küng built his case throughout the book: Atheism is not more rational than belief in God. Neither belief nor unbelief is provable; both are "basic decisions" on which everything else in a person's life rests.

Küng's appeal to "basic decisions" forms a part of the epistemological approach he calls "critical rationality." He believes this approach is more appropriate both to the modern scientific mind and to Christian belief than either critical rationalism or fideism.

"Critical rationalism" is that concept of reason stemming from Descartes and espoused in the twentieth century by Karl Popper and Hans Albert (among others), which insists on mathematical-like proofs and disproofs as the basis of true knowledge. It is akin to positivism in its view of empirical verification and falsification as criteria of truth. Küng argued that such an epistemology is inappropriate, for it assumes the existence of some Archimedean point of reference for rationality.[8] Belief in reason requires a certain superrational belief in the rationality of the universe. Consequently, he added, "All knowledge . . . contains a 'presupposition' that can be described as a 'matter of faith'."[9] Furthermore, Popper's critical rationalism ignores the "multiple dimensionality" and "complex stratification" of reality by reducing everything to empirical data.[10]

Irrationality, or fideism, is just as inappropriate as dogmatic rationalism. Therefore, Küng outlined a middle way between the two extremes, which he called "the way of critical rationality." This approach recognizes the fundamentally uncertain condition of reality and our human grasp of it, as well as the multiple varieties of reality, and builds from superrational fundamental decisions that can at best be rationally justified beliefs about the nature of reality. Such basic attitudes or commitments cannot be proved or disproved, conclusively verified or falsified, Küng acknowledged. Nevertheless, they are rationally justified insofar as they fit human experience as a whole.

In *Does God Exist?* Küng applied the method of critical rationality to belief in God. Building from Kant, he asserted that neither God's existence nor his nonexistence can be proved, for it lies beyond the grasp of human reason.[11] Nevertheless belief in God is not an irrational "leap of faith" or a "sacrifice of the intellect." Rather, it is a rationally justified fundamental trust that can be verified *indirectly* through the "experienced reality of man and the world."[12] In other words, if God exists, certain universal human questions are answered and certain universal human experiences are explained. Ultimately, uncertain reality itself receives coherence, meaning and a ground of being, if God exists; if God does not exist, reality remains uncertain, and there can be no ground, basis or support for fundamental trust.

The book represents a sustained *indirect* proof of the rationality of belief in God. That is certainly far from a proof of the existence of God in any traditional sense. However, Küng believes that all that is necessary today is to show that belief in God is not irrational, as many secularists claim, but rationally justified. Much of the force of his argument stems from his critique of atheism. While it is rationally irrefutable, he averred, "Denial of God implies an ultimately unjustified fundamental trust in reality," *unless* one wishes to be a sheer nihilist—an option that cannot be maintained consistently in practice.[13]

Küng's argument for theism's rationality begins with the necessity of taking an attitude toward uncertain reality: Reality is either ultimately trustworthy or untrustworthy.

Either the universe is a "home" for humanity full of meaning and value or it is a sheer happenstance devoid of any transcendent purpose. If we choose to believe the latter, we are by definition nihilists. But nihilism provides no ground for aesthetics or ethics; rather, everything is meaningless. Most people, however, do not believe that; they find "fundamental trust" a compelling option.

If we opt for fundamental trust, Küng averred, we must choose once more: Uncertain reality either has a ground and source that overcomes its absolute uncertainty, or it does not. It is ruled either by a divine providence or by chance. The choice to believe that reality is ruled by a personal transcendent-immanent God is rationally justified because it provides ground and support to fundamental trust, whereas atheism does not.

Compared to traditional natural theology and its opposite, Barthian defiance, Küng's approach is a modest one indeed. He placed his method of verifying the truth of God's existence "between Karl Barth and Vatican I."[14] He claimed, however, that this approach is the best one today, because it preserves both rationality and faith, something even natural science must do.[15]

A Postmodern Paradigm for Theology

Küng's reliance on critical rationality flowed over into his method of reinterpreting Christian belief for today. Not only apologetics but also systematic theology must be thoroughly critical, if it is to be taken seriously in modern culture, he argued: "In theological science, the rules are no different in principle from the rules of other sciences. Here, too, irrationality, unjustified reactions, subjectivist decisions, cannot be permitted."[16] At the same time, rationality must not be so absolutized that it becomes an ideology binding the transcendent Word of God at the outset. In systematic theology as in apologetics, Küng desired to inhabit a space between extremes.

The Catholic thinker has called for a new, postmodern paradigm for theology.[17] He borrowed the concept of paradigm from Thomas Kuhn, who wrote a landmark study in the philosophy of science entitled *The Structure of Scientific Revolutions* (1962 and 1971). Kuhn argued that scientific progress does not follow a smooth, rational path, but rather lurches forward through violent shifts in basic frameworks of meaning and interpretation (paradigms). These shifts constitute revolutions in scientific thought and happen when one paradigm, such as Newtonian physics, can no longer explain the data and gives way to a radically new and different paradigm, such as quantum physics. According to Kuhn, these scientific revolutions are not purely rational processes. Scientists are reluctant to give up old views of nature and methods for studying it. They only do so gradually or by sheer conversion when forced to by overwhelming evidence. In fact, it is usually "young Turks" in the scientific community who force such paradigm changes.[18]

Küng believes that Kuhn's analysis of paradigm change in natural science holds true in every science—including theology. The history of Christian theology can be analyzed in terms of shifts, not just from one type of theology to another, but from one "entire constellation of beliefs, values, and techniques" to another. An example of such a paradigm shift in Christian theology is the Protestant Reformation, which represented more than merely a shift of emphasis or interpretation. It was a radical change in the very foundations of theology away from medieval scholasticism and authoritarian traditionalism toward a concentration on Scripture and faith alone. Changing along with the Reformation involved more than just turning a new leaf or altering an opinion. It required a kind of conversion—albeit not an irrational leap.

In Küng's estimation, the Roman Catholic church and Christianity as a whole are ripe for a paradigm shift as radical as that of the Reformation. Any new paradigm, he argued in *Theology for the Third Millennium,* must be "postmodern," comprising "an immanent critique of modernity" and "sober, upright movement forward to the future."[19]

One of Küng's favorite concepts is the Hegelian idea of *Aufhebung,* a term for which there is no exact English equivalent. Küng's idea of postmodernity provides a good opportunity to explain the concept. A postmodern paradigm would be the *Aufhebung* of modernity (that is, culture based on the Enlightenment), in that it would transcend modernity without canceling it out. The enduring, positive values of modernity would be preserved, while its outmoded aspects would be transcended by something new. Modernity, Küng averred, must be "preserved, critiqued, and transcended" in a new postmodern paradigm of culture that includes philosophy and theology.[20]

Hence, Küng is not opposed to the Enlightenment; he even believes that it is impossible to go back behind it. The rise of critical reason, science and the historical-critical method of inquiry, and the Enlightenment emphasis on human freedom and autonomy can never be reversed. Theology must be among the first to acknowledge this. But such negative, even unscientific, elements of modern culture as dogmatic rationalism and the myth of inevitable progress must be transcended by a higher vision of reason and a more realistic assessment of experience. We have seen this basic response to the Enlightenment and modernity illustrated in Küng's idea of "critical rationality."

Küng called for a new, post-Enlightenment paradigm for theology, a "contemporary-ecumenical paradigm" resulting in a "critical ecumenical theology."[21] In *Theology for the Third Millennium* he did not provide a complete picture of the new paradigm that he saw struggling to be born in contemporary theology. But he did provide some principles, norms and guidelines for its birth.

Above all, like new scientific paradigms, the new theological paradigm must stand in both continuity and discontinuity with previous theological paradigms.[22] Küng brought to the fore a number of competing paradigms, attempting to expose their weaknesses while preserving their strengths. For example, "Catholic Traditionalism," represented especially by the nineteenth-century textbook theology of Denziger, was correct to preserve the unity and continuity of Christian teaching but wrong to make "sound Catholic teaching" the be-all and end-all of the Christian message.[23] Another alternative is that of Karl Barth. The Swiss Protestant initiated a change from the modern to the postmodern paradigm. But he would need to go further in embracing critical methodology and openness to the truth in world religions in order to establish his theology as the basic model for the third millennium.[24]

Theological Method

Küng laid down two basic poles between which a new theological paradigm must be equally balanced: "a theology from the perspective of Christian origins and the Christian center, against the horizon of today's world."[25] In other words, theology must work with two sources or norms: "God's revelatory speaking in the history of Israel and the history of Jesus,"[26] on the one hand, and "our own human world of experience"[27] on the other. Küng affirmed Tillich's method of correlation between these two sources/ norms of theology, while suggesting a significant alteration. He advocated a "critical correlation" in which there is sometimes genuine "critical confrontation" between them.[28] Hence, the theologian must not expect from the outset that there will always be smooth continuity and harmony between the gospel message, even as understood through the best historical-critical exegesis, and modern human experience. Sometimes conflict and confrontation will arise. This is why the paradigm is "postmodern" rather than "modern." When conflict happens the primacy must be given to the Christian message itself and not to the horizon of modern experience.

The strong emphasis on the primacy of the Christian gospel over the "horizon of human experience" marks a significant point of difference between Küng's methodology and both classical liberalism and neoliberalism. One can only wish that Küng would provide more in the way of concrete examples of such primacy. Generally he is more interested in discussing the importance of correlating the Christian message with human experience. Nevertheless, he insisted on this point of continuity with traditional paradigms of theology, both Catholic and Protestant:

> All this means that a drastic, paradigmatic upheaval can take place in Christian theology—if it is to be and remain Christian—always and only on the *basis* of the Gospel, and ultimately *on account of* the Gospel, but never *against* the Gospel. The Gospel of Jesus Christ himself—much as the testimonies to him must be deeply probed by means of historic-criticism—is no more at the theologian's disposal, to rule on its truth, than history is for the historian or the Constitution for the constitutional lawyer.[29]

Concretely, this means, for example, that Küng rejects the trend among certain Christian theologians to remove Jesus Christ from the center of Christianity and for the sake of interreligious understanding replace him with simply "God." The Catholic thinker considers this point a genuine watershed, "Caesar's Rubicon," which he cannot cross if he is to remain a Christian theologian.[30]

His emphasis on the primacy of the gospel in any new Christian theological paradigm does not mean, however, that Küng sides with conservatives or evangelicals who wish to base the gospel on the verbal inspiration of the Bible. He wishes to preserve as the primary source/norm of theology Jesus Christ as unique Lord and Savior of humanity, not the entire Bible. For Küng, believing the Bible is infallible is as much a mistake as regarding the pope as infallible. Infallibility belongs only to God; the writers of the Bible were merely fallible human witnesses to God's revelation in Israel and in Jesus Christ.

One must not elevate the Bible to the position of a "paper pope," as Küng believes has happened in Protestant fundamentalism and evangelicalism. Rather, we must make a clear distinction between even the New Testament and the gospel.[31] The gospel is imbedded in the New Testament in the person of Jesus Christ. Only sound "critico-historical method" can rediscover this *norma normans* (absolute norm) of theology, which norm must then be applied to the rest of the Bible.

Küng called for "a historic-critically responsible dogmatic theology" based on "historic-critically grounded exegesis."[32] As we will see, this raises the question, even for some of Küng's most sympathetic critics, of what the true *norma normans* of his critical ecumenical paradigm will be: the New Testament, as he has occasionally indicated in past writings,[33] the person of Jesus Christ, the "Gospel of Jesus Christ" or historic-critical methodology.[34]

As a Catholic, Küng must find a place for Christian tradition in his theological method. He relegates it to a secondary status within the overall source/norm of the Christian message. The gospel of Jesus Christ holds first place as *norma normans,* the touchstone of all truth, even over the Bible. The tradition of church teaching, including apparently even the Bible itself, as well as the church fathers, councils, popes and so forth, constitutes the *norma normata,* the secondary norm for determining the Christian message.[35] In his most recent writings Küng has notably neglected church tradition as constituting any essential ingredient in determining the structure and course of the new theological paradigm.

All of the immediately preceding material deals with Küng's view of the *first pole* or source/norm of the new "critical-ecumenical" paradigm of theology—the Christian message. Küng's account resembles that of dialectical theology, with a strong dose of critical-historical method thrown in. The core and touchstone of the Christian message is Jesus Christ plus the gospel message about him, which Küng has formulated in this way: "In the light and in the power of Jesus we can in the world of today live, act, suffer and die in a truly human way; utterly committed to our fellow-man because utterly sustained by God."[36] The Bible, and especially the New Testament, participates in this *norma normans* of theology as its historical vehicle, but it is not itself above criticism. Like the church as a whole, the Bible is "indefectible" in the whole, while not at all infallible. God makes his truth shine forth through the Bible's human mistakes. Church tradition helps in identifying the truth of the Christian message and should be respected as a secondary source/norm of theology, but is even more open to revision and reform than is the Bible.

The second pole and source/norm of the new critical-ecumenical theological paradigm is "the horizon of human experience," that is, "our present-day world of experience with all its ambivalence, contingency, and changeableness."[37] Among other things, the pole of experience establishes the necessity of critical reason in understanding and evaluating truth-claims, confirms the assumption of a scientific view of the natural world and its processes (that is, a "modern world view") and demands a generous, tolerant inclusivism of all faiths toward each other.

Küng worked out the correlation between the Christian message and critical rationality in *Does God Exist?* In *On Being a Christian* he explored the correlation between

Christian belief and the modern, scientific world view. In *Christianity and the World Religions* he discussed with representatives of the major faith traditions the relationship of Christian truth to other religions. In each case Küng managed to hold fast to Jesus Christ as the central source/norm of Christianity in the face of overwhelming objections and problems arising out of secular culture and non-Christian religions. At the same time, he also relativized, or outrightly denied, much of traditional Christian belief in favor of non-Christian truth-claims.

The "Historicity of God"

Like many twentieth-century theologians, Küng is concerned with overcoming the God/world dualism he sees implicit in much traditional theology, while avoiding any hint of pantheism. In other words, he seeks to discover God's transcendence *in* immanence. Küng worked out his doctrine of God primarily in critical dialog with Hegel, as is evident in his book *The Incarnation of God*. In spite of large areas of disagreement with Hegel, Küng is clearly dazzled by the German philosopher's overall vision of the dialectical unity of God and the world. Consequently he sought to delineate a "post-Hegelian" concept of God that would transcend-while-preserving *(aufheben)* both traditional Christian theism and Hegelian panentheism. Such a view of God would rule out any "naive anthropomorphic or even enlightened deistic picture of God on the basis of a supra- or even extra-terrestrial God deemed to exist alongside and over against this world and man."[38] At the same time, Küng's treatment would go beyond Hegel. It would lead to a new conception of the living God based on a dialectic of love, instead of Hegel's dialectic of knowledge, and would discover "*God* in the world, *transcendence* in immanence, the *beyond* in the here-and-now."[39]

Through a meticulous examination of Hegel's philosophical theology, Küng revealed his areas of agreement and disagreement with the great German thinker. He quickly discounted the charges of pantheism against Hegel, while acknowledging the truth of the charge of panentheism. In Hegel, God and the world—or God and humanity—are not "rolled into one." Nevertheless, they are united in intrinsic, reciprocal unity-in-differentiation, so that Hegel's God "is rarely described as a living, active person in an I-Thou relationship, but rather as a creatively present universal life and Spirit."[40]

Küng disagreed with the Hegelian diminution of God's personhood, as well as with the inevitable cancellation of grace that follows any intrinsic unity of God and humanity. Against Hegel, he declared, "What is entailed by a God of grace is a God who lives *in* the world itself, present but not caged within it, immanent within it yet also transcending it . . . close to and yet at the same time also other than the world."[41] Küng is likewise uncomfortable with Hegel's tendency to make God a prisoner of his own philosophical system and of the God-world totality ("monism of Spirit"). Apparently, God's freedom, which is presupposed by God's grace, is for Küng one of those non-negotiable items of the central core of the Christian message.

At the same time, Küng found much to embrace in Hegel's concept of God and God's relationship with the world. In contrast to the all-too-static and otherworldly God of traditional theism, Hegel's God is living, dynamic and capable of suffering, and he includes his antithesis in himself, rather than standing aloof from the world's history. This picture of God, Küng argued, is more compatible with and conducive to a full understanding of the Incarnation than is the Greek-inspired theism of much of traditional Christian theology. In the light of the Incarnation, the Catholic theologian asked, "Should not God's transcendence, immutability and unchangeability be subjected to a thoroughgoing reinterpretation?"[42] He answered his query in the affirmative, and declared that such a reinterpretation might be aided by "walking in Hegel's footsteps" (up to a point), because the German thinker's concept of God "is manifestly better suited to express what must be stated by a classical Christology which has been thought through to the end."[43]

Küng identified three key points where Hegel's concept of God could make a contribution to a renewed Christian doctrine of God: the suffering of God, the dialectic within God himself and God's involvement in becoming.[44] We will treat the three in reverse order, beginning with God's involvement in becoming.

In Küng's estimation, a major task for contemporary Christian thinking is to develop an understanding of God's historicality. In fact, the divine historicality is the main theme of *The Incarnation of God.* God's Incarnation, he affirmed, means that the divine attributes must be interpreted in the light of God's unity with Jesus' birth, life, suffering, death and resurrection. As Küng explained, "Man's salvation is entirely dependent on the fact that God himself does not hold aloof from this history and that it is God himself and not just a man who takes the stage in this man."[45] Consequently, the traditional affirmation of God's immutability and impassability, which Küng saw as based primarily on Greek metaphysics rather than on the Bible, must be reconsidered and revised in the light of God's presence in Jesus. This God is one who is capable of entering history and making it his own. He is a living, dynamic, historical God who becomes, not by necessity, but because he chooses to do so out of grace and overflowing love.

God's involvement in history does not signal a deficiency or even self-development, as if God *has* to become something to realize himself. In asserting this, Küng strenuously rejected both Hegel and Whitehead. A God who would need to become something would be "a pallid imitation of human wretchedness."[46] Nevertheless, God does really become, he added, and thus God possesses a "basic historicality" that flows out of his own inner dynamic life.

In his discussion of God's basic historicality Küng avoided the question as to whether God changes in his becoming. Yet by reading "between the lines" we can deduce something about Küng's attitude toward this crucial question. On the one hand, he rejected any notion of God's changeableness in the sense of being subject to change by necessity. He also has no use for any concept of irrational or capricious changeableness in God. On the other hand, he also rejected strict unchangeableness in the sense of being untouched by the history of pain and suffering in the world, especially in Jesus' life and death.

Once again, Küng's thinking is dialectical, moving between two false extremes. God can and does change, he declared, in full consistency with his own character by identification with finitude, temporality and suffering in Christ. Yet such change is not a denial or diminution of his deity, but constitutes its highest manifestation.[47]

Küng became more speculative when he delved into the hidden aspect of God's being, which makes such historicality possible. Hegel's second contribution, he argued, is the dialectic within God himself. God can become, because he always already includes finitude and imperfection in his own infinite being. This is a version of Hegel's idea of God as the *"wahrhaft Unendliche"*—the true infinite—that does not stand alongside the finite, but includes it. In Küng's words, "The living Christian God is therefore a God who does not exclude but includes his antithesis."[48] Greek metaphysics, he noted, upon which traditional Christian theism is largely based, could not conceive of such a God. For Küng, this dialectical unity of infinity and finitude within God's eternal being is the basis for God's self-humiliation in Christ. His entire thesis in *The Incarnation of God* is summed up in one passage dealing with this speculative vision of God's dynamic, dialectical being:

> God is not *forced*, but he is able to do what he does in history; and he has a power and ability to perform these acts which are rooted in his nature. The nature of the living God is a nature which is capable of self-humiliation, even though not compelled to take this path, a nature which contains within itself the power for gracious self-externalisation.[49]

These two theses concerning God, based on perceived "contributions of Hegel," form the foundation for Küng's revision of God's transcendence and immanence. Throughout his writings he repeatedly emphasized that a viable modern or postmodern concept of God must not separate God from the world: No worldless God and no godless world! God is to be conceived as present and revealed in the world and its history without being dissolved in them. God embraces the world in a loving gesture of self-abnegation, so that he becomes deeply imbedded in its history and its history becomes part of him. This is possible because God already contains the finite within himself.

But does that not lead back to Hegel's panentheism? Can Küng avoid it in any way other than by sheer assertion that it cannot be? Why does he not avail himself of the doctrine of the Trinity, as other contemporary theologians such as Moltmann and Jüngel have done, to explain how God can become in time and history without losing himself? In the final analysis, Küng's doctrine of God leans dangerously close to panentheism; he avoids the fallacy by simply asserting that to preserve God's freedom and grace the position cannot be true.

The emphasis on God's suffering is the third Hegelian contribution Küng embraced. Because God contains his antithesis in himself, he is able to suffer without being pathetic. Once again, Küng wended his way dialectically between two false opposites: God as apathetic and God as pathetic. The former extreme is the fault early Christianity inherited from Greek metaphysics. The latter is the error of process theology and other modern metaphysical conceptions of God that are based on the modern concept of the ultimacy of the category of change. The God of the Incarnation, Küng averred, is one who suffers freely and out of grace, not out of necessity or lack.[50]

That God suffers is almost a truism in contemporary theology. In a single theological generation the traditional doctrine of God's impassability has been overturned, so that it is now almost heresy to reassert it. Nevertheless, one must question whether Küng's account of the basis for God's suffering is better than that provided by process theology. God's suffering, for Küng, is based on his free choice to identify with Christ's sufferings. Yet it is also based on the divine inner dialectic, in which God always already includes the tension of antithesis within himself. He is the infinite that includes the finite, perfection that includes imperfection, life that includes death. Such a God would seem to be bound up with historicity and suffering. For such a God, involvement with the world and identification with its pain and misery would seem a given rather than gracious.

Küng accused Hegel of "sublating" the graciousness of God's relationship with the world in his philosophical system. Yet he also affirmed that the Christian God "is here *and* hereafter, distant *and* near, above the world *and* within the world, future *and* present. God is oriented to the world: There is no God without a world. And the world is wholly ordered to God: there is no world without God."[51] Küng's intention to balance the transcendence and immanence of God is reflected in the first part of this affirmation. The second part, however, raises the question as to whether Küng has fallen into Hegel's error of tying God too closely to the world, to the detriment of both.

It would be wrong to accuse Küng of emphasizing exclusively the immanence of God. He never tires of reasserting the transcendent freedom of God over the world. He is perfectly aware that the tendency toward immanentism in contemporary theology has led to a serious crisis in every area of theology. However, his ready acceptance of certain aspects of Hegel's ontology, such as the dialectical unity of the infinite and finite, pushes him unwittingly toward the pitfall of chaining God to the world and thus reducing the graciousness of the God/world relationship.

Christology

No aspect of Küng's theology has been as controversial outside of the Vatican as has his Christology. Even the German bishops of the Catholic church were more upset over it than over Küng's ecclesiology. His Christology was the straw that broke the proverbial camel's back. Although action was already underway to discipline him in some way, when *On Being a Christian* appeared in 1974 and church leaders had opportunity to evaluate Küng's statements on Jesus Christ, it seemed inevitable to many that he would receive a harsh sentence.

Yet Küng considers his theology radically christocentric. His intention in his Christology is to return to the earliest biblical teachings about Jesus Christ and place that testimony at the heart of the Christian message. As he explained, "Christianity is based not on myths, legends, or fairy tales, and not merely on a teaching . . . but primarily on a historical personality: Jesus of Nazareth, who is believed as God's Christ."[52] Why all the controversy, then?

Küng made clear in *On Being a Christian* that his approach to expounding the faith for today would be consistently "from below." He wanted to communicate Christian belief to modern men and women not by presupposing any dogmas of the church but by beginning with their questions and experiences, in order to provide a rational justification of faith today.[53] The Catholic thinker carried this approach into his Christology, investigating who Jesus is by following the path from the history of Jesus to the church's confession of him as the Christ—the same path traversed by the first disciples.[54]

There was nothing particularly new in this approach to the doctrine of Christ. Emil Brunner and Wolfhart Pannenberg, among others, had also followed it. The controversy was not over the method so much as over the results reached at the end of the process.

Küng spent hundreds of pages in *On Being a Christian* exploring the historical personality of Jesus. Jesus was not a "pious legalist" or a "revolutionary." Rather, in Küng's portrayal, he was a man totally consumed with God's cause—the well-being of others—a man who had a unique experience of God as his "Abba" and devoted himself without reservation to the kingdom of God. In the end, he was raised up by God and "exalted" to glory. (Küng made clear, however, that these are metaphors that can only give hints of what actually became of Jesus Christ after his death.) Clearly, the Catholic theologian considers Jesus a unique human person. Because of who he was, what he did and the fate he suffered, "the *true man* Jesus of Nazareth is for faith the real *revelation* of the one *true God*."[55] He is God's "representative, delegate, deputy" and "the living pointer to God the Father."[56]

What Küng's critics were looking for, however, was some positive statement of Jesus' divinity, some affirmation of the ontological Incarnation of God in Jesus, some acknowledgment that Jesus could be said to be God. This they could not find. In discussing Jesus' preexistence—an appropriate point for an affirmation of his divinity—Küng interpreted the doctrine as meaning only that Jesus' ultimate origin was from God.[57] This affirmation could be made about everyone and everything! It seemed that Küng was affirming a version of the "ideal preexistence" theory, that Jesus preexisted in the mind and will of God but not as the eternal second person of the Trinity.[58] In one brief passage Küng provided his "up-to-date positive paraphrase of the ancient Chalcedonian formula 'truly God and truly man.' " Once again he stated that Jesus was "God's advocate and deputy, representative and delegate" and the "permanently reliable ultimate standard of human existence."[59] This, he wrote, was to stand "against all tendencies to deify Jesus."[60]

Naturally, Küng was charged by his critics with adoptionism and christological reductionism. And rightly so, in that his Christology seems to be a model of a purely "functional" approach to the Incarnation—God working and acting in a man. Once again a contemporary theologian seems to be trying to speak of God by speaking of humanity in a very loud voice. Can Jesus be God incarnate merely by being God's human representative? Does being the paradigm of humanity add up to God in the flesh? Is it possible to keep from "crossing the Rubicon" of relativizing Jesus into another great prophet, if we refuse to affirm that he is in some real, ontological sense God?

Questions like these led the German bishops and others to take a stand against Küng.

Critical Evaluation

Hans Küng has been one of the twentieth century's most prolific and popular theologians. For many people, he has become the symbol of progressive Christian thought. For others he is the epitome of the arrogant academic rebel. Among those who know him and his theology indifference is rare. We have already indicated some of the strengths and weaknesses of Küng's theology.

Perhaps its greatest strength lies in its provision of an apologetic for a secular age. Few if any theologians have wrestled as profoundly or in as great detail with the challenges of atheism, agnosticism and nihilism as has Küng. The breadth and depth of his knowledge of these secular ideologies is amazing, as is his ability to probe their strengths and weaknesses. He approaches them with sympathy and candor while casting a critical eye toward their inner contradictions and their inconsistencies with experience.

For example, in *Does God Exist?* Küng discussed the views on the role of belief in God in society set forth by the influential Frankfurt school of social science and its spokesmen Adorno, Horkheimer and Habermas. In his treatment, he pitted Horkheimer against the other two, revealing the social scientist's sympathies toward belief in God as a necessary basis for objective ethics.

Creative dialog with modern and postmodern science and philosophy is Küng's forte. Through it he builds a convincing case that the rational credentials of unbelief are no stronger than those of belief and that to hold fast to God we need not sacrifice being enlightened, modern persons.

If apologetics is Küng's strength, theological method and interpretation of doctrine are his weaknesses. What does the Christian belief—the rationality of which he strove so mightily to defend—amount to? Does he allow it once again to be taken captive by a modern, or postmodern, world view? As we have already seen, even some of Küng's most sympathetic critics recognize an ambiguity in his theological method.

Nowhere is this ambiguity more evident than in his position concerning the theological norm. According to Küng, Scripture is supposed to stand over all ecclesiastical traditions, whether ancient or modern, as the *norma normans non normata* (supreme norm judging all norms) of Christian theology. Yet in his estimation Scripture is itself thoroughly historical and fallible; consequently it must be judged by rigorous historical-critical exegesis.[61] Once the historical-critical method of interpretation is introduced, Küng shifts his supreme norm of theology to the gospel within Scripture—Jesus Christ. But this norm must be drawn from Scripture and applied to Scripture and tradition by the historical-critical method. What is Küng's actual final criterion? Is it Scripture, the "gospel" within Scripture or the historical-critical method?

Catherine LaCugna correctly observed that a distinction must be made between Küng's theoretical methodology (his stated intentions) and his applied methodology (what he actually does).[62] After a rigorous investigation of the former she concluded, "Formally speaking . . . in Küng's theoretical theological methodology there appears to be a lively, if not difficult, tension between faith and history, in which the historical strand conditions but does not determine the strand of faith."[63] In other words, Küng cannot make up his mind which he will choose as the ultimate norm for theological truth, should a conflict arise between critical historical reason and clear biblical teachings about Jesus Christ. At least he never clearly opted for historical criticism over faith in the teachings of the Bible about the gospel.

LaCugna concluded, however, that in his applied methodology Küng gives undue weight to the historical-critical method. While Jesus Christ is supposed to be the criterion of all truth and truth itself, the "real Christ" seems to be accessible only through historical-critical analysis.[64] In practice, then, Küng elevates critical reason above, or at least alongside of, Jesus Christ himself, and certainly above both Scripture and tradition. But does not this approach serve to raise the individual critical exegete or some group of critical scholars above the absolute claim of the gospel, which is available only through Scripture and tradition? If so, then the charge that Küng is a "liberal Protestant" is largely sustained.

The charge of "liberal Protestant" arises more sharply than ever in relation to Küng's specific reconstructions of Christian doctrines. His account of the God/world relation leaves the prior actuality of God unclear. In several instances he indicated a marked preference for Hegel's "dialectical unity of God and the world." He likewise expressed strong distaste for the entire concept of the "supernatural" and blatantly denied that the concept of miracles, in the traditional sense of events that break the laws of nature, makes any sense at all: "Physically, a supernatural intervention by God in the world would be nonsense."[65] What should a Christian believe about such important dimensions of biblical piety as prayer, then? It comes as no surprise that Küng hardly discusses prayer in his major doctrinal or apologetic writings. Finally, Küng portrayed Jesus Christ as a special, even unique, human person, but not as God incarnate (in spite of the title of his most important book!).

After all the magnificent apologetics, we are left with a fairly weak, liberal Protestant theology in which historical criticism and the modern, scientific world view play the leading roles. Karl Rahner's judgment that Küng must be regarded as a liberal Protestant was quite correct.

9 TRANSCENDENCE WITHIN THE STORY:
Narrative Theology

*H*UMAN BEINGS ARE STORYTELLERS—PERHAPS BY NATURE. ALL TRIBES AND PEOPLES EX-
press their understanding of reality in terms of myths and stories. Some of these stories
are of a more personal nature. Since ancient times humans have recounted histories,
recalled testimonies concerning their lives and written autobiographies and biographies.

Beginning in the 1970s a specific approach to theology, which has gained a widespread following, is attempting to incorporate into the theological task recent discoveries concerning the importance of story for human self-understanding. This ap
proach, called "narrative theology," seeks to utilize the concept of story and the human
person as a storyteller as the central motif for theological reflection.

The move to story opens the way to a new means of conceptualizing the divine
transcendence while giving place as well to immanence, for its transcendence is the
transcendence of story. The new conceptualization developed by narrative theology
lifts the discussion beyond the purely temporal category that the theology of hope
introduced and that formed the basis for liberation theology's return to immanence.
The genius of narrative theology lies in its assertion that faith entails the joining of
our personal stories with the transcendent/immanent story of a religious community
and ultimately with the grand narrative of the divine action in the world. The divine
story mediated by the community of faith transcends our individual, finite narratives;
yet it is immanent both in the history of the world and by faith in the ongoing story
of the life of the believer.

Basic Characteristics

To be classified as a narrative, in the broadest sense of the term, a literary work need only contain a story and a storyteller. The newer narrative thinking, however, goes beyond this minimal definition of its subject matter. With respect to theological inquiry, narrative thinker Gabriel Fackre defined "story" as "an account of characters and events in a plot moving over time and space through conflict toward resolution."[1] Such narratives emerge from the human need to bring the past and the future into coherence with the present; they meet this need by ordering events in a way that conveys the sense that the chronology of time is not chaotic and insignificant, but rather has an ending.[2]

Like many other movements in modern theology, narrative thinkers begin with the question, What is the situation of being a human person in the world? For the key to the answer to this question, they look to narrative or story. Human experience, they argue, necessarily has a narrative form,[3] and as a result, it can only be understood in the form of a narrative.[4] Christian narrative theologians look to the particular historical events lying at the foundation of the Christian faith as recounted in the narratives of the Bible and Christian tradition, which, they claim, are redemptive when appropriated by individuals and thereby become the basis for personal identity and existence.[5]

This emphasis on telling one's story and meshing one's life into the story of a community is based on the contemporary assertion that nearly all our fundamental convictions, whether religious or nonreligious, are rooted in some narrative as the context in which they take on meaning. As a corollary to this assertion, narrative thinkers suggest that moral disagreements among people actually involve rival "histories of explanation."[6] Hence, narrative is crucial for theology, narrative theologians assert; it is central in the task of making intelligible and significant the religious convictions lying at the heart of theological reflection. According to Michael Goldberg, these thinkers share the primary assertion

> that in order justifiably to elucidate, examine, and transform those deeply held religious beliefs that make a community what it is, one must necessarily show regard for and give heed to those linguistic structures which, through their portrayal of the contingent interaction between persons and events, constitute the source and ground of such beliefs.[7]

Theological Background

Although the movement emerged only in the 1970s, the foundation for narrative theology was laid in developments earlier in the century. As with other new directions in theology, the move to narrative came as a response to perceived difficulties in older approaches to theology. More specifically, currents both in theology itself and in biblical studies concerning the nature of revelation and the authority and use of the Bible formed the basis for the newer movement. Narrative theology, then, may be viewed in part as the outworking of a crisis concerning the nature of the theological enterprise and the function of Scripture in theology that has come to characterize the modern era in its entirety.

The understanding of theology that predominated in the church throughout the Middle Ages and into the era of Protestant scholasticism viewed theology as the systematic presentation of revealed truth. Revelation, in turn, was treated largely as the deposit of true propositions. By the middle of the twentieth century, this approach had been fully eroded. Not only theologians but even many church people came to the conclusion that merely quoting from Scripture could not bridge the gap from the first to the twentieth century. A new way needed to be found to continue the task of theology apart from the appeal to propositional revelation. For some, biblical narrative offered a promising direction in which to turn.

The precursors to narrative theology, however, did not maintain that theology could simply dispense with the traditional task of setting forth abstract, propositional formulations[8] (even though some of their followers have moved beyond them at this point).[9] Rather, their thesis was simply that in its task of critical reflection theology dare not forget the narratives from which theological reflection draws its force. In other words, they emphasized that theology must move between narrative and systematic reflection on it.[10]

On this basis, however, narrative theologians did give primacy to story over doctrine in their work. In this way the movement sought to overturn the traditional emphasis on doctrine as central to revelation. As Stanley Hauerwas so poignantly declared, "Doctrines . . . are not the upshot of the stories; they are not the meaning or heart of the stories. Rather they are tools . . . meant to help us tell the story better."[11]

In addition to and perhaps as an outworking of this crisis concerning the nature of theology has been a second, the emergence of a crisis in Christian identity.[12] According to narrative theologian George Stroup, symptomatic of the presence of this crisis is the silence of Scripture in the church:

> the Bible no longer exercises anything like the authority it once did in many Christian communities. And in those communities where the Bible continues to exercise its traditional role there is little or no serious engagement with the problems of the twentieth century.[13]

This symptom is paralleled by the loss of other foundational resources in the life of the church: the loss of a sense that the believer and the community live out of a theological tradition and the loss of the importance of theology for church life.

As a result of these losses, Christians are unable to employ their faith as a basis from which to make sense out of their personal identity, Stroup theorized.[14] For an increasing number of church people neither the language of the Christian faith nor their participation in the community of faith now plays a prominent role in their "identity narrative," the way they identify themselves to others. Narrative theology arose in part to meet this challenge.

Basis in Neo-orthodoxy

In the midst of the challenges to the older understandings of theological methodology the way for narrative theology was paved by the growing prominence of the neo-orthodox understanding of revelation. Although many delineations of this theme appeared during the 1930s and 1940s, two were most influential and above the others provided the foundations for narrative theology. These were *The Meaning of Revelation* (1941) by Reinhold Niebuhr's brother H. Richard Niebuhr, and the first two installments of Karl Barth's monumental *Church Dogmatics*.

In his book, Niebuhr attempted to redirect theological attention to an overlooked, although obvious, characteristic of the Christian faith, namely, that the source and setting of the foundational Christian convictions lie within a historical framework[15]— within a framework determined by biblical narrative. Theology, he argued, is implicitly historical, and the revelation of God comes through the medium of history.[16] By articulating this thesis, Niebuhr became one of the first thinkers to address explicitly the significance of the fact that much of the Bible is cast in the form of story.[17]

Of central importance in the development of his thesis is the distinction Niebuhr drew between what he found to be the two aspects of history, the outer and the inner, or history as contemplated from the outside and history as lived from within.[18] Outer history consists of the objective events, whereas inner history designates the personal stories of individuals and communities. In contrast to outer history, inner history is concerned with personhood, values and time as a dimension of life.[19]

This twofold understanding of history set the stage for Niebuhr's view of revelation, for it provided the way of understanding how events can be revelatory—can be the workings of God—while remaining the objects of the analysis of the observer.[20] According to Niebuhr, revelation is that set of events, that part of inner history, which functions in a person or community as the basis for the interpretation of all other events,[21] and in this way is crucial for the formation of personal and group identity. Revelation, he argued, is what allows us to understand, remember and appropriate the past,[22] to explain contemporary personal or moral action[23] and to anticipate our future. As a result, revelation is an ongoing event, one "which happens over and over again when we remember the illuminating center of our history."[24]

His discussion of these themes allowed narrative theologians to look back to Niebuhr's book and find in it in embryonic form the salient points of their own proposal. "Niebuhr has directed our attention to the encounter which takes place between events in 'objective' or 'external' history and the personal histories of individuals and communities," concluded George Stroup. "It is in the context of this encounter between narratives that we have every reason to search for both the meaning of revelation and the structure of Christian identity." But beyond this, "Niebuhr made the provocative claim that revelation includes the appropriation of external event at the level of internal history and that this 'appropriation' necessarily assumes the form of a story, what Niebuhr referred to as 'the story of our life.' " The human response to the event of revelation compels the Christian in turn to confess faith by means of a narrative, Stroup concluded from Niebuhr.[25]

An additional aspect of Niebuhr's understanding of revelation was likewise important for the development of narrative theology.[26] Although it is an event that takes place in a person's inner history, revelation, as Niebuhr understood it, is not merely private. Rather, one's community is indispensable in the process of revelation, for it functions as the bearer of the narratives and the symbols, which when internalized by the individual become the occasion for revelation.

In the development of the narrative perspective, Karl Barth's discussion of revelation in the first two installments of his *Church Dogmatics* served to round out the picture presented by Niebuhr. Foundational for the new movement was Barth's widely known concept of the threefold nature of the Word of God—the Word incarnate, written and preached. This led in turn to his two-dimensioned concept of revelation. There is, of course, the objective dimension, the Incarnation of Jesus Christ as constituting the historical event in which God's Word became a visible reality. This forms the content of revelation, the "what" or "whom" that is revealed. Revelation, however, is likewise subjective, for it must occur in the present, in the experience of individuals and communities. This dimension describes how the Word of God becomes a reality in the midst of human words.

Barth's work provided a conceptual basis for the use of story as the vehicle of the divine-human encounter developed subsequently in narrative theology. In Stroup's words, "by giving priority to the doctrine of revelation Barth linked Christian faith and the identity of the events in which Christians believe they witness the presence and the activity of that reality Jesus called 'Abba.' "[27] Narrative theologians brought together this Barthian understanding with Niebuhr's in order to create a description of the event of revelation as what occurs in the collision between the personal history of an individual with that of a community.

Background in Biblical Studies

These monumental developments in theology were paralleled by equally important changes in the discipline of biblical studies. Just as theological questions concerning revelation and the nature of the Bible led to a theological crisis, so also biblical studies had been upset by a growing crisis concerning the historical-critical method that had been brewing since the beginning of the century.

The historical-critical approach to the Bible, which arose out of the Reformation, engages in exegesis by asking questions of a factual nature, especially the question concerning the actual historicity of the event as set forth by the biblical author. As a result of the dominance of the historical-critical method, there developed a growing tendency to see the question of the significance of a given text for today either as insignificant or as answered in the negative, with the assumed implication that if an event as told by the Bible did not happen it is no longer significant. This attitude led to a corresponding loss of the Bible's voice in the church. In the wake of this tendency, as World War 2 drew to a close biblical scholars devoted increasing attention to the problem of the ongoing importance of the Bible.

One key development in postwar biblical studies was the advent of what has come to be called the biblical theology movement, with its emphasis on the category of biblical history. An important voice in this development was that of G. Ernest Wright. Wright set forth the innovative thesis that at its core biblical theology is not primarily propositional dogmatics nor yet does it focus on the words, works and inner life of one personality. Above all, we must understand biblical theology in terms of "recital" or proclamation of the story of God's redemptive actions in history.[28] This thesis resulted in an important understanding concerning the nature of the Bible and its relationship to the narrative of history: "The Bible is not a static, but a living, book, in which the central figure is God and in which the central concern is to bear testimony to the story of what he has done to save man and to bring his kingdom into being on this earth."[29]

The biblical theology movement employed an understanding of history akin to that articulated by H. Richard Niebuhr and other neo-orthodox writers. For Wright "history" is a broad category, including "not only events of seeming impersonal significance, but also the lives of the individuals who compose it."[30] Further, he asserted that real historical events are involved in biblical theology, but that in themselves they do not "make" the biblical event. Rather, event plus interpretation are the constituent ingredients of history: "In the Bible an important or signal happening is not an event unless it is also an event of revelation, that is, unless it is an event which has been interpreted so as to have meaning."[31]

Wright's thesis carried profound implications for biblical studies. In the task of delineating biblical faith, he argued, the scholar ought not to begin with the history of the evolution of ideas in the Bible, but with history understood as the arena of God's activity. In biblical theology, believers confess their faith by reciting the formative events of their history "as the redemptive handiwork of God." The biblical theological framework viewed the facts of history as the facts of God.[32]

It was but a small step from Wright's thesis concerning biblical theology to the narrative approach to theology as a whole. He had set the stage for a renewed openness to read the Bible as story and then to tell one's own story on the basis of that reading:

> Since God is known by what he has done, the Bible exists as a confessional recital of his acts, together with the teaching accompanying these acts, or inferred from them in the light of specific situations which the faithful confronted. To confess God is to tell a story and then to expound its meaning.[33]

The crisis of the historical-critical method set the stage for the rise of another new, albeit related, methodology in biblical studies. The new methodology sought to move beyond the critical tools developed earlier in the twentieth century, such as form and redaction criticism, by utilizing what has sometimes been referred to as "canonical criticism." Less important to the work of canonical criticism is the actual historical facticity of the events narrated by the Bible. Rather, attention is given to the function of the genre of narrative within the context of Scripture.

An early statement of this direction came in Eric Auerbach's book, *Mimesis* (1946). Auerbach raised the question as to how biblical narratives compare to the literature of antiquity. His response to this query was unique. The Bible, he asserted, presents a vision of the way things are and issues a challenge to the reader to enter into the world of the text.[34] In this way, he urged the discipline of hermeneutics to move away from the widely followed program of seeking to bring the text into the world of the reader. The work of Auerbach and others has led to a renewed interest in concentrating on the final form of the biblical text, rather than on the history of its formation.

Narrative Approaches

Out of these developments in theology and biblical studies has emerged a loose coalition of thinkers who have found the category of narrative useful in addressing certain perennial or contemporary theological problems. Despite their agreement on the importance of the category, there is yet to emerge a consensus among narrative thinkers concerning precisely what the term *narrative* means.[35] And as is the case with the early stages of many new theological directions, members of the coalition have been moving in greatly diverse directions. Narrative theology has fostered a variety of specific expressions and a host of treatises, to the extent that sympathetic historians of the movement themselves cannot agree concerning its basic types.[36] This multiplicity of directions and expressions is in part the result of specific narrative thinkers taking upon themselves the challenges posed by the basic concerns that all participants in the movement share in common.

Structuralism

One such challenge has been that of relating the biblical stories to the perceived narrative structure of reality. In keeping with this concern, certain thinkers have explored what may be termed a "structuralist" approach to narrative theology. This orientation sees in the structure and form of the biblical story, in the words of Michael Goldberg, "the best guide for understanding the structure of reality."[37] The basic interest of these thinkers is *how* the "what" of a story is expressed, based on the supposition that how things are presented determines much of what is represented.

Some structuralists maintain that the truth of narrative may be noted in a somewhat general sense. The narrative structure, they argue, constitutes the universal inner form of human experience. Other structuralists are more cautious, focusing rather on the more specific function biblical narrative serves within the Christian community.[38]

Important in laying the foundations for the structuralist approach has been the work of Hans Frei of Yale[39] and of Sallie McFague of Vanderbilt.[40] Frei set himself to the goal of establishing a link between the general structure of the biblical narrative and the structure of reality. In his book *The Eclipse of Biblical Narrative* (1974), Frei argued that since the late seventeenth century, Western theologians have been guilty of a mistake of judgment. They have attempted to salvage the biblical story in the face of modern criticism by detaching the story's meaning from its truth, thereby separating the narrative from reality: "First in England and then in Germany the narrative became distinguished from a separable subject matter—whether historical, ideal, or both at once—which was now taken to be its true meaning."[41] By mistakenly attempting to detach the meaning of the biblical story from its truth, these thinkers created two separate and irreconcilable disciplines—biblical theology and historical criticism. In so doing, Frei declared, they undercut "all realistic narrative." He saw in all such systems of hermeneutics the danger of allowing the perspective of the reader, that is, the process of understanding itself, to set the terms on which the text is to be interpreted and thereby forcing the meaning of the text into that schematic mold,[42] so that "the focus of inquiry now became the unitary structure of understanding, rather than the written text itself."[43]

The point of Frei's attack is especially evident in the eighteenth- and nineteenth-century treatments of the narrative concerning Jesus. By detaching Jesus from his setting within the biblical narrative, theologians, he claimed, had exchanged the biblical story for another story, which they erroneously believed depicted reality in some truer manner.[44]

The solution Frei proposed to this unfortunate turn in thought is to become cognizant once again of the historylike nature of the biblical stories. A "realistic story" (that is, the biblical narrative), he noted, shares the same descriptive form found in historical accounts.[45] As a result, there is an important literary parallel between history writing and historylike writing:

> In each case narrative form and meaning are inseparable, precisely because in both cases meaning is in large part a function of the interaction of character and circumstances. It is not going too far to say that the story is the meaning or, alternatively, that the meaning emerges from the story form.[46]

For Frei, then, its relation to meaning demands that we pay attention to the structure of biblical narrative.

Frei claimed that this relation likewise opens the way to overcoming the debate concerning the actual historicity of the biblical narratives. Their relation to the shape of reality, and not their actual historicity, is the relevant question. Therefore, according to Frei, to take seriously the structural shape of biblical narrative means to take it as the shape of reality.[47]

In contrast to Frei's more general structuralism, McFague's interests were more limited, being narrowed to one specific structure, that of parable. Her proposal, which emphasizes the special importance of biblical parables, was articulated in the book *Speaking in Parables* (1975). Because the structure displayed by parable (and to some extent by metaphor) reflects the structure of human thought and thus of humanly perceived reality, she argued, it furnishes the basis for all human understanding of God, self and world. This has far-reaching results for the study of biblical narrative. According to McFague, the truthfulness of biblical narrative lies in its faithful depiction of the structure of reality, for the shape of the story goes hand-in-hand with the shape of experience.[48]

Story and Life

All narrative thinkers, of course, have some interest in moving beyond the narrative itself to the implications of story for life. This shared interest, however, has become the specific concern of a second group of narrative theologians. Rather than focus their efforts on the somewhat formal categories related to the structure of the story, they attempt to draw out the ethic expressed through the biblical narrative and its implications for life today. Thinkers that share the "ethicist" approach to narrative theology tend to emphasize certain key themes: the primacy of ethics in the theological task, the primacy of narrative for ethics and the primacy of certain concepts such as "character" and "community."

An early voice in the exploration of this approach has been that of the Baptist thinker James McClendon. His special interest in the 1970s, as evidenced in his book *Biography as Theology: How Life Stories Can Remake Today's Theology* (1974), was that of the contribution of one specific type of narrative—biography—to the theological task. His thesis was that biographical subjects contribute "to the theology of the community of sharers of their faith" and this especially "by showing how certain great archetypical images of that faith do apply to their own lives and circumstances, and by extension to our own."[49]

In the 1980s McClendon turned his attention more directly to the construction of a narrative ethic out of which systematic theology would emerge. His efforts crystallized in a treatise bearing the descriptive, albeit untraditional, title, *Ethics: Systematic Theology*.[50] McClendon emphasized the importance of character formation, or the development of virtues, for corporate human life and the necessity of narrative for the formation of such virtues.[51] As a result of this thesis, he offered an apologetic for the assertion that "a truly Christian ethics *must* be a narrative ethics."[52]

McClendon and other early voices[53] were joined by an articulate apologist for the ethicist approach to narrative theology, Stanley Hauerwas.[54] Paul Nelson considers Hauerwas to be "the most significant and influential exponent of narrative among contemporary Christian ethicists."[55]

Hauerwas found in narrative a "perennial category" by means of which he thought we could understand how the individual is formed by one's religious convictions.[56] Reminiscent of those structuralists who posited a real connection between the structure of narrative and the structure of human life, Hauerwas argued that stories are similar to human living in the world. A narrative account binds together in an intelligible pattern events and actors which are non-necessary and contingent. In this way they reflect the form of human action.[57] Further, Hauerwas maintained that the self is best understood in terms of being a narrative. Because of the conflicting roles and loyalties that confront the self during the course of life, the self requires the unifying dynamic offered by a narrative, with its intertwining of subplots and characters.[58]

Like McClendon, Hauerwas rejected two generally accepted understandings in theology and ethics. Against the traditional ordering of the two disciplines, he has concluded that ethics does not follow after a systematic presentation of the Christian faith, but must come at the beginning of Christian theological reflection.[59] This innovative move is related to his understanding of the nature of the ethical task, which is his second deviation from established procedures. In contrast to the more widely held orientation toward actions as the object of ethical deliberations, Hauerwas has consistently championed what may be termed an "ethics of virtue."[60] For him the central ethical question is not so much, What constitutes a good action? as What constitutes a good person? And the "good person," in turn, is related to the narrative community.

Hauerwas's prioritizing of ethics before theology arose out his understanding of the role convictions play in the life of the self. For him, neither the self nor personal character is static or a given reality; rather, they develop "through our history."[61] In this process convictions are crucial. Their task is not to provide a metaphysical answer concerning the constitution of the world,[62] but to "transform the self to true faith by creating a community that lives faithful to the one true God of the universe." This process, in turn, is related to truth: "When self and nature are thus put in right relation we perceive the truth of our existence." The fact that the attainment of such truth is connected to the transformation of the self forms the basis for the priority of as well as the narrative nature of ethics.[63]

In his writings Hauerwas has repeatedly moved among three interrelated concepts— character (or virtue), vision and narrative.[64] His definitions of these terms are quite precise. *Character* is the name we give to the cummulative source of human actions;[65] it is "our deliberate disposition to use a certain range of reasons for our actions rather than others," for our character is both revealed and molded through the process of forming actions according to chosen reasons.[66] But life is more than making rational choices, he argued; it also entails *vision*, which means "to see the world in a certain way and then to become what we see."[67] How we view the world and ourselves, in other words, influences what we are becoming.

This introduces the important concept of *narrative*. According to Hauerwas, our vision does not arise *sui generis;* rather, we view the world in accordance with story-related metaphors and symbols. Our vision is formed and given content by the narrative context in which we live, by "the stories through which we have learned to form the story of our lives."[68] For Hauerwas, then, stories evidence a certain didactic quality. In the words of Goldberg, "By allowing a particular story to direct our attention to the world in some specific way, we let it direct our activity in a certain manner."[69] Such paradigmatic narratives not only describe the world in the present but indicate how it ought to be changed.[70] They also challenge our own self-deceptions and mediate to us the courage "appropriate to human existence."[71]

It is no surprise that his emphasis on narrative led Hauerwas to a corresponding emphasis on the Christian community as the focal point of the development of a people of character and on social ethics in terms of the nature of the social responsibility of the church. In the 1980s he has given increased attention to this theme, as evidenced in books carrying titles such as *The Community of Character* (1981) and *The Peaceable Kingdom* (1983).

In his more recent writings Hauerwas sought to assist Christians in rediscovering that their most important social task is, in his words, "nothing less than to be a community capable of hearing the story of God we find in the scripture and living in a manner that is faithful to that story,"[72] that is, of being "a community capable of forming people with virtues sufficient to witness to God's truth in the world."[73] According to Hauerwas the narratives of the community—the stories of Israel and Jesus, which are to live through the lives of believers—are crucial to the fulfillment of this task.[74] In fact, the community lives from the foundational biblical narratives together with its own tradition, and hence from memory. Narrative is central to the explication of Christian existence, because the narrative structure displays human existence as the existence of contingent and historical beings, and because it is the form God has chosen to reveal himself. Because of the narrative character of God's activity and of our own lives, through these narratives we hear about God and ourselves.[75]

In Hauerwas's thinking the dependency of the community on narrative results in a reciprocal relationship between the Bible and the believing community. Scripture, he declared, is dependent on the community that it shapes:

> The authority of scripture derives its intelligibility from the existence of a community that knows its life depends on faithful remembering of God's care of his creation through the calling of Israel and the life of Jesus.[76]

At the same time, the Bible is authoritative for Christians, because they find in it the traditions through which they come to know the truth.[77] They look to the Bible in moral matters because of its power to help them remember the stories of God for the continual guidance of their corporate and individual lives.[78]

Narrative Systematic Theology

The relationship between narrative and the self-disclosure of God in history (the story of God) touched on by thinkers such as Hauerwas has become the specific interest of a final group of narrative thinkers, who have sought to employ the category of narrative as the principle material for the systematic elucidation of Christian faith. The goal of these theologians has been that of setting forth the major doctrines of Christian faith in a manner that reflects the normative importance of narrative in the expression of human experience in general and Christian faith in particular.

The extension of the category of narrative to the realm of functioning as a major motif for the construction of a systematic theology has been perhaps the most controversial development within the broader narrative movement. Not all narrative thinkers agree that this undertaking is possible, helpful or even desirable.[79] As we have seen, narrative thinkers generally agree that because human identity has a narrative structure, narrative plays a crucial role in the articulation of personal identity. Opponents of the use of narrative to construct a systematic theology, however, argue that the concept can serve only as an introduction or bridge to the constructive theological enterprise. "Narrative theology," they argue, is technically impossible, in that such a program confuses two forms of discourse, the first order language of faith and the second order rational reflection on the faith encounter.

Despite such criticisms, several theologians remain undaunted. They maintain that because of its essential relationship to our understanding of human identity, the category of narrative is useful beyond functioning as the introduction to the theological task; it is central to doctrinal theology itself. George W. Stroup,[80] Gabriel Fackre[81] and more recently Clark Pinnock[82] have defended or experimented with the implications of the concept of narrative for the systematic presentation of the Christian story. And it is perhaps this variety of narrative that holds the most promise for the ongoing task of theology.

Biography and Autobiography

In keeping with their common adherence to the usefulness of the category of narrative, nearly all narrative thinkers employ at one point or another the narrative literary form in their writings, either building from or at least incorporating religious (auto)biographies (that is, "confession"). The use of biography is not surprising, for it is in keeping with a central concern of narrative theology, namely, the concern for personal identity development. The biographies employed in narrative treatises are generally presented as emerging from the "collision" between the believer's personal identity narrative and the narrative of the Christian community. The study of life stories (biography or the depiction of the activity of a self through time), therefore, is central to the narrative thinker's perception of the theological task.[83]

Narrative theologians find a deeper purpose in a story than mere entertainment, however. By virtue of its plot, its ability to unfold or develop character, a story is able to offer insight into the human condition, as well as the origins and goal of human lives.[84] Beyond this dimension, religious (auto)biography serves as a reminder that the salvation of personal and communal histories is found in the Christian story; persons and communities cannot be redeemed without their histories, for their identity is inseparable from them. The goal of narrative theology, then, is to use the Christian faith as embodied in the church's narratives to reinterpret personal and social existence.

Personal Identity Development
The use of biography is based on a foundational concern present in narrative theology, that of human identity development. Identity development is related to narrative in such a manner that narrative is the necessary form for the articulation of personal identity. A narrative theologian who has reflected on the specific understanding of personal identity development required by this approach and whose presentation of this topic is indicative of that found in a variety of narrative theologians is George Stroup.[85]

According to Stroup, identity development refers not only to the persistency of the individual through time but also as the quality of personhood, what kind of person an individual is becoming. Hence, it is both historical and social. Because of its historical dimension, it is based on memory. Through the memory an individual selects certain events from one's past (that is, from one's personal history) and uses them as a basis for interpreting the significance of the whole of one's life. Personal identity, then, is the pattern that memory retrieves from the personal history and projects into the future.

Personal identity is not only created from the factual data of the events of one's life. Crucial as well is an "interpretive scheme," which includes such intangibles as personal values, ideals and goals. This interpretive framework, however, cannot be derived from the data of one's life. Here the other dimension of identity development—the social aspect—comes into play. In addition to being historical (based on the data of one's personal history), personal identity is also social. It develops within a social context or "tradition," which provides the categories for the individual interpretive framework. As a result, personal identity is never a private reality, but has a communal element, for it is shaped by the community of which the person is a participant.[86]

To describe the distinction between the data of one's life history and the interpretive framework Stroup employed the terms *chronicle* and *interpretation*. Both dimensions are important, he argued. Apart from interpretation, the chronicle of a person's life, the events and experiences of one's personal history, is meaningless, for without the interpretive context it lacks a "plot." Hence, it is the interpretation that makes a personal narrative "history" and thus gives rise to personal identity.

Connected with this basic understanding of personal identity development is the concept of self-deception. Self-deception goes beyond mere distorting of an event in the past. Drawing from the work of philosopher Herbert Fingarette, Stroup, like other narrative thinkers, employed the term to refer to the incoherent way a person lives in relation to the past and in anticipation of the future.[87] Reminiscent of the response of the fallen Adam and Eve to God in the Genesis story, self-deception entails a discrepancy between how a person lives in the world and the narrative he or she offers to others.

Similar to the idea of identity development, the concept of self-deception binds the individual to the corporate dimension of identity narratives, according to Stroup. The community forms a check on the human capacity for self-deception, for it calls to account the individual's interpretation and appropriation of the common social tradition.

Narrative and Community

Communities, and not merely individuals, tell stories and are characterized by narratives. Stroup's definition is typical of narrative theologians:

> A community is a group of people who have come to share a common past, who understand particular events in the past to be of decisive importance for interpreting the present, who anticipate the future by means of a shared hope, and who express their identity by means of a common narrative.[88]

This common narrative, the common corporate memory expressed in living traditions, is the glue that holds the members of a community together, for to belong to the group means to share the community narratives, to recite the same stories, and to allow them to shape one's identity.

Of greatest significance for Christian narrative thinkers is the specifically Christian community, which appeals to the biblical narratives as the indispensable resource for interpreting its identity and world. The community elevates the exodus and the Christ event, especially Jesus' passion and resurrection, as lying at the core of the biblical narrative. Stroup found in the Gospels themselves credence for his emphasis on the biblical story rather than abstract teachings. These writings, he noted, answer the questions of Jesus' identity and of the meaning of discipleship in terms of a decision-demanding narrative (the story itself), not by setting forth a doctrinal discourse. But Christian communities not only look to the biblical stories, they also accept church history as the history of the interpretation of Scripture. Narrative thinkers find in this phenomenon an attempt by the community of faith to bring the entire narrative history—the biblical and Christian stories—to bear on the contemporary world in order to understand the present in light of the resources of the past.

The narrative understanding of the nature of a community sets the stage for the final significant set of categories in Stroup's presentation, the "collision of stories" leading to "conversion" and "faith." According to narrative theology the genius of a life story lies in its potential for revision. A story is intended to empower, even to force, the individual to be self-critical, to look at his or her story from the perspective of other stories.

The hearing of a different story can lead to a crisis experience. In such a situation the individual is confronted with the meaning-scheme of another community that calls into question his or her previous interpretation of the personal story. Stroup termed this experience a "collision of narratives." As the new community narrative causes the individual to sense "disorientation," to sense that the world as he or she knows it is coming apart, the process of faith begins. Because one's identity has been called into question by the new story, the person must reinterpret the personal story in accordance with the categories of the new narrative.

Stroup employed the traditional term *conversion* to refer to the personal acceptance of the new narrative categories as the conceptual framework by which to reinterpret one's own story. Faith comes to completion, he argued, as the individual seeks to become a part of the community's life by reconstructing his or her own personal identity by means of the community's narratives and symbols.

For this understanding of the nature of faith Stroup built on Karl Barth's discussion of the dynamics of faith found in his *Church Dogmatics*.[89] According to Barth the human activity of faith may be viewed under three moments. The first is acknowledgment *(Anerkennen)*, the acceptance of and obedience to Jesus Christ as the object of faith. The second moment is recognition *(Erkennen)*, seeing Jesus Christ as *pro me* (for me). This entails the existential knowledge of Jesus Christ that arises as the believer's self-understanding is altered and the history of Jesus Christ comes to be re-enacted in the history of the believer. Finally, confession *(Bekennen)*, the recognition that one's redemption is found in Jesus Christ, marks the "moment" when the believer, supported by the community, reconstructs his or her personal identity by means of what is acknowledged to be the truth about Jesus Christ.[90]

Revelation and Scripture

Stroup's emphasis on story in narrative theology led him to a specific, albeit basically neo-orthodox, understanding of the nature of revelation and scriptural authority, typical of narrative theology as a whole.

> God's Word refers to those moments in which Christian narrative becomes disclosive, those moments when Christian narrative ceases to be merely an object for historical curiosity, when its horizon collides with that of the reader and hearer, when the process of understanding commences, and acknowledgement, recognition, and confession become a possibility, when the human words of Christian narrative witness to Jesus Christ.[91]

For Stroup, therefore, the Christian narrative itself does not constitute divine revelation. Rather, it is the context in which Christians believe they hear the Word of God.

As a result of this understanding of revelation, Stroup offered a functional interpretation of the authority of Scripture. The Bible's authority is to be seen in terms of its function in the life of the Christian community, he argued, and not in some intrinsic property of the book itself.[92] The Bible is authoritative as a witness to the events that form the basis of the church's proclamation and that form the focus around which the community gathers. This witnessing dimension of Scripture arises because of the writers' proximity to the events reported and because their writings report what was real to the biblical authors, namely, the history of salvation. As a result, the Bible may be true without being at all points historically accurate.[93]

But as is indicative of many narrative theologians, for Stroup the Bible's authority does not lie simply in its relationship to past events. He also ascribed to the Bible an ongoing normative authority. Scripture provides the narratives and symbols to which the community continually returns in order to understand anew the substance of its faith.[94]

Criticisms of Narrative Theology

To their credit, narrative theologians have not only engaged in constructive proposal in view of what they have perceived to be the shortcomings of alternatives; they have also been willing to be self-critical. Michael Goldberg stands as an example. From his study of the movement, he drew three critical issues any narrative theology must face:

(1) the relationship between stories and experience—the question of truth; (2) the hermeneutic involved for understanding stories rightly—the question of meaning; and (3) the charge of moral relativism—the question of rationality.[95]

Paul Nelson concluded that "narrative is not a universal solvent for all theological problems or disagreements."[96] Among the several tasks yet outstanding he cited the need of spelling out what the term *narrative* means, what significance subnarratives (the stories of minority peoples) have within the larger cultural narrative, how ultimate truth-claims fit within the basic narrative approach, and how and on what basis we are able to choose among the various stories that claim our allegiance.[97]

Such criticisms point to the central question posed by narrative theology. As a yet young and not fully developed movement, it offers promise for the future. It rightly calls theology and ethics to consider the role of the Christian community in the formation of believers as people of character. And the delineation of conversion as the result of a collision of narratives, typical of narrative theology, discloses an important dimension of the process of coming to faith. But narrative theologians have yet to articulate fully the understanding of God's relation to the world that underlies their approach. Narrative theology looks for the transcendent God within the story of the community of faith. Whether or not the eternal truth of the transcendent God can emerge from the competing religious narratives found within the human story remains a yet unanswered question.

10 REAFFIRMING THE BALANCE: *Evangelical Theology Coming of Age*

ALTHOUGH THE TWENTIETH CENTURY HAS BEEN CHARACTERIZED BY MANIFOLD ATTEMPTS by theological visionaries to chart new directions, theologians who saw themselves as conserving and carrying forward the theological orientation of the Reformation remained a potent force as well. During the course of the century these theologians charted a course independent of the currents outlined thus far in this book.

Despite setbacks, conservative theology was never engulfed by other theological movements. It always remained a force to be reckoned with in the church, even when it appeared to have been abandoned in the more academic settings. Sometimes conservative theologians held themselves aloof from the debates of their peers in the mainline seminaries and universities. At other times, they entered the foray, debating points of methodology and calling for a return to doctrines they sensed had been discarded by contemporary thinkers.

In the second half of the century, certain conservative theologians formed a loose coalition under the banner of the evangelical movement. Their overarching concern was to articulate theological statements that remained true to the Bible and to the heritage of the church, especially as set forth in the Reformation. Although committed to "the faith once committed to the church" and hence to the maintenance of theological orthodoxy, evangelical theologians were nevertheless interested in engaging in dialog with proponents of the modern theological currents with which they disagreed.

The background for the formation of the evangelical coalition lay in the events that racked the church in the United States and Canada at the turn of the century. In contrast to the situation in Europe, American Protestantism had retained a strong Reformation flavor throughout the nineteenth century. However, as the century was coming to a close, the winds of change that had been blowing in European theology since the Enlightenment began to be felt in the New World as well. Especially important were the newer higher-critical methodologies employed in biblical studies and the attempts of European theologians to come to terms with Darwinian theories concerning human origins.

As an increasing number of American theologians came to accept higher criticism, Darwinism and liberal theology, a heated controversy ensued. Opponents of the newer ideas, those who desired to preserve classical Christianity, or the "fundamentals" of the Christian faith, came to be known as "fundamentalists." Increasingly, the fundamentalists found themselves on the defensive, and when the dust had settled the leading denominational seminaries lay in the control of the "modernists."

After these initial defeats during the early years of the century, many conservatives withdrew from the mainline denominations and formed alternative ecclesiastical structures, as well as Bible colleges and seminaries. This retreat, while fostered in the name of separating from error for the sake of doctrinal purity, led to an unfortunate by-product—the hardening of fundamentalism into a theologically rigid and socially separatistic outlook toward Christianity.

By mid-century, however, new breezes had begun to enliven the sterile soil of fundamentalism. Younger voices were calling for a new presence in the marketplace of ideas by those who were committed to classical Protestant orthodoxy. These thinkers criticized their fundamentalist forebears of abandoning society to the liberals and of seeking to shield themselves and the gospel by forming enclaves of purity that were nothing more than "holy ghettos."

One voice calling for change was that of a young professor at Northern Baptist Seminary in Chicago, Carl F. H. Henry. His short treatise, *The Uneasy Conscience of Modern Fundamentalism* (1947),[1] exploded like a bombshell in the fundamentalist camp. Henry chastised his fellow fundamentalists for several sins of omission. The basic problem as he saw it was that fundamentalism lacked a social program; its humanitarianism—its benevolent regard for the interests of humankind—had evaporated.[2] As a result, the movement failed to raise the voice of the gospel toward world political or economic conditions, it divorced the Christian faith from the great social reform movements, it shied away from preaching the kingdom of God as a present reality, and it withdrew from the task of shaping the mindset of society.

Although he knew full well the danger of attempting to "perform surgery" on fundamentalism at a time when it was already under vicious attack, Henry feared that unless someone spoke out, fundamentalism would soon be reduced to an insignificant sect having no impact on the wider culture. Therefore he boldly challenged his colleagues with a call to action, claiming that "the hour is ripe now, if we seize it rightly, for a rediscovery of the Scriptures and of the meaning of the Incarnation for the human race."[3] He envisioned nothing less than the reemergence of "historic Christianity" as a vital "world ideology," and this because of his conviction that "the redemptive message has implications for all of life."[4]

Those who heeded the call to reenter the discussion eventually came to be known as "evangelicals," in distinction from the older fundamentalism. The differences between the two movements is not so much one of doctrine. Evangelicals have generally defended the same basic theological system as fundamentalists.[5] Rather, the chief point of difference is one of spirit or mood. In contrast to the separatistic, nonengagement stance that fundamentalism had come to adopt, evangelicals sought to enter into discussion with contemporary theology and to avoid what Carl Henry termed the "harsh temperament," the "spirit of lovelessness and strife"[6] of many mid-century fundamentalist leaders.

Since the 1940s and 1950s, many capable and articulate theologians have set forth the stance and concerns of the newer evangelicalism. But two theologians—Carl F. H. Henry and Bernard Ramm—serve as representative voices. Both happen to be Baptists. While their denominational affiliation does carry impact on their theology, each of them articulates a position that goes beyond any one confessional group and is representative of the thinking of elements in the broader evangelical coalition. Hence, it is their participation in evangelicalism as a whole, not their denominational preference, that has most shaped their understanding of the Christian faith.

Each of these theologians represents a basic orientation that has been prevalent within the evangelical movement. While sharing the broader evangelical concern for dialog with alternative viewpoints, Carl Henry ranks among those who are cautious in this process. He represents evangelicals who turn their faces away from modern theology in any form. Henry has been highly critical of the various attempts—even the more conservative attempts from Karl Barth[7] to narrative theology[8]—to reformulate the Christian faith in the context of the contemporary situation. Bernard Ramm offers an alternative evangelical approach. He represents those who have turned their faces toward modern theology, in his case the neo-orthodoxy of Karl Barth. Rather than reject Barth, as did evangelical thinkers such as Cornelius Van Til and Carl Henry,[9] Ramm hoped to find in aspects of his brand of modern theology assistance in reformulating evangelical theology in order to move beyond fundamentalism. This is evidenced in his book, *Beyond Fundamentalism*, which extols the virtues of Barth for the future of theology.

CARL F. H. HENRY:
THE EVANGELICAL ALTERNATIVE TO MODERNISM

The most prominent evangelical theologian of the second half of the twentieth century is without a doubt Carl Henry. In 1983 he was hailed as "the prime interpreter of evangelical theology, one of its leading theoreticians, and . . . the unofficial spokesman for the entire tradition."[10] More recently he was termed "one of the theological luminaries of the twentieth century."[11] Yet Henry published no systematic theology. Rather than delineate the theology of evangelicalism, he devoted the bulk of his career to being a type of theological journalist, describing and critiquing theological currents as they emerged. His career reached its climax with the publication of his magnum opus, a six-volume treatise entitled *God, Revelation and Authority,*[12] in which Henry sought to lay the methodological groundwork for evangelical theology.

Henry's Pilgrimage

Just as his theology broadly depicts that of the movement as a whole, so Henry's spiritual pilgrimage,[13] focusing as it does on his experience of the "new birth," is typical of that of many evangelicals.

Henry was born on January 22, 1913, the oldest of eight children in a German immigrant household in New York City, although the family later moved to Long Island. His childhood religious exposure was minimal, even though his father, a pastry chef, was Lutheran, and his mother Roman Catholic. He was confirmed in the Episcopal church as a teenager, but then left the church, although not before gaining some awareness of Christianity through the prayer book and before managing to steal a pew Bible, which he occasionally read in subsequent years.

Conversion came to Carl Henry as a result of Christian influences from outside his parental home. His contacts as a promising young journalist with a local newspaper included a godly elderly Methodist woman, whom Henry came affectionately to call "Mother Christy," and several members of the evangelistically oriented Oxford Group, including Gene Bedford. Through the prodding of these persons and as an outworking of his fascination with the biblical accounts of Jesus' resurrection, young Carl experienced conversion on June 10, 1933.[14]

Henry's conversion was typical of the experience of many in the evangelical movement. It included prayer for forgiveness and for the presence of God in his life; a sense of inner assurance of forgiveness and Jesus as his personal Savior; a committing of his entire life into God's hands that included a willingness to follow wherever God would lead; and a zeal to tell others of his new-found relationship with God. His conversion was likewise typically evangelical in that it transcended any specifically denominational orientation or loyalty. Henry had become a believer, not an Episcopalian, a Methodist, a Presbyterian or a Baptist. He later enumerated the "plurality of contributory factors" in his conversion: "a pilfered Bible, fragmentary memories of the Episcopal prayer book, a Methodist friend's insistence on the new birth, an Oxford Grouper's daring call for changed lives, all coalescing around my need for vocational direction and crowned by the Holy Spirit's work of grace and inner assurance."[15]

In the months that followed, Henry discovered that his commitment would mean a change in career plans. Partly through circumstances, partly through an inner sense and partly through the prodding of a Presbyterian pastor, Peter Joshua, God was steering Henry away from secular journalism and into theological studies. Finally, in the fall of 1935 he enrolled in Wheaton College. One factor in this choice was his positive impression of a lecture delivered by Wheaton's president, J. Oliver Buswell, in which he set forth the importance of reason to faith and the resurrection as a historical event.[16] The move to Wheaton was no easy matter economically for a young man of simple means in the midst of the depression, but Henry experienced the miraculous provision of God.

The years at Wheaton set the direction of Henry's subsequent life. Above all, they solidified Henry's relationship to evangelicalism. During this time, he established friendships with several persons who would later become respected leaders in the evangelical movement, including Billy Graham and Harold Lindsell. But most significant, Wheaton—especially its philosophy professor, Gordon Clark, who was perhaps the single most important intellectual influence on Henry's thought—strengthened his basically rationalist-oriented evangelical world view.

The interdenominational flavor of Wheaton also provided the context for other important life decisions. There Henry met his future wife, Helga Bender, the daughter of pioneer German Baptist missionaries to Cameroon. His studies likewise led him to embrace what he found to be the distinctives of the Baptists, including believer's baptism by immersion and especially the primacy of Scripture.

After graduation in 1938, Henry entered Wheaton's M.A. program, while simultaneously beginning studies at nearby Northern Baptist Theological Seminary, which had been founded by fundamentalists within the Northern Baptist Convention (now the American Baptist Churches) as an alternative to the liberal course set by the University of Chicago Divinity School. Significant events followed each other in rapid-fire succession—marriage (1940), the M.A. from Wheaton (1941), a B.D. from Northern (1941), ordination at Chicago's Humbolt Baptist Church (1941) and a Th.D. from Northern (1942).

Armed with these credentials, he was ready to launch an academic career, which began at Northern Seminary. His commitment to the evangelical movement, however, soon took the Henrys to Pasadena, California, for Carl had been invited to join the faculty of the fledgling Fuller Theological Seminary. While at Fuller, Henry completed a second doctorate, a Ph.D. at Boston, and wrote nine books.

Editor

But the context for Henry's greatest contribution to evangelicalism was not to be that of the seminary classroom. In 1956, he moved to Washington, D.C., to become the founding editor of a new evangelical effort, the journal *Christianity Today*. This publication was launched in response to the dream of several evangelical leaders (such as Billy Graham and Harold Ockenga) and leading Christian businessmen (including J. Howard Pew) for a conservative alternative to the older but more liberally oriented *Christian Century*. The choice of Henry for the post of editor was obvious. He had credentials in both journalism and theology. And he was articulate and solidly conservative in theology, yet conversant in contemporary theological currents.

The twelve-year tenure at *Christianity Today* was a time of growing influence and prominence for Henry among evangelicals. Despite yeoman service as its founding editor, disagreements among its leaders concerning the direction of the journal led to his departure in 1967.[17] The lifting of the heavy editorial responsibilities gave Henry the opportunity to engage in research and writing, teaching at evangelical seminaries and traveling throughout the world. Although no longer at the helm of the leading evangelical journal, his voice continued to be heard, especially through his many publications, including his monumental *God, Revelation and Authority,* produced during the years 1976 to 1983. Even into retirement Carl Henry has continued his lecturing and writing activities and thereby has served as an elder statesman for evangelicalism.

The Commentator on Contemporary Theology

Carl F. H. Henry has been an articulate shaper and defender of evangelical theology. Yet he has never been a systematic theologian. His literary production is phenomenal, but he has never produced a systematic theology. Rather than a systematician, Henry is perhaps better characterized as a commentator on the fortunes of theology in the twentieth century from a conservative or evangelical perspective, as well as a commentator on the fortunes of evangelicalism.[18] This role has been the central motivation and basis for many of his articles[19] and books.[20] It is prominent even in his most systematic-theological work, the mammoth six-volume *God, Revelation and Authority.* Even here Henry cannot but repeatedly engage in analysis of contemporary theological currents.

His activities as a theological commentator fit well with what Henry perceived to be the malaise of evangelicalism. Writing in 1964, he bemoaned as the weakness of the movement its tendency "to neglect the frontiers of formative discussion in contemporary theology." As a result, he added, evangelicals "forfeit the debate at these points to proponents of subevangelical points of view, or to those who assert evangelical positions in only a fragmentary way." He likewise chastised evangelical theological writing for its lack of "an air of exciting relevance." "The problem is not that biblical theology is outdated;" he explained, "it is rather that some of its expositors seem out of touch with the frontiers of doubt in our day."[21] One explicit goal of Henry's literary activities was to alter this situation.

More disturbing to him than the problems of evangelicalism, however, were the tragic losses Henry perceived in mainline Protestantism. Throughout his career he was driven by a thesis foundational to all his efforts as a Christian theologian, namely, that to its own peril the twentieth-century mindset had forsaken its rootage in the earlier commitment to divine revelation. Already in the 1940s he pinpointed the years 1914-1946 as marking "the midnight of modern culture."[22] By this he meant that during this period, the tragedy of two world wars had led to widespread questioning of the assumptions of modernity: the inevitability of human progress, the inherent goodness of humankind, the ultimate status of nature and the basic animality of humanity.[23]

Biblical Authority

His perception of the problems of modern theology leads to a related area of Henry's contribution. Equally important as his role in offering commentary on theological trends of the day has been Henry's passion to set forth the foundations for a truly valid theology. He has continually argued that only a return to the basic evangelical perspective can solve the current difficulty in theology. For him, the foundation for theology can be nothing other than the revelation of God as deposited in the Scriptures.[24] As a result, the single most prominent theme delineated in Henry's writings is that of biblical authority.

The emphasis on the authority of the Bible reflects a concern that lies at the heart of evangelicalism. Its importance to both Henry and the movement as a whole was born out by a survey conducted soon after the founding of *Christianity Today*, which indicated that "two out of three evangelical scholars think biblical authority is the main theological theme now under review in conservative circles in America." After citing this survey in *Frontiers of Modern Theology*, Henry went on to lament in typically evangelical fashion "the compromise of the authority of the Bible" noticeable in mainstream Protestantism and the "surrender of scriptural perspectives to modern critical speculations" that have led to "doubts over historical and propositional revelation, plenary inspiration, and verbal inerrancy."[25] Henry's career has been devoted to the defense of these dimensions of the conservative doctrine of Scripture.

For Henry and others the focus on biblical authority is not an end in itself. Rather, its importance rests in the perception that "the doctrine of the Bible controls all other doctrines of the Christian faith."[26] As a result, evangelicals fear that any diluting of this emphasis will remove the Bible as the authoritative voice in theology, thereby endangering central principles such as salvation by grace and even the authority of Jesus Christ and crucial doctrines such as anthropology and Christology.[27]

The emphasis on revelation that pervades Henry's writings is not uniquely his. On the contrary, neo-orthodoxy and to some extent even twentieth-century theology as a whole have been interested in this category. What sets Henry apart from these various movements is his understanding of the nature of revelation. For him revelation means that God has both acted in history and spoken to humankind. God's speaking is crucial to God's acting, he argued, for it provides the rationale and meaning of the divine historical acts.[28] Through God's interpretation God's activity gains meaning for us.[29] In keeping with this emphasis, Henry defined revelation as

> that activity of the supernatural God whereby he communicates information essential for man's present and future destiny. In revelation God, whose thoughts are not our thoughts, shares his mind; he communicates not only the truth about himself and his intentions, but also that concerning man's present plight and future prospects.[30]

Revelation as Rational

For Henry, its spoken nature means that in a very important way, revelation is rational and hence propositional. In his magnum opus Henry went to great lengths to develop the thesis that "God's revelation is rational communication conveyed in intelligible ideas and meaningful words, that is, in conceptual-verbal form."[31] He agreed with the modern emphasis on the functional, dynamic and teleological dimensions of revelation, but argued that these cannot be separated from the propositional. For him, the reality that God has spoken means that the intellect plays an integral role in the revelatory process.[32] Revelation, in other words, is objective,[33] conceptual,[34] intelligible and coherent.[35] Christianity, rather than being an escape from rationality, is oriented toward the intellect.[36]

But this thesis was not developed in a theological vacuum. Lying behind the rational character of the Christian faith Henry found "the rational living God"[37] who "addresses man in his Word."[38]

The Christian revelation, therefore, is "rationally consistent and compelling," for "rationality has its very basis in the nature of the Living God."[39] The concepts of revelation, reason and Scripture coalesced in what for Henry was his foundational epistemological axiom:

> Divine revelation is the source of all truth, the truth of Christianity included; reason is the instrument for recognizing it; Scripture is its verifying principle; logical consistency is a negative test for truth and coherence a subordinate test. The task of Christian theology is to exhibit the content of biblical revelation as an orderly whole.[40]

In typically Henry fashion he asserted that to omit the rational dimension would leave theology with "a stuttering deity, a transcendental self who roams about in a super-rational sphere not fully subject to the categories of thought."[41]

The emphasis on the propositional dimension of revelation so prominent in Henry's thought finds its supplement in his anthropology. In keeping with the rationalist tradition in theology, Henry elevated reason to the status of being the foundational dimension of the human person, a view, he argued, that was universally held prior to the modern era.[42] In fact, he found in the biblical concept of the image of God the explanation for the phenomenon of divine revelation.[43]

Despite the Fall, this divine image, which Henry viewed as including a certain knowledge of God, rational competence and ethical accountability, was present in some measure in every human being.[44]

Although acknowledging the presence of the divine image in everyone and the doctrinal importance of general revelation,[45] Henry rejected any attempt to construct a natural theology.[46] For him theology could be based only on the self-disclosure of God found in the Bible. In this way, he set himself apart not only from the Thomist tradition but also from evangelical "evidentialists," those apologists who sought to ground Christian faith on arguments from reason and empirical evidence. Henry, followed the "presuppositionalist" approach,[47] basing all theology solely on the presupposition of the truthfulness of the Bible.[48]

Inspiration and Inerrancy

Commitment to the truthfulness of Scripture means for Henry, as for many evangelical thinkers, that the Bible is divinely inspired and therefore inerrant.[49] He saw these two dimensions of the doctrine of Scripture intimately related. Inspiration asserts that God is the ultimate author of Scripture, with the result that the divine revelation in the Bible is free from error. More specifically, "the Holy Spirit superintended the scriptural writers in communicating the biblical message . . . safeguarding them from error."[50] Henry defined inspiration as "a supernatural influence upon divinely chosen prophets and apostles whereby the Spirit of God assures the truth and trustworthiness of their oral and written proclamation."[51] The Bible is essential in this context in that "it inscripturates divinely revealed truth in verbal form."[52]

While affirming the standard conservative position, Henry avoided some of the more radical positions found in certain fundamentalist circles. He was quick to reject any suggestion that the Bible was the product of divine dictation.[53] Nor did inerrancy imply such features as modern technical precision or exactitude in New Testament quotations from the Old.[54]

More important, although he advocated inerrancy, Henry did not go so far as to make adherence to this doctrine a test of evangelical authenticity, as did some of his colleagues,[55] and this for quite pragmatic reasons. "The somewhat reactionary elevation of inerrancy as the superbadge of evangelical orthodoxy," he lamented, "deploys energies to this controversy that evangelicals might better apply to producing comprehensive theological and philosophical works so desperately needed in a time of national and civilizational crisis."[56] Consequently, he distanced himself from evangelical leaders such as Harold Lindsell, who, he claimed, erroneously elevated inerrancy over authority and inspiration as the first claim to be made for the Bible.[57] For Henry, issues such as revelation and culture, hermeneutics, and propositional revelation were at least as important as inerrancy.

The Doctrine of God

Henry's concern for the category of propositional revelation leads quite naturally to the final major feature of his thought, his emphasis on the doctrine of God as the linchpin of theology. The link between revelation and God was forged by Henry's concept of the *Logos* as the mediating agent of the divine self-disclosure.[58] In his understanding, therefore, the Word of God comes from beyond the world, being "transcendentally given, and not immanent in man as a conception or abstraction achieved by human imagination or reflection."[59] Because of this emphasis on the transcendent nature of revelation mediated through the *Logos,* Henry could assert that the question concerning Scripture was in the final analysis not an issue concerning the Bible but concerning God. His conclusion was inescapable: "If one believes in a sovereign divine mind and will, in God who personally speaks and conveys information and instruction, then the presuppositions of scriptural inspiration lie near at hand."[60]

The emphasis on the centrality of the doctrine of God, like so many other themes in Henry's thought, was carved out early in his career. In 1946 he wrote, "From a certain vantage point, the concept of God is determinative for all other concepts; it is the Archimedean lever with which one can fashion an entire world view."[61]

For Henry, what is of fundamental importance about God, the dimension of the divine reality from which God approaches his creatures in act and rational speech, is the divine transcendence. Henry claimed that the emphasis on divine immanence so prominent in contemporary theologies was only a partial answer to the major concern of these theologies, namely, the gnawing question concerning how God acts in the world.[62] Equally important was God's transcendence, which meant that "nature is always and everywhere open to his purpose, a purpose that he expresses freely either in repetitive cosmic processes and events, or in once-for-all acts."[63] Henry, therefore, found God's disclosure of his "purposive presence" equally in the regularities of nature and in the miraculous.[64]

Henry bemoaned the unfortunate loss of this dimension of God in modern thought.[65] Precisely a regaining of transcendence is crucial for the future fortunes of humankind, he asserted. Pulling together the themes of transcendence, reason and salvation, he offered this assessment in 1964:

> If Christianity is to win intellectual respectability in the modern world, the reality of the transcendent God must indeed be proclaimed by the theologians—and proclaimed on the basis of man's rational competence to know the transempirical realm. Apart from recognition of the self-revealed Redeemer of a fallen humanity, who vouchsafes valid knowledge of the transempirical world, the modern Athenians are left to munch the husks of the religious vagabonds.[66]

The transcendence of God was vital for Henry, because it is out of his transcendence that God speaks to humankind. God does not only act; he is also a speaking God. Henry was convinced that the Bible is the message of God and that the authoritive source of the biblical message "was, is and forever remains the transcendent God."[67]

Henry's Magnum Opus

The nature of this God and the content of God's self-disclosure received extended treatment in the six volumes of Henry's magnum opus. After an introductory statement concerning the nature of theology in the opening volume, he turned his attention in installments two, three and four to a delineation of fifteen foundational theses concerning the divine revelation. These were followed in volumes five and six by the development of a largely classically orthodox approach to the doctrine of God.[68]

The order of these two major topics in *God, Revelation and Authority* is instructive. By placing his discussion of revelation prior to the delineation of the doctrine of God, Henry intended to make clear that what may be said about the being and attributes of the deity arises solely out of the divine self-disclosure found in the Scriptures. God is who God shows himself to be in the Bible.

In the nine-hundred-page presentation of the doctrine of God, Henry discusses the traditional questions concerning the relationship between the essence and existence of God, presents the classical understanding of the Trinity, and then delineates the traditional divine attributes (such as eternality, omniscience, immutability, omnipotence, holiness and love), encompassed within which are likewise such matters as the doctrine of creation and the problem of evil. In the whole Henry's concern remains that which characterized his entire corpus, namely, to show the rationality of God and the reasonableness of the Christian position in the midst of an increasingly irrationally oriented intellectual climate. He was convinced that only by returning to the classical position and its emphasis on the reasonableness of the faith could we hope to experience a revitalization of theology in our day.

Social Ethics

The revitalization of theology Henry envisioned did not end with the purely intellectual realm, however. Rather, the renewal of biblical authority in theology was to lead to a reengagement with the world. As a result, he did not confine his interests to pure theology, but entered into the discussions in the realm of social ethics as well.[69]

Henry set forth the thesis that Christianity ought to foster social transformation in realms such as politics, business and work. What he saw as "the Biblical view" finds indispensable both individual conversion and social justice,[70] understood not only in terms of ministry to the victims of injustice but as the remedying and eliminating of the causes of that injustice.[71] He even called evangelicals to voice an "authentic challenge to the status quo" in the name of fidelity to the social and political implications of the biblical message.[72]

Henry's thesis, of course, put him at odds with the fundamentalism of the mid-twentieth century, which he claimed had no social program;[73] therefore he called on evangelicals to move beyond it.[74] But his interest in setting a social agenda did not move Henry to the position articulated by many voices in mainline Protestantism. In contrast to much of the social activism advocated by theologians in this century, Henry maintained that social change must begin with the individual, rather than on the corporate level. The church, he declared, "must rely on spiritual regeneration for the transformation of society."[75] Among other implications, this principle means that the church avoids attempting to wield direct pressure on government or public agencies to adopt specifically church-approved programs, but rather looks to its individual members "to fulfil their duties as citizens of two worlds."[76]

Henry's concern for social justice dovetailed naturally with his central theological orientation. For him efforts on behalf of justice flow out of the proclamation of divine supernatural revelation and the historical resurrection of Jesus Christ. These principles, together with the vision of the kingdom of God, provide the transcendent basis for justice[77] as well as for making moral choices permanently significant.[78]

Critical Evaluation

Carl Henry has offered to the evangelical movement an example of academically informed critique of the developments within the wider stream of twentieth-century theology. He articulated well the typically evangelical assessment of the crisis in modern thought as a crisis in our understanding of divine revelation, behind which lay a crisis in our perception of God. In the midst of the challenge posed by contemporary theology, Henry boldly sought to reaffirm the orthodox emphasis on the reality of the transcendent God who comes to humankind from beyond the world through his self-disclosure. The transcendent God speaks, he asserted, through a divine revelation that is coherent and reasonable and therefore may be grasped by humans who are made in the divine image.

As one whose primary purpose was to level a critique of the modern mentality and set forth an evangelical alternative, Henry never tackled the challenge of delineating a complete systematic theology. As a result, his writings reflect certain glaring omissions.[79] In his defense it ought to be said that Henry's goal was a more modest one, that of providing the foundation on which other evangelicals could construct a solid theological system.

Henry's critics have also found him to be overly concerned with reason and propositional revelation. Some have rejected him as a type of throwback to an earlier, even pre-Enlightenment, era in theological history.[80] Others, including Clark Pinnock, have assessed as an impossible task his attempt to set forth the infallible Scripture as the foundational axiom of theology.[81]

In the midst of such criticism, Henry remained convinced that theology took a wrong turn at an earlier fork in the road. Only by returning to that point and once again reaffirming the older orthodox conception of the transcendent God who discloses himself in the Bible can the crisis in theology be overcome. Whether the traditional balance of transcendence and immanence can be reconstituted in the manner advocated by Henry—that is, in terms of the God who speaks to us from beyond the world—without employing the spatial categories scorned by the movement of twentieth-century thinkers remains the unresolved dilemma of evangelical theology.

BERNARD RAMM:
EVANGELICALISM IN DIALOG WITH MODERN THOUGHT

The conservative theologians who heeded Carl Henry's call to reenter the discussion with secular culture and who therefore joined together under the banner of evangelicalism sought to articulate theological statements that remained true to the Bible and the heritage of the church, especially as set forth in the Reformation, in the aftermath of the Enlightenment. Despite this similarity of broad purpose among them, evangelical theologians reflect great diversity in matters including theological method and basic outlook.

The diversity within the broader unity of the evangelical movement is made starkly apparent by the differing attitude toward modern theology displayed by Bernard Ramm when compared to that of Carl Henry. In contrast to Henry's generally cautious stance toward, and even negative rejection of, current trends in theology, Bernard Ramm offers a second evangelical approach. He represents those who have turned their faces toward modern thinking, in his case, toward contemporary scientific advances and the approach to modern learning advocated by neo-orthodoxy, especially by Karl Barth. Rather than join his colleagues in decrying Barth as the epitome of a "new modernism," as his career progressed Ramm grew progressively appreciative of the Swiss theologian, until finally he embraced Barth as providing a paradigm for evangelical theology in the wake of the Enlightenment.

Ramm did not come to this conclusion lightly nor painlessly, however. His evangelical roots insured an initially cautious stance toward this theology from the Continent. Yet his generally more appreciative view of modern learning provided the link that would allow Ramm to move beyond the tighter categories of others in the evangelical movement and at the end of his career call for his colleagues to embrace a basically Barthian paradigm for theology "after fundamentalism."

Ramm's Life and Career

Carl Henry's chief contribution to evangelical theology came through his efforts to set forth its prolegomenon through an extended study of the concept of revelation and the doctrine of Scripture distilled in his magnum opus, *God, Revelation and Authority*. Bernard Ramm likewise devoted himself to these topics. But his major contribution came through a somewhat different direction. Ramm attempted to move evangelicalism further than Henry did in the task of engaging in dialog with the modern mindset. His central interest was that of showing the interface of the Bible—that is, of Bible-centered theology—with the totality of human knowledge, which in the twentieth century has been focused primarily on the realm of science.

Just as Henry's background in journalism provided him with the tools to serve as an evangelical commentator on the fortunes of theology in the twentieth century, especially as editor of *Christianity Today*, so also Bernard Ramm was especially positioned to take up the challenge of relating biblical theology to modern knowledge. He was raised on the modern thinking of the day, but he underwent a deeply felt, evangelically oriented conversion to Christ.

From "early youth" Ramm, who was born in 1916 in the mining city of Butte, Montana (location of the Montana State School of Mines), was interested in science. The household of one of his boyhood friends, the son of an immigrant engineer, continually buzzed with talk of Einstein, relativity theory, atomic theory and chemistry.[1] Young Bernard always assumed that he would grow up to become a scientist. By his own account he was a typical high school graduate of the 1930s, "with a mind stocked with what practically all high school graduates have when they leave high school—a profound respect for the sciences, a hope for a newer and better civilization, a toleration and mild respect for religion, a delight in sports and entertainment, and a desire 'to make good' in the world."[2]

Although raised in an environment that prized secular science, Ramm came to be a Christian in a typically evangelical fashion, for he was visited with a conversion experience that altered the direction of his life. Sometime during the summer prior to his planned entrance to the University of Washington, in part through the instrumentality of his bother, John, to whom he later dedicated his book *The Evangelical Heritage*, "the gospel came to him."[3] His conversion was instantaneous, radical, and life-transforming. Describing it in the third person, he later declared:

> In one three-minute period his entire life perspective and basic personality were changed. He experienced the inflowing grace and transforming power of the grace of God. In a few moments he received a new philosophy, a new theology, a new heart, and a new life.[4]

Ramm never lost the evangelical fervor this experience mediated to him.

After completing university studies in speech and philosophy in 1938, Ramm entered the B.D. program at Eastern Baptist Theological Seminary in Philadelphia, a school that had been founded to carry the conservative banner among the academic institutions sponsored by the Northern Baptist Convention (now the American Baptist Churches). In 1941 Ramm completed his work at Eastern, the final year of which included graduate studies at the University of Pennsylvania and an interim pastorate in New York City. Then followed two short pastorates on the West Coast—Seattle (1942-1943) and Glendale, California (1943-1944).[5]

Ramm's contribution to evangelicalism, however, was not to be in the pastorate. In 1943 he launched what would be a lengthy and successful academic career, becoming professor of biblical languages at the Los Angeles Baptist Theological Seminary. The next academic year, he changed both institutions and fields, shifting to what would become a major focus of his life work. He became head of the department of philosophy and apologetics at the Bible Institute of Los Angeles (BIOLA), where he taught until 1951.

Ramm's formal education was not yet completed when he launched into teaching. From his vantage point in Los Angeles, he studied philosophy at the University of Southern California, earning the M.A. in 1947, followed by the Ph.D. in 1950. The keen interest in science that had laid just beneath the surface while he was in seminary and the pastorate now resurfaced. Ramm combined this interest with philosophy by choosing the field of philosophy of science for his educational track. This merging of disciplines with his Christian commitment became evident in his doctoral dissertation, "An Investigation of Some Recent Efforts to Justify Metaphysical Statements from Science with Special Reference to Physics"[6] and again later in one of his early major books, *The Christian View of Science and Scripture* (1954).

Additional institutional changes in the 1950s—Bethel College and Seminary (1951-1954) and Baylor University (1954-1959)—brought Ramm to the American Baptist Seminary of the West (ABSW, formerly the California Baptist Theological Seminary), the location of his longest tenure of service (1959-1974, 1978-1986), albeit one that was interrupted by a brief sojourn at his alma mater, Eastern Baptist Seminary (1974-1977). In addition, Ramm taught courses at several schools, including Fuller and Mennonite Biblical Seminary, and throughout most of his career he instructed young people at Young Life summer institutes.

The Irenic Evangelical

Through his teaching and writing, Ramm made an important contribution to the development of the evangelical movement. Many have looked to him as a thoughtful conservative, one who was able to meet the contemporary intellectual challenges with integrity. Wesley H. Brown, former president of ABSW, summarizes this dimension of his impact:

> Part of Bernard Ramm's great appeal has been his ability to express the Christian faith and relate to contemporary issues with theological competence and intellectual integrity. Far too often evangelicals have been viewed as anti-intellectual, as lacking historical perspective, or as failing to understand the struggles of the scientific

community when talking of matters of faith. Bernard Ramm dispelled those stereotypes for many young Christians, who found in his writing and speaking that they did not need to close their minds nor sacrifice their integrity when thinking and talking about their faith.[7]

Ramm's overarching passion was the pursuit of Christian theology in the aftermath of the Enlightenment. He sought to take the Enlightenment seriously, demonstrating an understanding of the radical changes that era of human intellectual history produced, and at the same time to reaffirm the classical doctrines of Christianity. As a result, he repeatedly called evangelicals to engage in the positive construction of Christian truth while avoiding what he termed "obscurantism," the hindering of knowledge or the active resistance of progress, especially in the areas of critical biblical scholarship and science.[8] In fact, for Ramm a dividing line between evangelicalism and fundamentalism lies just at this point. "Fundamentalism," he noted, "attempts to shield itself from the Enlightenment," whereas "the evangelical believes that the Enlightenment cannot be undone."[9] Ramm's personal task was that of demonstrating how Christians can be intellectually responsible in the face of the Enlightenment—that is, without either making the concessions characteristic of modern theology or resorting to the blind faith or hyper-rationalism of fundamentalism. And he has been a continual example and voice of admonition to his colleagues concerning this enterprise.

His vision of an enlightened Christianity led Ramm to an openness to modern theology uncharacteristic of many of his peers. He was willing to be convinced by the findings of biblical critics. Hence, he could say, "Whenever biblical critics seem to make a real case in which there is close to universal, international agreement, the evangelical has no other course than to assent."[10] In the same way he cautioned his colleagues to avoid accepting "trashy theology, substandard by all academic criteria, as evangelical, and to brand as nonevangelical some great biblical theology."[11]

In the construction of a nonobscurantist theology, Ramm looked not only to the Bible but also to the great theological heritage of the church,[12] including the patristic era, but above all the Reformation[13] (and its continuing legacy in persons such as the Dutch Calvinist theologian-statesman, Abraham Kuyper), which in his view formed "the greatest periods of theological creativity."[14] Ramm found in classical Christianity the fundamental truth for life. The challenge he acknowledged, however, was how a Christian could defend the classical faith of the church in today's world. In Clark Pinnock's words, the question Ramm faced was,

> How can a person as knowledgeable and honest as Ramm is—aware of the humanity of the Bible, of historical and cultural relativity, of the flow of history as a natural process—hold onto traditional convictions, if he really faces up to these challenges?[15]

Ramm, therefore, epitomizes the gentle, irenic side of evangelicalism.[16] Yet this spirit was not inborn; it developed over his career. In fact, his life has been termed one of the "paradigmatic models of evangelical development,"[17] for it depicts a journey charted by many of his colleagues from fundamentalism to what Mark Lau Branson has termed "a learned and thoughtful evangelicalism." This pilgrimage was sparked by the inability of Ramm's fundamentalist roots to bear the insights that he discovered through his openness to science and the scientific method.

Apologetics

The journey of Bernard Ramm into irenic evangelicalism was paralleled by the moves he completed during his academic career—from the fundamentalism of BIOLA to the open posture of ABSW (which participates in the Graduate Theological Union at Berkeley, California). Perhaps more significantly, however, this journey is reflected in his numerous books and, more specifically, in the topics that have been the objects of his research. Although the scope of his writing was not limited to these, three major concerns—apologetics, the Bible and science, and scriptural authority—consumed most of his energies.[18] Although each of these remained a focus of interest throughout of his career, his treatment of them showed progression of thought, albeit always within the broad parameters of the evangelical categories he had accepted. In fact, not only in the conclusions he drew but even in his choice of subjects for exploration, Ramm remained typically evangelical, despite the controversies several of his works have sparked within the evangelical movement.

From the beginning of his career, Ramm was concerned with apologetics. Perhaps this concern was sparked by his early interest in science followed by his shift to philosophy as the subject of his academic training. Perhaps Ramm sensed a need to reconcile reason and faith in his own life and as a result sought to inform his readership that philosophy has an important place in the Christian task.[19] In any case, in typically evangelical fashion his writings reveal an interest in reconciling Christian faith with human knowledge.

Ramm decried the prevalent attitude that sees religion as purely a matter of faith and hence a personal matter. Against this "superficial" view, he declared that "all human disciplines," which for Ramm included religion, "must come to terms with truth."[20] He saw this as opening the way for the work of Christian apologetics, which Ramm defined as "the conscious, deliberate defense and vindication of Christian theology as truth. It is deliberately interacting with the critical criteria of truth in order to show that the realities of which the Christian faith speaks are indeed true realities."[21] This, however, necessitated concern for philosophy: "The Christian apologist is forced to enter the field of philosophy if he is to face the question of truth in genuine integrity of both spirit and methodology."[22]

Although his basic approach to apologetics was typical of evangelicals in general, he deviated from the presuppositionalism of thinkers such as Carl Henry. At least early in his career, Ramm chose another classical approach, sometimes termed "evidentialism." This strategy set forth actual evidences for the truth of the Christian faith drawn from data (Ramm called them "facts") that could be observed or verified, at least in theory, by everyone.

As its title indicates—*Problems in Christian Apologetics*[23]—his first book, a distillation of the mid-year lectures he delivered at Portland's Western Conservative Baptist Seminary, was devoted to apologetics. At this beginning stage in his career, he approached the topic from a problematic, almost combative, manner. This early probing was followed four years later (1953) by two further studies, *Types of Apologetic Systems* and *Protestant Christian Evidences,* and then after a nineteen-year gap by yet a fourth title, *The God Who Makes a Difference* (1972).

In *Types of Apologetic Systems*[24] Ramm viewed the major options in methodology as arising from the starting point and foundation for the apologetical task. Ramm cited these as either apologetics based in "subjective immediacy," which moves from the inward experience of grace through the gospel (Pascal, Kierkegaard, Brunner); apologetics based in "natural theology," which asserts that human rational powers are able to find the truth about religion (Aquinas, Joseph Butler, F. R. Tennant); or apologetics based in divine revelation, which follows the dictum, "faith precedes understanding" (Augustine and contemporary evangelicals Cornelius Van Til and Edward John Carnell).[25]

In these foundational works, Ramm asserted that a proper Christian apologetic must be based on revelation, that is, on the divine self-disclosure "in creation, in the nature of man, in the history of Israel and the Church, in the pages of Holy Scripture, in the incarnation of God in Christ, and in the heart of the believer by the gospel."[26] Only this approach, which Ramm claimed constitutes historic Christianity in contrast to "modernism" or Protestant liberalism, leads to a defensible statement of the faith. Ramm answered his call in his own textbook in the field, *Protestant Christian Evidences,* a treatise he directed toward both critically thinking Christians and persons outside the faith "who still have enough flexibility in their mentality to hear a case on its own merit."[27]

Important to Ramm's delineation of his position is the distinction he drew between "apologetics" itself as the verification of the Christian system of belief or "the strategy of setting forth the truthfulness of the Christian faith and its right to the claim of the knowledge of God,"[28] and "evidences" as the subdivision of this discipline directed toward "the demonstration of the *factuality* of the Christian religion."[29] He believed that this factuality, this relationship between Christianity and reality, could be demonstrated. To this end, he harnessed the traditional evidences of fulfilled biblical prophecy and biblical miracles, Jesus' character and resurrection, and Christian experience. All of these, coupled with the Bible's perennial ability "to grip profoundly the human soul,"[30] work together to witness to the divine inspiration of the Bible, so that the supernatural character of the Bible forms the final verification of Christianity.[31]

Already in 1958 Ramm appeared to be moving toward a course correction in his approach to apologetics. In an article entitled "The Evidence of Prophecy and Miracle," he sought to correct any misunderstanding that would assert that evidences alone could stir the heart.[32] To do so, he built from the Augustinian and Calvinist differentiation between "the inner and outer witness," which declares that religious certitude about the truth is derived directly from God. With this in view, Ramm argued from the inner and outer nature of Christianity that the inner work of the Spirit and evidences such as fulfilled prophecy and miracles work together to assure the Christian of the validity of belief. Thus he could conclude:

The fulfilled promise of a prophetic word, the miraculous act of an apostle, are part of the divine *indicia* which inform the believing heart that the religion he holds within his heart by reason of the witness of the Spirit in the Word exists also in the world (prior to his personal experience) by the supernatural acts of the Living God.[33] A step beyond the evidentialism of his earlier days came in *The God Who Makes a Difference* (1972). His basic thesis that apologetics must be grounded in revelation remained. But now, because "individual facts, no matter how many of them, do not constitute effective knowledge,"[34] he offered Christianity (specifically the Reformed faith as its best expression) as a postulate or hypothesis. The evidences cited in his earlier works were reorganized and presented in terms of three concentric circles (the persuasion of the Holy Spirit, the action of God in creation and history, and a "synoptic vision" or integrative view of humanity, the world and God).

Building from his earlier differentiation between the inner and outer witness, Ramm the apologist now also differentiated between "certitude" and "certainty." On the basis of Scripture and the internal witness of the Spirit the believer may have "full spiritual certitude" concerning the great truths of personal salvation.[35] The historical dimension of Christian faith, however, can never be known with certainty, but only with a high degree of probability. In a manner that was a precursor to his later advocacy of Barth as the paradigm for theology, he concluded:

> The Christian apologist then says that spiritually, inwardly, convictionally he rests his faith in full certitude; in reference to the objective historical, factual, etc., basis of the Christian revelation, he believes with a high degree of probability.[36]

It was precisely here that the fundamentalists had gone astray, he claimed. They erroneously sought rational religious certainty for the history narrated by the Bible.[37]

After 1972 Ramm turned away from apologetics as such and began to struggle more intensely with issues of systematic theology. Yet he never left behind his interest in the discipline. Even his more purely theological treatises in the 1980s never lost the apologetic dimension. Thus, for example, when he presented his theology of sin in *Offense to Reason* (1985), he wrote with a view toward the modern mindset and the totality of human knowledge. His thesis is that despite its offensive nature or apparent unreasonableness, the doctrine of sin is not a parochial Christian topic, but is wrestled with by humans in many ways and in many disciplines of thought. As a result, this doctrine is necessary in order to understand human existence in the world. His thesis, of course, sets forth an apologetic for this aspect of the Christian view of humanity and the world. In the same way, in his final book, *An Evangelical Christology,* Ramm remained the apologist who finds it necessary to reply to the various objections to the classical doctrine.

Despite the continued orientation to apologetics demonstrated by these later works, it is clear that Ramm the apologist had steadily moved away from the evidentialism of much of evangelicalism. This movement was in many ways merely the natural outworking of his own thinking as it came to be influenced by Augustine, the Reformers and finally Karl Barth. Ramm came to agree with Barth's dictum (which he claimed Barth drew from Luther and Calvin) that "if something external to the Word of God is necessary to establish the Word of God as true, then it is greater than the Word of God."[38]

Bible and Science

The desire to interact with the sciences (in addition to literature and philosophy) evident in *Offense to Reason* is indicative of a second lifetime concern of Bernard Ramm. He was continually concerned to explore the interface of the Bible and biblical truth with modern knowledge, especially science. This interest resulted in his involvement with the American Scientific Affiliation, a professional society comprised of evangelicals committed both to faith and to the scientific enterprise.

The major distillation of Ramm's attempt to bring the Bible and science into dialog came in the book that catapulted him as a young thinker into the evangelical limelight, *The Christian View of Science and Scripture* (1954). Although not wanting to capitulate to the modern scientific mindset found in Protestant liberalism, Ramm's chief intent in this work was to avoid the fundamentalist approach to the issue that pitted Christianity against scientific findings. He described this "ignoble tradition" as one that "has taken a most unwholesome attitude toward science, and has used arguments and procedures not in the better traditions of established scholarship."[39] In its stead he hoped "to call evangelicalism back to the noble tradition,"[40] to the view that asserted that God was the author of both creation and redemption and that therefore built from the assumed agreement between true science and the Bible.[41] Ramm claimed that this tradition had enjoyed ascendancy in the closing years of the nineteenth century, but had been buried by "a narrow bibliolatry, the product not of faith but of fear."[42]

In keeping with the older "noble tradition" Ramm was convinced that no ultimate contradictions could be found between science and the Bible. Problems arise only when specialists do not keep to their proper spheres or through the element of human sin. Thus he wrote with almost the naive optimism of an earlier era that had not yet acknowledged the subjective dimension necessary to all scientific advance:

> If the theologian and the scientist had been careful to stick to their respective duties, and to learn carefully the other side when they spoke of it there would have been no disharmony between them save that of the non-Christian heart in rebellion against God.[43]

As a reflection of this conviction, his study led to a most positive conclusion:

> We have tried to show that no man of science has a proper reason for not becoming a Christian on the grounds of his science. We have tried to show the inoffensive character of the Biblical statements about Nature; the relevance of so much of Biblical truth to fact; and the credibility of the miraculous. We have not tried to force a man to Christ by these chapters, but if a man is a Christian, a scientist cannot question on scientific grounds the respectability of that man's faith.[44]

Although important in its own right, the program displayed in *The Christian View of Science and Scripture* was not an interest totally separate from that of apologetics. On the contrary, the former fit within and was an integral part of the latter. At its heart, this discussion attempted to show "the correlation of Christianity with *material fact*,"[45] which Ramm had set forth in his earlier apologetics textbook as one of the three types of facts pursued by Christian evidences.[46]

Despite Ramm's laudable intent, *The Christian View of Science and Scripture* triggered a commotion. While at points he simply harmonized science with Scripture, he nevertheless boldly declared that the Bible contained culturally conditioned statements. The biblical writers, he asserted, simply were not teachers of science in the modern sense. As a result, Ramm suggested that theories such as a local flood, a figurative "long day of Joshua" and an ancient earth, if confirmed by science, were plausible from biblical grounds. He even went so far as to allow for "theistic evolution" (God employed evolution in bringing the various life forms, including humankind, into existence), although he himself preferred the expression "progressive creation."[47]

To fundamentalists, of course, all this smacked of pure accommodation. Liberals, however, were equally unconvinced, accusing him of inconsistency in failing to follow his theses to their logical conclusions.[48]

The hermeneutics employed in *The Christian View of Science and Scripture* had been spelled out in a widely read early work, *Protestant Biblical Interpretation* (1950).[49] Its theological basis was subsequently delineated in *Special Revelation and the Word of God* (1961). Articulating a foundational theme of his entire career, Ramm asserted in the earlier work that "only a full-fledged, intelligent Biblicism is adequate to the present day situation in science, philosophy, psychology, and religion.[50] This "Biblicism" included not only traditional Reformation premises such as the clarity of Scripture (that is, the interpreter can know what the Bible is saying), but also the principle that revelation is accommodated. This latter principle meant that Scripture has an "anthropomorphic character" that the exegete must acknowledge.[51]

In *His Way Out*, Ramm applied his hermeneutical approach to a specific biblical book—Exodus. In this nontechnical, lay-oriented work, the author illustrated his mediating stance between "the capitulation to the modern post-Enlightenment mentality presenting itself as scientific" he found in liberalism and the pure supernaturalism of many fundamentalists. Thus, for example, Ramm asserted that the miracles described in the biblical narrative "represent some sort of conjunction of divine power and natural phenomena associated with the land of Egypt."[52]

One of the most thorny problems evangelicals must deal with in any attempt to relate the biblical accounts with scientific findings is that of human origins, that is, the question of Adam. Again at this point, Ramm sought a mediating position. Near the beginning of his career, he set the stage for this position. In *The Christian View of Science and Scripture,* he opted neither for the rejection of geological findings that point to a great age of humankind nor for a purely mythological interpretation of the biblical narrative. Instead Ramm pointed to the features that geology and Scripture share.

At the end of his career, in *Offense to Reason,* Ramm still advocated a mediating position, albeit one that emphasizes even more strongly the *theological* rather than the *historical* character of the Genesis narrative. Genesis 1—3 is a "divinely inspired reconstruction" and "theology by narration."[53] It is Hebrew reflection on creation and on the nature and origin of sin expressed by telling a story. As a result, Adam, he declared, is both "a generic figure and the person who in Jewish history is the head of both the Jewish people and the human race."[54] The Bible and science, therefore, are both correct, when viewed within the proper perspective of each.

Authority

Finally, Ramm devoted himself to the question of Scripture, revelation and theological authority. As the 1950s gave way to the 1960s, the evangelical theologian churned out three books dealing with these topics: *The Pattern of Authority* (1957, but republished the next year as *The Pattern of Religious Authority*), *The Witness of the Spirit* (1959) and *Special Revelation and the Word of God* (1961). Like his concern for the interface of the Bible and science, this interest was not pursued as separable from the task of apologetics[55] but served the same goal, namely, the demonstration of the truth of the Christian faith.

As in the other aspects of his thought, Ramm's intent here was to chart a middle course.[56] In this dimension of theology, he sought to avoid both subjectivism, such as results from the emphasis on religious experience as the final authority, found in liberalism,[57] and authoritarianism. He accomplished this task by locating ultimate authority in the divine revelation (which in the final analysis is Christ) and by seeking a balance between the inspired Scripture and the illumined reader—between the outer and the inner, the objective and the subjective dimensions.[58] For this, Ramm appealed to the Reformation,[59] asserting that the Protestant principle of authority is "the Holy Spirit speaking in the Scriptures which are the product of the Spirit's revelatory and inspiring action."[60]

Ramm's doctrine of Scripture follows. The primary principle of authority—God in the divine self-disclosure—produces the immediate principle of authority—the Spirit speaking in the Scriptures.[61] As a result, final authority lies neither in the book itself nor in the Spirit, but in the revelation (Jesus Christ) to which the Bible witnesses as the Spirit effects illumination.[62] Consequently, the New Testament is authoritative in the church, because it is the witness of the apostles (and those associated with them) to the revelation of God in Christ.[63]

His affirmation of what he saw as the full Reformation understanding formed the basis for Ramm's rejection not only of the liberal alternative but also of fundamentalism.[64] He found three errors in the latter. First, fundamentalists had become so concerned to defend the inspiration of the Scriptures that they lost track of the more comprehensive Reformation doctrine of revelation and thereby failed to understand that "inspiration lives on revelation and not vice versa."[65] Second, by losing the perspective of the instrumental character of Scripture—that is, its role as the document the Spirit uses in enlightening the believing reader[66]—fundamentalism gave Scripture a life of its own independent of the Spirit. They equated the expression "the Word" with the Bible, thereby making it equivalent with the Reformation expression "Word and Spirit."[67] Finally, despite their abhorrence for accommodation to science, fundamentalists "let the spirit of science permeate their apologetic" by seeking to demonstrate scientifically the inspiration of Scripture[68] (rather than understanding that the

Scriptures are self-authenticating).[69]

As a result of his nonrationalistic approach, Ramm never entered into the debate about the Bible that shackled the evangelical movement. He affirmed the concept of "inerrancy."[70] But for him, it was a broad, nonrestrictive category, and he indicated that debates concerning it "pay no great dividends."[71] Rather than any doctrine of inspiration or even Scripture itself, Ramm elevated as the "first line of defense" the content of Scripture, namely, Jesus Christ.[72] It is therefore not without significance that his last book dealt with Christology. But already in 1961 he articulated this theme in no uncertain terms:

> The temptation of biblicism is that it can speak of the inspiration of the Scriptures *apart from* the Lord they enshrine. . . . There can be no formal doctrine of inspiration; there can be only a Christ-centered doctrine of inspiration.[73]

For this reason, Ramm could have no part with conservatives who tended to view their understanding of the doctrine of Scripture integral to the essence of Christianity.[74]

For Ramm, inspiration must always be subservient to revelation. Inspiration has the function of preserving revelation in a trustworthy and sufficient form.[75] Revelation, then, moves from God to God's spokesperson, to God's people, and finally it is cast in written form through divine inspiration.[76] But even here, Ramm avoided any naive equating of the inspired product with the words of the Bible. Instead, he argued that inspiration relates to units of meaning, not isolated words.[77] Hence, he made a distinction between the external form—the words of the original documents in their original languages—and the internal form—the inspired meaning of the text, which is in the final analysis the Word of God.[78]

Ramm and Barth

Ramm's concern to set forth credible theology in the post-Enlightenment situation as expressed in his work in apologetics, the interface of Bible and science, and in the doctrine of revelation eventually led him to Karl Barth. In 1983 his lifelong intrigue with the writings of the Swiss theologian climaxed with his controversial open embracing of Barth's approach as the paradigm for evangelicalism in the contemporary world.

The affirmation of Barth is perhaps the greatest development in Ramm's thinking.[79] At the beginning of his career he joined the evangelical chorus that dismissed the Swiss theologian. In 1953, for example, he asserted, "The Christ of atheism, of liberalism, and of Barthianism is not the Christ of the historical documents."[80] By 1971, his stance had begun to mellow, in part due to study in Basel during the academic year 1957-1958.[81] Ramm concluded his article on "Biblical Interpretation" with a mixed review of Barth, declaring that his "particular exegesis" may be questioned, "but his notion of exegesis" is sound.[82] One year later, however, he admitted Barth's influence on his own thinking in the area of apologetics.[83] Finally, in his 1983 book, *After Fundamentalism,* Ramm broadened his acknowledgment of Barth's importance to the crucial area of theological method.

What drew Ramm to Barth was his discovery of a kindred spirit in the Swiss theologian. Ramm had come to discover that Barth was doing exactly what Ramm had himself set out to do—engage in classical theology in full view of the Enlightenment. Thus, he concluded: "Barth's theology is a restatement of Reformed theology written in the aftermath of the Enlightenment but not capitulating to it."[84]

Constructive Theology

In the wake of this monumental discovery, Ramm spent the remainder of his career seeking to engage in theology through the employment of the basically Barthian model. It was as if he could now finally turn his attention away from its former focus on issues of theological foundation—apologetics, Bible and science, revelation—and engage in constructive theology. As a result, his final two volumes dealt with two core Christian doctrines, sin and Christ.

Although treatises on major doctrines came only at the end of his career, Ramm articulated his understanding of the nature of theology earlier, in *Special Revelation and the Word of God*. According to Ramm this task is pursued with a view toward both its possibilities and its limits. Theology is possible because it is related to the knowledge of God that arises out of God's self-disclosure. As a result he saw a crucial connection between theology and divine revelation: "The theologian does not treat God *in himself,* but God *in his revelation.*"[85] More specifically, the theologian sets out the genesis and the structure of God's ectypal revelation—"that segment of the archetypal knowledge of God [that is, God's self-knowledge] which God wishes man to know"[86]—given to humankind by God in special revelation ("God's word in a concrete form to a specific person or group").[87]

At the same time, however, Ramm knew the limits of theology. These limits arise from two divergent directions, the incomprehensibility of God and human sinfulness. He linked the divine incomprehensibility with God's transcendence. As finite beings standing before the transcendent God, we simply cannot adequately conceive of God or properly describe God in human language, he declared.[88] God must condescend to us, if we are to know the Divine One. This is what God does in revelation, coming to us from the transcendent realm, choosing thereby to impart to us partial knowledge of the divine reality.

Human sinfulness likewise places limits on theological engagement. In the words of William Herzog, Ramm "never forgot how close at hand sin lay, awaiting the opportunity to turn any fruitful endeavor into distorted consequence."[89] Ramm himself spoke of the necessity for a limited pessimism in evangelicalism due to its "inherent serious doctrine of sin," with the result that "the evangelical believes in amelioration (things may be made better) but not in utopia (things may be made perfect)."[90] Yet given the choice of elevating sin or human possibility, Ramm preferred the latter. In this sense, he reflects the Calvinist emphasis on the doctrine of creation as mediated to him by Abraham Kuyper, who asserted that despite its terrible effect, the entrance of sin did not negate God's original purpose for humankind.[91]

Critical Evaluation

The genius of Bernard Ramm lay in his attempt to move beyond fundamentalism. The evangelical thinker found the Achilles' heel of the movement in its inadequate acknowledgment of the limits of theology. For him, the revelation that lay at the genesis of theology encompasses a mystery. But the rationalism of fundamentalism "reads the revelation of God as a transcript without mystery."[92] In his theologizing, in contrast, Ramm sought to capture a profound sense of this aspect of revelation: "The mystery and wonder of grace is that the transcendent God has willed to reveal himself. The incomprehensible God has spoken and in this speaking we understand that he is incomprehensible."[93]

Ramm's entire approach to theology, therefore, was built on the premise that the transcendent One had condescended to humankind revealing thereby the divine reality to God's sinful creatures. He believed that this divine revelation was not in competition with the best of modern learning, but on the contrary that the two coalesced. In this way, the transcendent One was also immanent—present as the truth of all human knowledge. It was to the exploration of this divine self-disclosure, pursued in the context of the contemporary, post-Enlightenment situation and for the purpose of knowing the self-disclosing, transcendent God, that Ramm offered his life in service.

With his more profound understanding of the positive contributions of the Enlightenment, Ramm was able to move beyond the backward-looking approach of Carl Henry. In so doing, he provided the foundation for a generation of younger evangelical thinkers who would build on the freedom to think critically and engage in positive dialog with modern culture. Evangelical theology had begun to come of age.

But for the younger thinkers, Ramm had not moved far enough. Although he sought new ways to reaffirm the grand evangelical axiom that God speaks to us from beyond the world, the evangelical innovator seemed to have drunk too deeply from the traditional theological well with its employment of the now discredited spatial metaphor of transcendence and immanence. Despite his significant contribution to the movement, Ramm had not totally resolved the evangelical dilemma.

CONCLUSION:
Past Contributions and Future Prospects in the Quest for a Theology of Transcendence and Immanence

*I*N EVERY ERA THEOLOGY HAS BEEN CONFRONTED WITH THE CHALLENGE OF ARTICULATING the Christian understanding of the nature of God in a manner that balances, affirms and holds in creative tension the twin truths of the divine transcendence and the divine immanence. The biblical God is self-sufficient apart from the world, is above the universe and comes to creation from beyond. But the God of the Bible is also present to creation, active within the world and involved with the historical and natural processes.

In the twentieth century theologians attempted to engage in the theological task in the wake of the imbalance bequeathed to them by their forebears. The situation under which they labored was the product of the demise of the medieval consensus that occurred at the hands of the Enlightenment.

The medieval thinkers sought to balance the divine transcendence and immanence by appeal to spatial categories. God dwelt in heaven above, but nevertheless was present in the world beneath the heavens. This God had made himself present to humans first as their Creator "in the beginning" and then as their Redeemer in the Incarnation of Jesus. The medieval model found the presence of God in the world now mediated primarily through the church, which served as the link between heaven above and earth below. Through the activities of the church, especially the celebration of the sacraments, the situation on earth came to reflect the deeper realities of heaven.

The Enlightenment, however, erased the gulf that separated the two realms. It brought the creature into direct contact with the Creator, a contact that required only the mediation of reason with its power to uncover the *Logos* it shared with the universe. Because reason could perceive the underlying *Logos,* it could delve into the mysteries of reality. The age of reason shaped the mindset that we today label "modern," a world view that searches for, and at times even claims to have discovered, absolute knowledge and certitude.

The thinkers of the nineteenth century sought to transcend the rationalism of the Enlightenment. But for all their good intentions, the theologians of that era could not escape from the immanentalism they inherited from the age of reason, nor were they sure that they wanted to do so. Consequently, they bequeathed to the twentieth century the task of determining how theology could speak of the transcendence of the imma-nent God and thereby forge a new and more adequate balance between immanence and transcendence.

The challenge twentieth-century theologians accepted was no small matter. On the contrary, theirs has been the job of determining whether or not any such balance is even possible, given the impact of the Enlightenment on the modern mindset and the unsatisfying submergence of God within the world they found in the theological con-structions of the nineteenth century. Beginning with Barth's rebellion, thinkers searched for new models, new ways of constructing theology for the era beyond the Enlightenment. As we have seen, the solutions these theologians offered bear witness to the instability introduced whenever transcendence and immanence are out of kilter. The lopsided emphasis on one will indeed eventually lead to attempts to redress the imbalance by moving too far in the other direction.

As the century has drawn to its close, we have been left wondering if any progress has been made. Rather than create a balanced theology, the efforts of the last decades seem only to have increased the tension between immanence and transcendence. In fact, only in the twentieth century have loud voices emerged from the ranks of aca-demic theologians despairing of the entire task and calling for the demise of the discipline. Could an age that began on a hopeful note—with a man who undertook the writing of one of the most massive constructions of theology of all time—end with a whimper, with the deconstruction of the systematic theological enterprise as a whole? This question indicates that not only the creation of a theology that adequately bal-ances the truths of immanence and transcendence but even the defense of the theo-logical task as it has traditionally been understood remain major problems to be tackled by thinkers in the twenty-first century.

For all the difficulties encountered, however, the theologies that emerged during the twentieth century did indeed make certain contributions. Although no single signpost pointing the way forward emerged, at least its shadow may nevertheless lie across our pathway. The theological history of the century does offer some indication of what must be considered by any future attempt to delineate a balanced theology.

The twentieth century began with a protest against the emphasis on immanence so important for the Western mindset since the Renaissance. Hence, its genesis lay in a rebirth of transcendence. As we have seen, immanentalist theology did not fade from view. On the contrary, throughout the century theologians of immanence and advocates of transcendence sought to redress each others' overemphases. Nevertheless, in the end the greatest lasting legacy of this century of theology is its recovery of the importance of the transcendence theme. The message of transcendentalists from Karl Barth onward is clear: At the foundation of every theology that remains true to its task must lie the desire to be attentive to the word from the God of heaven. Theology, in other words, must always remain Barth's "happy science," anticipating even in the most despairing circumstances that God has spoken and does speak, and that the voice of God can still be heard.

Yet the interpretive challenge remains. How are we to understand "word," "God" and "heaven"? In what sense does God's voice collide with our world? Who is this God who addresses us in this manner? And from where does God speak? These are the questions with which twentieth-century theologians have struggled. And each of the major theological movements has offered a specific contribution to the whole.

Neo-orthodoxy, of course, sounded the theme of the Word of God coming to our world from beyond. But in addition, this movement also served a chastening function. It reminded us of the classical Christian doctrine of sin, which should give theologians pause, lest we become overwhelmed by the hubris of the modern age and believe we are able to capture ultimate truth by our rational constructs. Barth may have overstated his case for a categorical rejection of natural theology. Yet the somber note he, together with other neo-orthodox thinkers, struck in response to the apparently unbridled optimism of classical liberalism is of lasting value. Our fallenness does preclude our solving the human predicament by the employment of innate human capabilities. We stand in need of resources that transcend our world. Contra Barth there may indeed be a point of contact between the in-breaking Word and the human receptacle; yet in the final analysis the resource that invades our world is of a categorically different order.

The resurgent liberalism of the century was likewise not without its message. Paul Tillich reminded us that the Word from beyond does not invade our world in some capricious manner, but comes as the answer to the fundamental questions posed by the reality of the world and by human existence. Furthermore, if we are to communicate the truth of the faith, we can no longer envision the "beyond" that invades our present in terms drawn from the old spatial metaphor. Although he offered no satisfying alternative, he eloquently posed the problem, a problem that the theologies of the 1960s tackled.

Process theology articulated a thesis that all subsequent theologies have adopted, even if they adapted it to their own perspectives. Reality is dynamic, not static. The theological implication of this thesis is far-reaching. Whatever else is said about the divine reality must be based on the fundamental dictum that in some sense God participates with us in the dynamic process of the universe. This dictum, of course, has been variously interpreted.

The radical theologies of the 1960s sounded the final death peal of the older spatial model of the divine relationship to the world. The model of a God who existed in heaven above the world is dead, they announced. If God does speak, the divine address is the immanent voice submerged within the modern secular realm.

The thesis of the theologians of secularity did not mark the death of transcendence, however. Instead it paved the way for a new metaphor of God and the world, the temporal metaphor introduced by the theologians of hope. Rather than invade our turf from above, God comes to us from the temporal beyond, they argued. God participates in our present from the vantage point of the future. In this way Moltmann, and with greater success Pannenberg, attempted a renewal of a balance in theology not seen since the undermining of the medieval consensus.

In the wake of the promise of a possible new consensus employing the temporal metaphor, the liberation theologies reminded us that the shift to the temporal, while not fundamentally incorrect, does carry certain dangers. Above all, the new balance may be inherently unstable and unsatisfying, especially if it becomes simply another version of the old "pie in the sky by-and-by" theology. The theology of hope declared that God cannot be the God of the present without being the God of the future; liberation theologians cautioned that God cannot be the God of the future unless that God is the Liberating One active in the present. Any correct theology, in other words, must exercise an impact on life and on life in the here-and-now.

The fledgling loose coalition of thinkers that forms the movement known as narrative theology has in a sense sought to tie these strands together, with the addition of yet one more theme. God is a dynamic reality who participates with us on the journey of life. But the focus of the divine participation is story. God calls us to join our story— our history—with the broader story of the divine activity in history.

In the past, representatives of the conservative Western traditions—Roman Catholics and conservative Protestants—have tended to stand apart from developments within the innovative sectors of Protestant theology. But in recent decades this has become increasingly less and less the case. As we have seen, in the mid- to late twentieth century, Catholic thinkers sought to add their contributions to the ongoing theological discussions. They have struggled with the question that plagued their Protestant counterparts, the tension between immanence and transcendence, which traditional Catholic theology knows as the problem of nature and grace: How can the human being be naturally open to God's self-communication without that natural openness preconditioning or limiting the freedom of that self-communication? Our representative Catholic thinkers reminded us that the key to the answer to this query can be found only within the human spirit.

During the last half of the century the evangelical movement within conservative Protestantism also entered into the broader theological discussions. Several evangelical thinkers joined their efforts with the struggle to determine the meaning of the Christian faith in the aftermath of the Enlightenment, as is indicated by the two representatives treated in this volume.

Whatever their short-comings may be, evangelicals have provided a necessary corrective to what at times has become the unbridled innovations of others. They have been untiring in their reminder that theology must direct its efforts toward the vision of the balance between immanence and transcendence. And they have been unabashedly committed to biblical authority. In our search for new models and paradigms, the evangelical tradition cautions, let us keep a biblical perspective. For this reason, the commitments of evangelicalism offer an orientation point for the laying of a firm foundation for theology in the twenty-first century.

In these pages we have not exhausted the theological options presented during the last decades. On the contrary, a host of other thinkers struggled with the major and minor theological issues of the century and made their unique contributions to the flow of thought. Some of these contributors could be subsumed under the predominant crosscurrents we have outlined and for which we have provided only representative spokespersons. Others may have charted somewhat independent courses, but for various reasons—whether rightly or wrongly—never found their way into the central weave of the tapestry of the century. And certain gropings for new directions that have emerged in recent years are still too new to venture some evaluation as to whether or not they will influence the future or merely be relegated to the dust bin of passing theological interests and fads.

One interest that will shape theology in the twenty-first century, at least initially, is the question of postmodernism. The twentieth century may be viewed as a transitional era. During the ten decades that comprise it, Western culture moved somewhat haltingly, yet relentlessly, beyond the modernity that constituted the inheritance of the Enlightenment. But where this movement is leading—what will be the marks of postmodernity—remains an open question. To date the gurus of postmodernism have engaged only in the task of deconstructing the modern mindset. Of one thing they are sure, modernity's quest to achieve heaven on earth has ended in failure. Whatever may eventually characterize the postmodern mind, it will be an outlook toward ourselves and the world chastened by the realism thrust upon us by the experiences of a century of failure and unmet expectations.

In a sense, then, the twentieth century ends by repeating the lesson with which it began. Despite our good intentions, by our innate human ability we cannot transform earth into heaven. For many today, this awareness can lead to only one conclusion: There is no heaven, no transcendency, no beyond—whether above us or in front of us; we are imperfect selves imprisoned on an imperfect earth.

Although the emerging postmodern mind may appear to put faith on the defensive, it actually marks a new day of opportunity for theology. Postmodernism indicates that the theological history of the century has had some impact on the Western mind. When true to its foundations, Christian theology has always proclaimed that human attempts to create the new human order are doomed. But this does not spell the demise of faith and hope. Our inability to bring heaven to earth only opens the door to a greater possibility, God coming to us in creating a new world.

At the transition between the modern and the postmodern eras, therefore, theology has the opportunity to articulate anew and in new ways the Christian conviction of the reality of the transcendent-immanent God. This God invades our present circumstances from the vantage point of the transcendent *telos* of the whole of reality. At the same time, this God is immanent in our circumstances, sharing our present, just as God invites us to look beyond our imperfection to the as yet unattained perfection. In short, theology must accept the verdict of the experience of the twentieth century: earth cannot become heaven. But it must then add the message of hope: "on earth" can be "as it is in heaven." The God who addresses us from beyond—from the then-and-there—is the God who is with us in the present—in the here-and-now. Our realization of this truth lies at the heart of the theological balancing of the divine immanence with the divine transcendence.

Notes

1 The Enlightenment: The Shattering of the Classical Balance

[1] For this reason, Hampshire claims that Bacon "was rather the last philosopher of the Renaissance than the first philosopher of the seventeenth century." Stuart Hampshire, *The Age of Reason 17th Century Philosophers* (New York: The New American Library of World Literature, 1956), 17, see also 19-20.

[2] See, e.g., ibid., 11.

[3] William C. Placher, *A History of Christian Theology* (Philadelphia: Westminster, 1983), 237-38.

[4] Carl L. Becker, *The Heavenly City of the Eighteenth-century Philosophers* (New Haven: Yale University Press, 1932), 7.

[5] The roots of this change lay likewise in the Renaissance. De Santillana credits Erasmus as the one who transformed the meaning of rationalism from the medieval to the modern. Giorgio de Santillana, *The Age of Adventure* (New York: New American Library of World Literature, 1956), 27.

[6] Ibid., 46.

[7] This opinion is voiced, e.g., by Descartes' translator, Laurence J. Lafleur. Translator's Introduction, in René Descartes, *Discourse on Method and Meditations*, trans. Laurence J. Lafleur (Indianapolis: Bobbs-Merrill, 1960), vii, xvii. See also Hampshire, *Age of Reason*, 12.

[8] Hampshire, *Age of Reason*, 17.

[9] For a succinct summary of the lasting importance of Descartes, see Lafleur, Translator's Introduction, viii-xiv.

[10] Justo L. Gonzáles, *A History of Christian Thought* (Nashville: Abingdon, 1975), 3:297.

[11] Hampshire, *Age of Reason*, 12-13. Isaiah Berlin, *The Age of Enlightenment* (New York: Mentor, 1956), 16-17.

[12] John Herman Randall, Jr., Introduction, in Isaac Newton, *Newton's Philosophy of Nature*, ed. H. S. Thayer (New York: Hafner, 1953), xiv.

[13] In his helpful study of theological history, Paul Tillich characterizes the Enlightenment mindset by means of the first four of these principles. See *A History of Christian Thought* (New York: Simon and Schuster, 1968), 320-41.

[14]Immanuel Kant, *Foundations of the Metaphysics of Morals* and *What Is Enlightenment?* (New York: Liberal Arts Press, 1959), 85.

[15]Becker, *Heavenly City*, 65.

[16]Berlin, *Age of Enlightenment*, 14.

[17]Becker, *Heavenly City*, 118.

[18]Berlin, *Age of Enlightenment*, 29.

[19]In his *Christianity as Old as Creation*, Matthew Tindal (1655-1733), e.g., argued that the gospel is intended to show that a universal natural law lies at the basis of all religion.

[20]E.g., John Toland (1670-1722), *Christianity Not Mysterious*.

[21]An early articulation of the principle beliefs of natural religion was set forth by Lord Herbert of Cherbury in *De Religione Gentilium* (1663). For a delineation of these, see Arthur Cushman McGiffert, *Protestant Thought Before Kant* (London: Duckworth, 1911), 212; Placher, *History of Christian Theology*, 242.

[22]Gonzáles, *History of Christian Thought* 3:307.

[23]This view was articulated already in the seventeenth century by the Anglican archbishop John Tillotson (see McGiffert, *Protestant Thought*, 195), but was developed further by Tindal (McGiffert, 214).

[24]E.g., Tindal, *Christianity as Old as Creation*, and Thomas Chubb, *The True Gospel of Jesus Christ Asserted* (1738).

[25]E.g., Anthony Collins, *A Discourse on the Grounds and Reasons of the Christian Religion* (1724).

[26]E.g., the tracts of Thomas Woolston (1727) and especially David Hume's *Essay on Miracles* (1748).

[27]This position was argued by John Tillotson, John Locke and Samuel Clarke. See McGiffert, *Protestant Thought*, 195-210.

2 The Reconstruction of Transcendence: Immanence in Nineteenth-Century Theology
Immanuel Kant: The Immanence of God in Moral Experience

[1]David Hume was the exemplar of enlightened skepticism. For a discussion of this development, see Arthur Cushman McGiffert, *Protestant Thought Before Kant* (London: Duckworth, 1911), 230-51.

[2]Paradigmatic was the position of Gotthold Lessing. For a summary of Lessing's views, see William C. Placher, *A History of Christian Theology* (Philadelphia: Westminster, 1983), 249-50.

[3]McGiffert, *Protestant Thought*, 253.

[4]These arguments are put forth in Hume's essays, *Providence and a Future State* (1748), *Dialogues Concerning Natural Religion* (1779) and *Natural History of Religion* (1757).

[5]Hume agreed that such concepts were necessary for human knowing, but declared that they were deduced from experience. Kant, in contrast, claimed that these concepts "sprang from the pure understanding." Immanuel Kant, *Prolegomena to Any Future Metaphysics*, trans. and ed. Paul Carus (Illinois: Open Court, 1967), 7.

[6]Immanuel Kant, *Critique of Judgement*, trans. J. H. Bernard (New York: Hafner, 1968), 322.

[7]Immanuel Kant, *Critique of Pure Reason*, trans. Norman Kemp Smith (New York: St. Martin's, 1929), 29.

[8]Immanuel Kant, *Fundamental Principles of the Metaphysic of Morals*, trans. Thomas K. Abbott (Indianapolis: Bobbs-Merrill, 1949), 38.

[9]Another well-known formulation of the categorical imperative emphasized treating humans always as ends, never as means: "So act as to treat humanity, whether in thine own person or in that of any other, in every case as an end withal, never as means only." Ibid., 46.

[10]Immanuel Kant, *Religion within the Limits of Reason Alone* (New York: Harper and Row, 1960), 5-6.

[11]This is the conclusion of Paul Tillich, *A History of Christian Thought*, ed. Carl Braaten (New York: Simon and Schuster, 1968), 363.

[12]Kant, *Religion within the Limits*, 32.

[13]G. E. Michaelson, Jr., "Moral Regeneration and Divine Aid in Kant," *Religious Studies* 25/3 (1989):265.

[14]Kant, *Religion within the Limits*, 54.

[15]Ibid., 56, 59.

[16]Ibid., 105.

[17]Ibid., 123.

[18]Ibid., 78.

[19]Ibid., 123.

[20]Ibid., 158.

[21]Ibid., 190.

[22]E.g., ibid., 130.

G. W. F. Hegel: The Immanence of God in Speculative Reason

[1]Carl J. Friedrich, Introduction, in G. W. F. Hegel, *The Philosophy of Hegel*, ed. Carl J. Friedrich (New York: Random House, 1954), xiv.

[2]For a basic biography of Hegel's life, see Franz Wiedmann, *Hegel: An Illustrated Biography*, trans. Joachim Neugroschel (New York: Pegasus, 1968). Hegel's intellectual development is delineated in the monumental study by Hans Küng, *The Incarnation of God* (New York: Crossroad, 1987).

[3]Friedrich, Introduction, xx.

[4]G. W. F. Hegel, Preface to *The Philosophy of Right and Law*, in *Philosophy of Hegel*, ed. Friedrich, 224.

[5]Quentin Lauer, *Hegel's Concept of God* (Albany: SUNY, 1982), 79. Hegel set forth this thesis in his work *The Science of Logic*.

[6]Henry D. Aiken, *The Age of Ideology* (New York: Mentor, 1956), 72.

[7]Friedrich, Introduction, xvii.

[8]G. W. F. Hegel, *The Phenomenology of Mind*, trans. J. B. Baillie (New York: Harper and Row, 1967), 86.

[9]G. W. F. Hegel, *The Science of Logic (The First Part of the Encyclopedia of the Philosophical Sciences)*, trans. William Wallace (Oxford: Clarendon, 1892), #160, 288. Wallace entitled his translation *The Logic of Hegel*.

[10]In Hegel's words, the whole is "the essential nature reaching its completeness through the process of its own development." Ibid., 81. Hence, for Hegel, in the process truth and being coalesce. See ibid., 97.

[11]Hegel, *Phenomenology of Mind*, 807-8. See also his poetic statement, ibid, 91.

[12]George Lichtheim, Introduction, in Hegel, *Phenomenology of Mind*, xxvi.

[13]Lauer, *Hegel's Concept of God*, 190.

[14]Lichtheim, Introduction, xxiv.

[15]Friedrich, Introduction, xliii.

[16]This is described in J. B. Baillie, Translators Introduction, in *Phenomenology of Mind*, 37-39.

[17]Hegel, *Phenomenology of Mind*, 88.

[18]Friedrich, Introduction, xxxiv.

[19]Ibid., xxxvi.

[20]Hegel, *Phenomenology of Mind*, 683-785.

[21]Hegel develops this in *Phenomenology of Mind*, 767-85. For a helpful summary of Hegel's understanding of Christian doctrine, see James C. Livingston, *Modern Christian Thought—From the Enlightenment to Vatican II* (New York: Macmillan, 1971), 150-56.

[22]Hegel's understanding of the Trinity is delineated in his *Philosophy of Mind*, together with the Zusätze in Boumann's Text, trans. A. V. Miller (London: Oxford, 1971), #381 Zusätze, 12; #567, 299.

[23]According to Hegel, humankind knows God because in humanity God knows himself. See, e.g., G. W. F. Hegel, *Lectures on the Philosophy of Religion: Together with a Work on the Proofs of the Existence of God*, trans. Rev. E. B. Speirs and J. Burdon Sanderson (London: Routledge and Kegan Paul, 1962), 3:303.

[24]Hegel, *Phenomenology of Mind*, 781.

[25]Ibid.

[26]Baillie, Translator's Introduction, 64.

[27]Lichtheim, Introduction, xxx.

[28]This is the conclusion of many Hegel critics, including Lichtheim, Introduction, xxiii.

Friedrich Schleiermacher: The Immanence of God in Religious Feeling

[1]Brian Gerrish, *A Prince of the Church: Schleiermacher and the Beginnings of Modern Theology* (Philadelphia: Fortress, 1984), 20.

[2]Richard R. Niebuhr, *Schleiermacher on Christ and Religion* (New York: Scribner, n.d.), 6.

[3]Robert R. Williams, *Schleiermacher the Theologian: The Construction of the Doctrine of God* (Philadelphia: Fortress, 1978), 1.

[4]Keith W. Clements, *Friedrich Schleiermacher, Pioneer of Modern Theology* (London and San Francisco: Collins, 1987), 7.

[5]Ibid., 24.

[6]Ibid., 33.

[7]Martin Redeker, *Schleiermacher: Life and Thought*, trans. John Wallhausser (Philadelphia: Fortress, 1973), 213.

[8]Clements, *Friedrich Schleiermacher*, 11.

[9]Ibid., 15.

[10]Terrence N. Tice, Introduction, in Friedrich Schleiermacher, *On Religion: Addresses in Response to its Cultured Critics*, trans. Terrence N. Tice (Richmond: John Knox, 1969), 12.

[11]Friedrich Schleiermacher, *On Religion: Addresses in Response to its Cultured Critics*, trans. Terrence N. Tice (Richmond: John Knox, 1969), 79.

[12]Ibid.

[13]Schleiermacher's discussion of the "Essence of Religion" is found in *On Religion*, 67-176.

[14]Ibid., 77.

[15]Ibid., 80.

[16]Ibid., 81-82.

[17]"Christian doctrines are accounts of the Christian religious affections set forth in speech." Friedrich Schleiermacher, *The Christian Faith*, 2d ed., ed. H. R. Mackintosh and J. S. Stewart (Philadelphia: Fortress, 1928), 76.

[18]Schleiermacher, *On Religion*, 140.

[19]Ibid., 300.

20Schleiermacher, *Christian Faith*, 76. For the exact quote see n. 17 above.

21Ibid., 98.

22Ibid., 125.

23Ibid., 390.

24Claude Welch, *Protestant Theology in the Nineteenth Century, Volume 1, 1799-1870* (New Haven and London: Yale University Press, 1974), 72.

25Schleiermacher, *Christian Faith*, 265.

26Ibid., 594.

27Ibid., 609.

28Ibid., 608.

29Ibid., 194.

30Ibid., 200.

31Ibid., 335. Schleiermacher rejects belief in the reality of Satan or demons. Both are simply personifications of evil thoughts that resist the good. See ibid., 156-70.

32Ibid., 178-79.

33Ibid., 180.

34Ibid., 183.

35Ibid., 739.

36Ibid., 393.

37Ibid., 379. For a good discussion of this see Niebuhr, *Schleiermacher on Christ and Religion*, 219-28.

38Schleiermacher, *Christian Faith*, 367.

39Ibid., 385.

40Ibid., 425.

41Ibid., 424.

42Quoted in Karl Barth, *The Theology of Schleiermacher* (Grand Rapids, Mich.: Eerdmans, 1982), 186.

43Barth's criticisms of Schleiermacher are scattered throughout his writings. However, a volume of lectures Barth delivered on Schleiermacher contains some of his most trenchant criticisms: see ibid.

44Schleiermacher, *Christian Faith*, 156. Schleiermacher states that God transcends the contradiction between freedom and necessity. Thus it cannot be said that God might *not* have created the world.

45Ibid., 412.

Albrecht Ritschl and Classical Liberal Theology: The Immanence of God in Ethical Culture

1Claude Welch, *Protestant Thought in the Nineteenth Century, Volume 1, 1799-1870* (New Haven and London: Yale University Press, 1972), 142.

2Bernard M. G. Reardon, *Liberal Protestantism* (Stanford: Stanford University Press, 1968), 10.

3Albrecht Ritschl, *The Christian Doctrine of Justification and Reconciliation*, trans. H. R. Mackintosh and A. B. Macaulay (Edinburgh: T. & T. Clark, 1900), v.

4Ritschl's explanation of these two realms of knowledge may be found in ibid., 203-13. There Ritschl admits that even science inevitably includes some value judgments because it is impossible for the scientist or philosopher to be purely objective. However, he makes a distinction between "concomitant" and "independent" value judgments. Religion, he avers, moves only in the realm of the latter, which are perceptions of moral ends or moral hindrances.

5Ibid., 398.

[6]Albrecht Ritschl, "Theology and Metaphysics: Towards Rapproachement and Defense," in *Three Essays*, trans. Philip Hefner (Philadelphia: Fortress, 1972), 164.

[7]David L. Mueller, *An Introduction to the Theology of Albrecht Ritschl* (Philadelphia: Westminster, 1969), 45-47.

[8]Ibid., 33.

[9]For a good discussion of Lotze's influence upon Ritschl see Philip Hefner, "Albrecht Ritschl: An Introduction" in *Three Essays*, 27-28.

[10]Ritschl, *Christian Doctrine*, 282.

[11]Ibid., 236, 281.

[12]Ritschl's formal definition of the kingdom of God is rather lengthy and complicated: "the uninterrupted reciprocation of action springing from the motive of love—a kingdom in which all are knit together in union with every one who can show the marks of a neighbour; further it is that union of men in which all goods are appropriated in their proper subordination to the highest good." Ibid., 334-35.

[13]Ibid., 282. Here Ritschl refers to the kingdom of God as God's own glory and personal end.

[14]Ibid., 329.

[15]Ibid., 350.

[16]Ibid., 398.

[17]Ibid., 413.

[18]This is an interpretation of Ritschl's account of Jesus' divinity as it is presented at great length and complexity in "The Doctrine of Christ's Person and Life-Work," chap. VI of *Christian Doctrine*, 385-484.

[19]Ibid., 469.

[20]Ibid., 477-78.

[21]James Richmond, *Ritschl: A Reappraisal. A Study in Systematic Theology* (London: Collins, 1978), 203.

[22]Renewed interest in Ritschl appears in books such as those by Mueller and Richmond cited above. Another person responsible for it is Lutheran theologian Philip Hefner, translator and editor of some of Ritschl's works and author of an important sympathetic study of Ritschl entitled *Faith and the Vitalities of History* (New York: Harper and Row, 1966).

[23]Richmond, *Ritschl: A Reappraisal*, 105.

[24]Ibid., 114.

[25]Ibid., 120.

[26]Ibid., 172.

[27]Mueller, *Introduction to Albrecht Ritschl*, 170.

[28]Hugh Ross Mackintosh, *Types of Modern Theology, Schleiermacher to Barth* (New York: Charles Scribner's Sons, 1937), 165.

[29]Ritschl, *Christian Doctrine*, 465.

[30]Richmond, *Ritschl: A Reappraisal*, 205.

[31]Martin Rumscheidt, "Introduction: Harnack's Liberalism in Theology: A Struggle for the Freedom of Theology," in *Adolf von Harnack, Liberal Theology at Its Height*, ed. Martin Rumscheidt (London: Collins, 1989), 24.

[32]Adolf Harnack, *What Is Christianity?*, trans. Thomas Bailey Saunders (New York: G. P. Putnam's Sons, 1901), 13.

[33]Ibid., 154.

[34]Ibid., 55.

[35]Ibid., 216-20.

[36]Ibid., 122.

[37]Claude Welch, *Protestant Theology in the Nineteenth Century, Volume 2, 1870-1914* (New Haven and London: Yale University Press, 1985), 261.

[38]Walter Rauschenbusch, *Christianity and the Social Crisis* (New York: Macmillan, 1907), xi.

[39]Walter Rauschenbusch, *A Theology for the Social Gospel* (Nashville: Abingdon, 1978), 142.

[40]Ibid., 174-75.

[41]Ibid., 99.

[42]H. Richard Niebuhr, *The Kingdom of God in America* (New York: Harper and Row, 1959), 193.

3 The Revolt against Immanence: Transcendence in Neo-orthodoxy
Karl Barth: Transcendence as God's Freedom

[1]Colin Brown, *Philosophy and the Christian Faith* (London: Tyndale, 1968), 128.

[2]William E. Hordern, *A Layman's Guide to Protestant Theology,* rev. ed. (New York: Macmillan, 1968), 114.

[3]Søren Kierkegaard, *Concluding Unscientific Postscript,* trans. David F. Swenson and Walter Lowrie (Princeton, N.J.: Princeton University Press, 1968), 182.

[4]Søren Kierkegaard, *Philosophical Fragments,* trans. David F. Swenson (Princeton, N.J.: Princeton University Press, 1962).

[5]Eberhard Jüngel, *Karl Barth, A Theological Legacy,* trans. Garrett E. Paul (Philadelphia: Westminster, 1986), 22.

[6]Eberhard Busch, *Karl Barth, His Life from Letters and Autobiographical Texts,* trans. John Bowden (Philadelphia: Fortress, 1976), 12.

[7]Ibid., 31.

[8]Karl Barth, *The Word of God and the Word of Man,* trans. Douglas Horton (Boston: The Pilgrim Press, 1928), 43.

[9]Karl Barth, *God, Gospel and Grace,* trans. James S. McNab, *Scottish Journal of Theology Occasional Papers No. 8* (Edinburgh: Oliver and Boyd, 1959), 57.

[10]Karl Barth, *The Epistle to the Romans,* trans. Edwyn C. Hoskyns (London: Oxford University Press, 1933), 1.

[11]Ibid., 28.

[12]Ibid., 10.

[13]Karl Barth, *Anselm: Fides Quarens Intellectum,* trans. Ian W. Robertson (London: SCM, 1960), 34.

[14]Ibid., 40.

[15]Karl Barth, *Church Dogmatics* II/1, *The Doctrine of God,* Part 1, trans. T. H. L. Parker et al. (Edinburgh: T. & T. Clark, 1957), 139-40.

[16]Ibid., 173.

[17]Karl Barth, *Church Dogmatics* I/1, *The Doctrine of the Word of God,* Part 1, trans. G. W. Bromiley (Edinburgh: T. & T. Clark, 1975), 222.

[18]Karl Barth, *Church Dogmatics* II/2, *The Doctrine of God,* Part 2, trans. G. W. Bromiley et al. (Edinburgh: T. & T. Clark, 1957), 191-92.

[19]Barth, *Church Dogmatics* I/1, 241.

[20]Ibid., 109.

[21]Ibid., 113.

[22]Karl Barth, *Church Dogmatics* I/2, *The Doctrine of the Word of God,* Part 2, trans. G. T. Thomson and Harold Knight (Edinburgh: T. & T. Clark, 1956), 534-35.

[23]Ibid., 540.

[24]Barth, *Church Dogmatics* I/1, 287.

[25]Ibid., 311.

[26]Barth, *Church Dogmatics* II/1, 5.

[27]Barth, *Church Dogmatics* I/1, 309.

[28]Ibid., 301.

[29]Barth, *Church Dogmatics* I/2, 151.

[30]Ibid.

[31]Barth, *Church Dogmatics* I/1, 350-51.

[32]Barth, *Church Dogmatics* II/1, 318.

[33]Barth, *Church Dogmatics* II/1, 273.

[34]Ibid., 274.

[35]Barth, *Church Dogmatics* IV/1, *The Doctrine of Reconciliation*, Part 1, trans G. W. Bromiley (Edinburgh: T. & T. Clark, 1956).

[36]Barth, *Church Dogmatics* II/1, 351-439.

[37]Ibid., 280.

[38]Ibid., 281.

[39]Ibid., 275. Of course for Barth this "before" of God's inner-trinitarian love is not temporal but logical.

[40]Ibid., 302.

[41]Ibid., 311.

[42]Ibid., 440-677.

[43]Ibid., 274.

[44]Barth, *Church Dogmatics* IV/1, 50.

[45]Ibid., 7.

[46]Barth, *Church Dogmatics* II/2, 123.

[47]Ibid., 163.

[48]Ibid., 167.

[49]Ibid., 319-20.

[50]Ibid., 319.

[51]Quoted by Eberhard Jüngel, *Karl Barth, A Theological Legacy*, 44-45. For Barth's direct statements on *apokatastasis* and universalism see *Church Dogmatics* II/2, 417-18, and Karl Barth, *The Humanity of God*, trans. Thomas Wieser and John Thomas (Richmond: John Knox, 1960), 61-62.

[52]Hans Urs von Balthasar, *The Theology of Karl Barth*, trans. John Drury (New York, Chicago, San Francisco: Holt, Rinehart and Winston, 1971), 163.

[53]L. Harold DeWolf, *The Religious Revolt Against Reason* (New York: Harper and Row, 1949). Although he should not be characterized as a liberal, Wolfhart Pannenberg has presented some of the most cogent arguments against Barth's theological method from this basic perspective. In his view, it contributes to subjectivism in contemporary Christianity and therefore diminishes Christianity's influence in the world. See Wolfhart Pannenberg, *Theology and the Philosophy of Science*, trans. Francis McDonagh (Philadelphia: Westminster, 1976), 265-76.

[54]Clark Pinnock, "Karl Barth and Christian Apologetics," *Themelios* (May 1977): 66-71.

[55]Bernard Ramm, *After Fundamentalism, The Future of Evangelical Theology* (San Francisco: Harper and Row, 1983).

[56]Wentzel van Huyssteen, *Theology and the Justification of Faith: Constructing Theories in Systematic*

Theology, trans. H. F. Snijders (Grand Rapids, Mich.: Eerdmans, 1989), 22.

[57]von Balthasar, *Theology of Karl Barth*, 170.

[58]Klaas Runia, *Karl Barth's Doctrine of Holy Scripture* (Grand Rapids, Mich.: Eerdmans, 1962), 174-88.

[59]Wolfhart Pannenberg, "Die Subjektivität Gottes und die Trinitätslehre," *Grundfragen systematischer Theologie, Band 2* (Göttingen: Vandenhoek & Ruprecht, 1977).

[60]Barth, *Church Dogmatics* I/1, 348-68, esp. 350.

[61]Ibid., 382.

[62]Barth, *Church Dogmatics* IV/1, 200-201.

[63]G. C. Berkouwer, *The Triumph of Grace in the Theology of Karl Barth*, trans. Harry R. Boer (Grand Rapids, Mich.: Eerdmans, 1956), 279.

Emil Brunner: Transcendence in Divine-Human Encounter

[1]Paul King Jewett, *Emil Brunner's Concept of Revelation* (London: James Clarke, 1954), 12.

[2]Emil Brunner, *The Christian Doctrine of God*, vol. I of *Dogmatics*, trans. Olive Wyon (London: Lutterworth, 1949), 155.

[3]Emil Brunner, *Natural Theology, Comprising 'Nature and Grace' and the Reply 'No!' by Dr. Karl Barth*, trans. Peter Fraenkel (London: Geoffrey Bles, The Centenary Press, 1946).

[4]One of Brunner's final words on this came toward the end of his *Dogmatics:* "We do not believe it is right to say that Christ has closed the gates of Hell for ever." In *The Christian Doctrine of the Church, Faith, and the Consummation*, vol. III of *Dogmatics*, trans. David Cairns and T. H. L. Parker (London: Lutterworth, 1962), 421.

[5]Emil Brunner, *Truth as Encounter*, trans. Amandus Loos, David Cairns and T. H. L. Parker (London: SCM, 1964), 60.

[6]Martin Buber, *I and Thou*, trans. Ronald Gregor Smith (New York: Charles Scribner's Sons, 1958).

[7]This work, cited in n. 5 above, was first published in German in 1938. It was first published in English in 1943 as *The Divine-Human Encounter* and then revised and reprinted in 1963 as *Truth as Encounter.*

[8]Brunner, *Truth as Encounter*, 24.

[9]Emil Brunner, *The Christian Doctrine of Creation and Redemption*, vol. II of *Dogmatics*, trans. Olive Wyon (London: Lutterworth, 1952), 8-9.

[10]Brunner, *Dogmatics* I:16.

[11]Ibid., 20.

[12]Ibid., 29.

[13]Ibid., 30.

[14]Jewett, *Brunner's Concept of Revelation*, 72.

[15]For a fine philosophical and theological critique of the idea of nonpropositional revelation see Paul Helm, *The Divine Revelation* (Westchester, Ill.: Crossway, 1982), 21ff. For a very positive survey and evaluation of the idea see John Baillie, *The Idea of Revelation in Recent Thought* (New York: Columbia University Press, 1956).

[16]Brunner, *Dogmatics* I:25.

[17]Ibid., 27.

[18]Ibid., 41.

[19]Ibid., 35-43.

[20]Ibid., 45.

[21]Ibid., 34.

[22]Ibid., 28.

[23]Ibid., 44.

[24]Ibid., 47.

[25]Jewett, *Brunner's Concept of Revelation,* 157-73.

[26]Ibid., 158.

[27]Ibid.

[28]Ibid., 162.

[29]Brunner, *Dogmatics* I:33.

[30]Jewett, *Brunner's Concept of Revelation,* 164.

[31]Ibid., 168.

[32]Virtually the same point is made by Harold E. Hatt in his very sympathetic study of Brunner's theology, *Encountering Truth: A New Understanding of How Revelation Yields Doctrine* (Nashville: Abingdon, 1966), 194: "Faith which is exercised in complete disregard of knowledge, if there be such faith, is merely blind and meaningless faith, not trust. Interpretation is not inimical but essential to encounter with God. Encounter is not free of but dependent on I-It elements."

[33]Brunner, *Natural Theology,* 32-33.

[34]Ibid., 58

[35]Ibid., 59.

[36]Ibid., 72.

[37]Ibid., 71-72.

[38]Ibid., 90.

[39]Ibid., 79.

[40]Ibid., 121.

[41]Ibid., 128.

[42]Brunner, *Dogmatics* I:236.

[43]Ibid., 349.

[44]Ibid., 312.

[45]Ibid., 353.

[46]Ibid., 320.

[47]That he may recently be receiving some of the attention due him is indicated by an excellent article celebrating the centennial of his birth: I. John Hesselink, "Emil Brunner: A Centennial Perspective," *The Christian Century* (December 13, 1989): 1171-74.

Rudolf Bultmann: Transcendence of the *Kerygma*

[1]Norman J. Young, *History and Existential Theology* (Philadelphia: Westminster, 1969), 39.

[2]See "Liberal Theology and the Latest Theological Movement," in Rudolf Bultmann, *Faith and Understanding,* ed. Robert W. Funk, trans. Louise Pettibone Smith (New York: Harper and Row, 1969), 1:29.

[3]See his "Autobiographical Reflections," in Rudolf Bultmann, *Existence and Faith,* trans. Schubert M. Ogden (Cleveland: Meridian, 1960), 283-88.

[4]For Bultmann's own account of his heritage, see ibid., 283-84.

[5]Ibid., 286.

[6]For examples of his statements, see Walter Schmithals, *An Introduction to the Theology of Rudolf Bultmann* (Minneapolis: Augsburg, 1968), 295-99.

[7]Ibid., 197.

[8]Martin Kähler, *The So-Called Historical Jesus and the Historic Biblical Christ,* trans. and ed. Carl E.

Braaten (Philadelphia: Fortress, 1964), 66.

[9]Rudolf Bultmann, *Jesus Christ and Mythology* (New York: Charles Scribner's Sons, 1958), 84; see also Rudolf Bultmann, *Kerygma and Myth,* ed. Hans Werner Bartsch (New York: Harper and Row, 1961), 211.

[10]Bultmann explicitly refuted this charge in his "Reply," in *The Theology of Rudolf Bultmann,* ed. Charles W. Kegley (New York: Harper and Row, 1966), 274.

[11]See his discussion of the historic event of the cross in "A Reply to the Theses of J. Schniewind," in Bultmann, *Kerygma and Myth,* 110. For this interpretation of Bultmann, see also Young, *History and Existential Theology,* 119-20.

[12]Ruldolf Bultmann, *Primitive Christianity in its Contemporary Setting* (New York: Meridian, 1957), 71.

[13]Rudolf Bultmann, *Theology of the New Testament* (New York: Charles Scribner's Sons, 1951), 1:3.

[14]Bultmann, *Christ and Mythology,* 14.

[15]E.g., ibid., 32-34.

[16]Bultmann develops and defends his program of demythologizing in *Jesus Christ and Mythology* and in "New Testament and Mythology" in *Kerygma and Myth.*

[17]See, e.g., Bultmann's development of this gulf in "New Testament and Mythology," in *Kerygma and Myth,* 1-8; *Christ and Mythology,* 14-16.

[18]Bultmann, *Christ and Mythology,* 15.

[19]The appeal to the New Testament is summarized in ibid., 33-34, and developed in various sections of *Theology of the New Testament,* e.g., 1:258-59, 300-308; see also Rudolf Bultmann, *The Presence of Eternity: History and Eschatology* (New York: Harper and Brothers, 1957), 40-50.

[20]Bultmann, *Christ and Mythology,* 51; see also "Is Exegesis Without Presuppositions Possible?" in *Existence and Faith,* 289-96; *Presence of Eternity,* 113-14.

[21]Bultmann, *Christ and Mythology,* 53.

[22]Ibid., 55.

[23]See, e.g., "New Testament and Mythology," in *Kerygma and Myth,* 1-8; *Christ and Mythology,* 11-32.

[24]Bultmann, *Presence of Eternity,* 95-96.

[25]Bultmann, *Christ and Mythology,* 71.

[26]That for Bultmann theology is not simply anthropology is argued persuasively by Young, *History and Existential Theology,* 66-72. See also Bultmann, *Christ and Mythology,* 70.

[27]Introduction to *Existence and Faith,* 19.

[28]Young, *History and Existential Theology,* 48.

[29]Ibid., 47.

[30]Bultmann rejected this criticism in "New Testament and Mythology," in *Kerygma and Myth,* 25.

[31]On this matter, see John Macquarrie, *An Existentialist Theology* (London: SCM, 1955), 5-6.

[32]Ibid., 14.

[33]E.g., Bultmann, *Christ and Mythology,* 56.

[34]Rudolf Bultmann, "Humanism and Christianity," *Journal of Religion* 32 (1952): 83. See also Young, *History and Existential Theology,* 134.

[35]Bultmann, *Presence of Eternity,* 43-44, 140-41, 152.

[36]See Morris Ashcraft, *Rudolf Bultmann,* in *Makers of the Modern Theological Mind,* ed. Bob E. Patterson (Waco, Tex.: Word, 1972), 35.

[37]See, e.g., the discussion in *Presence of Eternity,* 117-22. Bultmann's understanding is explained in Young, *History and Existential Theology,* 23-24.

[38]Bultmann outlined his differences with existentialism in "New Testament and Mythology," in

Kerygma and Myth, 22-33. See also *Presence of Eternity*, 149-52.

[39]Bultmann, "New Testament and Mythology," in *Kerygma and Myth*, 38-39.

[40]Rudolf Bultmann, *Jesus and the Word* (New York: Charles Scribner's Sons, 1958), 213.

[41]Bultmann, "New Testament and Mythology," in *Kerygma and Myth*, 37.

[42]Ibid., 39, 42.

[43]Schmithals, *Introduction to Theology of Bultmann*, 145.

[44]Bultmann, "New Testament and Mythology," in *Kerygma and Myth*, 41.

[45]Intriguing as well is his application of this principle to historical studies; see, e.g., *Presence of Eternity*, 122.

[46]In addition to the literature cited elsewhere, see Robert C. Roberts, *Rudolf Bultmann's Theology* (Grand Rapids, Mich.: Eerdmans, 1976). A sympathetic treatment is offered in Andre Malet, *The Thought of Rudolf Bultmann*, trans. Richard Strachan (Garden City, N.Y.: Doubleday, 1971).

[47]Young, *History and Existential Theology*, 154.

[48]Jürgen Moltmann, *Theology Today* (Philadelphia: Trinity, 1988), 65.

[49]This problem has been repeatedly noted. See, e.g., Klaus Bockmuehl, *The Unreal God of Modern Theology* (Colorado Springs: Helmers and Howard, 1988), 74-76.

[50]E.g., Bultmann wrote, "From the statement that to speak of God is to speak of myself, it by no means follows that God is not outside the believer." *Christ and Mythology*, 70.

[51]Ibid., 43.

[52]Ibid., 78-83.

[53]Macquarrie, *Existentialist Theology*, 243.

[54]Bultmann, *Christ and Mythology*, 82.

[55]Ibid., 80.

[56]For a penetrating discussion of this dimension of the failure of Bultmann's program, see Hans Jonas, "Is Faith Still Possible? Memories of Rudolf Bultmann and Reflections on the Philosophical Aspects of His Work," *Harvard Theological Journal* 75/1 (1982): 1-23.

Reinhold Niebuhr: Transcendence Revealed through Myth

[1]See, e.g., Niebuhr's opening comments to his "Intellectual Autobiography," in *Reinhold Niebuhr: His Religious, Social, and Political Thought*, vol. 2 of *The Library of Living Theology*, ed. Charles W. Kegley and Robert W. Bretall (New York: Macmillan, 1961), 3.

[2]Reinhold Niebuhr, *Justice and Mercy*, ed. Ursula M. Niebuhr (New York: Harper and Row, 1974), 1.

[3]Niebuhr, "Intellectual Autobiography," in Kegley and Bretall, *Reinhold Niebuhr*, 3.

[4]Ibid., 4.

[5]D. R. Davies, *Reinhold Niebuhr: Prophet From America* (New York: Macmillan, 1948), 14.

[6]Paul Jersild, "Reinhold Niebuhr: Continuing the Assessment," *Dialogue* 22/4 (Fall 1983): 284.

[7]See, e.g., William Hordern, *A Layman's Guide to Protestant Theology*, rev. ed. (New York: Macmillan, 1968), 150.

[8]For a concise discussion of Niebuhr's relation to Barth, see Ronald H. Stone, *Reinhold Niebuhr: Prophet to Politicians* (Nashville: Abingdon, 1972), 122-25.

[9]Niebuhr, "Intellectual Autobiography," in Kegley and Bretall, *Reinhold Niebuhr*, 5. For another statement by Niebuhr concerning the development of his thinking, see Reinhold Niebuhr, "Ten Years that Shook the World," *The Christian Century* 56/17 (April 26, 1939): 545.

[10]Niebuhr, "Intellectual Autobiography," in Kegley and Bretall, *Reinhold Niebuhr*, 6.

[11]Niebuhr's prayer as found at the beginning of *Justice and Mercy*. The concept of change forms

the central motif for an intellectual biography of Niebuhr. See June Bingham, *Courage to Change* (New York: Charles Scribner's Sons, 1961).

[12]Stone, *Reinhold Niebuhr,* 10.

[13]Ibid., 11. See also Reinhold Niebuhr, *An Interpretation of Christian Ethics,* Living Age ed. (New York: Meridian, 1956), 27-28.

[14]Davies concludes that this is the connecting theme of Niebuhr's entire work *(Reinhold Niebuhr,* 95).

[15]Reinhold Niebuhr, *Christian Realism and Political Problems* (New York: Charles Scribner's Sons, 1953), 1.

[16]Niebuhr, "Intellectual Autobiography," in Kegley and Bretall, *Reinhold Niebuhr,* 3.

[17]Ibid., 17.

[18]Ibid., 19.

[19]Ibid., 20.

[20]For a development of the presence of this dimension in Niebuhr's thought, see Hans Hofmann, *The Theology of Reinhold Niebuhr,* trans. Louise Pettibone Smith (New York: Charles Scribner's Sons, 1956), 73.

[21]Davies, *Reinhold Niebuhr,* 80.

[22]See, e.g., his "Intellectual Autobiography," in Kegley and Bretall, *Reinhold Niebuhr,* 15.

[23]Davies, *Reinhold Niebuhr,* 72.

[24]For an example of Niebuhr's description of the phrase "impossible possibility," see *Interpretation of Christian Ethics,* 97-123.

[25]Ibid., 110.

[26]William John Wolf, "Reinhold Niebuhr's Doctrine of Man," in Kegley and Bretall, *Reinhold Niebuhr,* 230.

[27]In contrast to Wolf, Paul Lehmann writes, "By Reinhold Niebuhr's own admission, however, Christology has been and is the principle passion and purpose of his theological work." Paul Lehmann, "The Christology of Reinhold Niebuhr," in Kegley and Bretall, *Reinhold Niebuhr,* 253.

[28]Niebuhr, *Christian Realism and Political Problems,* 3.

[29]Niebuhr, *Interpretation of Christian Ethics,* 23.

[30]Reinhold Niebuhr, *The Nature and Destiny of Man,* Scribner Library ed. (New York: Charles Scribner's Sons, 1964), 1:12-18.

[31]See his "Intellectual Autobiography," in Kegley and Bretall, *Reinhold Niebuhr,* 11, 18.

[32]This is set forth by Hofmann, *Theology of Niebuhr,* 104. Hofmann argues that Niebuhr claimed that each person has a twofold obligation—toward God and toward others. This in turn led to his emphasis on faith and society (145), so that the mistrust of God and social injustice are intertwined and reciprocal (195).

[33]Ibid., 16-17.

[34]See his essay "The Truth in Myths," in Reinhold Niebuhr, *Faith and Politics,* ed. Ronald H. Stone (New York: George Braziller, 1968), 24-25.

[35]Hofmann makes a similar point, *Theology of Niebuhr,* 107-9.

[36]Niebuhr, *Nature and Destiny of Man* 1:147.

[37]Ibid., 242-64.

[38]Stone, *Reinhold Niebuhr,* 133. See also Niebuhr, *Nature and Destiny of Man* 2:viii.

[39]Reinhold Niebuhr, *Man's Nature and His Communities* (New York: Charles Scribner's Sons, 1965), 106.

[40]Niebuhr, *Nature and Destiny of Man* 1:182-83, 251-52.

[41]See ibid., 228-40.

[42]Ibid., 186-203.

[43]Ibid., 208.

[44]Edward J. Carnell, *The Theology of Reinhold Niebuhr* (Grand Rapids, Mich.: Eerdmans, 1951), 37.

[45]Niebuhr, *Nature and Destiny of Man* 1:126.

[46]Ibid., 127.

[47]See, e.g., his essay, "Coherence, Incoherence, and Christian Faith," in Niebuhr, *Christian Realism and Political Problems*, 175-203.

[48]E.g., Niebuhr, *Nature and Destiny of Man* 1:267.

[49]Gordon Harland argues this point in *The Thought of Reinhold Niebuhr* (New York: Oxford, 1960), 118, where he appeals to Niebuhr, *Nature and Destiny of Man* 2:67.

[50]Niebuhr, *Nature and Destiny of Man* 2:66; see also Reinhold Niebuhr, *The Self and the Dramas of History* (New York: Charles Scribner's Sons, 1955), 71.

[51]For a discussion of Niebuhr's differing understanding of myth, see Hofmann, *Theology of Niebuhr*, 74-83.

[52]Niebuhr, *Self and Dramas of History*, 97.

[53]Reinhold Niebuhr, *Moral Man and Immoral Society* (New York: Charles Scribner's Sons, 1932), xi. This thesis was stated in embryonic form already in 1927 in Reinhold Niebuhr, *Does Civilization Need Religion?* (New York: Macmillan, 1928), 129-34.

[54]Niebuhr, *Moral Man and Immoral Society*, xi.

[55]Ibid., 25.

[56]Ibid., 257.

[57]Niebuhr, *Interpretation of Christian Ethics*, 9.

[58]Niebuhr, "Intellectual Autobiography," in Kegley and Bretall, *Reinhold Niebuhr*, 9.

[59]Niebuhr, *Interpretation of Christian Ethics*, 155.

[60]Ibid., 110.

[61]Niebuhr's argument is concisely summarized in Harland, *Thought of Niebuhr*, 44-46.

[62]Niebuhr, *Nature and Destiny of Man* 2:vii.

[63]See, e.g., Reinhold Niebuhr, *Beyond Tragedy* (New York: Charles Scribner's Sons, 1937), 4.

[64]Ibid., ix.

[65]See his essay, "The Truth in Myths," in *Faith and Politics*, 17-18.

[66]"The Christian Church in a Secular Age," in Reinhold Niebuhr, *Christianity and Power Politics* (New York: Charles Scribner's Sons, 1940), 221.

[67]Niebuhr, *Self and Dramas of History*, 242.

[68]See Reinhold Niebuhr, *Faith and History* (New York: Charles Scribner's Sons, 1949), 152.

[69]Stone argues this point; see *Reinhold Niebuhr*, 225.

[70]See Niebuhr, *Faith and History*, 112-13.

[71]Niebuhr, *Self and Dramas of History*, 242.

[72]Niebuhr, *Faith and History*, 137.

[73]Ibid., 151.

[74]See Harland, *Thought of Niebuhr*, 20.

[75]Niebuhr, *Nature and Destiny of Man* 2:68.

[76]Niebuhr, *Christianity and Power Politics*, 210.

[77]Niebuhr, *Faith and History*, 125. Niebuhr explicates the Christian understanding in its contrast to that of ancient Greece in "Christianity and Tragedy," in *Beyond Tragedy*, 155-69.

[78]Niebuhr, "Truth in Myths," in *Faith and Politics*, 31.

[79]Lehmann develops this point in "Christology in Niebuhr," in Kegley and Bretall, *Reinhold Niebuhr*, 270-74.

[80]Niebuhr, *Nature and Destiny of Man* 2:68.

[81]Ibid., 212.

[82]Niebuhr, *Beyond Tragedy*, 229.

[83]Ibid., 237.

[84]Niebuhr, *Faith and History*, 113.

[85]Ibid., 215; *Christianity and Power Politics*, 200.

[86]This understanding lay behind Niebuhr's political realism. See, e.g., "Why the Christian Church is not Pacifist," in *Christianity and Power Politics*, 21.

[87]Niebuhr, *Nature and Destiny of Man* 2:288.

[88]For a discussion of these symbols, see ibid., 287-98.

[89]For Niebuhr's presentation of an understanding of the resurrection in terms of the human self, see *Self and Dramas of History*, 237-42.

[90]Niebuhr, *Nature and Destiny of Man* 2:320.

[91]Ibid., 321.

[92]For a related criticism, see Robert E. Fitch, "Reinhold Niebuhr's Philosophy of History," in Kegley and Bretall, *Reinhold Niebuhr*, 297.

[93]See the criticism offered by Daniel D. Williams, "Niebuhr and Liberalism," in Kegley and Bretall, *Reinhold Niebuhr*, 209.

[94]Lehman, "Christology in Niebuhr," in Kegley and Bretall, *Reinhold Niebuhr*, 279.

[95]Hofmann, *Theology of Niebuhr*, 246.

[96]Lehmann, "Christology in Niebuhr, in Kegley and Bretall, *Reinhold Niebuhr*, 277. For a book-length development of this thesis, see Rachel Hadley King, *The Omission of the Holy Spirit from Reinhold Niebuhr's Theology* (New York: Philosophical Library, 1964).

[97]Jersild, *Reinhold Niebuhr*, 285.

[98]See ibid., 286.

[99]Reinhold Niebuhr, *The Children of Light and the Children of Darkness* (New York: Charles Scribner's Sons, 1944, 1960), xiii.

[100]Fitch raises a related question. If Christian doctrine is a reminder of the ultimate character of sin and evil, is it not also a revelation of an ultimate good? See "Reinhold Niebuhr's Philosophy of History," in Kegley and Bretall, *Reinhold Niebuhr*, 295.

[101]Benton Johnson applied this point to the national situation in "Taking Stock: Reflections on the End of Another Era," *Journal of the Scientific Study of Religion* 21/3 (September 1982): 189-200.

4 The Deepening of Immanence: Reformulations of the Liberal Tradition
Paul Tillich: The Immanence of the "God Above God"

[1]Robert W. Schrader, *The Nature of Theological Argument: A Study of Paul Tillich* (Missoula, Mont.: Scholar's Press, 1975), 73-74.

[2]D. MacKenzie Brown, ed., *Ultimate Concern: Tillich in Dialogue* (New York and Evanston: Harper and Row, 1956), 88-89.

[3]Thor Hall, *Systematic Theology Today: State of the Art in North America* (Washington, D.C.: University Press of America, 1978), 94.

[4]Most of the biographical material here is taken from the very authoritative biography of Tillich by Wilhelm and Marion Pauck: *Paul Tillich, His Life and Thought*, vol. I, *Life* (New York: Harper

and Row, 1976). Wilhelm Pauck was one of Tillich's students and became one of his most intimate friends. There are several biographies of Tillich including one by his wife, Hannah, entitled *From Time to Time* (New York: Stein and Day, 1973), which has created a great deal of morbid fascination and controversy. Since this chapter is intended to be an introduction to Tillich's theology, the details of his private life, however fascinating, must be left aside—especially since so much of it is conjecture.

[5]Pauck and Pauck, *Paul Tillich*, 198.

[6]Ibid., 219.

[7]Ibid., 250.

[8]Ibid., 275.

[9]Ibid., 274.

[10]Ibid., 251.

[11]For a balanced, if somewhat overgenerous, account of Tillich's marriage and infidelities see Pauck and Pauck, *Paul Tillich*, 85-93.

[12]Paul Tillich, *Systematic Theology*, vol. I, *Reason and Revelation, Being and God*, three volumes in one (New York: Harper and Row; Evanston: University of Chicago Press, 1967), 3-4. Hereafter references to Tillich's systematic theology will read *Theology* plus volume and number. The pagination for the volumes in the "three-in-one" edition is the same as for the separate volumes, which were published by the University of Chicago Press.

[13]Ibid., 7.

[14]Paul Tillich, *Biblical Religion and the Search for Ultimate Reality* (Chicago: University of Chicago Press, 1955), 7-8. This little book, comprising only eighty-five pages, constitutes a major exposition and defense of theology's use of philosophy. It should be read carefully once before and once after reading his systematic theology.

[15]Ibid., 85.

[16]Tillich, *Theology* I:18.

[17]Ibid., 20.

[18]Tillich, *Biblical Religion*, 6.

[19]Tillich, *Theology* I:20.

[20]Ibid.

[21]Ibid., II:67.

[22]Ibid., I:62.

[23]Ibid., II:27.

[24]Ibid., I:21.

[25]Ibid., 22.

[26]Ibid., 25. See also Tillich, *Biblical Religion*, 64-66.

[27]Tillich, *Theology* I:176, 260; II:23, 120.

[28]Ibid., I:176.

[29]For a good critique by a sympathetic philosopher, see John Herman Randall, Jr., "The Ontology of Paul Tillich" in *The Theology of Paul Tillich*, ed. Charles W. Kegley and Robert W. Bretall (New York: Macmillan, 1964), 132-61.

[30]Reinhold Niebuhr gently criticizes Tillich for subverting biblical drama to ontological speculation in "Biblical Thought and Ontological Speculation in Tillich's Theology," in Kegley and Bretall, *Theology of Tillich*, 216-27. Kenneth Hamilton accuses Tillich of allowing a philosophical system of ontological speculation ("*logos* philosophy") to predetermine and control the content of the Christian message. See Kenneth Hamilton, *The System and the Gospel, A Critique of Paul*

Tillich (New York: Macmillan, 1963), esp. 227-39.

[31]The analysis and criticism of this conflation is the subject of Adrian Thatcher's excellent book *The Ontology of Paul Tillich* (Oxford: Oxford University Press, 1978).

[32]Tillich, *Theology* I:60.

[33]Ibid., 64-65.

[34]Ibid., 65.

[35]Ibid.

[36]Ibid.

[37]Ibid.

[38]Ibid., 65-66.

[39]Ibid., 64.

[40]Ibid.

[41]The terms "autonomy," "heteronomy" and "theonomy" are crucial to Tillich's thought. The first refers to the rule of the self or individual over itself. The second refers to the rule of another over the self. The third refers to the self and other united in God, the ground of being.

[42]George F. Thomas, "The Method and Structure of Tillich's Theology," in Kegley and Bretall, *Theology of Tillich,* 104.

[43]Ibid.

[44]Hamilton, *System and Gospel,* 124.

[45]John Jefferson Davis, "Tillich—Accurate Aims, Alien Assumptions," *Christianity Today* 20/23 (1976): 8.

[46]Tillich, *Theology* I:147.

[47]Ibid., 94.

[48]Thatcher, *Ontology of Tillich,* 99-116. Here Thatcher discusses the various philosophical traditions that deal with concepts such as essence and existence and concludes that although Tillich's use draws on several of them the Platonic interpretation is dominant (109).

[49]Tillich, *Theology* I:80.

[50]Ibid., 72.

[51]Ibid., 82.

[52]Ibid., 105.

[53]Ibid., 155.

[54]Ibid., 94.

[55]Ibid., 124.

[56]Ibid., 118.

[57]Ibid., 157.

[58]Ibid., 159.

[59]Ibid., 158-59.

[60]Ibid., 132.

[61]Ibid., 147-55.

[62]Ibid., 135-36.

[63]Ibid., 135.

[64]Gnosticism was a heretical movement within early Christianity that, among other aberrations, believed that Jesus Christ was not truly human. "Docetism," held by some of Gnostics, is the view that Jesus only *appeared* to be human and was not even a physical being at all but purely spiritual. The majority of Gnostics, however, held to a dualistic Christology. That is, they believed that the man Jesus of Nazareth was nothing more than the instrument of the heavenly redeemer

"Christ" who came down from heaven to teach gnosis or wisdom to the spiritual ones. This Christ-spirit left Jesus before he died on the cross. The claim being made here is not that Tillich's Christology is full-blown Gnosticism in this sense, but that it echoes the dualistic view of Jesus Christ that the early church condemned as heresy.

[65] In his excellent study of Tillich's Christology entitled *Paul Tillich and the Christian Message* (New York: Charles Scribner's Sons, 1962), George Tavard accuses it of being docetist (131-37). However, the actual heresy he seems to describe and attribute to Tillich is not so much docetism as dualism. Nowhere does Tillich deny that Jesus of Nazareth was human. What he seems to do is deny the importance of Jesus' humanity except as it is negated and sacrificed to a purely spiritual power called the Christ.

[66] Tillich, *Theology* I:156.

[67] Ibid., 205.

[68] One of the harshest attacks on Tillich is by Leonard F. Wheat in *Paul Tillich's Dialectical Humanism, Unmasking the God Above God* (Baltimore and London: Johns Hopkins University Press, 1970), the basic thesis of which is that "Tillich is an atheist, in the broadest sense of the word" (20).

[69] The "God above God" is a phrase Tillich used in *The Courage to Be* (New Haven and London: Yale University Press, 1952), 186-90. It is meant to designate the God who transcends the supposedly finite God of theism because he is not *a* being but being itself.

[70] Mark Kline Taylor, *Paul Tillich, Theologian of the Boundaries* (San Francisco: Collins, 1987), 23.

[71] Tillich, *Theology* I:163.

[72] Ibid., 189.

[73] Ibid., 235.

[74] Ibid., 202-5.

[75] Ibid., 237.

[76] Ibid., 238-39. Tillich's use of the term *infinite* is highly ambiguous if not contradictory. In some places he distinguishes God as being-itself from infinity and places him above the finite-infinite split (e.g., 191). In other places, however, he says that "that which is infinite is being itself" (239)! In another place he says that God is infinite but includes the finite in himself and therefore is not strictly infinite (252). This is closely akin to Hegel's concept of the "truly infinite" as opposed to "bad infinity."

[77] Ibid., 238.

[78] Ibid., 243-45.

[79] Ibid., 252.

[80] Ibid., 263.

[81] Taylor, *Paul Tillich*, 23.

[82] Thatcher, *Ontology of Tillich*, 87.

[83] Tillich, *Theology* III:422.

[84] Ibid., 421.

[85] G. W. F. Hegel, *Lectures on the Philosophy of Religion*, Vol. I, trans. E. B. Speirs and J. Burden Sanderson, ed. E. B. Speirs (New York: Humanities, 1962), 200.

[86] Tillich, *Theology* II:86.

[87] Ibid., I:245.

[88] Tillich, *Biblical Religion*, 83.

[89] Tillich, *Theology* I:286.

[90] Ibid., II:40.

[91]Ibid., 44.

[92]Ibid., 29.

[93]Ibid., 44.

[94]Ibid., 35.

[95]Ibid., 36.

[96]Ibid., 120.

[97]Ibid., 114.

[98]Ibid., 95.

[99]Ibid., 94.

[100]Ibid., 126.

[101]Ibid., 148.

[102]Ibid., 123.

[103]Ibid., 145-46.

[104]Ibid., 157.

[105]Ibid., 158-64.

[106]For Tillich's view of paradox in theology and especially the paradox of the New Being see ibid., 90-92.

[107]Ibid., 147-48.

[108]Tavard, *Tillich and the Christian Message*, 132.

Process Theology: Immanence Within the Process

[1]"Parmenides," in William L. Reese, *Dictionary of Philosophy and Religion* (Atlantic Highlands, N.J.: Humanities, 1980), 412-13.

[2]As quoted in Rex Warner, *The Greek Philosophers* (New York: Mentor, 1958), 26. Warner's source is John Burnet, *Early Greek Philosophy*, 4th ed. (New York: Macmillan, 1930), 132-41.

[3]Eduard Zeller, *Outlines of the History of Greek Philosophy*, 13th ed., rev. Wilhelm Nestle, trans. L. R. Palmer (New York: Meridian, 1957), 61. Some historians, however, have questioned this interpretation of Heraclitus. "Can Heraclitus really have thought that a rock or a bronze cauldron, for example, was invariably undergoing invisible changes of material?" ask G. S. Kirk and J. E. Raven, *The Presocratic Philosophers*, corrected reprint (Cambridge: Cambridge University Press, 1963), 197.

[4]"Heraclitus," in Reese, *Dictionary*, 219.

[5]For a discussion of the developments away from the static concept of reality from a process perspective, see Bernard E. Meland, *The Realities of Faith* (New York: Oxford University Press, 1962), 109-36.

[6]"Henri Bergson," in Reese, *Dictionary*, 55. A concise summary of Bergson's views is offered by Thomas A. Gouldge, Editor's Introduction, in Henri Bergson, *An Introduction to Metaphysics*, rev. ed., trans. T. E. Hulme (Indianapolis: Bobbs-Merrill, 1955), 9-20.

[7]"William James," in Reese, *Dictionary*, 263.

[8]See Alfred North Whitehead, *Science and the Modern World*, Mentor Books ed. (New York: Mentor, 1948), 130.

[9]These dimensions of contemporary life as the context for process theology are noted in Lonnie D. Kliever, *The Shattered Spectrum* (Atlanta: John Knox, 1981), 44-46.

[10]See, e.g., the discussion by Teilhard de Chardin's disciple, Eulalio R. Baltazar, *God Within Process* (Paramus, N.J.: Newman, 1970), 1-23.

[11]See, e.g., Alfred North Whitehead, *Science and the Modern World*, 165.

[12]John B. Cobb, Jr., and David Ray Griffin, *Process Theology* (Philadelphia: Westminster, 1976), 8-9. See also Norman Pittinger, "Process Thought as a Conceptuality for Reinterpreting Christian Faith," *Encounter* 44/2 (1983): 113.

[13]In fact, Whiteheadian process theologians generally set forth an understanding of the divine reality in which God and the world are intricately related. E.g., this theme is set forth by Schubert Ogden, "Toward A New Theism," revised from "Love Unbounded: The Doctrine of God," *The Perkins School of Theology Journal* 19/3 (Spring 1966): 5-17. Reprinted in Delwin Brown, Ralph E. James, Jr. and Gene Reeves, eds., *Process Philosophy and Christian Thought* (Indianapolis: Bobbs-Merrill, 1971), 173-87.

[14]The importance of the reconciliation of transcendence and immanence as a basis for process theology is set forth by Walter E. Stokes, "God for Today and Tomorrow," in Brown, James and Reeves, eds., *Process Philosophy*, 244-45.

[15]Helpful summaries of Teilhard's life are found in Julian Huxley, Introduction, in Pierre Teilhard de Chardin, *The Phenomenon of Man*, Harper Torchbook ed. (New York: Harper and Row, 1961), 21-26, and Doran McCarty, *Teilhard de Chardin*, in *Makers of the Modern Theological Mind*, ed. Bob E. Patterson (Waco, Tex.: Word, 1976), 16-24. For a book-length treatment of his life and thought, see Robert Speaight, *The Life of Teilhard de Chardin* (New York: Harper and Row, 1967).

[16]Teilhard de Chardin, *Phenomenon of Man*, 283-85.

[17]Ibid., 55.

[18]Ibid., 278.

[19]Concerning Teilhard's involvement in this task, Julian Huxley concluded, "Through his combination of wide scientific knowledge with deep religious feeling and a rigorous sense of values, he has forced theologians to view their ideas in the new perspective of evolution, and scientists to see the spiritual implications of their knowledge. He has both clarified and unified our vision of reality." Huxley, in *Phenomenon of Man*, 26.

[20]Teilhard de Chardin, *Phenomenon of Man*, 61.

[21]Ibid., 65.

[22]See ibid., 67-74.

[23]Ibid., 77-160.

[24]Ibid., 165.

[25]Ibid., 220.

[26]Ibid., 214. For Teilhard, this awesome realization means that the world had entered a crucial phase that allows only two alternatives: absolute optimism or absolute pessimism; see *Phenomenon of Man*, 232. For a discussion of the current "crucial phase," see "Life and the Planets," in Pierre Teilhard de Chardin, *The Future of Man*, trans. Norman Denny (New York: Harper and Row, 1964), 113-20.

[27]Teilhard de Chardin, *Phenomenon of Man*, 244. Foundational to this vision is his thesis that the emergence of humankind had brought a new law of nature into force, convergence, resulting in the phenomenon of "reflexion." Whereas previous phyla of life forms had spread out in fanwise fashion, breaking into subspecies and falling into stagnation, humankind coils inward and thus generates new, spiritual energies. (See "The Formation of the Noosphere," in *Future of Man*, 165. This definition of "reflexion" is offered by Norman Denny in his Translator's Note, 9.) Based on this principle and his understanding of the nature of consciousness, he anticipated a future "involution" to the point that he termed "Omega."

[28]Teilhard de Chardin, *Phenomenon of Man*, 257-63.

[29]Ibid., 243-53. This term is the focus of his essay, "A Great Event Foreshadowed: The Planetisation

of the Mankind," in *Future of Man,* 124-39.

[30]See *Phenomenon of Man,* 270-71.

[31]Teilhard de Chardin, "Life and the Planets," in *Future of Man,* 123-24.

[32]Teilhard de Chardin, "The Formation of the Noosphere," in *Future of Man,* 180-81. See also his "The End of the Species," in *Future of Man,* 302.

[33]Christopher F. Mooney, *Teilhard de Chardin and the Mystery of Christ* (New York: Harper and Row, 1964), 54. Mooney claims that in 1949 Teilhard's mode of conceiving of Omega underwent a sudden change of mode from the exclusively eschatological to an emphasis on the present reality.

[34]Teilhard de Chardin, *Phenomenon of Man,* 291-98. See also "The Human Rebound of Evolution," in *Future of Man,* 208, and "Turmoil or Genesis?" in *Future of Man,* 223-25.

[35]Mooney traces this path in Teilhard's thought through three stages *(Teilhard de Chardin and the Mystery of Christ,* 65-66).

[36]Rosemary T. Curran offers a succinct summarization of Whitehead's philosophy in "Whitehead's Notion of the Person and the Saving of the Past," *Scottish Journal of Theology* 36/3 (1983): 363-85. Also important has been the work of Charles Hartshorne. A short but helpful summary of Hartshorne's contribution is found in Alan Gragg, *Charles Hartshorne,* in Patterson, Makers of Modern Theological Mind.

[37]"Whitehead," in Reese, *Dictionary,* 622.

[38]See Alfred North Whitehead, *Adventures of Ideas,* Mentor Books ed. (New York: Mentor, 1955), 147-50, 158. Alfred North Whitehead, *Religion in the Making,* Meridian Books ed. (New York: World, 1960), 76, 83.

[39]Whitehead, *Adventures of Ideas,* 223. See also the discussion in Alfred North Whitehead, *Process and Reality,* Harper Torchbook ed. (New York: Harper and Row, 1960), 4-26.

[40]In accordance with the new physics, Whitehead abandoned "the notion that simple location is the primary way in which things are involved in space-time. In a certain sense, everything is everywhere at all times." *Science and the Modern World,* 87.

[41]Whitehead, *Adventures of Ideas,* 188.

[42]In *Science and the Modern World* Whitehead offered his system of "organic mechanism" as a replacement for scientific materialism (76).

[43]Whitehead, *Process and Reality,* 80.

[44]Ibid., v.

[45]Whitehead, *Adventures of Ideas,* 177-78. This view is elaborated throughout *Process and Reality,* e.g., 246.

[46]Whitehead, *Adventures of Ideas,* 83, 252-53, 268. He wrote, "apart from the experiences of subjects, there is nothing, nothing, nothing, bare nothingness" (254).

[47]Whitehead, *Process and Reality,* 28.

[48]Huston Smith, "Has Process Theology Dismantled Classical Theism?" *Theology Digest* 35/4 (1988): 310.

[49]Whitehead postulates no reality for any principles except insofar as they are exemplified by actual occasions. This is what he meant by his widely known "ontological principle," which states that "actual entities are the only reasons; so that a search for a reason is a search for one or more actual entities." *Process and Reality,* 37.

[50]See, e.g., *Religion in the Making,* 87-88.

[51]Ibid., 87.

[52]Whitehead, *Process and Reality,* 43.

[53]Ibid., 28.

[54]Gragg, *Charles Hartshorne*, 31.

[55]Whitehead, *Process and Reality*, 38. See also Victor Lowe, *Understanding Whitehead* (Baltimore: Johns Hopkins University Press, 1962), 38-41.

[56]Whitehead, *Process and Reality*, 309.

[57]Ibid., 35.

[58]Stokes makes this connection in "God for Today and Tomorrow," in Brown, James and Reeves, *Process Philosophy*, 257.

[59]Whitehead, *Process and Reality*, 34.

[60]Ibid., 130, 374.

[61]The immortality of every actual entity is required by Whitehead's "ontological principle," for "everything in the actual world is referable to some actual entity." God functions as the onto-logical principle that fulfills this necessity. See *Process and Reality*, 373.

[62]"God is not to be treated as an exception to all metaphysical principles, invoked to save their collapse. He is their chief exemplification." Ibid., 521.

[63]Whitehead delineates the dipolar nature of God in relation to the world in *Process and Reality*, 519-33. He also referred to God as displaying a threefold character: primordial, consequent and superject (134-35).

[64]In Whitehead's words, God is "the unlimited conceptual realization of the absolute wealth of potentiality. . . . Not *before* all creation, but *with* all creation." Ibid., 521.

[65]Whitehead, *Religion in the Making*, 148.

[66]Whitehead, *Process and Reality*, 287.

[67]Norman Pittinger, "Whitehead on God," *Encounter* 45/4 (1984): 329.

[68]See "Whitehead" in Reese, *Dictionary*, 624.

[69]Whitehead, *Process and Reality*, 523.

[70]Ibid., 532.

[71]Ibid., 529. Whitehead adds, "the World's nature is a primordial datum for God; and God's nature is a primordial datum for the World."

[72]Whitehead, *Process and Reality*, 30. *Adventures of Ideas*, 204.

[73]See Whitehead, *Process and Reality*, 156ff.

[74]Whether Whitehead thought of God as an unbounded society or an actual entity has been debated by subsequent process thinkers. See Gene Reeves and Delwin Brown, "The Develop-ment of Process Theology," in Brown, James and Reeves, *Process Philosophy*, 39-40.

[75]For a discussion of the relationship between God and creativity, see John B. Cobb, Jr., *A Christian Natural Theology* (Philadelphia: Westminster, 1965), 203-14.

[76]Whitehead, *Process and Reality*, 31-32. Whitehead concluded *Process and Reality* by delineating four phases of creativity in the process of the actualizing of the universe. The first is the phase of conceptual origination, which lies in the primordial God. Next comes the temporal phase of physical origination, the rise of individual occasions lacking in solidarity. This is followed by the phase of perfected actuality, as the many are unified in the immediate consciousness of God. The final is the phase of the completion of the creative activity, as the "perfected actuality" is passed back to the temporal world so that each temporal actuality may include it "as an imme-diate fact of relevant experience." This, Whitehead added, is the love of God for the world. Ibid., 532.

[77]Ibid., 143.

[78]Ibid.

[79]Pittinger, "Whitehead on God," 328.

[80]Whitehead, *Process and Reality*, 525.

[81]Lewis S. Ford, "Divine Persuasion and the Triumph of Good," *The Christian Scholar* 50/3 (Fall 1967): 235-50. Reprinted in Brown, James and Reeves, *Process Philosophy*, 298.

[82]Whitehead, *Process and Reality*, 520.

[83]For a summary of the development of process theology and the views of representative theologians, see Gene Reeves and Delwin Brown, "The Development of Process Theology," in Brown, James and Reeves, *Process Philosophy*, 21-64. For a representative recent attempt to delineate a statement of Christian doctrine from a process perspective, see Marjorie Hewitt Suchocki, *God-Christ-Church* (New York: Crossroad, 1984).

[84] See Ted Peters, "John Cobb, Theologian in Process" (1) *Dialogue* 29 (1990): 210.

[85]In *Christian Natural Theology*, Cobb writes: "By theology in the broadest sense I mean any coherent statement about matters of ultimate concern that recognizes that the perspective by which it is governed is received from a community of faith" (252).

[86]Ibid., 261-62.

[87]However, not even all process thinkers agree with Cobb that it is proper to speak of a *Christian* natural theology. See, e.g., Schubert M. Ogden, "A *Christian* Natural Theology?" from "A Review of John B. Cobb's New Book: *A Christian Natural Theology*," *Christian Advocate* 9/18 (September 23, 1965): 11-12. Reprinted in Brown, James and Reeves, *Process Philosophy*, 111-15.

[88]Cobb, *Christian Natural Theology*, 104.

[89]John B. Cobb, Jr., *God and the World* (Philadelphia: Westminster, 1965), 42-66.

[90]Cobb and Griffin, *Process Theology*, 41-62.

[91]Cobb summarizes his Christology in *Process Theology*, 95-110. For a fuller treatment, see John B. Cobb, Jr., *Christ in a Pluralistic Age* (Philadelphia: Westminster, 1975).

[92]Cobb and Griffin, *Process Theology*, 22.

[93]Ibid., 98-99.

[94]Cobb develops this theme in *Christ in a Pluralistic Age*.

[95]Cobb and Griffin, *Process Theology*, 102.

[96]Ted Peters, "John Cobb, Theologian in Process" (2), *Dialogue* 29 (Autumn 1990): 292.

[97]Ibid., 113-14.

[98]This is evidenced, e.g., in his response to Wolfhart Pannenberg's *Anthropology in Theological Perspective* delivered at the annual meeting of the American Academy of Religion, 1986.

[99]See, e.g., John B. Cobb, Jr., *Beyond Dialogue: Towards a Mutual Transformation of Christianity and Buddhism* (Philadelphia: Fortress, 1982), ix.

[100]See ibid., 113.

[101]John B. Cobb, Jr., *Process Theology as Political Theology* (Philadelphia: Westminster, 1982).

[102]John B. Cobb, Jr., and Charles Birch, *The Liberation of Life* (Cambridge: Cambridge University Press, 1981), 65.

[103]John B. Cobb, Jr., and Herman E. Daly, *For the Common Good* (Boston: Beacon, 1989).

[104]Cobb also remains true to Whitehead here. See *Process Theology*, 117-18.

[105]Ford, "Divine Persuasion," reprinted in Brown, James and Reeves, *Process Philosophy*, 287-304.

[106]Pittinger, "Process Thought as a Conceptuality," 117.

[107]That this is the case in Whitehead is uncontestable. For a similar judgment concerning Teilhard, see McCarty, *Teilhard de Chardin*, 55.

[108]For a development of this idea, see Charles Hartshorne, *Man's Vision of God and the Logic of Theism* (Hamden, Conn.: Archon, 1964), 12-21.

[109]That this is the case in Teilhard is asserted by McCarty, *Teilhard de Chardin*, 63.

[110]A helpful interaction with several central difficulties of process theology from a sympathetic perspective is found in Bernard M. Loomer, "Christian Faith and Process Philosophy," *The Journal of Religion* 29/3 (July 1949), as reprinted in Brown, James and Reeves, *Process Philosophy*, 70-98.

[111]Smith, "Has Process Theology Dismantled Classical Theism?" 304-6. Bernard E. Meland cautioned Schubert Ogden against "a closed rationalism." He declared, "Something that will continually register the shock of *reality over reason* is needed to keep reasonable men from becoming victims of their own mental enclosures, and thus open to the judgment and grace of the living God." "Analogy and Myth in Postliberal Theology," *Perkins School of Theology Journal* 15/2 (Winter 1962), as reprinted in Brown, James and Reeves, *Process Philosophy*, 127.

[112]See, e.g., Royce G. Gruenler, "Reflections on the School of Process Theism," *TSF Bulletin* 7/3 (1984): 8.

[113]Smith, "Has Process Theology Dismantled Classical Theism?" 306-9.

[114]McCarty, e.g., finds this to be the greatest problem in Teilhard's proposal (*Teilhard de Chardin*, 81).

[115]Meland, e.g., asserts that in the contemporary concept of emergent evolution what Kant perceived as radical evil "takes on an even darker and more subtle turn" in "the demonry of personality itself." *Realities of Faith*, 131.

[116]For this theme in Teilhard, see McCarty, *Teilhard de Chardin*, 135. For Whitehead, note the discussion by Ford in Brown, James and Reeves, *Process Philosophy*, 294.

[117]See Peters, "John Cobb," 217.

[118]Wolfhart Pannenberg, "A Liberal Logos Christology: The Christology of John Cobb," in *John Cobb's Theology in Process*, ed. David Ray Griffin and Thomas J. J. Altizer (Philadelphia: Westminster, 1977), 142.

[119]Bruce A. Ware, "An Exposition and Critique of the Process Doctrines of Divine Mutability and Immutability," *Westminster Theological Journal* 47/2 (1985): 175-96.

[120]For this conclusion with respect to the position of Teilhard, see McCarty, *Teilhard de Chardin*, 134.

[121]Joseph A. Bracken, "The Two Process Theologies: A Reappraisal," *Theological Studies* 46/1 (1985): 127.

[122]That process theists do reject *creatio ex nihilo* is evident in their writings. See, e.g., Cobb, *Christian Natural Theology*, 205.

[123]Jürgen Moltmann, *God in Creation* (San Francisco: Harper and Row, 1985), 78.

[124]Peters, "John Cobb," 215.

[125]Smith, "Has Process Theology Dismantled Classical Theism?" 315-16.

[126]This criticism has been voiced from the feminist perspective. In the words of Jean Porter, the "feminine God" of process theology "reinforces an image of femininity that is antithetical to women's true interests," whereas the Judeo-Christian understanding "insists that God has entered into our community, has taken up our interests and made a commitment to protect the weakest among us." Jean Porter, "The Feminization of God: Second Thoughts on the Ethical Implications of Process Theology," *Saint Luke's Journal of Theology* 29/4 (1986): 256.

[127]Process theologians intend to take divine transcendence seriously, albeit by reformulating the classic notion. See, e.g., Loomer, who asserts that the basic meaning of transcendence is ethical, relating to the problem of perfection ("Christian Faith and Process Theology," 83). Ogletree, in contrast, offers a more "metaphysical" understanding, viewing transcendence in terms of

God's ability to be a creative factor in the world process. Thomas W. Ogletree, "A Christological Assessment of Dipolar Theism," *The Journal of Religion* 47/2 (April 1967), as reprinted in Brown, James and Reeves, *Process Philosophy*, 345.

[128]Smith, "Has Process Theology Dismantled Classical Theism?" 309.

[129]For a criticism of process theology at this point, see Peters, "John Cobb," 218.

[130]Ibid., 298.

[131]Daniel Day Williams, *God's Grace and Man's Hope* (New York: Harper and Brothers, 1949), 121.

5 Immanence Within the Secular: The Radical Movement
Dietrich Bonhoeffer: Transcendence in the Midst of Life

[1]The changing theological climate of the 1960s gave birth to a series of yearly anthologies, published from 1965 to 1974, devoted to tracking the new experiments in theology by means of reprinting significant current articles that were indicative of the directions being explored by leading thinkers. Martin E. Marty and Dean G. Peerman, eds., *The New Theology*, 10 vols. (New York: Macmillan, 1964-1973).

[2]Ibid., 4:10.

[3]See Martin E. Marty and Dean G. Peerman, "The Turn from Mere Anarchy," in *New Theology* 3:15.

[4]On this, see Martin E. Marty and Dean G. Peerman, "Beyond the Secular: Chastened Religion," in *New Theology* 4:9-15.

[5]Bonhoeffer's student and friend, Eberhard Bethge, has provided the most complete biographical work. For a basic overview, see Eberhart Bethge, *Costly Grace: An Introduction to Dietrich Bonhoeffer* (San Francisco: Harper and Row, 1979). His definitive biography, however, appeared as *Dietrich Bonhoeffer: Theologian, Christian, Contemporary*, trans. Eric Mosbacher, ed. Edwin Robertson (London: Collins, 1970), translated from Eberhard Bethge, *Dietrich Bonhoeffer: Theologe, Christ, Zeitgenosse* (Munich: Christian Kaiser Verlag, 1967).

[6]G. Leibholz, "Memoir," in Dietrich Bonhoeffer, *The Cost of Discipleship*, trans. R. H. Fuller (New York: Macmillan, 1948), 10.

[7]Dietrich Bonhoeffer, *No Rusty Swords: Letters, Lectures and Notes, 1928—1936*, trans. Edwin H. Robertson and John Bowden (New York: Harper and Row, 1965), 89.

[8]Eberhard Bethge, "The Challenge of Dietrich Bonhoeffer's Life and Theology," *The Chicago Theological Seminary Register* (February 1961): 4.

[9]Leibholz, "Memoir," in *Cost of Discipleship*, 11

[10]Cited in Edwin H. Robertson, Introduction, in *No Rusty Swords*, 22. See also *Gesamelte Schriften* 1:320.

[11]Wolf-Dieter Zimmerman and Ronald Gregor Smith, eds., *I Knew Dietrich Bonhoeffer*, trans. Kaethe Gregor Smith (New York: Harper and Row, 1966), 232.

[12]Leibholz, "Memoir," in *Cost of Discipleship*, 26.

[13]Heinrich Ott, *Reality and Faith: The Theological Legacy of Dietrich Bonhoeffer*, trans. Alex A. Morrison (Philadelphia: Fortress, 1972), 65.

[14]Eberhard Bethge, "Dietrich Bonhoeffer: Person and Work," in *Die muendige Welt* 1:16-23.

[15]Kenneth Hamilton, *Life in One's Stride* (Grand Rapids, Mich.: Eerdmans, 1968), 55.

[16]Ott, *Reality and Faith*, 368. Many interpreters of Bonhoeffer agree with this assessment, namely, that "Christology is the key to Bonhoeffer's thought." Edwin H. Robertson, "Bonhoeffer's Christology," in Dietrich Bonhoeffer, *Christ the Center*, trans. John Bowden (New York: Harper and Row, 1966), 12.

[17]Ott, *Reality and Faith*, 167. Bonhoeffer explicitly raised this question in his lectures on Christology. See Bonhoeffer, *Christ the Center*, 30-31.

[18]In his Christology lectures, Bonhoeffer dealt with the question, Where is Jesus Christ today? He argued that Christ is at the center of human existence, of history and of nature. *Christ the Center*, 61-67.

[19]E.g., *No Rusty Swords; The Communion of Saints: A Dogmatic Inquiry into the Sociology of the Church*, trans. R. Gregor Smith (New York: Harper and Row, 1963), 85; *Act and Being*, trans. Bernard Noble (New York: Harper and Row, 1961), 120; *Christ the Center*, 59-61. Phillips elevates this dimension to the center of Bonhoeffer's thinking, calling "Christ exists as the church" "the theme of Bonhoeffer's work." John A. Phillips, *Christ for Us in the Theology of Dietrich Bonhoeffer* (New York: Harper and Row, 1967), 48.

[20]Ott, *Reality and Faith*, 222.

[21]Phillips sees in this move a dramatic step in Bonhoeffer's thinking: "In this manner he seeks to free his Christology from his ecclesiology in order to describe a Christ moving about freely in the world; no longer a Christ identified with a church fighting against the world for her existence" *(Christ for Us, 137).*

[22]Hamilton, *Life in One's Stride*, 24.

[23]See, e.g., Bonhoeffer's characterization of Seeberg's position in *Act and Being*, 44-48.

[24]Hamilton, *Life in One's Stride*, 50.

[25]E.g., Bonhoeffer, *Communion of Saints*, 88-89.

[26]Bonhoeffer, *Cost of Discipleship*, 38.

[27]Ibid., 42.

[28]Dietrich Bonhoeffer, *Letters and Papers from Prison*, trans. Eberhard Bethge (London: Collins, Fontana Books, 1953), 91.

[29]Ibid., 107.

[30]Ibid., 114-15.

[31]Ibid., 92.

[32]Ibid., 117.

[33]Ibid., 108.

[34]Ibid., 110.

[35]Ibid., 118.

[36]For this interpretation of Bonhoeffer's understanding of religion, see Gerhard Ebeling, *Word and Faith*, trans. James W. Leitch (London: SCM, 1960), 148ff.

[37]Bonhoeffer, *Letters and Papers*, 120.

[38]Ibid., 93.

[39]Ibid., 104.

[40]Ibid., 122.

[41]Ibid.

[42]Ibid., 93.

[43]Ibid., 112.

[44]Ibid., 56.

[45]See Phillips' claim to this effect *(Christ for Us, 236).*

[46]Bonhoeffer, *Letters and Papers*, 138-39.

[47]Ibid., 166.

[48]Ibid., 125.

[49]Ibid., 131.

⁵⁰See Dietrich Bonhoeffer, *Ethics*, trans. Neville Horton Smith, Macmillan paperback edition (New York: Macmillan, 1965), 142.

⁵¹See Bonhoeffer, *Letters and Papers*, 92.

⁵²Bonhoeffer, *Ethics*, 133.

⁵³For a discussion of Bonhoeffer's understanding of the secret discipline, see Regin Prenter, "Bonhoeffer and Karl Barth's Positivism of Revelation," in *World Come of Age*, ed. Ronald Gregor Smith (Philadelphia: Fortress, 1967), 104. See also Phillips, *Christ for Us*, 225-37; Ott, *Reality and Faith*, 149; Hamilton, *Life in One's Stride*, 72-76.

⁵⁴Bonhoeffer referred to the secret discipline on two occasions in the prison letters. See *Letters and Papers*, 92, 95.

⁵⁵Bonhoeffer, *Cost of Discipleship*, 134-48.

⁵⁶Bonhoeffer, *Letters and Papers*, 160.

⁵⁷Ibid., 95.

⁵⁸Ibid., 165. Note in this rendition of the text, "thou" has been substituted for "thing" in Bonhoeffer's definition of transcendence. For the basis of this change, see Bethge, "Challenge of Bonhoeffer's Life," 32.

Secular Theology: The Submergence of God within the Modern World

¹Kenneth Hamilton points out that this movement reasserted major theses of liberalism, but it could not simply return to the older theology because of the intervening era of Karl Barth. Kenneth Hamilton, *Revolt Against Heaven* (Grand Rapids, Mich.: Eerdmans, 1965), 39.

²For a summary of Barth's positive contribution to the secular theology movement, see William Hordern, *Introduction*, vol. 1 in *New Directions in Theology Today*, ed. William Hordern (Philadelphia: Westminster, 1966), 116-22.

³John Macquarrie, *God and Secularity*, vol. 3 of *New Directions in Theology Today*, ed. William Hordern (Philadelphia: Westminster, 1967), 40.

⁴Karl Barth, *Church Dogmatics* III/2, *The Doctrine of Creation*, Part 2, trans. G. W. Bromiley et al. (Edinburgh: T. and T. Clark, 1960), 410.

⁵Karl Barth, *Church Dogmatics* III/3, *The Doctrine of Creation*, Part 3, trans. G. W. Bromiley and R. J. Ehrlich (Edinburgh: T. and T. Clark, 1960), 255-56.

⁶For a discussion of Gogarten's importance, see Ronald Gregor Smith, *Secular Christianity* (New York: Harper and Row, 1966), 151-55.

⁷Macquarrie, *God and Secularity*, 38.

⁸Martin E. Marty and Dean G. Peerman voice this opinion in "Beyond the Secular Chastened Religion," in *The New Theology*, ed. Martin E. Marty and Dean G. Peerman, 10 vols. (New York: Macmillan, 1964), 4:11.

⁹William Hamilton and Thomas Altizer are generally considered the two main proponents of the "death-of-God" movement, although other theologians expressed their own versions of it. Two others who are often included as death-of-God theologians are Gabriel Vahanian and Paul van Buren. For a detailed analysis and critique of the entire phenomenon of death-of-God theology see *The Death of God Debate*, ed. Jackson Lee Ice and John J. Carey (Philadelphia: Westminster, 1967).

¹⁰William Hamilton, "American Theology, Radicalism and the Death of God," in Thomas J. J. Altizer and William Hamilton, *Radical Theology and the Death of God* (Indianapolis: Bobbs-Merrill, 1966), 3.

¹¹Ibid., 27-28.

¹²Thomas J. J. Altizer, *The Gospel of Christian Atheism* (Philadelphia: Westminster, 1966), 102.

[13]For a brief biography and updating of Hamilton's career to 1989 see Lloyd Steffen, "The Dangerous God: A Profile of William Hamilton," *Christian Century* 106/27 (September 27, 1989): 844-47.

[14]For a poignant and revealing look into Hamilton's thought about radical Christianity see "Thursday's Child" in *Radical Theology and the Death of God*, 87-93.

[15]Quoted in Steffen, "Dangerous God," 844.

[16]William Hamilton, *On Taking God Out of the Dictionary* (New York: McGraw-Hill, 1974).

[17]Quoted in Steffen, "Dangerous God," 845.

[18]Ibid., 846.

[19]Altizer, *Gospel of Christian Atheism*.

[20]Altizer and Hamilton, *Radical Theology and the Death of God*, 31-32.

[21]Altizer, *Gospel of Christian Atheism*, 10.

[22]Ibid., 22

[23]Ibid.

[24]Ibid., 23.

[25]Ibid., 89-90.

[26]Ibid., 132-57.

[27]Ibid.

[28]Peter L. Berger, *Rumor of Angels* (Garden City, N.Y.: Doubleday, 1969).

[29]Langdon Gilkey, *Naming the Whirlwind* (Indianapolis: Bobbs-Merrill, 1969).

[30]Ibid., 148

[31]Ibid.

[32]Paul M. van Buren, *The Secular Meaning of the Gospel* (New York: Macmillan, 1963).

[33]This evaluation is shared by many observers, including Macquarrie, *God and Secularity*, 29. In 1966 Marty and Peerman cite Robinson's book as "certainly the most popular theological work of the decade." *New Theology* 3:13.

[34]Following his tenure as bishop of Woolwich, Robinson returned to the academic setting and to his scholarly discipline. He then set himself to a study of the dates of the canonical New Testament writings. See John A. T. Robinson, *Redating the New Testament* (Philadelphia: Westminster, 1976).

[35]See John A. T. Robinson, "The Debate Continues," in *The Honest to God Debate*, ed. David L. Edwards (Philadelphia: Westminster, 1963), 233.

[36]John A. T. Robinson, *Honest to God* (Philadelphia: Westminster, 1963), 7-8.

[37]Ibid., 139.

[38]For Robinson's own subsequent reflection on the importance of these three authors for his influential work, see John A. T. Robinson, *Exploration into God* (Stanford: Stanford University Press, 1967), 15-20. See also his essay "Not Radical Enough?" in John A. T. Robinson, *Christian Freedom in a Permissive Society* (Philadelphia: Westminster, 1970), 232-40. This article was originally written for the series, "How My Mind Has Changed," *Christian Century* 86 (November 12, 1969).

[39]Robinson, *Honest to God*, 123.

[40]The Anglican bishop interacted with contemporary doubts about various traditional Christian doctrines in a later work. John A. T. Robinson, *But That I Can't Believe!* (London: Fontana Books, 1967).

[41]Robinson, *Honest to God*, 44.

[42]Ibid., 130-31.

[43]Ibid., 49.

[44]Ibid., 55.

[45]Ibid., 87.

[46]John A. T. Robinson, *The New Reformation?* (Philadelphia: Westminster, 1965), 33.

[47]Ibid., 40.

[48]Ibid., 46.

[49]Ibid., 49.

[50]Ibid., 92.

[51]Robinson, *But That I Can't Believe,* 125-26.

[52]Ibid., 124.

[53]John A. T. Robinson, *The Human Face of God* (Philadelphia: Westminster, 1973), 241.

[54]Robinson, *Exploration Into God,* 111.

[55]Ibid., 81.

[56]Ibid., 145.

[57]Ibid., 159-60.

[58]Ibid., 161.

[59]"For ten years now I have promised myself that my next book would be on Christology," he wrote in the preface to the work. Robinson, *Human Face of God,* vii.

[60]Ibid., 240-41.

[61]Ibid., 244.

[62]For a sketch of the secular point of view as set forth by the secular theologians, see Macquarrie, *God and Secularity,* 43-49. See also Charles C. West, "Community—Christian and Secular," in *The Church Amid Revolution,* ed. Harvey Cox (New York: Association, 1967), 228-56.

[63]Harvey Cox, *The Secular City* (New York: Macmillan, 1965), 60, 69.

[64]Ibid., 72.

[65]Ibid., 20.

[66]Ibid., 21.

[67]William O. Fennell, "The Theology of True Secularity," *Theology Today* 21 (July 1964), reprinted in Marty and Peerman, *New Theology* 2:33.

[68]Ibid.

[69]Ibid., 37.

[70]Cox, *Secular City,* 17.

[71]Ibid., 128. See also 121.

[72]Ibid., 191.

[73]Ibid., 114.

[74]Ibid., 109.

[75]Ibid., 110, 116.

[76]Ibid., 125-48.

[77]Ibid., 146.

[78]Elsewhere Cox speaks of his indebtedness to Bonhoeffer. See Harvey Cox, *God's Revolution and Man's Responsibility* (Valley Forge, Pa.: Judson, 1965), 81-99; *The Seduction of the Spirit* (New York: Simon and Schuster, 1973), 123-31.

[79]Cox, *Secular City,* 241-69.

[80]Ibid., 255.

[81]Ibid., 262.

[82]For a similar interpretation of this enigmatic phrase, see Steven S. Schwarzschild, "A Little Bit

of a Revolution?" in Daniel Callahan, ed., *The Secular City Debate* (New York: Macmillan, 1966), 151.

[83]For a similar appraisal, see Marty and Peerman, *New Theology* 3:15.

[84]David L. Edwards, "Looking Forward," *Student World* 59 (1966): 180.

[85]For a discussion of this phenomenon, see Marty and Peerman, *New Theology* 3:16-18.

[86]Cox, e.g., was criticized as being but a revival of Walter Rauschenbusch and the social gospel. In response, he acknowledged the validity of the comparison, but declared that "we all stand today in the shadow of Karl Barth." Cox, *God's Revolution and Man's Responsibility,* 10.

[87]Charles W. West, "What It Means to Be Secular," in Callahan, ed., *Secular City Debate,* 62.

[88]Ibid., 62.

[89]James H. Smylie, "Sons of God in the City," in ibid., 11.

[90]Cox, *God's Revolution and Man's Responsibility,* 94.

[91]Daniel Callahan, "Toward a Theology of Secularity," in *Secular City Debate,* 97, 99. A similar point is raised by Claude Welch, "Reflections on the Problem of Speaking about God," 163-67; and by Harmon R. Holcomb, "How to Speak of God in a Secular Style," 174-76, both in *Secular City Debate.*

[92]See, e.g., Michael Novak's suggestion that Cox erroneously left no distinction between love for God and love for neighbor in "An Exchange of Views," in *Secular City Debate,* 112.

[93]See Harvey Cox, *The Feast of Fools* (Cambridge, Mass.: Harvard University Press, 1969).

[94]Note the autobiographical format of Cox, *Seduction of the Spirit* and Harvey Cox, *Just As I Am,* in *Journeys of Faith,* ed. Robert A. Rains (Nashville: Abingdon, 1983).

[95]See Harvey Cox, *Religion in the Secular City* (New York: Simon and Schuster, 1984).

[96]See Harvey Cox, *Many Mansions* (Boston: Beacon, 1988).

[97]Harvey Cox, Afterward, in *Secular City Debate,* 181-82, 185-86.

[98]Cox, *Feast of Fools,* vii.

[99]Ibid., 129.

[100]Ibid., 131-38.

[101]Cox, *Seduction of the Spirit,* 26.

[102]Harvey Cox, "*The Secular City* 25 Years Later," *Christian Century* 107/32 (November 7, 1990): 1029.

[103]See Cox, Afterword, in *Secular City Debate,* 197-203. See also Harvey Cox, "The Death of God and the Future of Theology," in Harvey Cox, *On Not Leaving It to the Snake* (New York: Macmillan, 1967), 3-13. Cox was commissioned by Herder & Herder to provide the introduction for a translation of a selection of Bloch's writings. See Harvey Cox, "Ernst Bloch and the 'Pull of the Future,' " in Marty and Peerman, eds., *New Theology* 5:191-203.

[104]Cox, Afterward, in *Secular City Debate,* 197.

[105]See, e.g., the sharp critique offered by Schwarzschild, "A Little Bit of a Revolution?" in *Secular City Debate,* 145-55; and Cox's reply, Afterword, 183-85.

6 The Transcendence of the Future: The Theology of Hope
Jürgen Moltmann: The Transcendence and Immanence of the Future

[1]Jürgen Moltmann, *Theology of Hope,* trans. James W. Leitsch (New York: Harper and Row, 1967). The original publication of the book was in Germany in 1965.

[2]Carl E. Braaten, "Toward a Theology of Hope," in *The New Theology,* ed. Martin E. Marty and Dean G. Peerman, 10 vols. (New York: Macmillan, 1968), 5:90-92.

[3]Ibid., 94.

[4]Jürgen Moltmann, *The Experiment Hope,* trans. M. Douglas Meeks (Philadelphia: Fortress, 1975), 50.

⁵No biography of Moltmann exists, but brief autobiographical reflections provide some information about his life. See "Why Am I a Christian?" in *Experiences of God* (Philadelphia: Fortress, 1980), 1-18, and "An Autobiographical Note" in A. J. Conyers, *God, Hope, and History: Jürgen Moltmann and the Christian Concept of History* (Macon, Ga.: Mercer University Press, 1988), 203-23.

⁶Moltmann, "Autobiographical Note" in Conyers, *God, Hope, and History,* 203.

⁷Jürgen Moltmann, *Anfänge der dialektischen Theologie,* 2 vols. (Munich: Christian Kaiser Verlag, 1962, 1963).

⁸For a definitive study of Moltmann's reception of and reaction to Barth, see M. Douglas Meeks, *Origins of the Theology of Hope* (Philadelphia: Fortress, 1974), 15-53.

⁹Moltmann, *Theology of Hope,* 16.

¹⁰Jürgen Moltmann, "Theology as Eschatology," in *The Future of Hope, Theology as Eschatology,* ed. Frederick Herzog (New York: Herder & Herder, 1970), 9.

¹¹M. Douglas Meeks claims that "Iwand's theology must be considered the most crucial generating force in the theology of hope." *Origins of the Theology of Hope,* 34.

¹²Marcel Neusch, *The Sources of Modern Atheism: One Hundred Years of Debate Over God,* trans. Matthew J. O'Connell (New York: Paulist, 1982), 189.

¹³Jürgen Moltmann, *God in Creation: A New Theology of Creation and the Spirit of God,* trans. Margaret Kohl (San Francisco: Harper and Row, 1985), 180.

¹⁴Jürgen Moltmann, "Hope Without Faith: An Eschatological Humanism without God," trans. John Cummings, in *Is God Dead? Concilium,* vol. 16, ed. Johannes Metz (New York: Paulist, 1966), 37-40.

¹⁵Ibid., 36.

¹⁶Neusch, *Sources of Modern Atheism,* 211.

¹⁷Meeks, *Origins of the Theology of Hope,* 18.

¹⁸Moltmann, "Autobiographical Note," in Conyers, *God, Hope, and History,* 222.

¹⁹Ibid., 204.

²⁰Moltmann, *Theology of Hope,* 84.

²¹Moltmann, *Experiment Hope,* 9.

²²Moltmann, *Theology of Hope,* 92.

²³Moltmann, *God in Creation,* 202.

²⁴Moltmann, "Theology as Eschatology," 11.

²⁵Moltmann, *Theology of Hope,* 35-36.

²⁶Ibid., 282.

²⁷Moltmann, *God in Creation,* 64.

²⁸Moltmann, *Experiment Hope,* 8.

²⁹Moltmann, *Theology of Hope,* 32.

³⁰Ibid., 95-229.

³¹Ibid., 99-102.

³²Ibid., 228.

³³Ibid., 102.

³⁴Ibid., 100.

³⁵Ibid., 139-40.

³⁶Ibid., 203.

³⁷Ibid.

³⁸Ibid.

[39]Moltmann, *Experiment Hope,* 8.

[40]Ibid., 7.

[41]Jürgen Moltmann, "The Fellowship of the Holy Spirit—Trinitarian Pneumatology," *Scottish Journal of Theology* 37 (1984): 278.

[42]Moltmann, *Theology of Hope,* 85.

[43]Ibid., 84.

[44]Ibid., 105.

[45]Ibid., 227.

[46]Moltmann, "Theology as Eschatology," 10.

[47]Ibid.

[48]Jürgen Moltmann, *The Crucified God,* trans. R. A. Wilson and John Bowden (New York: Harper and Row, 1974), 244.

[49]Ibid., 249.

[50]Jürgen Moltmann, "The 'Crucified God': God and the Trinity Today," in *New Questions on God,* ed. Johannes Metz (New York: Herder & Herder, 1972), 35.

[51]Jürgen Moltmann, "The Trinitarian History of God," *Theology* 78 (December 1975): 644.

[52]Moltmann, *God in Creation,* 79. For an excellent comparison and contrast of Moltmann's doctrine of God with process theology, see John J. O'Donnell, *Trinity and Temporality, The Christian Doctrine of God in the Light of Process Theology and the Theology of Hope* (Oxford: Oxford University Press, 1983), 159-200.

[53]Moltmann, *God in Creation,* 82.

[54]Ibid., 84.

[55]Ibid., 86.

[56]Ibid., 91.

[57]Ibid., 98-103.

[58]Christopher Morse, *The Logic of Promise in Moltmann's Theology* (Philadelphia: Fortress, 1979), 119.

[59]Moltmann, *Crucified God,* 207.

[60]Ibid., 240. Rahner's statement and a fuller explanation of it is to be found in Karl Rahner, *The Trinity* (New York: Seabury, 1974), 22. For those unfamiliar with these theological terms, the "immanent Trinity" is the eternal Trinity in which God exists *in himself* as Father, Son and Holy Spirit before he expresses himself outwardly in the "economic Trinity" in history through the Incarnation and sending of the Spirit.

[61]For a thorough discussion of the development of and tensions within Moltmann's doctrine of the immanent Trinity, see Roger Olson, "Trinity and Eschatology: The Historical Being of God in Jürgen Moltmann and Wolfhart Pannenberg," *Scottish Journal of Theology* 36 (1983): 213-27.

[62]Jürgen Moltmann, *The Trinity and the Kingdom,* trans. Margaret Kohl (San Francisco: Harper and Row, 1981), 17.

[63]Ibid., 64.

[64]Ibid., 175.

[65]Ibid., 183.

[66]Ibid., 160.

[67]Ibid., 161.

[68]Ibid.

[69]Ibid.

[70]Moltmann, *God in Creation,* 258.

[71]Ibid., 150.

[72]Ibid., 279.

[73]Moltmann, *Trinity and the Kingdom,* 221.

[74]Ibid., 191-92.

[75]Peter Fumiaki Momose, *Kreuzestheologie: Eine Auseinandersetzung mit Jürgen Moltmann* (Freiburg: Herder, 1978), 87. Translation is the writer's.

Wolfhart Pannenberg: Transcendence in Reason and Hope

[1]For his own account of these experiences, see Wolfhart Pannenberg, "God's Presence in History," *Christian Century* 98 (March 11, 1981): 260-63.

[2]Ibid., 261.

[3]Wolfhart Pannenberg, "Die Theologie und die neuen Fragen nach Intersubjektivität, Gesellschaft, und religiöser Gemeinschaft," *Archivio di Filosofia* 54 (1986): 422-24.

[4]Pannenberg, "God's Presence in History," 263.

[5]Wolfhart Pannenberg, *Introduction to Systematic Theology* (Grand Rapids, Mich.: Eerdmans, 1991), 18-19.

[6]Richard John Neuhaus, "Wolfhart Pannenberg: Profile of a Theologian," in Wolfhart Pannenberg, *Theology and the Kingdom of God,* ed. Richard John Neuhaus (Philadelphia: Westminster, 1969), 16.

[7]Wolfhart Pannenberg, *Revelation As History* (with Rolf Rendtorff, Trutz Rendtorff, and Ulrich Wilkens), trans. David Granskow (New York: Macmillan, 1968), German ed., 1961.

[8]This conclusion is articulated in Neuhaus, "Wolfhart Pannenberg," 38.

[9]For a critique of the World Council of Churches, see "Unity of the Church—Unity of Mankind: A Critical Appraisal of a Shift in Ecumenical Direction," *Mid-Stream* 21 (October 1982); 485-90.

[10]Wolfhart Pannenberg, *The Church,* trans. Keith Crim (Philadelphia: Westminster, 1983), 165; Wolfhart Pannenberg, *Faith and Reality,* trans. John Maxwell (Philadelphia: Westminster, 1977), 138.

[11]See the discussions in Wolfhart Pannenberg, *The Apostles' Creed in the Light of Today's Questions,* trans. Margaret Kohl (Philadelphia: Westminster, 1972), 152-55; *Jesus—God and Man,* trans. Lewis L. Wilkins and Duane A. Priebe, 2d ed. (Philadelphia: Westminster, 1977), 372-73; see also *Theology and the Kingdom,* 72-101.

[12]Pannenberg's fight against grounding theology on a "decision of faith" and on the attempt to create a separate sphere for theology alongside scientific endeavor is well known, for the topic is broached in many of his essays. See "Insight and Faith," in Wolfhart Pannenberg, *Basic Questions in Theology,* trans. George H. Kelm (Philadelphia: Fortress, 1971), 2:43; "Faith and Reason," in *Basic Questions* 2:52-53; "Eschatology and the Experience of Meaning," in Wolfhart Pannenberg, *The Idea of God and Human Freedom,* trans. R. A. Wilson (Philadelphia: Westminster, 1973), 208. This concern arises in part from his interest in speaking to the contemporary atheistic alternative to belief, a topic he discusses in several essays. See, e.g., "Types of Atheism and their Theological Significance" and "The Question of God" in *Basic Questions* 2:184-233, and "Anthropology and the Question of God" and "Speaking about God in the Face of Atheist Criticism" in *Idea of God,* 80-115.

[13]See "The Crisis of the Scripture Principle," in Wolfhart Pannenberg, *Basic Questions* 1:1-14.

[14]See, e.g., Wolfhart Pannenberg, *Anthropology in Theological Perspective,* trans. Matthew J. O'Connell (Philadelphia: Westminster, 1985), 71-73.

[15]See, e.g., Pannenberg, *Introduction to Systematic Theology,* 4-5.

[16]Ibid., 6.

[17]See Wolfhart Pannenberg, "What Is Truth?" in *Basic Questions* 2:1-27.

[18]Ibid., 2:1-27.

[19]See "On Historical and Theological Hermeneutic" and "What Is a Dogmatic Statement?" in ibid., 1:137-210.

[20]This characterization of Pannenberg's theology is delineated in Stanley J. Grenz, *Reason for Hope: The Systematic Theology of Wolfhart Pannenberg* (New York: Oxford University Press, 1990).

[21]See, e.g., Pannenberg, *Theology and the Kingdom*, 51-54.

[22]Pannenberg, "Faith and Reason," in *Basic Questions* 2:52-53.

[23]Wolfhart Pannenberg, *Systematische Theologie* (Göttingen: Vandenhoeck and Ruprecht, 1988), 70-72. See also *Basic Questions* 2:1-27.

[24]Pannenberg, *Introduction to Systematic Theology*, 8

[25]See, e.g., Pannenberg, *Theology and the Kingdom*, 55-56.

[26]Pannenberg, *Introduction to Systematic Theology*, 10.

[27]Ibid., 12.

[28]Wolfhart Pannenberg, *Theology and the Philosophy of Science*, trans. Francis McDonagh (Philadelphia: Westminster, 1976), 151-52.

[29]Pannenberg, *Systematische Theologie*, 121-32.

[30]For a development of this theme, see Wolfhart Pannenberg, *What Is Man?* trans. Duane A. Priebe (Philadelphia: Fortress, 1970), chap. 1, and *Anthropology in Theological Perspective*, chap. 2.

[31]Pannenberg, *Systematische Theologie*, 133-205. See also "Toward a Theology of the History of the Religions," in *Basic Questions* 2:65-118.

[32]See, e.g., the conclusion Pannenberg reached in *Systematische Theologie*, 280-81.

[33]See, e.g., Pannenberg, "God's Presence in History," 263.

[34]Pannenberg sets this forth in *Systematische Theologie*, 283-483.

[35]For a methodological preview of Pannenberg's doctrine of the Trinity, see Wolfhart Pannenberg, "The God of History," *Cumberland Seminarian* 19 (Winter/Spring 1981). Roger E. Olson discusses Pannenberg's doctrine of the Trinity in "Trinity and Eschatology: The Historical Being of God in Jürgen Moltmann and Wolfhart Pannenberg," *Scottish Journal of Theology* 36 (1983): 213-27; and in Roger E. Olson, "Wolfhart Pannenberg's Doctrine of the Trinity," *Scottish Journal of Theology* 43 (1990): 175-206.

[36]See Pannenberg, *Jesus—God and Man*, 181-83, 340.

[37]The concept of field is set forth in Wolfhart Pannenberg, "Theological Questions to Scientists," *Zygon* 16 (1981): 65-77; and in "The Doctrine of Creation and Modern Science," *East Asia Journal of Theology* 4 (1986): 33-46.

[38]Pannenberg, *Systematische Theologie*, 401-16.

[39]Pannenberg, *Introduction to Systematic Theology*, 43-47. The basis for his development of pneumatology is outlined in "The Spirit of Life," in Wolfhart Pannenberg, *Faith and Reality*, trans. John Maxwell (Philadelphia: Westminster, 1977), 32-37.

[40]Pannenberg, "Spirit of Life," 33.

[41]Cf. Wolfhart Pannenberg, "Spirit and Mind," in *Mind in Nature*, ed. Richard Q. Elvee, Nobel Conference 17 (New York: Harper and Row, 1982), 143.

[42]Pannenberg, *Anthropology in Theological Perspective*, 226-29, 235-36, 240, 384.

[43]See Pannenberg, "Spirit and Mind," 137.

[44]Pannenberg, *Anthropology in Theological Perspective*, 85-96.

[45]Pannenberg, *Systematische Theologie*, 433-43.

[46]E.g., Pannenberg, *Introduction to Systematic Theology*, 48.

[47]Ibid., 49.

[48]Ibid.

[49]Pannenberg, *Jesus—God and Man*.

[50]Ibid., 324-49.

[51]Pannenberg, *Introduction to Systematic Theology*, 61.

[52]Pannenberg has been accused of minimizing the Bible as divine revelation. See, e.g., Fred H. Klooster, "Aspects of Historical Method in Pannenberg's Theology," in *Septuagesimo Anno: Festschrift for G. C. Berkouwer*, J. T. Bakker et al. (Kampen, the Netherlands: Kok, 1973), 116.

[53]Even with respect to the history of Jesus, the biblical texts "allow themselves to be questioned," Pannenberg wrote in 1964. "On Historical and Theological Hermeneutic," in *Basic Questions* 1:155. He delineated the importance of Scripture and its use in essays such as "Hermeneutic and Universal History" and "What Is a Dogmatic Statement?" *Basic Questions* 1:155, 184-98.

[54]For a criticism of Pannenberg's position, see Daniel Fuller, *Easter Faith and History* (Grand Rapids, Mich.: Eerdmans, 1965), 186.

[55]Hence, Ted Peters, "Pannenberg's Eschatological Ethics," in *The Theology of Wolfhart Pannenberg: Twelve American Responses*, ed. Carl E. Braaten and Philip Clayton (Minneapolis: Augsburg, 1988), 264.

[56]See, e.g., David P. Polk, "The All-Determining God and the Peril of Determinism," in *Theology of Wolfhart Pannenberg*, 158-68.

7 The Renewal of Immanence in the Experience of Oppression: Liberation Theologies
Black Liberation Theology: Immanence in the Black Experience

[1]For a discussion of Negro spirituals from the perspective of the Black theology of the 1960s, see Joseph R. Washington, Jr., *Black Religion*, Beacon Paperback ed. (Boston: Beacon, 1966), 206-20.

[2]E.g., James H. Cone, *Speaking the Truth* (Grand Rapids, Mich.: Eerdmans, 1986), 144-45.

[3]Benjamin May, *The Negro's God as Reflected in His Literature* (New York: Russell and Russell, 1968), 245-55.

[4]The renewed interest in the theology of Negro spirituals is reflected in the writings of James H. Cone. See, e.g., *The Spirituals and the Blues* (New York: Seabury, 1972). Cone declared the central theme of the spirituals to be "slavery contradicts God, and he will therefore liberate black people" (72).

[5]For the case of Black theology, see Gayraud S. Wilmore and James H. Cone, eds., *Black Theology: A Documentary History, 1966—1979* (Maryknoll, N.Y.: Orbis, 1979), 16.

[6]"Statement by the National Committee of Black Churchmen, June 13, 1969," reprinted in Wilmore and Cone, *Black Theology*, 101.

[7]James H. Cone, *For My People* (Maryknoll, N.Y.: Orbis, 1986), 72.

[8]For an early evaluation of the relationship between James Cone and Jürgen Moltmann, see G. Clarke Chapman, Jr., "Black Theology and Theology of Hope: What Have They to Say to Each Other?" in Wilmore and Cone, *Black Theology*, 193-219.

[9]Cone, *For My People*, 68-70.

[10]Wilmore and Cone, *Black Theology*, 4-9. See also Cone, *For My People*, 24-28, 108, 110.

[11]Wilmore and Cone, *Black Theology*, 25.

[12]Ibid., 108-9.

[13]See ibid., 26.

[14]Ibid., 110.

[15]Ibid., 27-28.

[16]Ibid., 110.

[17]For a statement of this evaluation, see James H. Cone, "Epilogue: An Interpretation of the Debate among Black Theologians," in Wilmore and Cone, *Black Theology,* 609. While expressing reservations concerning Washington's book as a whole, Cone affirms it as "the first text to demonstrate the uniqueness of black religion." *For My People,* 75.

[18]Washington, *Black Religion,* 149.

[19]Ibid., 234.

[20]Ibid., 267.

[21]Ibid., 289.

[22]Ibid., 291.

[23]Even Washington himself came to repudiate his earlier position. See Joseph R. Washington, Jr., *The Politics of God: The Future of the Black Churches* (Boston: Beacon, 1967).

[24]Wilmore and Cone, *Black Theology,* 67-68.

[25]Albert B. Cleage, Jr., *The Black Messiah,* Search Book ed. (New York: Sheed and Ward, 1969), 9.

[26]Ibid., 111.

[27]Ibid., 89-91.

[28]Ibid., 174.

[29]Wilmore and Cone, *Black Theology,* 251-52.

[30]"The Black Manifesto," reprinted in Wilmore and Cone, *Black Theology,* 84.

[31]Gayraud S. Wilmore, "A Black Churchman's Response to the Black Manifesto," in Wilmore and Cone, *Black Theology,* 93.

[32]Wilmore and Cone, *Black Theology,* 70.

[33]Ibid., 76-77.

[34]Ibid., 75.

[35]For a helpful summary of this debate and the different voices party to it, see Deane William Ferm, *Contemporary American Theologies: A Critical Survey* (New York: Seabury, 1981), 44-58.

[36]Statements from Black evangelicals included Tom Skinner, *Words of Revolution* (Grand Rapids, Mich.: Zondervan, 1970); Columbus Salley and Ronald Behm, *Your God Is Too White* (Downers Grove, Ill.: InterVarsity Press, 1970). For summary discussions of the contribution of Black evangelicals, see Ronald C. Potter, "The New Black Evangelicals," and William H. Bentley, "Factors in the Origin and Focus of the National Black Evangelical Association," in Wilmore and Cone, *Black Theology,* 302-21.

[37]In August 1977, at the Theology in the Americas Conference, James Cone noted that an awareness of the importance of expanding the horizon of Black theology was already present: "the need for a global perspective, which takes seriously the struggles of oppressed peoples in other parts of the world, has already been recognized in black theology." However, he admitted that the road to such solidarity had not been without difficulties and differences of understanding due to the diverse context in which liberation theologies have developed. James H. Cone, "Black Theology and the Black Church: Where Do We Go from Here?" reprinted in Wilmore and Cone, *Black Theology,* 358. For an account of the struggles and accomplishments of this dialog, see Wilmore and Cone, 445-62.

[38]For Cone's own recounting of his background, see James H. Cone, *God of the Oppressed* (New York: Seabury, 1975), 5-7; James H. Cone, *My Soul Looks Back* (Maryknoll, N.Y.: Orbis, 1986), 17-92.

[39]James H. Cone, *Black Theology and Black Power* (New York: Seabury, 1969), 1.

[40]Ibid., 6.

[41]See Cone's discussion of violence in ibid., 138-43.

[42]Ibid., 8.

[43]Ibid., 39.

[44]Ibid., 117.

[45]Ibid., 120.

[46]Ibid., 68-69.

[47]Ibid., 151-52.

[48]James H. Cone, *A Black Theology of Liberation* (Philadelphia: Lippincott, 1970), 20-21.

[49]Ibid., 65.

[50]Ibid., 91.

[51]Ibid., 76.

[52]In the preface to the second edition of the book, Cone expresses his unhappiness with its structure and dependency on Barth. *Black Theology of Liberation*, 2d ed. (Maryknoll, N.Y.: Orbis, 1986), xxi.

[53]Cone, *Black Theology of Liberation*, 1st ed., 115.

[54]Ibid., 121.

[55]Ibid., 170.

[56]Ibid., 183.

[57]Ibid., 202.

[58]Ibid., 220. For his more fully developed Christology, see Cone, *God of the Oppressed*, 108-37.

[59]See, e.g., Cone's statement in *Speaking the Truth*, 1.

[60]For his comments on his use of Barth and other White theologians, see his autobiographical work, *My Soul Looks Back*, 80-83.

[61]Cone, *God of the Oppressed*, 148-49.

[62]Ibid., 8. For a concise description of Cone's liberation hermeneutic, see 81-82.

[63]Ibid., 32.

[64]Ibid., 17.

[65]See, e.g., Cone's statement in *My Soul Looks Back*, 110.

[66]See, e.g., Cone, *For My People*, 88-96.

[67]Cone, *Black Theology of Liberation*, 141.

[68]Ibid., 144.

Latin American Liberation Theology: Immanence in Liberation

[1]Robert McAfee Brown, *Gustavo Gutiérrez, An Introduction to Liberation Theology* (Maryknoll, N.Y.: Orbis, 1990), 11.

[2]For a description of the roles of Medellín and Puebla in the rise and development of liberation theology, see Brown, *Gutiérrez*, 11-21.

[3]Gustavo Gutiérrez, *The Power of the Poor in History*, trans. Robert R. Barr (Maryknoll, N.Y.: Orbis, 1983), 205.

[4]Ibid., 195.

[5]For a representative work by Metz see Johann Baptist Metz, *Faith in History and Society, Toward a Practical Fundamental Theology*, trans. David Smith (New York: Seabury, 1980).

[6]For the full instruction and commentary on it see *Origins: NC Documentary Service*, published by the National Catholic News Service, 14/13 (September 13, 1984).

[7]For the full text of the "Instruction on Christian Freedom and Liberation" see *Origins: NC*

Documentary Service 15:44 (April 17, 1986). For an analysis of the instruction from the viewpoint of liberation theology see Brown, *Gutiérrez*, 146-48.

[8]For Brown's own original work on liberation theology see Robert McAfee Brown, *Theology in a New Key. Responding to Liberation Themes* (Philadelphia: Westminster, 1978). For one of the best, if most fawning, commentaries on liberation theology see Brown, *Gutiérrez*.

[9]Gustavo Gutiérrez, *The Theology of Liberation*, rev. ed., trans. and ed. Sister Caridad Inda and John Eagleson (Maryknoll, N.Y.: Orbis, 1988). All quotations are taken from this 15th anniversary ed.

[10]José Míguez Bonino, *Christians and Marxists: The Mutual Challenge to Revolution* (Grand Rapids, Mich.: Eerdmans, 1976).

[11]José Míguez Bonino, *Doing Theology in a Revolutionary Situation* (Philadelphia: Fortress, 1975).

[12]José Míguez Bonino, *Toward a Christian Political Ethic* (Philadelphia: Fortress, 1983).

[13]Dermot A. Lane, *Foundations for a Social Theology: Praxis, Process and Salvation* (New York and Ramsey, N.J.: Paulist, 1984), 77.

[14]For a basic overview of "critical theory" and its influence on liberation theology, see ibid., 43-56.

[15]Gutiérrez, *Power of the Poor*, 186.

[16]Ibid., 193.

[17]Ibid.

[18]Míguez Bonino, *Doing Theology*, 86.

[19]Brown, *Gutiérrez*, 52. The rest of the statistics cited here are also from this and surrounding pages.

[20]Quoted from Leonardo Boff in Dean William Ferm, *Profiles in Liberation* (Mystic, Conn.: Twenty-Third Publications, 1988), 125.

[21]Brown, *Gutiérrez*, 39.

[22]Gutiérrez, *Theology of Liberation*, 151.

[23]Míguez Bonino, *Doing Theology*, 16.

[24]Gutiérrez, *Theology of Liberation*, 54.

[25]Gutiérrez, *Power of the Poor*, 28.

[26]Unfortunately it is not possible here to give a detailed account of the liberation theologians' criticism of capitalism. For the best brief statement of it see Míguez Bonino, *Doing Theology*, 21-37.

[27]Gutiérrez, *Theology of Liberation*, 18.

[28]Ibid., xxxviii.

[29]Míguez Bonino, *Doing Theology*, 112.

[30]Brown, *Gutiérrez*, 60.

[31]Gutiérrez, *Theology of Liberation*, xxix.

[32]Míguez Bonino, *Doing Theology*, 81.

[33]Míguez Bonino explains: "Truth is not found in the contemplation of a Platonic world of ideas or in the exploration of subjective consciousness but in the scientific analysis of the activity of human beings within the conditions of their social situation." Míguez Bonino, *Christians and Marxists*, 93.

[34]Gutiérrez, *Theology of Liberation*, 156.

[35]Ibid., 10.

[36]Gutiérrez, *Power of the Poor*, 13.

[37]Gutiérrez, *Theology of Liberation*, xxxiv.

[38]Ibid., 116.

[39]Míguez Bonino, *Christians and Marxists*, 116.

[40]Gutiérrez, *Theology of Liberation*, 83.

[41]Ibid., 116.

[42]Ibid., 118.

[43]Gutiérrez, *Power of the Poor*, 64.

[44]Gutiérrez, *Theology of Liberation*, 104.

[45]Míguez Bonino, *Doing Theology*, 121-31.

[46]Gutiérrez, *Power of the Poor*, 28.

[47]Ibid., 196.

[48]Brown, *Gutiérrez*, 155.

[49]See Max L. Stackhouse, "Torture, Terrorism and Theology: The Need for a Universal Ethic," *Christian Century* (October 8, 1986): 861-63.

[50]See P. T. Bauer, "Western Guilt and Third World Poverty," *Commentary* (January 1976): 31-38.

[51]Sam A. Portaro, Jr., "Is God Prejudiced in Favor of the Poor?" *Christian Century* (April 24, 1985): 404-5.

[52]Wolfhart Pannenberg, "Christianity, Marxism, and Liberation Theology," *Christian Scholar's Review* 18/3 (March 1989): 215-26.

[53]J. Andrew Kirk, *Liberation Theology: An Evangelical View from the Third World* (Atlanta: John Knox, 1979), 193.

[54]Ibid., 198.

[55]Gutiérrez, *Theology of Liberation*, 110.

Feminist Theology: The Immanence of God in Women's Experience

[1]Rosemary Radford Ruether, *Women-Church: Theology and Practice of Feminist Liturgical Communities* (San Francisco: Harper and Row, 1986), 137.

[2]Rosemary Radford Ruether, *Sexism and God-Talk: Toward a Feminist Theology* (Boston: Beacon, 1983), 193-94.

[3]Pamela Dickey Young, *Feminist Theology/Christian Theology: In Search of Method* (Minneapolis: Fortress, 1990), 60.

[4]Ibid., 15-17.

[5]Anne E. Carr, *Transforming Grace. Christian Tradition and Women's Experience* (San Francisco: Harper and Row, 1988), 146.

[6]Elisabeth Schüssler Fiorenza, *In Memory of Her: A Feminist Reconstruction of Christian Origins* (New York: Crossroad, 1984).

[7]Letty M. Russell, *Human Liberation in a Feminist Perspective—A Theology* (Philadelphia: Westminster, 1974).

[8]Letty M. Russell, *Household of Freedom: Authority in Feminist Theology* (Philadelphia: Westminster, 1987).

[9]Carr, *Transforming Grace*, 7-9.

[10]Rosemary Ruether, "Feminist Theology in the Academy," *Christianity and Crisis* 45/3 (March 4, 1985): 59.

[11]Young, *Feminist Theology/Christian Theology*, 13.

[12]Ruether, "Feminist Theology in the Academy," 61.

[13]Ruether, *Sexism and God-Talk*, 173.

[14]Carr, *Transforming Grace*, 136.

[15]Ruether, "Feminist Theology in the Academy," 59.

[16]Ruether, *Sexism and God-Talk*, 61.

[17]Ibid., 94-99.

[18]Fiorenza, *In Memory of Her,* 154.

[19]See, e.g., Patricia Wilson-Kastner et al., *A Lost Tradition: Women Writers of the Early Church* (Lanham, Md.: University Press of America, 1981).

[20]Ruether, *Sexism and God-Talk,* 178.

[21]Carr, *Transforming Grace,* 30.

[22]Young, *Feminist Theology/Christian Theology,* 53-56.

[23]Carr, *Transforming Grace,* 127.

[24]Ruether, *Sexism and God-Talk,* 13.

[25]The exposition of these three approaches to feminist theological method is deeply indebted to Pamela Dickey Young, who provides an exceptionally clear analysis in *Feminist Theology/Christian Theology,* 23-48.

[26]Ruether, *Sexism and God-Talk,* 18.

[27]Ibid., 29.

[28]Ibid., 23.

[29]Ibid., 32.

[30]Russell, *Household of Faith,* 20.

[31]Ibid., 41.

[32]Ibid., 43.

[33]Ibid., 51.

[34]William Oddie, *What Will Happen to God? Feminism and the Reconstruction of Christian Belief* (London: SPCK, 1984), 19.

[35]Carr, *Transforming Grace,* 109.

[36]This is a cursory summary of a key element of Ruether's critique of traditional theology in *Sexism and God-Talk* and other writings. One important passage where this critique of patriarchy as dualism is found is in *Sexism and God-Talk,* chap. 3: "Woman, Body, and Nature: Sexism and the Theology of Creation," 72-92.

[37]Ibid., 188.

[38]Ibid., 112.

[39]Ibid., 67.

[40]Ibid., 69.

[41]Quoted in Mary Hembrow Snyder, *The Christology of Rosemary Radford Ruether. A Critical Introduction* (Mystic, Conn.: Twenty-Third Publications, 1988), 107.

[42]Ruether, *Sexism and God-Talk,* 86-87.

[43]Ibid., 71.

[44]Russell, *Human Liberation,* 139.

[45]Ruether, *Sexism and God-Talk,* 116.

[46]Ibid., 135.

[47]Ibid., 137.

[48]Ibid., 138.

[49]Ibid., 8.

[50]Ibid.

[51]Ibid., 11.

[52]Donald G. Bloesch, *The Battle for the Trinity: The Debate Over Inclusive God-Language* (Ann Arbor: Servant Publications, 1985), 84.

[53]Ibid., 85.

[54]Young, *Feminist Theology/Christian Theology*, 74.

[55]Ibid., 77.

[56]Elizabeth Achtemeier, "The Impossible Possibility: Evaluating the Feminist Approach to Bible and Theology," *Interpretation* 42 (January 1988): 57.

8 The Transcendence of the Human Spirit: The New Catholic Theology
Karl Rahner: The Transcendence of Human Subjectivity

[1]Karl Rahner, *I Remember. An Autobiographical Interview with Meinhold Krauss*, trans. Harvey D. Egan, S.J. (New York: Crossroad, 1985), 19.

[2]George Vass, *The Mystery of Man and the Foundations of a Theological System*, vol. 2 of *Understanding Karl Rahner* (Westminster, Md.: Christian Classics, 1985), 118.

[3]Herbert Vorgrimler, *Understanding Karl Rahner. An Introduction to His Life and Thought*, trans. John Bowden (New York: Crossroad, 1986), 99.

[4]*Karl Rahner in Dialogue. Conversations and Interviews, 1965-1982*, ed. Paul Imhof and Hubert Biallowons, trans. Harvey D. Egan (New York: Crossroad, 1986), 22.

[5]Ibid., 147.

[6]Karl Rahner, *Foundations of Christian Faith. An Introduction to the Idea of Christianity*, trans. William V. Dych (New York: Seabury, 1978), 87.

[7]Karl Rahner, *Hearers of the Word*, trans. Michael Richards (New York: Herder & Herder, 1969), 17.

[8]Rahner, *Foundations*, 12.

[9]Rahner, *Hearers*, 53.

[10]Michael J. Buckley, "Within the Holy Mystery," in *A World of Grace. An Introduction to the Themes and Foundations of Karl Rahner's Theology*, ed. Leo J. O'Donovan (New York: Seabury, 1980), 34.

[11]Rahner, *Hearers*, 56.

[12]Ibid., 57.

[13]Ibid., 59-60.

[14]Ibid., 53.

[15]Ibid., 155.

[16]Ibid., 161.

[17]Ibid., 101.

[18]Ibid., 65-66.

[19]Roberts declares that for Rahner, "Man exists only by virtue of the fact that he is always on his way to God, whether he knows it explicitly or not and whether he wills it or not." Louis Roberts, *The Achievement of Karl Rahner* (New York: Herder & Herder, 1967), 37.

[20]George Vass, *A Theologian in Search of a Philosophy*, vol. 1 of *Understanding Karl Rahner* (Westminster, Md.: Christian Classics, 1985), 20.

[21]Rahner, *Hearers*, 112.

[22]Ibid., 114.

[23]For Rahner's formal discussion of the problem of nature and grace and his argument against extrinsicism, see "Nature and Grace," in Karl Rahner, *Theological Investigations*, vol. IV, trans. Kevin Smyth (Baltimore: Helicon, 1966), 165-88.

[24]O'Donovan, ed., *World of Grace*, 191.

[25]Rahner, *Foundations*, 116.

[26]Ibid., 129.

[27]Ibid., 123-24.

[28]Ibid., 116.

[29]Ibid., 131.

[30]Ibid., 123.

[31]Karl Rahner, "Anonymous Christians," in *Theological Investigations*, vol. VI (London: Darton, Longman and Todd, 1969; New York: Seabury, 1974), 390-91, 393-95.

[32]Rahner, *Foundations*, 152.

[33]This conclusion is reached by George Vass in his two-volume analysis and critique of Rahner's theology. See especially *The Mystery of Man* (vol. 2), 59-83.

[34]Rahner, *Foundations*, 60-61.

[35]Ibid., 171.

[36]Ibid.

[37]Ibid.

[38]Ibid., 173.

[39]Ibid., 174.

[40]Ibid., 158.

[41]Ibid., 161.

[42]Rahner's connection of Christ, and especially the Incarnation, with human evolution parallels the theology of Teilhard de Chardin in many ways. Teilhardian motifs are especially evident in the section of *Foundations* entitled "Christology within an Evolutionary View of the World" (178-206).

[43]Ibid., 74.

[44]Ibid., 75.

[45]Ibid., 74.

[46]Ibid., 78.

[47]Vass, *Theologian in Search of a Philosophy*, 59.

[48]Rahner, *Foundations*, 62.

[49]Vass, *Theologian in Search of a Philosophy*, 61.

[50]Rahner, *Foundations*, 63.

[51]Karl Rahner, *The Trinity*, trans. Joseph Donceel (New York: Seabury, 1974), 22. The term *Rahner's Rule* was coined by Ted Peters in "Trinity Talk, Part I," *Dialog* 26 (Winter 1987): 46.

[52]Ibid., 99-101.

[53]Rahner, *Foundations*, 220.

[54]Ibid., 223.

[55]Ibid., 228-29.

[56]Ibid., 296.

[57]Ibid., 279.

[58]Ibid., 280.

[59]Ibid., 300-301.

[60]Ibid., 228.

[61]Ibid., 303.

[62]Ibid., 249.

[63]Ibid., 224-27.

[64]Ibid., 225.

[65]Ibid., 226.

[66]Vass, *Mystery of Man*, 99.

Hans Küng: Striking the Balance Between Immanence and Transcendence

[1] Hans Küng, *Justification: The Doctrine of Karl Barth and a Catholic Reflection,* trans. Thomas Collins et al. (New York: Thomas Nelson & Sons, 1964), 282.

[2] Hans Küng, *Infallible? An Inquiry,* trans. Edward Quinn (Garden City, N.Y.: Doubleday, 1971), 181.

[3] Robert Nowell, *A Passion for Truth. Hans Küng and His Theology* (New York: Crossroad, 1981), 194.

[4] Küng communicated this to the author in personal conversation in Houston, Texas, in March 1989.

[5] Ibid.

[6] Hans Küng, *Reforming the Church Today. Keeping Hope Alive,* trans. Peter Heinegg et al. (New York: Crossroad, 1990), 64-71.

[7] Hans Küng, *Does God Exist? An Answer for Today,* trans. Edward Quinn (Garden City, N.Y.: Doubleday, 1980), 403.

[8] Ibid., 449.

[9] Ibid., 464.

[10] Ibid., 124.

[11] Ibid., 544.

[12] Ibid., 550.

[13] Ibid., 571.

[14] Ibid., 536

[15] Ibid., 111

[16] Ibid., 337.

[17] Küng, of course, is not the only contemporary theologian to use the term *postmodern* to describe a new approach to theology in the light of a culture-wide critique of certain aspects of modernity. There is, however, no consensus about what postmodern theology actually is. Küng is one theologian who is seeking to fill the concept with content. For other attempts, see David Ray Griffen, William A. Beardslee and Joe Holland, *Varieties of Postmodern Theology* (Albany: State University of New York Press, 1989).

[18] For an excellent discussion of paradigm change in both natural science and in theology, see Hans Küng, *Theology for the Third Millennium. An Ecumenical View,* trans. Peter Heinegg (New York and London: Doubleday, 1988), 123-69.

[19] Ibid., 6.

[20] Ibid., 8-9.

[21] Ibid., 127.

[22] Ibid., 154.

[23] Ibid., 185.

[24] Ibid., 190-91.

[25] Ibid., 106.

[26] Ibid., 108.

[27] Ibid., 116.

[28] Ibid., 122.

[29] Ibid., 159.

[30] From personal conversation in Houston, Texas, March 1989.

[31] Küng, *Theology for the Third Millennium,* 193.

[32] Ibid., 194.

[33]Ibid., 59.

[34]Catherine Mowry LaCugna, *The Theological Methodology of Hans Küng* (Chico, Calif.: Scholar's Press, 1982), 182-83.

[35]For an excellent, detailed discussion of Küng's view of tradition, see ibid., 95-103.

[36]Quoted in Nowell, *Passion for Truth*, 246.

[37]Küng, *Theology for the Third Millennium*, 166. It is interesting that Küng reversed the order of these two poles in the two places in this book where they are explicitly mentioned in relation to each other.

[38]Ibid., 237.

[39]Ibid.

[40]Ibid., 133.

[41]Ibid., 288.

[42]Ibid., 455.

[43]Ibid., 457.

[44]Ibid., 458.

[45]Ibid., 449.

[46]Ibid., 455.

[47]Ibid., 450-51.

[48]Ibid., 452.

[49]Ibid.

[50]Ibid., 445-46.

[51]Küng, *On Being a Christian*, 306.

[52]Küng, *Theology for the Third Millennium*, 111.

[53]Küng, *On Being a Christian*, 83.

[54]Küng, *Incarnation of God*, 493.

[55]Ibid., 444.

[56]Ibid., 391-92.

[57]Ibid., 447.

[58]Küng's doctrine of the Trinity is underdeveloped and extremely vague. It seems that for him the "Spirit" is the presence of God the Father and the "Son" is Jesus. Thus, there is no immanent, eternal, ontological Trinity, but only a historical and functional Trinity. However, this can only be surmised because he provides very little to go on in interpreting his concept of God's triunity. See *On Being a Christian*, 477.

[59]Ibid., 449-50.

[60]Ibid., 449.

[61]LaCugna, *Theological Methodology*, 85.

[62]Ibid., 174.

[63]Ibid., 178.

[64]Ibid., 194-95.

[65]Küng, *Does God Exist?* 653.

9 Transcendence within the Story: Narrative Theology

[1]Gabriel Fackre, *The Christian Story*, rev. ed. (Grand Rapids, Mich.: Eerdmans, 1984), 5.

[2]See Paul Nelson, *Narrative and Morality: A Theological Inquiry* (University Park, Pa.: Pennsylvania State University Press, 1987), 100, who cites Frank Kermode, *The Sense of an Ending: Studies in the Theory of Fiction* (New York: Oxford University Press, 1967), 7.

[3]Stephen Crites, "The Narrative Quality of Experience," *Journal of the American Academy of Religion* 39/3 (September 1971): 291-311.

[4]James William McClendon, Jr., *Biography as Theology* (Nashville: Abingdon, 1974), 190.

[5]See, e.g., George W. Stroup, *The Promise of Narrative Theology* (Atlanta: John Knox, 1981), 17.

[6]Stanley Hauerwas, *Truthfulness and Tragedy* (Notre Dame: University of Notre Dame Press, 1977), 15. See also Michael Goldberg, *Theology and Narrative* (Nashville: Abingdon, 1982), 36.

[7]Goldberg, *Theology and Narrative*, 35.

[8]Even Hauerwas finds some (albeit secondary) importance to propositions about God and propositional doctrines. See Stanley Hauerwas, *Vision and Virtue* (Notre Dame: Fides Publishers, 1974), 46; *The Peaceable Kingdom* (Notre Dame: University of Notre Dame Press, 1983), 26.

[9]James William McClendon, Jr., e.g., places narrative theology at odds with the older propositional theology. See *Biography as Theology*, 188, 197-98.

[10]See Goldberg, *Theology and Narrative*, 151-52.

[11]Hauerwas, *Peaceable Kingdom*, 26.

[12]This crisis is presented in Stroup, *Promise of Narrative Theology*, 21-38.

[13]Ibid., 26.

[14]Ibid., 36.

[15]H. Richard Niebuhr, *The Meaning of Revelation* (New York: Macmillan, 1946), 21.

[16]Ibid., 46-48.

[17]Goldberg, *Theology and Narrative*, 147.

[18]Niebuhr, *Meaning of Revelation*, 59-60.

[19]Ibid., 65-73.

[20]Ibid., 82, 86.

[21]Ibid., 93.

[22]Ibid., 110-21.

[23]Ibid., 125-26.

[24]Ibid., 132, 177.

[25]Stroup, *Promise of Narrative Theology*, 69.

[26]Ibid., 63-64.

[27]Ibid., 50.

[28]G. Ernest Wright, *The God Who Acts: Biblical Theology as Recital* (London: SCM, 1952), 11-13.

[29]G. Ernest Wright and Reginald H. Fuller, *The Book of the Acts of God,* Anchor Books ed. (Garden City, N.Y.: Doubleday, 1960), 43.

[30]Wright, *God Who Acts*, 13.

[31]Wright and Fuller, *Book of the Acts of God*, 11.

[32]Wright, *God Who Acts*, 38.

[33]Ibid., 85.

[34]Erich Auerbach, *Mimesis,* Anchor Books ed. (Garden City, N.Y.: Doubleday, 1957), 11-20.

[35]George Strong, "Theology of Narrative or Narrative Theology? A Response to *Why Narrative?*" *Theology Today* 47/4 (January 1991): 425.

[36]Compare the threefold categorization schemes of Goldberg, *Theology and Narrative*, 155-84, and Stroup, *Promise of Narrative Theology*, 71-84. Nelson offers a twofold division in *Narrative and Morality*, 65-78. Gary L. Comstock likewise presents a twofold delineation, differentiating between "pure narrativism" and "impure narrativism." "Truth or Meaning: Ricoeur versus Frei on Biblical Narrative," *Journal of Religion* 66/2 (1986): 117-40; "Two Types of Narrative Theology," *Journal of the American Academy of Religion* 55/4 (1987): 687-717.

[37]Goldberg, *Theology and Narrative,* 155.

[38]Nelson distinguishes between the experiential-expressive and the cultural-linguistic uses of *Narrative and Morality,* 69-78. Related to this understanding is George Lindbeck's assertion that doctrines function in a regulatory sociological role in the church so that the task of theologians is that of telling stories about the functions of beliefs. George Lindbeck, *The Nature of Doctrine: Religion and Theology in a Postliberal Age* (Philadelphia: Westminster, 1984), 19.

[39]For a succinct summary of Frei's contribution, see William C. Placher, "Hans Frei and the Meaning of Biblical Narrative," *Christian Century* 106/18 (May 24-31, 1989): 556-59.

[40]Both Goldberg, *Theology and Narrative,* 156-64, and Stroup, *Promise of Narrative Theology,* 81-84, agree that Frei and McFague are to be included among the narrative thinkers.

[41]Hans Frei, *The Eclipse of Biblical Narrative: A Study in Eighteenth and Nineteenth Century Hermeneutics* (New Haven: Yale University Press, 1974), 51.

[42]Ibid., 322-23.

[43]Ibid., 323.

[44]Ibid., 230.

[45]Ibid., 27.

[46]Ibid., 280.

[47]Goldberg finds this to be Frei's basic thesis; *Theology and Narrative,* 162.

[48]Sallie McFague TeSelle, *Speaking in Parables* (Philadelphia: Fortress, 1975), 36, 45, 138-39.

[49]McClendon, *Biography as Theology,* 96.

[50]James William McClendon, *Ethics: Systematic Theology,* vol. 1 (Nashville: Abingdon, 1986).

[51]Ibid., 171.

[52]Ibid., 328ff.

[53]Another noteworthy writer who has espoused similar themes as those of the narrative ethicists is John Howard Yoder. His most influential statement to date has been *The Politics of Jesus* (Grand Rapids, Mich.: Eerdmans, 1972).

[54]Hauerwas describes the development of his approach in "The Testament of Friends," *Christian Century* 107/7 (February 28, 1990): 212-16.

[55]Nelson, *Narrative and Morality,* 109.

[56]Hauerwas, *Truthfulness and Tragedy,* 8.

[57]Ibid., 75-77.

[58]Stanley Hauerwas, *The Community of Character* (Notre Dame: Notre Dame University Press, 1981), 144.

[59]Hauerwas, *Peaceable Kingdom,* 16, 54.

[60]For a description of an ethics of doing versus an ethics of being, see William Frankena, *Ethics* (Englewood Cliffs, N.J.: Prentice-Hall, 1973), 61-69.

[61]Hauerwas, *Vision and Virtue,* 67.

[62]Hauerwas, *Truthfulness and Tragedy,* 73.

[63]Hauerwas, *Peaceable Kingdom,* 16.

[64]Ibid. See also Hauerwas, *Vision and Virtue,* 2-3. The centrality of these concepts in Hauerwas' thought has been noted as well by Goldberg, *Theology and Narrative,* 174.

[65]Hauerwas, *Truthfulness and Tragedy,* 29.

[66]Hauerwas, *Vision and Virtue,* 59.

[67]Ibid., 29, 36.

[68]Ibid., 74.

[69]Goldberg, *Theology and Narrative,* 176.

[70]Hauerwas, *Vision and Virtue*, 73.

[71]Hauerwas, *Truthfulness and Tragedy*, 80.

[72]Hauerwas, *Community of Character*, 1.

[73]Ibid., 3.

[74]Ibid., 4, 95-96.

[75]Hauerwas, *Peaceable Kingdom*, 24-30.

[76]Hauerwas, *Community of Character*, 53, 55.

[77]Ibid., 63.

[78]Ibid., 66.

[79]This is acknowledged by narrative systematic theologian Stroup, *Promise of Narrative Theology*, 84.

[80]Ibid., 99-261.

[81]Fackre, *Christian Story*.

[82]Clark Pinnock, *Tracking the Maze* (San Francisco: Harper and Row, 1990), 190-211.

[83]Two examples are James McClendon, *Biography as Theology*, and James W. Fowler, *Trajectories in Faith* (Nashville: Abingdon, 1980). For a summary and evaluation of these two quite different approaches to biography, see Goldberg, *Theology and Narrative*, 66-95.

[84]Hauerwas, *Truthfulness and Tragedy*, 30, 36.

[85]Stroup, *Promise of Narrative Theology*, 101-98.

[86]For his understanding of this dimension, Stroup draws from the work of Hans-Georg Gadamer, especially his book *Truth and Method* (New York: Seabury, 1975), as well as from George Herbert Mead (see *Promise of Narrative Theology*, 109-10, nn. 23, 24).

[87]Stroup, *Promise of Narrative Theology*, 127. See also Goldberg, *Theology and Narrative*, 107-13; Hauerwas, *Truthfulness and Tragedy*, 87.

[88]Stroup, *Promise of Narrative Theology*, 132-33.

[89]Ibid., 186-93, citing Karl Barth, *Church Dogmatics*, IV/1 (Edinburgh: T. and T. Clark, 1956), 740-79.

[90]Goldberg offers a somewhat different triad of faith. The process of faith includes acknowledgment of what one was in the past—conversion—acceptance of what one is in the present—reconciliation—and willingness to take responsibility for what one will become in the future—transformation; *Theology and Narrative*, 129.

[91]Stroup, *Promise of Narrative Theology*, 241.

[92]Ibid., 249.

[93]Pinnock, *Tracking the Maze*, 161-62

[94]See, e.g., Stroup, *Promise of Narrative Theology*, 252.

[95]Goldberg, *Theology and Narrative*, 192.

[96]Nelson, *Narrative and Morality*, 142.

[97]Ibid., 149-51.

10 Reaffirming the Balance: Evangelical Theology Coming of Age

Carl F. H. Henry: The Evangelical Alternative to Modernism

[1]Carl F. H. Henry, *The Uneasy Conscience of Modern Fundamentalism* (Grand Rapids, Mich.: Eerdmans, 1947). For his later reflections on the problematic areas of fundamentalism and the need for evangelicals to move beyond it, see Carl F. H. Henry, *Evangelical Responsibility in Contemporary Theology*, Pathway Books (Grand Rapids, Mich.: Eerdmans, 1957).

[2]Henry, *Uneasy Conscience*, 16.

[3]Ibid., 9.

[4]Ibid., 68.

[5]See, e.g., Henry's reaffirmation of the five points of fundamentalism in *Evangelical Responsibility*, 66.

[6]Ibid., 43.

[7]Henry's criticisms of Barth were set forth in a series of articles published in *Christianity Today*. Carl F. H. Henry, "Between Barth and Bultmann," *Christianity Today* 5/6 (May 8, 1961): 24-26; "The Deterioration of Barth's Defenses," *Christianity Today* 9/1 (October 9, 1964): 16-19; "The Pale Ghost of Barth," *Christianity Today* 15/10 (February 12, 1971): 40-43; "Wintertime in European Theology," *Christianity Today* 5/5 (December 5, 1960): 12-14. Henry described an encounter with Barth at George Washington University in Carl F. H. Henry, *Confessions of a Theologian* (Waco, Tex.: Word, 1986), 210-11. Richard Albert Mohler presents an appraisal of Henry's rejection of Barth in "Evangelical Theology and Karl Barth: Representative Models of Response" (Ph.D. diss., Southern Baptist Theological Seminary, 1989), 107-34.

[8]E.g., Carl F. H. Henry, "Narrative Theology: An Evangelical Appraisal," *Trinity Journal* 8 (1987): 3-19.

[9]Henry followed Van Til's dismissal of Barth. See, e.g., Carl F. H. Henry, *Fifty Years of Protestant Theology* (Boston: Wilde, 1950), 96.

[10]Bob E. Patterson, *Carl F. H. Henry*, in *Makers of the Modern Theological Mind*, ed. Bob E. Patterson (Waco, Tex.: Word, 1983), 9. Patterson notes that in 1978 *Time Magazine* named Henry evangelicalism's "leading spokesman."

[11]R. Albert Mohler, "Carl Ferdinand Howard Henry," in *Baptist Thinkers*, ed. Timothy George and David S. Dockery (Nashville: Broadman, 1990), 518.

[12]Carl F. H. Henry, *God, Revelation and Authority*, 6 vols. (Waco, Tex.: Word, 1976-1983).

[13]For Henry's own recounting of his pilgrimage, see *Confessions of a Theologian*.

[14]Ibid., 44.

[15]Ibid., 47.

[16]Ibid., 55.

[17]For Henry's perspective on the developments at *Christianity Today*, see *Confessions of a Theologian*, 264-301.

[18]E.g., Carl F. H. Henry, *Evangelicals in Search of Identity* (Waco, Tex.: Word, 1976). Even his autobiography concludes with a presentation of his perspective on "The Evangelical Prospect in America." *Confessions of a Theologian*, 381-407.

[19]E.g., Carl F. H. Henry, "Crosscurrents in Contemporary Theology," in *Jesus of Nazareth: Saviour and Lord*, ed. Carl Henry (Grand Rapids, Mich.: Eerdmans, 1966), 3-22.

[20]E.g., Carl F. H. Henry, *Frontiers in Modern Theology* (Chicago: Moody, 1964).

[21]Ibid., 140-41.

[22]Carl F. H. Henry, *The Protestant Dilemma* (Grand Rapids, Mich.: Eerdmans, 1949), 18. See also Carl F. H. Henry, *Remaking the Modern Mind* (Grand Rapids, Mich.: Eerdmans, 1946), 26. He delineated the misfortunes of liberalism from a mid-century vantage point in *Fifty Years of Protestant Theology*.

[23]Henry, *Remaking the Modern Mind*, 26, 265. For an alternate list, see *Protestant Dilemma*, 18-21.

[24]For an early statement of this theme, see Henry, *Protestant Dilemma*, 225.

[25]Henry, *Frontiers in Modern Theology*, 134-35.

[26]Ibid., 138.

[27]Ibid., 138-39. See also *Protestant Dilemma*, 221-24.

[28]Henry, *Protestant Dilemma*, 95-96.

[29]Ibid., 217.

[30]Henry, *God, Revelation and Authority* 3:457.

[31]Ibid., 3:248-487.

[32]Henry, *Protestant Dilemma*, 97.

[33]Henry, *God, Revelation and Authority* 4:426.

[34]Ibid., 3:173.

[35]Henry, *Protestant Dilemma*, 99.

[36]Henry, *Remaking the Modern Mind*, 213.

[37]Henry, *God, Revelation and Authority* 1:244.

[38]Ibid., 199.

[39]Carl F. H. Henry, "The Fortunes of Theology" (3) *Christianity Today* 16/18 (June 9, 1972): 30 [874].

[40]Henry, *God, Revelation and Authority* 1:215.

[41]Henry, *Protestant Dilemma*, 115.

[42]Henry, *Remaking the Modern Mind*, 247.

[43]Henry, *God, Revelation and Authority* 1:394.

[44]Ibid., 405; 2:136.

[45]Ibid., 2:83-85.

[46]Ibid., 123.

[47]For a lengthier discussion of this label and its significance in Henry's thought, see Patterson, *Carl F. H. Henry*, 58-83.

[48]Henry lays down the thesis of the Bible as the sole foundation for theology in *God, Revelation and Authority* 1:181-409.

[49]Henry set forth his understanding of inspiration, inerrancy and infallibility in ibid., 4:103-219.

[50]Ibid., 4:166-67.

[51]Ibid., 129.

[52]Ibid.

[53]Ibid., 138.

[54]For Henry's discussion of what inerrancy does and does not imply, see ibid., 4:201-10.

[55]Mohler notes this point in *Carl Henry*, 528, and cites Henry's discussion of the issues in R. Albert Mohler, *Conversations with Carl Henry: Christianity for Today* (Lewiston, N.Y.: Edwin Mellon, 1986), 23-30.

[56]Carl F. H. Henry, "Reaction and Realignment," *Christianity Today* 20/20 (July 2, 1976): 30 [1038].

[57]See, e.g., the interview with Carl Henry, "The Concerns and Considerations of Carl F. H. Henry," *Christianity Today* 25/5 (March 13, 1981): 19.

[58]This theme forms thesis nine in Henry's magnum opus. See *God, Revelation and Authority* 3:164-247.

[59]Ibid., 174.

[60]Ibid., 428.

[61]Henry, *Remaking the Modern Mind*, 171.

[62]E.g., *God, Revelation and Authority* 6:49.

[63]Ibid., 6:50.

[64]Ibid.

[65]E.g., *Remaking the Modern Mind*, 209-10; Carl F. H. Henry, *The God Who Shows Himself* (Waco, Tex.:

Word, 1966), 4.

[66]Henry, *Frontiers in Evangelical Theology*, 154-55.

[67]Henry, *God, Revelation and Authority* 6:51.

[68]For a helpful overview of these volumes, see Patterson, *Carl F. H. Henry*, 84-159.

[69]In addition to scattered discussions in *God, Revelation and Authority*, Henry's most important statements concerning social ethics are his book, *Aspects of Christian Social Ethics* (Grand Rapids, Mich.: Eerdmans, 1964), and certain essays in *A Plea for Evangelical Demonstration* (Grand Rapids, Mich.: Baker, 1971), *The Christian Mindset in a Secular Society* (Portland: Multnomah, 1984) and *God Who Shows Himself.* Also important is his lengthier, more general treatise on ethics, *Christian Personal Ethics* (Grand Rapids, Mich.: Eerdmans, 1957).

[70]*Plea for Evangelical Demonstration*, 107; *God Who Shows Himself,* 31. For an extended discussion of justice, see *God, Revelation and Authority* 6:402-54.

[71]Henry, *Plea for Evangelical Demonstration*, 115.

[72]See, e.g., Henry, *God, Revelation and Authority* 4:573-77.

[73]Henry set forth this claim in 1947 in *The Uneasy Conscience of Modern Fundamentalism.* He later concluded that fundamentalism had been guilty of reductionism in the realm of personal ethics as well. See *Evangelical Responsibility*, 70.

[74]Henry issued this call repeatedly, including in *Evangelical Responsibility,* esp. 69-78.

[75]Henry, *Aspects of Christian Social Ethics*, 16.

[76]Henry, *Plea for Evangelical Demonstration*, 46-47. For an extended discussion of Christian political duty, see *God, Revelation and Authority* 6:436-54.

[77]Henry, *God Who Shows Himself*, 67; *God, Revelation and Authority* 6:418-35.

[78]Henry, *God, Revelation and Authority* 1:408.

[79]Mohler, for example, chastises Henry for lacking a developed ecclesiology, a problem he finds indicative of evangelicalism as a whole. See Mohler, "Carl Henry," 530.

[80]See, e.g., the appraisal of fellow evangelical Bernard Ramm, *After Fundamentalism* (San Francisco: Harper and Row, 1983), 26-27.

[81]Pinnock, *Tracking the Maze*, 46-47.

Bernard Ramm: Evangelicalism in Dialog with Modern Thought

[1]Bernard L. Ramm, *The Christian View of Science and Scripture* (Grand Rapids, Mich.: Eerdmann, 1954), 7.

[2]Bernard L. Ramm, *Protestant Christian Evidences: A Textbook of the Evidences of the Truthfulness of the Christian Faith for Conservative Protestants* (Chicago: Moody, 1953), 220.

[3]Ibid.

[4]Ibid., 220-21.

[5]See Wilbur M. Smith's preface to Bernard L. Ramm, *Protestant Biblical Interpretation* (Boston: Wilde, 1950), xvi-xvii.

[6]See Ramm, *The Christian View of Science and Scripture,* 8.

[7]Wesley H. Brown, "Bernard Ramm: An Appreciation," in *Perspectives on Theology in the Contemporary World: Essays in Honor of Bernard L. Ramm,* ed. Stanley J. Grenz (Macon, Ga.: Mercer University Press, 1990), 6.

[8]See Bernard Ramm, "Are We Obscurantists?" *Christianity Today* 1/10 (February 18, 1957): 14.

[9]Bernard L. Ramm, *The Evangelical Heritage* (Waco, Tex.: Word, 1973), 70.

[10]Bernard L. Ramm, *His Way Out* (Glendale, Calif.: Regal, 1974), Introduction.

[11]Bernard L. Ramm, "Is 'Scripture Alone' the Essence of Christianity?" in *Biblical Authority,* ed.

Jack Rogers (Waco, Tex.: Word, 1977), 115.

[12]For his understanding of the importance of theological history, see Bernard L. Ramm, *The Pattern of Religious Authority* (Grand Rapids, Mich.: Eerdmans, 1959), 56-62.

[13]See esp. Ramm, *Evangelical Heritage*, 23-63.

[14]Ramm, *Pattern of Religious Authority*, 60.

[15]Clark H. Pinnock, "Bernard Ramm: Postfundamentalist Coming to Terms with Modernity," in Grenz, *Perspectives on Theology*, 15.

[16]Ramm's irenic tone is exemplified in *The Devil, Seven Wormwoods and God* (Waco, Tex.: Word, 1977), in which he points out what evangelicals can learn from seven modern thinkers who are generally "bad-mouthed" as the devil's "hacks."

[17]R. Albert Mohler, "Bernard Ramm: Karl Barth and the Future of American Evangelicalism," in Grenz, *Perspectives on Theology*, 26.

[18]Ramm's other interests as reflected in the books he authored include the doctrine of glorification *(Them He Glorified* [Grand Rapids, Mich.: Eerdmans, 1963]), ethics *(The Right, the Good and the Happy* [Waco, Tex.: Word, 1971]) and the contemporary controversy concerning the Holy Spirit *(Rapping about the Spirit* [Waco, Tex.: Word, 1974]).

[19]This thesis is set forth by J. Deotis Roberts, "Bernard L. Ramm: Apologetic Use of Philosophy," in Grenz, *Perspectives on Theology*, 42.

[20]Bernard L. Ramm, *The God Who Makes a Difference: A Christian Appeal to Reason* (Waco, Tex.: 1972), 15.

[21]Ibid., 16.

[22]Ibid.

[23]Bernard L. Ramm, *Problems in Christian Apologetics* (Portland, Oreg.: Western Baptist Theological Seminary, 1949).

[24]Bernard L. Ramm, *Types of Apologetic Systems: An Introductory Study to the Christian Philosophy of Religion* (Wheaton, Ill.: Van Kampen, 1953). This work was subsequently revised as *Varieties of Christian Apologetics* (Grand Rapids, Mich.: Baker, 1961).

[25]In the revised version, Ramm substitutes Calvin and Abraham Kuyper for Van Til and Carnell.

[26]Ramm, *Protestant Christian Evidences*, 33.

[27]Ibid., 7.

[28]Ramm, *Varieties of Christian Apologetics*, 13

[29]Ramm, *Protestant Christian Evidences*, 13.

[30]Ibid., 224.

[31]Ibid., 249.

[32]Ramm soon revised his appeal to prophecy and miracles. Bernard L. Ramm, "The Evidence of Prophecy and Miracles," in *Revelation and the Bible*, ed. Carl F. H. Henry (Grand Rapids, Mich.: Eerdmans, 1958), 253-63.

[33]Ibid., 263.

[34]Ramm, *God Who Makes a Difference*, 32.

[35]Ibid., 73. For the background of this certainty as lying in the concept of the *testimonium*, see Bernard L. Ramm, *The Witness of the Spirit* (Grand Rapids, Mich.: Eerdmans, 1959), 84-87.

[36]Ramm, *God Who Makes a Difference*, 73.

[37]Ramm, *Special Revelation and the Word of God* (Grand Rapids, Mich.: Eerdmans, 1961), 99.

[38]Bernard L. Ramm, *After Fundamentalism* (San Francisco: Harper and Row, 1983), 61.

[39]Ramm, *Christian View of Science and Scripture*, 8.

[40]Ibid., 9.

[41]See, e.g., ibid., 25-29.

[42]Ibid., 9.

[43]Ibid., 43.

[44]Ibid., 244-45.

[45]Ibid., 29-30. See also 43, 169, 238, 244.

[46]Ramm, *Protestant Christian Evidences,* 17-25.

[47]Ramm, *Christian View of Science and Scripture,* 76-78.

[48]See, e.g., George Marsden, *Reforming Fundamentalism: Fuller Seminary and the New Evangelicalism* (Grand Rapids, Mich.: Eerdmans, 1987), 158; James Barr, *Fundamentalism* (Philadelphia: Westminster, 1977), 94-98, 244-47.

[49]Bernard L. Ramm, *Protestant Biblical Interpretation: A Textbook for Conservative Protestants* (Boston: Wilde, 1950). This book went through two revisions, the third edition published by Baker in 1972. See also Bernard L. Ramm, "Biblical Interpretation," in *Hermeneutics* (Grand Rapids, Mich.: Baker, 1971), 5-28.

[50]Ramm, *Protestant Biblical Interpretation,* 3d ed. (Grand Rapids, Mich.: Baker, 1972), 95.

[51]Ibid., 99-101. See also Ramm, *Special Revelation and the Word of God,* 33, 36-40, 74.

[52]Ramm, *His Way Out,* 33.

[53]Bernard L. Ramm, *Offense to Reason* (San Francisco: Harper and Row, 1985), 68-69.

[54]Ibid., 72.

[55]In his final treatment of apologetic, Ramm cites the three volumes devoted to the doctrine of revelation as also related to this topic. See *God Who Makes a Difference,* 11.

[56]Ramm, *Pattern of Religious Authority,* 18.

[57]Ibid., 73-84.

[58]E.g., Ramm, *Witness of the Spirit,* 33.

[59]For Ramm's fullest treatment of the Reformation heritage on the nature of authority, see ibid., 11-27.

[60]Ramm, *Pattern of Religious Authority,* 28.

[61]Ibid., 38.

[62]Ibid., 36; *Witness of the Spirit,* 62-65. In fact, the internal witness of the Spirit can be operative in situations where there is no written word, such as through sermon, song or Christian literature. Ramm, *Witness of the Spirit,* 98-99.

[63]Ramm, *Pattern of Religious Authority,* 54.

[64]Ramm, *Witness of the Spirit,* 124-27.

[65]Ibid., 124.

[66]Ramm, *Special Revelation and the Word of God,* 120.

[67]Ramm, *Witness of the Spirit,* 125.

[68]Ibid., 126.

[69]Ibid., 107.

[70]See Ramm, *Protestant Biblical Interpretation,* 3d ed., 201-14.

[71]Bernard L. Ramm, "Welcome Green-Grass Evangelicals," *Eternity* 25 (March, 1974): 13. See also "Is Scripture Alone the 'Essence of Christianity'?" in Rogers, *Biblical Authority,* 107-23.

[72]See Bernard L. Ramm, *An Evangelical Christology: Ecumenic and Historic* (Nashville: Thomas Nelson, 1985), 202.

[73]Ramm, *Special Revelation and the Word of God,* 117.

[74]See Ramm, "Is 'Scripture Alone' the Essence of Christianity?" in Rogers, *Biblical Authority,* 122-23.

[75]Ramm, *Special Revelation and the Word of God,* 176.

[76]See, e.g., *His Way Out,* 36.

[77]Ramm, *Special Revelation and the Word of God,* 177.

[78]Ibid., 196.

[79]For a summary of Ramm's encounter with Barth, see Mohler, in Grenz, *Perspectives on Theology,* 29-37.

[80]Ramm, *Protestant Christian Evidences,* 180.

[81]For Ramm's own account of the influence of Barth on his thinking, see Bernard Ramm, "Helps from Karl Barth," in *How Karl Barth Changed My Mind,* ed. Donald K. McKim (Grand Rapids, Mich.: Eerdmans, 1986), 121-25.

[82]Ramm, "Biblical Interpretation," in *Hermeneutics,* 28.

[83]Ramm, *God Who Makes a Difference,* 12.

[84]Ramm, *After Fundamentalism,* 14.

[85]Ramm, *Special Revelation and the Word of God,* 14.

[86]Ibid., 141, 145.

[87]Ibid., 17.

[88]Ibid., 21.

[89]William R. Herzog II, "A Commendation of Professor Bernard L. Ramm," in Grenz, *Perspectives on Theology,* 8.

[90]Ramm, *Evangelical Heritage,* 135.

[91]Bernard Ramm, *The Christian College in the Twentieth Century* (Grand Rapids, Mich.: Eerdmans, 1963), 78.

[92]Ramm, *Special Revelation and the Word of God,* 23-24.

[93]Ibid., 24.

Bibliography

Achtemeier, Elizabeth. "The Impossible Possibility: Evaluating the Feminist Approach to Bible and Theology." *Interpretation* 42 (January 1988).

Aiken, Henry. *The Age of Ideology.* New York: Mentor Books, 1956.

Altizer, Thomas J. J. *The Gospel of Christian Atheism.* Philadelphia: Westminster, 1966.

Ashcraft, Morris. *Rudolf Bultmann.* The Makers of the Modern Theological Mind. Edited by Bob E. Patterson. Waco, Tex.: Word, 1972.

Auerbach, Erich. *Mimesis.* Garden City, N.Y.: Doubleday, Anchor Books, 1957.

Bakker, J. T., et al. *Septuagesimo Anno: Festschrift for G. C. Berkhouwer.* Kampen, the Netherlands: Kok, 1973.

Baltazar, Eulalio R. *God Within Process.* Paramus, N.J.: Newman, 1970.

Barr, James. *Fundamentalism.* Philadelphia: Westminster, 1977.

Barth, Karl. *Anselm: Fides Quarens Intellectum.* Translated by Ian W. Robertson. London: SCM, 1960.

———. *Church Dogmatics* I/1, *The Doctrine of the Word of God,* Part 1. Translated by G. W. Bromiley. Ediburgh: T. & T. Clark, 1975.

———. *Church Dogmatics* II/1, *The Doctrine of God,* Part 1. Translated by T. H. L. Parker et al. Edinburgh: T. & T. Clark, 1957.

———. *Church Dogmatics* II/2, *The Doctrine of God,* Part 2. Translated by G. W. Bromiley et al. Edinburgh: T. & T. Clark, 1957.

———. *Church Dogmatics,* III/2, *The Doctrine of Creation,* Part 2. Translated by G. W. Bromiley et al. Edinburgh: T. & T. Clark, 1960.

———. *Church Dogmatics,* III/3, *The Doctrine of Creation,* Part 3. Translated by G. W. Bromiley and R. J. Ehrlich. Edinburgh: T. & T. Clark, 1960.

———. *The Epistle to the Romans.* Translated by Edwyn C. Hoskyns. London: Oxford University Press, 1933.

———. *God, Gospel and Grace.* Translated by James S. McNab. *Scottish Journal of Theology Occasional Papers No. 8.* Edinburgh: Oliver and Boyd, 1959.

———. *The Humanity of God.* Translated by Thomas Wieser and John Thomas. Richmond: John Knox, 1960.

————. *The Theology of Schleiermacher.* Grand Rapids, Mich.: Eerdmans, 1982.

Bauer, P. T. "Western Guilt and Third World Poverty." *Commentary* (January 1976).

Becker, Carl L. *The Heavenly City of the Eighteenth-century Philosophers.* New Haven: Yale University Press, 1932.

Berger, Peter L. *Rumor of Angels.* Garden City, N.Y.: Doubleday, 1969.

Bergson, Henri. *An Introduction to Metaphysics.* rev. ed. Translated by T. E. Hulme. Indianapolis: Bobbs-Merrill, 1955.

Berkouwer, G. C. *The Triumph of Grace in the Theology of Karl Barth.* Translated by Harry R. Boer. Grand Rapids, Mich.: Eerdmans, 1956.

Berlin, Isaiah. *The Age of Enlightenment.* New York: Mentor Books, 1956.

Bethge, Eberhard, "The Challenge of Dietrich Bonhoeffer's Life and Theology." *The Chicago Theological Seminary Register* (February 1961).

————. *Costly Grace: An Introduction to Dietrich Bonhoeffer.* San Francisco: Harper and Row, 1979.

————. "Dietrich Bonhoeffer: Person and Work," in *Die mündige Welt.*

————. *Dietrich Bonhoeffer: Theologe, Christ, Zeitgenosse.* Munich: Christian Kaiser Verlag, 1967.

————. *Dietrich Bonhoeffer: Theologian, Christian, Contemporary.* Translated by Eric Mosbacher. Edited by Edwin Robertson. London: Collins, 1970.

Bingham, June. *Courage to Change.* New York: Charles Scribner's Sons, 1961.

Bloesch, Donald G. *The Battle for the Trinity: The Debate Over Inclusive God-Language.* Ann Arbor: Servant Publications, 1985.

Bockmuehl, Klaus. *The Unreal God of Modern Theology.* Colorado Springs: Helmers and Howard, 1988.

Bonhoeffer, Dietrich. *Act and Being.* Translated by Bernard Noble. New York: Harper and Row, 1961.

————. *The Communion of Saints: A Dogmatic Inquiry into the Sociology of the Church.* Translated by R. Gregor Smith. New York: Harper and Row, 1963.

————. *Ethics.* Translated by Neville Horton Smith. New York: Macmillan, Macmillan paperback edition, 1965.

————. *Letters and Papers from Prison.* Translated by Eberhard Bethge. London: Collins, Fontana Books, 1953.

————. *No Rusty Swords: Letters, Lectures and Notes, 1928—1936.* Translated by Edwin H. Robertson and John Bowden. New York: Harper and Row, 1965.

Braaten, Carl E. "Toward a Theology of Hope." In *The New Theology.* Edited by Martin E. Marty and Dean G. Peerman. New York: Macmillan, 1968.

Bracken, Joseph A. "The Two Process Theologies: A Reappraisal." *Theological Studies* 46/1 (1985).

Brown, Colin. *Philosophy and the Christian Faith.* London: Tyndale, 1968.

Brown, D. MacKenzie, ed. *Ultimate Concern: Tillich in Dialogue.* New York and Evanston: Harper and Row, 1956.

Brown, Delwin, Ralph E. James, Jr., and Gene Reeves, eds. *Process Philosophy and Christian Thought.* Indianapolis: Bobbs-Merrill, 1971. (Hereafter cited as Brown, James and Reeves.)

Brown, Robert McAfee. *Gustavo Gutiérrez: An Introduction to Liberation Theology.* Maryknoll, N.Y.: Orbis, 1990.

————. *Theology in a New Key: Responding to Liberation Themes.* Philadelphia: Westminster, 1978.

Brunner, Emil. *Dogmatics, Vol. I: The Christian Doctrine of God.* Translated by Olive Wyon. London: Lutterworth, 1949.

————. *Dogmatics, Vol. II: The Christian Doctrine of Creation and Redemption.* Translated by Olive

Wyon. London: Lutterworth, 1952.

————. *Dogmatics, Vol. III: The Christian Doctrine of the Church, Faith, and the Consummation.* Translated by David Cairns and T. H. L. Parker. London: Lutterworth, 1962.

————. *Natural Theology, Comprising 'Nature and Grace' and the Reply 'No!' by Dr. Karl Barth.* Translated by Peter Fraenkel. London: Geoffrey Bles, The Centenary Press, 1946.

————. *Truth as Encounter.* Translated by Amandus Loos, David Cairns and T. H. L. Parker. London: SCM, 1964.

Buber, Martin. *I and Thou.* Translated by Ronald Gregor Smith. New York: Charles Scribner's Sons, 1958.

Buckley, Michael J. "Within the Holy Mystery." In *A World of Grace: An Introduction to the Themes and Foundations of Karl Rahner's Theology.* Edited by Leo J. O'Donovan. New York: Seabury, 1980.

Bultmann, Rudolf. *Existence and Faith.* Translated by Schubert M. Ogden. Cleveland: Meridian, 1960.

————. *Faith and Understanding.* Edited by Robert W. Funk. Translated by Louise Pettibone Smith. New York: Harper and Row, 1969.

————. *Jesus and the Word.* New York: Charles Scribner's Sons, 1958.

————. *Jesus Christ and Mythology.* New York: Charles Scribner's Sons, 1958.

————. *Kerygma and Myth.* New York: Harper and Row, 1961.

————. *The Presence of Eternity: History and Eschatology.* New York: Harper and Brothers, 1957.

————. *Primitive Christianity in its Contemporary Setting.* New York: Meridian, 1957.

————. *The Theology of Rudolf Bultmann.* Edited by Charles W. Kegley. New York: Harper and Row, 1966.

————. *Theology of the New Testament.* New York: Charles Scribner's Sons, 1951.

Burnet, John. *Early Greek Philosophy.* 4th ed. New York: Macmillan, 1930.

Busch, Eberhard. *Karl Barth, His Life from Letters and Autobiographical Texts.* Translated by John Bowden. Philadelphia: Fortress, 1976.

Callahan, Daniel, ed. *The Secular City Debate.* New York: Macmillan, 1966.

Carnell, Edward J. *The Theology of Reinhold Niebuhr.* Grand Rapids, Mich.: Eerdmans, 1951.

Carr, Anne E. *Transforming Grace: Christian Tradition and Women's Experience.* San Francisco: Harper and Row, 1988.

Cherbury, *De Religione Gentilium.* 1663.

Cleage, Albert B., Jr. *The Black Messiah.* New York: Sheed and Ward, Search Books, 1969.

Clements, Keith W. *Friedrich Schleiermacher, Pioneer of Modern Theology.* London and San Francisco: Collins, 1987.

Cobb, John B., Jr. *Beyond Dialogue: Towards a Mutual Transformation of Christianity and Buddhism.* Philadelphia: Fortress, 1982.

————. *Christ in a Pluralistic Age.* Philadelphia: Westminster, 1975.

————. *A Christian Natural Theology.* Philadelphia: Westminster, 1965.

————. *God and the World.* Philadelphia: Westminster, 1965.

————. *Process Theology as Political Theology.* Philadelphia: Westminster, 1982.

Cobb, John B., Jr., and Charles Birch. *The Liberation of Life.* Cambridge: Cambridge University Press, 1981.

Cobb, John B., Jr., and David Ray Griffin. *Process Theology.* Philadelphia: Westminster, 1976.

Cobb, John B., Jr., and Herman E. Daly. *For the Common Good.* Boston: Beacon, 1989.

Comstock, Gary L. "Two Types of Narrative Theology." *Journal of the American Academy of Religion* 55/4 (1987).

_____ . "Truth or Meaning: Ricoeur versus Frei on Biblical Narrative." *Journal of Religion* 66/2 (1986).

Cone, James H. *Black Theology and Black Power*. New York: Seabury, 1969.

_____ . *A Black Theology of Liberation*. Philadelphia: Lippincott, 1970.

_____ . *For My People*. Maryknoll, N.Y.: Orbis, 1986.

_____ . *God of the Oppressed*. New York: Seabury, 1975.

_____ . *My Soul Looks Back*. Maryknoll, N.Y.: Orbis, 1986.

_____ . *Speaking the Truth*. Grand Rapids, Mich.: Eerdmans, 1986.

_____ . *The Spirituals and the Blues*. New York: Seabury, 1972.

Conyers, A. J. *God, Hope, and History: Jürgen Moltmann and the Christian Concept of History*. Macon, Ga.: Mercer University Press, 1988.

Cox, Harvey. "Ernst Bloch and the 'Pull of the Future.' " In *The New Theology*. Edited by Martin E. Marty and Dean G. Peerman. New York: Macmillan, 1968.

_____ . *The Feast of Fools*. Cambridge, Mass.: Harvard University Press, 1969.

_____ . *God's Revolution and Man's Responsibility*. Valley Forge, Pa.: Judson, 1965.

_____ . *Just As I Am*. In *Journeys of Faith*. Edited by Robert A. Rains. Nashville: Abingdon, 1983.

_____ . *Many Mansions*. Boston: Beacon, 1988.

_____ . *On Not Leaving It to the Snake*. New York: Macmillan, 1968.

_____ . *Religion in the Secular City*. New York: Simon and Schuster, 1984.

_____ . *The Secular City*. New York: Macmillan, 1965.

_____ . *"The Secular City* 25 Years Later." *Christian Century* 107/32 (November 7, 1990).

_____ . *The Seduction of the Spirit*. New York: Simon and Schuster, 1973.

Crites, Stephen. "The Narrative Quality of Experience." *Journal of the American Academy of Religion* 39/3 (September 1971).

Curran, Rosemary T. "Whitehead's Notion of the Person and the Saving of the Past." *Scottish Journal of Theology* 36/3 (1983).

Davies, D. R. *Reinhold Niebuhr: Prophet from America*. New York: Macmillan, 1948.

Davis, John Jefferson. "Tillich—Accurate Aims, Alien Assumptions." *Christianity Today* 20/23 (1976).

de Santillana, Giorgio. *The Age of Adventure*. New York: New American Library of World Literature, 1956.

DeWolf, L. Harold. *The Religious Revolt Against Reason*. New York: Harper and Row, 1949.

Ebeling, Gerhard. *Word and Faith*. Translated by James W. Leitch. London: SCM, 1960.

Edwards, David L. "Looking Forward." *Student World* 59 (1966).

Fackre, Gabriel. *The Christian Story*. Rev. ed. Grand Rapids, Mich.: Eerdmans, 1984.

Fennell, William O. "The Theology of True Secularity." *Theology Today* 21 (July 1964). Reprinted in *The New Theology*. Edited by Martin E. Marty and Dean G. Peerman. New York: Macmillan, 1968.

Ferm, Deane William. *Contemporary American Theologies: A Critical Survey*. New York: Seabury, 1981.

_____ . *Profiles in Liberation*. Mystic, Conn.: Twenty-Third Publications, 1988.

Fiorenza, Elisabeth Schüssler. *In Memory of Her: A Feminist Reconstruction of Christian Origins*. New York: Crossroad, 1984.

Ford, Lewis S. "Divine Persuasion and the Triumph of Good." *The Christian Scholar* 50/3 (Fall 1967): 235-50. Reprinted in Brown, James and Reeves.

Fowler, James W. *Trajectories in Faith*. Nashville: Abingdon, 1980.

Frankena, William. *Ethics*. Englewood Cliffs, N.J.: Prentice-Hall, 1973.

Frei, Hans. *The Eclipse of Biblical Narrative: A Study in Eighteenth and Nineteenth Century Hermeneutics.* New Haven: Yale University Press, 1974.

Friedrich, Carl J. "Introduction." In G. W. F. Hegel, *The Philosophy of Hegel.* Edited by Carl J. Friedrich. New York: Random House, 1954.

Fuller, Daniel. *Easter Faith and History.* Grand Rapids, Mich.: Eerdmans, 1965.

Gadamer, Hans-Georg. *Truth and Method.* New York: Seabury, 1975.

Gerrish, Brian. *A Prince of the Church: Schleiermacher and the Beginnings of Modern Theology.* Philadelphia: Fortress, 1984.

Gilkey, Langdon. *Naming the Whirlwind.* Indianapolis: Bobbs-Merrill, 1969.

Goldberg, Michael. *Theology and Narrative.* Nashville: Abingdon, 1982.

Gonzales, Justo L. *A History of Christian Thought.* Nashville, Abingdon, 1975.

Gragg, Alan. *Charles Hartshorne.* The Makers of the Modern Theological Mind. Edited by Bob E. Patterson. Waco, Tex.: Word, 1973.

Grenz, Stanley J., ed. *Perspectives on Theology in the Contemporary World: Essays in Honor of Bernard Ramm.* Macon, Ga.: Mercer Univ. Press, 1990.

———. *Reason for Hope: The Systematic Theology of Wolfhart Pannenberg.* New York: Oxford, 1990.

Gruenler, Royce G. "Reflections on the School of Process Theism." *TSF Bulletin* 7/3 (1984).

Gutiérrez, Gustavo. *The Power of the Poor in History.* Translated by Robert R. Barr. Maryknoll, N.Y.: Orbis, 1983.

———. *The Theology of Liberation.* Rev. ed. Translated and edited by Sister Caridad Inda and John Eagleson. Maryknoll, N.Y.: Orbis, 1988.

Hall, Thor. *Systematic Theology Today: State of the Art in North America.* Washington, D.C.: University Press of America, 1978.

Hamilton, Kenneth. *Life in One's Stride.* Grand Rapids, Mich.: Eerdmans, 1968.

———. *Revolt Against Heaven.* Grand Rapids, Mich.: Eerdmans, 1965.

———. *The System and the Gospel, A Critique of Paul Tillich.* New York: Macmillan, 1963.

Hamilton, William. "American Theology, Radicalism and the Death of God." In Thomas J. J. Altizer and William Hamilton, *Radical Theology and the Death of God.* Indianapolis: Bobbs-Merrill, 1966.

———. *On Taking God Out of the Dictionary.* New York: McGraw-Hill, 1974.

Hampshire, Stuart. *The Age of Reason: 17th Century Philosophers.* New York: The New American Library of World Literature, 1956.

Harland, Gordon. *The Thought of Reinhold Niebuhr.* New York: Oxford, 1960.

Harnack, Adolf. *What Is Christianity?* Translated by Thomas Bailey Saunders. New York: G. P. Putnam's Sons, 1901.

Hartshorne, Charles. *Man's Vision of God and the Logic of Theism.* Hamden, Conn.: Archon Books, 1964.

Hatt, Harold E. *Encountering Truth: A New Understanding of How Revelation Yields Doctrine.* Nashville: Abingdon, 1966.

Hauerwas, Stanley. *The Community of Character.* Notre Dame: University of Notre Dame Press, 1981.

———. *The Peaceable Kingdom.* Notre Dame: University of Notre Dame Press, 1983.

———. "The Testament of Friends." *Christian Century* 107/7 (February 28, 1990).

———. *Truthfulness and Tragedy.* Notre Dame: University of Notre Dame Press, 1977.

———. *Vision and Virtue.* Notre Dame: Fides Publishers, 1974.

Hefner, Philip. "Albrecht Ritschl: An Introduction." In *Three Essays.* Philadelphia: Fortress, 1972.

———. *Faith and the Vitalities of History.* New York: Harper and Row, 1966.

Hegel, G. W. F. *Lectures on the Philosophy of Religion*. Vol. I. Translated by E. B. Speirs and J. Burden Sanderson. Edited by E. B. Speirs. New York: The Humanities Press, 1962.

———. *Lectures on the Philosophy of Religion: Together with a Work on the Proofs of the Existence of God*. Translated by Rev. E. B. Speirs and J. Burden Sanderson. London: Routledge and Kegan Paul, 1962.

———. *The Phenomenology of Mind*. Translated by J. B. Baillie. New York: Harper and Row, 1967.

———. *Philosophy of Mind: Being Part Three of the Encyclopedia of the Philosophical Sciences*. Translated by William Wallace, together with the Zusatze in Boumann's Text, translated by A. V. Miller. London: Oxford, 1971.

———. Preface to *The Philosophy of Right and Law*. In *The Philosophy of Hegel*. Edited by Carl J. Friedrich. New York: Random House, 1953.

———. *The Science of Logic (The First Part of the Encyclopedia of the Philosophical Sciences)*. Translated by William Wallace. Oxford: Clarendon Press, 1892. Wallace entitled his translation *The Logic of Hegel*.

Henry, Carl F. H. *After Fundamentalism*. San Francisco: Harper and Row, 1983.

———. *Aspects of Christian Social Ethics*. Grand Rapids, Mich.: Eerdmans, 1964.

———. "Between Barth and Bultmann." *Christianity Today* 5/6 (May 8, 1961).

———. *The Christian Mindset in a Secular Society*. Portland, Ore.: Multnomah, 1984.

———. *Christian Personal Ethics*. Grand Rapids, Mich.: Eerdmans, 1957.

———. "The Concerns and Considerations of Carl H. Henry." *Christianity Today* 25/5 (March 13, 1981).

———. *Confessions of a Theologian: An Autobiography*. Waco, Tex.: Word, 1986.

———. "Crosscurrents in Contemporary Theology." In *Jesus of Nazareth: Savior and Lord*. Edited by Carl Henry. Grand Rapids, Mich.: Eerdmans, 1966.

———. "The Deterioration of Barth's Defenses." *Christianity Today* 9/1 (October 9, 1964).

———. *Evangelical Responsibility in Contemporary Theology*. Grand Rapids, Mich.: Eerdmans, Pathway Books, 1957.

———. *Evangelicals in Search of Identity*. Waco, Tex.: Word, 1976.

———. *Fifty Years of Protestant Theology*. Boston: W. A. Wilde, 1950.

———. "The Fortunes of Theology." *Christianity Today* 16/18 (June 9, 1972).

———. *Frontiers in Modern Theology*. Chicago: Moody, 1964.

———. *God, Revelation and Authority*. 6 vols. Waco, Tex.: Word, 1976-1983.

———. *The God Who Shows Himself*. Waco, Tex.: Word, 1966.

———. "Narrative Theology: An Evangelical Appraisal." *Trinity Journal* 8 (1987).

———. "The Pale Ghost of Barth." *Christianity Today* 15/10 (February 12, 1971).

———. *A Plea for Evangelical Demonstration*. Grand Rapids, Mich.: Baker, 1971.

———. *The Protestant Dilemma*. Grand Rapids, Mich.: Eerdmans, 1949.

———. "Reaction and Realignment." *Christianity Today* 20/20 (July 2, 1976).

———. *Remaking the Modern Mind*. Grand Rapids, Mich.: Eerdmans, 1946.

———. *The Uneasy Conscience of Modern Fundamentalism*. Grand Rapids, Mich.: Eerdmans, 1947.

———. "Wintertime in European Theology." *Christianity Today* 5/5 (December 5, 1960).

Hesselink, I. John. "Emil Brunner: A Centennial Perspective." *The Christian Century* (December 13, 1989).

Hoffman, Hans. *The Theology of Reinhold Niebuhr*. Translated by Louise Pettibone Smith. New York: Charles Scribner's Sons, 1956.

Hordern, William. *Introduction*. Vol. 1 in *New Directions in Theology Today*. Edited by William

Hordern. Philadelphia: Westminster, 1966.

Hume, David. Essays: *Providence and a Future State* (1748), *Dialogues Concerning Natural Religion* (1779), and *Natural History of Religion* (1757).

Huxley, Julian. "Introduction." In Pierre Teilhard de Chardin, *The Phenomenon of Man*. New York: Harper and Row, Harper Torchbook edition, 1961.

Ice, Jackson Lee, and John J. Carey, eds. *The Death of God Debate*. Philadelphia: Westminster, 1967.

Imhof, Paul, and Hubert Biallowons, eds. *Karl Rahner in Dialogue: Conversations and Interviews, 1965-1982*. Translated by Harvey D. Egan. New York: Crossroad, 1986.

James, Richmond. *Ritschl: A Reappraisal. A Study in Systematic Theology*. London: Collins, 1978.

Jersild, Paul. "Reinhold Niebuhr: Continuing the Assessment." *Dialogue* 22/4 (Fall 1983).

Jewett, Paul King. *Emil Brunner's Concept of Revelation*. London: James Clarke, 1954.

Johnson, Benton. "Taking Stock: Reflections on the End of Another Era." *Journal of the Scientific Study of Religion* 21/3 (September 1982).

Jonas, Hans. "Is Faith Still Possible?" *Harvard Theological Journal* 75/1 (1982).

Jüngel, Eberhard. *Karl Barth, A Theological Legacy*. Translated by Garrett E. Paul. Philadelphia: Westminster, 1986.

Kähler, Martin. *The So-Called Historical Jesus and the Historic Biblical Christ*. Translated and edited by Carl E. Braaten. Philadelphia: Fortress, 1964.

Kant, Immanuel. *Critique of Judgement*. Translated by J. H. Bernard. New York: Hafner, 1968.

————. *Critique of Pure Reason*. Translated by Norman Kemp Smith. New York: St. Martin's, 1929.

————. *Foundations of the Metaphysics of Morals* and *What Is Enlightenment?* New York: Liberal Arts Press, 1959.

————. *Fundamental Principles of the Metaphysic of Morals*. Translated by Thomas K. Abbott. Indianapolis: Bobbs-Merrill, 1949.

————. *Prolegomena to Any Future Metaphysics*. Translated and edited by Paul Carus. Illinois: Open Court, 1967.

————. *Religion within the Limits of Reason Alone*. New York: Harper and Row, 1960.

Kegley, Charles W., and Robert W. Bretall, eds. *Reinhold Niebuhr: His Religious, Social, and Political Thought*. Vol. 2 of The Library of Living Theology. New York: Macmillan, 1961.

Kermode, Frank. *The Sense of an Ending: Studies in the Theory of Fiction*. New York: Oxford, 1967.

Kierkegaard, Søren. *Concluding Unscientific Postscript*. Translated by David F. Swenson and Walter Lowrie. Princeton, N.J.: Princeton University Press, Princeton Paperback edition, 1968.

————. *Philosophical Fragments*. Translated by David F. Swenson. Princeton, N.J.: Princeton University Press, 1962.

King, Rachel Hadley. *The Omission of the Holy Spirit from Reinhold Niebuhr's Theology*. New York: Philosophical Library, 1964.

Kirk, G. S., and J. E. Raven. *The Presocratic Philosophers*. Corrected reprint. Cambridge: Cambridge University Press, 1963.

Kirk, J. Andrew. *Liberation Theology: An Evangelical View from the Third World*. Atlanta: John Knox, 1979.

Kliever, Lonnie D. *The Shattered Spectrum*. Atlanta: John Knox, 1981.

Klooster, Fred H. "Aspects of Historical Method in Pannenberg's Theology." In *Septuagesimo Anno: Festschrift for G. C. Berkouwer*. Edited by J. T. Bakker et al. Kampen, The Netherlands: Kok, 1973.

Küng, Hans. *Does God Exist? An Answer for Today*. Translated by Edward Quinn. Garden City, N.Y.: Doubleday, 1980.

————. *The Incarnation of God*. New York: Crossroad, 1987.

———. *Infallible? An Inquiry.* Translated by Edward Quinn. Garden City, N.Y.: Doubleday, 1971.

———. *Justification: The Doctrine of Karl Barth and a Catholic Reflection.* Translated by Thomas Collins et al. New York: Thomas Nelson & Sons, 1964.

———. *Reforming the Church Today: Keeping Hope Alive.* Translated by Peter Heinegg et al. New York: Crossroad, 1990.

———. *Theology for the Third Millennium: An Ecumenical View.* Translated by Peter Heinegg. New York and London: Doubleday, 1988.

LaCugna, Catherine Mowry. *The Theological Methodology of Hans Küng.* Chico, Calif.: Scholar's Press, 1982.

Lafleur, Laurence J., trans. René Descartes, *Discourse on Method and Meditations.* Indianapolis: Bobbs-Merrill, 1960.

Lane, Dermot A. *Foundations for a Social Theology: Praxis, Process and Salvation.* New York and Ramsey, N.J.: Paulist, 1984.

Lauer, Quentin. *Hegel's Concept of God.* Albany: SUNY, 1982.

Leibholz, G. "Memoir." In Dietrich Bonhoeffer, *The Cost of Discipleship.* Translated by R. H. Fuller. New York: Macmillan, 1948.

Lindbeck, George. *The Nature of Doctrine: Religion and Theology in a Postliberal Age.* Philadelphia: Westminster, 1984.

Livingston, James C. *Modern Christian Thought—From the Enlightenment to Vatican II.* New York: Macmillan, 1971.

Lowe, Victor. *Process and Reality, Understanding Whitehead.* Baltimore: Johns Hopkins University Press, 1962.

McCarty, Doran. *Teilhard de Chardin.* Makers of the Modern Theological Mind. Edited by Bob E. Patterson. Waco, Tex.: Word, 1976.

McClendon, James William, Jr. *Biography as Theology.* Nashville: Abingdon, 1974, 1980.

———. *Ethics: Systematic Theology.* Vol. I. Nashville: Abingdon, 1986.

McGiffert, Arthur Cushman. *Protestant Thought Before Kant.* London: Duckworth, 1911.

Mackintosh, Hugh Ross. *Types of Modern Theology, Schleiermacher to Barth.* New York: Charles Scribner's Sons, 1937.

Macquarrie, John. *An Existentialist Theology.* London: SCM, 1955.

———. *God and Secularity.* Vol. 3 of *New Directions in Theology Today.* Edited by William Hordern. Philadelphia: Westminster, 1967.

Marsden, George. *Reforming Fundamentalism: Fuller Seminary and the New Evangelicalism.* Grand Rapids, Mich.: Eerdmans, 1987.

Marty, Martin E., and Dean G. Peerman. "Beyond the Secular Chastened Religion." In *The New Theology.* Edited by Martin E. Marty and Dean G. Peerman. New York: Macmillan, 1964.

Marty, Martin E., and Dean G. Peerman, eds. *The New Theology.* 10 vols. New York: Macmillan, 1964-1973.

May, Benjamin. *The Negro's God as Reflected in His Literature.* New York: Russell and Russell, 1968.

Meeks, Douglas. *Origins of the Theology of Hope.* Philadelphia: Fortress, 1974.

Meland, Berd E. *The Realities of Faith.* New York: Oxford, 1962.

Metz, Johann Baptist. *Faith in History & Society, Toward a Practical Fundamental Theology.* Translated by David Smith. New York: Seabury, 1980.

Michaelson, G. E., Jr. "Moral Regeneration and Divine Aid in Kant." *Religious Studies* 25/3 (September 1989).

Míguez Bonino, José. *Christians and Marxists: The Mutual Challenge to Revolution.* Grand Rapids,

Mich.: Eerdmans, 1976.

———— . *Doing Theology in a Revolutionary Situation.* Philadelphia: Fortress, 1975.

———— . *Toward a Christian Political Ethic.* Philadelphia: Fortress, 1983.

Mohler, R. Albert. "Carl Ferdinand Howard Henry." In *Baptist Thinkers.* Edited by Timothy George and David S. Dockery. Nashville: Broadman, 1990.

———— . *Conversations with Carl Henry: Christianity for Today.* Lewiston, N.Y.: Edwin Mellon, 1986.

———— . "Evangelical Theology and Karl Barth: Representative Models of Response." Ph.D. dissertation, Southern Baptist Theological Seminary, 1989.

Moltmann, Jürgen. *Anfänge der dialektischen Theologie.* 2 vols. Munich: Christian Kaiser Verlag, 1962, 1963.

———— . "An Autobiographical Note." In A. J. Conyers, *God, Hope, and History: Jürgen Moltmann and the Christian Concept of History.* Macon, Ga.: Mercer University Press, 1988.

———— . *The Crucified God.* Translated by R. A. Wilson and John Bowden. New York: Harper and Row, 1974.

———— . "The 'Crucified God': God and the Trinity Today." In *New Questions on God.* Edited by Johannes Metz. New York: Herder & Herder, 1972.

———— . *The Experiment Hope.* Translated by M. Douglas Meeks. Philadelphia: Fortress, 1975.

———— . "The Fellowship of the Holy Spirit—Trinitarian Pneumatology." *Scottish Journal of Theology* 37.

———— . *God in Creation: A New Theology of Creation and the Spirit of God.* Translated by Margaret Kohl. San Francisco: Harper and Row, 1985.

———— . "Hope Without Faith: An Eschatological Humanism without God." In *Is God Dead?* Vol. 16 of *Concilium.* Edited by Johannes Metz. Translated by John Cummings. New York: Paulist, 1966.

———— . "Theology as Eschatology." In *The Future of Hope, Theology as Eschatology.* Edited by Frederick Herzog. New York: Herder & Herder, 1970.

———— . *Theology of Hope.* Translated by James W. Leitsch. New York: Harper and Row, 1967.

———— . *Theology Today.* Philadelphia: Trinity, 1988.

———— . *The Trinity and the Kingdom.* Translated by Margaret Kohl. San Francisco: Harper and Row, 1981.

———— . "Why Am I a Christian?" In *Experiences of God.* Philadephia: Fortress, 1980.

Momose, Peter Fumiaki. *Kreuzestheologie: Eine Auseinandersetzung mit Jürgen Moltmann.* Freiburg: Herder, 1978.

Mooney, Christopher F. *Teilhard de Chardin and the Mystery of Christ.* New York: Harper and Row, 1964.

Morse, Christopher. *The Logic of Promise in Moltmann's Theology.* Philadelphia: Fortress, 1979.

Mueller, David L. *An Introduction to the Theology of Albrecht Ritschl.* Philadelphia: Westminster, 1969.

Nelson, Paul. *Narrative and Morality: A Theological Inquiry.* University Park, Pa.: Pennsylvania State University Press, 1987.

Neuhaus, Richard John. "Wolfhart Pannenberg: Portrait of a Theologian." In Wolfhart Pannenberg, *Theology and the Kingdom of God.* Philadelphia: Westminster, 1969.

Neusch, Marcel. *The Sources of Modern Atheism: One Hundred Years of Debate Over God.* Translated by Matthew J. O'Connell. New York: Paulist, 1982.

Niebuhr, H. Richard. *The Kingdom of God in America.* New York: Harper and Row, Harper Torchbook edition, 1959.

———— . *The Meaning of Revelation.* New York: Macmillan, 1946.

Niebuhr, Reinhold. *Beyond Tragedy*. New York: Charles Scribner's Sons, 1937.

————. *The Children of Light and the Children of Darkness*. New York: Charles Scribner's Sons, 1944, 1960.

————. *Christian Realism and Political Problems*. New York: Charles Scribner's Sons, 1953.

————. *Christianity and Power Politics*. New York: Charles Scribner's Sons, 1940.

————. *Does Civilization Need Religion?* New York: Macmillan, 1928.

————. *Faith and History*. New York: Charles Scribner's Sons, 1949.

————. *Faith and Politics*. Edited by Ronald H. Stone. New York: George Braziller, 1968.

————. "Intellectual Autobiography." In *Reinhold Niebuhr: His Religious, Social, and Political Thought*. Vol. 2 of *The Library of Living Theology*, edited by Charles W. Kegley and Robert W. Bretall. New York: Macmillan, 1961.

————. *Justice and Mercy*. Edited by Ursula M. Niebuhr. New York: Harper and Row, 1974.

————. *Man's Nature and His Communities*. New York: Charles Scribner's Sons, 1965.

————. *Moral Man and Immoral Society*. New York: Charles Scribner's Sons, 1932.

————. *The Nature and Destiny of Man*. New York: Charles Scribner's Sons, Scribner Library edition, 1964.

————. *The Self and the Dramas of History*. New York: Charles Scribner's Sons, 1955.

Niebuhr, Richard R. *Schleiermacher on Christ and Religion*. New York: Scribner, n.d.

Nowell, Robert. *A Passion for Truth: Hans Küng and His Theology*. New York: Crossroad, 1981.

O'Donnell, John J. *Trinity and Temporality, The Christian Doctrine of God in the Light of Process Theology and the Theology of Hope*. Oxford: Oxford University Press, 1983.

Oddie, William. *What Will Happen to God? Feminism and the Reconstruction of Christian Belief*. London: SPCK, 1984.

Ogden, Schubert. "Toward A New Theism." Revised from "Love Unbounded: The Doctrine of God." *The Perkins School of Theology Journal* 19/3 (Spring 1966). Reprinted in Brown, James and Reeves.

Ogletree, Thomas W. "A Christological Assessment of Dipolar Theism." *The Journal of Religion* 47/2 (April 1967). Reprinted in Brown, James and Reeves.

Olson, Roger E. "Trinity and Eschatology: The Historical Being of God in Jürgen Moltmann and Wolfhart Pannenberg." *Scottish Journal of Theology* 36 (1983).

————. "Wolfhart Pannenberg's Doctrine of the Trinity." *Scottish Journal of Theology* 43 (1990).

Ott, Heinrich. *Reality and Faith: The Theological Legacy of Dietrich Bonhoeffer*. Translated by Alex A. Morrison. Philadelphia: Fortress, 1972.

Pannenberg, Wolfhart. *Anthropology in Theological Perspective*. Translated by Matthew J. O'Connell. Philadelphia: Westminster, 1985.

————. *The Apostles' Creed in the Light of Today's Questions*. Translated by Margaret Kohl. Philadelphia: Westminster, 1972.

————. *Basic Questions in Theology*. Translated by George H. Kelm. 2 vols. Philadelphia: Fortress, 1971.

————. "Christianity, Marxism, and Liberation Theology." *Christian Scholar's Review* 18/3 (March 1989).

————. *The Church*. Translated by Keith Crim. Philadelphia: Westminster, 1983.

————. "The Doctrine of Creation and Modern Science." *East Asia Journal of Theology* 4 (1986).

————. *Faith and Reality*. Translated by John Maxwell. Philadelphia: Westminster, 1977.

————. "The God of History." *Cumberland Seminarian* 19 (Winter/Spring 1981).

————. "God's Presence in History." *Christian Century* 98 (March 11, 1981).

———— . *The Idea of God and Human Freedom.* Translated by R. A. Wilson. Philadelphia: Westminster, 1973.

———— . *Introduction to Systematic Theology.* Grand Rapids, Mich.: Eerdmans, 1991.

———— . *Jesus—God and Man.* 2d ed. Translated by Lewis L. Wilkins and Duane A. Priebe. Philadelphia: Westminster, 1977.

———— . "A Liberal Logos Christology: The Christology of John Cobb." In *John Cobb's Theology in Process.* Edited by David Ray Griffin and Thomas J. J. Altizer. Philadelphia: Westminster, 1977.

———— . *Revelation As History* [with Rolf Rendtorff, Trutz Rendtorff and Ulrich Wilkens]. Translated by David Granskow. New York: Macmillan, 1968 [German ed., 1961].

———— . "Spirit and Mind." In *Mind in Nature,* edited by Richard Q. Elvee. Nobel Conference 17. New York: Harper and Row, 1982.

———— . "Die Subjektivität Gottes und die Trinitätslehre." *Grundfragen systematischer Theologie, Band 2.* Göttingen: Vandenhoek & Ruprecht, 1977.

———— . "Theological Questions to Scientists." *Zygon* 16 (1981).

———— . "Die Theologie und die neuen Fragen nach Intersubjektivität, Gesellschaft, und religiöser Gemeinschaft." *Archivio di Filosofia* 54 (1986).

———— . *Theology and the Kingdom of God.* Edited by Richard John Neuhaus. Philadelphia: Westminster, 1969.

———— . *Theology and the Philosophy of Science.* Translated by Francis McDonagh. Philadelphia: Westminster, 1976.

———— . *The Theology of Wolfhart Pannenberg.* Edited by Carl E. Braaten and Philip Clayton. Minneapolis: Augsburg, 1988.

———— . *What Is Man?* Translated by Duane A. Priebe. Philadelphia: Fortress, 1970.

Patterson, Bob E. *Carl F. H. Henry.* In Makers of the Modern Theological Mind. Edited by Bob E. Patterson. Waco, Tex.: Word, 1983.

Pauck, Wilhelm and Marion. *Paul Tillich, His Life and Thought.* Vol. 1: *Life.* New York: Harper and Row, 1976.

Peters, Ted. "John Cobb, Theologian in Process." *Dialog* 29 (1990).

———— . "Trinity Talk, Part I." *Dialog* 26 (Winter 1987).

Pinnock, Clark. "Karl Barth and Christian Apologetics." *Themelios* (May 1977).

———— . *Tracking the Maze.* San Francisco: Harper and Row, 1990.

Pittinger, Norman. "Process Thought as a Conceptuality for Reinterpreting Christian Faith." *Encounter* 44/2 (1983).

———— . "Whitehead on God." *Encounter* 45/4 (1984).

Placher, William C. "Hans Frei and the Meaning of Biblical Narrative." *Christian Century* 106/18 (May 24-31, 1989).

———— . *A History of Christian Theology.* Philadelphia: Westminster, 1983.

Portaro, Sam A., Jr. "Is God Prejudiced in Favor of the Poor?" *Christian Century* (April 24, 1985).

Porter, Jean. "The Feminization of God: Second Thoughts on the Ethical Implications of Process Theology." *Saint Luke's Journal of Theology* 29/4 (1986).

Prenter, Regin. "Bonhoeffer and Karl Barth's Positivism of Revelation." In *World Come of Age.* Edited by Ronald Gregor Smith. Philadelphia: Fortress, 1967.

Rahner, Karl. "Anonymous Christians." In *Theological Investigations.* Vol. VI. London: Darton, Longman and Todd, 1969, and New York: Seabury, 1974.

———— . *Foundations of Christian Faith: An Introduction to the Idea of Christianity.* Translated by William V. Dych. New York: Seabury, 1978.

_____ . *Hearers of the Word.* Translated by Michael Richards. New York: Herder & Herder, 1969.

_____ . *I Remember: An Autobiographical Interview with Meinhold Krauss.* Translated by Harvey D. Egan, S.J. New York: Crossroad, 1985.

_____ . "Nature and Grace." In *Theological Investigations.* Vol. IV. Translated by Kevin Smyth. Baltimore: Helicon, 1966.

_____ . *The Trinity.* Translated by Joseph Donceel. New York: Seabury, 1974.

Ramm, Bernard L. *After Fundamentalism, The Future of Evangelical Theology.* San Francisco: Harper and Row, 1983.

_____ . "Are We Obscurantists?" *Christianity Today* 1/10 (February 18, 1957).

_____ . "Biblical Interpretation." In *Hermeneutics.* Grand Rapids, Mich.: Baker, 1971.

_____ : *The Christian College in the Twentieth Century.* Grand Rapids, Mich.: Eerdmans, 1963.

_____ . *The Christian View of Science and Scripture.* Grand Rapids, Mich.: Eerdmans, 1954.

_____ . *The Devil, Seven Wormwoods and God.* Waco, Tex.: Word, 1977.

_____ . *An Evangelical Christology: Ecumenic and Historic.* Nashville: Thomas Nelson, 1985.

_____ . *The Evangelical Heritage.* Waco, Tex.: Word, 1973.

_____ . "The Evidence of Prophecy and Miracles." In *Revelation and the Bible.* Edited by Carl F. H. Henry. Grand Rapids, Mich.: Eerdmans, 1958.

_____ . *The God Who Makes a Difference: A Christian Appeal to Reason.* Waco, Tex.: 1972.

_____ . "Helps from Karl Barth." In *How Karl Barth Changed My Mind.* Edited by Donald K. McKim. Grand Rapids, Mich.: Eerdmans, 1976.

_____ . *His Way Out.* Glendale, Calif.: Regal, 1974.

_____ . "Is 'Scripture Alone' the Essence of Christianity?" In *Biblical Authority.* Edited by Jack Rogers. Waco, Tex.: Word, 1977.

_____ . *Offense to Reason.* San Francisco: Harper and Row, 1985.

_____ . *The Pattern of Religious Authority.* Grand Rapids, Mich.: Eerdmans, 1959.

_____ . *Problems in Christian Apologetics.* Portland, Ore.: Western Baptist Theological Seminary, 1949.

_____ . *Protestant Biblical Interpretation: A Textbook for Conservative Protestants.* Boston: Wilde, 1950. 3d ed. Grand Rapids, Mich.: Baker, 1972.

_____ . *Protestant Christian Evidences: A Textbook of the Evidences of the Truthfulness of the Christian Faith for Conservative Protestants.* Chicago: Moody, 1953.

_____ . *Rapping about the Spirit.* Waco, Tex.: Word, 1974.

_____ . *The Right, the Good and the Happy.* Waco, Tex.: Word, 1971.

_____ . *Special Revelation and the Word of God.* Grand Rapids, Mich.: Eerdmans, 1961.

_____ . *Them He Glorified.* Grand Rapids, Mich.: Eerdmans, 1963.

_____ . *Types of Apologetic Systems: An Introductory Study to the Christian Philosophy of Religion.* Wheaton, Ill.: Van Kampen, 1953.

_____ . *Varieties of Christian Apologetics.* Grand Rapids, Mich.: Baker, 1961.

_____ . "Welcome Green-Grass Evangelicals." *Eternity* 25 (March 1974).

_____ . *The Witness of the Spirit.* Grand Rapids, Mich.: Eerdmans, 1959.

Randall, John Herman, Jr. "Introduction." In Isaac Newton, *Newton's Philosophy of Nature.* Edited by H. S. Thayer. New York: Hafner, 1953.

_____ . "The Ontology of Paul Tillich." In *The Theology of Paul Tillich.* Edited by Charles W. Kegley and Robert W. Bretall. New York: Macmillan, 1964.

Rauschenbusch, Walter. *Christianity and the Social Crisis.* New York: Macmillan, 1907.

_____ . *A Theology for the Social Gospel.* Nashville: Abingdon, 1978.

Reardon, Bernard M. G. *Liberal Protestantism*. Stanford: Stanford University Press, 1968.

Redeker, Martin. *Schleiermacher: Life and Thought*. Translated by John Wallhausser. Philadelphia: Fortress, 1973.

Reese, William. "Parmenides." In *Dictionary of Philosophy and Religion*. Atlantic Highlands, N.J.: Humanities, 1980.

Ritschl, Albrecht. *The Christian Doctrine of Justification and Reconciliation*. Translated by H. R. Mackintosh and A. B. Macaulay. Edinburgh: T. & T. Clark, 1900.

————. "Theology and Metaphysics: Towards Rapproachement and Defense." In *Three Essays*. Translated by Philip Hefner. Philadelphia: Fortress, 1972.

Roberts, Louis. *The Achievement of Karl Rahner*. New York: Herder & Herder, 1967.

Roberts, Robert C., *Rudolf Bultmann's Theology*. Grand Rapids, Mich.: Eerdmans, 1976.

Robertson, Edwin H. "Bonhoeffer's Christology." In Dietrich Bonhoeffer, *Christ the Center*. Translated by John Bowden. New York: Harper and Row, 1966.

Robinson, John A. T. *But That I Can't Believe!* London: Fontana, 1967.

————. *Christian Freedom in a Permissive Society*. Philadelphia: Westminster, 1970.

————. "The Debate Continues." In *The Honest to God Debate*, edited by David L. Edwards. Philadelphia: Westminster, 1963.

————. *Exploration into God*. Stanford: Stanford University Press, 1967.

————. *The Human Face of God*. Philadelphia: Westminster, 1973.

————. *The New Reformation?* Philadelphia: Westminster, 1965.

————. "Not Radical Enough?" In *Christian Freedom in a Permissive Society*. Philadelphia: Westminster, 1970. (This article was originally written for the series, "How My Mind Has Changed," *Christian Century* 86 [November 12, 1969].)

————. *Redating the New Testament*. Philadelphia: Westminster, 1976.

Ruether, Rosemary Radford. "Feminist Theology in the Academy." *Christianity and Crisis* 45/3 (March 4, 1985).

————. *Sexism and God-Talk. Toward a Feminist Theology*. Boston: Beacon, 1983.

————. *Women-Church. Theology and Practice of Feminist Liturgical Communities*. San Francisco: Harper and Row, 1986.

Rumscheidt, Martin, ed. "Introduction: Harnack's Liberalism in Theology: A Struggle for the Freedom of Theology." In *Adolf von Harnack, Liberal Theology at its Height*. London: Collins, 1989.

Runia, Klaas. *Karl Barth's Doctrine of Holy Scripture*. Grand Rapids, Mich.: Eerdmans, 1962.

Russell, Letty M. *Household of Freedom: Authority in Feminist Theology*. Philadelphia: Westminster, 1987.

————. *Human Liberation in a Feminist Perspective—A Theology*. Philadelphia: Westminster, 1974.

Salley, Columbus, and Ronald Behm. *Your God Is Too White*. Downers Grove, Ill.: InterVarsity, 1970.

Schleiermacher, Friedrich. *The Christian Faith*. 2d ed. Edited by H. R. Mackintosh and J. S. Stewart. Philadelphia: Fortress, 1928.

————. *On Religion: Addresses in Response to its Cultured Critics*. Translated by Terrence N. Tice. Richmond: John Knox, 1969.

Schmithals, Walter. *An Introduction to the Theology of Rudolf Bultmann*. Minneapolis: Augsburg, 1968.

Schrader, Robert W. *The Nature of Theological Argument: A Study of Paul Tillich*. Missoula, Mont.: Scholar's Press, 1975.

Skinner, Tom. *Words of Revolution.* Grand Rapids, Mich.: Zondervan, 1970.

Smith, Huston. "Has Process Theology Dismantled Classical Theism?" *Theology Digest* 35/4 (1988).

Smith, Ronald Gregor. *Secular Christianity.* New York: Harper and Row, 1966.

Snyder, Mary Hembrow. *The Christology of Rosemary Radford Ruether: A Critical Introduction.* Mystic, Conn.: Twenty-Third Publications, 1988.

Stackhouse, Max L. "Torture, Terrorism and Theology: The Need for a Universal Ethic." *Christian Century* (October 8, 1986).

Steffen, Lloyd. "The Dangerous God: A Profile of William Hamilton." *Christian Century* 106/27 (September 27, 1989).

Stokes, Walter E. "God for Today and Tomorrow." In *Process Philosophy and Christian Thought.* Edited by Delwin Brown, Ralph E. James, Jr., and Gene Reeves. Indianapolis: Bobbs-Merrill, 1971.

Stone, Ronald H. *Reinhold Niebuhr: Prophet to Politicians.* Nashville: Abingdon, 1972.

Strong, George. "Theology of Narrative or Narrative Theology? A Response to *Why Narrative?*" *Theology Today* 47/4 (January 1991).

Stroup, George W. *The Promise of Narrative Theology.* Atlanta: John Knox, 1981.

Suchocki, Marjorie Hewitt. *God-Christ-Church.* New York: Crossroad, 1984.

Tavard, George. *Paul Tillich and the Christian Message.* New York: Charles Scribner's Sons, 1962.

Taylor, Mark Kline. *Paul Tillich, Theologian of the Boundaries.* San Francisco: Collins, 1987.

Teilhard de Chardin, Pierre. "Life and the Planets." In *The Future of Man.* Translated by Norman Denny. New York: Harper and Row, 1964.

TeSelle, Sallie McFague. *Speaking in Parables.* Philadelphia: Fortress, 1975.

Thatcher, Adrian. *The Ontology of Paul Tillich.* Oxford: Oxford University Press, 1978.

Tice, Terrence N. "Introduction." In Friedrich Schleiermacher, *On Religion: Addresses in Response to its Cultured Critics.* Translated by Terrence N. Tice. Richmond: John Knox, 1969.

Tillich, Paul. *Biblical Religion and the Search for Ultimate Reality.* Chicago: University of Chicago Press, 1955.

––––––. *The Courage to Be.* New Haven and London: Yale University Press, 1952.

––––––. *A History of Christian Thought.* Edited by Carl Braaten. New York: Simon and Schuster, Touchtone Book edition, 1968.

––––––. *Systematic Theology.* Vol. I: *Reason and Revelation, Being and God.* Three volumes in one. New York: Harper and Row; Evanston: University of Chicago Press, 1967.

Vahanian, Gabriel, and Paul van Buren. *The Death of God Debate.* Edited by Jackson Lee Ice and John J. Carey. Philadelphia: Westminster, 1967.

Van Buren, Paul M. *The Secular Meaning of the Gospel.* New York: Macmillan, 1963.

Van Huyssteen, Wentzel. *Theology and the Justification of Faith: Constructing Theories in Systematic Theology.* Translated by H. F. Snijders. Grand Rapids, Mich.: Eerdmans, 1989.

Vass, George. *The Mystery of Man and the Foundations of a Theological System.* Vol. 2 of *Understanding Karl Rahner.* Westminster, Md.: Christian Classics, 1985.

––––––. *A Theologian in Search of a Philosophy.* Vol. 1 of *Understanding Karl Rahner.* Westminster, Md.: Christian Classics, 1985.

Von Balthasar, Hans Urs. *The Theology of Karl Barth.* Translated by John Drury. New York, Chicago, San Francisco: Holt, Rinehart and Winston, 1971.

Vorgrimler, Herbert. *Understanding Karl Rahner: An Introduction to His Life and Thought.* Translated by John Bowden. New York: Crossroad, 1986.

Ware, Bruce A. "An Exposition and Critique of the Process Doctrines of Divine Mutability and

Immutability." *Westminster Theological Journal* 47/2 (1985).

Warner, Rex. *The Greek Philosophers.* New York: Mentor, 1958.

Washington, Joseph R., Jr. *Black Religion.* Boston: Beacon, Beacon Paperback edition, 1966.

―――. *The Politics of God: The Future of the Black Churches.* Boston: Beacon, 1967.

Welch, Claude. *Protestant Theology in the Nineteenth Century,* Volume 1: *1799-1870.* New Haven and London: Yale University Press, 1974.

―――. *Protestant Theology in the Nineteenth Century,* Volume 2: *1870-1914.* New Haven and London: Yale University Press, 1985.

West, Charles C. "Community—Christian and Secular." In *The Church Amid Revolution.* Edited by Harvey Cox. New York: Association, 1967.

Wheat, Leonard F. *Paul Tillich's Dialectical Humanism, Unmasking the God Above God.* Baltimore and London: Johns Hopkins University Press, 1970.

Whitehead, Alfred North. *Adventures of Ideas.* New York: Mentor, 1955.

―――. *Process and Reality.* New York: Harper and Row, Harper Torchbook edition, 1960.

―――. *Religion in the Making.* New York: World Publishing, Meridian Books edition, 1960.

―――. *Science and the Modern World.* New York: Mentor, 1948.

Wiedmann, Franz. *Hegel: An Illustrated Biography.* Translated by Joachim Neugroschel. New York: Pegasus, 1968.

Williams, Daniel Day. *God's Grace and Man's Hope.* New York: Harper and Brothers, 1949.

Williams, Robert R. *Schleiermacher the Theologian: The Construction of the Doctrine of God.* Philadelphia: Fortress, 1978.

Wilmore, Gayraud S., and James H. Cone, eds. *Black Theology: A Documentary History, 1966-1979.* Maryknoll, N.Y.: Orbis, 1979.

Wilson-Kastner, Patricia, et al. *A Lost Tradition: Women Writers of the Early Church.* Lanham, Md.: University Press of America, 1981.

Wright, G. Ernest. *The God Who Acts: Biblical Theology as Recital.* London: SCM, 1952.

Wright, G. Ernest, and R. H. Fuller. *The Book of the Acts of God.* Garden City, N.Y.: Doubleday, Anchor Books edition, 1960.

Yoder, John Howard. *The Politics of Jesus.* Grand Rapids, Mich.: Eerdmans, 1972.

Young, Norman J. *History and Existential Theology.* Philadelphia: Westminster, 1969.

Young, Pamela Dickey. *Feminist Theology/Christian Theology: In Search of Method.* Minneapolis: Fortress, 1990.

Zeller, Eduard. *Outlines of the History of Greek Philosophy.* 13th ed. Revised by Wilhelm Nestle. Translated by L. R. Palmer. New York: Meridian Books, 1957.

Zimmerman, Wolf-Dieter, and Ronald Gregor Smith, eds. *I Knew Dietrich Bonhoeffer.* Translated by Kaethe Gregor Smith. New York: Harper and Row, 1966.

Author and Name Index

Subject Index